Cases on Cultural Implications and Considerations in Online Learning

Andrea Edmundson
eWorld Learning, USA

Managing Director: Lindsay Johnston
Senior Editorial Director: Heather A. Probst
Book Production Manager: Sean Woznicki
Development Manager: Joel Gamon
Assistant Acquisitions Editor: Kayla Wolfe
Typesetter: Nicole Sparano
Cover Design: Nick Newcomer

Published in the United States of America by
Information Science Reference (an imprint of IGI Global)
701 E. Chocolate Avenue
Hershey PA 17033
Tel: 717-533-8845
Fax: 717-533-8661
E-mail: cust@igi-global.com
Web site: http://www.igi-global.com

Library of Congress Cataloging-in-Publication Data

Cases on cultural implications and considerations in online learning / Andrea Edmundson, Editor.
pages cm
Summary: "This book presents teaching cases that address multiple critical cultural challenges faced in a global online learning environment"--Provided by publisher.
ISBN 978-1-4666-1885-5 (hardcover) -- ISBN 978-1-4666-1886-2 (ebook) (print) -- ISBN 978-1-4666-1887-9 (print & perpetual access) 1. Virtual reality in education--Cross-cultural studies. 2. Internet in education--Cross-cultural studies. 3. Distance education--Computer-assisted instruction--Cross-cultural studies. 4. Multicultural education--Computer-assisted instruction. 5. Intercultural communication. I. Edmundson, Andrea, 1955-
LB1044.87.C368 2013
371.33'468--dc23

2012005075

British Cataloguing in Publication Data
A Cataloguing in Publication record for this book is available from the British Library.

Table of Contents

Section 2
Cultural Accessibility

Section 3
Content Globalization

Section 5
Institutional Globalization

Detailed Table of Contents

Web-based and self-paced learning modules have become a common-and sometimes primary-tool used by the Ethics & Compliance departments of global organizations to educate employees worldwide. These e-learning modules provide guidance around such topics as the company's Code of Conduct, specific policies or laws, globally applicable corporate standards, and how best to manage ethical dilemmas in a corporate environment. In this case, the authors describe the instructional design process that were used on various ethics and compliance courses to achieve a more global, regional, or country-specific applicability, including an overview of changes made to content and methodology that was originally perceived as "very American."

The contextual backdrop of the problem and goal of the study are based within the framework that the researchers wanted to be sure that the courses were unique in their appropriateness to their respective cultures; but they also wanted to see if the course adaptations provided cultural values and perspectives that were fairly consistent and appropriate across cultures and nations. The methodology is qualitative in nature, specifically focused upon development design research and narrative inquiry. The findings suggest that there were several levels of concern: learner concerns; instructional design or teaching concerns; management and organizational concerns; and, technology concerns. This study has addressed the question "what lessons could be learned from semiotic and philosophical instructional imperatives inclusion within e-learning environments?" As such, the interpretation of the findings of the study shed light on the importance of simple mediation tools, such as signs, symbols, and stories. The implications of the findings indicate that more research could shed light on how to help students feel comfortable enough to follow through and complete their e-learning courses. In viewing best practices for e-learning, students' existent knowledge can be bridged with what they need to know by using a variety of the semiotic tools discussed in this study.

Section 4
Instructional Globalization

This chapter looks at processes for conducting collaborative reflection in action and collaborative reflection on action. The authors examine this in the context of globally distributed inter-cultural course teams. From a review of the literature, they identify the significance of openness, structure and dialogue as factors that support collaborative reflection. The authors consider these factors in our own experience of global online teaching. They explore and focus upon one technique used in their collaborative inter-cultural reflective practice. This technique involves having one tutor maintain and share an online journal with the other tutors in the course team. This process combined reflective writing and discussion in action. The authors suggest that having one tutor author and share a learning journal may provide facilitation and structure that supports reflective dialogue in inter-cultural globally distributed teams. They consider the influence of cultural pedagogy on inter-cultural reflection. The authors' technique is culturally sensitive in that it respects the right of others to read the journal and to comment only if they wish. Finally, the authors close with a look at instrumentalist versus developmental collaborative reflective practice.

In this chapter the authors describe this interdisciplinary project focusing on the contribution in the teaching-learning process of students at the University of Valencia, in the context of the subject Marketing Research. Specifically, a series of photographs is selected in order to organize an exhibition in London and, to ensure the success of the exhibition, students of the subject Marketing Research have combined sources of secondary and primary data, and have become familiar with databases of business information from the Library of the University of Valencia as well as with the commonly used software for data processing. In general, students have very much appreciated this activity as a facilitator of learning in the field.

Section 5
Institutional Globalization

As information and communication technology (ICT) evolves, the scope of social interactions expands globally through the Web, and knowledge has become a key source for economic production. The capacity to understand diverse cultures and the ability to utilize ICT for knowledge acquisition and application have become critical to increasing and sustaining global solidarity, peace and development. Accordingly, society expects educational institutions to provide students with cultural learning opportunities and ICT skills. In an effort to address these issues, a cross-cultural virtual classroom exchange program using an online course management system was introduced to public schools in Korea and the USA. By investigating technological, pedagogical, and organizational factors, this paper analyzes the adaptability of public schools in Korea and the USA with respect to integrating cross-cultural virtual exchange activities within their respective curricula. Ultimately, this case recommends solutions for increasing adaptability, and invites international collaboration among education stakeholders to disseminate the cross-cultural virtual learning worldwide.

This chapter examines international collaboration in distance education in Sub-Saharan Africa (SSA), focusing on efforts aimed at utilizing technology. It identifies a number of significant collaborative endeavors. The collaborative efforts observed have a similar goal of pooling together ICT resources and expertise towards improving educational outcomes. The prevalence of teacher education and training across the initiatives, in the context of the Millennium Development Goals, is noted. Institutions outside Africa are actively involved in the funding and provision of expertise. Also, the AVU consortium model seems to be a viable approach to collaboration, with notable results seen. With the challenges facing technology-focused collaboration, such as a lack of enabling policies and the digital divide, the chapter suggests that African countries and institutions should pursue a culture of change and be more flexible. More formal training in distance education, utilizing Africans in the Diaspora and promoting dialogue across international spectrums are also recommended.

Preface

INTRODUCTION

In the mining industry, geologists typically do not find gemstones like diamonds and sapphires in areas associated with metallic minerals like gold, silver, and copper simply because gemstones do not form in the same geologic environment. However, there are exceptions to that condition when there are tectonic juxtapositions of diverse rock types. Such conditions raise the possibility that they could find both types of commodities at the same time. For example, finding gold also paves the way to the discovery of precious gems.

Such is the condition that led to the development of this book, *Cases on Cultural Implications and Considerations in Online Learning.* The cases were originally compiled as 'gold' in their original publications because they offered essential insights into cultural challenges of online learning. Subsequently, upon further exploration, we have discovered that they were also valuable gemstones because they inadvertently addressed multiple critical cultural challenges faced in a global online learning environment. For example, in the chapter, *Developing a Grassroots Cross-Cultural Partnership to Enhance Student Experiences,* the authors' intent was to reveal how they enhanced the student experience in an online course on how to market environmental products to American versus French consumers. However, in pursuit of that goal, they also revealed a creative technique for globalizing course content so that it was more acceptable to learners across multiple cultures. While the author's goal in *Integrated Cross-Cultural Virtual Classroom Exchange Program: How Adaptable Public Schools are in Korea and the USA* was to document the benefits of cross-cultural virtual classrooms worldwide for improving intercultural competence, he also revealed institutional barriers and constraints to implementing online learning.

Thus, as you read each of these cases, refer to the section to which they have been assigned; *Cultural Expectations, Cultural Accessibility, Content Globalization, Instructional Globalization,* or *Institutional Globalization*, to discover which gemstones were found with the gold.

SECTION 1: CULTURAL EXPECTATIONS

Which topic logically comes first, access or cultural expectations? If access were only related to technological challenges, I would naturally address it first. However, this is not the case. Access to online learning is culture-bound, meaning that you cannot address access until you understand the underlying cultural differences. Thus, it makes more sense to discuss cultural expectations before access because online educators need to understand what expectations they are facing before they can facilitate access. Expectations – of life, work, education, etc. – are rooted in cultural values.

However, even with the best of intentions, (embracing the benefits of providing online courses to globally distributed learners), the cultural expectations of learners will continue to challenge educators. Why?; because online learning is a cultural artifact, imbedded with the preferences and nuances of the 'designing' culture. However, the targeted learners often have markedly different expectations with respect to how they are taught and how they learn. Moreover, no approach is wrong, just different. However, if educators, (instructors, instructional designers, and institutions), are unaware that these expectations even exist, they cannot address or accommodate them, and subsequently, they will fail in their efforts to provide global online learning. Moreover, they will fail in a multitude of ways; failing to effectively transfer knowledge and skills to learners; failing to create online learning in resource-effective ways; and failing to preserve the reputation of online institutions by ignoring cultural differences. Let's look at the examples of cultural expectations in this section. Recognizing and exploring cultural expectations establishes a foundation of understanding upon which you learn how to address and accommodate them, as covered in subsequent sections of the book.

In *Designing Culturally Appropriate E-Learning for Learners from an Arabic Background: A Study in the Sultanate of Oman*, author Andrea Hall describes how the Sultanate of Oman recognized the benefits of online learning and how this format could be used to address national educational goals. Hall describes how the first iteration of an online course sought to avoid passive learning – a cultural expectation in Oman - by using tools such as discussion forums, chat rooms, wikis, e-portfolios and blogs. These methods represented a significant departure from the lecture format and the traditional roles of learners and instructors in Oman. From the outset of the course, learners expressed discomfort with the social community, the lack of structure, and the lack of obligatory accountability. For example, participants used the forums to post information instead of for reflection and building upon each others' contributions. In addition, instructors did not use the interactivity functions to augment communicative and collaborative aspects of learning as prescribed; instead, they reverted to traditional didactic approaches. All of these culturally nuanced factors compromised learning outcomes. Subsequently, armed with the findings of their analysis, the authors redesigned the course to better facilitate the use of the learning tools. Yet, even though there was some improvement in the acceptance of the second iteration of the course, it still fell short of students' expectations. What does this signify for educators? It signifies that, even when we have recognized and accommodated cultural expectations, they are difficult to affect. It illustrates that the nature of culture – of deeply imbedded, learned behaviors – is a substantial challenge that requires continuous effort and *time*.

In *Collabor8: Online and Blended Cross-Cultural Studios*, author Ian McArthur further underscores the challenge of addressing cultural expectations when The Collabor8 Project (C8) challenged design students from universities and colleges in Australia and China to collaborate online. As in Hall's case, adapting to the range of issues encountered in collaborative interactions between very different groups of undergraduate and postgraduate art and design students required two iterations of the course to accommodate learners' expectations. MacArthur illustrates how C8 evolved to integrate blended pedagogical strategies that enabled stronger collaborative relationships to develop and to identify cultural preferences and tendencies regarding the use of media. To address different cultural backgrounds and expectations, McArthur encourages instructional designers to recognize different styles of knowledge production and to present content in the students' language using culturally inclusive methodologies.

In *Chinese Postgraduate Students Learning Online in New Zealand: Perceptions of Cultural Impact*, Yan Cong and Kerry Earl approach the challenge of recognizing cultural expectations from a different angle. Instead of identifying them 'post-implementation', they actively sought the Chinese students' perceptions of the impact of their culture on their online learning, especially from the perspective of how instructional design supported learning and achievement. In other words, they addressed the expectations directly of the non-designing culture. In their investigation, they uncovered first; the Chinese students' understanding of online learning; second, their perceptions as to whether their cultures influenced their online learning, and finally, what they recommended to online teachers and students. The first-hand, real-time feedback from these students offered rich insights into their cultural expectations. In addition, the expectations of American students contrasted with those of the Chinese offer the reader insights into how our own cultural expectations can 'block' knowledge of others'.

Cultural expectations affect more than how instructional approaches and technological tools are used. In *Incorporating "World View" into the LMS or CMS is Best*, Katherine Watson asserts that cultural expectations – worldviews – affect the design and use of learning and content management systems (LMSs and CMSs, respectively). She effectively illustrates how American-centric systems render subject matter design and delivery, as well as assignment formulation, scheduling, and grading, difficult for educators with alternate worldviews. She recommends that to resolve these disparities, "...institutional control, identity, and contextualization must be addressed, while unique-to-the subject matter identity and contextualization are also considered." In many cases, LMSs and CMSs are imposed upon educators and learners; thus, the challenges she describes may be considered 'unchangeable' but her proposed modifications extend from temporary ones (can be affected by instructors on a course-by-course basis) to long-term ones (requiring redesign and deployment by developers).

SECTION 2: CULTURAL ACCESSIBILITY

Understanding and accepting different cultural expectations are preliminary steps to making online courses more accessible to global audiences. Cultural accessibility encompasses several concepts. First, despite the proliferation of online learning technologies, many learners lack access to them (completely or intermittently) or have no way in which to support the use of certain technologies (like multimedia). In contrast, some technologies, such as mobile phones, have not been used or optimized for suitable locations. Content may also be culturally inaccessible if it is not localized to be relevant and useful to the targeted learners. Localization can encompass language issues (utilizing global English, translation challenges) as well as visual components (images, signs, and symbols). It also encompasses instructional approaches, from the types of activities used to the types of assessments imposed.

In the case by Pauline Hope Cheong and Judith N. Martin, *Cultural Implications of E-Learning Access and Divides: Teaching an Intercultural Communication Course Online,* in addition to focusing on how to effectively provide an intercultural communications online, they illustrate how they surmounted the multifaceted barriers to course access. You should ask: What characteristics or situations prevent learners from accessing an online course? Instinctively, most people would offer responses related to the technologies themselves, the 'digital divide' that can be created by lack of technologies or infrastructure. However, the barriers identified by these authors are characterized as *technocapital,* such as mental access (what motivates learners), how materials are accessed, what skills are needed to access courses, and usage characteristics. Rohas, Straubhaar, Roychowdhury, and Okur,(2004) describe techno-capital as "a specific form of cultural capital encompassing the acquired knowledge, skills, and dispositions to use information technologies (personal computers plus the Internet) in ways that are considered personally empowering or useful (p. 115)." With respect to mental access and motivation, for example, the authors ask how courses could be altered to meet the challenges of students' various learning styles and culture-specific communication styles. How can universities ensure that students can have equitable access to materials, via hardware and software? Research also shows that considerable variance exists in the way and time in which individuals access and find information. A lack of technical skills and assistance has been noted as a barrier to *persistence* in online courses. This case offers a deeper reflection on what characteristics the term 'access' truly comprises in online learning.

In *Blended Learning Internationalization from the Commonwealth: An Australian and Canadian Collaborative Case Study* by Shelley Kinash and Susan Crichton, the authors discuss how blended learning can address the multitude of factors that make online learning culturally inaccessible. According to their experiences, these problems tend to be exacerbated by the fact that universities are not using "culturally inclusive teaching and assessment strategies." The case focuses on the four pedagogic areas identified by De Vita (2007): Communications, with a particular focus on language difficulties; academic skills; teaching and learning stance, and; constructivism. For example, barriers to effective intercultural communication included stereotyping, language fatigue (for both second-language speakers and listeners) and misunderstandings due to the unqualified use of colloquialisms, idiomatic expressions and analogies. They found cross-cultural awareness gaps in approaches to essay writing. There were cultural clashes between learning and teaching styles, exemplified by issues such as the reluctance by some international students to participate in collaborative and student-cantered activities. In addition, there were transitional difficulties for students moving from dependence on rote learning to autonomous learning skills. In the case, the authors illustrate how two universities facilitated culturally accessible teaching and learning of international students through blended learning.

Author Gemma Baltazar, in *Developing an E-Learning Course for a Global Legal Firm,* describes the considerations, challenges, and lessons learned in developing an online course for a global legal firm. The firm's risk management course needed to accommodate lawyers speaking more than 75 languages (i.e., many of them were non-native English speakers), belonging to a variety industry groups, with different local laws and legal environments, and coming from various cultural backgrounds. Noting that research identifies accessibility as one of the top motivating factors for effective elearning, Baltazar describes how the project was managed to accommodate overall end users' learning experience, including: accessing the course online, speed of load, performance of the technology, and obtaining adequate and timely user support when needed. For example, she describes steps taken by the firm to avoid the frustrations arising from problems such as buttons or links not working, pages loading slowly (or not at all), computer hardware not meeting requirements of the program, and so forth. In addition, the firm took concrete steps to avoid frustrations related to not knowing who to ask for help, lack of motivation due to lack of interactivity, and language usage (British versus American English). Readers will benefit from reviewing the challenges faced by a corporation, how they creatively addressed them, and the project management required to facilitate the development of accessible online learning.

Ray Archee and Myra Gurney, in *Integrating Culture with E-Learning Management System Design,* describe ways in which the asynchronous learning platform, WebCT, is culturally inaccessible. They state that "[t]he evolution of the Web from a text-based medium to an interactive, multimedia platform has created the need to consider the audience of websites in more sophisticated and nuanced ways."

In their research, they asked students to comment on their preferences for three uniquely different WebCT pages intentionally designed with near-identical content. In contrast to what most Americans might expect, the students showed a definite preference for sparse, menu-driven webpages as opposed to a colorful, congested, all-in-one interfaces, or the bare-bones WebCT interface. In addition, the majority of the sites sampled used WebCT primarily for posting course material, with a minority using the interactive capabilities of discussion boards, drop boxes or online assessment. This finding is indicative of both the limitations of the WebCT interface as well as the limitations of the technical web skills of the academic staff, both representing implications for the issue of cultural accessibility. The authors argue that template-driven web portals like WebCT are culturally one-dimensional and that the architecture, the tools and the interface tend to reflect the orientation of the culture (usually Western) that has developed and marketed them. In conclusion, Archee and Gurney describe five 'lessons learned,' addressing the design and functions of the WebCT system itself, as well as how universities and instructors use its functions. For any organization contemplating a singular web-based solution for multinational audiences, this chapter is a must-read because many factors related to culture could restrict accessibility.

SECTION 3: CONTENT GLOBALIZATION

Given that learners and instructors come from different cultural backgrounds, we might suspect that not all course content may be relevant in all environments. In contrast, we also make assumptions that certain content is understandable and relevant to all learners. How can we identify 'inappropriate' content and adapt it to suit the needs of our targeted learners? Typically, to globalize content, course developers rely upon localization techniques. What is localization? For online learning, localization represents more than translating words and using appropriate images; instead, it's creating culturally appropriate *content* and using culturally preferred *instructional techniques*. This section discusses content localization; in the subsequent one, instructional approaches.

Content localization is important because it shows learners that you are aware of their unique environments and context. For example, U.S. laws on disabilities will not be relevant in India. In a case study on the ethics of giving and receiving business gifts, an image of a bottle of wine would be irrelevant in an Arab culture. Even language needs to be localized (spelling localised?). For example, many American business terms, such as 'the bottom line,' have no meaning in other cultures. In addition, they create costly translation challenges. Almost all courses designed by one culture and destined to use in another require some level of localization. However, before submitting our courses to localization experts, we can take action as instructors or course designers to globalize the content. In this section, in the course of designing effective instructional strategies, the authors also discovered multiple ways in which to globalize their content. In other words, the same techniques they used to instruct could serve to localize course content!

Not surprisingly, for-profit companies have used localization in advance of educational institutions, primarily because it was a business and marketing decision. Thus, we can extrapolate their experiences to our needs. In *Developing a Grassroots Cross-Cultural Partnership to Enhance Student Experiences*, the authors Iryna Pentina and Veronique Guilloux reveal how students collaborated to globalize their marketing content so that it would appeal to two different cultural groups, Americans and French. While the authors focused on how they used problem-based learning and team collaboration to sell environmental products and services across two cultures, what they also revealed was an excellent approach to discovering: First, *how* content might vary across cultures; and subsequently, how to *localize* it. In their approach, learners identified their assumptions about what would appeal to both groups and then, by addressing the different cultural values, adapted the content to suit learner expectations. For example, Americans were more interested in how a product saved them money, gas, or other resources; whereas, the French were more interested in how the products saved the planet or contributed to the beauty of their country. Thus, this case reveals how the targeted learners themselves assisted with content localization.

In *Cultural Adaptation of E-Learning Courseware: An Ethics & Compliance Example* by Randall Stieghorst and Andrea Edmundson, the authors provide very explicit examples of how they globalized the content of self-paced online courses by focusing on content integrity, values integrity, contextualization, modified language, and appropriate multimedia and images (actual and metaphoric). They illustrate ways in which they identified what content required cultural adaptation and how they accomplished it via systematic analysis and research. Moreover, they stress the importance of including end-users (targeted learners) in confirming and testing their proposed modifications. Lastly, they recommend changes to the instructional design and development processes for online courses, including the training of production staff (instructional designers, scriptwriters, multimedia experts, graphic designers, etc.), so that cultural adaptation (localization) becomes a systematized process and not a post-development course revision (the latter being more expensive and time consuming). For you as the reader, the systematic approach (the Cultural Adaptation Process Model) allows you to localize course content even when you are uninformed about cultural differences.

Authors Caroline M. Crawford and Ruth Gannon Cook have researched and published many articles on *semiotics*, the study of signs and symbols as elements of communicative behavior; the analysis of systems of communication, as language, gestures, or clothing (www.dictionary.com). In *Culturally Significant Signs, Symbols, and Philosophical Belief Systems within E-Learning Environments,* they illustrate the "students' inability to succeed in taking an online course, in learning how to navigate the course, and in getting used to the isolation of online courses" because courses lacked culturally recognized signs and symbols. The goal of their study was to see if the inclusion of semiotic tools, signs, symbols, stories, and tools would support learners' understanding of the subject matter. In addition, they explored whether semiotic tools helped students feel more comfortable and subsequently, whether that comfort helped them to persist in completing assignments and finishing the course. The findings of the student feedback revealed that, while students participated in the primarily text-based online courses, they seemed to prefer the course modules embedded with signs, symbols, and narrative. In their list of "lessons learned," the authors stated that semiotics affected the online environment more than they previously considered. They recommend that educators recognize the benefits of scaffolding learning with semiotic tools as illustrated in their case study.

SECTION 4: INSTRUCTIONAL GLOBALIZATION

Across cultures, learners – and instructors - have preferred approaches to learning and teaching, different learning styles, and unique teacher-student role models. These culturally embedded characteristic influence how teachers and students interact and how students interact with each other. For example, in hierarchical cultures such as many Asian cultures, the instructor is the 'expert' and students expect to learn from the expert, not their colleagues. They tend to learn from lecture and rote memorization. They typically do not question the 'expert' nor challenge any teachings. In contrast, American instructors often assume the role of 'facilitator' and expect students to learn from research, collaboration, interaction with each other, and application of learning to real world situations. Facilitators expect and welcome questions and challenges. Thus, you can see why it would be important to have a repertoire of instructional techniques that benefit – and are accepted by – multicultural audiences. In these chapters, authors address instructional approaches such as problem-based learning, virtual role-play (including virtual learning environments or VLEs and synthetic characters), and simpler techniques such as mentoring via email: How they work (or not) across cultures and how they can be adapted to be effective for targeted learners.

As was done in the chapter on content globalization (*Developing a Grassroots Cross-Cultural Partnership to Enhance Student Experiences*), authors Nicholas Bowskill and David McConnell use feedback and cultural assumptions provided by the learners themselves to localize their online course. In *Collaborative Reflection in Globally Distributed Inter-Cultural Course Teams*, they illustrate how they used the technique of reflective writing – using shared online journals – to help course tutors from the United Kingdom and China to overcome cultural differences in their approaches to teaching. According to research, using collaborative reflection techniques helps people to detect different perspectives of a topic while providing a system of checks and balances on one's private views. In this course, using the shared online journal helped tutors improve their knowledge of local and global teaching practices and showed them how to deliver learning and teaching *with* people from other cultures, not *to* them. Thus, in addition to their own professional development – a better understanding of another culture- they also discovered very authentic ways in which to globalize their instructional approaches.

A Multidisciplinary Project Integrating Marketing Research, Art, and Spanish Language for Social Sciences by Manuel Cuadrado-García, María-Eugenia Ruiz-Molina, and Lourdes Hernández-Martín is another example of how marketing courses and/or research can lead educators to a better understanding of the need for globalized instructional techniques. While challenged with conducting a complex project for a marketing course, the authors report on the benefits of using problem-based learning to motivate students and to improve involvement and performance online. "Problem-based learning [is] an instructional learner-centered approach that empowers learners to conduct research, integrate theory and practice, and apply knowledge and skills to develop a viable solution to a defined problem." In the online course, students from two universities (in Spain and the United Kingdom) participated in an interdisciplinary project based on a real decision-making process. The project had positive effects on students' motivation, involvement and performance because of the approaches used in the project. The results illustrated that, even if there were low extrinsic reward for project participation, students became actively involved in the problem-based situations because they perceived them as exciting, challenging and useful for solving a real-world problem. Via cooperative activities, the students not only benefitted directly (by achieving the desired learning objectives), they benefitted indirectly by improving their language skills.

To date, few online courses for adults use techniques such as virtual role-playing. In fact, research may prove that it's an instructional technique better assimilated by younger learners, but that remains to be evidenced. In *ORIENT: The Intercultural Empathy through Virtual Role-Play*, the authors (Enz, Zoll, Vanninim, Lim, Schneider, Hall, Paiva, and Aylett) illustrate how virtual learning environments (VLEs) increased opportunities for practice, exploration, experimentation, and construction in a safe learning environment in an online course for 12-14 year olds. Noting the lack of empirical evidence on the relationship between virtual worlds and the effectiveness and efficiency of knowledge acquisition, the authors worked on the premise that, once a positive relationship is established between the "agent" (like an avatar) and learner, motivation and interest would be enhanced, and in fact, their study illustrated the development of such relationships. However, they felt that to be more effective, the VLEs required some sort of reflective activity in order to reinforce and imbed the experience in the learners' minds. In addition, the authors learned that while integrating multiple technologies such as mobile phones and WII to create the VLEs had positive rewards, the techniques themselves required too much focus on the mechanics (more than most instructors would be willing to accept).

Learning in Cross-Cultural Online MBA Courses: Perceptions of Chinese Students by Xiaojing Liu and Richard J. Magjuka is valuable to the reader because it offers not only candid feedback from students (the non-dominant culture, Chinese) in the online course, but their recommendations on how to improve the online course by removing perceived cultural barriers. The authors wanted to explore and identify cultural barriers that could affect the performance and satisfaction of the international students (Chinese) in an America (dominant culture) course. A feeling of 'cultural discontinuity' (defined as "a lack of contextual match between the conditions of learning and a learner's socio-cultural experiences" by Wilson, 2001) led students to feel discombobulated and ineffective in this culturally different situation. In particular, they commented on course aspects of time management, time zone differences, language, case-based instruction, collaboration, instructional design, academic conduct, instructional scaffolding, and academic integrity. Time-related challenges are not a surprise, yet the students felt that instructors could do more to accommodate the differences. In addition, language issues were expected, yet, instructors did little to accommodate the needs of non-native English speakers. (Instructors erroneously tend to assume that 'English speaking' means that Chinese students used American English as adeptly as their American counterparts did.) Particularly useful to you the reader are the students' comments on instructional techniques, which tend to contrast significantly from what Chinese students experience in their own country. Lastly, the comments related to academic integrity raised definite cultural differences in which one cultures' concept of plagiarism was different from another's.

SECTION 5: INSTITUTIONAL GLOBALIZATION

Even before courses can be built or placed online, the institutions offering these courses need to be prepared for the global, multicultural environment into which they are about to enter. However, too many institutions make the mistake of ignoring key factors of success and in particular, dismissing the inevitable cultural differences associated with global online courses. In this section, we present two cases, from very different parts of the world (the U.S., Korea), that illustrate what educational institutions need to consider before they globalize their courses or curricula because, across cultures, they will encounter significant differences in policies, infrastructure, laws, missions, and other high level differences that should be addressed at the organizational level.

In this case, *Integrated Cross-Cultural Virtual Classroom Exchange Program: How Adaptable Public Schools are in Korea and the USA*, the author Eunhee Jung O'Neill describes the barriers and constraints to implementing the International Virtual Elementary Classroom Activities (IVECA). IVECA is an online classroom exchange program where K-12 school students in the United States and Korea shared their thoughts and ideas through a web based, course management system (CMS). The goal of the researcher was ultimately to document the benefits of cross-cultural virtual classrooms worldwide for improving intercultural competence. O'Neill identified three types of barriers to this goal: Technological, pedagogical, and organizational (see Figure 1). The technological and pedagogical barriers were similar to those discussed in previous chapters; however, this case offers unique insights into *organizational* barriers – some predictable; others surprising. For example, the two country's public schools systems differed significantly; the American model being decentralized in contrast to Korea's very centralized one. In addition, school policies on the use of information and communication technologies (ICTs) were incompatible. (Interestingly, the Korean policies assured that ICT usage and infrastructure was standardized in the public schools; whereas, in the US, each school was equipped differently and had different resources available to them.) Predictable barriers were different classroom management styles, school schedules, teacher availability. Less predictable were the different paces at the schools, school goals, the ICT literacy level of teachers, and so forth. For example, the American schools' goals were to facilitate students' achievement (test scores) and to conform to the NCLB Act regulations (No Child Left Behind). This mission conflicted with the typical Asian goal of educating students to better everyone' life. A figure from the case illustrates the barriers addressed in IVECA via communication and sharing and understanding one another's values.

Figure 1. Barriers of cross-cultural virtual classrooms for improving intercultural competence

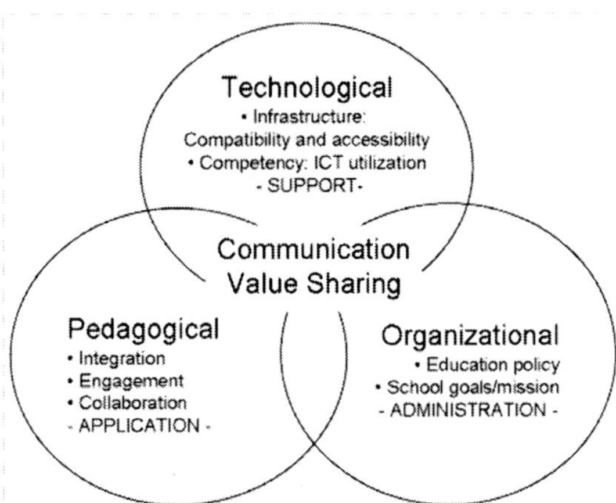

In addition, some barriers were local (i.e., within participating schools, infrastructure, ICT competency, etc.). The author concludes with recommendations on globalizing online courses that are relevant to any globalizing institution.

As evident from the discussion thus far, ICTs are necessary for the realization of wider access to global online courses. However, given the infrastructure and limited or inequitable capacities (human, technical, and organizational) across the globe, the realization of international collaboration in ICT-use will remain a challenge for a considerable time into the future. In this final chapter, *International Collaboration in Distance Education in Sub-Saharan Africa: Trends, Trials and Tomorrow's Thrusts* by Gbolagade Adekanmbi and Bopelo Boitshwarelo, the authors talk about the 'digital divide' in African countries, particularly in tertiary education. "Digital divide refers to the gaps between individuals, communities and nations in their capacity to utilize, and the extent to which they have access to or own various forms of Information and Communication Technologies (ICTs). This also refers to imbalances which occur as a result of the availability or non-availability of resources or skills which individuals require to operate new technologies." In Africa, the absence of technology policies in many countries is a major hindrance to online education. Developing such policies could help identify resources (and resource gaps), users, and opportunities for collaboration (internationally and globally). Subsequently, the creation, adoption, and sharing of policies could further educational and economic goals. As the author illustrates, certain global 'movements' (The *Millennium Development Goals,* the African Virtual University, etc.) are playing positive roles in increasing access to online learning; however, more concerted efforts are needed to truly globalize online learning for all countries. Read this chapter as a treatise on the international collaboration that is required for success globalization of education.

CONCLUSION

As stated in the introduction, these cases were originally compiled as 'gold' in their original publications because they offered essential insights into cultural challenges of online learning. Subsequently, upon further exploration, we discovered that they are also valuable gemstones because they addressed other cultural implications and considerations in online learning. For example, many of the online courses discussed in these cases were designed to teach intercultural skills; however, they also introduced ways to address cultural expectations, improve course accessibility, and globalize course content and instructional approaches. In addition, in the process of implementing these courses, the researchers discovered that often their organizations needed 'globalization' as well, to prepare them for online course delivery.

Across the chapters, the targeted audiences varied greatly: Youth and adults; University, corporate, and public versus private schools; and economically advantaged or disadvantaged. Course content and purpose varied greatly, as well: Art, marketing, communications, interculturalism, law, and so forth. Nonetheless, what did not vary was that all of the cases illustrated ways in which to reach and engage learners across cultures by using online learning that accommodates cultural differences and preferences. For example:

Motivation was typically increased by:

- Enhanced experiences
- Active involvement
- Real world applications

Courses often addressed the preferences of non-traditional learners.

Courses provided for the tangential development of skills:

- Improved language capacity
- Increased computer competence
- Richer cross-cultural knowledge and skill
- Use of new resources, techniques, and technologies

Courses identified differences in values and perceptions manifested in content (i.e., environmental concerns of U.S. and French) and approaches to learning (group collaboration versus instructor-led)/

I think you'll agree that the original gold in these cases paved the way to the discovery of these precious gems. I've given you a map - Enjoy the mining!

Section 1
Cultural Expectations

Chapter 1
Designing Culturally Appropriate E-Learning for Learners from an Arabic Background:
A Study in the Sultanate of Oman

Andrea Hall
Sultan Qaboos University, Sultanate of Oman

EXECUTIVE SUMMARY

Case studies on adult online learners in professional development courses in an Omani context found that cultural preferences had a significant impact on learning success. It was found that their preferences in the development of learning communities, for face-to-face needs, in online course flexibility, and interdependent learning were not accounted for in the learning design. Therefore, the problem identified was: how can learning be designed that accounts for culture in the design of learning for those from an Arabic cultural background, as in Oman? The research provided a solution in the form of design guidelines. These can be used as a practical and useful means for teachers and educators in designing online courses that are culturally compatible with the learning preferences in this context in the Sultanate of Oman.

DOI: 10.4018/978-1-4666-1885-5.ch001

BACKGROUND

For Omanis to compete in an increasingly globalised world, they need to be equipped with the skills needed to function effectively in the marketplace. This is no easy task for the Sultanate of Oman; in 1970 it had only three schools for a population of over half a million. Oil was discovered in the Sultanate of Oman in the 1960s, but for years after, the then Sultan, Said bin Taimar, did nothing to help his people modernise and they continued to live as the ancient Arabs did. However, in 1970, a coup d'etat took Oman "from feudalism almost into the ranks of developed nations in only a quarter of a century, [a feat] unparalleled in the developing world."(Curtiss, 1995, July/August para. 2). When Qaboos bin Said took over power from his father he began the building of the country and its virtually non-existent education system (Curtiss, 1995, July/August; UNESCO-UIE, 2002). Development of the government was through the formulation of five year plans, and in the fourth Five Year Plan from 1991 to 1995, the Omanisation Policy was developed to provide jobs for Omanis and to train them so they could develop the skills needed to take over positions held by expatriates (Al-Dhahab, 2003; Al-Lamki, 1998; Al-Lamki, 2000; Ministry of Information, 2000). However, the rate of Omanisation was slow, and it became obvious that training and education was key means for success of Omanisation, and therefore reform was needed to increase the quality of education and training.

Since the early nineties, there has been concern about the quality of education. The World Bank (2001) reported that in Oman it took 12.6 pupil years to produce a graduate of the nine year basic education system, and most of those who graduated from school with high marks still required an extra foundation year at university. There were also concerns about academic and pedagogical deficits. Tibi (1991, cited in Pollack, 1998 p. 9) commented that "A student …learns natural science or technology exactly as if it were sacral knowledge from the Koran or Hadith". Memorisation skills have been the main method of learning across the Arab world. Rabie (1979, cited in Pollack, 1998) commented:

Students are given thousands of facts to memorize instead of the research skills that will enable them to find the facts when needed. Teachers and professors tend to cling to specific innovations instead of applying the principles of innovation, thus rendering the system rigid and conservative. Memorization, together with the authoritarian method of instruction, serves to inhibit rather than encourage students' ability to think and take initiative. The students' ability to develop realistic and imaginative solutions to whatever problem they may have to deal with is very much limited.

Reform Recommended

Following World Bank studies (2001) on the effectiveness of their general education, it was realised that comprehensive educational reform was necessary to increase the quality of education. Some of the features of this reform included making the education more student-centred, with more interaction, participation and independent learning, as well as the use of technology in some of the classes (UNESCO, 2004). Other issues in the reform included providing a more complete assessment and follow up of each child, emphasizing more mathematics and science, providing more technology in teaching, and introducing English in the earlier grades. These reforms started in the elementary schools with plans to implement this approach in the secondary schools.

Higher Education

Rapid expansion occurred within higher education to provide sufficient places for increasing numbers of secondary school graduates. The first and only government university, Sultan Qaboos University (SQU), was completed by 1986. Private institutions were encouraged as it was believed that there should be more reliance on investment from local and international sources (Al-Lamki, 2000), and subsidies were provided by the government. By the 2006- 2007 academic year there were nearly 17,000 students enrolled in a total of sixteen private colleges and three private universities (Khan, 2007). However, the Omani population growth rate indicates the escalating need for a greater expansion in higher education than is occurring. Forty percent of the population is 15 years of age and under. The annual growth rate is 0.2 for developed nations and 1.9 for the less developed. For Gulf countries, including Oman it was between 3 to 7 percent (Kapiszewski, 2000) and number of places available for secondary school graduates has not kept up with the number of graduates. For example, in 2005, there were 63,000 school graduates and only approximately 15,000 places available in higher education in Oman (Khan, 2007).

Challenges Facing Higher Education

Education in Oman has shown incredible development over the last 40 years, but there are still significant challenges that need to be met, primarily that of quality and access to higher education. These are also issues that were addressed by the World Bank (2001) which commented that the education system is facing the "twin challenges of the need for quality and the need for expanding opportunities in the higher education system"(p. 15).

Although higher education has been provided at a phenomenal rate, there are still insufficient places for school leavers in a rapidly increasing population, and for university graduates and others in the workplace desiring further education. Continuing higher education must be provided if Oman is to compete internationally with those who consider life long learning to be a normal part of professional life (Al-Lamki, 2002).

Omanisation plans focused on the need to increase the quality of the education, which would prepare Omani citizens more effectively for life and work, to help develop skills for the globalised market place. As Oman's Minister of Education commented: "To survive in a globalised world, countries need creative and flexible citizens who are technologically literate, can engage in critical thinking and are skilled communicators" (ONA, 2005). Elementary and secondary schools are aware of the need to reform their educational approach and provide more interactive participatory student-centred learning. In an international conference in Oman on reform in secondary schools, it was noted that schools and the labour market need to understand what today's requirements are and how the secondary school education system could meet these needs (Ghailani, 2002). This approach needs to be within higher education as well. All graduates, whether directly from high school or higher education, need to develop the skills required in the work place, such as problem solving, developing communicative skills, independent learning, being able to work in teams, and having a motivated attitude to work.

This type of approach to teaching and learning is not found in most higher education settings; the lecture is the standard form of teaching; and although this may be one way to deliver large amounts of information, students are often passive and do not develop the desired skills needed as professionals. Therefore reform is necessary not only in schools but in higher education, to address both quality and access in learning.

Using Technology to Address Issues of Quality and Access

The main recommendations of the World Bank (2001) for improving educational outcomes in Oman focused on increased parental involvement and the use of various assessment schemes. Technology was mentioned as being a necessary tool to learn, but the specific benefits of using technology as a tool for quality teaching and as a means to provide education for a higher number of students does not appear in these recommendations. Technology can be used to respond to these challenges and make a difference in teaching and learning in Oman. However the technology must be used effectively.

Using Technology to Make a Difference

Technology can be used to make a difference to learning and teaching, especially technology developed for online learning. The online learning environment provides access to the internet and to an online social network. This environment has different qualities from the face-to-face classroom increasing flexibility in learning. However, technology may not always enhance the learning process; it is a tool, and therefore needs to be used to support sound teaching practices; a deciding factor in the quality of learning. For example, this online environment provides the opportunity for enhancing the communicative and collaborative aspects of learning through using tools such as discussion forums, chat rooms, wikis, e-portfolios and blogs.

Benefits of Online Learning

The benefits of online learning can be envisaged in two categories, that of increased access and increased quality of learning:

Increased Access to Courses

- Access for large numbers of students in a class. Classroom-based teaching can mean a course is taught multiple times. Twigg (2003) gives examples of multiple repeats of a classroom-based course being changed into one course that was accessed by 800 to 1,500 students. This would not be possible in traditional classroom teaching.
- Use of methods that help decrease the amount of time faculty spend teaching, for example by using automatic marking and grading in online quizzes.
- Use of reusable learning objects which can save time in the design of new courses but can increase course quality, as the designer is usually an expert in that topic (Wiley, 2000).

However, studies have shown that teaching online has resulted in increased teaching hours, usually attributed to increase time in interacting with students (Cavanaugh, 2003; Lazarus, 2003). Teachers need new strategies in teaching so that greater access does not mean a significant increase their time teaching online.

Increased Learning Quality

Online learning can support teaching strategies that increase the quality of learning. It can:

- Provide learning contexts that enable learners to be actively engaged and can enable authentic problems to be designed in the learning environment, and therefore increasing learning quality (Jonassen, Hernandez-Serrano & Jonassen, 2003; Jonassen, 1998).
- Promote a social networking between peers and with the tutor in individual, group and class interaction, helping learners to use professional language and work collaboratively in an authentic environment (Brown, Collins & Duguid, 1989; McLoughlin & Luca, 2000).

Addressing Oman's Higher Education Challenges

Thus online learning can benefit learning through addressing the issues of quality and access for both campus-based and online learning courses, and therefore help respond to the challenges of higher education in Oman. However, these benefits are not automatic. There are several issues that need to be addressed to adequately support the use of online learning. These include the following:

- Adequate and reliable administrative and technical infrastructure support systems
- Sufficient professional development and support for teachers in the design of pedagogically sound online courses that help learners build their cognitive and collaborative skills.
- Knowledge on how to design and implement courses that meet the needs of learners in their own particular learning context. The learners' individual needs may include several issues, such how the learners' cultural values and preferences affect the success of their learning.

Oman would need to address all these issues if it intends to use the online environment to respond to its teaching and learning challenges. However, the final point is the focus of this chapter. This is because there is little available in the literature concerning the impact of cultural values and preferences on learning, and therefore on how to design effective courses with culture in consideration. If the impact is significant, learning may be compromised. Therefore suitable culturally appropriate course designs are necessary so that all learners have the opportunity for a successful learning experience. The question is asked, how can online courses be designed that are culturally suitable for learners from a context in the Sultanate of Oman.

CULTURAL PREFERENCES AND ONLINE LEARNING IN OMAN

The Omani culture has been influenced both by its geography and history. The dry arid environment resulted in Arabs forming tight family-based communities in areas where water could be found, and Oman today is still hierarchical, based on family connections. This resulted in strong loyalty and a strong social life based around family commitments, and with cousins usually being the first choice as a marriage partner. Since Oman's renaissance, equal opportunities have been encouraged for females in employment as well as in education, including higher education.

As has been stated, higher education in the Sultanate of Oman consists of one public university, and several private universities and institutes. The public university accepts virtually only Omani students. The private universities and institutes accept expatriate students, but the vast majority is still Omani. Faculty are from a multicultural background, with the government university having the greatest number of Omani faculty members.

There is little in the literature on the concerns and perceptions of faculty about cultural challenges in teaching in Oman. However, personal observations and verbal comments by other practitioners provide some anecdotal evidence of perceptions and challenges concerning cultural values in online learning. This includes the following:

- Many students memorise course materials instead of focusing on understanding. This characteristic is the most often noted in this culture. Some courses encourage this type of approach to course work; others aim to build cognitive skills.
- Many students do not read for pleasure, many of them come from homes with few books, and Oman has no public libraries, yet most courses require significant amounts of reading.
- Traditional teaching tends to have a formal approach in the traditional classroom, but after teaching time, students frequently spend time on an informal basis with faculty in their offices.
- This community is visual and highly relationship orientated; yet teaching approaches tend to be text-based and individualistically orientated.

Personal observations also suggest that many of these characteristics could be explained by cultural values and worldviews of the Arabic society; that the learners' values and expectations did not match those of the course designer or teacher. It is also observed that many practitioners comment on the way learners respond to their courses, without seeking to explain this from the learners' perspectives.

Although this evidence is only anecdotal, and therefore has limited value, it is consistent with the comments made by other researchers and practitioners (Dunn

& Marinetti, 2005; Ziguras, 1999). This suggests that in the Sultanate of Oman, cultural values and preferences are not considered in the design of teaching and learning, and therefore the learning process may be compromised. If technology does act as a cultural amplifier (McLoughlin, 1999), then it is even more important to find a means to design courses for the e-learning environment that are culturally appropriate.

CASE DESCRIPTION

In the attempt to determine the question of how to design culturally appropriate learning designs for a context in Oman, research was done with nine faculty members studying on a two-month course designed to prepare faculty to teach online. This course was offered twice. The first included three research participants, and the second the remaining six participants. Table 1 shows demographic information regarding each participant, using pseudonyms to protect their identity.

Research Approach

The case studies were done within a Design-based Research approach. The case study strategy provided the means for the data collection and analysis. As the aim of the research was to provide guidelines for learning design, the Design-based research approach provided the framework for testing and modifying prototype guidelines. That is, the responses of the cases helped determine the cultural appropriateness of the guidelines, and how they could be modified.

Design-Based Research Approach

The Design-based Research approach developed from the work of Ann Brown (1992) and Allan Collins (1992), who believe that education theory should be tested and shaped in sustained authentic practice, as this is the best environment to determine

Table 1. Case data

Case	1 Amal	2 Badar	3 Dawood	4 Faiza	5 Issa	6 Nasser	7 Majid	8 Salim	9 Talib
Gender	F	M	M	F	M	M	M	M	M
Age	52	40	35	26	42	50	48	45	37
Years Teaching	25	12	2	1	15	19	15	14	8

if the research has been able to improve teaching and learning. They describe the key features of Design-based Research as:

- Researching problems in authentic contexts with practitioners,
- Testing theoretical solutions, and
- Using the research approach to refine both the learning environment and the design principles

This type of research focuses on both the practical aspect in learning as well as the theory that drives the learning design. This has several consequences:

- There are two products, the learning environment that has been refined through the research process; and the design principles, which may be used in other contexts.
- The theory is modified through the research process and through the response of learners in the learning environment. This means the theory is modified by practice, and practice is driven by tested theory, and can result in improving " theoretical accounts (The Design-Based Research Collective, 2003 p. 7), or "propositions about teaching and learning" (Bannan-Ritland, 2003 p. 21).

Modifications to theory tested in this manner can contribute to the knowledge about particular theories, and can therefore enable these theories to be practical tools that improve teaching and learning (Cobb, Confrey, diSesssa, Lehrer & Schauble, 2003; Collins, Joseph & Bielaczyc, 2004; Reeves, 2000)

Data Collection

During the implementation of the online courses, data were collected in several research cycles from the case studies, using several tools, including participant observation, interviews, and statistical data from the Moodle Virtual Learning Environment. Data analysis was used to modify design guidelines, and these were used to modify the course. This meant that over time, the course was modified several times to more effectively represent a design where the learners preferred to learn. During the research process, learners' cultural preferences were also identified, as is described in a later section.

Learner Responses to their Courses

The online courses used for the research were developed on pedagogically sound principles and used an active learning-centred approach. The case study findings are now described, using four main themes that can be identified from an analysis of the research data. As there were two courses investigated, with two sets of cases studied, the analysis from each course is presented separately.

Implementation of the First Online Course

Development of the Learning Community

There were problems for these participants in feeling a sense of community. From the outset of the first course, no one sensed any social community in their on the course. Amal and Badar had made direct comments to others in the welcome or help forums and Amal had received a response from other people on the course, which she acknowledged. Dawood also recognised at least one other person on the course. However none of these efforts were sufficient for them to feel part of the community. The emails from the facilitator and welcoming notices did provide the desired sense of belonging either. Amal commented that she felt "alone and on my own"; Badar noted, "At the moment I feel I am working alone"; and Dawood said, "I feel alone so far".

All three participants preferred a course that would provide more physical presence, especially in the beginning. For example, Amal said she wanted the "human touch", for the course to become a place where people "love to communicate"'. Badar want to "build bridges" between people and did not want to "miss the train"; and Dawood wanted to feel part of "the family of the course". Amal and Dawood suggested a meeting at the beginning to get to know each other, and all three felt that they would like to have a structured time when they know everyone is online together, and have a chat at that time. Dawood also noted that having people on the course who he already knew could help build the sense of community. Badar also believed that this structure or support would provide the means to enhance the communication. This indicates that these participants wanted to work with others, but found the online environment was a difficult place to sense the presence of others, and anything that helped the feeling of others being there, such as synchronous chats, would help.

Interdependent Learning

Participants also expressed their preference for accountability to others in learning. Both Badar and Dawood commented on the necessity of accountability to others for interacting in the course, as Badar mentioned "I am trying to contact (a participant on the course who messaged him) to chat with and I hope that will make me feel more accountable." Badar expressed similar concerns: "We all have to be more genuine or enthusiastic because in doing so we are effectively helping each other". Neither Badar nor Dawood contributed significantly to the online discussion forums, and were not able to build good relationships with others on the course, and both dropped out. This need for accountability to others appeared to be a significant factor in successful completion of the course.

Flexibility

The participants found difficulty working with the flexible nature of learning online. All commented on requiring more structure, for example in organizing chats at a particular time for them to interact together, as has already been noted. Amal and Badar both mentioned issues with time, both mentioned being interrupted by students coming into the office while they were working on the course, and often could not find time finish what they intended to do. As Badar commented," I have time management crises ...... I just need to sort myself out and manage my time properly". Some of the participants expected that the facilitator would provide more deadlines and reminders to help them manage their time so they could complete course tasks.

Course Orientation

Exemplars in context were preferred for orientation. The first unit of the course contained reading material to orientate learners to the learning-centred style for the online environment. All three participants found that reading this material was a negative part of the course. Amal thought it was "background" and implied that not all of it needed to be read, Badar was selective, and Dawood found it was "not encouraging" or "off-putting". It was subsequently found that the online activities were not used in a learning-centred manner as had been explained in the orientation material. For example, the forums were used by participants to post information instead of using them for reflecting and building on other's contributions. This compromised the learning as the outcomes of the forums were needed for their projects.

Implementation of the Second Online Course

The analysis of the findings was used to make changes to the course. This included provision of more interaction to help develop a social community, such as more chats, forums and face-to-face time. The orientation was changed from a reading format to an exemplar one where participants could learn how use the active learning tools by doing exemplar activities in an initial face-to-face session. Six participants were investigated during implementation of this second course.

Development of the Learning Community

Analysis of the discussion forums in this course showed a low level of interaction. The extra online interaction provided was not able to help learners develop a sense of community; "When e-learning starts to feel easier I will interact more" commented Issa. Groups were set up in the course, but there was only a small amount of group interaction in the face-to-face orientation workshop and the lack of interaction between group members online indicated the difficulty of developing relationships online. However it was found that chats were preferred to forums because the immediate replay made the others feel closer, "When you have something to ask it is better to immediately get the answer like in the chat, not the next day" stated Talib. The lack of interaction suggests there should be more focus on relationship development in the face-to-face environment at the beginning of the course. Most cases recommended the face-to-face environment as being important for developing friendships first, as most either felt uncomfortable online or did not envisage how relationships could be developed in that environment, as is shown in a comment by Talib:

In a lot of courses you meet people from other colleges and they are active, you do the work with them and a friendship started from there, but the thing with this course is that everything is done remotely, that type of relationship is not built. Friendship is most likely built only in the face to face situation

Salim also felt that the initial part of the course is very important:

I think if you want to make a successful group in the course, make the social group before the beginning. It may be that if the networks were built beforehand it would be easier to meet online

The lack of relationship may be why most participants felt reluctant to make the kind of personal disclosures needed to maintain a caring community online, and sharing was at a more formal level. Issa commented, "Maybe because they didn't know each other so it was formal", and Majid said "You keep out your private life when you don't know how they will react to it."

Interdependent Learning

The case studies showed that there was a relationship between interaction and accountability, as Faiza stated, "I felt obliged to do [interact] it because there are other people whose work depends on everybody's showing up". Nasser felt accountable to Salim who was in his department. He organised a chat with Salim where he gave him advice. By contrast, Issa, Majid, Salim and Talib felt no sense of accountability or commitment to others. Majid commented that he felt no social obligations to meet online when promised, "I probably don't meet them so I don't feel embarrassed", and Nasser said, "We need to make some kind of commitment". It was found that where there was no accountability, there was also minimal interaction online and poor performance in project work.

For most of the participants it was found that the face-to-face orientation time was important in developing responsible relationships. Majid stated, "If you get them to know each other at the beginning and talk, personally, I think they will have more obligation to be online later in the course". Thus responsibility to others is a key issue in learners achieving success online; and probably needs to be developed from initial sessions in a face-to-face environment.

The group situation may be the preferred learning community, as all six cases were found to prefer to work in groups. Faiza commented, "I felt that like when I see a contribution done by [my] group I felt like this is from somebody in my group so I have to read it really well and contribute to that". For five of the six case studies, group responsibility did not develop online, and initial face-to face sessions may require more emphasis on the social aspects so that group formation can occur in the classroom. This suggests that the participants preferred interdependent learning, not autonomous learning; and they preferred to learn where they were accountable to one another, as this may provide motivation to learn.

Flexibility

It was found in most cases that increased support was preferred, for example, to help meet deadlines, as commented by Majid, "It will force us to follow deadlines. If you are flexible, they become more flexible". Salim also preferred to have his teaching hours arranged to match others in his online course to provide structure for working in the online environment, "Everyone has the same time free, to decrease the obstacles in their timing for doing the required study". Talib was also concerned that flexibility in courses would result in deadlines not being met, "They will relax more, sink in their chair and not do the work" he said.

There were other time management issues during the course. The assignment deadlines were posted on the course home page and in the course calendar but in only few met the deadlines. Committed responsible relationships were a key to motivate participants to go online and complete the course, not the provision of increased structure and external incentives. This means that extra support may be helpful for some online course participants, but that responsibility to other may be a more effective means to enable learners to meet deadlines. Thus flexibility in online courses may not be helpful for learners from this cultural background unless they are able to develop committed and responsible relationships with others.

Learners' Responses and Arabic Cultural Values

The responses of these cases were compared to Arabic cultural values from the literature, and it was found that there was strong correlation. This shows that the preferences found were probably cultural preferences. Thus the findings can be used to describe the type of environment where people from an Arabic cultural background may prefer to learn.

Two strong features of the Arabic society, as in the Sultanate of Oman, identified in the literature are that it is a collectivist culture and has oral cultural values (Hofstede, 2003; Ong, 1982; Zaharna, 1995). A collectivist culture emphasizes group goals over individual ones, and relationships have a high priority. Commitment to others more than to individual needs means that the group would provide the support and responsibility; therefore the individual may look to others for goals and expectations (Shkodriani & Gibbons, 1995; Wu & Rubin, 2000). This is evident in an Omani society today. The Arabic culture is also described as an oral culture (Havelock, 1986; Ong, 1982; Pollack, 1998; Zaharna, 1995). Oral cultures are those that value their language as a spoken language, even though they have a written language, as with the Arabic language. For example in the appreciation of its pleasure to the ear, and in the value placed on memorisation and recitation of the Qur'an. Ong (1982) proposes that the way a language is used affects the way people think, because this would determine how knowledge, skills and traditions are transmitted within the society. These values are evident in the society with preferences for communication characteristics that resemble an oral culture such as rhetoric, exaggeration and a preference for imagery over accuracy (Zaharna, 1995). As knowledge in an oral culture is not abstract but more human-related, learning therefore is more situational and centred around activities and with other people. People from an oral background tend to use more visual methods of learning. Zaharna (1995) explains that this is because they are more people or event-orientated, where objects are seen, not as discrete linear objects, but within the context of their environment.

This study did not intend to identify cultural values specific for an Omani or Arabic society. Its purpose was to identify preferred ways of learning for those in a particular context, regardless of whether these values or preferences were unique to this one society. It was found that the preferences identified in the research could be aligned with many of the cultural values of collectivist and oral societies such as the Arabic society as is in Oman (Hall, 2009). These preferences are summarised in Table 2.

As these findings suggest that the preferences identified were in fact cultural preferences, it means that the findings from the study can be used to help design courses that reflect the values of the Arabic society as is found in the Sultanate of Oman.

Table 2. Arabic cultural values and learning preferences

Cultural Values	Preferences identified in the case studies
Collectivist	• Prefer to work in community in responsible relationships • Prefer to work in groups instead of individually • Extrinsic motivation; provided by others • Prefer structure more than flexibility
Oral Language	
Visual imagery	• Language should be used to develop rich mental images. • Other visual tools may be required
Story-based	• Learn in context, not through abstract reading (as in the orientation)
People-related	• Prefer face-to-face for relationships, or any tool that helps make online relationships feel like face-to-face

SOLUTIONS AND RECOMMENDATIONS

The design of the research used enabled the collection of course guidelines that were developed during the empirical phase of the study. Each time the case studies were analysed, refinements were made to the guidelines that had been used to design the original course. This meant that by the end of the study, the modified guidelines represented the preferences of the learners, and as described above, most of these preferences are cultural. Therefore the guidelines developed during the research provide a design solution for designing courses for learners from Arabic cultural backgrounds such as the Sultanate of Oman. The complete set of design guidelines developed in the study are shown in Table 3.

The guidelines provided in the table may be used by educators or learning designers as a set of hints or recommendations whilst developing online courses for Omani learners. This section provides practical examples of the use of some of these guidelines, as they relate to the themes identified in this chapter.

Designing for a Learning Community

As has been stated, the Arabic society places great value on the community. This was found to be an extremely important component for the online environment, and for many participants it was not possible to develop this community without a face-to-face component in the course. This means that great emphasis needs to be placed on the development of the learning community from the first week of the course or it may not develop at all. Guidelines 3.1 to 3.4 provide suggestions on how to develop this community. Guideline 3.1 suggests that while the learners are new to learning online, courses should start in the classroom. For example, for learners who are new to each other, this may require at least two sessions. The classroom

Table 3. Guidelines for Culturally-suitable Online Courses in Oman

Designing the Tasks	
1.1	Use a learning-centred design, where the focus is on learners actively engaged in performing tasks.
1.2	Provide activities where learning is gained from peers or other sources, but also provide the direction and support from the teacher.
1.3	Design activities that are integral to the course structure, in that they help achieve the learning outcomes.
1.4	Design most tasks as group work, and give responsibilities to the group leader
1.5	Design interaction as an integral part of course design but participant commitment to the course and each other must be developed before interaction will occur.
1.6	Use both discussion forums and chat but chat is the preferred option.
1.7	Base the collaborative work on learning issues if the goal is to develop deeper learning at the conceptual level but commitment should be developed before this task can be successful
1.8	Use separate roles or functions for some collaborative work, but commitment and responsibility must be developed before this can be successful.
Designing Orientation	
2.1	Provide orientation for students in how to use discussion boards and chat in the context of use, from a technical and educational perspective, as well as training as moderators.
2.2	Provide orientation for learners to help them understand the benefits of a learning-centred environment.
2.3	Provide examples or activities that help learners to understand the type of learning that is expected of them in learning- centred courses
2.4	Provide orientation for learners on the style of communication used in an interactive online classroom.
Designing the Development of the Learning Community during Orientation	
3.1	Provide initial classes face-to-face for learners who are not sufficiently experienced interacting in the online environment
3.2	Design groups, using participants' social networks or from people within a close circle.
3.3	Provide opportunities for participants to develop relationships and share personally in the initial part of the course.
3.4	Help learners to first be committed and accountable to others, as this can help them become responsible in completing the work.
Designing Tools to Scaffold Learning	
4.1	Use a variety of tools and support, including visual tools.
4.2	Design cognitive tools or scaffolds in such a way that helps learners to understand how to apply them.
Implementatiown: Teacher Responsibilities	
5.1	Develop the sense of commitment and responsibility where the frequency of interaction is low
5.2	Use soft or spontaneous scaffolding through monitoring student learning.
5.3	Ensure that the tools are sufficient, suitable and are being used. If not, then modify the tools or provide training, and focus on the learning benefits.
5.4	Build a sense of teacher immediacy through the use of individual messages
5.5	Provide more support and scaffolding in the learning environment through, emailed assignment due dates or calendar of deadlines and time management suggestions

setting and lesson plan would need to provide maximum opportunity for interaction, such as using informal seating arrangements, use of laptops where participants can talk with each other at the same time as working online. The orientation activities used in these sessions should include interactivity to help participants get to know each other online and face-to-face at the same time.

As suggested in Guideline 3.2, participants should work in groups, and therefore meet and get to know others in their group from the first face-to-face session. If the participants sit with their group members, then this can provide the opportunity for them to get to know each other, and perhaps share personally. Exchanging phone numbers and email addresses can all help build up the relationships, as is suggested in Guideline 3.3.

In many situations, it may be difficult for a whole class to meet at the same time or even meet at all. Therefore the course facilitator may need to be creative in meeting this need. For example groups that are selected based on geography may be able to meet together, or use a weekend day together for the initial part of the course. Otherwise, visual or synchronous technology could be used, such as video-conferencing, video Skype and Gmail, or telephones.

This design solution for Arabic communities is different from that recommended from the general literature (Wegerif, 1998), which suggests that the development of a learning community happens as a result of frequent interaction online. In the Arabic cultural setting, the development of the relationships must happen first otherwise interaction may not occur. Therefore these initial face-to-face sessions may be more important in this culture than some others.

Interdependent Learning

Autonomous learning is often described as an important skill to be developed in online learners. However, in this society, as has been stated, community is valued over individuality, and people prefer not to work, act or live alone. In this research it was found that learners from this cultural background wanted to learn within committed responsible relationships; and where these relationships did not form, the learners either did not complete the course or their learning was compromised. Therefore it is suggested that courses are designed to help participants to learn interdependently, that is independent of the facilitator but dependent on each other, for example in using group work.

As the initial face-to-face meeting is important time for participants to get to know one another sufficiently to develop responsible relationships, this initial class can be designed to help develop group responsibility. The facilitator can encourage the participants to perceive their group members as those who will both support them and be the ones they are responsible for, in helping achieve course success. Envisaging their group as one where there is commitment and responsibility may make the difference for them, as is recommended in Guideline 3.4 in Table 3.

According to Guideline 5.1, the facilitator is should monitor the amount of interaction. If interaction is low, then commitment and responsibility between group members should be encouraged for example by helping groups organize a face to face meeting to discuss their projects and deadlines. This would then enable participants to learn in an environment that is culturally familiar to them.

Flexibility in Course Implementation

The participants in the research found difficulty in working in a flexible learning environment and preferred a more structured one. A collectivist society, such as this, is motivated by extrinsic values, and would therefore prefer others to provide deadlines. The participants were not able to spend sufficient time online and most had difficulty meeting deadlines. Two solutions were identified in the research, as explained be Guidelines 3.4 and 5.5 in Table 3. These suggest that courses be designed with extra support and structure, including email reminders from the facilitator. However, the research also suggested that the development of effective responsible group relationships can be used to provide the structure that is needed to help meet course requirements. These findings suggest that learners from an Arabic cultural background would prefer to study on courses that have prescribed start and finish dates, and not those where there is open enrolment for *'any where any time'* courses.

Designing Orientation

Orientation to using online learning is important for ensuring the learners can use the technology comfortably and confidently and in a way that enhances the educational outcome; for example, by using discussion forums not to just post, but to reply in a reflective manner. As suggested in Guideline 2.2, a separate unit or module can be designed for the beginning of the course for orientation to all the tools used in the course. For learners from an Arabic cultural background, it is recommended in Guideline 2.3 that readings are not used for orientation, but instead examples should be used to orientate them, such as using a task on a wiki to exemplify how wikis are used. Orientation using readings was not successful in this research, but exemplar use of these tools was. The high-context culture such as the Arabic society understands objects within their context, and therefore the necessity to learn about tools within their context of use. For example, where the chat or forum question is placed, there should also be some hints explaining how to use the tool effectively as suggested in Guideline 2.1.This means the information is provided exactly at the time the activity is performed.

As is recommended in the design guidelines of 1.1 to 1.8, engaged learning designs should be used, but also learners need to know how to use them, as the approach is different from traditional teaching. Therefore orientation time should also be used for learners to reflect on how they learned during that session, for example in a classroom discussion. This can help learners to see how they learned in interactive or reflective work, as is suggested in Guideline 2.2., so they may learn how to use the tools effectively during the rest of the course.

LESSONS LEARNED

This research has developed guidelines aimed at supporting educators and learning designers in the development of pedagogically-based cultural-appropriate courses for their students. The guidelines are intended as a practical tool that does not need the presence of expert educators or researchers to interpret their meaning. It is hoped that these guidelines will provide an easy means for educators to develop more culturally suitable designs for online courses in the Sultanate of Oman, and other contexts where learners are from an Arabic cultural background. As these guidelines were designed in a specific context, they should be refined and modified in each situation to enable them to more effectively match the cultural values of the learners.

There were some lessons learned during the research:

- The effect of culture in learning is more significant than had been previously assumed. Of the 25 guidelines from this case study, 23-24 of them could be aligned to cultural values identified in the literature
- The effect of culture on learning success was more significant than had been assumed. Learning was compromised for eight out of the nine cases studied. Extrapolation of this to world-wide online courses has sobering implications.
- The significance of the social aspects of learning was the most impacted by cultural preferences. In online learning, this is very significant, as the development of social networking and community is more difficult than in face-to-face classrooms.

CHALLENGES

The research did not provide a final solution as 'an answer'. There were five research cycles and with each cycle, more modifications were made to the guidelines and to the course. This of course suggests that had the research continued, modifications would have continued, and the guidelines may have been different from what is presented in this chapter. However, what was found was that the guideline modifications matched the cultural values in the literature, and met the criteria for this research. Therefore it was concluded that this was a working solution for designing guidelines, and that evaluation of the learning design should be an integral part of any course.

A significant challenge in designing such guidelines is where the learner group may have a variety of cultural backgrounds, which is probably the more common finding in most online courses. Each study provides building blocks for the next, and therefore each study will take us closer to finding 'the answer' for culturally-appropriate learning design.

REFERENCES

Al-Lamki, S. (2000). Omanization: A three tier strategic framework for human resource management and training in the Sultanate of Oman. *Journal of Comparative International Management, 1*(3).

Al-Lamki, S. (2002). Higher education in the Sultanate of Oman: The challenge of access, equity and privatization. *Journal of Higher Education Policy and Management, 24*(1), 75–86. doi:10.1080/13600800220130770

Bannan-Ritland, B. (2003). The role of design in research: The integrative learning design framework. *Educational Researcher, 32*(1), 21–24. doi:10.3102/0013189X032001021

Brown, A. L. (1992). Design experiments: Theoretical and methodological challenges in creating complex interventions. *Journal of the Learning Sciences, 2*(2), 141–178. doi:10.1207/s15327809jls0202_2

Brown, J. S., Collins, A., & Duguid, P. (1989). Situated cognition and the culture of learning. *Educational Researcher, 18*(1), 32–42.

Cavanaugh, J. (2003). Teaching online-a time comparison. *Online Journal of Distance Learning Administration, 3*(1). Retrieved April 25, 2008, from http://www.westga.edu/~distance/ojdla/spring81/cavanaugh81.htm

Cobb, P., Confrey, J., diSessa, A., Lehrer, R., & Schauble, L. (2003). Design experiments in educational research. *Educational Researcher, 32*(1), 9–13. doi:10.3102/0013189X032001009

Collins, A. (1992). Towards a design science of education. In Scanlon, E., & O'Shea, T. (Eds.), *New directions in educational technology* (pp. 15–22). Berlin, Germany: Springer. doi:10.1007/978-3-642-77750-9_2

Collins, A., Joseph, D., & Bielaczyc, K. (2004). Design research: Theoretical and methodological issues. *Journal of the Learning Sciences, 13*(1), 15–42. doi:10.1207/s15327809jls1301_2

Curtiss, R. H. (1995, July/August). Oman: A model for all developing nations. *The Washington Report on Middle East Affairs.* Retrieved August 21, 2009, from http://www.wrmea.com/backissues/0795/9507049.htm

Dunn, P., & Marinetti, A. (2005). Cultural adaptation: Necessity for global e-learning. *New Economy e-Magazine.* Retrieved June 21, 2009, from www.linezine.com/7.2/articles/pdamca.htm

Ghailani, J. (2002, December 24). Quality of secondary education and labour market requirements. *Oman Daily Observer, Supplement,* (p. 3).

Hall, A. (2009). *Designing online learning environments for local contexts, as exemplified in the sultanate of Oman.* EdD thesis, Faculty of Education, University of Wollongong. Retrieved April 20, 2009, from http://ro.uow.edu.au/theses/272

Havelock, E. (1986). *The muse learns to write: Reflections on orality and literacy from antiquity to the present.* New Haven, CT: Yale University Press.

Hernandez-Serrano, J., & Jonassen, D. H. (2003). The effects of case libraries on problem solving. *Journal of Computer Assisted Learning, 19*(1), 103–111. doi:10.1046/j.0266-4909.2002.00010.x

Hofstede, G. (2003). Geert Hofstede™ cultural dimensions. Retrieved March 31, 2009, from http://www.geert-hofstede.com/

Jonassen, D. (1998). Designing constructivist learning environments. In Reigeluth, C. M. (Ed.), *Instructional theories and models* (2nd ed., pp. 215–239). Mahwah, NJ: Erlbaum.

Kapiszewski, A. (2000). *Population, labour and education dilemmas facing GCC states at the turn of the century.* Paper presented at the Crossroads of the New Millennium, Abu Dhabi, UAE.

Khan, N. (2007). The business of education. *Education.* Retrieved April 5, 2007, from http://www.apexstuff.com/bt/200703/education.asp

Lazarus, B. D. (2003). Teaching courses online: How much time does it take? *Journal of Asynchronous Learning Networks, 7*(3), 47–54.

McLoughlin, C. (1999). Culturally responsive technology use: Developing an online community of learners. *British Journal of Educational Technology, 30*(3), 231–243. doi:10.1111/1467-8535.00112

McLoughlin, C., & Luca, J. (2000). *Cognitive engagement and higher order thinking through computer conferencing: We know why but do we know how?* 9th Annual Teaching Learning Forum. Retrieved September 20, 2008, from http://lsn.curtin.edu.au/tlf/tlf2000/mcloughlin.html

ONA. (2005, March 1). Sulaimi: Constant increase in schools, students, teachers. *Times of Oman,* (p. 1).

Ong, W. J. (1982). *Orality and literacy: The technologizing of the world.* London, UK: Routledge. doi:10.4324/9780203328064

Pollack, K. M. (1998). *Arab culture and Arab military performance: Tracing the transmission mechanism.* Ideas, Culture and Political Analysis Workshop. Retrieved October 14, 2002, from http://www.ciaonet.org/conf/ssr01/ss01af.html

Reeves, T. (2000). Socially responsible educational technology research. *Educational Technology, 40*(6), 19–28.

Shkodriani, G. M., & Gibbons, J. L. (1995). Individualism and collectivism among university students in Mexico and the United States. *The Journal of Social Psychology, 135*(6), 765–780. doi:10.1080/00224545.1995.9713979

The Design-Based Research Collective. (2003). Design-based research: An emerging paradigm for educational inquiry. *Educational Researcher, 32*(1), 5–8. doi:10.3102/0013189X032001005

Twigg, C. (2003). *Expanding access to learning: The role of virtual universities.* Retrieved June 14, 2004, from http://www.center.rpi.edu/PewSym/mono6.html

UNESCO. (2004). *Quality education in Oman.* Retrieved March 21 2009, from http://www.ibe.unesco.org/International/ICE47/English/Natreps/reports/oman_part_2.pdf

UNESCO-UIE. (2002). *Literacy exchange: World resources on literacy: Oman.* March 21, 2004, from http://www.rrz.uni-hamburg.de/UNESCO-UIE/literacyexchange/oman/omandata.htm

Wegerif, R. (1998). The social dimension of asynchronous learning networks. *Journal of Asynchronous Learning Networks, 2*(1), 34–49.

Wiley, D. A. (2000). Connecting learning objects to instructional design theory: A definition, a metaphor, and a taxonomy. In Wiley, D. A. (Ed.), *The instructional use of learning objects: Online version.*

World Bank. (2001). *The Sultanate of Oman cost effectiveness study for the education sector.* Muscat, Oman: World Bank.

Wu, S.-Y., & Rubin, D. L. (2000). Evaluating the impact of collectivism and individualism on argumentative writing by Chinese and North American college students. *Research in the Teaching of English*, *35*(2), 148–179.

Zaharna, R. S. (1995). Bridging cultural differences: American public relations practices & Arab communication patterns. *Public Relations Review*, *21*(3), 241–255. doi:10.1016/0363-8111(95)90024-1

Ziguras, C. (1999). *Cultural diversity and transnational flexibility delivery*. ASCILITE Conference, Brisbane, Australia.

This work was previously published in Cases on Globalized and Culturally Appropriate E-Learning: Challenges and Solutions edited by Andrea Edmundson, pp. 94-113, copyright 2011 by Information Science Reference (an imprint of IGI Global).

Chapter 2
Collabor8: Online and Blended Cross-Cultural Studios

Ian McArthur
The College of Fine Art, University of New South Wales, Australia

EXECUTIVE SUMMARY

The rapid advancement of online communication technologies is reconfiguring the creative industries through globally networked and interdisciplinary modalities of practice. These inescapable shifts are challenging most of our assumptions about the nature of creative processes. Consequently art and design educators are impelled to teach students in ways that mirror contemporary creative processes. This inevitably includes collaboration in online environments. Instigated in 2003, The Collabor8 Project (C8) responds to these conditions by challenging design students from universities and colleges in Australia and China to collaborate online. Recently, C8 has evolved to integrate blended pedagogical strategies that enable stronger collaborative relationships to develop. This chapter provides a comparative analysis of two project iterations conducted during 2008 and 2009. Using data collected through observation, interviews, questionnaires, discussions, and specific research tasks within creative briefs, it identifies, discusses, and offers insights relating to a range of issues encountered in collaborative interactions between very different groups of undergraduate and postgraduate art and design students.

DOI: 10.4018/978-1-4666-1885-5.ch002

BACKGROUND

The creative industries are undergoing significant transformation as societal and industrial changes reshape them into hitherto unforeseen multidisciplinary hybrids. In a marketplace where strong disciplinary skills are taken as given and problem-solving abilities, communication skills, collaborative strengths, creative and innovative thinking have become mandatory, individuals must master the abilities required to coordinate synchronized parallel processing while immersed in complex, unstructured problems (McArthur, McIntyre, Watson, 2007). If graduates are to compete in this increasingly globalised economic landscape then appropriate transnational pedagogic models facilitated by digital communication channels are needed. Given the speed of the changes underway however it is unsurprising that educationalists to date have been slow to respond (DiPaola, Dorosh and Brandt, 2004).

Additionally, China's increasingly integral position in relation to industry (a key factor influencing this study) is creating an urgent need for culturally based education for both eastern and western students as they enter a globally networked world of work (Buchanan, 2004). However, although the case for such approaches is clear, the reality of facilitating networked educational experiences related to east-west co-creation online is complex and fraught with challenges. It is widely acknowledged that cultural factors present significant challenges to effective learning and teaching in online contexts. Visual, auditory and environmental cues to communication and understanding are known to diminish in digital environments, even amongst students from the same cultural backgrounds. In Confucian Heritage Culture (CHC) contexts educational paradigms are usually more teacher-centered than western learning and teaching models further compounding the issues educators face. Historically, western styles of education have attracted significant suspicion within eastern contexts as an inappropriate challenge to educational traditions (Zhang 2007; Ziguras 2001). An effective, if superficial analogy, might be drawn related to the perceived (and rightly challenged) notion of 'east' and 'west' as a dichotomy representing student-centered (western) and teacher-centered (CHC) learning modes. This context does not provide the scope to deconstruct the discourse of Orientalism (Said, 1978) but a dearth of contemporary literature regarding culture in relation to online modes of art and design education suggests strongly that little work using network technologies to foster intercultural co-creation online has occurred.

Theories about Culture

Many contemporary ideas about cultural differences are based on anthropologists Hall and Hall's theory (1990) of a continuum of cultural dimensions ranging from high context to low context. Asian cultures such as Japan and China tend to be high context cultures while western societies such as Germany, USA and Australia are low context cultures. In high-context cultures, everyone knows how to behave in a variety of situations without explicit instructions. In low context cultures people constantly negotiate to formulate ad-hoc solutions (Aoki, Aydın, 2006). Morse (2003, p. 51) asserted that in online courses, "integration of high context participants is made more difficult by technology differences as well as the communication norms implicit in their cultural background. Many online learning environments are typically low-context, particularly those that are text-based (Stirling, 2005). The other key cultural theory relevant to this study is Hofstede's (2001) notion of a range of five cultural dimensions: 1. Power distance; 2. Uncertainty avoidance; 3. "Individualism versus collectivism"; 4. "Masculinity vs. femininity"; 5. Long-term orientation, (Hofstede, 2001, p. 29).

Others have offered perspectives on the role of culture in online learning. Bonk and Kim (2002), and Bonk and Wisher (2000) acknowledged the role of culture in research examining, "collaborative learning to address student online construction of knowledge, social interactions, and critical thinking." Hewling (2005) asserted a model based on a "culture of doing". Kim, Kim, Park and Rice (2007) conducted a study into configurations of communication relationships in Korea through face-to-face, email, instant messaging, mobile phone, and SMS media.

Issues Associated with Language

English is recognized as a standard language for international communications - but this presents issues of understanding and communication across culture. Luna, Peracchio and de Juan (2002) and De Groot (1992) argue that a psycholinguistic framework known as "the conceptual feature model" (CFM) points to language as a cultural symbol whereby individuals use language to, "...express concepts and values embedded in culturally bound cognitive schemas". According to the CFM, words in each language activate a series of conceptual features. Features activated by a word in one language may not correspond to schemas activated by the same word in literal translations – even where the recipients are bilingual." Cognitive structures are therefore affected by cultural cues as well as language. However, as Cassell and Tversky (2005) have stated (2005), "The literature is particularly sparse on the topic of how language functions in cross-cultural communities online."

The Need for Further Research

Ziguras (2001) highlighted that, "Since its emergence in the late 1980s, trans-national higher education in South East Asia has commonly involved Western educators teaching offshore using educational approaches developed for local students with very little effort to tailor teaching for offshore students." The need for empirical research in this area has also been identified by academics working in the online education field (e.g. Kim & Bonk, 2002; Hewling, 2005; Hart & Freisner, 2004). Aoki and Aydın (2006) suggest different cultural groups respond well in learning environments that offer media corresponding to cultural mores, values and modes of understanding the world.

Research into cultural factors specifically impacting on online education to date has established that further work is essential as industry and education become more global. Chase, Macfadyen, Reeder and Roche (2002) suggest that, "Despite rapid advances in information and communications technology (ICT) approaches to networked learning, relatively little is known about actual experience in the field using these technologies to facilitate communications between individuals and groups from different cultural backgrounds."

The Collabor8 Project (C8) provides a vehicle for students, educators and industry from eastern and western cultural contexts to explore ways of working together by leveraging the potential of digital networks and tools. Since it's inception C8 has typically consisted of online lectures informing a brief, discussion forums and galleries allowing students to conceptualize individually and in groups, discuss and compare their ideas, and display concepts and outputs. The students are encouraged to collaborate across culture with the objective of finding new ways of working together using the network. Through its consideration of cultural dimensions and the challenges of working in different geographic locations C8 emulates, in an intensive mode, contemporary real-world practices across the global creative industries.

SETTING THE STAGE

C8 began as a small experimental project where students exchanged information and images via email and has developed through the use of Omnium Software™, a product of the Omnium Research Group at the University of New South Wales (UNSW), into a more sophisticated online platform. C8 has also collaborated with a diverse range of academic and industrial partners. The most recent iteration of C8 has involved working with influential Australian artist and architect Professor Richard Goodwin's Porosity Studio. The Porosity Studio was established by Goodwin in 1996 and has since successfully offered intensive studios in diverse locations around the world. The studio builds on Goodwin's practice and research providing a potential component of a student's major study in final years from a range of disciplines: Fine Art, Design, Media Studies, Architecture, Urban Design and Engineering. The impact of this collaboration has been significant in the integration of blended pedagogy into the C8 online model.

C8 is closely affiliated with COFA Online (COL) an academic unit (established 2003) at The College of Fine Arts (COFA), UNSW. COL is responsible for the development and management of thirty fully online undergraduate courses, and an online multidisciplinary postgraduate degree. In recent years COL developed blended undergraduate courses for implementation across the various schools within COFA. COL specializes in propagating online learning and teaching approaches offering students educational experiences that parallel evolving work practices in the creative industries. Teachers and students in it's courses are dispersed widely around the globe and as such recognition of the need to develop culturally sensitive approaches is high, as is acknowledgement that students should develop skill-sets that include cultural literacy.

To date universities and colleges in China and Australia participating in C8 have included Donghua University (DHU), Fudan University (SIVA), East China Normal University (ECNU), Jinan University School Of Applied Design, Shandong University Of Art & Design, Wuhan University, Beijing Institute of Technology, Beijing Communication University Of China, The University of Sydney, The University of Technology (UTS) and Raffles University. Involvement has ranged from small numbers of students participating in the projects through interest, to students enrolled formally into elective subjects. C8 continues to develop and invest in mutually beneficial relationships with a number of these universities. It is widely documented (Deng 2004; Ngor 2001; Wang 2007) that online education in China is seen as a potential panacea for the significant challenges that the government faces in meeting the demand for education most particularly across the central and western regions of the country. Art and design education is also seen as a high priority.

Now the central government is developing a design policy to help China move beyond a manufacturing economy and forward in implementing cross-disciplinary education and bridging left- and right-brained thinking. As in other sectors, schools are beginning to train a new wave of design managers "with Chinese characteristics" who can apply design thinking in a context that fits China's commercial and political landscape. (Wong, V., (2009))

Industry involvement is crucial in the C8 methodology. The project has attracted involvement from innovators across multidisciplinary practice. Amongst others, IDEO (Shanghai), Map Studio (Hong Kong), Moving Cities (Beijing), De-Luxe & Associates (Sydney), Innovation Lab (Copenhagen), Futurebrand (Australia) have all contributed content or acted as mentors to students.

CASE DESCRIPTION

Overview

This case description refers to iterations of C8 conducted during 2008 and 2009. Both projects are underpinned by a research agenda designed to develop effective strategies for successfully implementing cross-cultural art and design pedagogy online and developing real and mutually beneficial relationships at student, teacher and institutional levels. A range of processes, the primary issues faced, and the lessons learnt are discussed. Opportunities for future research and development are also highlighted.

1. C8 2008: A Fully Online Cross-Cultural Collaboration

In 2008, C8 attracted ninety-four Visual Communications and Graphic Design students from nine universities across Australia and China to participate in a fully online project for eight weeks. Awareness of the project was created by a series of lectures in Shanghai, Beijing and Sydney and accompanying online promotion. Twenty-six academics and practitioners worked as lecturers and mentors. The research aims underpinning the project were specifically to:

- Examine the impact of cultural background on the effectiveness of the online learning experience by determining cultural preferences and tendencies regarding the use of media.
- Identify which media are more effective in improving student cognition of course materials across cultures.
- Propose key considerations for design of online course content in regard to media for cross-cultural delivery.

C8 2008 used a pedagogic approach adapted from a model for Online Collaborative Creativity (OCC) by Omnium founder Rick Bennett (2007) comprised of five phases: (1) Access and Socialization; (2) Gathering; (3) Identifying; (4) Distilling and Abstracting (5) Resolving. Each phase contained a brief that contributed to a final collaborative project outcome. The Omnium Software™ used in the project provides digital tools for online discussion, collaborative team areas, downloadable resources, live chat, galleries, links, and file sharing.

Lectures were provided in a range of media formats including PowerPoint, audio podcast, video, text and image, PDF and HTML. The student were placed in twelve teams and encouraged to respond to creative briefs requiring either individual or group responses that were released at the beginning of each phase using a range of media. The initial focus of interactions was on information sharing about Chinese and Australian culture through text and image. Immediately it became apparent that, in the words of one Mainland Chinese participant, "…there are some culture difference, some people are not used to post their profile online…" The Australian students tended to be more forthcoming in posting profile information. This has proved to be the case in each C8 project.

In week 3 of the project, on May 12 2008, the devastating Sichuan Earthquake occurred significantly impacting the behavior and focus of most C8 students in Mainland China, and altering the direction and nature of the project. The brief was subsequently augmented so students had the opportunity (as an option) to develop design solutions addressing the human need that had arisen so dramatically. This reflexive strategy was successful with several teams beginning to research, brainstorm and identify potential earthquake related design solutions.

Post-earthquake activity from the students located in China however subsided noticeably. Some Chinese lecturers working with students in the project set alternative projects related to the emergency. Students in Australia at this point experienced confusion because Mainland Chinese students in their teams were not responding to their communications to them. They felt this limited the opportunity to collaborate, something they saw as integral to the project. In effect the 'silence' was difficult for them to understand and assimilate. However, data collected regarding number of daily logins to the website (see Fig. 1 & 2) indicated significant numbers of students from Mainland China continued to log in but not actively, or visibly participate by posting, suggesting that other forces were impacting on the process.

The project concluded with a range of interesting products exhibiting differing levels of cross-cultural collaboration being developed. The final outcomes must be acknowledged as *both* individual and collaborative. One team was particularly successful in producing a concept for a post-earthquake school facility. In some instances collaboration was between students in Mainland China working with students located in Australia. In other projects collaboration was between students based in Australia only. Where students found they were not able to collaborate, the work posted reflects an individual effort.

Data was collected over the eight-week period and triangulated through observation of behavioral indicators (quality of engagement, participation, use of media types and levels of collaborative interaction), student interviews, and integration of targeted research questions into discussion points. An online questionnaire gathered qualitative and quantitative responses to questions on aspects of cultural background, cross-cultural design education; levels of cognition and participation; accessibility; preferences for media used in C8; aspects of collaboration in C8; and general feedback.

Corresponding with studies by Doctoroff (2007) that demonstrate Chinese youths experience the web more intensely than their western peers, the findings related to the research aims indicated that Australian respondents were more ambivalent toward the media used to present content. In contrast CHC students were more decisive in their preferences for particular media types than their Australian counterparts. For Chinese students, image files and PDF documents were most popular followed closely by web-based material. Text files were the least favored by this group. Text and image files were preferred by students in Australia followed by, web media. Audio was more popular in China but both groups were equally ambivalent towards video as a delivery format due to the accessibility issues inherent in large file downloads. Media was found to be a significant factor, however it is only part of a more complex picture.

Anecdotal reports from Australian students suggested that informally, and outside the C8 interface, levels of communication between Chinese and Australian students using MSN were much higher and more frequent than inside C8 itself. This 'back channel' – outside C8, became a means for students to communicate, form friendships and discuss the project. The immediacy of 'chat' appeared to be conducive to higher levels of communication.

Unsurprisingly, the role of lecturers within each cultural context proved a critical factor. Our findings suggested that successful online collaboration between Western and CHC students may be achieved only if Eastern and Western academics recognise its importance and can collaborate themselves to develop a pedagogy representative of all relevant cultural inputs. If online content can be presented to students using their own language and delivered in a way that is consistent with their culturally derived experiences of learning environments, it is likely they will subsequently have a stronger basis for collaborating with others. Educational designers must be cognisant of the cultural implications inherent in teacher and student expectations of what learning is, and respond using appropriate, *inclusive methodologies* if cross-cultural collaboration between east and west is the objective. This cultural adaptivity implies:

- Collaborative involvement from lecturer's representative of the cultures involved.
- Content presented to students in their own language.
- Processes that acknowledge culturally based student expectations of learning environments and different styles of knowledge production.

Overall, the need to establish *common ground* where collaboration and intercultural cooperation might occur online was emphasized. This in turn prompted questions of how we might identify and deconstruct difference through finding similarity in shared understandings and experiences.

2. PorosityC8 2009: Blended Cross-Cultural Collaboration

Collaboration with Professor Goodwin's Porosity Studio in 2009 pushed C8 into new territory. The outcomes of C8 2008 identified the need for identifying strategies that would enable greater levels of involvement from academics and institutions in China. After a series of meetings in Shanghai the project was scheduled and the decision taken to involve four lecturers from Donghua and four lecturers from COFA representing a range of disciplines from each school – Digital Media, Design, Sculpture, Environments, Product Design and Visual Communication. Through the integration of Porosity's multidisciplinary studio component, an important opportunity for making comparisons between the effectiveness of a fully online collaboration, and what might be achieved between students who meet in the 'real' world as well as online was forged. Correspondingly, the collaboration represented an opportunity to extend Porosity Studio's vision further toward creative practice within hybrids of real and digital space. The aims of this project pertaining to online pedagogy included:

- Development of processes reflecting trends in creative practice through inclusive interaction between remote collaborators and students in an intensive studio.
- Stimulation of strategies promoting collaborative practice between cultural spaces both 'real' and digital.
- Integration of online technologies as armatures for conceptualization, communication and collaborative interaction and documentation of outputs.
- Development of deeper cooperation between Australian and CHC institutions and academics to develop culturally appropriate and adaptive pedagogy for online and blended collaboration.
- Provision of clearly defined opportunities for students to express and share cultural identity in blended environments where deeply embedded cultural norms are given due consideration.
- Establishment of adaptive pedagogy encompassing the student's expectations of educational contexts and their respective styles of knowledge production.

A specially developed bi-lingual version of Omnium Software™ was used as the primary delivery platform in concert with Twitter, Vimeo, Facebook, Google Translate and Google Maps which were used to promote, develop and distribute content and to influence collaborative activity.

Due to the differences in the structure, obligations and processes required by the collaboration between Porosity Studio and Collabor8 the process was conducted over a full 12-week semester for COFA students. Donghua University students engaged in the online process after returning from a semester break. In September 2009 after eight weeks of working together online, 25 students and five staff from COFA travelled to Shanghai to engage in a two-week long intensive blended studio with a similar number of students and lecturers from Donghua University. The project was self-funded by students, research grants and in-kind support made available from both universities.

The first week of the Shanghai studio contained a series of face-to-face lectures and workshops by high profile academics, artists and architects. The workshops focused on conceptual development and finding collaborators through small group work with tutors and mentors. Lectures in video format, images documenting studio activity, and other supporting video material were uploaded to the project website regularly for remote students to review. The focus of the second week was on realizing the collaborative projects and the staging of an exhibition of the work produced.

Students were initially required to make two preliminary presentations. The first presentation was a Petcha Kutcha-style self-introduction, and the second outlined their individual thinking in response to the studio brief. Collaboration was encouraged in accordance with the kinds of concepts students developed rather than directly placing students in teams and compelling them to work together. The distinction between teamwork and collaboration was clearly stated. A number of students worked remotely from Sydney and explored how they might engage with the studio remotely using information, images, video content and student presentations regularly posted to the web. They were encouraged to collaborate remotely, to hijack projects occurring in the studio or to develop their own solutions to the brief as a group or as individuals.

Supported by a program of appropriately considered lecture content highlighting similarity over culturally specific differences and a studio workshop led by designers from global design agency IDEO brainstorming solutions to the issues of cross-cultural collaboration, most students in the studio opted to collaborate. The significantly higher levels of cross-cultural collaboration achieved during this process can at least in part be attributed to a strategy more reflective of pure collaboration where each participant brings their own content, skills, interests and ideas to the relationship rather than be forced into a potentially incompatible partnership.

The preliminary outcomes documented confirm that students from COFA were significantly more active and 'vocal' in their use of the online medium as a channel for communication. Their comfort in using discussion to share ideas and information, and to disclose information about themselves and their processes, is in marked contrast to students from Donghua. Notwithstanding this very apparent difference, students from Donghua were also active, consistently sending emails to the lecturers requesting clarifications and assistance and logging on to the project website frequently as the project progressed to review the material posted. Interviews with students from Donghua revealed that they perceived the website not as a site for discussion but rather as a suite of learning resources to be studied. This differing use of the project website by each group of students reflects our understandings of differences in pedagogy inherent in each culture and supports the notion of boundary objects (Star, and Griesemer 1989) arising out of the interactions of different communities of practice – in this case the respective groups of students each from a different cultural context.

The project concluded with a successful exhibition and all students and teachers from both universities expressing high levels of satisfaction with the outcomes. The subsequent activity on the project website has seen a significantly higher level of visible activity from students at Donghua University who have continued to post comments and images related the work carried out in the studio. In the weeks following the intensive studio the online component of the project was used to reflect and document the process and the outcomes achieved as well as the social interaction that occurred. An exhibition is scheduled in Sydney showcasing re-contextualized work from the project and a book will be published in mid-2010. At the level of the institutions and academics involved a stronger relationship was forged in working together. The shared input of resources and co-operation between lecturers and administrators was at a higher level than in any previous C8 related project. This mutual investment in the project to ensure its success forms a stronger basis for ongoing development of future projects in both online and blended modes.

Language

In China C8 has been seen by teachers and students as an opportunity to practice written and verbal communication in English. Throughout both projects, translation assistance was available to all students. Rather than not communicate, students in China were encouraged to express themselves in their own language. The extent to which language differences were a factor in levels of cognition, interactions and collaborations between participants in both C8 projects was initially ambiguous. There are a range of considerations and experiences related to the language abilities of individuals.

Participant (Donghua 2009): *Language and culture is no barrier – it's the level of people – in many cases I have less communication with my friends and family but doing this I am very happy - this is the most interesting and happy course during my university life…*

Participant (COFA 2009): *It's an issue but I think it is also an issue if you speak the same language, you get almost more miscommunications in your own language. And I always think you can express yourself a lot with movement and emotions – we use actually way too many words – if you go back to the beginning when we started it was just ooh and aahh...you don't need so many words...and because there is so much space in way you communicate here you can only smile at the end and you become really happy – because its actually really funny and there is no judgment or expectation...*

Participant (COFA 2009): *A lot of the burden of communicating the ideas lies very strongly on one half of our relationships...we have to work so hard to communicate and things come from that...*

Research into the role of language and communication within cross-cultural online communities is lacking. Even where participants in a community are bilingual the specific meanings of words (especially terminology) may be unclear (Cassell & Tversky, 2005). Cognitive structures are affected by cultural cues as well as language and this is likely to impact students' ability to collaborate despite bilingual ability. Even with translation support both online and in the studio, many students suggested that language was the number one impediment to their work together. Conversational English was not generally a problem but discipline specific communication and terminology along with the expression of abstract ideas was cited as a significant challenge. It is clear however that Chinese students possess much higher levels of bilingual ability than their most of their Australian peers.

In 2008 a Shanghai-based academic commented via email that the real language challenge in C8 was not to the students, but to their teachers, who found the level of English difficult. This is very significant within a teacher-centered CHC context. The inability of western teachers in C8 to communicate effectively in Chinese was equally a limiting factor foregrounding the need for effective accessible translation.

Culturally Based Expectations of Learning Environments

The nature of pedagogy in C8 is open-ended and flexible, acknowledging that project-based approaches encouraging discovery, divergence and reflection are most appropriate for teaching design thinking. Within C8 2008 students from Australian backgrounds, and to a potentially lesser extent Chinese students being educated in Australia, the creative brief and the format of lectures was familiar in that they understood they should engage with the problem in a manner which required them to find a solution through research, discussion, brainstorming and other creative thinking strategies. At the end of C8 2008 it was not clear if there was a perception in China that the process had imposed an overly Western mode of learning and teaching, however this online chat with a participant in Shanghai (C8 2008) suggests this is a possibility...

Participant (Shanghai): *we do not have the space to be ourselves as chinese*

IM: *in C8?*

Participant (Shanghai): *no, i mean always in our really life*

Participant (Shanghai): *so chinese students get lost in C8*

IM: *so how to make them see they can have that space in there IM:?*

IM: *that may be very important*

IM: *as it is a deep cultural thing*

Participant (Shanghai): *like what i said, give them a story, design a situation for them, give them a boundary*

Participant (Shanghai): *you might think it's weird*

Participant (Shanghai): *but boundary is a good way to give space*

Participant (Shanghai): *ppl need that*

Participant (Shanghai): *now they lost in air... no earth, no sky, nothing to hold*

Participant (Shanghai): *it's normal for western ppl,*

Participant (Shanghai): *but for us, i think it's not really comfortable (Transcript from online chat, McArthur, I., (2008))*

This exchange can be contrasted with the response of a Donghua student in 2009 when asked what he had learned in the blended studio.

Participant (Donghua 2009): *"The (western) teachers give me space to let me think... they don't tell me what I must do ...they just give me some suggestions to make my project better...a lot of Chinese students usually follow their teacher's thinking... the teachers said what they must do...(the western professors) they don't tell me what I must do but they give me some useful suggestions to improve my project – they let me think about my project...I think it is the most important thing I learnt."*

Pedagogy, learning styles and cognition are thus highlighted as issues and remind us to consider more closely the educational environments students in China and Australia are accustomed to. Although referring specifically to face-to-face contexts it has been well documented that,

"In China, students have most of their classes in the form of lectures rather than discussions... They may participate quite actively mentally, but not with their mouths. Most Western teachers expect students to show their participation with their mouths, or at least with body language. Even in lectures there is often time left for discussion. This is one of the cultural differences." (Amity Teachers Program Handbook, How to be an effective teacher in China: A Chinese teacher's insight, Prof. Sun Yunzhong (Nanjing University of Traditional Chinese Medicine), November 1996 http://www.amityfoundation.org/page.php?page=512)

Evidence supporting the notion that this 'active silence' (McArthur, 2008) on the part of the students in China might translate into the online context is found in data collected from both projects indicating significant numbers of students from China log into and spend time on the website but do not actively or visibly participate. This may not ultimately be the problem it might first seem to the western educator. Zembylas & Vrasidas (2007) suggest that silence is an aspect of online interactions not yet well researched. Within C8, silence is now seen as evidence of the use of the web interface as a boundary object where the interface is perceived and used by the students from each country in different ways. It was noted in the blended studio that the Donghua students and teachers referred to the website as "the resources". This can be contrasted with the use of the asynchronous aspects of the website by COFA students and staff as a tool for dialogue. Data gathered in 2009 indicated that, as in 2008, Chinese students regularly visited the site but little discussion or visible use of the site was recorded prior to the studio. Donghua students became more active online only after actually meeting and working with the COFA students in the studio.

SOLUTIONS AND RECOMMENDATIONS

Fully Online vs. Blended Modes

Within C8 the higher levels of cross-cultural co-creation achieved using the blended model suggest that the fully online delivery format is less effective in generating the profound human connection and interactions needed to produce exceptional work. This reflects the nature of collaboration in industry contexts, as remote processes often start with, or at some point include, face-to-face meetings with counterparts, partners and colleagues that establish a stronger connection between the parties concerned. This is evident in comparisons between the level of collaborative interaction, mutual cultural understanding and real friendships occurring in C8 2008 and PorosityC8 2009 and implies that blended delivery offers significant opportunities for more effective collaborative learning online between different cultural groups.

Language Resources

Despite some assertions to the contrary in both projects, in most instances of collaboration between eastern and western students and faculty, language is a major consideration. Although many Chinese students learn English and have good levels of conversational English, the realities of articulating complex concepts and the specific terminology associated with creative disciplines become difficult and time consuming.

Participant (Donghua 2009): *There are some difficulties in our talking – maybe it wastes a lot of time...*

This is compounded by the inability of most teachers we have worked with (including ourselves) to converse bilingually to any great depth. In CHC contexts this intersects with trust, teaching styles and issues of institutional support. Translation as a form of scaffolding is therefore a major benefit in ensuring all parties understand what is happening. Online text should as far as possible be bilingual and in blended modes lectures must be supported by translators. It is important to budget for this in preparation for such projects.

Establish Trust through Institutional Relationships

After C8 2008 it became very clear that further progression of the C8 methodology relied on establishing more focused and formal long-term relationships and material support from the Chinese universities involved. By gaining institutional support for

C8, ties between the universities are strengthened and more resources able to be elicited via research funding and other administrative mechanisms further ensuring the viability of the process. Great care must be taken to enhance the mutually beneficial nature of the project. It is important to note that the foundations of trust important to such formal relationships can be developed over time in less formal activities that demonstrate commitment to a particular concept – in this case cross-cultural collaboration in art and design between east and west. Where the level of institutional acknowledgement and support is higher, the subsequent involvement of relevant faculties has resulted in more positive results. In the successive C8 projects to date the level of institutional engagement has increased steadily proving to be crucial to successful implementation of the project but challenging to achieve.

Formal engagement with Chinese universities has become from the author's perspective and experience perhaps the single most crucial aspect that can ensure the process of collaboration can actually happen. It may seem obvious to suggest that the development of strong institutional links is a prerequisite for transnational cross-cultural collaborations. However innovations such as C8 are very often the result of teacher led initiatives at grass-roots level. This is certainly the case in relation to C8. It is one thing to establish a teacher-led initiative funded by research grants and work with interested teachers (the origins of C8), but success in a CHC educational context relies heavily on such support due to the teacher-centered nature of classroom interactions. Whereas in a western university a student may engage with projects relevant to their own study or research focus with relative autonomy, this is less the case in CHC contexts. Much of this constraint lies in culturally embedded pedagogical and institutional processes.

Additionally, given the academic world's perceptions of China as a giant education market there is some evidence of fatigue and frustration on the part of Chinese academics subject to ongoing deluge of interactions with western universities based on a subtext of establishing relationships in order to tap into the potential market for Chinese students studying abroad. This is compounded because many interactions between western and eastern academics prove to be fleeting or one-off. This can be attributed to the fact that CHC emphasize interpersonal norms where trust holds an especially significant status as a foundation on which relationships are built (Osland 1990; Wu, 1994). In this context trust development requires an investment of time not familiar to most westerners with many unwilling to engage in this activity (Thorelli, 1990). If due attention and time is invested in this area the interactions between students are more likely to be richer and more meaningful.

Multiple Realities

Throughout both projects, online discussions, responses to lectures, online chat, posts to galleries and other interactions both inside and outside the C8 interface increasingly reflected the range of participant profiles. The online discussion areas in particular make visible user experiences and responses distinguished by a diversity of cultures, student expectations of learning environments, experience of academia and industry practice, and level of study.

The overall assumption was initially that students, lecturers, mentors and industry guests would interact in these discussion spaces. Over time the actual transactions that occurred took on particular characteristics increasingly indicative of the particular user groups. These interactions highlight the existence of sub-communities identified by (among other attributes) the depth and amount of discussion and responses to events, or in contrast, by their relative silence. This pointed to the potential for complex multifaceted learning communities, in the words of one astute mentor during an online chat between students and teachers in 2008, "…to harbor multiple realities and have them positively interact with each other…". 'Reality' is not used here to denote the more philosophic associations of the term. Rather it should be seen as representative of cultural perspectives, values, experiences, circumstances, attitudes and understandings that in turn might shape, drive, or inhibit, interactions with others online.

The Boundary Object

The issues inherent in 'active silence' and 'multiple realities' reflect our assumptions about the ways students will perceive and use online tools to learn and to collaborate. In both projects described, students in Australia have used the online interface as a space in which to converse, discuss ideas, respond to talking points posted by lecturers and develop their profiles. In contrast students and lecturers in China have referred to the website as 'the resources', and have used them largely as a text for reference. Their discourse has been limited, but their activity has been consistent. This aligns both with well-documented evidence of resistance to dialogue on the part of Chinese students and notions of boundary objects (Star, & Griesemer, 1989).

Marick (2003) provides a clear definition of the circumstances in a learning community where boundary objects may emerge:

A community of interest can expect to face more communication problems than a community of practice.... Arias and Fischer (2000) write, "Fundamental challenges facing communities of interest are found in building a shared understanding of the task at hand (which often does not exist upfront, but is evolved incrementally and collaboratively...). Members of communities of interest need to learn to communicate with and learn from others who have a different perspective and perhaps a different vocabulary for describing their ideas. [They need to] establish a common ground and a shared understanding." (p.1)

Ellen Christiansen (2005, p. 3) argues that boundary objects cannot be designed. Her assertion that, "You can never predict use, hence designed structures must have an open end." resonates with the experiences to date in C8. This challenges any assumption students in China will interpret and use the online materials and tools provided in the same way that the community of students based in Australia will.

Appropriate Technologies

The appropriateness of particular online technological forms for the purpose of cross-cultural collaboration requires consideration. Responses from students highlight the difficulties experienced in navigating large amounts of text. Students in both projects alluded to the desirability of direct interaction through synchronous rather than asynchronous technologies. In C8 2008, MSN and other forms of instant chat were acknowledged as the site where most interactions took place – outside the project interface itself.

Participant (Sydney): *Although my team didn't work together on the final outcome (as far as I know) we did a lot of chatting about our ideas via msn and the chat function.*

Drag and drop facilities for image sharing, Skype-like VoIP communications and instant messaging echo real-world interactions and offer alternatives to dense textual information and reliance on asynchronous push-technologies requiring students to both 'consume' and generate content. The correspondence between live interaction the real classroom is clear. The potential is that respective communities of learners might use and interpret the learning environment in ways that are more likely to engender the requisite mutual empathy established in face-to-face encounters.

LESSONS LEARNED

Emphasize Pedagogy over Technology

COFA Online, Omnium Research and The Collabor8 Project actively promote approaches to online and blended learning emphasizing the development of strong pedagogy over the embrace of technology for its' own sake. It is essential that educators have a clear rationale for adopting online or blended modalities of educational delivery. Adoption of technologies should reflect and accommodate educational strategy rather than the inverse. A key early question might be whether online or blended methodologies are appropriate at all for the purposes of a particular project.

Where the educational experience is to be transnational or cross-cultural it is also essential that extensive research into the relative cultural dynamics pertaining to the groups involved. If at all possible it is highly advisable to involve a range of respected educators from each cultural group in the development of educational strategy. This is not always easy but it will certainly add to the potential for successful learning outcomes.

Develop Strategies to Address Language Differences

Development of a bilingual online interface is highly recommended. Where complex conceptual or discipline-specific jargon is to be used there are considerable language challenges to face. This is the case in both fully online and blended modes. Therefore serious consideration has to be given to the role and function of translation in both online and studio environments. This of course is dependent on the language abilities of students and staff that (in our experience) are almost always diverse in terms of capability.

Participant (Donghua 2009): *Translators are not necessary – we are all students studying design and art and we can understand each other well...sometimes translators cannot understand the meaning or the logic of art and design.*

In the case of China and Australia we have found that students from Chinese universities are the most bilingual participants in the projects. Australian students and staff and the Chinese lecturers are often not bilingual and need assistance to communicate verbally or in writing. Translation services are highly specialized and in many instances it is difficult to locate translators well versed in the terminology or conceptual underpinnings of a particular creative discipline. Translation services are also expensive and need to be well budgeted for.

Design for Diverse Student Expectations and Styles of Knowledge Production

Cultures as divergent as those of China and Australia are embodied in the microcosm of the classroom. Students are acculturated according to the dominant ethos of the institution and their expectations of learning are shaped by their experiences in the educational environment. In C8 these divergences have manifested themselves as multiple realities characterized by the cultural milieu of classroom, community and society. These learned responses appear to translate from the real into the digital and consequently classroom behaviors and interpretations of learning materials presented online are shaped accordingly. The notion of boundary objects fits this scenario and although the boundary object cannot be 'designed' as such it may be possible to create open-endedness that has the potential to cater to different learning styles and modalities of knowledge production. Assumptions about how students will learn and collaborate are often challenged by the realities that emerge. Openness and flexibility in accommodating this has become an increasingly central tenet of the C8 methodology.

Create the Possibility for Intensive Blended Studio Workshops

When we compare the levels of collaborative interaction and the quality of creative outputs realized in C8 2008 and Porosity C8 2009 it is evident that face-to-face studio interaction where issues related to culture and collaboration and potential solutions are brainstormed is a transformative experience for students resulting in profound learning experiences that lead to in the words of one Chinese student "fire" - meaning that the dynamic effect is powerful releasing creative synergies otherwise unavailable. Subsequent online interaction is likely to be greater being based in a mutually shared reality and experience. This in itself reflects the processes of industry where remote teams meet at various points in order to develop rapport and collegiality. Therefore communication challenges of online environments can be somewhat ameliorated by inclusion of face-to-face studios. By using this strategy mutual trust forms and higher levels of subsequent interaction occur online.

CURRENT, FUTURE, OR RELATED CHALLENGES

To the foreigner Chinese culture is, despite the plethora of rhetorical and confidently expressed theory, hyperbole and "knowledge", mystery shrouded in the clouds of Confucianism, orientalism, post-colonialism. Directly engaging with CHC is an ambiguous undertaking not familiar or comfortable to most western minds. In many senses as suggested by Kishar Mahbubani we are limited by own heritage as westerners.

The Western mind is a huge world, but even in that huge world, you are actually trapped in a mental box. For those who live in the West, you assume that you can understand the world just by looking at it through Western perspectives, which gives you gives you a limited view of the world. (Kishore Mahbubani (2004), Retrieved August 29 2009 from http://www.cceia.org/resources/transcripts/123.html)

However, as Mahbubani asserts, we do need a fusion of civilizations not a clash of civilizations if we are to survive as a species. It is young artists and designers from east and west who might lead the way by presenting new ways to see the world making the objective of creating such fusions through education a highly attractive objective. Underpinned by a shifting globalized landscape the contemporary paradigm presents creative practitioners with immense challenges and opportunities. Graduates require a skill-set enabling them to operate effectively in this environment. It is clear however that the long-term objective of developing an adaptive pedagogy able to be applied in a consistent and reliable manner in cross-cultural collaborative art and design practice is still some way off.

Key challenges remain even in the convincing of funding bodies, institutions and colleagues that to pursue such 'ambitious' plans is viable or worthwhile. The securing of ongoing support at local level for projects that innovate and form trans-national relationships, but face funding challenges, is a high priority. The outcomes emerging from the blended studio in 2009 are re-orientating the agenda of this research significantly. C8 is currently working to accommodate a wider range of academic inputs at institutional level with university partners in China and Europe to further establish a formal basis upon which to launch more focused collaborative and technological inputs reflecting the findings and experiences of lecturers and students in the project to date.

The increasing availability of new and more flexible technologies both synchronous and asynchronous is opening up considerable potential for innovative educational approaches that reflect the realities of contemporary multidisciplinary practice. When wielded with sensitivity, culturally adaptive pedagogies based around technological interactions and collaboration present the possibility to open up opportunities for students, educators and institutions to transcend our differences and find our similarities to further enable the development of creative solutions to the issues we face as a planet. The lessons learnt to date in the evolution of C8 present convincing arguments that this is the case. There is however much more to be done.

REFERENCES

Bateson, G. (2002). *Mind and nature. A necessary unity.* New Jersey: Hampton Press.

Bennett, R. (2007). *Omnium five-stage process for online collaborative creativity (OCC).* Omnium Research Group. Retrieved August 28, 2008, from http://www.omnium.net.au/research

Buchanan, R. (2004). Human-centered design: Changing perspectives on design education in the East and West. *Design Issues*, *20*(1), 30–39. doi:10.1162/074793604772933748

Cassell, J., & Tversky, D. (2005). The language of online intercultural community formation. *Journal of Computer-Mediated Communication, 10*(2). Retrieved September 12, 2007, from http://jcmc.indiana.edu/vol10/issue2/cassell.html

Christiansen, E. (2005). *Boundary objects, please rise! On the role of boundary objects in distributed collaboration and how to design for them*. Retrieved September 2, 2009, from http://redesignresearch.com/chi05/EC%20Boundary%20Objects.pdf

Deng, Y. (2004). Network-based distance education in Chinese universities. *The UKEU reports*. UK eUniversities Worldwide Limited. Retrieved June 27, 2007 from http://www.matic-media.co.uk/ukeu/UKEU-r04-china-2005.doc

DiPaola, S., Dorosh, D., & Brandt, G. (2004). *Ratava's line: Emergent learning and design using collaborative virtual worlds*. Retrieved October 22, 2007, from http://www.digitalspace.com/papers/sig2004-paper-ratava/index.html

Doctoroff, T. (2007). *Young digital mavens*. Beijing: IAC-JWT Worldwide.

Mackie, C., Macfadyen, L., Reeder, K., & Roche, J. (2002). Inter-cultural challenges in networked learning: Hard technologies meet soft skills. *First Monday, 7*(8). Retrieved September 12, 2007, from http://firstmonday.org/issues/issue7_8/chase/index.html

Mahbubani, K., & Myers, J. J. (2004). *Can Asians think? Understanding the divide between East and West*. Carnegie Council for Ethics in International Affairs. Retrieved August 29, 2009, from http://www.cceia.org/resources/transcripts/123.html

Marick, B. (2003). *Boundary objects*. Retrieved September 2, 2009, from http://citeseerx.ist.psu.edu/viewdoc/download?doi=10.1.1.110.3934&rep=rep1&type=pdf

McArthur, I. (2008). *East-West collaboration in online education*. Conference Proceedings, DesignEd 2008, 9-10 Dec 2008. School of Design, Hong Kong Polytechnic University.

McArthur, I., McIntyre, S., & Watson, K. (2007). *Preparing students for the global workplace: An examination of collaborative online learning approaches*. ConnectEd Conference Proceedings. The University of New South Wales, Australia.

Ngor, A. (2001). The prospects for using the Internet in collaborative design education with China. *Higher Education*, *42*, 47–60. doi:10.1023/A:1017529624762

Osland, G. E. (1990). Doing business in China: A framework for cross-cultural understanding. *Marketing Intelligence & Planning*, *8*(4), 4–14. doi:10.1108/02634509010141194

PorosityC8. (2009). e-SCAPE studio. Retrieved August 28, 2009, from http://porosity.c8.omnium.net.au/outline/

Said, E. (1978). *Orientalism*. New York, NY: Pantheon.

Star, S. L., & Griesemer, J. R. (1989). Institutional ecology, translations and boundary objects: Amateurs and professionals in Berkeley's Museum of Vertebrate Zoology, 1907-39. *Social Studies of Science*, *19*, 387–420. doi:10.1177/030631289019003001

Wang, Q. (2007). Evaluation of online courses developed in China. *The Asian Journal of Distance Education*, *5*(2), 4–12.

Waves, C. - Collabor8. (2008). *Omnium research group*. Retrieved August 28, 2008, from http://creativewaves.omnium.net.au/c8/

Wong, V. (2009). China's new focus on design. *Business Week*. Retrieved October 9, 2009, from http://www.businessweek.com/

Wu, W. P. (1994). *Guanxi and its managerial implications for western firms in China: A case study*. Paper presented at the International Conference on Management Issues for China in the 1990s. University of Cambridge, UK.

Yunzhong, Y. (1996). How to be an effective teacher in China: A Chinese teacher's insight. In *Amity Teachers Program Handbook, Nanjing University of Traditional Chinese Medicine*. Retrieved June 21, 2003, from http://www.amityfoundation.org/page.php?page=512

Zembylas, M., & Vrasidas, C. (2007). Listening for silence in text-based, online encounters. *Distance Education*, *28*(1), 5–24. doi:10.1080/01587910701305285

Zhang, J. (2007). A cultural look at information and communication technologies in Eastern education. *Educational Technology Research and Development*, *55*(3), 301–314. doi:10.1007/s11423-007-9040-y

Ziguras, C. (2001). Education technology in trans-national higher education in South East Asia: The cultural politics of flexible learning. *Education Technology and Society, 4*(4). Retrieved September 12, 2007, from http://globalism.rmit.edu.au/publications/CZ_EducationalTechnology.pdf

KEY TERMS AND DEFINITIONS

Active Silence: Active Silence refers to the use of web resources by CHC students in ways that are not overtly visible. Typically this is represented by the consumption of learning resources but does not include activity such as posting, discussion or responding to the posts of others.

Boundary Object: Boundary objects are flexible interfaces/objects able to be adapted by the different groups who use them in ways that suit their own needs and understandings.

Blended: Educational approaches where the process is carried out both online and in face-to-face contexts. Both strategies are intended to compliment and support each other.

Collaboration: Unlike teamwork, which implies hierarchy collaboration is a process requiring individuals to bring their experience and ideas together to co-create.

Cross-Cultural: In the context of this text specifically refers to the interactions of students from different cultural backgrounds

Multidisciplinary: The cross-pollination of ideas and practices from different disciplines within the creative industries e.g. sculpture, architecture, design, digital arts

Multiple Realities: This term is used as representative of cultural perspectives, values, experiences, circumstances, attitudes and understandings that in turn might shape, drive, or inhibit, interactions with others online. Online groups form communities around such understandings.

This work was previously published in Cases on Globalized and Culturally Appropriate E-Learning: Challenges and Solutions, edited by Andrea Edmundson, pp. 187-206, copyright 2011 by Information Science Reference (an imprint of IGI Global).

Chapter 3
Chinese Postgraduate Students Learning Online in New Zealand: Perceptions of Cultural Impact

Yan Cong
University Of Waikato, New Zealand

Kerry Earl
University Of Waikato, New Zealand

EXECUTIVE SUMMARY

Based on the two fully online papers making up a Postgraduate Certificate in e-education (University of Waikato, New Zealand), this study researched Chinese students' perceptions of the impact of their culture on their online learning. The key questions were:

- *What are Chinese students' understandings of online learning?*
- *What are their perceptions of whether Chinese culture has impacts on their online learning?*
- *What are these students' recommendations to eTeachers and other Chinese students about eTeaching and eLearning?*

Findings presented explore the Chinese cultural influence, aspects of instructional design that supported learning and achievement, and the influence of the culture in which they were learning. Lessons for the teaching staff, learning design staff and others involved in online learning for students of other cultures are outlined.

DOI: 10.4018/978-1-4666-1885-5.ch003

ORGANIZATION OR SITUATION BACKGROUND

The School of Education at the University of Waikato focuses on pre-service and in-service professional development and accreditation of teachers. The University of Waikato was the first in New Zealand to connect to the Internet in 1989 and the School of Education has been offering undergraduate and graduate programs online since 1996. At the time the Post Graduate Certificate in eEducation was developed, the university had a key strategy of "leadership in e-learning". This was designed "to assist educators to explore eEducation research and development and plan, develop and evaluate online learning" (School of Education, 2002, p.1). It was introduced in 2003. The certificate was designed to provide opportunities for teachers at all levels (in universities, polytechnics, primary & secondary teachers and industry training organizations), and others in relevant roles (such as librarians and instructional designers), to "examine the potential of this medium and investigate and upskill themselves in its use" (School of Education, 2002, p.1). The program has a focus on preparing these people to work in online environments "utilizing the potential of information communication technologies to create effective eLearning opportunities"(School of Education, 2002, p.1).

The Post Graduate Certificate Programme consists of two 500 level papers. The first, PROF521A (NET) *eEducation Research and Development*, emphasizes current research and development of eEducation, and the second, PROF522B (NET) *The Professional Practice of eTeaching*, focuses on the professional practice of eTeachers. Both papers are compulsory for the certificate and both are taught entirely online. In the eEducation Research and Development paper, students explore the history of distance education, open learning, and flexible and mixed modes of teaching or delivery. Examining the research and literature in this field, students consider the context of eEducation in New Zealand and internationally, and orientate their own personal and professional experiences to this field. Students critically examine the rhetoric, trends and challenges for all levels; teachers, students, parents, school leaders, managers, commercial interests, policy makers and government. This paper looks at an historical perspective on eEducation, themes and trends, the role of eEducation in the current learning landscape, and the challenges facing institutions.

In the second paper, The Professional Practice of Teaching, the emphasis is on aspects of professional teaching practice in online environments, reviewing research and literature on pedagogy, instructional design, issues, and trends to identify what is good practice when teaching online. Specifically, this paper looks at needs and opportunities of online environments, planning and preparation for teaching, good practice and evaluating online environments. Students develop confidence in learning in an online environment and understand the challenges and choices that face eTeachers.

This program has been running since 2003 and has attracted a diverse group of students including foreign students from a range of Asian-Pacific nations, New Zealand teachers currently working overseas but looking to return to New Zealand, teachers looking for learning to support their moves to increased responsibility and senior management, librarians in tertiary institutions, lecturers in tertiary institutions, and IT and technology specialists looking to be more involved in training. However, at the time of this study there were also a number of Chinese students from Hebei Province on a professional development program for teachers arranged between local Chinese Government and School of Education, University of Waikato. These students were very interested in eEducation because some were secondary and high school teachers and university tutors. Their purpose in taking on online paper studies, particularly these two papers, was to obtain knowledge of eEducation and experience so that they could apply this to their future teaching as well as enhancing Chinese education professional development on their return to China (Organizing Committee of China International Distance Education, 2007). The Chinese government's needs for developing eLearning and eTeaching may be considered as a main reason why these participants chose to undertake this programme in New Zealand.

The rapid growth in Internet use and telecommunications in China is powered in part by China's economic boom. The latest report from Chinese Ministry of Industry and Information showed that the Internet population in China had reached 221 million by the end of February in 2008 (Xinhua, 2008, para.1). China Mobile has become the world's first mobile operator to pass the half a billion subscriber milestone. In a brief customer update on its website, the Chinese market-leader said it had reached 503 million customers by the end of August. It added 5.3 million customers (net additions) in August (China Mobile Limited, 2009). From these statistical reports, it can be expected that China could probably become a huge online learning market, and also has great potential in online learning and teaching development, which perhaps will create a strong need for online teachers and professionals. According to the invitation from the Organizing committee of China International Distance Education Conference (2007), online education in China is developing rapidly under its promotion by the government. The scale of online education of ordinary universities and colleges expands continuously and has become the mainstream for adult and continuing education. Many enterprises introduce eLearning, and more and more of them set up their own corporation university.

SETTING THE STAGE

New Zealand is a western capitalist society. Ideals in this society revolve around egalitarianism, equal access and opportunity, and individualism (O'Neill & O'Neill,

2007). Although a generalization, the role of Teachers in New Zealand is increasingly seen as being a facilitator, moderator, organizer, counselor, coach, supervisor, and problem solver. The key role for Teachers is to engage students and help them to construct knowledge from the combination of prior knowledge and new learning rather than content delivery or transmission. The learner-centred approach is an important teaching pedagogy. The main principle of this approach is that students discover and construct knowledge through active participation and the effective interactions rather than receiving knowledge passively. To tailor to students' different interests, abilities, and needs is stressed in the learner-centred approach (Cong, 2008).

The development of the Postgraduate Certificate in eEducation, University of Waikato, and the design of the two papers was lead by Nola Campbell (1946-2005). Campbell believed that "it is not possible to take a traditional course and 'put it on line' and expect the transition for teachers or students to be smooth without consideration of pedagogical, organizational and institutional issues" (1998, p. 11).

However, Campbell also believed in the similarities of good teaching practice across formats (face-to-face or online). Pallof and Pratt (1999) described the implementation of successful online education as "a process of taking our very best practices in the classroom and bringing them into the new [online] arena even though the practices might not look exactly the same" (p. 6). The focus for teachers working online would not be on technological skills and competencies but the relational aspects of teaching and learning, the quality of the content (Peters, 1999), and the level of interaction (Berge, 2000; Harasim, 2000). Campbell believed that "reflective, effective teaching is something possible regardless of time, place or geographical location" (Campbell, 2003, p.12). To be successful as an online teacher, she summarized what you need as being a positive attitude, a desire to be an active agent of change and, as Toffler (1991) discussed, to be able to "learn, unlearn and relearn" including modes of teaching.

The design of the Post Graduate Certificate in eEducation was based on the following learning design principles:

- To teach confidently and effectively, online teachers benefit from the opportunity to be immersed in quality online learning and teaching experiences as learners
- Students need support to be comfortable and develop confidence in what it takes to be a successful online learner
- The presence of the teacher through their visibility in the online class is very important for student engagement and retention
- Learning takes place through discussion, and asynchronous discussion allows students the greatest opportunity to participate

- Working online takes a great degree of time management, so dividing study and assignment work into smaller sections supports student success.
- It is important to give students opportunities to contribute and exercise choice to maximize individual learning
- Teachers working online need to work smarter not harder

Students' Need for Support

Students' need for support begins with getting started. The importance of students starting the paper prepared and with a degree of confidence was addressed by both PROF521 and PROF522 being open for students to explore and post their first post (an introduction) two weeks before the official start of the paper. The teacher also put in an introduction as a model. There was a welcome letter posted by mail in advance with instructions on how to access the learning management system, and class space, and how to work through the online module guide to using this system. There was also a frequently asked question and answer section in anticipation of expected student questions from those studying online for the first time. Allowing this extra time for students helped overcome any initial technical or enrollment issues and to familiarize themselves with the environment, the paper content and expectations, structure and how to contribute supports students in starting off promptly on the first day of class.

This support continued with the posting of a weekly notice to outline for students the focus and activities they should be undertaking for the week. This notice used a template that made it easy for the teacher to finalize for posting each week and was:

- A signal of teacher presence and leadership
- A support to ensure expectations were clear
- A support for student's time management

Other features included to support online students in these papers were:

- The teaching staff took time to plan ahead and think paper through carefully. All information and material students needed to complete the papers was provided upfront from the start of the paper. This material needs to be proof read carefully especially for consistency throughout the material of deadline dates for assignments. Students can quickly loose confidence and trust if confused
- Both class business areas in open forum and individual one-to-one space were used. If asked a question privately that would benefit the class then the teacher posted the question and answer in the general area, editing as appropriate

- Information areas were kept separate from discussion or activity areas for clarity and to cue and meet student expectations
- Students were encouraged to keep communication with teachers about the paper areas (and out of individual teacher's email inboxes). This kept records of student-teacher interaction within the forum, accessible by other teachers and for later reference by teachers and students

Teacher Presence

An online teacher needs to work to make him/herself visible online. The visible presence of the teacher is enhanced through such posts as weekly notices and news items, responding to general and individual questions and regular posts to discussions. An appropriate level of teacher participation allows monitoring of discussion, often catching distractions, misunderstandings or confrontational messages early enough to redirect and refocus student contributions. This visibility also provides a good role model in terms of regularity of participation and nature and content of posts (tone, length, focus).

Translating normally non-verbal feedback into a visual presence can be helped through timeliness of feedback. The use of templates helped the teacher with timeliness of feedback, assignment marking and workload management.

It is also very important for teachers to be explicit about when students can expect them to be online. It was the policy in these papers that teachers let the class know if they would be absent for longer than 24 hours for any reason.

Discussion Participation

The teachers in this course believed that learning takes place through discussion and in the value of class discussion for developing knowledge and understanding (drawing on prior knowledge and experiences, posing and responding to questions, considering implications for self and other stakeholders and demonstrating skills). An asynchronous format was chosen.

Asynchronous discussion allows greater flexibility for both teachers and students to fit participation around other commitments and make time when it suits them and from a place that suits them. Because the discussion format was asynchronous, the students had time to consider, read and reread others' posts, reflect and draft, edit and proof read their own post, and have a greater voice in this setting. For each student, there is less dependence on ability with and/or confidence with English language, a factor that was very important for the varied population of the students enrolled in this certificate, particularly the number of Hebei students whose experience is the basis of this study.

Each paper was split into 4 modules of 3 weeks duration. For each module there were two discussions of 1½ weeks in length. The class was divided into groups of 12-14 participants (with participant access), and each group was also able to read the contributions in other groups' discussions (read-only access). Attached to contribution posts were photographs of learners and teachers. These were stamp-sized photographs attached alongside the text. These photos are the students' identification photos by default but students can substitute another photo of their choice. Pallof and Pratt (1999) encourage this visual identification. However, Salmon (2000) found some students found this a distraction. We found that teachers and students appreciated the visual cue amongst all the text within the forum and that the majority of students (greater than 80% on average) left their student identification (ID) photo up. Some students in each class swopped their ID photo for a personal one and a few (1-2) used a cartoon character. This substitution tended not to last for the duration of the paper as students developed a greater understanding of online identity building and presence over the course of the paper. As this understanding developed, any students using a cartoon replaced these with photograph of themselves.

Teachers started each discussion with a big question. Teachers had considered the desired coverage and understandings of the specific discussion topic both expected or intended, and also other potential aspects that may arise through student contributions. With this planning the teacher could let discussion develop naturally and pick up on specific points mentioned in contribution posts to follow teachable moments and create a clear trail through the duration of the discussion. Teachers used strategies such as providing a summary, posing of further questions linked to previous discussions and linking ahead to the discussions that would follow.

The importance of class discussions included aspects of support for students and feedback. Student discussion participation was assessed to reward students for participation in line with teachers' belief in the value of this practice. Specific guidance on participating in discussions was provided for students in the paper information area and often referred to by teachers.

Discussion participation was monitored and feedback provided at the conclusion of each module. Teachers were looking to encourage the development of a learning community through online conversation rather than simply a sequence of mini essays in response to discussion starter questions. Teachers were looking for:

- Contribution to knowledge and understanding
- Sharing of beliefs and experiences
- Responses to the reading of provided material
- Presentation of relevant materials discovered for other's to consider
- Responding to others and posing own questions
- Reflecting on roles and nature of own participation.

Participation was rewarded with 5% of marks per module, and 20% of the total marks in each paper were awarded for discussion contributions. (Note: If participation drops off without word from the student then individuals may be phoned if online and email contact gained no response).

However, misunderstandings still occurred. One Chinese male student confessed privately to the teacher that he was frustrated in preparing his post and waiting to post as number 4. It can only be speculated how much time this student had spent trying to post fourth before explaining this to the teacher so that this misunderstanding could be corrected,

Students were encouraged to reflect on their own participation. Guidance for this was provided. One form of this guidance was an adaption from Salmon (2002), where students likened their participation to animal characteristics. For example, a wolf (an irregular visitor but very active when participating), a mouse (visits once a week and contributes little) or a rabbit (lives online, prolific message writer, responds rapidly). Another form of this guidance was also to encourage a variety of content and types of posts through students taking on different roles (Earl & Ball, unpublished). Examples of the types of roles were the Literary Giant (is well read, ensures close links with what the current writing in the area is saying), Scenario writer (adds examples from personal experience, research, websites or imagination), Cultural advocate (cultural issues are paramount, wants people's voices to be heard), and Devil's advocate (argues against a cause or position, not as a committed opponent but simply for the sake of argument or to determine the validity of the cause or position).

Modules and Assignments

As mentioned earlier, each paper was split into 4 modules of 3 weeks duration. The assignment work also fitted into each module (being worth 20% with 5% for discussion). The intention of designing the assessment into bite-size lots was for several reasons:

- Supporting students in using and/or developing effective time management
- Giving students a sense of a 'fresh start' with the close of one module and the start of the next
- Spreading the load so that students experiencing difficulties at the time of one module still had other opportunities to achieve in the paper
- Allowing for a variety of assignments so that those with different strengths and interests had opportunities to show what they knew and could do
- Ease for teachers to mark online

Assignments were designed to encourage students to seek additional sources and resources and use their personal funds of knowledge. Providing choices was deliberate to increase relevance to each individual student's prior experience and professional contexts. Some assignments focused on academic skills and others allowed for more creativity. This variety was also intended to counter potential for plagiarism that occurs when assignments are of the standard essay type and the same each year. For some of the creative assignments, there was the opportunity for students to voluntarily share copies of these after marking was complete in the specific area for this purpose. An example of student assignment choice is called 'scenario planning'.

SCENARIO PLANNING

Select ONE of the following scenarios that relates most closely to you own workplace situation or is of particular interest to you. Respond to your chosen scenario by answering the following questions. Place your response and reference list in the Module Two area of your eFolio.

Personal Response

A. How would you feel if you were involved in this situation?
B. How might you accommodate the challenges you might face as an employee if you were involved in this situation?

Issues and Influences

A. What are the significant positive issues evident in this scenario?
B. What are the significant negative issues in this scenario?
C. Describe how you think this scenario will unfold over the next year.

Scenario # One presents a situation where senior staff in Early Childhood organisations in New Zealand are required to upgrade their qualifications to a minimum of a relevant Bachelors degree. The way in which this will be done is not yet clear but what has been made known is that it will all be online. What are some likely scenarios for this 'everyone will do it' approach and the mode of teaching and learning based on your own reading and understanding of the needs of teachers and the workplace demands?

Scenario # Two presents a situation where your school has decided to collaborate with other schools in the region and produce a 'cookie-cutter' type approach to the development of online aspects of classroom programmes. Schools will use learning objects developed by The Learning Federation in Australia for New Zealand and Australian Schools. The New Zealand Ministry of Education has put $7 million into the project. You wonder about some likely reactions to this 'cookie-cutting' approach based on your own reading and understanding of some of the current trends in eEducation.

Scenario # Three presents a situation where the Kaitaia Town Library has announced that it is to become a centre for community online education in the region and is seeking funding to establish the project. This has come at a time when many small schools are being closed in this area and the communities are feeling angry about the way the government has responded to their concerns. What are some likely scenarios for this type of community development based on your own reading and understanding of what could be possible given the financial and community support for such a project?

CASE DESCRIPTION

Consideration of the variety of students typically enrolling in these two papers making up this qualification had been a feature of the learning design decisions. However, with a large group of Chinese students enrolled, it was seen as important to take the opportunity to seek feedback on the influence of culture, and the identification of online course features that worked for them.

Introduction to the Research

The research was an investigation into Chinese tertiary students' perceptions of the impact of Chinese culture in online learning. The aim of this research was to look at Chinese students' understanding of online learning, investigate how Chinese students perceived the cultural impact on students' online learning attitude, behavior, participation and achievement, and seek their recommendations for eLearning and eTeaching guidelines and/or professional development.

The research took place in 2007 and involved eight Chinese students' participation through email surveys. Three of these Chinese students also participated in the individual interviews. All the participants were past graduates of the Postgraduate Certificate in eEducation. They all had an experience and interest in eTeaching as a student and as a teacher. The researcher (Yan Cong) also had undertaken one of these Postgraduate Certificate papers. Having been a student in this online paper helped the researcher to reflect on the difference in culture and teaching and learning style between two countries (New Zealand and China) as well as to understand how other Chinese students perceived this online learning program and the impact of Chinese culture on their online learning.

Research Methodology

This study used a qualitative research framework that examined participants' words and perceptions. Participants in this research were Chinese students studying in New Zealand who all had online learning experiences but were still different in other ways like gender, age, and personal study and employment experiences.

This study used the methods of email survey and interview. The email survey was chosen in this research with consideration of the advantages of speed, convenience, and economy. The advantages of email surveys were being economical and fast to create, convenient for researchers to send, convenient for participants who can respond at a time that suits them, and there being no need for special software or technical expertise. Although participants in this case study enrolled the online courses as on-campus students, many had returned to China at the time data was gathered. Using email surveys enabled the researcher to overcome a number of practical constraints such as cost, time, and travel distance. Email was a fast way to deliver information, and it was also very convenient and flexible for the researcher to use follow up questions about interesting points or points participants made that required clarifying. Additionally, it allowed participants to consider the questions and frame appropriate responses. Because most of participants for this research had a heavy workload or study load, responding to the survey through email gave them more time to reflect on their answers.

In this email survey, an email message introducing the usage of email surveys with the questionnaire as an attachment was sent to each participant, and participants completed their questionnaires and emailed them back as attachments. This email survey used some dichotomous questions, more multiple choice and rating scale questions for obtaining direct answers from participants, and open-ended questions designed for gathering in-depth data.

Using interviews in this study was designed to go deeper into the motivations of respondents and their reasons for responding as they did in the email surveys. Most of the interview questions were designed as open-ended questions which allowed unexpected or unanticipated answers that may suggest hypotheses. Some other questions were designed according to specific interviewees' email survey responses.

RESULTS

This section looks at these Chinese students' perceptions of the influence of culture, aspects of learning design and the influence of host culture, in this case New Zealand.

Influence of Chinese Culture

According to the research findings, half of the participants agreed that Chinese culture has an impact on their online learning. Their explanations of their agreement indicated that they had seen the Chinese culture has an impact on their online learning in both positive and negative ways. Chinese students being able to provide information in a different context to other students who are not Chinese was valued as a positive influence. The negative impact was explained as Chinese students being used to specific instructions from teachers and being passive in making their own voice in online discussion as well as unconfident in expressing their own ideas. However, other participants disagreed with the cultural impact on their online learning and they perceived that cultural impact cannot be generalized because students who are from the same culture differ from each other. In other words, they believed not all the Chinese students are likely to be shy or silent in online communication forums.

The research also investigated some specific aspects that may be cultural such as hard work. Most participants agreed that Chinese students generally study harder than other students, and believed that the success in online learning comes from students' efforts. To spend more time on overcoming the language barrier was perceived as a one of reasons why Chinese students study hard, and they also explained that a financial burden, including the huge a amount of tuition fees and living expenses in New Zealand, was also a motivation for them to study hard. The relevant literature suggests that under the influence of Confucian culture, Chinese people believe that success comes from hard work, self-effort, and willpower. They also think that studying hard determines high grades, and could potentially reward them with power, wealth, social status, a good career, and a good life in the future, and help them to succeed in the competitive Chinese society (Lee, 1996; Tang & Biggs, 1996; Wang, 2006). Therefore, the findings on participant's perceptions of Chinese student being a hard worker is consistent with the literature, but the individual differences in learning such as learning strategies and approach were also acknowledged.

In regard to their perceptions of the level of comfort when they post different opinions to the lecturers and peers, the majority of the participants indicated that they felt comfortable when they posted different opinions to eTeacher and peers in the online discussion. It is interesting that the literature suggests that Chinese students might not be comfortable with expressing contrary opinions to peers and teachers in the discussion (Gao & Ting-Toomey, 1998; Mao, 1994). According to the Confucian culture, questioning the teacher is viewed as disrespectful to teachers or showing off, so it is not encouraged, and students should keep silent during a conversation (Tsui, 1996). Also, Chinese culture places a value on maintaining group harmony which is achieved by showing politeness and maintaining face, both one's own and others', so, in order to avoid conflicts, students show an unwillingness to provide critical feedback and express different ideas (Carson & Nelson, 1996; Gao & Ting-Toomey, 1998; Mao, 1994). However, Chinese students in this research saw challenging lecturers' and peers' ideas as a positive and meaningful thing because different ideas could attract others' attention and enlighten others' thinking as well. They also realized that it is normal that students who are from a different cultural background have different thinking. Posting different ideas to others in the online discussion was acknowledged as a positive way of learning, and was thought of as to be encouraged. Perhaps this finding showed that these Chinese students made an effort to adapt to a new culture and a western learning style.

Chinese students' comments about the relationship between themselves and the lecturers in New Zealand showed their appreciation of such a relationship which made them more willing to communicate with teachers. They also believed that a more equal relationship between teachers and students has positive influences on students' online learning.

Aspects of Learning Design

The purpose of these Chinese students taking an online paper, particularly these two papers, was to obtain knowledge of eEducation and experience working online so that they could apply this experience to their future teaching as well as enhancing Chinese education professional development on their return to China. As one participant indicated "the course was very helpful for my future teaching" (Cong, 2008, p.38). Another participant from Hebei Radio and Television University commented that this experience being good for their career development was one of the reasons considered by him/her, "The distance education is one of the most important components of my university in China, so I think it is necessary for me to have some learning experience and also to learn how to run an online course." (Cong, 2008, p. 39).

Participants were asked to rank learning design features for helpfulness: clear introductions, ongoing access to records of discussion, having librarian assistance, and all material such as course and assignment information being available online. The majority of Chinese students agreed that these features were helpful. However, they indicated that the level of helpfulness of these features varied. Clear introduction of participation, and the ongoing access to discussion records were rated as the most helpful features. Having asynchronous discussions allowed Chinese students to re-read peers' and lecturers' posts so they could have more time to edit and proof read the English language in their posts as well as reflecting on the content.

As mentioned earlier, online discussion participation was worth 20% of the total marks in each paper. All the Chinese students agreed that online discussion should be marked, and they commented that marks for participating in the online discussion is a kind of encouragement, and receiving a mark for participating in online discussion reflects whether students meet the course and lecturer's requirements as well as being part of the learning process. So perhaps, as graduate level students, these Chinese students were not only concerned about online learning outcomes, but also sought to pursue knowledge and gain good experiences in their online learning process.

Despite these students deliberately electing to enroll in an online paper for the experience, some Chinese students in this research indicated that having less cultural contact was one of the negatives of studying online as a Chinese student. One of Chinese student even commented that "It's like wasting money if I only come to New Zealand for studying online."(Cong, 2008, p. 43) Chinese students came to New Zealand for their studies not only for obtaining knowledge and qualifications from New Zealand, but also expecting to have more understanding of New Zealand culture during their studies. This would be difficult to achieve through learning online. So, studying online for these Chinese students had both pros and cons. They acknowledged the benefits of being a Chinese student choosing online learning such as improving their written English, more time to reflect on questions as well as less pressure in online participation, but less contact with New Zealand culture was perceived as a negative for Chinese students. To some extent, this perception may suggest that some changes of the course content with the increased cultural content might appeal to more Chinese students and encourage them to choose courses in the future. This study may also suggest to those Chinese students who are intending to choose fully online papers in New Zealand in the future, that they need to take both the positives and negatives of studying online into account when deciding to enroll in online courses.

Participants were asked about their perceptions of the skills they developed through learning online. Their responses clearly indicated that they perceived that studying online did improve their written English. However, they also pointed out that there was "less improvement in their oral English." The assignments gave opportunities for these Chinese students to improve their written English skills although they had an expectation of improving both oral and written English skills. This finding was consistent with how participants perceived the benefits of learning online as a Chinese student. According to their responses, being able to have more time to reflect on questions was rated as the most beneficial aspect about studying online. It is understandable that because they face English language difficulties, learning online gave them more time to reflect on questions and prepare the online participation as well as the assignments, which was perhaps less stressful than the instant interaction in a face-to-face course.

This research also investigated how Chinese students perceived the features of being an effective eTeacher. Participants were asked to rate the features of being an effective eTeacher. These features are helpful feedback, good at explaining things, encouraging individuals to participate, enthusiasm, clear expectations, being approachable, good technical skills, and choosing interesting subjects. The majority of participants agreed with all these features. However, the level of importance of these features also varied. Helpful feedback is one of these features all participants agreed was important and rated as the most important feature. Participants acknowledged that effective online teaching pedagogies should come first, and feedback is more important than technical skills and other features. This is consistent with the literature which suggests that to provide feedback is an element of effective online teaching (Bischoff, 2000), and prompt and positive feedback is important in increasing students' learning enthusiasm (Bender, 2003; Young, 2006). In regard to these two online papers, lecturers made the effort to participate in the online discussion and provided helpful feedback in order to monitor the online discussion, catch the misunderstandings as well as re-direct students. The use of templates also helped the teacher to provide timely feedback to students' online discussion and assignments, and students appreciated the prompt and positive feedback from the teacher. These students recognized and appreciated that the design of these two online papers gave students opportunities to contribute and exercise choice. They believed that these aspects were helpful for their learning.

Influence of New Zealand Culture

This research clearly identified that Confucian culture had some impact on Chinese students' beliefs of hard work, success from effort, and the desire for achieving high grades. However, this study also suggested that the Chinese cultural influence cannot be generalized because for one thing, individuals differ in their beliefs although they are from the same culture. In particular, participants in this study argued that some Chinese students were more willing to adapt to a new culture and learning environment. Some participants in this study believed that although they had studied in New Zealand for a short time period, they needed to be willing to learn from New Zealand culture and try to accept the western ways of learning in order to be successful. This finding is consistent with the literature. Xun Lu described this ideological attitude towards foreign culture as 'come essence', which has strongly influenced Chinese people's ideas and attitude towards a new culture (Chen, 2001). Lu's ideology tells Chinese people to take the essence of a new culture, and learn from the other culture so that they can adapt to the new culture. Therefore, in an online learning context, it may be expected that some Chinese students acknowledged that to be willing to share ideas with peers, to be open in communication, to speak out in their own voices is important and applicable to online learning, so they could probably learn better in New Zealand universities.

The study raised the issue of how quickly these Chinese students adapted to New Zealand culture and a new learning environment. Clearly, they showed their appreciation of a western learning style such as speaking their own thoughts rather than relying on teachers' instructions, and being willing to share ideas as well as being critical in their thinking. It seemed that New Zealand culture and a western teaching and learning style had more impact on Chinese students who had better English proficiency and those with greater English proficiency were more willing to adapt to New Zealand culture.

RECOMMENDATIONS

This case study sought Chinese students' recommendations for eLearning, eTeaching and learning design guidelines and/or professional development. Four recommendations were made.

- Lecturers should make efforts to include relevant context information for the variety of student backgrounds.

Participants appreciated that some assignment design in this program allowed students a choice of several assignment questions. However, these participants suggested the inclusion of some context specific assessment tasks. Participants indicated that they had a lack of knowledge about New Zealand culture, so they probably had difficulties in understanding some online course content related to a New Zealand context or culture when they first started the program. So, these students suggested that starting with more familiar examples or contexts would be helpful for these Chinese students to get into the online course. Participants explained that this recommendation may also mean that using a Chinese context in online learning could bring more information to other students who are not Chinese for the purpose of broadening their minds. This recommendation is interesting because assignments were designed to be easily modified for different contexts and students were encouraged to do this. It was the teachers' observation that the Chinese students did not easily select one assignment when given a choice, even when this choice was limited. These students also seemed to have difficulty understanding that they could adapt the context to suit their experience. For example, the scenario looking at one country using the materials and programs developed in another country (in the paper this was New Zealand institutions using Australian programs) could easily be adapted. In fact, this scenario was actually happening in China at the time, with

Chinese universities buying Australian programs. The more able Chinese students developed assignment responses reflecting their own context with explicit guidance and reassurance. Acknowledging students' differences including interests and cultural background, and the diversity of student needs is part of catering for students in a learner-centred approach (Bender, 2003: Shea-Schultz & Fogarty, 2002)

- Relevant material about online learning in a Chinese language version should be provided.

Technical support guides and library guides were available online but were not available in languages other than English. Participants suggested eTeachers could provide some relevant material in a Chinese version, and give more information about online learning before they start the course. Apart from considering Chinese students' English language difficulties, these participants suggested that having more information about what online learning is could help them make better preparation so that they could have a better start in online learning. It should be noted that a basic instruction regarding the use of specific online learning management system (Classforum) was available when students logged in. However, students were unlikely to be aware of this guidance until the decision to enroll had been made. These participants pointed out that this recommendation would allow students to be better informed in their decision making when choosing to enroll in online papers.

- Timely feedback should be given.

Some literature about students' perceptions of online interaction stressed the link between the online interaction, feedback and students' enthusiasm (Bender, 2003; Donaghy, McGee, Ussher & Yates, 2003). In particular, researchers have emphasized the importance of prompt and positive feedback (Bender, 2003; Young 2006). Prompt feedback is needed because students expect their contributions to be acknowledged, and they need to know what they have done well and what needs to be improved. In this case study, participants also perceived that to give prompt feedback was one of the most important features of being an effective eTeacher.

- The lecturer should organize student-to-student time and space beside course work.

Apart from the online student-student interaction, Chinese students suggested that lecturers to make an effort to organize student-to-student group meetings and this would perhaps provide them with additional support from other students. The two papers of this qualification were conducted fully online to enable students from a variety of countries to enroll and participate fully. It is interesting that the Chinese students who were participants in this study saw the organization of informal support meetings for students as the role of the teacher. Any offline work within the paper would be unlikely so as not to be seen as disadvantaging those students who, because of distance, would be unable to attend. However, the teachers can explicitly encourage students to make informal contacts and meet face-to-face if they wish to do this.

LESSONS LEARNED

It is clear that meeting student needs is not easy, and that modifying any learning design to better cater for the needs of one student group needs to be considered in light of the impact of these changes on other student groups. The different perceptions of intentions, problems and solutions by teachers and students, and between and within different student groups, means that there is no perfect online course design or facilitation.

The following five lessons stand out: attend to student voice, learn about student backgrounds, encourage student contributions, be explicit, and utilize available expert support.

- Attend to student voice

Increasingly, researchers are attending to the student voice in their research (Motteram & Forrester, 2005; Morrow, 1999; Tayor, 2000; Young, 2006) and promoting awareness of student needs in their teaching (Bender, 2003; Engvig & White, 2006; Laurillard, 2002; Palloff & Pratt, 2001; Palloff & Praff, 2003). The aim of this case study was to attend to Chinese students' voices in order to cater for their needs as well as enhancing this online program in the future.

- Learn about students' backgrounds

This can be done through the use of introductions, encouraging sharing of experiences in discussion and providing opportunities for individual students to take a lead and share what they can do. This will help the teachers understand students.

To understand these Chinese student's background and their purpose for enrolling in the program, and to know that Chinese students are facing English language difficulties and a new culture, it would be helpful for eEducators in order to cater for their needs. For example, the majority of Chinese students in this study agreed that grades are an important part of their achievement for an online course because they perceived that grades indicated whether they met the course requirement and reflected how well they had studied. However, some of them paid more attention to the learning process, experience, and improvement rather than only having the desire for high grades. Perhaps because these participants were graduate level students, their attitude towards online learning tended to be more mature. As explained earlier, some of the participants were secondary, high school, and online tutors at the universities in China before they studied in New Zealand, so it may be expected that they may have a deeper understanding about learning. Although they all believed that online discussion should be marked, interestingly, their reasons for such an agreement were not about grades themselves, but about acknowledging that grades can reflect whether students met the course requirements as well showing their improvement.

- Encourage student contributions.

Students need to feel they are making a contribution to the class (Tomlinson, 2000). Aside from this, student contributed sources and materials also provide immediate support for other students during the course and for the eTeacher to review for potential future use. For example, Chinese students attaching relevant articles by Chinese authors or organizations, in English or otherwise, provides potential resource material to support future Chinese students in these papers.

- Be explicit

Online teachers need to be explicit about the intentions, options and opportunities for students. There was considerable support for the online classroom environment in these papers including teacher facilitation of discussion and student-to-student interaction in the responses from the students in this study. Participants also clearly valued teacher support and feedback and highly appreciated the relationship between themselves and the teachers.

- Utilise available expert support such as librarians

The involvement of librarian assistance was also appreciated. However, this occurred at a late stage of this case study. Therefore, the early involvement of librarian assistance was suggested as being needed and important so that Chinese students could get support when they started the online course.

Although the learning design of the online papers had intentionally taken account of the typical variety of students enrolled in these papers, when the majority of the class was going to be Chinese, the opportunity arose to gather Chinese student opinion on the impact of culture on their learning, features of design and recommendations. It was interesting that some of the features that the teachers believed were important (such as modulising the learning) went largely unnoticed by these students. The features these students did identify as important were often seen as important for different reasons. It is important to gather student perceptions in order to appropriately evaluate and develop the teaching and learning in online papers. Such information is likely to reflect cultural influences but it would be a mistake to generalize broadly as different individuals have different perceptions even within the one cultural group. Because the role of the teacher online is seen as a key factor, any developments to support learning need also to consider supporting teacher effectiveness through strategies for working smarter not harder.

CURRENT, FUTURE, OR RELATED CHALLENGES

The involvement of a librarian as an information coach was introduced about half way through PROF521 during the occurrence these participants were involved in. Since then, having a librarian involved, using an identified 'Information coach' area, has been a regular feature of these papers.

In 2007, the University of Waikato shifted to using Moodle as the Learning Management System. This involved decisions about levels of the online forum and changes to the way the papers' content and activities were divided up. Teacher knowledge and up-skilling with the new system was needed in order to make these decisions.

As the numbers of students enrolling changes, so does the involvement of different teaching staff. The induction of new staff into the beliefs that are the foundation of these papers as well as maintaining an openness to new ideas remains a challenge.

Teaching staff are also challenged to keep up to date in the field of eEducation and the use of developing digital technologies and features for the benefit of teaching and learning.

As the only consistent re student enrollments is the mixture of students typically taking these papers, the evaluation of appropriate modifications to design, facilitation and assignments for specific student groups remains an ongoing challenge.

REFERENCES

Bender, T. (2003). *Rethinking learning theory within in the online class. Discussion-based online teaching to enhance students learning* (pp. 16–33). Sterling, VA: Stylus Publishing.

Berge, Z. (2000). New roles for learners and teachers in online higher education. In Heart, G. (Ed.), *Readings and resources in global online education* (pp. 3–9). Melbourne, Australia: Whirlgig Press.

Bischoff, A. (2000). The elements of effective online teaching: Overcoming the barriers to success. In White, K. W., & Whight, B. H. (Eds.), *The online teaching guide: A handbook of attitudes strategies, and techniques for the virtual classroom* (pp. 57–72). Boston, MA: Allyn and Bacon.

Campbell, N. (1998). Learning to teach online: A case for support. *Computers in New Zealand Schools, 10*(1), 11–13.

Campbell, N. (2003). So you want to teach online? It won't happen overnight but it can happen. *Computers in New Zealand Schools, 15*(1), 11-13, 25.

Carson, J., & Nelson, G. (1996). Chinese students' perceptions of ESL peer response group interaction. *Journal of Second Language Writing, 5*(1), 1–19. doi:10.1016/S1060-3743(96)90012-0

Chen, F. J. (2001). Analysis of Lu Xun used the dialectics: Dialectic among

China Mobile Limited. (2009). *Customer data for August 2009.* Retrieved October 3, 2009, from http://www.chinamobileltd.com/

Cong, Y. (2008). *The impact of Chinese culture in online learning: Chinese tertiary students' perceptions*. Unpublished master's thesis, University of Waikato, New Zealand.

Donaghy, A., McGee, C., Ussher, B., & Yates, R. (2003). *Online teaching and learning: A study of teacher education students' experiences*. Hamilton, New Zealand: The University of Waikato.

Earl, S. K., & Ball, T. (2007). *Roles for discussion. An update of one of Nola Campbell's online class activities. Unpublished document for class use in PROF521 and PROF522*. New Zealand: School of Education, University of Waikato.

Engvig, M., & White, M. (2006). The students' perspectives. In Engvig, M. (Ed.), *Online learning: All you need to know to facilitate and administer online courses* (pp. 37–84). Cresskill, NJ: Hampton Press.

Gao, G., & Ting-Toomey, S. (1998). *Communicating effectively with the Chinese*. Thousand Oaks, CA: Sage.

Harasim, L. (2000). Shift happens: Online education as a new paradigm of learning. *The Internet and Higher Education, 3*(1-2), 41–61. doi:10.1016/S1096-7516(00)00032-4

Laurillard, D. (2002). *Designing teaching materials. Rethinking university teaching* (pp. 181–198). London, UK: Routledge Falmer. doi:10.4324/9780203304846

Lee, W. O. (1996). The cultural context for Chinese learners: Conceptions of learning in the Confucian tradition. In David, W. A., & John, B. B. (Eds.), *The Chinese learner: Cultural, psychological and contextual influences*. Hong Kong: Comparative Education Research Centre.

Lu-Xun's Fetchtism. *Guangxi Business College Journal, 4*. Retrieved May 26, 2008, from http://scholar.ilib.cn/Abstract.aspx?A=gxsygdzkxxxb200104018

Mao, L. (1994). Beyond politeness theory: Face revisited and renewed. *Journal of Pragmatics, 21*, 451–486. doi:10.1016/0378-2166(94)90025-6

Morrow, V. (1999). It's cool… 'cos you can't give us detentions and things, can you?!: Reflections on research with children. In Carolin, B., & Milner, P. (Eds.), *Time to listen to children: Personal and professional communication* (pp. 203–215). London, UK: Routledge.

Motteram, G., & Forrester, G. (2005). *Become an online distance learner: What can be learned from students' experiences of induction to distance programmes?* ProQuest.

O'Neill, A. M., & O'Neill, J. (2007). How the official curriculum shapes teaching and learning. In St. George, A., Brown, S., & O'Neill, J. (Eds.), *Facing the big questions in teaching: Purpose, power and learning* (pp. 3–113). Melbourne, Victoria, Australia: Cengage.

Organizing Committee of China International Distance Education. (2007). *Conference invitation*. Retrieved 28 May, 2008 from http://www.chinaonlineedu.com/2007/English.asp

Palloff, R. M., & Pratt, K. (1999). *Building learning communities in cyberspace: Effective strategies for the online classroom*. San Francisco, CA: Jossey-Bass.

Palloff, R. M., & Pratt, K. (2001). *Working with in the virtual student. Lessons from the cyberspace classroom* (pp. 107–124). San Francisco, CA: Jossey-Bass.

Palloff, R. M., & Pratt, K. (2003). *Who is the virtual student? The virtual student: A profile and guide to working with online learners* (pp. 3–14). San Francisco, CA: Jossey-Bass.

Peters, O. (1999). The paradigm shift in distance education and its meaning for teacher training. *Indian Journal of Open Learning, 8*(1), 5–7.

Salmon, G. (2002). Creating e-tivities. *eTivities the key to active online learning* (pp.87-105). London, UK: Kogan Page School of Education. (2002) *Postgraduate certificate in e-education*, version 5/4/02. Unpublished new qualification proposal, University of Waikato, New Zealand.

Shea-Schultz, H., & Fogarty, J. (2002). *Online learning today: Strategies that work.* San Francisco, CA: Berrett-Koehler.

Tang, C., & Biggs, J. (1996). How Hong Kong students cope with assessment. In David, W. A., & John, B. B. (Eds.), *The Chinese learner* (pp. 159–182). Hong Kong: Comparative Education Research Centre.

Taylor, A. S. (2000). The UN convention on the rights of the child: Giving children a voice. In Lewis, A., & Lindsay, G. (Eds.), *Researching children's perspectives* (pp. 21–33). Buckingham, UK: Open University Press.

Toffler, A. (1991). *Future shock.* New York, NY: Bantam Books.

Tomlinson, C. (2002). Invitations to learn. *Educational Leadership, 60*(1), 6–10.

Tsui, A. (1996). Reticence and anxiety in second language teaching. In Bailey, K., & Nunan, D. (Eds.), *Voices from the language classroom* (pp. 145–167). Cambridge, UK: Cambridge University Press.

Wang, T. (2006). *Understand Chinese culture and learning.* Paper presented at Conference of the Australian Association for Research in Education, Melbourne, Australia. Retrieved February 1, 2008, from http://search.informit.com.au.ezproxy.waikato.ac.nz:2048/search;action=doSearch

Xinhua. (2008, April). *China's Internet users hit 221m, rank world's first.* Retrieved May 27, 2008, from http://www.chinadaily.com.cn/china/2008-04/24/content_6641838.htm

Young, S. (2006). Student views of effective online teaching in higher education. *American Journal of Distance Education, 20*(2), 65–77. doi:10.1207/s15389286ajde2002_2

This work was previously published in Cases on Globalized and Culturally Appropriate E-Learning: Challenges and Solutions, edited by Andrea Edmundson, pp. 73-93, copyright 2011 by Information Science Reference (an imprint of IGI Global).

Chapter 4
Incorporating "World View" into the LMS or CMS is Best

Katherine Watson
Coastline Community College, USA

EXECUTIVE SUMMARY

"Linguistic relativism" leads people of different cultures to define, explain, and even see reality in images framed by their diverse languages. The most readily available and commonly used online educational materials are often scaffolded in unyielding structures shrouded in American standards and expectations. These Americano-centric course management and learning management systems render subject matter design and delivery, as well as assignment formulation, scheduling, and grading, difficult for educators who understand the importance of imbuing their materials with atypical alternative views of reality expressed in the worldviews of languages and cultures beyond the borders of the United States.

ORGANIZATION BACKGROUND

Coastline Community College, based in Fountain Valley, CA has learning and study centers located throughout multi-lingual Orange County. For more than three decades, Coastline has been offering educational programs via television; more recently, the College has placed itself in the forefront of the online learning movement. Coastline serves more than 20,000 students each semester, with well

DOI: 10.4018/978-1-4666-1885-5.ch004

over half of them enrolled exclusively in distance learning programs in art, science, literature, language, technology, and business. Students range in age from high school homeschoolers to senior citizens; they may be incarcerated or in the United States military; they may sign up for courses part-time or full-time, although the vast majority of them are part-timers with jobs and families. In light of the College's interest in remaining responsive to ever-fluctuating economic shifts and altering student demands, a unique Course Management/Learning Management System (CMS/LMS) was conceived within the institution. This CMS/LMS, *Seaport*, has benefited from faculty, administrative, and student input, but, like most CMSs and LMSs, it retains certain Americano-centric inflexibilities that keep it from being as malleable, frustrating the educator who would use it as an interface to international thought or expression. That is, like other CMSs and LMSs designed in the United States within American information technology (IT) firms, the Coastline system has been conceived in the American English dialect, its preferred format for quizzes and assignments is objective, and its scheduling is regulated in accordance with strict dates. Marcus and Gould (2000), among others, have noted that CMS/LMS design created outside the United States can offer insights into alternative worldviews; just as artists and philosophers, writers and educators from other countries may prefer to think in languages other than English, to argue in a vermicular fashion, and to leave assigned tasks open-ended and amendable, so do CMSs and LMSs originating from elsewhere often allow unrestricted and subjective evaluations, loose scheduling, and default dialects other than the American. At Coastline, French language and culture courses offered online exemplify an effort to incorporate Marcus and Gould-style observations in courses that would internationalize the insular.

"Linguistic relativism" depends upon the notion that, for instance, "We dissect nature along lines laid down by our native languages" (Whorf, 1956); that is, observers of reality who speak different languages will define and describe that reality in divergent ways. Moreover, reality itself is expressed, viewed, and valued in a manner convergent with linguistic expression. In the United States, educational materials delivered online are almost always embedded in what might be termed an Americano-centric interface. For example, online-delivered materials deploy buttons labeled in American English, top-down models designed by outside decision-makers who are often not the users, and shapes and colors that harmonize with an American point of view (Marcus and Gould, 2000). Paulsen (2003) notes that American CMS/LMS designs all seem to be similar to one another in these respects even as they appear to have been created "top-down", for institutional ease rather than for educator or student interactivity. As an instructional technology professional, Paulsen points out that distance education is booming in areas outside the United States, and there is an increasing demand for the "bottom-up", where teachers and learners may meet in a zone of cyberspace that is not necessarily similar to the American model.

The educators who would teach a "foreign", non-English, language or culture online in the United States must, therefore, work hard to impart an alternative worldview through an American institutional CMS/LMS; to suffuse an alternative, small sector of cyberspace with systems that encourage learners from the outset to think, to reason, to write, to do their assignments and research in atypical ways – in ways that are different from American ones .

At Coastline Community College, online learners of French language and culture are encouraged from the beginning of each course term to see and to reason through a French perspective integrated into their American coursework; they start right away to conceive things not just hierarchically, but from a bottom-up, user-centered, argumentative and interactive vermicular fashion, *à la française*.

AN EXAMPLE

Online learning at Coastline Community College - like Web-based education at most institutions - is embedded in systems. This is reality online in America. And Americano-centric course management and learning management systems present problems to the educator who would imbue his materials with a non-American, linguistically/culturally fitting interface, an essentially alternative reality that would enrich communicability (Faiola and Matei, 2005). In addition, United States institutional requirements make course design, assignment formulation, scheduling, and grading difficult for the instructor who would value unconventional viewpoints of these three subtle, but significant aspects of learning as part of the target language/culture learning process. Thus, for example, it remains difficult in the United States to teach French language and culture through a francophone perspective - incorporating the French worldview as it appears in francophone institutional interfaces (e.g., http://www.u-cergy.fr/index.php) - which are judged and marketed for their beauty, ergonomics, and accessibility more than for their practicality or consistency (Blond, et al., 2009). American CMS/LMS design is conceived in a top-down manner (Wolfe, et al., 2003); that is, it is relatively fixed, standardized, made to be apolitical, practical, and without nuance (e.g., http://www.u-cergy.fr/rubrique1328.html). The standard American CMS/LMS does not allow for the artistic air—"le Webdesign" is considered an art in France---; nor is it decorated with the historical monuments and individuals that headline many francophone-generated sites (e.g., French version http://www.univ-paris5.fr/ and Anglophone version http://www.univ-paris5.fr/spip.php?article2677). Neither does most American CMS/LMS design exhibit the sort of "small-country syndrome" that francophones display in their institutional sites, dotting their data with tastes of news from the world and global, alternative perspectives in a stimulus-rich, bottom-up way (e.g. francophone media and resource sites: http://www.rfi.fr/ and http://www.bnf.fr/fr/acc/x.accueil.html vs. United States media and resource sites: http://www.cbsradio.com/index.html and http://www.loc.gov/index.html (Wolfe, et al., 2003). Even so, political and world-aware francophone thinking is integrated online into Coastline College's *Seaport* CMS/LMS as much as possible in French language and culture courses, so that learners discover with only a few mouse clicks that their target language defines in detail a culture dependent on history, interested in the written word, argumentation, and the prolix. Learners are encouraged from the outset to think, to reason, to write, to do their assignments and research in an unsymmetrical manner, without attention to the school's top-down-imposed "due dates" and with a mind set to operate *à la française*.

It should be noted that two principal, opposing factors affect full, satisfactory resolution of the problem of how best to teach a non-American mode of thinking and reasoning online in a country that depends upon American systems. That is, institutional control, identity, and contextualization must be addressed, while unique-to-the subject matter identity and contextualization must also be considered. The question turns, therefore, on whether it is recognizable institutional markers that are most important, or whether it is, alternatively, cultural or linguistic features of a language/culture learning site that are most important.

Technology Concerns

Technological questions often revolve around ease of use, consistency, and requirements. Technicians prefer not to deal with the unusual or the exceptional in a day when bugs and viruses, hacking and downtime can cause frustration, if not system failure; indeed, educators and students like to keep things technologically simple, too.

The technological question of language learning online has much to do with what technology in the USA will permit from other linguistic/cultural backgrounds, from scripts and accent marks to text-v.-image-v.-open page area questions, color, font, line thickness and straightness, and the like. Many CMSs and LMSs fabricated in the USA do not permit "foreign" accentuation or writing systems, not to mention right-to-left or top-to-bottom script or the sorts of alternative esthetics that often underlie francophone-designed Web pages (Auré, 2010). Too, although Coastline's *Seaport* system has met many student and instructor demands for the malleable, it remains "Microsoft-centric", rendering it difficult to access from either Macintosh equipment or from computers using Mozilla Firefox or Google Chrome, for example.

Learner Concerns

Rarely do students have a role in deciding what they want to learn and when and how. At Coastline, most Distance Learning Department students are self-selected self-motivated, self-directed adults; they want to learn as much as possible as fast as possible, whatever it takes. Notably, however, thousands of these learners are not native speakers of English, and so the language of the electronic interface should not impede their learning; indeed, they do not attend fully to the effects that an Americano-centric interface might have upon learnability.

Instructional Design and Teaching Concerns

Instructional designers prefer model consistency for practical reasons; it is easier to fix technical problems if there are only a few limited options. Institutional designers are generally tasked to set forth an institutional air; all courses delivered online at a particular institution bear a kind of electronic signature, a college identity. Moreover, technical designers know how much each element of Web design costs in time and money; they make decisions with this in mind, as well as with an eye on ADA requirements, federal standards, and the like. For their part, the teachers who must use these institutional designs tend to want two competing things: On the one hand, they would like to have to create from scratch as little as possible, enjoying the ease of template use; but on the other hand, they want to be able to customize their courses, giving them a personal or subject-matter imprint.

Management and Organizational Concerns

The managerial question in online course development, design, and presentation at Coastline has often to do with *hierarchy*: Is it the institution's administration, the Web design and technical staff, or the instructor who gets to choose how what kinds of materials are to be presented in a course? The organizational question in online-delivered French language and culture courses has to do with cultural values: Is material to be presented in a beads-on-a-string, American-design fashion, with assignments delivered at set times and withdrawn later, for example, or is it to be presented all in a mass, with no timeline, calling upon students to learn to schedule themselves as they must do in French institutions? Are assignments to be designed with ease of scoring in mind, largely in the objective mode, or are they to be open-ended, reflective, demanding individual attention to their subjectivity?

And is grading to be done in an add-up-the-points-for-the-parts manner, or is it to be a more holistic affair, incorporating the way in which students have arrived at their answers, rather than just the answers themselves?

SOLUTIONS AND RECOMMENDATIONS

The challenges of adapting to others' world views - of how best to train learners to move about in a new reality, using an alternative mode of thinking in a language other than English - has led to a solution of compromise. That is, the institutional CMS/LMS is retained, but it is used mostly as a portal to elsewhere.

Page design is rendered as subject-matter friendly as possible, with images exhibiting francophone-style curved lines and harmonious colors, for instance, integrated into the *Seaport* CMS/LMS. Students are directed immediately from their *Seaport* homepage into francophone-designed alternative areas, where all buttons, hyperlinks, directions, and the rest are written in French, conceived with emphases on the artistic and the user-centered, even "multi-dimensional", as francophone designers would have them be (Auré, 2010, and Duverneuil, 2007).

Indeed, use of as much authentic francophone-sourced material as possible in an online learning environment has proven productive at Coastline.

In order to encourage the timeless, serendipitously teachable-moment nature of learning online, French language and culture course assignments are presented from semester Day One altogether as a mass for students to schedule as they wish; no due date is assigned but the end of each course term. E-mail messages are scheduled weekly from the instructor to encourage students to design their own work plans, as is done in francophone institutions.

Coastline online learners of French language and culture have, during the past fifteen years of participation in online courses in French at the College, learned to appreciate francophone reasoning and perspectives as they have improved their technological skills and their linguistic awareness, including fluency. Students report being "able to think in French", finding themselves "thinking of that word in French", "imagining (themselves) seeing this from a French point of view", for instance. Use of the French interface in E-mail and in assignments has led to reduced distractability; rather than being invited by familiar Anglophone advertising or interfaces, students remain "on task" while immersed in francophone cyberspace.

Alternatively, the use of Anglophone materials can be useful as a guide into the francophone, but it poses the risk of being a crutch. As *Converge* magazine states in its 14 July, 2009, issue, immersion is still the *nec plus ultra* of learning models, and as Coastliners have found, immersion is easy to perform online. The francophone resources available in cyberspace are vast, and most of them are free.

LESSONS LEARNED

Three particular lessons have been learned: One must, in online learning environments:

1. **Use "The System":** Find the advantages, the things that work for you, the instructor, and poll students informally and regularly to find out which features of the course/learning management system work best for them; use those most often. Frequently, learners from varying sociocultural, economic, and/or linguistic backgrounds will address and interact with institutional systems in diverse ways. Find out how who is looking at what: are students looking at things in an analytical, sequential way or in a synthetic, holistic manner, for instance---and cognitively---are they influenced by a high-context, high risk-averse society or a low-context one, for instance, and is their time orientation a long-term one or a short-term one? Students may need more than one version of the CMS/LMS designed by technologists from more than one cultural background. Open Source materials are popular in many countries; Scandinavian-based ones are some of the many that may be used easily and free, without automatically changing instructor or student work into English with an Anglophone text editor, for instance.
2. **Tweak "The System":** Find out how much wiggle room is available within the system, so as to customize it as much as possible. This may mean that the aforementioned alternative versions of course sites bear different looks, various arrangements on a Webpage of the same course content, not just translated from English but transmuted into an authentic alternative that harmonizes with alternative cognitive styles (Holzl, 1999). Moreover, either alongside such alternatives or in addition to them, embedded links may be necessary to lead learners to areas where materials have been created by technologists who see and interact with the world in complementary ways; it may mean that surfing experiences to far-away Web sites or to institutions employing vastly distinct CMSes or LMSes may be required. As Paulsen (2003), among others, has noted, online education across borders can be rendered difficult by a country's citizens' strong preference to use their own language, as well as their own cognitive patterns. Best practices in this realm warrant examination. It may mean collaborating not just within an institution but everywhere, including with institutions across the globe and with students from one's own institution and beyond.
3. **Never Stop Integrating:** Learners from diverse backgrounds, especially adults, have learned how to learn in varying ways, some preferring formal or informal oral communication, others preferring collaborative learning, and still others favoring individual research or coursework by correspondence. Indeed,

> educators would do well to remain constantly aware of their goals: Does the principal effort comprise, as Holzl (1999) summarizes it, an attempt to meet the student in his own realm of learning preferences, or does it, alternatively, entail a endeavor to change a student's cognitive style into one that conforms with either the institutional worldview or the perspective of the educator? Holzl (1999) holds that *constructivist learning environments* may be the best suited to the integration of the alternative, approaching the sort of cognitive flexibility that would at once meet learners where they are mentally, and lead them into a new domain with realia.

Converge magazine cites in its 14 July issue two confirmations of twenty-first century linguistic/cultural immersion techniques using electronic media, including audio and video capabilities; integrating these along with the perpetually-self-renewing features of electronic and social media, such as live news feeds, podcasts, wikis, and blogs, can keep coursework new and fresh while at the same time training learners in the technologies and in the discursive manners of reasoning that define non-American societies, particularly the rich vermicular argumentation models of the francophone.

CURRENT, FUTURE, AND RELATED CHALLENGES

It has been said that the past is prologue. In online learning of foreign language and culture, the future shall be epilogue. That is, in a world that is increasingly multi-cultural, the end game should be mutual understanding. Understanding among individuals will occur more rapidly and more readily if those others feel a sense of inclusion, which will begin with a sense of familiarity with layout, framework, and design, and which will lead, in the most serendipitous case, to an inviting learnability in CMS or LMS (Marcus and Gould, 2000). And the principal lesson learned in French language/culture course design, development, and delivery is that compromise and mutual respect, attained through listening, dialogue, and continuing interactivity, must be sustained among all parties, if education is to take place. The work done to implement a successful program in French language/culture delivered online should have local and global long-term impact: Locally, other area foreign language instructors can use this work as a *manuel d'études*, a study guide, on the one hand, and as a warning of pitfalls on the other. Globally, institutions worldwide can use this reported sequence of events as a classic case study, not just for the teaching of foreign languages but for the customization of course materials to fit a particular subject matter in a particular marketplace of ideas, of human interaction.

REFERENCES

Ash, R. (1999). The Sapir-Whorf hypothesis. New York, NY: Payne. Retrieved 14 July, 2010, from http://www.angelfire.com/journal/worldtour99/sapirwhorf.html

Auré, L. (2010). Lisibilité des sites Web. In *All for Design*. Retrieved 4 April, 2010, from http://all-for-design.com/afd-le-theme

Blond, M.-V., Marcellin, O., & Zerbib, M. (2009). *Lisibilité des sites Web*. Paris, France: Eyrolles.

Converge. (2009, 8 July). Podcast projects promote literacy. *Converge Magazine*. Retrieved from http://www.convergemag.com/literacy/Podcast-Projects-Promote-Literacy.html

Duverneuil, B. (2007). *Webdesign: Passé, present, et...présent*, p.3. World Wide Web Consortium SlideShare presentation. Retrieved 3 April, 2010, from http://www.slideshare.net/bduverneuil/webdesign-passe-present-et-present-part3

Faiola, A., & Matei, S. (2005). Cultural cognitive style and Web design: Beyond a behavioral inquiry into computer-mediated communication. *Journal of Computer-Mediated Communication, 11*(1), 18. doi:10.1111/j.1083-6101.2006.tb00318.x

Hall, E. (1976). *Beyond culture*. New York, NY: Anchor Books.

Holzl, A. (1999). Designing for diversity in online learning environments. In *ASCILITE Proceedings*, Brisbane, Australia. Rertrived 23 March, 2010, from http://www.ascilite.org.au/conferences/brisbane99/papers/holzl.pdf

Marcus, A., & Gould, E. (2000). Cultural dimensions and global Web user interface design: What? So what? Now what? *Proceedings 6th Conference on Human Factors and the Web*, 19 June 2000, University of Texas, Austin, TX.

Michael, L. (2002). Reformulating the Sapir-Whorf hypothesis: Discourse, interaction, and distributed cognition. Austin, TX: University of Texas. Retrieved 14 July, 2010, from http://studentorgs.utexas.edu/salsa/proceedings/2002/papers/michael.pdf

Napier, J. (2009, 10 July). Breaking language barriers. *Converge Magazine*. Retrieved from http://www.convergemag.com/literacy/Breaking-Language-Barriers.html

Paulsen, M. (2003). *Global e-learning in a Scandinavian perspective*. Oslo, Norway: NKI Forlaget.

Straker, D. (2008). *Changing minds*. London, UK: Syque.

Whorf, B. (1956). *Language, thought, and reality: Selected writings of Benjamin Lee Whorf* (Carroll, J., Ed.). Cambridge, MA: MIT Press.

Wolfe, J.M., Butcher, S., Lee, C., & Hyle, M. (2003). Changing your mind: On the contributions of top-down and bottom-up guidance in visual search for feature singletons. *Journal of Experimental Psychology*, *29*(2), 483–502.

KEY TERMS AND DEFINITIONS

Course Management System (CMS): A software platform provided by an educational institution for delivery of academic course materials to students online

Learning Management System (LMS): A software application that automates administration, tracking, and student interaction with institutional Web-delivered materials

Distance Learning: A form of education employing technology to deliver academic materials to learners who may be separated by time or distance, or both, from the source of those materials

Interface: The external, explicit gateway into the electronic, including typeface, color, movement, text-image ratio, ease of navigability, for instance

Portal: An internet gateway providing access in a single place to multifarious bits of information and to multiple diverse Web-based resources

Vermicular Reasoning: A type of argumentation process that tends to the circuitous, rather than the top-down direct, access to a conclusion

This work was previously published in Cases on Globalized and Culturally Appropriate E-Learning: Challenges and Solutions, edited by Andrea Edmundson, pp. 326-337, copyright 2011 by Information Science Reference (an imprint of IGI Global).

Section 2
Cultural Accessibility

Chapter 5
Cultural Implications of E-Learning Access (and Divides):
Teaching an Intercultural Communication Course Online

Pauline Hope Cheong
Arizona State University, USA

Judith N. Martin
Arizona State University, USA

EXECUTIVE SUMMARY

This chapter presents a case study of developing and teaching an intercultural communication (IC) course online, within the context of a department in a large research University in the U.S. In so doing, we discuss a broadened and recursive model of cultural access and divides in E-learning. Expanding on Van Dijk's (2005) framework, the authors present several ways in which their IC course attempts to address multiple pathways of E-learning access, including motivational, material, skills and usage access. They describe both the successes and challenges of meeting the goals of e-learning access with specific examples of the content, activities, assignments, pedagogical strategies, and student assessment in this online course. Finally, they identify challenges of this e-learning at the micro and macro level context—in the course, university writ large and in the communication discipline.

DOI: 10.4018/978-1-4666-1885-5.ch005

INTRODUCTION: UNDERSTANDING E-LEARNING ACCESS

Increasing numbers of students are enrolling in online courses in institutions worldwide (Allen & Seaman, 2007). The internationalization of higher education and popularity of applying a global approach to education is increasingly facilitated by the use of communication technologies in E-learning (Burbules, 2000). An important topic in new media use is the issue of access, related to the 'digital divide' or the technological chasm between information haves and have-nots which is of concern among policy makers and educators both in the United States and abroad (Warschauer, 2003). As van Djik (2005) and others suggest, the digital divide is more than just a question of access to computer software, but rather includes technocapital on many levels including: mental, material, skills, and usage. Furthermore, in many places in the world, technocapital is in competition with basic necessities of life (Olaniran & Agnello, 2008).

There is a research gap in considering the cultural implications of E-learning access and (on the flip side, divides). In particular, there are cultural aspects of socio-technical divides that tend to be overlooked in E-learning (Ess & Sudweeks, 2005; Schwartzman, 2007). E-learning technologies should not be considered *fait accompli* but recursively constructed and defined by a host of psychological, social and political influences and actors (Dutton, Cheong & Park, 2004). In this paper, we present a case study of developing and teaching an intercultural communication (IC) course online, within the context of a department (subsequently referred to as 'the department') in a large research University ('the University') in the U.S. In doing so, we discuss a broadened and recursive model of cultural access in E-learning, to encompass access to communication technologies, information, people and services associated with online pedagogy. This paper has theoretical and practical implications for educators' curricula design and implementation of E-learning courses.

BACKGROUND AND SETTING THE STAGE

We begin by first discussing the backdrop and circumstances leading to this IC course development. The online course was first delivered as a face-to-face course (Elements of Intercultural Communication), an integral part of the department's offerings - a popular major choice among undergraduates. The course is designed "as an introduction to the basic concepts, principles, and skills for improving communication across racial, ethnic and cultural differences." The course has been offered each semester since Fall 2006. The course is always enrolled to the maximum capacity (30 students) and there is usually a waiting list of students. While the course is designed as an introductory level course, most of the students are juniors and seniors, a few sophomores and occasionally one or two freshmen. This is due to the fact that courses in this department are impacted in general and students are not able to enroll in required courses until late in their college career. The students in this online course have a variety of majors. Most are business or pre-business majors, a few communication students and the remainder represent a range of majors including pre civil engineering, anthropology, music, art, biotechnology. The cultural backgrounds of the student usually reflect the make up of the University (approximately 65% white, 35% international students, and ethnic and racial minorities)—the largest minority group is Latino and the smallest American Indian.

Spurred by the following factors, this course was first developed in 2004 and offered Fall semester 2006. At the time of the course's inception, the University was undergoing a period of rapid expansion and growth, and the leadership was promoting a philosophy of "access, excellence and impact". Like many academic institutions, the University saw potential income in online courses. The department had been at the forefront of online courses, offering a very successful course since 1996 and was eager to expand its offerings. Consonant with its mission, from 2000-2005 the University provided monetary incentives and technology assistance to faculty interested in developing new online courses. The initial proposal to put the existing IC course online included the following rationale: "Our undergraduate students will benefit as we will be able to expand our offerings of IC to students who are not traditional students, who may be off campus students. Secondly, our graduate students and faculty who teach this course will benefit by having a competitive edge in this aspect of curriculum delivery. Finally, from a scholarly point of view, gaining expertise in this new area of communication research will enhance our visibility in the field." In this light, this online course can be seen to be part of the overall curriculum infrastructure to open up opportunities for students to access intercultural courses and complete their degree.

An interview with the Director of Online Programs revealed the extent of the University support for online programs, as well as information about the administration philosophy, culture and practices.[1] She reported that the numbers of online courses are steadily increasing and gave four reasons for the University support: 1) The University is focused on access and bringing education to more people. As she noted "Online degree programs are a way to bring a University education to those who may not be able to physically make it to a campus"; 2) Students want online courses, so the University is meeting student demand by offering increasing online course options; 3) the University believes that online courses can be as *effective* for student learning and in large classes can be *more efficient* than face-to-face classes (due to technological advances, students in courses with high enrollment of several hundred students receive the same lecture material from the professor as in face-to-face class, can have *more* interaction with each other and the professor and *more* access to supplemental materials like online quizzes, video examples, learning activities). In addition, there are better retention checks—a major priority for the University, e.g. when an assignment is missed, there is prompt communication and follow-up with the student by the professor. There is also a new "lockdown browser" in development which will provide better control for online exams (cheating is a huge problem in a 500 student class); and 4) Today's students learn better with new media than students in the past because they are comfortable with technology.

She described the specific ways in which the University offers support. For example, her office offers technical as well as pedagogical assistance for existing online courses and those in development, and thus serves as a type of e-learning quality control. While it is not mandatory for instructors to work with her office staff, most do take advantage of the available expertise. She and her staff work with faculty who already teach online but want to improve the design and delivery of their courses—e.g. incorporate the latest technology in testing, discussion board and lecture delivery.

While the macro organizational culture was supportive of E-learning, and believes that e-learning can be as effective as traditional instruction, there were and continue to be a number of challenges. In a recent review of online programs, Bejerano (2008) notes that (1) e learning is not for everyone, that some college students need the physical presence of instructors and other students to socially and intellectually integrate and adapt to the college experience, (2) success in online courses require discipline which not all students possess, and 3) there is little evidence of higher-order learning, e.g. evaluation and synthesis, in online instruction.

For these and other reasons, some faculty were at first hesitant to transfer the IC course online. They knew that developing and teaching online courses takes an enormous commitment. Early estimates were that it takes 500 hours to put an existing course online (Santovec, 2003), and teaching online is as time-consuming as teaching a traditional course (Akintunde, 2006; Carnes, Awang & Marlow, 2003; Sieber, 2005; Young, 2005). Also, some faculty perceived that an online intercultural communication course could not replicate the richness of experiential learning that takes place in the face-to-face course. Many of the department's students are white, middle class, with little intercultural experience, and the course was intended to deliver theoretical concepts and provide exposure to intercultural experiences. However, as online courses became more prevalent and it was apparent that students (and faculty) live increasingly mediated lives, this IC course, as explained below, was developed to incorporate meaningful experiential learning activities.

CASE DESCRIPTION: EXAMINING MULTIPLE LAYERS OF E-LEARNING ACCESS

There exists a need to address the dialectics of access in terms of technology adoption to minimize the disparities in Internet use for education (Natriello, 2001). Dominant discourse in digital divide research is grounded in a functionalist approach, focusing on the binary nature between the technologically rich and poor (Warschauer, 2003). The lion's share of digital divide research consists of quantitative data analyses with various studies concluding that socio-demographic factors like age, gender, and race play a significant part in access disparities in terms of Internet adoption. However, leading conceptualizations of digital inclusion rarely consider the social embeddedness of the Internet and the dynamic interactions between technological and social inequalities (Selwyn, 2004). According to Van Dijk (2005), digital access to information technology should be theorized as cumulative and recursive, including motivational, material, skills and usage access. Past survey studies employ measures of Internet use to reveal summary data differences in access but quantitative data may enshroud how cultural vectors dynamically affect the situated experiences of certain populations, including how college students grapple with various layers of with E-learning access.

In the next section, we present several ways in which our IC course attempts to address multiple pathways of E-learning access. As we do not want to essentialize instructors, administrators or students' behavior to group membership in our presentation, we note that various dialectics characterize peoples' relationships with E-learning technologies, (Martin & Nakayuma, 1999) that may simultaneously engender digital bridges and divides. A consideration of these related and oppositional logics illustrate how E-learning in this IC course case study may bridge multiple layers of access, albeit incompletely within the context of the larger department and University.

Material Access

As Mitchell (1999) argues, bridging the digital divide entails access to electronic appliances as "equitable access" requires access to fast digital connections, the affordable appliance, user-friendly software and the skills and motivation to learn and benefit from the new technologies (Mitchell, 1999, p. 151). In our case, several efforts have been made on the University and department level to provide parity in students' connections with regards to access to a panoply of digital resources to fulfill their educational goals.

The role of social institutions, including the University, is significant in shaping technological access (Kerckhoof, 1995), as the "political will" of governing organizations can help turn past divides into present and future digital opportunities (Koss, 2001). In recent years, the University has advanced several steps to build physical and technological infrastructure to create a wired and wireless campus. Computer laboratories in multiple buildings and student residential halls on campus provide free computing facilities. To provide equal access in computer facilities across campus for qualified students with disabilities, the University ensures federally mandated physical and program access for students with disabilities in all computer laboratory facilities commensurate with the general student population. Furthermore, the University provides wireless coverage throughout the campus. A 'mobile initiative 1:1' has been launched in partnership with Apple, Dell and Verizon Wireless. This initiative provides discounts on laptop purchases and also provides opportunities for students from financially disadvantaged households to apply for a $500 (locally endowed) scholarship toward a new laptop purchase. Additionally, operating software is provided gratis by the University as students can download popular applications like Microsoft Word, SPSS, Photoshop, Microsoft Access, Acrobat Professional, and Microsoft Powerpoint, needed to complete their coursework. On the departmental level, there are several computers available to students. To the extent that differences in family resources and environment play a part in students' using computers to benefit their academic pursuits (Attewell, 2001), the University's plan to provide various channels of digital connections to students serves as an entry point for them to gain technical access to electronic appliances and software to log on to course materials.

Every student is provided access to the University's virtual E-learning environment and electronic course management system, Blackboard, where course materials for online courses are housed. This IC course is hosted on Blackboard which is integrated into the students' personalized start page from which they can access their University email, receive messages from various University offices (e.g. library, messages about registration, etc), and a number of other Internet resources. As soon as they register, this course is immediately listed on their personal start page and they click on the course listing which takes them to the course website.

E-learning allows students to experience a sense of continuous dialogue – they can post anytime; discussions and insight are not confined to the classroom. A student may send a paper or post a message after school hours, a unique characteristic of online instruction. However, it should be noted that gaps may still exist in terms of technical access, for example, in online connectivity. Regular, if not monthly maintenance may disrupt online services. Dutton, Cheong & Park (2004b) highlight in their case study that technological glitches on electronic course management systems like Blackboard represent a more substantial barrier to Internet use than anticipated by students and faculty, including slow response times and trouble uploading course materials. A recent Pew Internet and American life survey, entitled 'When technology fails' also points to technical limitations that are a facet of digital divides as 39% of American adults surveyed with desktop or laptop computers reported to have had their machines not work properly at some time in the previous year (Horrigan & Jones, 2008).

Therefore, it is noteworthy that technical problems may still exist despite advances in courseware upgrades and the wiring of classrooms. When the course was first offered, the electronic course system was frequently unavailable for periods of time due to technological failure. This created anxiety for the students if the breakdowns happened to occur when an assignment was due. Course exams have also been the source of some problems since a technical glitch could cause the exam to close before students have completed it. The course policy is that once an exam is started it cannot be reopened (to prevent students from opening the test, copying it and then taking the exam later). When a test is prematurely closed (because of technical breakdowns or less legitimate reasons) the instructor makes a judgment as to whether to open the exam again.

In order to deal with the current occasional technological glitch and the challenges for first time online students, the IC instructor is readily available and open to student contact—particularly at the beginning of the semester and the University maintains a 24- hour help desk that students can call, email or chat electronically if they have technical problems. In addition, the University maintains a website with useful information—including a tutorial for first time students, which walks them through the details and logistics of their course website. This information about the website, helpline, and instructor contact information is posted prominently in the IC course syllabus, and students are instructed who to contact for various problems they might encounter (the help desk for technical problems, the instructor for answers to questions about grading etc). On the IC course syllabus, students are advised to submit their assignments early before the stipulated deadline and to always keep a copy of their assignments until they have received their grades. The IC course also allows for one missed assignment to allow students a little leeway if they are not used to online courses, or in the case of technical failure which might inhibit a student from submitting an assignment on time.

Motivational and Mental Access

Besides access to physical electronic gadgetry and the Internet, intellectual access is another dimension of E-learning. Stanley (2003) in an ethnographic research among marginalized populations highlights how individuals' "self-concept", "fear", and the "relevance" of the Internet interfere with their motivation to engage and thus potentially benefit from electronic technologies. With regard to E-learning, prior studies on student motivation and their attitudes toward online pedagogy highlight connections between learning style preferences and particular cultural groups (Aragon, Johnson & Shaik, 2003). For instance, one way of framing learning styles is according to field independence/dependence (Witkin, Moore, Goodenough, & Cox, 1977). Field independent learners prefer to work alone, with narrow focus; they impose structure on environment and have self-defined goals. In contrast, field-dependent learners rely more on the context for clues about information, they prefer structure and experience environment more holistically and globally; they are also interested in people and learn better in more social settings. For example, Mestre (2006) notes that African American students tend to prefer experiential learning and minimal structure, while Native Americans and Latinos prefer relational, social learning. All three groups tend to be more field-dependent learners while Asian Americans and white males tend to field independent learners. Notwithstanding the complexity of online communication (Hewling, 2005), these insights raise significant issues for E-learning instructors to address in order to encourage fruitful participation for students of diverse educational and cultural backgrounds.

This IC course was designed to take into account various learning styles so as to maximize students' motivational access. Typically, online learning situations stress logical, text-based, passive learning, more suited to those students who prefer abstract conceptualization and reflection, as well as field-independent learning (Mestre 2006). Thus, in addition to information delivery, this IC course was designed to provide opportunities for experiential learning practices via several course assignments that prompt students to apply IC theories to real life situations. For example, the initial assignment asks students to create and share their cultural profile: Where they grew up, their language background, any intercultural experiences they've had (e.g overseas travel or study, and family members and friends from different religious, ethnic, national cultures). This exercise helps students and instructor to get to know each other in a more personal way, which is especially important for relational learners who learn best through interpersonal connections. A second assignment that connects real life to intercultural concepts is the family history interviews. Students are instructed to investigate their family's immigration history by interviewing the oldest members of their family (Martin & Davis, 2001). They write a paper summarizing this history and then post discussion messages ("After writing your family history paper, what did you learn about your family that might help you understand today's immigrants better?"). Through this exercise students learn from their own and others' histories about the complexities of intercultural communication in an immigration context. A third assignment asks students to interview someone in an intercultural relationship, to identify and describe the benefits and challenges of their relationship, and to connect their findings to concepts discussed in the course materials. Results of this assignment also form the basis for a discussion board forum where students are asked to discuss among themselves what they learned from those interviews that they might apply to their own relationships. Students seem to learn a lot from this experience that they can apply to their own lives. As one student reported:

It was great to learn more about [intercultural relationships] because I have many friends who are in intercultural relationships and I cannot always relate. I feel that learning in depth about intercultural relationships can definitely be applied to my own life. The interviews that we conducted as well as discussion posts that I was able to read from my fellow classmates has given me some insight that I can apply to the important people in my own life who are currently in an intercultural relationship.

Furthermore, various aspects of the course design caters to what Mestre (2006) identified as the "global learners" and "millennium learners"; new, emerging types of learners who are ethnically diverse, used to digital environments, used to multi-tasking, visual learning and interactivity via mobile computing and online social networking tools. Online courses may provide increased opportunities for interactivity where there is more student-student and teacher-student interaction than in traditional classrooms (Akintunde, 2006; Merryfield, 2001).

Many E-learning studies suggest that the most effective discussions are student-centered where the role of instructor is not as authority but as facilitator (Dennen, 2005; Kelly, Ponton, & Rovai, 2007), however there is little agreement on the specifics of optimum instructor participation (Mandernach, Gonzalez & Garrett, 2006). This IC course provides very structured, specific questions to encourage student reflection on their own knowledge and opinions (e.g. often students must complete a prior activity before posting messages to the discussion board). The IC instructor participates little during the actual discussion but provides a weekly summary of each discussion board, highlighting the main points in the discussion, often quoting particular students' messages, and reinforcing class norms of respectful, thoughtful discussion posts. In this way, students learn quickly that the instructor consistently monitors the discussions and that their contributions play a significant role in what they learn and the grade they earn. However, sometimes students remark that they would like more consistent instructor input during discussions. This remains a challenge for the course instructor to know how to achieve optimal input, given the variety of student personal preferences and learning style.

The course evaluation is designed to encourage honest and open discussions as students earn credit/no credit points for the discussion section of the course. In order to received credit, the students must: 1) post messages on different days during the unit, so that a *discussion* takes place and it's not just every student posting two messages on the last day of the unit; 2) address the questions listed in the assignment, 3) demonstrate that they have completed a prior activity, if required, 4) make a substantive contribution that moves the discussion forward (they can't just say "I agree") and 5) Be respectful of others in their postings. On the syllabus, it is stated that "Some of the topics we cover in this course can lead to emotionally intense discussions. One of the goals of the course is to help us become more aware of how people from different backgrounds think and experience life. This learning cannot occur when people feel threatened or defensive. If postings are deemed by me to be hostile or demeaning to others, the message will be removed and the sender will not receive credit".

Research shows that students who are too shy or anxious to talk in face-to-face classes may feel freer to speak up in online discussion (Merryfield, 2001; Thompson & Ku, 2005). This IC course was designed to encourage equitable power dynamics by structuring discussion assignments so as "move the center," creating a space wherein all learners feel they are the center of instruction. Merryfield (2001) describes how international students and students of color are often marginalized in classroom discussions (even online), while white U. S. students dominate the discussion. She describes how class interaction changed after she "shifted the center" in her online teacher education course by requiring that each student post the exact same number of discussion messages: "I found a lack of dominance of any one group in initiating new ideas.....there is no obvious pattern of one group of teachers (students) controlling the discourse or silencing others. Nor did I find evidence that people chose to interact with others like themselves" (p. 295). In this IC course, the instructor maintains an awareness of students who may feel marginalized (e.g., non-native English speakers, ethnic/racial minorities, gay students) and attempts to make a legitimate space for them in class discussion, particularly in the early days of the course. This is done by quoting *these* students in the instructor discussion summaries and/or explicitly reinforcing the opinions/feelings that these students express during discussions so that not one group of students seems to control the discourse.

While online pedagogy does not easily afford opportunities for skill practice (Doo, 2006), in this IC course, students have been asked to engage in experiential activities to gain intercultural experience and develop intercultural communication skills. For example, in one assignment, students experientially explore the role of nonverbal communication in prejudicial thinking. Using Breeze Plug-in technology, they close their eyes and listen to the audio recording of their instructor telling them to image a U. S. student and Japanese student interacting in front of the student union. Then they are asked to open their eyes and describe the U. S. student very specifically (how tall, what color eyes, hair, appearance, clothing etc)—in a written paragraph. They then look at their description and are asked to write about who they did NOT see as U. S. American (e.g., Latino/a, disabled person, old person, heavy person?) and then write about and later post their ideas on the discussion board about the implications of intercultural interactions (e.g., if we only "see" certain people as "Americans" what does that say about how we interact with people we meet)? This exercise has proven to be very effective and has led to many majority (and some minority) group students to insights about how ingrained and pervasive prejudice and discrimination are. As one student reported:

I have learned how easily I and everyone else stereotype people. I realized this from the assignment that we did when you had us visualize two people from different cultures having a conversation. I was surprise at the fact I did that. ...After that assignment I realized that I need to be careful on how I view others before I get to know them. Now, before I go and talk to someone I make sure I do not prejudge what they are going to be like based on their outer appearance. .... I believe I am a better communicator with those that are culturally different from me because I keep an open mind and do not prejudge how I think they should act.

Students in this IC course are also required to participate in two different virtual collaborations, one with other classmates and one with students in a similar course in an overseas University. Recognizing that there may be cultural differences in students' online collaborative behaviors (Kim & Bonk, 2002), students are asked to reflect on their own participating and cultural learning—particularly in their collaboration with overseas students. One written assignment asks the students to analyze the intercultural communication that took place in their online collaboration—relating their own success and challenges in terms of what they have learned in the course about intercultural skills and effectiveness. In addition, the IC instructor maintains an awareness of cultural differences that may impact the performances of students and on occasion meets with or maintains email contact with students who have particular challenges in meeting course expectations.

In sum, this IC course provides motivational and mental E-learning access in the aforementioned ways, yet it should be noted that divides may continue to exist for some students, dependent on their backgrounds and experiences. Several scholars have highlighted the potential impact of different communication styles in online communication, using the frameworks of E. T. Hall (1959, 1966; low/high context communication style) and communication styles reflecting Hofstede's (1980, 1997) values framework (individualism/collectivism, power distance, masculinity/femininity, high/low uncertainty avoidance). For instance, Olaniran (2001) notes that conversations between low and high-context communicators may be difficult online as the low-context communicator may be comfortable being direct about feelings and opinions, whereas the high-context communicator might feel rather constrained by computer-mediated communication.

In this course, several strategies are used to motivate all students. If a student seems to "disappear" from discussion fora or fails to turn in more than one assignment, the instructor contacts the student, asks if everything is alright. However, it is a challenge to assist students when they disappear from an online course. As Stanford-Bowers (2008) reminds us, there are many factors beyond the instructors' control that affect student persistence in online courses, and often require attention to minute details that are sometimes overlooked or taken for granted.

Having about 50% of the evaluation credit/no credit points in the course also helps motivate all students, regardless of communication style or prior knowledge. They just need to show up and participate. Furthermore, students participate actively in evaluation; they are asked to evaluate themselves and others in their virtual team assignment. They assign points to themselves and others and the Instructor does not add any additional evaluation. Therefore, students know from the beginning that there will be consequences if they do not actively contribute to the course's project.

Technological Skills Access

Another related area of mental access relates to the students' online skills. According to Warschauer (2003), technological "literacy" involves the development of relevant understandings of devices, content, skills, understanding, and social support in order to engage in meaningful pedagogical practices. Literacy also links to a "second- level" digital divide in terms of online skills as past experiments show that there exists a considerable variance in the way and time in which individuals access and find information that they need online (Hargattai, 2002). Lack of technical skills and assistance is noted as a barrier to persistence in online courses (Stanford-Bowers, 2008). Cheong's research among Asian college students also highlight another chasm differentiating highly versus lowly skilled Internet users, in terms of their daily computer and Internet problem solving behaviors which has implications for users' productivity and potential benefits that can be reaped from the Internet. Contrary to popular conceptualizations of Asian youths as a cohort of technically savvy experts, findings from survey and interview data show considerable variance in participants' Internet expertise and problem solving behaviors, with some demonstrating limited knowledge of Internet use and awareness of troubleshooting strategies (Cheong, 2008). Among American adults, findings show that about half the population surveyed needed help from others to set up new devices or to show them how they function (Horrigan & Jones, 2008), illustrating the significance of computing skills for literacy access and divides.

Among the steps taken on the University level to increase computer literacy and improve students' online skills was the formation of the E-learning network in 2001. The technology-based learning and research unit, as part of the College of education, partnered with Cisco systems to develop online networking and IT curriculum. Students can earn credit from the University by completing modules on topics related to hardware and networking called the "basic fundamentals approach technology" online courses that include graphics, video, hands-on virtual labs and stimulations.

As noted earlier, students in the IC course are provided technical help from the University helpdesk; on occasions when students have problems accessing the discussion board, or submitting their papers to the course "digital dropbox". In each instance students contacted the technical staff and were given assistance. In one case a student taking an exam in a computer lab insisted that the system has inexplicably closed his exam and that the action was seen by a lab attendant. The instructor contacted the lab attendant who verified that the action had occurred as described by the student and the exam was reset.

As people in many professions find themselves increasingly working in globally distributed environments (Connaughton & Shuffler, 2007); this IC course requires students to work in virtual teams and complete an assignment where they develop a powerpoint presentation on a particular relevant topic, which is then posted on the course website. This assignment is designed to provide students with transferable technical skills which should serve them well in future professional situations, particularly in contexts where they are working with culturally diverse teams. Each virtual team has their own communication "center" on the course website, where they can post documents, exchange emails etc. The course also provides exposure to different kinds of Internet resources and interactions. For example, students learn to post messages on a discussion board, learn when to start new discussions on the fora, use a digital drop box to submit assignments, and listen to Breeze powerpoint presentations with audio posted by the instructor.

Content Access

A fourth facet of E-learning access is the availability of content appropriate to students as past content analyses of websites through the most popular Internet portals revealed the dearth of inadequate content for traditionally disadvantaged communities; newer immigrants and ethnic minorities in the U.S. (Lazarus & Mora, 2000). In this IC course, the assignments cover a wide range of cultural knowledge; many are topics that all students can relate to regardless of ethnic/racial background (e.g., cultural dimensions of nonverbal communication, conflict, relationships), and in addition some topics (e.g. code-switching, multicultural identities, managing intercultural transitions), tap particular knowledge and expertise held by students not generally privileged in many University classes—those who are bi/multilingual, those with minority cultural backgrounds, those who have direct experiences with prejudice and discrimination, and those who have learned to navigate different cultures in their everyday life.

Merryfield (2003) points out that "online technologies increase the depth of study and the meaningfulness of academic content" (p. 162), in part because students have time to think and reflect in asynchronous interactions and also because writing, in contrast with spoken discussion, encourages deeper, more thoughtful analysis. This IC course provides structured online intercultural experiences for students to reflect upon in undergraduate courses, particularly where there is little cultural diversity among the students. Online dialogue can be an effective way of engaging students in discussion about race and ethnicity, specifically "the use of an online platform can facilitate one's learning about 'others' in a more engaged, open and accommodating manner, which goes beyond the traditional classroom teaching and learning of intercultural communication" (Kanata & Martin, 2007, p. 1).

The course also provides access to students overseas as one assignment pairs each IC course student with a student from a similar course in another university in either Europe or Asia. Each student pair conducts an "ethnographic" research project on cultural differences/similarities of a communication practice (e.g. workplace conflict, Internet relationships). Each student interviews 5 of their friends on the topic, the two students then compare their ethnographic data, draw some conclusions about cultural similarities/differences between the two cultural groups and speculates on the reason for their findings, using course materials to guide their analyses and conclusion. A final assignment asks the students to reflect on their own intercultural behavior with the overseas student, what they learned from the experience and what they can take from the experience that may help them in their future work and social relations. One student describes what he learned in the virtual collaboration assignment:

The Virtual Collaboration experience was very rewarding... I learned several important things that I will use in the future when working on projects such as this. Firstly, language barriers and time zone differences can increase the time it takes to complete common tasks. Realistic timelines need to allow extra time for the completion of tasks due to these factors. In addition, proper planning and frequent communication is essential. Clarification on issues can often take 24 hours or more to resolve. However, the unique perspective that collaboration with people from differing cultures produces is often a better result than either is capable of alone.

CURRENT CHALLENGES

This chapter has addressed multiple access/divide dialectics, in the case of an online IC course, in order to illuminate the multifaceted nature of E-learning access. While the delivery of this IC course seems to have met many of the challenges of access, a few challenges remain. Starting at the most local level, concerning material access—while the University has addressed this issue in many ways, there are still some students who cannot afford home Internet access and many nontraditional students have difficulty accessing the University computers because of child-care issues, work schedules, or lack of reliable transportation. Concerning mental access, while a great deal of effort is extended to motivate all students and to adequately meet the challenges of students' various learning styles and culture-specific communication styles, this course could be altered to incorporate more student input and suggestions concerning this goal. Similarly with issues of content access, it is possible that the content could be altered to be more explicitly inclusive of cultural issues, i.e., while cultural communication issues of race, ethnicity, age, and religion are fairly explicitly addressed, issues concerning disabilities are not.

At a more macro level, administrative challenges remain. As noted, while the course seems successful and desired, issues at the departmental level remain to prevent increasing access—i.e. adding more sections. The extant and looming economic crisis in the U.S. has also recently impacted the University in various ways (e.g. mandatory revertment of funds to the State) and may lead to the implementation of more bottom-line and cost-cutting philosophies to manage future technical and administrative support for E-learning. There are also challenges at the University level, described by the Director of Online Programs quoted earlier. One challenge is the evaluation of the effectiveness of existing courses which led to a recent initiative "Midterm Course Design Survey" where students were asked to evaluate the design of and materials in online courses, what technologies were most beneficial, and which activities were most helpful in student learning. These results will be useful in helping faculty and administration to improve the quality of online courses. A second challenge is to get the word out to faculty that technological and pedagogical support exists. She noted that while most instructors are open to teaching courses online, there are some who are resistant. Finding ways to persuade faculty to become involved in E-learning remains a challenge.

Finally, a word about the broader disciplinary context. It is important to context this case study in the larger scholarly endeavors of cultural and communication research. Historically, intercultural communication scholars have focused on face-to-face encounters and there is a dearth of research investigating the relationship between culture and mediated communication; theory lags substantially behind practice. Everyday, millions of people communicate online with culturally different others in social networking sites (SNS), on blogs, through email, in virtual teams—and communication scholars have only begun to scratch the proverbial surface of knowledge. Concomitantly, most intercultural communication courses are offered in face-to-face contexts. There has been some recent interest in online instruction, some institutions are supportive, but as we have shown in this paper, the issues of culture and access in E-learning processes are complex and multi-layered.

REFERENCES

Akintunde, M. (2006). Diversity.Com: Teaching an online course on white racism and multiculturalism. *Multicultural Perspectives*, *8*(2), 35–45. doi:10.1207/s15327892mcp0802_7

Allen, I. E., & Seaman, J. (2007). *Online nation: Five years of growth in online learning*. Needham, MA: The Sloan Consortium. Retrieved September 22, 2008 from http://www.sloan-c.org/publications/survey/pdf/online_nation.pdf

Aragon, S. R., Johnson, S. D., & Shaik, N. (2003). The influence of learning style preferences on student success in online versus face-to-face environments. *American Journal of Distance Education*, *16*(4), 227–243. doi:10.1207/S15389286AJDE1604_3

Attewell. (2001). The first and second digital divides. *Sociology of Education, 74*(3), 252-259.

Bejerano, A. R. (2008). The genesis and evolution of online degree programs: Who are they for and what have we lost along the way? *Communication Education*, *1*(3), 408 – 414.

Burbules, N. C. (2000). Does the Internet constitute a global educational community? In Burbules, N. C., & Torres, C. (Eds.), *Globalization and education: Critical perspectives* (pp. 323–355). New York: Routledge.

Carnes, L. W., Awang, F., & Marlow, J. (2003). Can instructors ensure the integrity and quality of online courses? *Delta Pi Epsilon Journal*, *45*, 162–172.

Cheong, P. H. (2008). The young and techless? Internet use and problem solving behaviors among young adults in Singapore. *New Media & Society*, *10*(5), 771–791. doi:10.1177/1461444808094356

Connaughton, S. L., & Shuffler, M. (2007). Multinational and multicultural distributed teams: A review and future agenda. *Small Group Research*, *38*, 397–412. doi:10.1177/1046496407301970

Dennen, V. P. (2005). From message posting to learning dialogues: Factors affecting learner participation in asynchronous discussion. *Distance Education*, *26*(1), 127–148. doi:10.1080/01587910500081376

Doo, M. Y. (2006). A problem in online interpersonal skills training: do learners practice skills? *Open Learning*, *21*(3), 263–272. doi:10.1080/02680510600953252

Dutton, W. H., Cheong, P. H., & Park, N. (2004). An ecology of constraints on e-learning in higher education: The case of a virtual learning environment. *Prometheus*, *22*(2), 131–149. doi:10.1080/0810902042000218337

Dutton, W. H., & Cheong, P. H. & Park, N. (2004b). The social shaping of a virtual learning environment: The case of a university-wide course management system. *Electronic Journal of e-Learning, 2*(1), 69-80.

Ess, C., & Sudweeks, F. (2005). Culture and computer-mediated communication: Toward new understandings. *Journal of Computer-Mediated Communication*, *11*(1), 179–191. doi:10.1111/j.1083-6101.2006.tb00309.x

Hall, E. T. (1959). *The silent language*. Garden City, NY: Anchor Press.

Hall, E. T. (1966). *The hidden dimension*. Garden City, NY: Anchor Press.

Hargittai, E. (2002). Second-Level Digital Divide: Differences in People's Online Skills. *First Monday, 7*(4), Retrieved Sep.2002 from http://firstmonday.org/issues/issue7_4/hargittai/index.html

Hewling, A. (2005). Culture in the online class: Using message analysis to look beyond nationality-based frames of reference. *Journal of Computer-Mediated Communication*, *11*(1), 337–356. doi:10.1111/j.1083-6101.2006.tb00316.x

Hofstede, G. (1980). *Culture's consequences: International differences in work-related values*. Beverly Hill, CA: Sage.

Hofstede, G. (1997). *Cultures and organizations: Software of the mind* (Rev. Ed.). New York: McGraw-Hill.

Horrigan, J., & Jones, S. (2008). *When technology fails*. Retrieved Nov. 15, 2008 from: http://www.pewinternet.org/pdfs/PIP_Tech_Failure.pdf

Kanata, T., & Martin, J. N. (2007). Facilitating dialogues on race and ethnicity with technology: Challenging "Otherness" and promoting a dialogic way of knowing. *Journal of Literacy and Technology*, *8*(2), 1–40.

Kelly, H. F., Ponton, M. K., & Rovai, A. P. (2007). A comparison on student evaluations of teaching between online and face-to-face courses. *The Internet and Higher Education*, *10*(2), 189–101. doi:10.1016/j.iheduc.2007.02.001

Kerckhoff, A. C. (1995). Institutional Arrangements and Stratification Processes in Industrial Societies. *Annual Review of Sociology*, *21*, 323–347. doi:10.1146/annurev.so.21.080195.001543

Kim, K., & Bonk, C. J. (2002). Cross-cultural comparisons of online collaboration. *Journal of Computer-Mediated Communication*, *8*(1).

Lazarus, W., & Mora, F. (2000). *Online content for low-income and underserved Americans: The digital divide's new frontier*. CA: The Children's Partnership.

Mandernach, B. J., Gonzales, R. M., & Garrett, A. L. (2006). *Journal of Online Learning and Teaching*, *2*(4). Retrieved February 23, 2009 from http://jolt.merlot.org/vol4no1/Vol2_No4.htm

Martin, J. N., & Davis, O. Idriss. (2001). Conceptual foundations for teaching about Whiteness in Intercultural Communication courses. *Communication Quarterly*, *50*, 298–313.

Martin, J. N., & Nakayama, T. K. (1999). Thinking dialectically about culture and communication. *Communication Theory*, *9*, 1–25. doi:10.1111/j.1468-2885.1999.tb00160.x

Merryfield, M. (2003). Like a veil: Cross-cultural experiential learning online. *Contemporary Issues in Technology & Teacher Education*, *3*(2), 146–171.

Merryfield, M. M. (2001). The paradoxes of teaching a multicultural education course online. *Journal of Teacher Education*, *52*(4), 283–299. doi:10.1177/0022487101052004003

Mestre, L. (2006). Accommodating diverse learning styles in an online environment, (Guest Editorial). *Reference and User Services Quarterly*, *46*(2), 27–32.

Natriello, G. (2001). Bridging the second digital divide: What can sociologists of education contribute? *Sociology of Education*, *74*(3), 260–265. doi:10.2307/2673278

Olaniran, B. A. (2001). The effects of computer-mediated communication on transculturalism. In Milhouse, V. H., Asante, M. K., & Nwosu, P. O. (Eds.), *Transcultural realities: Interdisciplinary perspectives on cross-cultural relations* (pp. 83–105). Thousand Oaks, CA: Sage. doi:10.4135/9781452229430.n5

Olaniran, B. A., & Agnello, M. F. (2008). Globalization, educational hegemony, and higher education. *Multicultural Education & Technology Journal*, *2*(2), 68–86. doi:10.1108/17504970810883351

Santovec, M. L. (2003). A model for evaluating online courses. *Distance Education Report*, *7*(8), 7–8.

Schwartzman, R. (2007). Refining the question: how can online instruction maximize opportunities for all students? *Communication Education*, *56*(1), 113–117. doi:10.1080/03634520601009728

Selwyn, N. (2004). Reconsidering Political and Popular Understandings of the *Digital Divide. New Media & Society*, *6*(3), 341–362. doi:10.1177/1461444804042519

Sieber, J. E. (2005). Misconceptions of and realities about teaching online. *Science and Engineering Ethics*, *11*, 329–340. doi:10.1007/s11948-005-0002-7

Stanford-Bowers, E. (2008). Persistence in online classes: As study of perceptions among community college stakeholders. *Journal of Online Learning and Teaching*, *4*(1). Retrieved February 23, 2009 from http://jolt.merlot.org/vol4no1/stanford-bowers0308.htm

Stanley, L. D. (2003). Beyond Access: Psychosocial Barriers to Computer Literacy. *The Information Society*, *19*, 407–416. doi:10.1080/715720560

Thompson, L., & Ku, H.-Y. (2005). Chinese graduate students' experiences and attitudes toward online learning. *Educational Media International*, *42*(1), 33–47. doi:10.1080/09523980500116878

van Dijk, J. (2005). *The Deepening Divide*. Thousand Oaks, CA: Sage.

Warschauer, M. (2003). *Technology and Social Inclusion: Rethinking the Digital Divide*. Cambridge, MA: MIT Press.

Witkin, H. A., Moore, C. A., Goodenough, D. R., & Cox, P. W. (1977). Field-dependent and field-independent cognitive styles and their educational implications. *Review of Educational Research*, *47*(1), 1–64.

Young, J. R. (2005, August 12). Professors give mixed reviews of Internet's educational impact. *Chronicle of Higher Education*. Retrieved August 21, 2005 from http://chronicle.com/weekly/v51/i49/49a03201.htm

ENDNOTE

1 Interview with Jill Schiefelbein, Director of Online Programs in the College of Liberal Arts and Sciences, November 26, 2008.

This work was previously published in Cases on Successful E-Learning Practices in the Developed and Developing World: Methods for the Global Information Economy, edited by Bolanle A. Olaniran, pp. 78-91, copyright 2010 by Information Science Reference (an imprint of IGI Global).

Chapter 6
Blended Learning Internationalization from the Commonwealth:
An Australian and Canadian Collaborative Case Study

Shelley Kinash
Bond University, Australia

Susan Crichton
University of Calgary, Canada

EXECUTIVE SUMMARY

This case depiction addresses the contentious issue of providing culturally and globally accessible teaching and learning to international students in universities in the Commonwealth nations of Australia and Canada. The chapter describes the university systems and cultures, the barriers to authentic higher education internationalization, and the problems frequently experienced by international students. Two university cases are presented and analysed to depict and detail blended learning approaches (face-to-face combined with e-learning) as exemplars of culturally and globally accessible higher education and thereby ideologically grounded internationalization. Lessons learned are presented at the systems level and as teaching and learning solutions designed to address pedagogical problems frequently experienced by international students in the areas of communication, academic skills, teaching and learning conceptualization, and moving from rote learning to critical thinking. The blended learning solutions are analysed through the lens of critical theory.

DOI: 10.4018/978-1-4666-1885-5.ch006

SITUATION BACKGROUND

The *cultural and global accessibility* of a university's teaching and learning is a direct measure of whether the university's development mission is to promote intercultural education and worldwide networks or whether that higher education institution recruits international students primarily as lucrative export-industry goods. *Culture* is the overall mindset shaped in a time and place and shared by a group of individuals. When individuals such as international students leave their group they typically carry a mindset with them from their culture of origin to their culture of study. This definition of culture is grounded in Hofstede's (2001) model. He defined culture as "collective programming of the mind" (p. 1). He explained that "it manifests itself not only in values, but in more superficial ways: in symbols, heroes, and rituals" (p. 1). *Cultural accessibility* means that faculty members actively design their teaching to ensure that *all* of their students are learning, through interaction with the instructor, their student peers and with globally responsible and responsive content (McBurnie, 2000). Lanham and Zhou (2003) wrote, "the inclusion of multiple cultures in university courses means that a more flexible approach should be taken with the design of these courses to ensure that all students are able to reach their course goals" (p. 278). Cultural accessibility can only be understood against the backdrop of internationalization which is a conflicted interplay between economy, pedagogy, and ideology (Meiras, 2004).

Surging in the mid 1990s, enrolment of international students in developed Commonwealth nations became a profitable industry (Davies & Harcourt, 2007; De Vita, 2007; Poole, 2001). The economic advantage of international student enrolment drove an operational or business stance on internationalization (De Vita & Case, 2003; Edwards et.al., 2003). De Vita and Case contrasted the economic stance of universities "expand[ing] their financial base by using international students as a source of revenue" with the ideological stance in which the primary work of universities is "preparing students to live and work in a multicultural society through greater understanding and respect for other cultures" (p. 385). While cultural accessibility is a laudable goal, there is a great deal of contemporary discourse presenting universities as more interested in capitalism than knowledge emancipation (Cimbala, 2002; Gunn, 2000; Huff, 2006; Murray & Dollery, 2005; Versluis, 2004).

Numerous critical theorists argue that administrators have paid so much attention to the profitability of internationalization that universities have not supported the needs of the international student nor benefitted from the knowledge and understanding brought by students from diverse cultures. In short, critics argue that issues of economic viability have diverted attention from the student experience. Davies and Harcourt (2007) wrote, "...considerable funds are spent on marketing and raising expectations when in fact the relationship between the academic staff member and the student is a key source of satisfaction" (p. 122). Brown and Jones (2007) wrote, "...to date, recruitment of international students has been seen by many primarily as a source of income generation, a 'cash cow', and often diverse students, once recruited, were problematised by the academy and seen as needy of support in a kind of deficit model" (p. 2). Brown and Joughin (2007) wrote that once in-program, international students are perceived as "bearers of problems" whereas universities would benefit from perceiving them as "bearers of culture" (p. 58). Post-secondary providers are metaphorically accused of rolling out the red carpet for international student entry, leading to the teaching and learning equivalent of a dungeon rather than palace once the students are inside. This might be as subtle as expectations of references and examples that are institutionally recognized rather than student experienced or as overt as food and dress standards that smell or look correct to the mainstream population.

From May through September 2009, Australia saw a hotbed of media activity reporting accounts of mistreatment of international students and the government's response. Waters and MacBean (May 29, 2009) for *ABC News*; Millar and Doherty (June 1, 2009) for *The Age*, and; Wong (July 13, 2009) as a guest contributor to the *Research School of Pacific and Asian Studies at Australian National University* made seven key points. First, post-secondary education of international students is a $15.5 billion industry making it Australia's third largest *export* industry earner after minerals and agricultural products. Second, there have been a large number of recent violent attacks on international students from India, and third, some students from China. Fourth, there were arguments regarding whether these attacks were racially targeted or whether the higher incident of attacks on Indian students was statistically proportionate, exacerbated by lifestyle factors that make attacks on students more likely. Fifth, there was dissatisfaction regarding Australian officials' response and perceived inaction to these assaults. Sixth, students held protest marches in Melbourne and Sydney, some of which resulted in physical confrontation between police and protesters. Seventh, Indian parents, officials, and the general public were distressed, resulting in negative public relations regarding Australian international education. These reports were followed by Wendy Carlisle's current affairs inquiry called *Holy Cash Cows*, aired on television July 27, 2009 by Australian Broadcasting Corporation's *Four Corners.* The show exposed: vocational training schools where the student experience did not match what was advertised to students, leaving them without career credentials upon graduation, and; crooked migration agents who were selling falsified certificates of visa requirements. The next surge of media reports addressed the Australian government's response to the allegations and events. In *World News Australia* on July 29, 2009 Julia Gillard, Deputy Prime Minister, was quoted as stating, "The Australian government is absolutely committed to providing quality education for all students, and we have taken steps to improve the experience for overseas students" (Para 9). The Australian Government Department of Education, Employment and Workplace Relations published a media release on August 19, 2009 introducing an Amendment Bill to the *Education Services for Overseas Students Act 2000* and warning "education providers that they risk being shut down if they don't comply with rules relating to international students" (Para 1). Glidden, for the *Melton Leader* (September 12, 2009) reported that Gillard visited India to restore international relations and ameliorate fears about the safety of students in Australia. Ja and Symons-Brown (September 14, 2009) wrote an article for the *Brisbane Times* stating that Gillard was holding roundtable discussions with international students. Perhaps Australian post-secondary educators are now outside the eye of the media storm, but the imperative of culturally accessible teaching and learning is heightened.

Neither has Canada been immune to criticism regarding treatment of international students. Reitmanova (2008) addressed Canadian universities' failure to provide equitable no-cost health care insurance to international students. The author referenced other inequities in international student benefits and experiences in such domains as childcare and employment. She wrote that while Canadian universities' rhetoric is of internationalization, "...it seems that the vision for such an environment is a narrow one, focused more on increasing the number of international students and organizing annual international food and craft fairs rather than on safeguarding students' rights" (p. 10). Guo and Jamal (2007) indicated that Canadian universities have not achieved cultural accessibility of teaching and learning in that the unconscious pervasive notion that *white is right* has not been adequately surfaced and addressed in attitude, policy and procedure, meaning that students' differences are treated as problems and deficits. What might be conceived of as an unsettled and transitional stage in internationalization, both necessitates and is indicated by, an emphasis on marketing and international student recruitment (Cudmore, 2005).

Perhaps what is most evident from the above summary of popular media and academic literature is that it is necessary but not sufficient to enroll international students in order to achieve internationalization. Higher education internationalization has numerous elements, and in this paper we are operationally defining internationalization as quality education for students who enrol in an Australian or Canadian university who do not have citizenship in the respective country. There are numerous stress factors of intercultural study, one of the most significant of which is conversational language (Briguglio, 2000; Patron, 2009; Patron, 2007; Ter-Minasova, 2005) at least in part because language and culture are so embedded that the incoming international student is continually adapting, accommodating and reconciling culture as much as those students from non-English speaking backgrounds are learning to use the mechanics of English (Liddicoat, 2005). For the purposes of this chapter we adopt Leask's (2007) definition of higher education internationalization as learning "...in which students from a variety of cultural and linguistic backgrounds come together in a predominantly English-speaking environment and are taught in English (e.g. in ... Australia, ... Canada and the US)" (p. 86). Higher education internationalization is not achieved merely by recruiting international students. The institution must also foster a pedagogical stance of cultural appreciation and therefore facilitate culturally accessible teaching and learning.

Being an international student to a Commonwealth country has inherent challenges. De Vita (2007) presented an overview of the internationalization literature, focusing on the experience of international students, particularly in the context of the United Kingdom. His appraisal revealed pedagogic problems of international students as a predominant theme. These problems are exacerbated by the fact that universities are not using "culturally inclusive teaching and assessment strategies" (p. 159). De Vita listed the primary problems of international university students as:

1. Barriers to effective intercultural communication, such as cultural stereotyping, language fatigue (for both second-language speakers and listeners) and misunderstandings due to the unqualified use of colloquialisms, idiomatic expressions and analogies;
2. A cross-cultural awareness gap in approaches in essay writing, in terms of discourse structures, academic literacies and referencing practices;
3. A cultural clash of learning and teaching styles, exemplified by issues such as the reluctance by some international students to participate in class discussions and in other collaborative and student-centred activities;
4. Transitional difficulties in moving from dependence on rote learning to developing intellectual independence, critical thinking, the synoptic capacity and autonomous learning skills. (p. 158)

The literature documents intercultural problems of international students beyond the teaching and learning components, such as a discomfort with the Western *drink culture* (consumption of alcohol as a form of entertainment) and the resulting social isolation that can occur (Midgeley, 2009; Patron, 2009). Or, in the case of Canada, an expectation that international students can cope with the climate (extreme winter conditions) and afford the costs associated with dressing appropriately and safely for the varied seasons. While it is important to acknowledge the wide and significant scope of international student concerns, the non-academic problems are beyond the scope of this chapter. The focus of the remainder of this chapter is on the four pedagogic areas identified by De Vita (2007) as identified in the literature as the key problem focuses: communications, with a particular focus on language difficulties; academic skills; teaching and learning stance, and; constructivism.

This chapter describes the solution that two Commonwealth universities have found to facilitate culturally accessible teaching and learning of international students through blended learning. While there are numerous analyses contributing to the specificities of the definition of blended learning in higher education, most authors agree on the basic elements that: a combination of face-to-face and digital teaching and learning approaches are offered to the students; the tools and approaches are deliberately chosen for their capacities and affordances, and; the design requires original creation versus tacking digital elements onto an existing face-to-face scenario or vice versa (Aspden & Helm, 2004; Boyle, 2005; Denis, 2003; Ellis & Calvo, 2004; Kirkley & Kirkley, 2004; Macdonald & Mcateer, 2003; Moore, 2005; O'Toole & Absalom, 2003; Osguthorpe & Graham, 2003; Stacey & Gerbic, 2007). Jelfs, Nathan and Barrett (2004) added an intriguing element to the definition in that blending also connotes *blending into students' lives*. Kerres and de Witt (2003) elaborated that designing pedagogically grounded blended learning means attending to content, communication, and student construction of learning. Lanham and Zhou (2003) specifically applied blended learning within the context of cultural accessibility. They argued that the "benefit of blending is that it allows students from different cultures the ability to select the delivery format of their learning content, hence improving their interaction with the environment" (p. 287). As presented in the cases that follow, it is this flexibility that is the key determinant of culturally and globally accessible higher education.

CASE DESCRIPTIONS

Putting aside geography and history momentarily, the two universities reflected in these cases have something unique to demonstrate in the field of higher education in that both have developed exemplar approaches to culturally and globally accessible teaching and learning. Both have common and disparate elements of higher education in Australia and Canada as Commonwealth nations which make them compelling for analysis. The case description is presented in three parts. The first part paints a picture of Australian and Canadian national and university culture in order to contextualize the relative cultural accessibility of the institutions. The second and third parts depict the case of a single university in each of these countries. The Bond University case focuses on the pedagogic problems frequently experienced by international students and the teaching and learning solutions that the university has put into place in order to address these challenges. The University of Calgary case is situated in the interface between learners and university programs and addresses the problems and solutions (where possible) of the Graduate Division of Educational Research within the Faculty of Education. Readers should note that blended learning is operationalized differently within the two cases. At Bond University, the blend of face-to-face and digital approaches is within every course, whereas within the University of Calgary case, the blend occurs within the program overall.

Australian and Canadian National and University Culture

Bourne (2000) wrote about the contemporary irony that universities have a heightened role to play in worldwide socio-economic development within the age of the globalized knowledge economy, and yet universities are devalued commodities. He argued that the solutions to worldwide declining esteem and support for universities lie in alliances, networks and collective action between Commonwealth nations (developed and developing). As academics within two universities in two of the five wealthiest Commonwealth nations (after Singapore and United Kingdom and before New Zealand) we believe that collaborative efforts to communicate cultural accessibility of higher education teaching and learning such as conveyed through this chapter are worth prioritizing.

Miller (1995) compared and contrasted university culture in the United Kingdom, Australia and Canada. For the purposes of this current analysis, only the results for Australia and Canada will be described. Overall, Miller's inquiry revealed that between universities in these two nations, "the ideas that inform the dominant political discourses have much common ground" (p. 41). Miller highlighted a number of similarities between Australian and Canadian nations and university culture, many of which define them as distinct from many other university systems. Both nations have a colonial (as opposed to imperial) history. In both, there is a notable absence of 'ancient collegial' universities such as Oxford and Cambridge in the United Kingdom. In both nations, there is an increased percentage of society pursuing higher education with the effect of lowered aptitude entry scores. Both are suffering troubled economies. This can be seen in the decline of public funding to universities and the intensification of marketing and enrolment schemes. There is increasing pressure to adopt instrumentalist vocational pedagogical models. There is reduced research funding and intensive competition between universities for these funds. The majority of funded research explicitly addresses national economic priorities and has the potential to generate private industry contribution.

While both nations administrate universities through federal as opposed to unitary systems, herein are the primary contrasts. Miller described the Australian case as a 'hard' federal case. "The Commonwealth government in Canberra, through the exercise of financial, administrative and political power, has been able to take increasing control over universities and those who work in them" (p. 44). On the other hand, while higher education is ultimately federal in Canada, distribution of funds is handled provincially. Canada is a "federal state of ten provinces and two territories[1], whose constitution recognizes higher education as a matter of provincial jurisdiction and control" (p. 44). Miller explained that the federal government distributes block funding to the provinces who may then distribute the overall money at provincial government members' discretion including, for example, acting upon a decision to allocate a higher proportion to health care leaving less for higher education. Miller's analysis revealed Australian and Canadian university systems as more similar than different, and as developed Commonwealth nations, distinct from other higher education systems.

The paragraphs above presented a primer to Australian and Canadian university systems. Because this chapter is part of a collection about cultural accessibility, the next question then, is what about culture? How similar are Australia and Canada culturally? The premier authority on culture is Geert Hofstede. His (2001) second edition of *Culture's Consequences* presents the most-pervasive and well-respected cultural factors and model despite the fact that his data was primarily collected between 1967 and 1973, and that his theory has been critiqued as static, essentialist and over focused on nation as the sole determinant of culture (Chiang, 2005; Min-Sun, 2007). While it is important to acknowledge these criticisms, Hofstede's model is used here because his data is consistent with the authors' case observations. Hofstede described his primary research method as follows.

The base data for the study discussed in this book were collected in a large multinational corporation: IBM. The company's international employee attitude survey program began between 1967 and 1973 in two survey rounds produced answers to more than 116,000 questionnaires from 72 countries in 20 languages. The analysis focused on country differences in answers on questions about employee values" (p. 41).

For the purposes of this chapter, each of Hofstede's five dimensions is briefly described, and the scores for Australia and Canada compared and contrasted. As a metaphoric yardstick for American readers, scores from the USA are included in the analysis. For international readers, the high and low country on each measure is identified. The implications of each cultural dimension on higher education are introduced.

The higher the score on the individualism / collectivism scale (out of a possible 100 points), the more motivated persons of that nation are by personal gain – hence higher individualism scores. They make their decisions based on what will benefit themselves personally over the good of the nation or society. Australia has the second high score in this category (90). USA, the high scorer, exceeded Australia's score by only one point. Canada falls somewhat lower in the national comparison, but is still highly individualistic at 80 points. The smallest score on this scale was by Guatemala, meaning that persons from this nation are more likely to put others over themselves. As an illustration of the complexity of higher education cultural accessibility, one can imagine the group-work dynamics when a Guatemalan student is assigned to work with students from the USA and Australia.

The second dimension is power distance. A high score in power distance means that there are large degrees of separation between ranks or castes in society. Persons from cultures who score high in this category honour and revere their superiors in social status and rank. Australia, Canada, and the United States all scored well below the midpoint of this scale at 36, 39, and 40 respectively. This means that by most counts they are egalitarian societies. It is not surprising that of the three, Australia scored lowest, as Australians have low tolerance for people who "big note" themselves, including and perhaps especially, university academics. The high culture on this measure is Malaysia and the low is Austria. The implications for higher education are that Malaysian students are likely to experience discomfort with expressing critical thinking if the line of argument runs counter to what their professor has lectured. The tendency of students from south-east Asia to listen rather than speak, and to seek and explicitly follow the professor's instructions is well documented by authors such as Gerbic (2005), Gu (2005), Skyrme (2005), and Thorpe (2006). Notably, international students beyond Asia (e.g. France) struggle with similar cultural dissonance with respect to pedagogical stance (Patron, 2009).

The third dimension is masculine / feminine. In a masculine culture, *men are men and women are women*. In other words, there is high traditional gender role definition. Feminine cultures, on the other hand, are much more flexible and allow diversity within gender characteristics and roles. A high score on this measure indicates a more masculine culture. On this scale, Australia and United States are once again very similar. The scores were 61 and 62 respectively. Canada, on the other hand, is close to the midpoint at 52. The high (masculine) culture is Japan and the low (thereby feminine culture) is Sweden. In other words, Japanese students are likely to feel at home in Australian higher education with a dominant discourse that authors such as Currie, Harris and Thiele (2000) call *masculinist*, where authority positions are considered to be biased towards men (Asmar, 1999) and where the majority of students are enrolled in traditionally gendered disciplines (Miller, Lietz, & Kotte, 2002).

The next cultural category is uncertainty avoidance. The people of countries who score low on this dimension (the lowest score going to Singapore) have low tolerance of the unknown. They like to identify, anticipate and control as many factors as possible. The high-scorer was Greece. With Australia's vernacular of "no worries" juxtaposed with a need to anticipate weather-related natural disasters, they fall almost exactly between the two ends of the continuum with a score of 51. Canada and United States are very close by, at 48 and 46 respectively. There is a higher education saying that goes – *the greatest university learning is to tolerate ambiguity.* Singaporean students do not subscribe to this sentiment. They tend to experience heightened frustration with Australian and Canadian educators with constructivist pedagogies.

The final category is about perspective and outlook with long-term on one end of the continuum and short-term on the other. Countries, who score highest such as Hong Kong, orient themselves to the distant future. The people of Hong Kong are capable of delayed gratification. On the other end of the scale, people from Pakistan are oriented toward short-term gains and rewards. Fortunately for the students from Pakistan, Australia and Canada both have fairly low scores on this domain (31 and 23 respectively), indicating that people of both of these cultures tend to cast their gaze upon the short-term. Similarly, the score for the United States is 29. Applying this domain to higher education, students from Pakistan tend to want assessment items earlier in the term with quick-turn-around on the feedback, whereas students from Hong Kong are willing to study for a large-scale final exam.

It is important to remember that there is a great deal of variation *within*, just as there is *between* cultures (Guo & Jamal, 2007). Some of the other impacting factors are age, gender and birth order. While Hofstede's model should not be used to homogenize, stereotype or to erect ceilings on students, the cultural dimensions do raise the salience of learning factors such as the dynamics of the relationship between the teacher and learner, the learners' relative needs for clear expectations, and desire for feedback. The means by which an Australian and a Canadian university developed solutions to address culturally accessible learning follow.

Bond University

Bond University opened in 1989 on the Gold Coast of Queensland, Australia. Bond was the only tertiary institution in Australia designed as an international university, as opposed to an Australian university with an enrolment of international students. As such, Bond has developed specialized programs and pedagogical initiatives to support a consistent enrolment of 40% international students and 60% Australian national students. The 2008 total student population was 3758, 27% of whom were postgraduate. Bond is a private, not-for-profit university with four faculties: business, technology, and sustainable development; health sciences and medicine; humanities and social sciences, and; law. Bond operates through three full compulsory semesters meaning that students complete a condensed degree. Since establishment, Bond has produced over 12,000 graduates and currently graduates 1500 people per annum.

As a newcomer to Australian higher education (Marginson, 2006), Bond University established and has maintained itself as distinctive in teaching and learning. Across the university, Faculty and school administrators, and academics design learning experiences and assessment items that catalyse the four graduate outcomes of: knowledge and critical thinking; leadership, initiative, and teamwork; communication skills, and; responsibility.

Teaching and learning at Bond University is distinctive in three ways. First, the ratio between academics and students is maintained at the uniquely low figure of ten to one. Small course sizes mean that Bond academics are able to meet the desirable pedagogical conditions of multiple means of representation, engagement, and expression. These principles of universal design for learning as described by Jardine, Friesen and Clifford (2006); Kinash (2006); Moulton, Huyler, Hertz, and Levenson (2002); Rose and Meyer (2002); Rose and Meyer (2006), and; Rose, Meyer, and Hitchcock (2005) are a means of meeting the needs of diverse learners through facilitating learning experiences, motivating, and encouraging students to demonstrate their learning in a variety of ways, including a blend of traditional paper-based, digital and multi-media pedagogies.

Second, Bond University is broadly and deeply connected to the community. Industry committees extensively informed the initial higher education curriculum, and the professions and professional accreditation continue to shape content and teaching processes. The students participate in work-integrated learning and all learning is conversely integrated through authentic work. Through research partnerships, internships, and a well-supported alumni network, Bond University maintains close ties to its corporate partners.

Third, Bond University has committed to blended learning through choosing a combination of face-to-face and e-learning across the university and for 100% of courses, unique in the field of higher education whereby the other Australian universities offer courses in each of the three modes of face-to-face, distance, and blended learning. In other words, at other universities some courses are offered as traditional lectures and tutorials without any interactive online components, other courses are offered entirely online through a learning moderation system and students never physically attend the campus, while still others are offered as a blend. The 100% blended nature of Bond University's pedagogy has proven effective.

Evidence of Bond University's quality is seen in a number of external awards. Most significant to this chapter, Bond is Australia's highest rating university, earning the most five-star ratings of any university across nine key performance indicators (including teaching quality, educational experience, and graduate outcomes) in the 2010 Good Universities Guide. The Law school's mooting team was the world champion of the 2009 International Criminal Court Trial Competition, defeating Yale and Utrecht University in the final of this prestigious competition. The Sustainable Development program is offered in the Mirvac School of Sustainability which won two of the 2009 Gold Coast Urban Design Awards and the 2009 Sustainability in the Built Environment Award. This building is Australia's first education pilot project to receive a six-green-star rating for design, thus demonstrating Bond University's commitment to authentic education of its students and leadership for global sustainability. Finally, Bond University is listed in the 2009 Industry, Company and Business Research's top 500 private companies. This bodes well for the Business students, many of whom prove to be successful entrepreneurs upon graduation.

The next focus is on Bond University's initiatives to foster culturally accessible teaching and learning through blended learning. These solutions are organised under the four headings of the key pedagogic problems of international students as presented by De Vita (2007). Only some of Bond University's many solutions to cultural pedagogical accessibility are addressed here. Because Bond's mission is as an international university, there is a pervasive intercultural attitude and approach throughout the Faculties, schools, and student support programs. The strategies are too numerous to create an exhaustive list here. In addition, academics, administrators, support staff, and the students themselves are always refining and creating approaches in a dynamic process. As such, some of the approaches that are thought to be especially creative and therefore may be new ideas to other universities will be described here.

1. The pedagogic problem of communication and in particular language and Bond University's blended learning solutions.

All Bond University students participate in face-to-face learning in pedagogically designed spaces. Student presence on campus presents informal opportunities to interact with their student colleagues. Bond University developers keep up to date on the latest research on learning spaces (e.g. Long & Ehrmann, 2005; Wedge & Kearns, 2005) so that campus spaces are richly connected and invite presence and collaboration. A prime example is the Multi-media Learning Centre always comfortably crowded with learners. The student attendance in the months June through August 2009 exceeded the main library visits by 30%. The space is technology-rich with computers loaded with software and with LCD projectors and screens, wireless internet, and plenty of electrical outlets for plugging in laptops and charging mobile devices. There are a variety of seating options including diner-booths, long counters with barstools, and a break-out room with kidney shaped couches.

It is not enough to leave student communication to chance. Even with conducive environments, fear of not being able to succeed with the language may still keep international students from communicating. The Bond University Career Centre enhances the opportunities for conversation by hosting regular chats designed for international students. Australian national students are also invited to attend, and frequently do. Students provide feedback that they look forward to these sessions, as it reduces the anxiety of approaching people cold and trying to create an opportunity to practice one's language skills through social conversation.

Because Bond University maintains a low instructor to student ratio, academics get to know their students well and are able to assess their particular needs and recommend solutions. It is suggested to students who experience heightened communication problems that they enroll in an elective called *Language and Drama*. This course was designed to address the communications needs of some of Bond University's international students, as drama is empirically demonstrated to yield more opportunities for conversational language than any other discipline (Gill, 1997). Students work in groups to plan short skits and perform them in front of one another. The instructor gives them assignments such as reading all of their lines very slowly, very quickly, or with deadpan or exaggerated expression so that the learners have extra practice with communications skills. The semester culminates with performance of a play in a theatre with an audience. The performance is filmed and students are given copies of the DVDs so that they have a record of their performance to take with them upon graduation.

Bond University offers instruction in four languages – Chinese, French, Japanese, and Spanish. Many of the international students choose to enrol in language courses, as studying a language brings salience to conventions such as grammar and intonation, thereby helping with their English learning. In 2009, Bond University initiated the first year of what will become annual language competitions. Students at all levels competed in the language(s) that they were learning. The adjudicators came from local embassies. The competitions were filmed and the resulting DVDs used to give learners multi-media feedback on their own progress and for other students' peer modelling in language development. Personal reports indicated that experiencing the challenge of learning a language heightened the empathy of Australian national students for their international student colleagues.

2. The pedagogic problem with academic skills and Bond University's blended learning solutions.

Student Learning Services (SLS) at Bond University offers a diverse menu of supports for students to develop their academic skills. The availability of these services is clearly advertised on digital signage. In addition, many of the instructors work together with the Manager of SLS to build trigger elements into early-semester assignments. Examples of trigger items might include proper in and end text referencing and synthesizing information. Through these trigger items, students who are at risk of academically struggling come to the early attention of their instructors, who then refer them to SLS for support. Online, SLS has developed an extensive student intra-net site with primers, exemplars, mind-maps, and digital games to practice academic skills. Face-to-face, SLS staff persons provide small-group workshops and one-on-one tutoring. They also provide workshops for academics in a train-the-trainer model.

3. The pedagogic problems of culturally dissonant conceptualisations of teaching and learning and Bond University's blended learning solutions.

As described above, culture is deep and enduring. We cannot expect students who have been taught to listen rather than speak, and rewarded for precise recall, to suddenly engage in Socratic dialogue with their instructor and frame their own arguments. Scaffolding is an educational metaphor that comes from the construction industry whereby supports are applied until a point of stability is reached. This approach of more intensive initial supports, removed over time when the student no longer needs them is effective in higher education (Rodríguez & Cano, 2006).

At Bond University, instructors from different schools and Faculties use the Podroom to scaffold learning through problem-based learning (PBL). The Podroom is a flexible, digitally enabled learning space. The work stations are designed for paired-learning. Each station has a single hard-drive and keyboard and two monitors. The central console is able to switch the images from station to station so that students can see the work being done at other stations without leaving their own. There are two LCD projectors and screens so that images from the central console and/or the stations can be centrally projected. In addition, there are kidney shaped couches and ottomans that are easily moved into comfortable group configurations.

The Podroom is ideal for problem-based learning (PBL). PBL begins with a problem, question or case. Instructors support students through progressive information and strategies to pose solutions (Venkatachary, Vasan, & Freebody, 2009). The flexible furnishings and spatial arrangements of the room allow the instructor to orient large group discussions. The pairing at the wireless work-stations allows students to support one another through searching, finding, analysing, and proposing. The instructors often pair international with Australian national students. The ability to project various images throughout the room and on the large screens allows peer-support and distribution of roles and stages of the process. The nature of PBL is grounded in scaffolded learning and students learn strategies and problem-solving skills that transcend the course and discipline.

4. The pedagogic problem of encouraging students to adopt a constructivist approach and Bond University's blended learning solutions.

As described above, one of the graduate attributes that Bond University has made a commitment to fostering is knowledge and critical thinking. It is imperative that students are supported to move from their comfort zone of rote learning to constructing their own frameworks, theories, and arguments. Bond University supports students' generation of knowledge through Web 2.0 technologies. Flew

(2008) presented and discussed a model of new media participation. The learners' new media actions listed in order from low to high engagement are, "read, favorite, tag, comment, subscribe, share, network, write, refactor, collaborate, moderate, lead" (p. 32). Web 2.0 technologies foster activity at the high end of the engagement scale. For example, through using WordPress, a blog publishing application, the instructor is not the sole member responsible for developing, posting and editing the learning resources. As adult learners, the students are also responsible for generating and sharing information, ideas, and critiques. Intercultural learning is fostered through activities such as asking students to generate examples and cases from their national contexts. Numerous communications tools are available through the application so that learners are conversing and pushing one another's thinking. The advantage of blended approaches is that there are face-to-face sessions in which to support learners who are new to Web 2.0 technologies.

University of Calgary, Faculty of Education

The University of Calgary (U of C) is a comprehensive university, ranked in the top seven of Canadian research universities, with 17 faculties and 30 research institutes, supporting more than 27,600 students in undergraduate, graduate and professional degree programs. U of C has a full complement of academic programs and encourages multi-disciplinary programs, meaning students can combine their interest areas and create an education that suits them. The university has a commitment to internationalization, recognizing it as an integral part of the economic, political and social realities of its campus and the wider community. There are over 2,100 international students from 100 countries at the U of C and approximately nine percent of undergraduate international students are exchange students, on-campus for only one or two semesters. Internationalization is a priority, and the university is committed to offering more students opportunities for study and travel abroad with over 125 active student exchange agreements as well as a number of field schools and group study opportunities. Currently more than 1000 undergraduates per year include study abroad as part of their degree program. For example, students in the final semester of their Bachelor of Education program can elect to participate in *Teaching Across Borders*, and complete their semester teaching in one of more than 10 countries around the world.

Owing to the size and complexity of the institution, it would be impossible to summarize the responsiveness of each faculty to the issue of internationalization and the inherent challenges identified earlier in this paper. For example, the Faculty of Nursing has opened a campus in Qatar, offering a bachelor's degree in Nursing, which is contextually based and driven by international standards (http://www.qatar.

ucalgary.ca/home/mission). Specifically, whereas the case of Bond University focussed on the entire university, this case will focus on the innovative programming of the Graduate Division of Education Research (GDER) – a division within the Faculty of Education.

GDER added distance delivery, in addition to and parallel with, its campus-based graduate programs, thereby extending its reach and access to a range of learners in various locations across Canada and the world. Application to both delivery options is viewed with the same rigorous admission standards. The difference between the two rests with the fees charged (distance delivery is more expensive); courses offered (of the 10 specialisations within GDER, two do not offer their courses online); and degrees offered (the PhD is not offered via distance delivery). Typically, graduate students enrol in a mixture of delivery options, choosing some distance education courses and others with face-to-face components. Most campus-based courses offer online activities, using a learning management system (Blackboard) or other social software such as blogs or WIKIS.

Because the University of Calgary (U of C) has identified itself as a research and inquiry-based institution, much of the pedagogical framework describing Bond University in the previous section is core to U of C's instructional design. Of particular interest are five concerns specific to U of C and the approach that GDER has taken to address them.

1. **The Value of a PhD Degree:** When the Faculty of Education conceptualized a distance delivery doctorial program, its purposes were clear; (1) to increase access to doctorial education for working professionals who could not stop their careers and pursue a degree fulltime and (2) to meet the needs of rural and remote students who could not leave their communities and move to Calgary full-time. The Faculty of Graduate Studies at U of C granted GDER permission to offer online doctorial studies but only for the specific program of Doctor of Education (EdD). This has proven problematic as some countries give priority to PhD degrees, viewing EdDs as less scholarly and more applied. Therefore, international students wanting a PhD must come to campus in Calgary, leaving work, families, friends and support networks while incurring substantial cost in terms of travel and relocation. At this point, there is absolutely nothing GDER can do to address this, as the decision was made by the Faculty of Graduate Studies. Ironically, Harvard University only offers EdD degrees so it seems the issue is really international perception of the value of the EdD.
2. **Difference in Fee Structure**: Completing a degree by distance delivery is almost double in cost. Further, few if any scholarship funds are available for distance delivery students. These issues have caused some distance students to feel that the distance program is a "cash grab" by the institution. Ironically,

even recognizing these price differentials, many local Calgary residents opt to take their program by distance delivery for the perceived convenience and flexibility. GDER is addressing the issue of scholarships for distance students, but the fee structure will probably not change in the near future as GDER is required to follow a cost recovery scheme to finance programs beyond the traditional model of campus based teaching and learning.

3. **Access to Resources**: University of Calgary has become a leader in access to digital resources to both support campus and distance students. The Faculty of Education is proud of the fact that it has provided library access to university colleagues in developing countries, offering them the same access to the U of C collection as campus faculty and students. Further, the U of C is building a digital library (http://www.ucalgary.ca/oncampus/weekly/oct14-05/digital-library.html) which will expand access to resources to a wider range of patrons - globally and locally.
4. **ICT Skills**: Even as technology becomes more pervasive and affordable, the deficiency and/or gap in skills and abilities of both students and faculty remains wide. GDER offers support and training sessions on everything from digital library access and database searching to basic ICT skills in the use of both asynchronous (Blackboard) and synchronous (Elluminate Live) software. While one might assume a gradual increase over the years in skills and awareness of both students and faculty, this has not proven to be true, and so students and faculty come to classes with various technological challenges and concerns. GDER has instituted an ICT support team; and the U of C has an IT department that handles technology and communication related issues, ranging for security to access, innovations to support for existing eLearning environments.
5. **eLearning Challenges**: So much has been written about the promises, potential and problems of eLearning, that they need not be addressed in this case other than to say issues of time zones for synchronous learning (for example, in a current distance course students are from across Canada, Greece, and Japan and Korea); cultural context (for example in the course mentioned previously, students are from Canada, Saudi Arabia, USA, Pakistan, and East Africa); and previous learning (previous degrees for graduate students in GDER have been obtained from countries around the world) significantly impact course design. To address these challenges, GDER has tried to balance synchronous and asynchronous class meetings recognizing that all students are not in the same time zone; has attempted to reflect a respectful stance to potentially controversial topics; and conforms to an international standard which translates degrees from various countries using a well recognized metric (International Handbook of Universities and Guide to Chinese Universities and Colleges).

While not claiming to have *gotten it totally right*, the Faculty of Education at the University of Calgary attempts to balance the competing interests of the institution, the faculty, faculty members and students. Students are offered regular opportunities to evaluate their program, courses and instructors. While not perfect, these evaluations do positively impact faculty merit and promotion, program direction, and external reports concerning student satisfaction.

ANALYSIS OF SOLUTIONS

The case universities' commitment to blended learning can best be understood through applying Postman's (2003) critique of the Internet in higher education. Pittinsky (2003), Chairman of Blackboard Inc. at the time of publication, invited six other people to write their responses to the question, "is the impact of e-learning on higher education transformative or simply evolutionary" (xiv). The responses of contributors such as the Columbia University Teacher's College President and a Wall Street Equity Analyst were very positive about the impact of the internet on higher education, leaving the reader with the question as to whether universities of the future would trade *clicks for bricks*, or in other words, whether all higher education would be conducted online rather than on physical campuses. Postman, New York University Professor and Social Critic, wrote what Pittinsky described as "the potential downside of technology's increasing impact on education" (xviii).

Postman (2003) posed six questions to consider about e-learning in higher education: what problem gets solved by this new technology; whose problem is it; what new problems are created after solving an old problem; who and what might be harmed by a technological solution; what changes are gained and lost with new technologies, and; who and what acquire power due to technological change.

The first question is – *what problem gets solved by this new technology*. Postman's (2003) goal in asking this question seemed to be to raise awareness that the technology *should* arise as a response to a problem rather than just because the developer or adopter is a techno-enthusiast. In the case of Bond University, the approach to blended learning was developed in response to authentic problems. The primary problem was that Bond University's commitment to maintaining a 60/40 ratio of national to international students meant that educators were trying to educate culturally diverse individuals together as one group. While Bond's problem was primarily one of cultural accessibility, the problem faced by the GDER program at the U of C was one of global accessibility. There was a growing need / want among overseas students for the type of education that the GDER program was offering.

The case universities considered three possible solutions. The three alternatives to culturally accessible teaching and learning are distance education, face-to-face learning, and blended learning. The pros of distance education are that it has the capacity to extend higher education teaching and learning to a geographically wider student population, although the reality is that any-time and any-place does not extend to any-one (Dhanarajan, 2001). Furthermore, if pedagogically-grounded, the flexibility of digital resources means that the needs of students at all ends of the continuum are addressed in multiple formats to accommodate learning styles (Rossiter, 2007). For example, while the primary goal of some students is to achieve the standard learning outcomes, others want or need enrichment or remedial skill development. The main con is that if they study while geographically situated in their home country, incoming international students may not receive the important cultural immersion and conversational English experience described as mandatory by researchers such as Briguglio, (2000), and Cruikshank, Newell and Cole (2003). The main pro of face-to-face learning is that academics have greater control over the learning experiences of students, who are required to attend lectures, tutorials, and labs for learning content and process - notwithstanding the claim from authors such as Rossiter that relinquishing the control to the students is actually one of the ultimate goals and potential benefits of infusing Web 2.0 technologies. The main cons of face-to-face teaching and learning without infused digital technologies are that students are denied the benefit of cognitive stimulation and dialogic engagement which are empirically demonstrated outcomes of infused educational technologies, and the teaching takes a one-size-fits-all approach. Both case universities have thereby elected blended learning whereby students reap the benefits of both face-to-face teaching and learning and of infused educational technologies including the internet, communications and multi-media tools (Dengler, 2008; Liu & Cheng, 2008; Panda, 2005; Pedró, 2005; Siritongthaworn, Krairit, Dimmitt, & Paul, 2006). At Bond University, blended learning takes the form of combined face-to-face and digital pedagogies for all students across all courses. At U of C, the blend of face-to-face and digital is across the GDER program as a whole.

The next question posed by Postman (2003) is – *whose problem is it.* The point that Postman is making through asking this question is that organizations often blame the victim. As described in the *situation background* above, international students are often recruited (for tuition fees) and then blamed for the problems that are inherent in being an international student. By making an intentional decision to maintain a ratio of 40% international students, Bond University accepted the problem of culturally accessible teaching and learning as an institutional responsibility. Their creative and multiple efforts as described above to address these problems through a blended learning pedagogy are evidence of taking responsibility for the solutions and thereby promoting a quality higher education experience for all learners. Within GDER, faculty members recognize the pressure on distance education students with respect to the differential fee structure and are actively working to be able to offer scholarships for these learners, provide increased digital resource options, and enhanced supervision / administrative support.

Postman (2003) asserted that problems and solutions in education are complex, and tend to have a dynamic and convoluted rather than a linear pattern. As such, he asked the question - *what new problems are created after solving an old problem.* The new problem at Bond University and at U of C is at the level of the academic. The e-learning components of blended learning are in place. Innovative learning spaces are built and well-equipped with hardware, software, and multimedia resources. Site licences have been purchased and staff persons' computers updated. However, the uptake of digital resources has not been universal, nor can one even say widespread, and many academics state that they perceive increased pressures experienced as expectations to learn and apply new technologies. These problems are not unique to the case universities. A sense of increasing pressure through ICT implementation is reported in the literature (Randaree & Narwani, 2009), as is not using educational technology to its full potential (Bell & Farrier, 2008; Norton & Hathaway, 2008; Reeves & Reeves, 2008).

While the response to Postman's (2003) previous question is in the domain of the educator, the answer to the next question is about the students. Postman asked - *who and what might be harmed by a technological solution.* While e-learning opens up opportunities and pedagogical inspiration for many learners, it also heightens the effect of the digital divide. The digital divide is particularly relevant when considering cultural accessibility, as many incoming students from developing nations do not have the exposure or experience to new technologies that come to play in the higher education environment (Babu, 2008; Enoch & Soker, 2006; Sims, Vidgen, & Powell, 2008). For example, a graduate student from Burundi came late in the semester to seek help with a distance course which was administered through a learning moderation system. He was able to access the discussion forums and regularly participated. However, he was increasingly discomforted by a sense of disorientation. He admitted that he was 'faking it' and really did not know what his student peers were talking about on the forum. The discovery was made that not only had he never accessed the course documents and multi-media materials, but he did not even know that these resources existed. He explained that prior to arriving at the University he had never used a computer. While this situation is diminishing as technology becomes more affordable, institutions cannot make the assumption that the digital divide has been bridged by all students in their programs.

There are two further aspects to accessibility and equitability. As a private university, Bond's higher fees leave little expendable income for some students to purchase needed technologies, and prevent some students from choosing Bond as their higher education provider. A similar problem exists for students enrolling in the distance education route through GDER. Further, if we are to embrace an authentic full-scale stance of accessibility for diverse learners, then we must also address the heightened digital divide experienced by students with disabling conditions, particularly with functional disabilities such as hearing or vision impairment (Konur, 2007; Steyaert, 2005).

Postman's (2003) fifth question is - *what changes are gained and lost with new technologies*. Postman was particularly interested in language changes because the new terms provide clues as to shifting perceptions and dynamics. Language is particularly relevant in the Australian context of internationalization of higher education because Australians are known for an expressive, colourful vernacular. The featured language is particularly intriguing in Davies and Harcourt's (2007) article, "No shonky, cappuccino courses here, mate. UK perspectives on Australian higher education." The article was written by two academic professionals from the United Kingdom. To interpret the article's title, *shonky* means of poor quality and the North American equivalent term would be *hokey*. *Cappuccino courses* are ones with low academic rigour and scholarship. *Mate* is a noun regularly used in greeting and conversation. There are subtle distinctions between when Australians insert the word *mate* as a term of endearment and when they use it to put others in their place, as is the case in the title of this article. Comparing the dynamics of the contemporary university between the United Kingdom and Australia, the authors wrote, "we discovered on our walkabout that although Australia distinguishes itself with a preference for flat whites and long blacks, like the UK it is a dynamic player in the global higher education market" (p. 122). *Walkabout* is a rite of passage for Aboriginal youth, connoting a voyage of discovery for the authors. Flat whites and long blacks are espresso drinks (Americano) the first with milk and the second without. This is in stark contrast to the article's title of cappuccino courses. The language of this article conveys a message about the motivations for higher education internationalization efforts in that the income and pedagogy need to stay entwined.

Postman's (2003) final question is - *who and what acquire power due to technological change*. Postman's conceptualization of power is consistent with Foucault's (1972 – 1979) notion of embedded power through actions and relationships. If designed, maintained, and grown as culturally accessible, blended learning has the potential to create the conditions to empower students and graduates who become social capital in the knowledge economy. Furthermore, universities become instruments, contributors and developers of diplomacy, global relationships, and equitable knowledge resources.

LESSONS LEARNED

The following is an abbreviated list of lessons from the cases.

1. **Communications**: Design learning spaces that are inviting, convenient, digitally useable and invite conversation and collaboration.
2. **Communications**: Invite international students to scheduled chats - opportunities for informal conversation.
3. **Communications**: Offer a *Language and Drama* elective to international students.
4. **Communications**: Offer language courses and host language competitions.
5. **Academic Skills**: Design early-semester trigger elements of assignments to alert instructors to students who might be at risk for academic problems.
6. **Academic Skills**: Develop online, small group workshops, and one-on-one student tutoring in academic skills.
7. **Academic Skills**: Host workshops for instructors showing them the academic skills strategies development for students.
8. **Conceptualisation of Teaching and Learning**: Design classrooms as flexible learning spaces with mobile furnishings and digital work stations.
9. **Conceptualisation of Teaching and Learning**: Scaffold students' learning through problem-based learning (PBL).
10. **Constructivism**: Consider Web 2.0 and 3.0 technologies such as blog publishing applications to encourage students to generate knowledge, resources, and understanding and explore virtual options (e.g. Second Life) for simulations and problem based learning.
11. **Naming Degrees**: Consider the status of degree designations (e.g. EdD) internationally (beyond the culture of the host institution).
12. **Fee Differentials**: If distance students are to pay higher fees for equivalent degrees, then investigate scholarships for the affected students.
13. **Global Information Access**: Provide library access to university colleagues in developing countries.
14. **ICT Skills**: Continue to assess and evaluate the match between ICT demands and abilities and facilitate timely and appropriate training and support accordingly.
15. **eLearning Challenges**: Balance asynchronous and synchronous communication tools, and be aware of culturally sensitive issues in order to maintain an expectation and practice of respect among students and faculty as well as bandwidth and time zones (for synchronous learning).

FUTURE CHALLENGES

Few would argue the future of higher education rests in embracing aspects of blended learning in current practice. "... it is clear ... blended learning is more than fashionable; it is training and educational delivery method of choice (Bonk & Graham, in press). While numerous issues, trends, and concerns have been identified, we will focus on seven ideas consistent across our cases and the literature.

1. Blended Learning options must be considered as a programmatic element. While this impacts bandwidth, access to current technology, and time zone issues, it appears blended learning is critical to student satisfaction and success.
2. Changed pedagogy is essential. Emerging technologies require changed pedagogies. Simply mapping existing face-to-face courses and instructional methods to distance delivery is poor practice.
3. Emerging technologies offer enhanced options for teaching and learning but also increase costs and user comfort. Every tool comes with a learning curve, suggesting faculty and students must commit to continuous learning and technology upgrading. Included in this is the emergence of handheld devices and the need to recognize that *mLearning* (mobile learning) will require its own pedagogical stance and instructional design.
4. Inclusion of multimedia to support multimodal learning is not only possible but essential to support core learning within blended courses. This will require universities to consider how they will support the development, delivery and storage of rich media.
5. Opportunities for eCollaboration will be expected. Facebook has well over 300 million subscribers worldwide. Social software and Web 2.0 and 3.0 are standard practice for learners with access to the Internet (Shih, 2009).
6. Faculty and students must rethink their roles. Faculty cannot embrace emerging technologies if learners refuse to acquire the necessary skills, abilities, and access to technology necessary to fully participate in distance delivery. While this will pass considerable cost on to universities, faculty members, and students, innovative practices, access to multimedia, exploration of virtual worlds such as *Second Life* and *Google Earth* will not be possible.

Learning is about preparing oneself for a changing world. If universities do not lead the way to innovation and technology enhanced teaching and learning, they risk finding themselves obsolete or irrelevant in an increasingly connected, global community. Internationalization allows students to make thoughtful choices about where they would like to receive their education. Blended learning, as suggested in this paper, encourages students to consider global educational experiences but reminds institutions there is more to internationalisation that attracting fee paying, non-resident students.

REFERENCES

Asmar, C. (1999). Is there a gendered agenda in academia? The research experience of female and male PhD graduates in Australian universities. *Higher Educator*, *38*(3), 255–273. doi:10.1023/A:1003758427027

Aspden, L., & Helm, P. (2004). Making the connection in a blended learning environment. *Educational Technology Research and Development*, *41*(3), 245–252.

Australian Government Department of Education. Employment and Workplace Relations. (August 19, 2009). *Media release: Measures to safeguard education for overseas students studying in Australia.* Retrieved September 23, 2009, from http://www.deewr.gov.au/ministers/gillard/media/releases/pages/article_090819_113519.aspx

Babu, D. R. S. (2008). Digital divide: Educational disparities in India. *ICFAI Journal of Public Administration*, *4*(3), 68–81.

Bell, M., & Farrier, S. (2008). Measuring success in e-learning–a multi-dimensional approach. *Electronic Journal of e-learning, 6*(2), 99-109.

Bonk, C., & Graham, C. (Eds.). (In press). *Handbook of blended learning: Global perspectives, local designs*. San Francisco, CA: Pfeiffer Publishing.

Bourne, R. (2000). Ivory towers or driving forces for change: The development role of Commonwealth universities in the 21st Century. *The Round Table*, *356*, 451–458. doi:10.1080/003585300225025

Boyle, T. (2005). A dynamic, systematic method for developing blended learning. *Education Communication and Information*, *5*(3), 221–232. doi:10.1080/14636310500350422

Briguglio, C. (2000). Language and cultural issues for English-as-a-second/foreign language students in transnational educational settings. *Higher Education in Europe*, *25*(3), 425–434. doi:10.1080/713669286

Brown, S., & Jones, E. (2007). Introduction: Values, valuing and value in an internationalised higher education context. In Jones, E., & Brown, S. (Eds.), *Internationalising higher education* (pp. 1–6). Abingdon, Oxon, UK: Routledge.

Brown, S., & Joughin, G. (2007). Assessment and international students: Helping clarify puzzling processes. In Jones, E., & Brown, S. (Eds.), *Internationalising higher education* (pp. 57–71). Abingdon, Oxon, UK: Routledge.

Carlisle, W. (July 27, 2009). Transcript: Holy cash cows. *Australian Broadcasting Corporation, Four Corners*. Retrieved September 23, 2009, from http://www.abc.net.au/4corners/content/2009/s2637800.htm

Chiang, F. (2005). A critical examination of Hofstede's thesis and its application to international reward management. *International Journal of Human Resource Management, 16*(9), 1545-1563.

Cimbala, S. J. (2002). Can teaching be saved? *International Journal of Public Administration, 25*(9-10), 1079–1095. doi:10.1081/PAD-120006126

Cruickshank, K., Newell, S., & Cole, S. (2003). Meeting English language needs in teacher education: A flexible support model for non-English speaking background students. *Asia-Pacific Journal of Teacher Education, 31*(3), 239–247. doi:10.1080/0955236032000149373

Cudmore, G. (2005). Globalization, internationalization, and the recruitment of international students in higher education, and in the Ontario colleges of applied arts and technology. *Canadian Journal of Higher Education, 35*(1), 37–60.

Currie, J., Harris, P., & Thiele, B. (2000). Sacrifices in greedy universities: Are they gendered? *Gender and Education, 12*(3), 269–291. doi:10.1080/713668305

Davies, J., & Harcourt, E. (2007). No shonky, cappuccino courses here, mate. UK perspectives on Australian higher education. *Perspectives, 11*(4), 116–122.

De Vita, G. (2007). Taking stock: An appraisal of the literature on internationalising HE learning. In Jones, E., & Brown, S. (Eds.), *Internationalising higher education* (pp. 154–168). Abingdon, Oxon, UK: Routledge.

De Vita, G., & Case, P. (2003). Rethinking the internationalisation agenda in UK higher education. *Journal of Further and Higher Education, 27*(4), 383–398. doi:10.1080/0309877032000128082

Dengler, M. (2008). Classroom active learning complemented by an online discussion forum to teach sustainability. *Journal of Geography in Higher Education, 32*(3), 481–494. doi:10.1080/03098260701514108

Denis, B. (2003). A conceptual framework to design and support self-directed learning in a blended learning programme. A case study: The DES-TEF. *Journal of Educational Media, 28*(2-3), 115–127. doi:10.1080/1358165032000165626

Dhanarajan, G. (2001). Distance education: Promise, performance and potential. *Open Learning, 16*(1), 61–68. doi:10.1080/02680510124465

Edwards, R., Crosling, G., Petrovic-Lazarovic, S., & O'Neill, P. (2003). Internationalisation of business education: Meaning and implementation. *Higher Education Research & Development, 22*(2), 183–192. doi:10.1080/07294360304116

Ellis, R., & Calvo, R. (2004). Learning through discussions in blended environments. *Educational Media International, 41*(3), 263–274. doi:10.1080/09523980410001680879

Enoch, Y., & Soker, Z. (2006). Age, gender, ethnicity and the digital divide: University students' use of Web-based instruction. *Open Learning, 21*(2), 99–110. doi:10.1080/02680510600713045

Flew, T. (2008). *New media: An introduction.* (3rd ed.). New York, NY: Oxford.

Foucault, M. (1972-1977). In Gordon, C. (Ed.), *Power/Knowledge: Selected interviews & other writings*. New York, NY: Pantheon.

Gerbic, P. (2005). *Chinese learners and computer mediated communication: Balancing culture, technology, and pedagogy*. Paper presented at the ASCILITE Conference 2005: Balance, Fidelity, Mobility: Maintaining the Momentum? Queensland University of Technology, December 4-7 2005. Retrieved 24 September, 2009, from http://www.ascilite.org.au/conferences/brisbane05/blogs/proceedings/27_Gerbic.pdf

Gill, C. (1997). Hands-on language learning through drama. In R. Ballantyne, J. Bain, & J. Packer (Eds.), *Reflecting on university teaching academics' stories* (pp. 1-12). Canberra, Australia: Commonwealth of Australia.

Gliddon, G. (September 12, 2009). Gillard calms Indian student fears. *Melton Leader.* Retrieved September 23, 2009, from http://melton-leader.whereilive.com.au/news/story/gillard-calms-indian-student-fears/

Gu, Q. (2005). Enjoy loneliness-understanding voices of the Chinese learner. *Humanising Language Teaching, 7*(6). Retrieved September 24, 2009, from, http://www.hltmag.co.uk/nov05/mart01.htm

Guo, S., & Jamal, Z. (2007). Nurturing cultural diversity in higher education: a critical review of selected models. *Canadian Journal of Higher Education, 37*(3), 27–49.

Hofstede, G. (2001). *Culture's consequences: Comparing values, behaviours, institutions and organizations across nations* (2nd ed.). Thousand Oaks, CA: Sage.

Huff, T. E. (2006). The big shift. *Society, 43*(4), 30–34. doi:10.1007/BF02687532

Ja, C., & Symons-Brown, B. (September 14, 2009). Gillard kicks off student roundtable. *Brisbane Times*. Retrieved September 23, 2009, from http://news.brisbanetimes.com.au/breaking-news-national/gillard-kicks-off-student-roundtable-20090914-fnct.html

Jardine, D. W., Friesen, S., & Clifford, P. (2006). *Curriculum in abundance*. Mahwah, NJ: Lawrence Erlbaum.

Jelfs, A., Nathan, R., & Barrett, C. (2004). Scaffolding students: Suggestions on how to equip students with the necessary study skills for studying in a blended environment. *Journal of Educational Media, 29*(2), 85–96. doi:10.1080/1358165042000253267

Kerres, M., & de Witt, C. (2003). A didactical framework for the design of blended learning arrangements. *Journal of Educational Media, 28*(2-3), 101–113. doi:10.1080/1358165032000165653

Kinash, S. (2006). *Seeing beyond blindness*. Greenwich, CT: Information Age.

Kirkley, S. E., & Kirkley, J. R. (2004). Creating next generation blended learning environments using mixed reality, video games and simulations. *TechTrends, 49*(3), 42–89. doi:10.1007/BF02763646

Konur, O. (2007). Computer-assisted teaching and assessment of disabled students in higher education: The interface between academic standards and disability rights. *Journal of Computer Assisted Learning, 23*(3), 207–219. doi:10.1111/j.1365-2729.2006.00208.x

Lanham, E., & Zhou, W. (2003). Cultural issues in online learning–is blended learning a possible solution? *International Journal of Computer Processing of Oriental Languages, 16*(4), 275–292. doi:10.1142/S0219427903000930

Leask, B. (2007). International teachers and international learning. In Jones, E., & Brown, S. (Eds.), *Internationalising higher education* (pp. 86–94). Abingdon, Oxon, UK: Routledge.

Liddicoat, A. (2005). Teaching languages for intercultural communication. In Cunningham, D., & Hatoss, A. (Eds.), *An international perspective on language policies, practices and proficiencies* (pp. 201–214). Belgrave, Australia: Fédération Internationale des Professeurs de Langues Vivantes.

Liu, J. N. K., & Cheng, X. (2008). An evaluation of the learning of undergraduates using e-learning in a tertiary institution in China. *International Journal on E-Learning, 7*(3), 427–447.

Long, P. D., & Ehrmann, S. C. (2005). Future of the learning space: Breaking out of the box. *EDUCAUSE Review*, *40*(4), 42–58.

MacDonald, J., & Mcateer, E. (2003). New approaches to supporting students: Strategies for blended learning in distance and campus based environments. *Journal of Educational Media*, *28*(2-3), 129–146. doi:10.1080/1358165032000165662

Marginson, S. (2006). Dynamics of national and global competition in higher education. *Higher Education*, *52*, 1–39. doi:10.1007/s10734-004-7649-x

McBurnie, G. (2000). Pursuing internationalization as a means to advance the academic mission of the university: An Australian case study. *Higher Education in Europe*, *25*(1), 63–73. doi:10.1080/03797720050002215

Meiras, S. (2004). International education in Australian universities: Understandings, dimensions and problems. *Journal of Higher Education Policy and Management*, *26*(3), 371–380. doi:10.1080/1360080042000290212

Midgeley, W. (2009). We are, he is and I am: The adjustment accounts of two male Saudi Arabian nursing students at an Australian university. *Studies in Learning, Evaluation. Innovation and Development*, *6*(1), 82–97.

Miller, H. (1995). States, economies and the changing labour process of academics: Australia, Canada and the United Kingdom. In Smyth, J. (Ed.), *Academic work: The changing labour* (pp. 40–59). Buckingham, UK: Open University Press.

Miller, L., Lietz, P., & Kotte, D. (2002). On decreasing gender differences and attitudinal changes: Factors influencing Australian and English pupils' choice of a career in science. *Psychology Evolution & Gender*, *4*(1), 69–92. doi:10.1080/1461666021000013670

Miller, P., & Doherty, B. (June 1, 2009). Indian anger boils over. *The Age*. Retrieved September 23, 2009, from http://www.theage.com.au/national/indian-anger-boils-over-20090531-brrm.html

Min-Sun, K. (2007). Our culture, their culture and beyond: Further thoughts on ethnocentrism in Hofstede's discourse. *Journal of Multicultural Discourses*, *2*(1), 26–31. doi:10.2167/md051c.2

Moore, M. G. (2005). Editorial: Blended learning. *American Journal of Distance Education*, *19*(3), 129–132. doi:10.1207/s15389286ajde1903_1

Moulton, G., Huyler, L., Hertz, J., & Levenson, M. (2002). *Accessible technology in today's business: Case studies for success*. Redmond, WA: Microsoft.

Murray, D., & Dollery, B. (2005). Institutional breakdown? An exploratory taxonomy of Australian university failure. *Prometheus, 23*(4), 385–398. doi:10.1080/08109020500350237

Norton, P., & Hathaway, D. (2008). Exploring two teacher education online learning designs: A classroom of one or many? *Journal of Research on Technology in Education, 40*(4), 475–495.

O'Toole, J. M., & Absalom, D. J. (2003). The impact of blended learning on student outcomes: Is there room on the horse for two? *Journal of Educational Media, 28*(2-3), 179–190. doi:10.1080/1358165032000165680

Osguthorpe, R., & Graham, C. (2003). Blended learning environments: Definitions and directions. *Quarterly Review of Distance Education, 4*(3), 227–233.

Panda, S. (2005). Higher education at a distance and national development: Reflections on the Indian experience. *Distance Education, 26*(2), 205–225. doi:10.1080/01587910500168868

Patron, M. C. (2007). Culture and identity in study abroad contexts: After Australia, French without France. In Chambers, H. (Ed.), *Cultural identity studies* (*Vol. 4*). Oxford, UK: Peter Lang.

Patron, M. C. (2009). *Diary of a French girl: Surviving intercultural encounters*. Gold Coast, Australia: Bond University Press.

Pedró, F. (2005). Comparing traditional and ICT-enriched university teaching methods: Evidence from two empirical studies. *Higher Education in Europe, 30*(3/4), 399–411. doi:10.1080/03797720600625937

Pittinsky, M. S. (2003). *The wired tower: Perspectives on the impact of the internet on higher education.* Upper Saddle River, NJ: Financial Times Prentice Hall. Poole, D. (2001). Moving towards professionalism: The strategic management of international education activities at Australian universities and their faculties of business. *Higher Education, 42*, 395-435.

Postman, N. (2003). Questioning media. In M. S. Pittinsky (Ed.), *The wired tower: Perspectives on the impact of the Internet on higher education* (pp. 181-200). Upper Saddle River, NJ: Financial Times Prentice Hall.

Randaree, K., & Narwani, A. (2009). Managing change in higher education: An exploration of the role of training in ICT enabled institutions in the United Arab Emirates. *The International Journal of Learning, 16*(4), 447–456.

Reeves, P. M., & Reeves, T. C. (2008). Design considerations for online learning in health and social work education. *Learning in Health and Social Care*, *7*(1), 46–58. doi:10.1111/j.1473-6861.2008.00170.x

Reitmanova, S. (2008). Unequal treatment of international students in Canada: Handling the case of health insurance coverage. *College Quarterly*, *11*(2), 10–10.

Rodríguez, L., & Cano, F. (2006). The epistemological beliefs, learning approaches and study orchestrations of university students. *Studies in Higher Education*, *31*(5), 617–636. doi:10.1080/03075070600923442

Rose, D. H., & Meyer, A. (2002). *Teaching every student in the digital age: Universal design for learning*. Alexandria, VA: ASCD.

Rose, D. H., & Meyer, A. (Eds.). (2006). *A practical reader in universal design for learning*. Cambridge, MA: Harvard Education Press.

Rose, D. H., Meyer, A., & Hitchcock, C. (Eds.). (2005). *The universally designed classroom: Accessible curriculum and digital technologies*. Cambridge, MA: Harvard Education Press.

Rossiter, D. (2007). Whither e-learning? Conceptions of change and innovation in higher education. *Journal of Organisational Transformation and Social Change*, *4*(1), 93–107. doi:10.1386/jots.4.1.93_1

Shih, C. (2009). *The Facebook era: Tapping online social networks to build better products, research new audiences, and sell more stuff*. Boston, MA: Pearson Education, Inc.

Sims, J., Vidgen, R., & Powell, P. (2008). E-learning and the digital divide: Perpetuating cultural and socio-economic elitism in higher education. *Communications of the Association for Information Systems*, *22*, 429–442.

Siritongthaworn, S., Krairit, D., Dimmitt, N. J., & Paul, H. (2006). The study of e-learning technology implementation: A preliminary investigation of universities in Thailand. *Education and Information Technologies*, *11*(2), 137–160. doi:10.1007/s11134-006-7363-8

Skyrme, G. R. (2005). *The reflective learner: Chinese international students' use of strategies to enhance university study*. Paper presented at the International Conference: Reflective Practice - The key to innovation in international education, Council for Research in International Education, Auckland, NZ, (23-26 June 2005). Retrieved 24 September 2009, from http://www.crie.org.nz/research_paper/G.Skyrme%20WP%2016.pdf

Stacey, E., & Gerbic, P. (2007). Teaching for blended learning–research perspectives from on-campus and distance students. *Education and Information Technologies, 12*, 165–174. doi:10.1007/s10639-007-9037-5

Steyaert, J. (2005). Web-based higher education: The inclusion/exclusion paradox. *Journal of Technology in Human Services, 23*(1/2), 67–78. doi:10.1300/J017v23n01_05

Ter-Minasova, S. (2005). Linguistic aspects of intercultural communication. In Cunningham, D., & Hatoss, A. (Eds.), *An international perspective on language policies, practices and proficiencies* (pp. 215–224). Belgrave, Australia: Fédération Internationale des Professeurs de Langues Vivantes.

Thorpe, K. (2006). *Report on responding to the needs of the Chinese learner in higher education: Internationalising the university.* Paper presented at the 2nd Biennial International Conference, University of Portsmouth, (15th & 16th July 2006). Retrieved September 24, 2009, from http://www.lass.soton.ac.uk/education/CLearnConfRpt.doc.

Venkatachary, R., Vasan, M. L., & Freebody, P. (2009). Training for learner-centred pedagogy and curriculum design agendas in staff development for problem-based learning (PBL). *Kritika Kultura, 12*, 81–99.

Versluis, A. (2004). Virtual education and the race to the bottom. *Academic Questions, 17*(3), 38–51. doi:10.1007/s12129-004-1017-2

Waters, J., & MacBean, N. (May 29, 2009). Anger grows over Indian student bashings. *ABC News.* Retrieved September 23, 2009, from http://www.abc.net.au/news/stories/2009/05/29/2583942.htm

Wedge, C. C., & Kearns, T. D. (2005). Creation of the learning space: Catalysts for envisioning and navigating the design process. *EDUCAUSE Review, 40*(4), 32–38.

Wong, R. (July 13, 2009). Problems in Australia's overseas student program. *New Mandala.* Retrieved September 23, 2009, from http://rspas.anu.edu.au/rmap/newmandala/2009/07/13/problems-in-australias-overseas-student-program/

World News Australia. (July 29, 2009). Government to crack down on student rip-offs. Retrieved September 23, 2009, from http://www.sbs.com.au/news/article/1061322/Government-to-crack-down-on-student-rip-offs

KEY TERMS AND DEFINITIONS

Blended Learning: In higher education means that: a combination of face-to-face and digital teaching and learning approaches are offered to the students; the tools and approaches are deliberately chosen for their capacities and affordances, and; the design requires original creation versus tacking digital elements onto an existing face-to-face scenario or vice versa.

Culture: The overall mindset shaped in a time and place and shared by a group of individuals. When individuals such as international students leave their group they carry the mindset with them from their culture of origin to their culture of study.

Cultural Accessibility: Higher educators actively design their teaching to ensure that *all* of their students are learning, through interaction with the instructor, their student peers and with globally responsible and responsive content.

Internationalization: (As defined within the parameters of this chapter) is quality education for students who do not have citizenship in the country in which they are studying.

ENDNOTE

1 Currently, Canada has three territories, as Nunavut was created in 1999.

This work was previously published in Cases on Globalized and Culturally Appropriate E-Learning: Challenges and Solutions, edited by Andrea Edmundson, pp. 141-167, copyright 2011 by Information Science Reference (an imprint of IGI Global).

Chapter 7
Developing an E-Learning Course for a Global Legal Firm

Gemma Baltazar
Baker & McKenzie Global Services LLC, USA

EXECUTIVE SUMMARY

Poor or nonexistent risk management processes can seriously impact law firms in many ways. Financial losses can be considerable, hard won reputations suffer, and in many cases key lawyers may have to separate from the firm. Risk management is particularly important in large, complex, multi—jurisdictional matters, which are the norm at global law firms such as Baker & McKenzie.

The Global Talent Management Team at Baker & McKenzie was tasked with designing and developing a training program around the existing Firmwide risk management approach. The approach has the objective of minimizing the Firm's practice and financial risk, and is based on ten core principles intended to provide guidance to our attorneys in managing some of the risk issues that they encounter in their daily practice. Developing an e-learning course, the core of this program, was envisioned to help achieve greater consistency in how the risk management approach is communicated internally, at the same time providing the Firm's lawyers with relevant information and resources at the right time.

In September 2008, The 10 Steps to Practical Risk Management interactive online course was launched globally within the Firm. The course was developed with guidance and subject matter expertise from the Firm's General Counsel and the Firm's Director of Professional Responsibility, and was developed by a team drawn from several geographies to help ensure global relevance. It identifies the principal

DOI: 10.4018/978-1-4666-1885-5.ch007

sources of risk and potential liability, the ethical standards expected of all of the Firm's lawyers, and the importance of providing high quality client representation that complies with the Firm's ethical obligations wherever it practices in the world. In addition to exploring some of the practical risk issues that the Firm's lawyers encounter in daily practice, this course allows lawyers to apply their knowledge by reacting to short questions and case studies, explores the issues from the perspectives of clients, lawyers and the Firm, and directs lawyers through hyperlinks to important sources of information and guidance.

This case study describes the considerations, challenges, and lessons learned in developing this online course, which is the foundation of an overall risk management training program for the Firm. Risk management is a very broad, deep, and complex topic which impacts the practice of law in many different ways. Recognizing that it is in meaningful discussions where learning most likely takes place, the project team's challenge was to design an e-learning course that allows sufficient interactivity to engage the learner and stimulate thinking around issues they encounter in whatever legal area, and at whatever level they practice.

ORGANIZATION OR SITUATION BACKGROUND

From its inception in 1949 Baker & McKenzie has always aimed to be global in reach. There are 3,900 locally admitted attorneys in 67 offices worldwide, operating as collaborative equals guided by shared values and common standards. The Firm's strength and culture is based on deep local roots and the experienced global perspective that comes from helping companies navigate sophisticated legal and business issues at home and across borders, cultures and practices around the world. The Firm's structure is characterized by:

- **Geography:** The Firm operates in 39 countries across the four regions of Asia Pacific, Europe and Middle East, North America, and Latin America;
- **Practice Group:** The Firm has 11 core practice groups (i.e. groups of lawyers practicing in the same specialist legal expertise areas): Antitrust & Competition, Banking & Finance, Dispute Resolution, Employment, Intellectual Property, Mergers & Acquisitions, Private Equity, Real Estate, Securities, Tax, Trade & Commerce
- **Industry Group:** The Firm focuses on 4 industry sectors: Energy, Mining & Infrastructure; Information Technology/Commercial; Pharmaceuticals & Healthcare.

Attorneys bring the knowledge, experiences and capabilities of a global law firm to domestic matters. The Firm's core brand idea is "*Fluency in the way we think, work and behave*", which means:

- Having an instinctively global perspective and a deep understanding of the language and culture of business all over the world.
- Having the ability to simplify legal complexity across practices and borders, bringing the right team and expertise regardless of location.
- Having a genuinely multicultural approach and is passionate about open and highly collaborative relationships.

The Firm is best known for its global footprint, and assisting clients transact business across borders. While such matters are an excellent foundation for the Firm's continued growth, they inherently carry the greatest degree of risk. Therefore, in an organization that expects its attorneys to think globally, effective risk management has always been at the forefront of Firm management priorities.

It is axiomatic that key to any successful law firm is having a combination of both experienced and young attorneys who are of the highest quality in terms of intelligence, skills and judgment. However, quality alone does not eliminate risk. (Zulkey 2009)

SETTING THE STAGE

Baker & McKenzie attorneys have a major part to play in managing and mitigating risk. broadly defined as an uncertainty; an unwanted event that may or may not happen. They must be aware of sources of reference and help, and of resources available to advise and assist on risk management related issues. Risk management is rarely covered in depth in law school curricula. Attorneys in the Firm need to better understand where their professional duties lie, sources of regulation of their activities and the potential exposure if they do not follow both ethical rules and internal Firm procedures. Moreover, even when following all rules and regulations, there are risk issues of which lawyers need be aware.

The Baker & McKenzie *Development Framework* (DF) is a competency model that defines what is required to be successful in Baker & McKenzie. A key performance area in the DF is "Matter Management", of which "Managing Risk" is an activity category. The DF makes it clear that all attorneys in the Firm are expected to adhere to the rules of the appropriate regulatory bodies, to follow the Firm's risk management procedures and to deliver a high quality of service that minimizes risk.

For Baker & McKenzie, it is vital that the Firm's risk management framework is clear to all attorneys, making them aware of potential sources of risk and liability, the ethical standards expected of them, and the importance of providing high quality client representation that complies with the Firm's ethical obligations wherever its lawyers practice in the world.

Risk management training had previously been delivered by the Firm in a variety of ways:

- Office orientation and other local training programs
- Global and regional Firm meetings
- Regional practice group meetings
- External Continuous Legal Education (CLE) programs
- Regional associates' meetings
- Online modules within the Development Framework's *Learning Resources*.

Coverage was not uniform; for example, not every associate meeting included a risk management session. Some attorneys might hear a substantially similar presentation two or three times, whether in the office or at a regional practice group event, while other attorneys might receive different training if their office happened to have their own programs in place.

To address this a plan was put in place to develop a comprehensive, Firmwide approach to risk management education, which was to be supported by course materials and training.

Main Considerations for Risk Management Training Program

Three main considerations were clear from the outset of this program:

1. Attorneys need to view risk management in the context of their daily practice, not merely as a matter for Firm management. They need to understand how the general principles apply to the situations they meet when advising their clients in their specialist area of practice.
2. Risk concepts need regular reinforcement. Risk management training should not be a 'one shot' solution; all attorneys need to be familiar with the key principles in this area, but they need to see how risk management issues manifest themselves in ways relevant to them (at the practice group level) as they take on greater responsibility for client matters and manage teams. As they progress in their careers, attorneys must become familiar with how risk arises in interactions with other attorneys and offices, clients outside their jurisdictions, and in cross-border transactional work, cross-border litigation and arbitration.

3. For this training program to be successful, it had to be designed and developed with regard to the structure of the Firm. Lawyers at all levels may be practicing in any combination of the following:
   - Geography
   - Practice Group
   - Industry Group

There are some core issues with which every attorney requires familiarity, and others which become more relevant according to an attorney's practice area and level of seniority. In developing the risk management training program, the team needed to consider the right time in an attorney's career to deliver the training. A junior associate needs to be able to recognize issues, and know when to escalate them to a partner and the Firm's Director of Professional Responsibility or General Counsel; a senior attorney has the responsibility to resolve issues with the help of Firm management. Professional responsibility issues therefore need to be covered in more depth at the more senior level, so that attorneys can apply Firm principles consistently.

The team anticipated that a partner level program would have a different emphasis from the core program, as partners need to be equipped to deal with risk issues in a different way from associates. The partner level program would incorporate a number of modules from the existing *Partner Learning Series* (comprised of 12 discrete programs targeted at building specific skills necessary for the Firm's partners, some of which deal with various aspects of risk management). The team planned to review and build upon the series' existing risk management and billing modules to ensure that partners receive regular refreshers of core principles.

Proposal for an Online Course

It was clear that in order to reach the widest possible audience that much of the course material would need to be delivered online.

The team therefore proposed the development of an online course that should also serve as a review and refresher for all attorneys, including partners, as part of their ongoing training program. Furthermore, the online course was to be an important aspect of the 'onboarding' and integration of lateral hires at any level, who need to get up to speed quickly with Firm procedures. The proposal recognized the need to promote existing training on managing the risk of "practice, time recording and billing" that were already developed, launched, and available in the Firm. The proposal also acknowledged that local offices should be able to build on this training, and cover any jurisdiction-specific and local Bar professional responsibility rules, in addition to Firm procedures (see Figure 1).

Figure 1. Screenshot on recognition of local rules

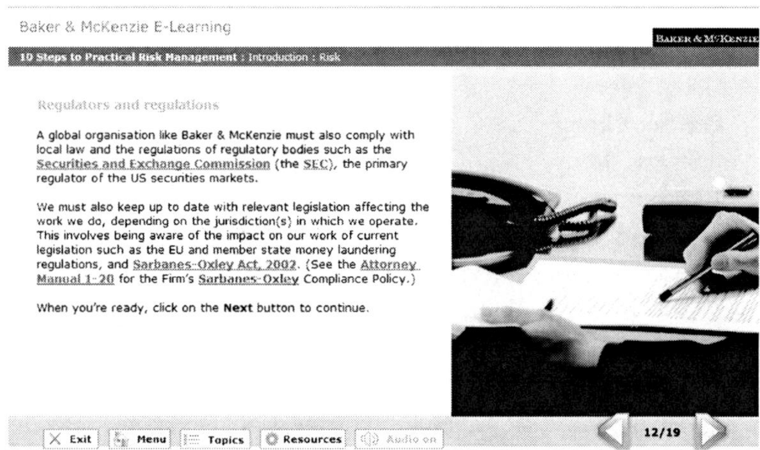

The team committed to developing facilitator guidance on the types of issues that may arise, and to recommending how offices might design and deliver training as part of local programs.

The team also proposed providing advice to practice groups on covering risk management issues as part of their curricula and regular training programs. Here, the principles covered in the core program would be placed in context and applied to practical everyday scenarios that attorneys in the practice group encounter.

One more thing to address was the fact that risk management is an agenda item for most regional associate meetings (i.e. meetings scheduled per year in varying frequency for new associates, midlevel associates, and/or senior associates in the regions). These meetings were ongoing while the risk management training program was in development. To facilitate as much alignment as possible to the materials being developed, the team proposed to provide materials and input for such sessions scheduled and assist in identifying facilitators.

For post-course launch, the team prepared updated in-person, facilitated session materials that would serve as the "core" content for local office and regional sessions. These include Facilitator Guide, slides, case studies and exercises tailored for specific job levels (i.e. junior associate, midlevel associate, senior associate, partner), and case studies and exercises tailored for specific practice groups. The team emphasized the need to ensure that these sessions are planned carefully across regional, and practice group offerings and do not duplicate the online course and office-based sessions, and that the risk management principles be applied to practical scenarios appropriate to the associates' job level.

In December 2007, the proposed program was approved and the team began the design and development of the e-learning course – the *The 10 Steps to Practical Risk Management* – and the risk management program as a whole.

In developing *The 10 Steps to Practical Risk Management*, the team had the following brief:

- To make attorneys aware of the rules of professional conduct which apply to all attorneys in the Firm, and how those rules affect individual attorneys in the representation of their clients
- To help attorneys understand risk management issues and how individual behaviour impacts the Firm's reputation and liability
- To make attorneys aware of and help them to understand the procedures and policies that the Firm has in place and why, and how they protect our clients' interests and the Firm's
- To help attorneys understand how to handle some difficult risk management? situations that may arise when representing new and existing clients

CASE DESCRIPTION

Project Planning

The Global Talent Management team prepared a Project Summary (a high level work plan that included scope, project team members, project goals, major milestones, and key deliverables) for the risk management program. At that time, while there were a variety of e-learning resources available through the Firm's Development Framework *Learning Resources* database, the risk management project team had not embarked on a similar e-learning endeavor. It was necessary to engage external e-learning development resources, within the approved scope and budget.

Project Team and Stakeholders

The risk management training program project team needed to consult with and obtain the support and commitment of key stakeholders as follows:

1. **General Counsel**: Sponsorship and subject matter expertise
2. **Director of Professional Responsibility (represents the Professional Responsibility and Policy Committee)**: Sponsorship and subject matter expertise
3. **Knowledge and Talent Management Committee**: For approval of global training projects, such as this program

4. **Regional Teams:** For support and buy-in for successful implementation
5. **Local Office Leadership and Staff**: For successful implementation, support and buy-in (especially of the Managing Partners), as well as feedback during design and development from Talent Management / Professional Development staff
6. **Practice/Industry Group Committees**: For support and subject matter expertise for the development of relevant examples and case studies
7. **Users**: For usability testing and feedback

The team involved the Firm's Global Information Services (GIS) team particularly in the following areas:

1. Request for Information (RFI) and vendor evaluation process
2. Purchasing
3. User testing
4. Network infrastructure integration

A key contact from the GIS team was identified to ensure smoother coordination and communications. From the Global Talent Management team, members included a Project Lead, Project Manager, and Product Manager / Instructional Designer. These roles were all based in various regions, and therefore had to work virtually as a team.

From the vendor side, the project team members were comprised of a Project Manager, Instructional Designer, Lead Developer, and an Account Manager. The vendor company was based in England and these roles were all based there, although they worked virtually as a team as well.

With members of the team identified, and a project scope and program objectives defined, the project team for the proposed risk management e-learning course set out to implement the project plan.

Cultural Accessibility Considerations

In order for all learners to achieve the same learning outcomes regardless of their country or culture of origin, globalized e-learning needs to be culturally accessible (Edmundson, 2009). One might argue that regardless of where training is delivered (classroom or online), cultural sensitivity is important for effective instruction, and is especially important for a self-driven online course which does not have the benefit of a facilitator to help draw out relevant discussions and make meaningful connections.

Thus, for a global Firm with lawyers speaking more than 75 languages (see Appendix A), belonging to any of a variety of practice and/or industry groups, adhering to local bar or local law society rules where they are admitted to practice, and coming from various cultural backgrounds, the project planning for the proposed online course required discussions around ensuring cultural accessibility.

But what are cultural issues in online education? In Wang and Reeves (as cited in Edmundson, 2007), they listed cultural issues identified by Joo (1999) which arise when using the Internet in classrooms, namely: 1) content of materials, 2) power of multimedia, 3) writing styles, 4) writing structures, and 5) web design (p. 7). In addition, they described research relating to a more holistic way of incorporating not just language and technology, but also learning styles and cultural dimensions with both local and global considerations, as well as pedagogical concerns in online education and cultural considerations in instructional design.

In fact, as the project team planned for the development of a culturally accessible online learning environment, they discussed considerations around:

1. Use of language
2. Use of graphics and images (ensuring diversity, cultural sensitivity, in addition to ensuring they comply with the Firm's Visual Identity Program guidelines)
3. Navigation features, including care in not making assumptions on what are "universal" navigation symbols and functionality
4. Culturally sensitive examples and case studies providing interactivity and opportunity to apply concepts
5. Assessments, not just for interactivity within the course modules and compliance considerations, but for knowledge checks across a multicultural audience
6. Use of audio and voice (whether to use for narration or voiceover of embedded role play scenarios, and if so, which accent/s)
7. Bandwidth and connectivity issues for some geographical locations
8. Need for learning paths or tracks (e.g. for partners vs. associates upon recognition of their user login)
9. Need for links to supplemental materials, as well as a Glossary of Terms, particularly the latter for those who may need assistance with English terminology
10. Evaluation and feedback mechanism to be aware of any issues raised by users – be they cultural or otherwise

These points are further described in the following sections on concerns around technology, learner and instructional design, and management and organization.

Technology Concerns

Olarinan (as cited in Edmundson, 2007) noted a study on attitude and perceptions of e-learning that showed that accessibility is one of the top motivating factors for effective e-learning, reported by almost half of participants, followed by course relevance to future career and user friendliness. The overall end users' learning experience should therefore be carefully considered – this includes: accessing the course online, speed of load, performance of the technology overall, and getting adequate and timely user support when needed. Frustration arising from problems with buttons or links not working, pages loading slowly or not at all, computer hardware not meeting requirements of the program, not knowing who to ask for help, lack of motivation due to lack of interactivity –will negatively impact the end user's learning (see Figure 2).

The internal project team's first task upon identifying the requirements for the course was to select the right vendor who could deliver on these requirements. In consultation with the technology group, the team completed the *Request for Information* (RFI) for prospective vendors which detailed the following end-user requirements

1. Baker & McKenzie (B&M) will supply the course content and questions.
2. B&M must be able to edit the course content and add new content sections or change the questions periodically.
3. All content is in English. There is no requirement to switch languages or host multiple sets of content in different languages.

Figure 2. Screenshot on sample interactivity

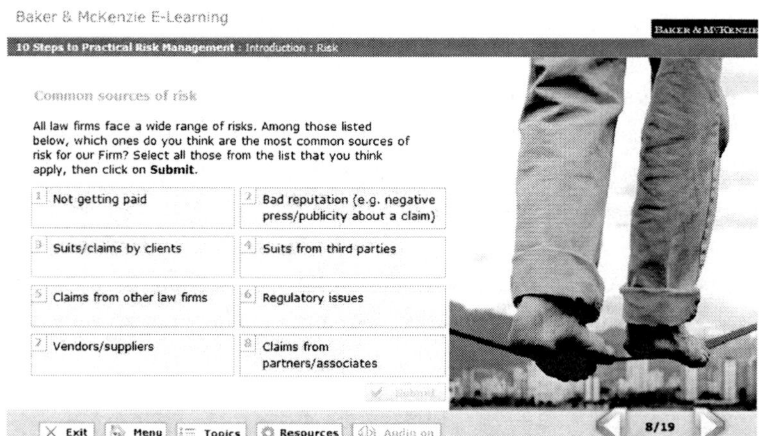

4. The course will incorporate audio.
5. The module will incorporate online help, instructional text and some animation.
6. Over 3,000 attorneys will complete the training provided within a 6 month period. Software must have a timeout so that the session is automatically saved and ended if the user walks away.
7. When the user has completed the module, their score must be recorded in a central database and a certificate generated in PDF format and sent to them in an email.

It also listed the following administrative tools requirements:

1. There must be a web-based reporting and administration module where the list of users required to take this training should be set up and where their results can be reported on centrally by authorized users.
2. Bi-weekly reports will be required detailing which attorneys have accessed the training module, whether they have completed it, and the score they obtain in the final assessment. Ideally, B&M administrators will also be able to access the information and generate reports.
3. It is a requirement that alerts to be sent to individual attorneys indicating the deadline for completing the course.
4. Detail is provided for timestamp record and log of user information when the user started/completed the course

A scoring system was used in the vendor selection process and eventually one clearly stood out in meeting most of the criteria and requirements. However, a challenge in particular was sorting out the hosting, reporting and administration of the module. The Firm does not have a learning management system (LMS) which this course can be integrated into. It does have a Learning Resources database as part of the Development Framework described earlier: its tracking system for access of online learning resources was limited to counting number of hits or visits to the sites and not tied to the users who accessed the sites. For this risk management course tracking a user's completion was critical, especially for programs where the course was a mandatory component. After some negotiation, the project team engaged the vendor's LMS partner's hosting services to provide the tracking and reporting requirement. This was beyond the scope and budget initially approved for the project, but was something that had to be put in place to monitor compliance.

In addition to the tracking limitation, other technology concerns had to be addressed. The project team coordinated two functional tests with users from all regions during the development of the e-learning course – one on the Alpha version of the course to report any issues, then a re-test on the Beta version to ensure fixes were complete. The tests aimed to determine:

- If the course was intuitive and easy to use
- What features of the course worked well
- What features of the course did not work well, or could be improved
- Any missing features

Specific questions around navigation, speed, design, text, images and graphics, and other technical problems were included.

It was key to get office representation from each region, and assess possible issues (technology or otherwise) unique to a region. Here are some highlights from feedback received:

- Speed issues in some offices outside of North America (i.e. course load and performance)
- Some users appreciated the audio feature, while others found it distracting and adding little value
- While navigation was for the most part fine, the tests revealed where fixes had to be made (e.g. some links not working etc.)

The team made a note of offices that have experienced load and performance issues, and consulted with the global technology group in improving network performance.

Despite conducting extensive user testing before the course was launched, the project team found that a small number of offices continued to experience slow connection to and performance of the course on their local networks, affecting their ability to deploy it locally.

There were also some issues relating to the external hosting solution provided through the vendor. These included:

- Reports not available when needed
- Reports not generated accurately, including users marked as "Incomplete" when they had actually completed the course

This enabled the project team to negotiate an extended hosting service for the course, thereby creating an extension for when the reports on tracking were made available and more time for the internal technology group to work on a more acceptable internal reporting solution.

Learner and Instructional Design Concerns

As indicated, the primary target audience for the online course included over 3,000 lawyers in 39 countries practising in different areas of law and industries. With the Firm's global reach, over 70 languages are spoken by the lawyers and staff.

As English is the official language of the Firm, the English language was used and there were no translations to other languages available, primarily for practical considerations. As described by Schell (in Edmundson, 2007), localization is unsustainable as a strategy for making online courses globally accessible, and that writing content in Global English is the best way to ensure that people from all linguistic backgrounds have a reasonable chance of understanding the material. While there was feedback from some users indicating preference for the course availability in their native language, making the course available in another one or more of the over 70 languages spoken in the Firm was not within the project's scope. It was helpful that the course was self-paced, so a non-native English speaking learner can control the amount of time spent reading and understanding the content as needed.

Apart from the use of the English language itself is the sensitivity to terminology, due to cultural and other considerations. In fact, Schell added that "in order to serve a worldwide audience, it is necessary to use *Global English* – English which is written in such a way that it can easily be understood by non-native speakers, as well as native speakers from diverse parts of the planet (p. 156). The use of British English as opposed to American English was debated, and in the end the project team went with British English (not because the e-learning developer vendor was based in England, but in the hope that its use would be more appealing for a larger group of users globally). Terms were carefully selected (e.g. where the word "trouble" was used initially by the vendor's instructional designer, the project team suggested that it be replaced with "problem" which may have less negative connotation in some cultures).

There were learners who liked the audio feature. The British accent was used primarily for the narration, and various accents were used for the role play voiceovers to add realism. Some users did not particularly like the audio feature as they tend to slow down the course. The project team decided to have this feature optional (i.e. can be turned on or off) (see Figure 3).

As mentioned earlier, a lawyer may be in any one combination of job level, Practice Group/Industry Group, and geography so consideration of relevance for each user in the target audience was critical. While the online course, which is the basis of the risk management program, has fixed content and to the extent possible generic examples and cases, there were case studies and examples provided to supplement the course targeted for specific job levels, practice and/or industry groups. There was feedback that some localization might be helpful (e.g. Local Bar

Figure 3. Screenshot on use of Japanese and British accents for voiceover, and ability to turn the audio on or off

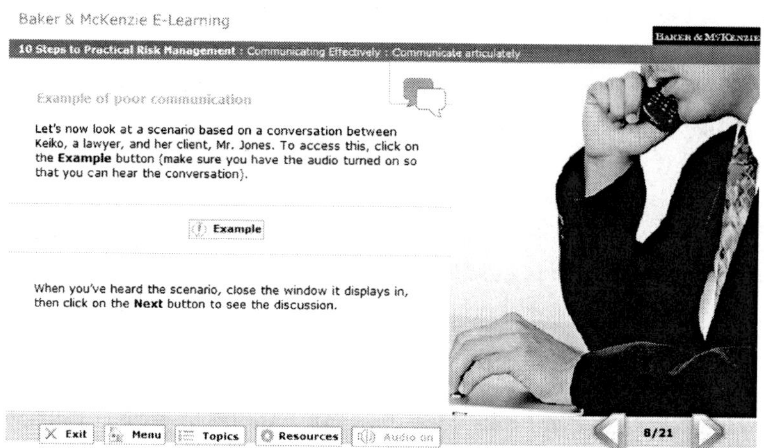

rules). Note that the course's "Introduction" module acknowledged that it is the responsibility of individual lawyers and employees to know about, and to comply with, all local bar or law society rules as well as the Firm's internal policies and rules; however, such localization was beyond the scope of the online course.

And still, there were learners who preferred other ways of learning. The online course was designed with exercises and quizzes for both interactivity and knowledge testing, as well as links to various sources for further information (e.g. to relevant sites in the Firm's intranet). Some learners would rather view a straightforward recorded PowerPoint presentation. Some learners appreciated group discussions around the issues presented. Some preferred viewing modules of the course in a group setting. And, some simply preferred the face to face approach over an online course.

Management and Organizational Concerns

Proper training and implementation are key in managing some of the risk areas. In addition, at the end of the day, a risk management approach will not be successful without a culture that not only fosters excellence but also fosters a spirit of compliance (Zulkey, 2009).

For the successful deployment of the course, leadership support and buy-in is critical. From the start the project team sought support from the relevant Leadership Committees by obtaining the proper sign-off and guidance. The General Counsel and the Director of Professional Responsibility's roles were critical in not just providing subject matter expertise but also in providing support and overall guidance for the e-learning course project.

Within the Global Talent Management team, there were regional team roles held by global team members (e.g., the Project Lead also held the role of Director of Talent Management for one of the regions), and their roles were critical in communicating with and providing consultation and support to the local offices. In global projects, and this project was no exception, there can sometimes be a tendency for local and regional priorities to take precedence. This required careful management in order to keep the global program on track.

We had positive participant feedback from delivering the course as part of new hire and lawyer orientation programs. Making the course a prerequisite to risk management sessions in regional meetings also added greater value to those sessions.

Lawyers completing the course in the United States receive Continuing Legal Education (CLE) credits, which facilitated the acceptance of the program by these lawyers. The project team worked with other jurisdictions with similar requirements for their lawyers, (for example, Hong Kong's Continuing Professional Development (CPD) requirements) to ensure a lawyer's participation earned the appropriate credit.

SOLUTIONS AND RECOMMENDATIONS

A major concern when delivering multimedia instruction via a network is bandwidth (the amount of data which can be delivered down the network at one time). While all offices have sufficient bandwidth for their day to day needs, streaming video and audio content can place severe stress on local office networks. To address these concerns, the project team identified offices likely to be subject to bandwidth limitations. CDs were supplied to these offices, and back up CDs to a number of others. Where offices run the course from their local servers, they were advised to set up appropriate systems for monitoring completion of the course, given that access other than from the main servers would not be reflected in the global usage reports.

Given the cost/benefit tradeoff of external hosting and tracking of the e-learning course, following the period negotiated with the vendor, the course was moved to an internal multimedia streaming server. Tracking access for this specific course was enhanced to include the user ID, pages visited and time spent by the user on the course. The reports are generated by the technology group manually, and therefore needs follow-up as opposed to an automatic reporting system. It is also not as straightforward as desired, although in the absence of a Learning Management System, it meets current expectations.

To address some language issues, there were offices, like the Bangkok office, where the online course (in English) was followed up with face-to-face sessions in the office in the local language. This improved uptake of the course considerably.

Additionally, the Bangkok office has created an assessment for local lawyers to test their understanding and application of the principles.

The project team worked with offices in jurisdictions where there were unique needs. For example, the Hong Kong/China offices needed to address Continuing Professional Development (CPD) tracking requirements by creating an online certificate of completion for users. While having an online certificate for all locations was part of the initial project plan, it was not implemented as it did not seem necessary; however, given the Hong Kong and China offices' needs, the team set this up.

The project team consulted with some of the Firm's larger offices (e.g. London, Australia, Chicago) that had existing risk management training in place. Partners and professional staff in those offices suggested that local practice group meetings would be an appropriate forum in which to discuss risk management issues, underlining the need that the project team had already identified for an updated collection of case study material for local and regional Practice Groups and Industry Groups to use and adapt in training.

A few months after the online course rollout, the project team released additional components of the Firm's risk management training program. Recognizing the need for blended learning or a more traditional approach in some contexts, the team produced a Facilitator Guide to provide guidance and recommendations on supplementing the online course with face-to-face and other moderated or structured training sessions. These sessions are delivered through local office, regional, or global meetings. Given the critical role that Firm Practice Groups and Industry Groups play in managing the Firm's risk of practice, the team also developed a Case Study Bank in May 2009 to supplement the *10 Steps to Practical Risk Management* Facilitator Guide. Its aim is to assist lawyers in running practice or industry specific training sessions, and in delivering relevant examples, exercises and case studies to their audience (see Figure 4).

LESSONS LEARNED

Following the e-learning development effort, the project team conducted an After Actions Review (AAR) activity with team members from the vendor side. The group thought that the overall course and content was well received. There was good project representation from the Firm and the vendor, overall good communication between the internal and external team members who also worked well virtually together despite some challenges along the way on staffing changes from the vendor side.

Asked if there were any "lessons learned" on the project or any part of the project process that should be identified as a "best practice" for future projects, the following were identified from the AAR:

Figure 4. Risk Management Training Program Deliverables

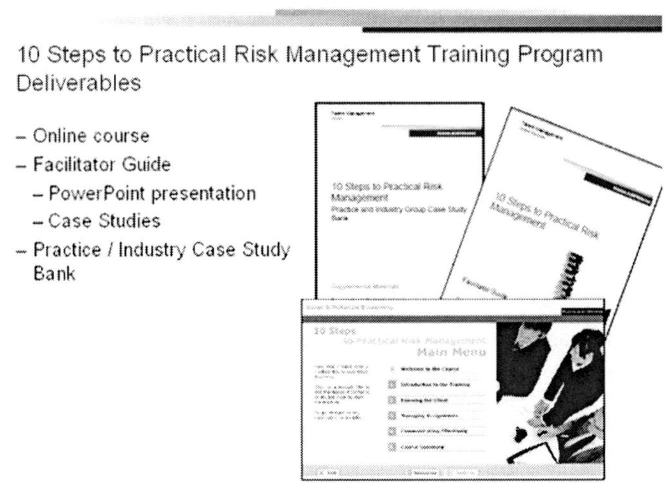

1. Managing scope is key; ensure proper sign-off

Managing scope is key. While there may be changes during the course of the project arising from various reasons, such as a change in priority, a realization of an unknown factor, clearer understanding of implications of something; best practice is to ensure there is as much clarity and agreement on scope as possible, before the project starts.

2. Set expectations for all phases of the project with all stakeholders

Ensuring proper agreement on scope facilitates setting expectations not just within the project team but also with stakeholders for all phases of the project. For example, the hosting service was an unforeseen cost to the project, and not part of the initial scope. The project team did not anticipate that a third party's services were needed to provide reports, therefore securing the external hosting service to allow tracking of access was necessary.

3. Allow more time for requirements gathering

As part of project planning, carefully consider all the features and functionalities required in designing and developing the e-learning course. A lot of this depends on existing technology infrastructure and limitations, within which the course will be integrated and need to perform successfully. Ask questions such as how will the course be accessed, where will the course reside, what global standards (if any) are there for computers (i.e. do all have sound cards?, what is the ideal screen resolution?, etc.). Allowing more time to define and agree on requirements and request for information from prospective vendors will facilitate the vendor selection process and help ensure that project needs are met.

4. Ensure proper cost management and communication

At the start, discuss with the vendor any possible deviation to the costs agreed upon, including impact of scope changes. If a requested change results in additional cost, ensure this is communicated and discussed between the appropriate Firm and the vendor team members immediately to eliminate any surprises.

5. Involve SMEs from the beginning of the project

The project team found it helpful that the subject matter expert (SME) was involved from the beginning of the project. The General Counsel, being the primary SME, attended initial meetings with the vendor in communicating his vision for the course and in understanding the process.

CURRENT, FUTURE, OR RELATED CHALLENGES

To date, feedback on the online course has been very positive, and in fact, 95% of respondents to the course evaluation rated the course excellent, very good, or good. Some participant comments are:

There were actual examples provided so that it could be very easy to understand what we were reading.

It enhanced my understanding of the possible risks the firm faces and my possible involvement. Thus, the course has better equipped me to prevent inadvertently committing any acts which may violate firm policy or bring possible claims against the firm.

I like the concept of the 10 steps. It is easy to follow and remember.

Useful links to further look into issues raised by the course.

The user-friendly electronic medium it was conducted in (was helpful).

The structure and the clarity (was helpful).

The cases and samples (were helpful).

Very clear and informative structure with lots of useful links.

The structure of the course combining audio and written materials, as well as general rules, study cases and tests, was right for me. The course is not overloaded with theoretical material, it provides clear ideas of the topic and their practical implementation, which are enhanced by study cases and tests.

The project team continues to centrally monitor usage of the online course, as well as feedback received from users. The team continues to promote the program and work towards increased course usage and program implementation overall. Continuing to recognize cultural differences among the target audience, the team is strategizing ways for wider implementation, and considers a variety of implementation angles (e.g. local office, regional, practice or industry group channels).

The team observed that most of the associates who have accessed the online course have done so in compliance with new hire orientation requirements or prerequisites to relevant meetings. The fact that some lawyers may have participated in local courses based on the content of the online course, or have accessed the course from local servers, should be considered in reviewing data since usage through these channels are not necessarily reflected in the usage reports tracked centrally.

Overall, we are currently reviewing the progress we have made in every region with the view to consider any additional steps we need to take to speed up implementation. Our General Counsel recently provided a status report to firm leadership and we have the full support of leadership to further embed the program throughout the firm.

ACKNOWLEDGEMENT

The author would like to acknowledge the contributions to this project of Kathryn Lippert, a former colleague and Director from Baker & McKenzie's Global Talent Management team, and Daljit Singh, Director of Talent Management in Baker & McKenzie (Asia Pacific).

REFERENCES

Edmundson, A. (2007). *Globalized e-learning cultural challenges*. Hershey, PA: Information Science Publishing.

Edmundson, A. (2009). Culturally accessible e-learning: An overdue global business imperative. *ASTD's Learning Circuits*.

Zulkey, E. (2009). *Risk management for law firms: From policy to practice, Chapter 4: Managing professional liability–a ten-point approach.* (pp. 27-31). Ark Group in association with Managing Partner.

KEY TERMS AND DEFINITIONS

After Action Review (AAR): An activity conducted after a project or major task to assess what went well, what can be improved, and lessons learned and best practices from the project.

Continuous Legal Education (CLE): Is also known as MCLE (mandatory/minimum continuing legal education), and is a requirement for attorneys in the United States to earn credits from education activities in order to maintain their ability to practice law in the states in which they are licensed to practice.

Development Framework (DF): Is the Firm's competency model and is based on extensive research into what it takes to be a successful, high performing lawyer at Baker & McKenzie. It sets out performance expectations for the Firm's lawyers at all levels based on the Key Performance Areas and Personal Qualities that have been identified as key contributors to high performance.

Professional Responsibility: Generally includes any matter or issues of ethical behaviour relating to the Firm or individual partners arising under the rules of professional conduct, Firm policies, and principles; including conflicts of interest, possible conflicts between clients, and matters of client selection.

Request for Information: A process conducted in seeking information from prospective service providers to help assess the extent they meet the Firm's requirements and serves as input for the vendor selection process.

Risk: Is an uncertainty, an event that may or may not happen. It is generally managed in one or a combination of four ways: acceptance, elimination, shifting, and mitigation. In the Firm, managing risk focuses on the elimination and mitigation of risk through following a ten-point approach.

Talent Management: In the Firm, defined as taking a coordinated approach to the related areas of recruitment, professional development, and career and performance management, using the Development Framework as the foundation. The emphasis is on recruiting people most likely to succeed in the Firm, providing challenging work, offering relevant development, coaching and support and ultimately differentiating rewards based on the level of performance displayed.

ENDNOTES

1. Aguateco is an indigenous Mayan language spoken in Guatemala.
2. Bahasa Malaysia or Bahasa Melayu is the official language of Malaysia.
3. Cebuano / Visayan is a language spoken by approximately one-fourth of the population of the Philippines.
4. Galician is a Romance language spoken in the northwest corner of Spain.
5. Gujarati is spoken by approximately 44 million people on the western coast of India and worldwide.
6. Hokkien (Fookien) is a dialect of Min Na Chinese spoken in southern Fujian, Taiwan and by many overseas Chinese throughout Southeast Asia.
7. Maori is one of the three official languages of New Zealand.
8. Marathi is the language spoken by the native people of the Indian state of Maharashtra, which includes Mumbai.
9. Nahuatl, the language of the Aztecs, is the most widely spoken indigenous language in Mexico.
10. Papiamento or Papiementu is the language spoken on the Caribbean islands of Aruba, Bonaire and Curaçao.
11. Putonghua is the name for standard Mandarin in mainland China, Hong Kong and Macau.
12. Shanghainese is a dialect of Wu Chinese spoken in the city of Shanghai.
13. Shona is a Bantu language native to the Shona people of Zimbabwe and southern Zambia.
14. Sindhi is an official language of both India and Pakistan.
15. Tagalog is the lingua franca of the Philippines.
16. Tajik is a form of Persian spoken in Tajikstan in Central Asia.
17. Tamil is the language spoken in Chennai (Madras) one of India's technology centers.
18. Telugu is a Dravidian language spoken in central India.
19. Tetum (Tetun) is one of the two official languages of East Timor.
20. Valencian is the name for the Catalan language as spoken in the Valencian community of Spain.

APPENDIX

The Firm's lawyers speak more than 75 languages, including all those used by the United Nations as well as the principal languages of the world's largest economies. Refer to Table 1 to see languages included.

Table 1. Languages spoken by firm lawyers

Afrikaans	Filipino	Kazakh	Sindhi[14]
Aguacateco[1]	Finnish	Korean	Slovak
Arabic	French	Latin	Slovenian
Armenian	Galician[4]	Latvian	Spanish
Azerbaijani	German	Maori[7]	Swahili
Bahasa Malaysia[2]	Greek	Mandarin	Swedish
Belarusian	Gujarati[5]	Marathi[8]	Tagalog[15]
Bengali	Haitian Creole	Nahuatl[9]	Taiwanese
Bulgarian	Hakka	Norwegian	Tajik[16]
Burmese	Hebrew	Panjabi (Punjabi)	Tamil[17]
Cantonese	Hindi	Papiamento[10]	Telugu[18]
Catalan	Hokkien / Fookien[6]	Polish	Tetum (Tetun)[19]
Cebuano / Visayan[3]	Hungarian	Portuguese	Thai
Croatian	Indonesian / Maylay	Putonghua[11]	Turkish
Czech	Irish (Gaelic)	Romanian	Ukrainian
Danish	Italian	Russian	Urdu
Dutch	Japanese	Serbian	Uzbek
English	Javanese	Shanghainese[12]	Valencian[20]
Farsi (Persian)	Kashmiri	Shona[13]	Vietnamese
			Welsh

This work was previously published in Cases on Globalized and Culturally Appropriate E-Learning: Challenges and Solutions, edited by Andrea Edmundson, pp. 223-244, copyright 2011 by Information Science Reference (an imprint of IGI Global).

Chapter 8
Integrating Culture with E-Learning Management System Design

Ray Archee
University of Western Sydney, Australia

Myra Gurney
University of Western Sydney, Australia

EXECUTIVE SUMMARY

Although it is a legal requirement of all organizations to permit sensorially, cognitively, and physically disabled persons equitable access to public website information, cultural factors are seldom considered as important in the design of online information content. But many tertiary institutions have a highly diverse, multicultural student body whose learning needs require special attention. Usually, instructors transform existing lectures and exercises, then adds links, and discussions to create Web-supported units, but without any real understanding of possible cultural artifacts or inherent limitations of their online interfaces. This study reports on the results of an action research study whereby students were asked to comment on their preferences for three uniquely different purpose-built WebCT pages which comprised near-identical content. The students showed a definite preference for a sparse, menu-driven webpages as opposed to a colorful, congested, all-in-one interface, or the bare-bones WebCT interface.

DOI: 10.4018/978-1-4666-1885-5.ch008

ORGANIZATION BACKGROUND

The University of Western Sydney is a large multi-campus metropolitan university. The campus involved in the study is located on the outskirts of Sydney and comprises students who come from highly diverse multicultural backgrounds. *Communication Research* is a core unit in the UWS Bachelor of Communication program taught by the School of Communication Arts. The unit introduces the modern process of communication research including critical review of research literature, argument and logic, data collection and analysis by Statistical Package for the Social Sciences (SPSS), writing the research report and research ethics. The unit is taught in a blended-learning environment, wholly within the university's computer labs. Students attend a two-hour, weekly workshop where course activities and material are situated within a specially-designed web page accessed from WebCT, and after initial instruction and discussion, work online with assistance from their tutor. Some activities are designed to be done in class with face-to-face instruction and support, while others can be completed in the student's own time.

SETTING THE STAGE

Over the past decade, e-learning has increasingly become a standard way of supporting students within higher education and in some cases, the sole method of instruction (Lee & Nguyen, 2007). While not always as attractive as traditional face-to-face instruction, e-learning does suit those students who prefer to work and study. Significantly, as cash-strapped tertiary institutions seek to broaden their market overseas, e-learning is being used with an ever-increasing proportion of students who originate from non-English speaking cultures.

Concomitant financial pressure from diminishing University funding has also driven the search for more efficient methods of course delivery. Thus course management systems such as WebCT, Blackboard, TopClass and Moodle have been widely embraced to provide easy, user-friendly ways of providing online material for tertiary students. At the University of Western Sydney, the most recent figures on the coverage of WebCT, show that more than 93% of units taught have an e-learning presence, with 1,800 staff who have sites set up for the purposes of supporting teaching and learning and that 35,000 students access these sites for their coursework (Rankine, 2009). Additionally, a 2009 UWS publication notes that the university is unique in the size, range and diversity of its student population, with cultural diversity being one of the more notable differences between UWS and other Sydney-based tertiary institutions. According to *Teaching@UWS 2009*:

In 2007, the domestic student cohort background represented more than 160 countries. One third of these domestic students were born overseas. International students were drawn from more than 100 countries and represented 11% of the University's total student population. Ten percent (10%) of the international students are studying offshore. (p. 7)

Adapting New Technologies for Multicultural Audiences

An unrecognized problem with using standardized methods of creating online materials is the issue of *accessibility* for a widely divergent student cohort – *cultural* accessibility being one of the most important. The evolution of the Web from a text-based medium to an interactive, multimedia platform has created the need to consider the audience of websites in more sophisticated and nuanced ways. The ability to include an increasing array of platforms such as Flash/Shockwave, video, sound and animation, have brought about both new potentials in web communication as well as new problems. Just as certain website designs may mitigate against users who are sensorially, cognitively or physically disabled (see Dey, 2002 for an accessibility audit of WebCT), websites may also varyingly attract or repulse some cultures more than others. Cultural accessibility is a website's potential to attract, to be understood, or to be used by members of other cultures. According to Wurtz (2005)

Cross-cultural web design nowadays requires dealing with design issues that include culture-specific color connotations, preferences in layout, animation, sounds, and other effects that are characteristic of today's generation of websites. (p. 2)

While intercultural communication has been the subject of hundreds of articles and books for decades, intercultural communication applied to online media has only recently begun to be studied. Further research on this phenomenon as applied to web use in an educational context, is only just beginning.

Limitations of the WebCT Template

Widely used across tertiary institutions worldwide, the WebCT platform, allows non-web literate authors to place learning material online. In the most recent review of WebCT use at the University of Western Sydney (UWS), Rankine and Malfroy (2006) studied WebCT use at UWS and noted that the majority of those sites sampled used the sites primarily for posting course material with a minority using the interactive capabilities of discussion boards, drop boxes or online assessment. This finding is indicative of both the limitations of the WebCT interface as well as the limitations of the technical web skills of the academic staff.

This in itself has implications for the issue of cultural accessibility. The proprietary interface allows users to select from a limited palette of choices in terms of its colors, navigation systems, graphic elements, or lack thereof, fonts and layout preferences. When these inbuilt WebCT elements are then published for a multicultural audience they yield unpredictable effects. For example, black text on a white background is used in Western cultures to represent purity, plainness, and professionalism. In many Asian countries, white is associated at a subconscious level with death, and feelings of grief (Scollon & Scollon, 2001). Thus, instructors who use default white backgrounds in WebCT pages are appealing to students from Western cultures, but psychologically inhibiting Asian student motivation to use these same pages. This effect may only be a small one for each web page, but the cumulative effect over dozens of pages and weeks of time may represent the differences between failure, ordinary marks or better than average marks.

Other color associations include blue for enlightenment (in India), red for prosperity and good luck (in China), yellow for royalty (Asian countries), and green for Catholicism (in Ireland). In European countries, red connotes communism, brown connotes Nazism, and black connotes death. It is easy to understand why many Asian websites use pastel colors, which are safe and neutral, but look so childish to the Western eye (Bernard, 2006). Various common web elements have regional variations even in the same language. The basic shopping cart used to purchase goods in US websites is known as the shopping basket in the UK, and shopping trolley in Australia. Thus the name of the shopping facility and the icon itself needs to be adapted for various international audiences.

A comparative cross cultural study of McDonald's websites by Wurtz (2005), noted that there were a number of significant visual and structural design differences between the company's websites across a range of different cultures. The study noted in particular, differences in the styles of navigation plus significant differences in many of the visual elements such as the use of animation, the use of music and sound effects, the use of text and the semiotic construction of the persuasive visuals. Wurtz assumed that McDonald's had performed extensive focus group testing of their websites and consequently customized each website to appeal to its user group in each target culture, to ensure that product communication was as efficient as possible.

With this study in mind, it can be argued that template-driven web portals like WebCT are culturally one-dimensional and that the architecture, the tools and the interface tend to reflect the orientation of the culture, (usually Western), which has developed and marketed them. These kinds of restraints make adapting an educational web presence to the needs and preferences of a culturally-diverse student cohort both difficult and challenging, especially when the web designers themselves have limited skills in design and usability.

CASE DESCRIPTION

Theories of Culture and Intercultural Communication

Theories of intercultural communication ultimately rely upon theories of culture, a term which has been defined many times in the research literature (see Giles & Middleton, 1999; Hall, 1976; Triandis, 1979; Williams, 1958). Researchers tend to adopt the most current or most popular definition in order to design research or explain findings. Within the fields of communication and human-computer interaction (and others), many scholars (e.g. Choi, Lee, Kim & Jeon, 2005; Marcus and Gould, 2000) have relied upon the Edward T. Hall's (1976) theory of high and low context cultures, and that of cultural anthropologist, Geert Hofstede (1991) who states that "culture is the collective programming of the mind that distinguishes the members of one human group from those of another. Culture, in this sense, is a system of collectively held values" (p. 5). This definition of culture has helped instructional designers to assess the impact of culture on user interface design (Kim & Lee, 2005). Following from this is a need to understand intercultural features such as user behaviors, preferences, attitudes and understandings.

In the field of intercultural communication, it is generally agreed that culture shapes, influences and determines how individuals perceive and experience the world (Hall, 1976; Hofstede, 1991; Trompenaars, 1998), but many web designers assume that both the medium and content of the web is culturally *neutral*, making communication transparent and universally understandable (Zhao et al, 2003). This ethnocentric assumption has been especially problematic for multinational companies using their websites to encourage and enhance global markets (McCool, 2006 Luna et al, 2002; Cook & Finlayson, 2005; Wurtz, 2005; Rose et al, 2003) as well as for educational institutions developing online courses for offshore programs comprising culturally diverse students (Tylee, 2002; Liang & McQueen, 1999).

A handful of recent studies have used the cultural dimensions articulated by Hofstede, Hall and Trompenaars to analyse the relationship between website layout, design, navigation and information architecture on usability for different cultures. One of the original and most widely cited cultural frameworks was developed and proposed by anthropologist Edward Hall (1976, 2000) in which he argued that cultures can be situated in relation to one another along a continuum which defines the styles with which they communicate. Hall labeled these styles *high-context* and *low-context*. Low-context (LC) communication styles occur predominantly through explicit statements in text and speech and cultures such as those of the Scandinavians, Germans and the Swiss are cited as examples. Low-context cultures tend to emphasise logic and rationality and linear processes of discovery and thinking. Communication in high-context (HC) cultures in contrast includes much more intrinsic and subtle cues such as body language and the use of silence. Integral to high-context communication is the context or situation in which a message occurs, not just the words or language used (Wurtz, 2005). Hall also considers that other important cultural variations are evidenced by different perceptions of time (monochronism vs polychronism) and space (proxemics). The implied impact of these differences, Wurtz notes, is that:

We might expect some similarities between the architecture of a website and the thought patterns belonging to a given culture. Logical, linear thinking patterns would imply linear navigation throughout the pages of the site, thus promoting a structured and timesaving quality. Parallel thinking patterns would imply a complex, less discernible navigation, offering subtle clues as to where the links will guide the visitor, Priority should be given to the aesthetic experience of the website in HC [high-context] cultures, rather than the informative function, which we would expect to be prioritised in LC [low-context] cultures (p. 7).

Hofstede's (1997) longitudinal study, undertaken between 1978-1983, of the comparative characteristics of global culture amongst employees of IBM in 53 countries determined what he believed were fairly consistent patterns of attitudes and behaviors. His theory, which has been widely debated yet remains highly influential, maintains that cultures vary across a spectrum of five consistent, fundamental dimensions. The impact of these cultural differences is manifested and can be measured, in terms of a culture's choices of symbols, heroes/heroines, rituals and values. However, both Hall's and Hofstede's oft-cited cultural dimensions have been criticized for being outdated given they were originally proposed in the 1970's and 1980's. A more substantial criticism was their underlying principles of determining cultural groups according to the geographic boundaries of nation-states.

Hall's and Hofstede's theories are not always invoked however, when culture is studied. In many educational fields, definitions of culture have wider meaning including sociological, anthropological and pedagogical perspectives (Chen, Mashhadi, Ang & Harkrider, 1999; Powell, 1997; Williams-Green, Holmes and Sherman, 1997). Culture can be said to be always present with Scheel and Branch (1993) offering a wide-ranging definition that encompasses the interdisciplinary nature of culture as:

...the patterns of behavior and thinking by which members of groups recognize and interact with one another. These patterns are shaped by a group's values, norms, traditions, beliefs, and artifacts. Culture is the manifestation of a group's adaptation to its environment, which includes other cultural groups and as such, is continually changing. Culture is interpreted very broadly here so as to encompass the patterns

shaped by ethnicity, religion, socio-economic status, geography, profession, ideology, gender, and lifestyle. Individuals are members of more than one culture, and they embody a subset rather than the totality of cultures identifiable characteristics (p. 7).

The latter definition overcomes one of the main criticisms of Hofstede's and Hall's theories, that individual nationals who belong to any one country may not be representative of that country. The above definition allows for a multiplicity of cultural groups (or sub-cultures) which may or may not share the country's assigned context or dimensional scores on Hofstede's scales. However this 'pan-cultural' definition introduces the problem as to how a researcher identifies an individual member of a culture for the purposes of performing research. Even more challenging, is the question of how an individual can themselves claim membership of a particular culture when they supposedly adhere to a multiplicity of cultural norms.

Student Webpage Preferences at UWS

Since the *Communication Research* unit was first introduced, the authors have developed a variety of online teaching modules which use a range and variety of online and traditional technologies including a bulletin board, podcasts for lectures as well as a series of Flash tutorials created using Adobe Captivate which give instruction on using SPSS and on writing and formatting the research report. A typical two-hour workshop is a seamless combination of short lecture, with accompanying Captivate, Powerpoint and/or Web presentation using computer projector, discussion, questions and student activities – all situated in UWS computer labs.

Given the cultural diversity of the UWS student cohort and the perceived structural limitations of WebCT, the authors undertook an action research project to answer the following questions:

- What are the learning effects of using WebCT with students from different cultural backgrounds?
- Are there any cultural preferences for WebCT tools, designs, structures or organization?
- Is there a way of optimizing online materials which maximises equitable access for all students?

After obtaining the required Human Ethics clearance, we created three different websites for *Communication Research.* All three websites were able to be accessed through WebCT links and comprised near-identical information and course material.

The three alternatives were:

1. A "Standard" menu-driven site (replicating our usual website driven units) and possibly more appealing to Australians; (Figure 1)
2. A "Non-standard" very congested, colorful site (replicating the busy, everything on the first-page approach found in many commercial sites) and possibly more appealing to an Asian audience; (Figure 2)
3. A plain vanilla site (replicating basic WebCT designs); (Figure 3)

In order to analyse student preferences, we employed an end of semester survey which asked students why they liked using the particular website/s for their access to the course support material. We obtained 341 surveys of a total 623 students who completed the unit over the two years, 2005 and 2006. We also assessed the web server logs to ascertain patterns of access for the unit over the two years.

Our survey consisted of 19 questions. Seven questions were demographic; 10 items were Likert-type scales and referred to user choices of site, color, navigation, graphics, and teaching features; two items were open-ended, general questions.

Since most of the students were Australian citizens, we soon realised that it was difficult to place participants into cultural groups. While the majority were locally-born Australian students, many had parents who were born overseas, and many spoke languages other than English. Thus, we asked participants "What is your culture?", but we also asked country of birth, maternal and paternal ethnicity, and languages spoken at home. This allowed us to formulate a "primary" culture and a "secondary" culture for each participant. Primary culture was usually the answer to "What is your culture?" whereas we determined a person's secondary culture from their answers to the other culturally relevant items. Data from the survey was analyzed using SPSS 13.

Three hundred and forty one (341) students participated in the survey during Nov 2005/2006. There were 56% female, and 44% males. In terms of age, 58% of the group was under 21, with 40% aged 21-25. A primary culture of "Australian" accounted for nearly 79% of the participants. This percentage dropped to 49% whose secondary culture was identified as Australian. There were another identified 42 cultures from the remaining 51% of students, with Filipino, Italian and Lebanese being the most popular.

The very large Australian component skewed both the culture variables. In particular, the Australian primary culture leads to very small percentages for the remaining 21% of the students, distorting statistical testing. Thus, we used the secondary culture as the main variable to distinguish the cultures of the participants for the rest of the study. From this, we created three new ethnic groups: Asian, European and Middle-Eastern by grouping various nationalities together facilitating comparisons to the Australians.

Figure 1. Standard Interface

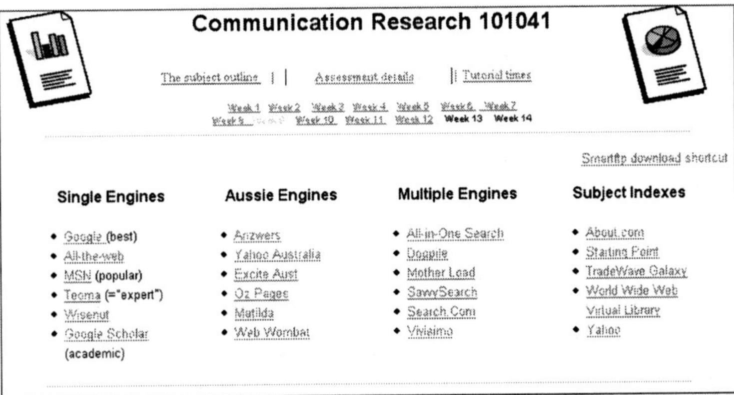

Figure 2. Non-Standard Interface

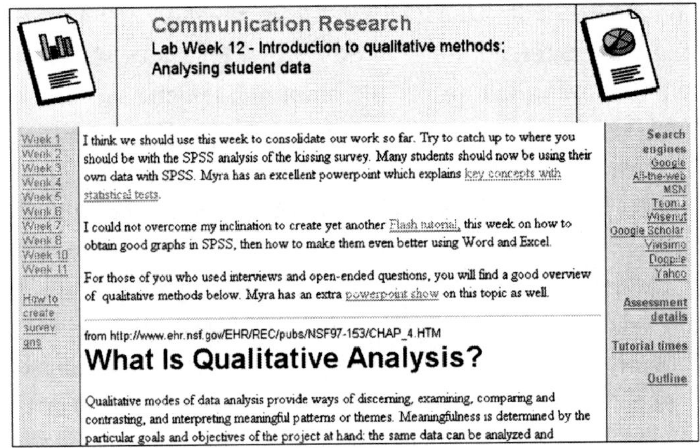

Figure 3. WebCT interface

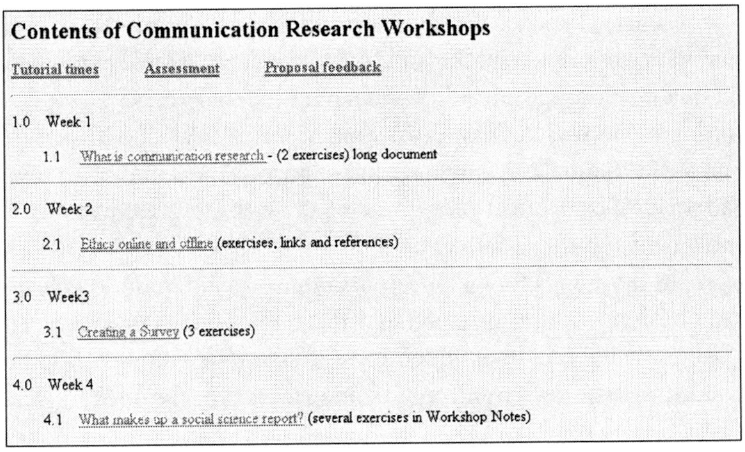

Contents of Communication Research Workshops

Tutorial times Assessment Proposal feedback

1.0 Week 1

1.1 What is communication research - (2 exercises) long document

2.0 Week 2

2.1 Ethics online and offline (exercises, links and references)

3.0 Week3

3.1 Creating a Survey (3 exercises)

4.0 Week 4

4.1 What makes up a social science report? (several exercises in Workshop Notes)

Overall summary statistics are given by Table 1 (low scores indicate more agreement). The main highlights of the summary statistics are all the small means and modal scores less than 2, namely "Having all the content on the first page was useful", "Use of Flash tutorials", "Design of WebCT pages was better than other sites" and "WebCT bulletin board was useful".

The main question we wished to answer was epitomized by the question, "Which web page did you prefer for your startup for the unit, *Communication Research*?" Percentages are shown in Table 2.

Table 2 shows the relative percentages of Australians, Asians, Europeans, and Middle-Easterners for "Which webpage did you prefer for startup". Europeans were very similar to Australians here. Since the standard page was very popular with Asians and Middle-Easterners, the non-standard page less popular for these two cultural groups. This is unusual since the non-standard page was seemingly a popular choice by many students who said that they liked having all the information they needed on the one colorful page. It could be the case that cultures from non-English speaking backgrounds were confused by the lack of structure of the non-standard web page, and in fact prefer the orderliness of the menu-driven standard page. The WebCT page is on par with no preference – all cultures seem unmoved by the WebCT basic interface.

If one inspects the actual server logs (Table 3) for the raw number of hits, a totally different picture arises however. The standard page is overwhelmingly the most popular choice for the majority of students. Nearly 60% of all the hits to the unit used the standard page. An anomaly can be seen here – if the standard page was so popular, then what accounts for the survey finding that Australians liked both the standard and non-standard pages almost equally? One explanation is that the dislike of the non-standard interface by other cultures led to this dramatic decrease in usage. Another explanation is that preference and usage are not the same thing and users do not always choose to use what they say they prefer. Habitual behavior probably plays a role in Internet usage. Perhaps users changed their minds when they were asked about their preferences at the end of the semester. A final explanation is that we did not obtain a true sample of all users over the two years.

Performing a one-way ANOVA (lowered alpha of 0.01 due to skewed sample sizes) on all the attitudinal scale items using culture as the main factor revealed that culture had a significant effect on two items: 1. website organization, 2. website design, and a near significant effect on 3. menu system.

If one graphs the means for the different cultures as in Figure 4, a clearer picture of how the different cultural groups rated these three items emerges. The design of the website was the one item which most divided the cultures. Middle-Eastern students valued website design and organization more than the others. Asian cultures

Table 1. Means and modes and standard deviations for all scale items

Survey Scale Item (7 point bipolar Likert scales)	Mean	Mode	Std. Dev
Website color did or did not play an important role in my preference	4.10	4	1.92
Menu system was or was not important factor in my choice	3.10	2	1.60
Website organization was or was not important	2.77	2	1.59
Website design was or was not important	2.89	2	1.55
I wanted or did not want more graphics	3.72	4	1.76
WebCT bulletin board was or was not important addition to learning	3.16	1	1.84
The use of flash tutorials helped or did not help me understand concepts	2.34	1	1.66
Having all the content on one web page was or was not useful	1.96	1	1.46
The design of the Communication Research WebCT pages was better or not better than most other sites	2.82	1	1.60

Table 2. Percentages of Australians, Asians, Europeans, and Middle-Easterners for "Which web page did you prefer for startup?"

Type of Web page	Australian	Asian	European	Middle-Eastern
Standard	41%	46%	40%	50%
Non-standard	42%	31%	43%	32%
WebCT	10%	11%	10%	9%
No preference	7%	12%	7%	9%
	100%	100%	100%	100%

Table 3. Popularity of interface by server hits

Type of Interface	TOTAL hits (%)
Standard	16,818 (59%)
Non-standard	6,130 (22%)
WebCT	5,338 (19%)
TOTAL	28,286 (100%)

Figure 4. Means of website organization, website design and menu system for Australian, Asian, European and Middle Eastern cultures (low means = stronger agreement)

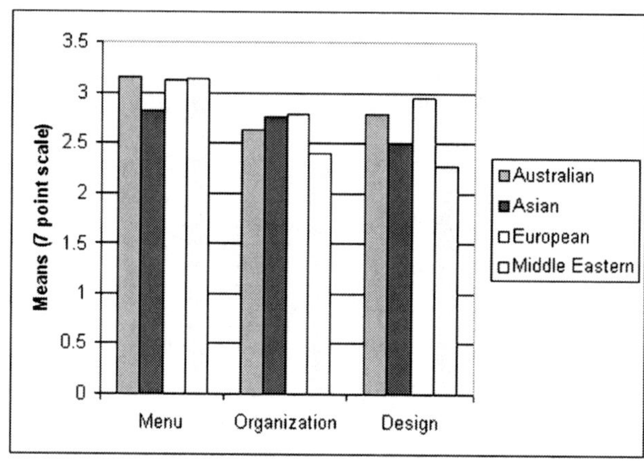

valued the menu system more than the other three cultures. It would seem that different cultures prefer different features of websites. Webpage color, bulletin boards, graphics, and type of content are equally valued by all cultures.

SOLUTIONS AND RECOMMENDATIONS

Our research project asked a number of specific questions.

1. "What are the learning effects of using WebCT with students from different cultural backgrounds?"

WebCT definitely enhances learning for all students since it allows a wealth of resources to be placed online for flexible access. The WebCT bulletin board system, online Flash tutorials, and 'having all information on one page' were seen as the most important benefits by students – but is WebCT the best possible choice? If you create alternate, well-designed startup pages, then students will predominantly use these in preference to the basic WebCT pages. We believe that the plain, and basic websites, which are the norm for most e-learning management systems, are only conducive to attracting students because they have no other choice. Students learn using a range of materials including books, lectures, notes, activities and WebCT. The issue is whether this learning can be optimised for the majority of cultures, and we believe that WebCT (and many other e-learning systems), is falling short of this mark.

WebCT allows novices to author Web-based materials, but this emphasis on the ease of use for authors is at the cost of usability for the user/student. Our experience is that WebCT-based learning materials acquire a captive audience, one that (we observe every day) is easily distracted by other online attractions such as instant messaging, hotmail, and better designed websites such as MySpace, which excels at organising resources.

2. "Are there cultural preferences or limitations for webpage color, design, structure and organization?"

Contrary to expectation, we found that website color was not an issue for any culture, since the means, modes and medians to the question, "Webpage color did or did not play an important role in my preference" were almost exactly 4, indicating no preference. We believe that there are two reasons for this: 1. students studying in host cultures adopted the preferences of that culture; and 2. there is an absence of native languages and familiar cultural contexts on test web pages – this lack of cultural milieu negated the normal effects of color for particular cultures.

We found that all cultures preferred well-organized, well-designed startup pages. We discovered that Middle-Eastern cultures significantly chose well-designed, well-organized pages to a greater extent than Australians, Asians or Europeans. Some cultures preferred the cluttered look of the non-standard page – Australians and Europeans stated they preferred the non-standard page and the standard page equally. This leads us to think that there is no way to predict preference for most students. We had originally thought that because pastel colored and cluttered webpages are the norm for many Asian commercial sites, then Asian cultures would also prefer this cluttered look. We failed to realize that lack of a cultural context and our use of English text (not Chinese, or Japanese or Korean), may have disrupted this natural predilection.

3. "Is there a way of optimizing online materials which maximizes equitable access for all students?"

We believe that the only way to ensure cultural equity is to produce a variety of e-learning webpages which can be selected by the students themselves. In a similar way to many European sites having a choice a several different languages, a choice of e-learning site could overcome much inherent cultural bias. However, this is not an option in current e-learning management systems, where limited templates create a standard look and feel across all WebCT-supported units, which inevitably merge into sameness.

There were problems which could have accounted for some anomalous findings:

- Locating the standard page icon on the extreme left of the WebCT icons may have inflated and influenced its choice in the server logs.
- The survey did not sample all students, whereas the server logs show a complete picture of the usage patterns. Perhaps many of the students who did not participate in the survey were avid users of the standard page and would have changed the survey preferences markedly in favor of that page if their opinions were also recorded.

LESSONS LEARNED

From performing this study, we learned five lessons:

1. E-learning management systems need to evolve and to provide choice and flexibility so that instructors can acknowledge and accommodate cultural differences by creating culturally diverse sites.
2. University decision makers need to understand that online learning is not simply a matter of placing course materials on to the Web as quickly and as easily as possible.
3. Instructors should aim to provide variety and interest wherever possible, not just information and resources arranged in boring lists.
4. All materials should be available in at least two different website designs.
5. Interactivity needs to be fostered, including the use of Flash tutorials, video, audio and simulations.
6. Identifying students' culture becomes an essential task for e-learning authors in order to allow them to customize online interfaces for widespread cultural access.

We also believe that university management and e-learning/IT decision makers need to consider the following when assessing the suitability and appropriateness of e-learning management systems for use with a culturally broad student cohort.

- The flexibility of the system in terms of layout, design, interface etc.
- The training of instructors/designers in principles of cultural accessibility and how to best use the system to ensure the best outcome for students.
- The recognition that the development of well-designed e-learning and blended-learning units, requires allocation of appropriate workloads for staff.
- Incorporation of regular measuring devices for feedback on cultural accessibility of e-learning systems across the institution.

CURRENT AND FUTURE CHALLENGES

This case study illustrates a range of problems and issues related to both the evolving use of the Web in education as well as the increased level of cultural diversity in university student populations. The broad issue is that in the rapid uptake of e-learning management systems in tertiary education, little, if any, attention has been paid to issues of cultural difference or the need to customize e-learning modes to take these into account, and thus ensure equity for all students. The template model of course management systems has been designed to encourage non-Web-literate designers and instructors to design blended-learning units and to publish online material for general student access. The downside of this is a lack of flexibility in terms of layout, design, interface, and color. In our project, only one of the three interface options available was created solely within WebCT, the other two used WebCT to link to an external web server which hosted the organized and congested interfaces. The WebCT interface was the plainest and lacked an integrated design – it was also the least popular. However, its layout was most similar to the majority of WebCT sites with which students would be familiar within the university. In fact, our experience has shown that even for academic designers such as ourselves who have above average skills, it is difficult to use the WebCT interface to achieve the same level of sophistication, integration and design.

A large proportion of academic users of WebCT may not be especially skilled in webpage design or cognizant of issues around online cultural accessibility and will use default modes for their material, many of which may unintentionally inhibit student motivation and engagement with the site. Additionally, increases in tertiary teaching and research workloads and the attending pressure for instructors to 'multi-skill', may impact on the ability of tertiary staff to develop appropriate levels of professional web design skills to address the issue of cultural accessibility in their online content.

The main challenge here is to have management and decision makers understand that e-learning is not simply a matter of permitting staff to place teaching materials on to a standardized webpage. While employing an e-learning management system is better than nothing, new software has made graphically-rich website creation much easier than ever before e.g. Web Studio, a totally graphically-based Web authoring tool. Such a multi-faceted approach using a variety of software will inevitably necessitate extra training and expenditure – an expense that management may find excessive. Student feedback forms will also need to be redesigned to incorporate feedback pertaining to online delivery and its improvement.

We believe that the e-learning management systems designers need to be aware of the limited cultural accessibility of their current designs and templates. Users of such systems also need to insist on change because their clients are not being equally supported by viewing Web pages that reflect a single cultural perspective.

We think that e-learning webpages themselves may be somewhat anachronistic. Given the popularity of social networking applications on the Internet, perhaps a much more interactive, socially active format for e-learning should be considered. One possibility is the growing interest in standalone interactive video tutorials such as those produced by Adobe Captivate. Others might include Second Life simulations, and Facebook-type student home pages. A third alternative might be some form of personal learning environment.

Ultimately, management needs to be aware that expensive e-learning systems may have only limited benefits for staff and students. In particular, while WebCT and similar platforms allow novices to author Web-based materials, we believe that this emphasis on the ease of use for authors is at the cost of usability for the user/student. Our experience is that WebCT-based learning materials acquire a captive audience, one that is easily distracted by other online attractions such as instant messaging, hotmail, and better designed websites such as Facebook, which excel at organizing resources.

In all cases, having a choice of webpage meant that students would exercise that choice and seek information elsewhere to the management system's offerings. We believe that the only way to ensure cultural equity is to produce a variety of e-learning webpages able to be selected by the students themselves. If the Europeans can cater for linguistic diversity by producing sites in several different languages, we should do the same by allowing a choice of e-learning interface in order to overcome cultural bias.

REFERENCES

Bernard, M. (2006). *Optimal Web design*. Retrieved 28 Sep, 2006, from http://psychology.wichita.edu/optimalweb/international.htm

Chen, A., Mashhadi, A., Ang, D., & Harkrider, N. (1999). Cultural issues in the design of technology-enhanced learning systems. *British Journal of Educational Technology*, *30*(3), 217–230. doi:10.1111/1467-8535.00111

Choi, B., Lee, I., Kim, J., & Jeon, Y. (2005). *A qualitative cross-national study of cultural influences on mobile data service design*. Paper presented at the Conference on Human Factors in Computing Systems, Portland, OR.

Cook, J., & Finlayson, M. (2005). The impact of cultural diversity on Web site design. *Advanced Management Journal*, *70*(3), 15–45.

Dey, A. (2002). *An accessibility audit of WebCT*. Retrieved 20 Sept, 2009, from http://ausweb.scu.edu.au/aw02/papers/refereed/alexander/paper.html

Giles, J., & Middleton, T. (1999). *Studying culture: A practical introduction*. Malden, MS: Blackwell Publishers.

Hall, E. T. (1976). *Beyond culture*. New York, NY: Doubleday.

Hall, E. T. (2000). Context and meaning. In Samovar, L. A., & Porter, R. E. (Eds.), *Intercultural communication: A reader* (9th ed., pp. 34–43). Belmont, CA: Wadsworth Publishing Co.

Hofstede, G. (1991). *Cultures and organizations: Software of the mind*. London, UK: McGraw Hill Book Company.

Kim, J., & Lee, K. (2005). *Cultural difference and mobile phone interface design: Icon recognition according to level of abstraction*. Paper presented at the Conference on Human Factors in Computing Systems, Portland, OR.

Lee, Y., & Nguyen, H. (2007). Get your degree from an Educational ATM: An empirical study in online education. *International Journal on E-Learning*, *6*(1), 31–40.

Liang, A., & McQueen, R. J. (1999). Computer assisted adult interactive learning in a multi-cultural environment. *Adult Learning*, *11*(1), 26–29.

Luna, D., Peracchio, L., & de Juan, M. (2002). Cross-cultural and cognitive aspects of website navigation. *Journal of the Academy of Marketing Science*, *30*(4), 397–410. doi:10.1177/009207002236913

Marcus, A., & Gould, E. (2000). Crosscurrents: Cultural dimensions and global Web user-interface design interactions. *ACM*, *7*(4), 32–46.

McCool, M. (2006). Information architecture: Intercultural human factors. *Technical Communication*, *53*(2), 167–183.

Powell, G. (1997). On being a culturally sensitive instructional designer and educator. *Educational Technology*, *37*(2), 6–14.

Rankine, L. (2009). *Personal e-mail* from E-Learning Manager, Univ of Western Sydney Teaching Development Unit, 22 September, 2009.

Rankine, L., & Malfroy, J. (2006). *The WebCT 100 project*. Retrieved 20 September, 2009, from http://tdu.uws.edu.au/elearning/referencesheets/TheWebCT100Project.pdf

Rose, G., Evaristo, R., & Straub, D. (2003). Culture and consumer responses to Web download time: A four-continent study of mono and polychronism. *IEEE Transactions on Engineering Management*, *50*(1), 31–44. doi:10.1109/TEM.2002.808262

Scheel, N. P., & Branch, R. C. (1993). The role of conversation and culture in the systematic design of instruction. *Educational Technology*, *33*, 7–18.

Scollon, R., & Scollon, S. W. (2001). *Intercultural communication: A discourse approach* (2nd ed.). Oxford, UK: Blackwell Publishers.

Smith, A., Dunckley, L., French, T., Minocha, S., & Chang, Y. (2003). A process model for developing usable cross-cultural websites. *Interacting with Computers*, *16*(1), 63–91. doi:10.1016/j.intcom.2003.11.005

Teaching Development Unit. (2009). *Teaching@UWS 2009*. Retrieved 21 September, 2009, from http://tdu.uws.edu.au/qilt/01_teachinguws/docs/Teaching@UWS.pdf

Triandis, H. C. (1979). *The handbook of cross-cultural psychology*. Boston, MA: Allyn and Bacon.

Trompenaars, F. (1998). *Riding the waves of culture: Understanding cultural diversity in global business* (2nd ed.). New York, NY: McGraw Hill.

Tylee, J. (2002). *Cultural issues and the online environment*. Retrieved 4 May, 2006, from http://www.csu.edu.au/division/celt/resources/cultural_issues.pdf

WebCT Australia and New Zealand. (2004). *A unified approach to e-learning at the University of Western Sydney*. Retrieved from http://www.webct.com/au_nz

Williams, R. (1958). Culture is ordinary. In McKenzie, N. (Ed.), *Convictions* (pp. 74–92). London, UK: MacGibbon and Kee.

Williams-Green, J., Holmes, G., & Sherman, T. (1997). Culture as a decision variable for designing computer software. *Journal of Educational Technology*, *26*(1), 3–18.

Wurtz, E. (2005). A cross-cultural analysis of websites from high-context cultures and low-context cultures. *Journal of Computer-Mediated Communication, 11*(1). Retrieved 18 July, 2006, from http://jcmc.indiana.edu/vol11/issue1/wuertz.html

Zahed, F., Van Pelt, W., & Song, J. (2001). A conceptual framework for international Web design. *IEEE Transactions on Professional Communication*, *44*(2), 83–103. doi:10.1109/47.925509

Zhao, W., Massey, B., Murphy, J., & Fang, L. (2003). Cultural dimensions of website design and content. *Prometheus*, *21*(1), 74–84. doi:10.1080/0810902032000051027

This work was previously published in Cases on Globalized and Culturally Appropriate E-Learning: Challenges and Solutions, edited by Andrea Edmundson, pp. 27-43, copyright 2011 by Information Science Reference (an imprint of IGI Global).

Section 3
Content Globalization

Chapter 9
Developing a Grassroots Cross-Cultural Partnership to Enhance Student Experiences

Iryna Pentina
University of Toledo, USA

Veronique Guilloux
UPEC IRG & EM Strasbourg (EA1347), France

EXECUTIVE SUMMARY

Increased globalization of the world economy makes international aspects of marketing an important priority. A growing number of business colleges provide cross-cultural experiences in marketing disciplines that help students better understand other cultures while applying their academic preparation to real-life settings. Today's students represent the first generation that has been born into the digital age, and freely use multiple technologies in preparing for classes, sharing notes, shopping, rating professors, and accomplishing multiple everyday tasks. This case discusses a class project on developing integrated marketing communications conducted by American and French cross-cultural student groups to promote environmentally-sustainable products in international markets. Modern social networking technologies were widely used both as tools for accomplishing the project, as means for presenting and displaying the results and as a medium for international marketing communications.

DOI: 10.4018/978-1-4666-1885-5.ch009

INTRODUCTION

Bringing real-world relevance into the classroom is a widely-acknowledged challenge for marketing educators (Bearden, Scholder, & Netemeyer, 2000). Media convergence and globalized markets present complex and unique problems to budding practitioners, requiring skills in innovativeness, problem-solving, resource optimization, and creativity. Business colleges and schools face more rigorous demands from both employers and students for adequate and cutting-edge workplace preparation. In addressing these challenges, marketing professors increasingly utilize innovative teaching methods that include simulations, qualitative interpretive research, interdisciplinary projects and innovative uses of technology (Albers-Miller, Straughan, & Prenshaw, 2001). Such emerging and rapidly developing content areas as corporate social responsibility, marketing ethics, digital and mobile marketing, globalization of marketing, and ecological sustainability are being incorporated in marketing curricula to reflect the changing business environment (Bridges & Wilhelm, 2008; Kelley, 2007; Jahan & Mehta, 2007). This paper reports on designing and implementing a cross-cultural student team project that answers the calls for comprehensive, realistic, and relevant teaching tools in marketing classrooms, which promote collaborative problem-solving using available technological advancements, and broaden students' perspectives on the global economy.

SETTING THE STAGE

The idea for the project was developed by the instructors as a result of sharing research papers and data online: both the French and the American marketing professors were using qualitative research in their investigation, and observed substantial cultural differences in student responses to similar questions. This finding led to an idea of having student teams create marketing communications campaigns using qualitative research data collected by their international teams with the goal to introduce and emphasize the concept of cross-cultural marketing and comparative marketing. The existence and wide availability of the Internet, the availability of overlapping instructional calendar schedule, as well as the requirement for the French students in their program to fluently speak English helped avoid frequently mentioned challenges for cross-cultural collaborations. The choice of the content area for the project was mutual: environmental sustainability has become a globally urgent issue that has yet to find its way into the marketing curriculum. The intensifying development of "green" start-ups, investment firms, political initiatives and regulations creates an imperative for business schools to prepare graduates for the sustainable business activities and practices, strategies and tactics. The project was conducted in the fall semester of 2008, with one pilot class of 30-35 students in each of the participating universities (in France and in the US).

CASE DESCRIPTION

Cross-Cultural Marketing Education

Increased globalization of the world economy makes teaching international aspects of marketing an important priority. The demand for international literacy and sensitivity among the business sector job applicants is reflected in AACSB requirements for international focus in business curricula. The major reason cross-cultural marketing education is necessary is that although globalization facilitates homogenization of tastes and fashions, strong national and local differences exist among cultures that warrant separate and different marketing campaigns, and brand and product development efforts. The ease of offering a product globally does not imply its universal acceptance. That is why globalization necessarily presupposes marketing with cultural sensitivity and understanding (Kelley, 2007). According to Morris et al. (1999), society can be analyzed using two different interpretations. The inside view considers constructs and ideas from a specific local perspective. This is the Emic view which relies on internal member's society criteria. In the outside view, the point of vantage is external and is called Etic. From the latter position, culture can be analyzed with universal categories. The two approaches are seen as either dichotomous or complementary and alternate in the process of cultural investigation. Thus, the ultimate goal of teaching cross-cultural marketing would be to teach students to evolve to the Etic interpretation through comparing various Emic approaches.

Harris and Moran's (1987) view on culture as a learned, shared and interrelated set of symbols, codes and values that justify human behavior informed our definition of cross-cultural marketing. Marketing across cultures means marketing to consumers whose culture is different in at least one fundamental aspect, such as values, lifestyle, social norms, religion, or language. Therefore, the strategic process of cross-cultural marketing should involve researching, planning and implementing all elements of the marketing mix (product, price, promotion, and distribution). In addition to studying how a particular culture may affect any marketing initiative, it is also important to ascertain the extent to which a company's marketing efforts may affect this culture (Hall, 1976) and the consequences of such changes. This, in turn, makes the process of cross-cultural marketing continually evolving, and the need for teaching and learning this are particularly pressing.

A growing number of business colleges provide study abroad experiences in marketing disciplines that help students better understand other cultures while applying their academic preparation to real-life settings. Recent reports indicate drastic increases in the number of study abroad tours among American students (100% increase over the past 8 years), with the most valued activities cited by the students being cultural activities, experiencing day-to-day life, and communicating with the locals (Koernig, 2007). The literature on study abroad mentions numerous potential difficulties and problems that can be encountered during the trip: managing large groups, overindulgence in parties, balancing academic content and cultural activities, etc. (Koernig, 2007). Additionally, with rising energy prices and weakening economic situation, the trips tend to be shorter and present a very sketchy and superficial introduction to different cultures and business environments. It appears that other methods may be used to achieve international emphasis in teaching marketing, in particular those using the available technology to connect students across the world.

The Roles of Technology and Team-Based Collaborative Problem-Solving

With the Internet penetration reaching 63.6% in the US, and 16.6% of the worldwide population (International Telecommunications Union, 2007), communicating and working across political and geographical borders have become unproblematic and universal. Email and chat, gaming and brand virtual communities, as well as medical, professional, social networks and political forums and blogs are being widely used; electronic commerce is booming; and mobile communications are becoming more available and affordable. Today's students represent the first generation that has been born into the digital age, and freely use multiple technologies in preparing for classes, sharing notes, shopping, rating professors, and accomplishing multiple everyday tasks. Such social networks as the Facebook and My Space allow its participants to literally share their lives with the selected referents. Any of these interfaces can be used by the project teams to meet, share ideas, and jointly work on the project using available collaboration software to track changes and make comments.

Group projects are considered a very effective pedagogical technique in marketing (Hernandez, 2002). They are used extensively in virtually all marketing classes as both a short, one class period-long technique (ad hoc clusters to discuss a question or solve a problem), and as longer formations to complete a case study or write a paper. The benefits stemming from utilizing group projects in advertising, marketing research, personal selling, public relations, and other marketing courses include exposure to applied near-work experiences, ability to work on larger and more complex projects, and higher student motivation and interest (McCorkle et al.,

1999, Williams et al., 1991). This project used formally assigned teams that were established for the whole duration of the assignment (from October until December of 2008). The teams were self-selected by the students and confirmed by instructors. Both the American and the French class formed 7 groups that were paired in cross-cultural teams according to their interest in one of the proposed "green" products (organic food, cosmetics, appliances, etc.). Thus, each joint cross-cultural group contained 4-5 American and 4-5 French students (for the total of 8-10 students). It has been noted that an optimal size for a team should be larger than 3 and fewer than 9 participants (Cooper, 1990; Smith, 1986). The suggested group size made in-country groups flexible enough to meet frequently, and cross-cultural groups – large enough to accomplish the assignment successfully. To avoid free-riding and prevent non-cooperation, peer evaluation was offered after the completion of the project, so that each member assessed the contribution of all members in their cross-cultural group. An additional benefit of using teams is an opportunity for inter-group competition. In this project, the marketing communications created by each team were subsequently rated by marketing students within respective Colleges of Business, and the winning cross-cultural team was announced and recognized within the College. Thus, the concept of cross-cultural virtual project teamwork has been created and implemented whereby technology (e-mail, social network, groupware) replaced face-to-face communications. In this type of project, cross-cultural teams are dedicated toward a target (here creation of an advertising) in delimited duration. The technology supports textual communication (e-mails) but also multimedia (through internet). Collaboration in this kind of environment requires trust and motivation to achieve the tasks.

Sustainability Marketing and its Role in Marketing Curriculum

Environmental concerns represent a prominent narrative in today's social, political, and economic life worldwide. The tasks of preserving and reproducing resources for future generations, reducing and eliminating toxic waste, and ensuring social justice are being put forward and prioritized by governments, non-governmental entities, and international bodies (Blackburn, 2007). In the business arena, firms are increasingly adopting a "green" image and employ public relations and advertising to promote and express their concern with the environment. More companies utilize independent certification and labeling in their products (e.g. organic, Energy-Star, natural, etc.) and release sustainability reports and accountability statements regarding key environmental performance indicators (Bridges & Wilhelm, 2008). Skills related to sustainability marketing and advertising appear to be in high demand by commercial and non-profit organizations.

For several decades the growing segment of environmentally-concerned consumers has presented both an opportunity and a challenge to marketers. Tracing its origin to the environmental activism of the 1960s and 1970s that led to the establishment of numerous environmental groups, creation of the Environmental Protection Agency, adoption of the Endangered Species Act, the Comprehensive Environmental Act (Menon & Menon, 1997), and other legislature, the concern about sustainable development has been steadily on the rise. The role of marketing in the process of social and environmental change was theoretically justified and legitimized in 1971. In the introduction to the *JM* special issue on the topic, Kelly (1971, p.1) stated:

Environmental deterioration is the social issue which will probably receive the greatest amount of business involvement. Business responsibilities toward improving the environment will become more important because a variety of ecological and social forces are stimulating a long-term national commitment to environmental protection.

In the same issue, Kotler and Zaltman introduced the concept of social marketing, which goes beyond influencing the acceptability of social ideas to "deal with the market's core beliefs and values" as opposed to "superficial preferences and opinions" (Kotler & Zaltman, 1971, p. 11). Since then, and in light of the increasing demand for environment-friendly products and more meaningful regulation policies and interventions, the need to understand the "green" consumers of the 21st century has become a priority for marketers. This understanding can help create meaningful marketing messages and help businesses modify their products and marketing strategies.

In accordance with a UN Human Environment report (World Commission on Environment and Development, 1987) on sustainable development, we define sustainable marketing as an integrative approach addressing environment, social equity, and economic/financial concerns in the development of marketing strategies (Bridges & Wilhelm, 2008). The concept of sustainable marketing incorporates environmentally sound vision, socially responsible business practices, and economic stability into traditional marketing strategies, tactics, and communications. A recent survey of business schools' commitment to teaching sustainability indicates that over half of the assessed business colleges require courses on sustainability. Among those courses there are a number of marketing electives that focus on new product and marketing communications sustainability; additionally, other marketing courses are adding content segments emphasizing environmental and social issues (Bridges & Wilhelm, 2008). Sustainable debates in France are emphasized, for example, by the ministry (Ministère de l'Ecologie, de l'Energie, du Développement durable et de la Mer) and through the implementation of the French law RNE (nouvelles régulations économiques) which imposes listed securities to write an annual report on their sustainable politics. Several research projects have been funded by the French government to analyze sustainable development. Academic association like Association Française du Marketing stimulates the creation of knowledge on that subject. Some French universities require pedagogical teams to integrate in each teaching module a session on sustainable development so that each student learns to be sensitive to ecological issues and to respect the planet. However, "current levels of student knowledge and comprehension regarding sustainability are low" (Bridges & Wilhelm 2008, p. 44) and calls are being issued to develop new pedagogical ideas, joint interdisciplinary projects and research endeavors that would move this content area to a more advanced level.

PROJECT OUTLINE

One Principles of Marketing Communications (US, 35 students) and one International Marketing Management (France, 40 students) class were selected for this cross-cultural project, the goal of which was to develop international and cultural understanding of environmental sustainability among future marketing professionals, promote analytical and creative thinking skills by engaging students in qualitative market research and interpretation, and provide hands-on opportunity to develop targeted marketing communications for international audiences and test their effectiveness. The selection of these classes was based on the objectives in their curricula emphasizing development of cross-cultural marketing understanding and skills. Additionally, the catalog descriptions of both classes emphasized the development of marketing communications campaigns as their intended deliverables. The project started in October and ended in December of 2008, the months during which academic schedules for both universities overlapped (Table 1).

At the beginning of the project, its objectives, structure, timeline, and the evaluation criteria were explained to both groups by their instructors (Figure 1).

They were then requested to voluntarily select their local team members based on common academic interests and convenience. Subsequently, local teams were paired with the respective foreign teams based on their interest in a particular sustainable, fair or green product category (Arthus-Bertrand, 2008; Canfin, 2008) from the following list: green transportation, personal care, clothes and accessories, organic food products, and household products (Table 2). By the third week of the project progression, the cross-cultural teams had established communications via email, discussion boards, and social networking sites and finalized their selection of products within their preferred categories.

Table 1. Outline of the Project

Date	Activity	Notes and Additional Readings
Oct 2008	Introduce the project and its goals	Students start selecting teams and product categories
	Module on Sustainability and its Global Implications	Clark 2007; McDonald et al. 2006; Mont and Plepys 2008; Oates et al. 2008;
	Confirm teams and products, assign international peer teams	Students establish electronic communications
	Module on Qualitative research and Depth Interviewing Techniques	McCracken 1988, LeCompte and Schensul 1999, Miles and Huberman 1994, Price, Arnould and Curasi et al. 2000, Pryor and Grossbart 2005
Nov 2008	Qualitative Research	Conduct depth interviews, record, translate and share transcripts
	Depth Interview Analysis	Code transcripts and analyze the results
	Work on Creative Campaigns	Students create marketing communications campaigns for both French and American audiences
Dec 2008	Compare US and French results and interpret them	Comparative analysis of campaign effectiveness and cultural differences

Figure 1. Objectives, structure, timeline and evaluation criteria for the project

This project provides you an opportunity to apply the concepts learned in this class to creating multi-cultural marketing communications campaigns for promoting "green" products. You will be working in international teams with marketing students in France (Paris). Initially you should select your local team members based on academic interests and logistical convenience (3-4 students), and then you will be paired with a French team based on common interests in particular "green" product categories. Each international team will then identify a product for which it will develop a **marketing communications campaign** embracing at least two communications venues (e.g. print and online) that would synergistically impact targeted consumers' behavior. Based on customer data obtained through depth interviews in both countries, each international team will develop one campaign for the American market, and one campaign for the French market.

The criteria for a successful marketing communications campaign are: proper audience selection and targeting, creativity, memorability, brand appeal, and competitive differentiation. In addition to a receiving grade, each campaign will be evaluated by other classes of marketing students in respective countries (or by actual target markets), based on brand recognition, brand recall, and purchase intentions. Winners in both countries will be recognized.

A proposal with your group's preliminary thoughts (no more than 1 page) is due no later than **October 25**. In the proposal you should: describe the selected "green" product (or service), describe the potential customers and competitors, and provide justification of your choice (e.g. changing consumption trends or technological breakthroughs).

Separate class meetings will focus on 1) sustainable consumption and its role in the world and 2) qualitative research techniques (specifically, on depth interviewing). Each team member will select a representative of the target market for their group's product and conduct a semi-structured depth interview (sample outline attached). French students should provide interview transcripts in English. Criteria for a good quality depth interview are: breadth of the domain tapped, number of new themes uncovered, information on motivations for acquiring the product, information on competitors' products perception, and suggestions for the group's Marketing communications creative and strategic solutions.

Table 2. List of the suggested environmentally sustainable product categories and the products selected

Product Category	Additional Information and Resources	Products Selected by Teams
Green Transportation	http://www2.ademe.fr http://www.cleanvehicle.org/ http://www.car-free.org/ http://www.sierraclub.org/transportation/	Tesla Roadster Honda Clarity Hybrid Ford Truck Solar-Powered Jet Skis
Personal care	http://www.greenpeople.org/OrganicSkinCare.html http://www.ecoseek.net/browse/personal-care/	Organic Cosmetics Bio-Detergent
Clothing and accessories	http://www.ams.usda.gov/AMSv1.0/nop http://www.buygreen.com/EcoGreenClothing.html http://www.ecoist.com/	Recyclable Flip-Flops Shoes from Tires Bio-Degradable Diapers
Organic Food Products	http://www.organic-europe.net http://www.organic.org/	Organic Beer
Household Products	http://www.guide-topten.com/ http://www.eco-label.com/default.htm http://www.ecohuddle.com/products/	Shower Filter Water Softener Solar Panels

Concurrently with team formation, students in both countries were offered a content module on sustainable consumption that included one class lecture and a general online discussion board supported by the US University's distance learning platform. The discussion was moderated by the instructors, based on the suggested readings (Table 1), and emphasized cultural differences in views on sustainability. The sustainability module served as a background that facilitated team and product selection and as an initial reference for collecting secondary data, and doing research on target markets and competitive environment.

At the beginning of the second month of the project the students were trained in depth interviewing and practiced compiling interview guides (Table 1). They proceeded to conduct depth interviews with consumers in their respective countries, which they transcribed and shared within their teams via email. The interviews followed a structured interview guide (Figure 2) and focused on consumer attitudes towards the selected product, the concept of sustainability in general, and the motivations of buying "green", with suggested probing questions on the role of information, communication and advertising in affecting buying decisions. The whole team was responsible for coding and categorizing the transcribed materials, as well as for coming up with marketing communications theme and creative decisions. The analysis was completed and submitted to the instructors by the end of the second month of the project. The third month was dedicated to team collaborations on creating marketing communications (advertising, web advertising, or a website)

Figure 2. Structured interview guide

This project provides you an opportunity to apply the concepts learned in this class to creating multi-cultural marketing communications campaigns for promoting "green" products. You will be working in international teams with marketing students in France (Paris). Initially you should select your local team members based on academic interests and logistical convenience (3-4 students), and then you will be paired with a French team based on common interests in particular "green" product categories. Each international team will then identify a product for which it will develop a **marketing communications campaign** embracing at least two communications venues (e.g. print and online) that would synergistically impact targeted consumers' behavior. Based on customer data obtained through depth interviews in both countries, each international team will develop one campaign for the American market, and one campaign for the French market.

The criteria for a successful marketing communications campaign are: proper audience selection and targeting, creativity, memorability, brand appeal, and competitive differentiation. In addition to a receiving grade, each campaign will be evaluated by other classes of marketing students in respective countries (or by actual target markets), based on brand recognition, brand recall, and purchase intentions. Winners in both countries will be recognized.
A proposal with your group's preliminary thoughts (no more than 1 page) is due no later than **October 25**. In the proposal you should: describe the selected "green" product (or service), describe the potential customers and competitors, and provide justification of your choice (e.g. changing consumption trends or technological breakthroughs).

Separate class meetings will focus on 1) sustainable consumption and its role in the world and 2) qualitative research techniques (specifically, on depth interviewing). Each team member will select a representative of the target market for their group's product and conduct a semi-structured depth interview (sample outline attached). French students should provide interview transcripts in English. Criteria for a good quality depth interview are: breadth of the domain tapped, number of new themes uncovered, information on motivations for acquiring the product, information on competitors' products perception, and suggestions for the group's Marketing communications creative and strategic solutions.

to promote the product. Each group worked on two types of communications: for French and for American audiences, analyzing and synthesizing their findings and realizing global advertizing principles learned in class. The final products of the project contained combinations of print, radio, video and/or social networks ads. They were posted online, and business students in both countries ranked them on quality and purchase intentions.

CHALLENGES FACING THE PROJECT

It is widely believed that college students learn better and report higher satisfaction with learning when they are actively involved in the process (Beckman, 1990). Working jointly on solving real-world problems fosters the development of communication and leadership skills, negotiation and persuasion abilities, as well as presentation and writing proficiencies (McCorkle et al., 1999). Being responsible for the group results stimulates independent contribution, increases student motivation to seek information and feedback from the instructor, and fosters organizational and time management capabilities (Paladino, 2008). Group projects are considered a very effective pedagogical technique in marketing (Hernandez, 2002). They are used extensively in virtually all marketing classes as both a short, one class period-long technique (ad hoc clusters to discuss a question or solve a problem), and as longer formations to complete a case study or write a paper. The benefits stemming from utilizing group projects in advertising, marketing research, personal selling, public relations, and other marketing courses include exposure to applied near-work experiences, ability to work on larger and more complex projects, and higher student motivation and interest (McCorkle et al., 1999, Williams et al., 1991). There are some potential downsides to utilizing project teams. Some frequently mentioned problems include potential lower exposure to the scope of the problem due to specialization of tasks, reduced quality of learning for free-riders (McCorkle et al., 1999), potential for inter-personal conflicts, etc. For a cross-cultural, electronically-mediated project, additional problems may arise with inability to get in touch, language and time differences, as well as cultural misunderstanding. Additionally, perceptions of sustainability have been historically different for Europe and the USA, with the European "green" movements enjoying much greater popularity and engagement among younger populations.

SOLUTIONS AND RECOMMENDATIONS

Participation in and fulfillment of this cross-cultural team assignment has provided students from both countries with hands-on experience with a foreign culture and understanding of the differences in approaches to sustainability, as well as analyzing different attitudes towards and expectations from marketing communications. For example, at the stage of product selection, French students reported that the market for pick-up trucks in France exists ONLY among small business owners, and is non-existent among general commuter drivers. Therefore, the French campaign was refocused to target small businesses with a hybrid pick-up truck. Similarly, the concept of solar-powered jet-skis was not familiar to the French students, and it took a sufficient amount of communications to be finalized as a "green" product of choice.

At the stage of interviewing and transcript sharing, the majority of teams found that the concept of sustainability and "green" consumption is perceived by the French markets as a duty, and by the American markets more in terms of convenience and savings these products may provide. Therefore, the campaigns for the French consumers overwhelmingly emphasized the cause-related appeals of saving the planet and making the country beautiful, while the same products for American consumers were focused on more pragmatic advantages, such as saving money and gas. It was also discovered that American respondents preferred learning about detailed and more technical product attributes and specifications (e.g. driving range of an electric vehicle or the number of shampoo bottles that one organic bar soap substitutes) while French customers were better persuaded by symbolic appeals and functional benefits within an ad (e.g. fashion for shoes from recycled tires and protesting animal testing for organic cosmetics).

The goals of the assignment were fulfilled: the cross-cultural groups created marketing communications campaigns, with the majority containing one social networks advertising and one print advertising, each utilizing the advantages of the respective medium and reflecting cultural differences of the target markets. In addition to formal grading by instructors, the campaigns were offered to other marketing students in both countries for comments that were subsequently discussed by the teams. The conclusions about campaign effectiveness were included into the final reports. While the project was very successful in achieving the predetermined educational goals, there were some unexpected issues and challenges in its execution. At the initial stage, the students enjoyed establishing connections and technology-mediated communications by sharing their photographs and becoming friends on social networks. As the project progressed, some groups experienced difficulties with on-time submission and sharing of ideas, suggestions, and depth interview transcripts that led to frequent instructor interventions. A solution to this may be arranging the project into modules by establishing deadlines and enforcing the submission of each deliverable increment to instructors. However, this approach may reinforce the timeliness at the expense of closer student collaboration and group norms development. Due to differences in academic schedules and academic levels, the final stage of the project (comparison and analysis of results) was less beneficial for the American participants who did not have sufficient time to reflect upon the outcomes. This issue can be addressed by more closely matching the educational level of the cross-cultural teams.

In order to more objectively assess the success of the project from the point of view of the students, the average class evaluation grade for the U.S. class was compared to the evaluation grade for the same Principles of Marketing Communications class that was taught by the same instructor in the Spring 2009 semester and did not offer a cross-cultural project. The class that contained the innovative project received the average evaluation of 4.2 out of 5, and the class without the innovation 4.0 out of 5. Additionally, both French and American students provided their verbal assessments of the project in their written comments. The responses (quoted below) were overwhelmingly positive and addressed the following learning outcomes:

Educational value added:

- "When compared to a similar project in another class based solely on secondary research, this joint research approach was an invaluable experience in that it gave me an opportunity to develop and test ideas based on dialog with students from France"
- "We not only studied theory, but had to use personal reflection and personal action"

- "The level of commitment was higher and we understand better, we learn better"
- "Very enriching, would be glad to do it again!"
- "In seven semesters at two different universities, I've never had another opportunity like that. I recommend the experience highly"
- "Having the ability to do a project with direct contact to students in another country should be a part of every student's college experience"

Higher level of analytical skills:

- "In case studies method, solutions are within easy reach, this project makes us think and draw conclusions based on our observations"
- "We used the same methods (e.g. SWOT analysis), but had to adapt it to fit the local conditions: e.g. the concept of recycling tires to make shoes is not new for the American consumers, but is an innovation for the French, so the whole business environment analysis is different"
- "Our ideas and work were compared, which helped to see different approaches in marketing and advertising in two countries"

High practical relevance and realism:

- "This project was a little bit like working for two different branches of the same company"
- "In the same project, there is not a sole answer but different ones linked to different cultures. French people want to dream while American advertising is more practically oriented – we achieve the same result by different means"
- "It was very enriching to perceive other views in a culture that seems very close to ours"
- "This project helped me to develop some skills in marketing and advertising for my scholarship in Bordeaux where I worked for a communications agency"

Intercultural competencies:

- "I got to know working habits of other cultures, which helps avoid ethnocentrism"
- "Now I will go to London for an internship … I have understood that a "French way" is not the only best way…I am ready to go to this English firm and be open to other perspectives"

- "Even in international business classes I have not been able to connect with another culture so easily and efficiently as in this assignment"

Some negative evaluations of the project concerned logistical difficulties mentioned above:

- "We did not have enough time in the course of the project to speak to our American colleagues"
- "The schedules did not allow us to compare the different reactions of both markets to the advertising campaigns"
- "The cultural objectives of the project were not clearly formulated ... but that was a first experience"

Based on the above comments, the instructional innovation can be considered a useful pilot test of cross-cultural collaborative teaching.

Due to the broad spectrum of skills it introduces and reinforces, this project can be successfully incorporated into International Marketing, Marketing Research, Marketing Strategy and other classes with various degrees of emphasis on its components. For example, instead of depth interviews, students can do secondary or survey research; instead of "green" products, non-profit services can be the focus; alternatively, the deliverables do not have to focus on communications campaign, but may be a marketing plan or a package design. A similar assignment can be offered to MBA classes, with the additional results assessment and analytical components. This project was intended to improve student knowledge and awareness in the areas of international marketing and advertising (e.g. standardization vs. localization), human values (universal vs. culture-specific, e.g. environmentalism), establishing comparability (emic and etic dilemma), and the emerging domain of online advertizing and marketing (Craig & Douglass, 2000). It also promoted research skills, creativity and accountability, as well as cross-cultural technology-mediated collaboration, ability to apply theoretical knowledge to practice, and capability to solve real-life problems. By addressing the above content areas and specific skills development, this project answered the calls for marketing educators to incorporate complex, real-life and creative assignments into marketing curriculum and prepare more aware and better marketing specialists. This cross-cultural study involved only two cultures (American and French). It could be interesting to conduct a similar project in countries that are more culturally distant from each other. Additionally, the idea of "sustainable development diffusion lag" between economically developed and developing countries (e.g. those in Africa) could be explored to better understand differential marketing approaches in those countries.

REFERENCES

Albers-Miller, N. D., Straughan, R. D., & Prenshaw, P. J. (2001). Exploring innovative teaching among marketing educators: Perceptions of innovative activities and existing reward and support programs. *Journal of Marketing Education*, *23*(3), 249–259. doi:10.1177/0273475301233010

Bearden, W. O., Scholder, P. E., & Netemeyer, R. G. (2000). Challenges and prospects facing doctoral education in marketing. *Marketing Education Review*, *10*(1), 1–14.

Beckman, M. (1990). Collaborative learning: Preparation for the workplace and democracy. *College Teaching*, *38*(4), 128–133.

Blackburn, W. R. (2007). *The sustainability handbook*. Washington, DC: Environmental Law Institute.

Bridges, C. M., & Wilhelm, W. B. (2008). Going beyond green: The why and how of integrating sustainability into the marketing curriculum. *Journal of Marketing Education*, *30*(1), 33–46. doi:10.1177/0273475307312196

Clark, G. (2007). Evolution of the global sustainable consumption and production policy and the United Nations environment programme's (UNEP) supporting activities. *Journal ofCleaner Production*, *15*, 492–498. doi:10.1016/j.jclepro.2006.05.017

Cooper, J. (1990). Cooperative learning and college teaching: Tips from the trenches. *Teaching Professor*, *4*(5), 1–2.

Craig, C., & Douglas, S. (2000). *International marketing research*. Wiley.

Hall, E. T. (1976). *Beyond culture*. New York, NY: Anchor Press-Doubleday.

Harris, P. R., & Moran, R. T. (1987). *Managing cultural differences* (2nd ed.). Houston, TX: Gulf.

Hernandez, S. (2002). Team learning in a marketing principles course: Cooperative structures that facilitate active learning and higher level thinking. *Journal of Marketing Education*, *24*(1), 73–85. doi:10.1177/0273475302241009

Jahan, K., & Mehta, Y. (2007). Sustainability across the curriculum. *International Journal of Engineering Education*, *23*(2), 209–217.

Kelley, C. A. (2007). Assessing the trends and challenges of teaching marketing abroad: A delphi approach. *Journal of Marketing Education*, *29*(3), 201–209. doi:10.1177/0273475307306885

Kelley, E. P. (1971). Marketing's changing social/environmental role. *Journal of Marketing, 35*(3), 1–2.

Kotler, P., & Zaltman, G. (1971). Social marketing: An approach to planned social change. *Journal of Marketing, 35*(3), 3–12. doi:10.2307/1249783

LeCompte, M. D., & Schensul, J. J. (1999). The ethnographic tool kit: *Vol. 5. Analyzing and interpreting ethnographic data*. Walnut Creek, CA: AltaMira Press.

McCorkle, D. E., Reardon, J., Alexander, J. F., Kling, N. D., Harris, R. C., & Vishwanathan, I. R. (1999). Undergraduate marketing students, group projects, and teamwork: The good, the bad, and the ugly? *Journal of Marketing Education, 21*(2), 106–117. doi:10.1177/0273475399212004

McCracken, G. (1988). Lois Roget: Curatorial consumer in a modern world. In *Culture and consumption* (pp. 44–56). Bloomington, IN: Indiana University Press.

McDonald, S., Oates, C. J., Young, C. W., & Hwang, K. (2006). Toward sustainable consumption: Researching voluntary simplifiers. *Psychology and Marketing, 23*(6), 515–534. doi:10.1002/mar.20132

Menon, A., & Menon, A. (1997). Enviropreneurial marketing strategy: The emergence of corporate environmentalism as marketing strategy. *Journal of Marketing, 61*, 51–67. doi:10.2307/1252189

Miles, M. B., & Huberman, A. M. (1994). *Qualitative data analysis*. Thousand Oaks, CA: Sage.

Mont, O., & Plepys, A. (2008). Sustainable consumption progress: Should we be proud or alarmed? *Journal of Cleaner Production, 16*(4), 531–537. doi:10.1016/j.jclepro.2007.01.009

Morris, M. W., Leung, K., Ames, D., & Lickel, B. (1999). Views from inside and outside: Integrating EMIC and ETIC insights about culture and justice judgment. *Academy of Management Review, 24*(4), 781–796.

Oates, C., McDonald, S., Alevizou, P., & Hwang, K. (2008). Marketing sustainability: Use of information sources and degrees of voluntary simplicity. *Journal of Marketing Communications, 14*(5), 351–365. doi:10.1080/13527260701869148

Paladino, A. (2008). Creating an interactive and responsive teaching environment to inspire learning. *Journal of Marketing Education, 30*(3), 185–188. doi:10.1177/0273475308318075

Price, L. L., Arnould, E. J., & Folkman, C. C. (2000). Older consumers' disposition of special possessions. *The Journal of Consumer Research, 27*(2), 179–201. doi:10.1086/314319

Pryor, S., & Grossbart, S. (2005). Ethnography of an American main street. *International Journal of Retail and Distribution Management, 33*(11), 806–823. doi:10.1108/09590550510629400

Smith, K. A. (1986). Cooperative learning groups. In Schmoberg, S. F. (Ed.), *Strategies for active teaching and learning in university classrooms*. Minneapolis, MN: Office of Educational Development Programs, University of Minnesota.

Williams, D. L., Beard, J. D., & Rymer, J. (1991). Team projects: Achieving their full potential. *Journal of Marketing Education, 13*(2), 45–53. doi:10.1177/027347539101300208

ADDITIONAL READING

Arthus-Bertrand, Y. (2008). *Le catalogue GoodPlanet.org 1000 façons de consommer responable*, ed de La Martinière.

Canfin, P. (2008). *Consommer responsable*. Flammarion.

Carlson, L., Grove, S., Kangun, N., & Polonsky, M. (1996). An international comparison of environmental advertising. *Journal of Macromarketing, 16*, 57–68. doi:10.1177/027614679601600205

KEY TERMS AND DEFINITIONS

Culture: A learned, shared and interrelated set of symbols, codes and values that justify human behavior

Cultural Emic vs. Etic Perspectives: The Emic view relies on internal member's society criteria, while in the Etic view, the point of vantage is external. From the latter position, culture can be analyzed with universal categories. The two approaches are seen as either dichotomous or complementary and alternate in the process of cultural investigation

Cross-Cultural Marketing: Marketing to consumers whose culture is different in at least one fundamental aspect, such as values, lifestyle, social norms, religion, or language.

Cross-Cultural Marketing Strategy: Researching, planning and implementing all elements of the marketing mix (product, price, promotion, and distribution).

Cross-Cultural Virtual Project Teamwork: Project in which technology (e-mail, social network, groupware) replaces face-to-face communications. In this type of project, cross-cultural teams are dedicated toward a target in delimited duration. The technology supports textual communication (e-mails) but also multimedia (through internet). Collaboration in this kind of environment requires trust and motivation to achieve the tasks.

Social Marketing Approach: Marketing that goes beyond influencing the acceptability of social ideas to deal with the market's core beliefs and values (as opposed to superficial preferences and opinions).

Sustainable Marketing: An integrative approach addressing environment, social equity, and economic/financial concerns in the development of marketing strategies.

This work was previously published in Cases on Innovations in Educational Marketing: Transnational and Technological Strategies, edited by Purnendu Tripathi and Siran Mukerji, pp. 183-195, copyright 2011 by Business Science Reference (an imprint of IGI Global).

Chapter 10
Cultural Adaptation of E-Learning Courseware: An Ethics & Compliance Example

Randall Stieghorst
Language & Culture Worldwide, LLC, USA

Andrea Edmundson
eWorld Learning, Inc., USA

EXECUTIVE SUMMARY

Web-based and self-paced learning modules have become a common-and sometimes primary-tool used by the Ethics & Compliance departments of global organizations to educate employees worldwide. These e-learning modules provide guidance around such topics as the company's Code of Conduct, specific policies or laws, globally applicable corporate standards, and how best to manage ethical dilemmas in a corporate environment. In this case, the authors describe the instructional design process that were used on various ethics and compliance courses to achieve a more global, regional, or country-specific applicability, including an overview of changes made to content and methodology that was originally perceived as "very American."

DOI: 10.4018/978-1-4666-1885-5.ch010

ORGANIZATION OR SITUATION BACKGROUND

Language and Culture Worldwide

Language and Culture Worldwide (LCW) offers training, translation, and consulting services for global organizations. LCW's training contextualization services evaluate and adapt learning tools and strategies so that they are more successful with multicultural and multilingual audiences (Language and Culture Worldwide, 2010).

eWorld Learning, Inc.

eWorld Learning, Inc. analyzes and revises training courses, particularly self-paced elearning courses, to align the content, instructional methods, and media/technology to the preferences of learners in other countries and cultures. eWorld Learning recommends critical modifications (those that could interfere with learning or learner acceptance) and tests those modifications with the targeted learners. Subsequently, we revise courses *before* they are translated, localized (from a technical and language perspective), or reproduced (eWorld Learning Inc., 2010).

Background

Web-based and self-paced learning modules have become a common -- and sometimes primary -- tool used by the Ethics & Compliance departments of global organizations to educate employees worldwide. However, as these courses are used more frequently outside of the United States, non-American learners protest that the courses are not acceptable or relevant to them, recognizing that many aspects reflect American culture, not theirs. Thus, e-learning designers must understand, anticipate, and adapt to cultural differences *before* courses are 'exported' to different cultures. In addition, ethics and compliance content must be accurate for the non-US regions or countries and placed in a context that is meaningful to them.

Typically, software being marketed to other countries is translated and localized before it is reproduced for international markets. Translation addresses specific dialects. Localization addresses obvious cultural differences, such as; spelling changes (localize to 'localise,' for example); replacing images and icons for local versions (replacing an American stop sign for a European one); and technical aspects (ensuring that the software supports expanded text, other alphabets, and so forth). However, elearning courseware, while it is technically software, is also a cultural artifact, imbedded with the cultural values, preferences, and nuances of the designing culture. Thus, for elearning courseware to be most effective for multinational and multicultural audiences, *cultural adaptation* beyond translation and localization becomes critical.

Cultural analysis of courseware is the foundation of cultural adaptation. Courses are analyzed to determine what needs to be changed, why and how, to best reflect the environment and learning preferences of the targeted learners. We analyze existing content (language, relevance, and context), pedagogy (instructional methods, activities, and assessments), and media/technology (acceptability, images and scenes, audio, etc.), so they align with regional and national expectations and cultural preferences.

The cultural analysis allows us to identify the characteristics that make the course 'too American' and subsequently, to at least neutralize or replace them with local or regional variations, depending upon where the courseware is to be launched. For example, a video scene in the American version of a module on Conflict of Interest portrayed casually dressed participants sipping coffee from Styrofoam cups outside of a hotel conference room. For the European version of the module, we replaced the scene with well-dressed participants sipping coffee from glass cups in a sophisticated hotel lobby with silver coffee urns (see Figure 1). This is an example of image localization, an integral part of cultural adaptation. However, in some instances, as you will see, we also make modifications to how the course is taught in order to accommodate learner preferences. Our goal is to remove or modify any course elements that could alienate learners, interfere with effective learning, or simply be incorrect or inaccurate in a different locale.

SETTING THE STAGE

While some organizations design their own classroom and web-based ethics and compliance learning, there are also numerous ethics and compliance training companies that offer a wide range of pre-packaged customizable e-learning products

Figure 1. US coffee break versus European

for global organizations. Driving the proliferation of such ethics and compliance training is legislation such as the Sarbanes-Oxley Act of 2002 (a bill enacted as a reaction to a number of major corporate and accounting scandals including those affecting Enron, WorldCom, etc.), the Federal Sentencing Guidelines, and the growth of global markets, offshoring, multinational corporations, etc.

CASE DESCRIPTION

In this case, we describe several approaches to modifying different modules in ethics and compliance courseware, on topics such as bribery and corruption, intellectual property, financial integrity, gifts and contributions, etc., which will be useful to other designers of ethics and compliance e-learning for international learners. Our client's customers were reporting that their course library lacked relevant content and context. For modules originally perceived as "very American," we discuss and provide examples of how we modified content and methodology to addressed global, regional, and country-specific applicability.

In our case, a series of elearning modules were being rolled out to various regions. From one standard template (the U.S. version), the client hoped to create several versions that looked and felt like they were local to the differing regions. In this case, suggestions for changes needed to be provided and incorporated into several versions, while maintaining the integrity of the content and a consistency within the series. We will focus on modifications made to the American version of courseware for a European audience. However, it is important to note that every region, sub-region, and even different industry groups, will require different modifications; but knowing what kinds of differences to look for is the first step of understanding the process of cultural analysis.

Content Concerns

1. Content Integrity

In the case of ethics and compliance learning, the content often consists of very specific laws and policies that apply to an organization and its employees. For designers of such elearning, it seems to be rather straightforward and low-context material – these are the rules and this is how we follow them. It is important to work through and explain, to the ethics and compliance leaders, any additional explanations which are necessary to localize a learning module for a specific region.

For example, in one elearning module on the Foreign Corrupt Practices Act (FCPA), certain additions were made to regionalized versions that compared the

FCPA to certain other national versions of the law. In addition, the punishments for violations were expanded to include ways in which non-US citizens (who are not necessarily subject to the jurisdiction of US laws when living in their home country) might feel the impact of an FCPA violation (e.g., when transiting the U.S. for personal travel, or on the impact on the community-at-large, should the organization be subject to a large monetary penalty.) Simple explanations of laws and rules may work well in a culture such as the U.S. (where people may feel that laws and rules must be enforced merely because the law or rule exists), but more robust explanations may be needed to provide greater context and additional justification for the value of such rules outside the U.S. Management needs to know that the rules and policies have been communicated successfully, but instructional designers need to ensure that the policies can be understood and the learner leaves with an understanding of such policies.

For example, not hiring young pregnant females has been acceptable business practice in some countries. In the module on Discrimination and Harassment, we added substantial explanation of why that practice would be unacceptable when working for the client's company.

Assumptions about groups of people or regions (geographically, politically, etc.) can lead to incorrect content. For example, law in China varies considerably—with a long-term, established legal framework for sexual harassment in Hong Kong - to newer statutes on the mainland. Thus, we also created 'sub-groups' of content for certain areas. In the module on Financial Integrity, we engaged European subject matter experts so that the revised content accurately reflected the rules on money laundering.

Maintaining a reference library for these variations, as well as designated space in the course templates for content placement, allow designers to easily update and modify courseware when these variations occur. In instructional design, such content chunks are termed 'reusable learning objects' because content 'objects' can be replaced based on the region or group of learners for whom the courseware is being designed.

In some cases, content can conflict with cultural norms. For example, in many European cultures, relationships take priority over work. Socializing, building relationships, and networking are ways of doing business. Thus, the wording in the module on Conflicts of Interest was carefully edited to clarify and reinforce what the client company expected with respect to 'doing favors.' Note that, while the employees may behave according to the company rules while within the company, it does not mean that they have dropped their cultural norms.

2. Context

Learners respond best to courses that are clearly designed for them, so written (and visual) content must be meaningful and relevant. For example, the module on Bribery and Corruption was going to be available in a country with an emerging economy, where bribery-type practices in the past had been considered appropriate ways in which to do business. Consider the situation: If you have always given money to an official to 'speed up' a process, you perceive it as an acceptable way to conduct business. Therefore, unless the courseware designer finds a way to connect with the learners in *their* context, the content seems "foreign" and learners may disregard the examples shown as "not relating to our reality." To strengthen this message, the content was 'scaffolded' by including phrases that recognized past practices, but introduced alternatives to corruption and bribery as more effective ways of doing business – ones that meet international standards (probably local standards as well) - and most importantly met company standards, regardless of what the standard practices may have been in the past.

For example, in the module addressing Business Relationships and Favoritism, the content encouraged learners not to make vendor choices based on relationships; however, we recommended the following extended explanation:

In addition to maintaining good customer relationships, a company's relationship with its suppliers is also of great strategic importance. Maintaining a good reputation with suppliers results when your company selects a supplier based on merit... avoids perceptions of favoritism...A company's procurement decisions reflect its best judgement about a supplier's technology, quality, responsiveness, and delivery capabilities, as well as cost. The supplier's financial stability, environmental performance, and track record are other factors that affect a company's decision. When companies invite potential suppliers to participate in a formal bidding process, they must stringently adhere to the procedures they define and announce for the same.

Some content may have no context whatsoever for non-U.S. audiences. For example, a video script mentioned "charitable contributions," a concept that is common in American corporations but not necessarily in other parts of the world, so it needs to be researched and determined where, if anywhere in Europe, it is a common practice.

In another module of client courseware, references were made to "protected classes", US legal terms relating to discrimination, understandable to a U.S. audience. For learners outside of the U.S. to connect to this content, it was necessary to remove the U.S.-specific term and include a more generic reference to groups which are protected against discrimination. In some cases where a country or region does not specifically address these groups, it was reinforced that this was company policy and not presented as a local legal requirement as well.

Figure 2. Wine gift versus DVD

Even the content of examples may require modification. In one scene of Gifts and Entertainment, the gift was a bottle of wine, which was inappropriate for learners in the Muslim regions. A change to an expensive watch or new technology gadget can create an example that is more realistic to local learners. In instructional design, we use 'cross-cultural learning objects (Edmundson, 2008).' These are reusable learning objects generated specifically to consistently address cultural differences. As in this example, there were different cultural representations of locally expected gifts (refer to Figure 2).

Our values can create assumptions about content and context. In the American version on discrimination, a Muslim woman was the subject of harassment and discrimination. However, in many European countries, the laws, as mentioned previously, may be different, and require investigation and confirmation.

In general, European law holds that harassment occurs when unwanted conduct related to the race, religion or disability of a person violates her dignity by creating an intimidating, hostile, degrading or offensive environment," Warnock said. "The burden of proof starts with the employee, who must establish facts supporting her claim. If a plaintiff can establish those facts, the burden switches to the employer, which must prove the law was not breached, he said. (Article from (Society for Human Resource Management (SHRM), 2009)

3. Values Integrity

In some of the courseware that was reviewed, certain value assumptions were made regarding the role of women as perpetrators of sexual harassment, something which did not serve as a good example in certain Asian contexts. In other cases, there is an American belief in the value of showing a diversity of races and nationalities

Figure 3. US diversity versus more common white male

Figure 4. Change from young female CEO to more mature

in the images, to represent the diversity of the U.S. This same demographic is not present in all countries and inclusion of such diversity again indicates to learners that the content was created elsewhere. Such differences need to be addressed as demographic differences and not seen as sexist or racist by U.S. instructional and creative designers (see Figure 3).

For example, in many parts of Europe, the percentage of the population that is non-white is less than 5%. This does not represent a values judgment, simply a regional demographic. Thus, the image of a diverse workforce was replaced with a more homogenous one. In addition, in Europe, fewer than 10% of C-level employees are female. Thus, we recommended modifying the scenario of a business meeting being led by a young female to one that was run by an older, white male. We ultimately agreed with the client that substituting a white (mature) female CEO would be acceptable, although the American courseware designers were reluctant because the situation was contrary to *their* values on diversity (refer to Figure 4). However, the goal was to create a course that addressed local expectations, not to create a 'statement.'

Values and context can overlap. In the module on Conflicts of Interest, a scene presented to learners portrayed a sporting event where a manager encounters one of his vendors. He accepts a dinner invitation from the vendor. The course feedback stated that learners should avoid this potential conflict of interest. However, sports and socializing are common business practice in many countries and you would be an outsider if you did not participate. Thus, just like the aforementioned scaffolding of the bribery example, the revised feedback included "In some countries, where socializing is part of the business environment, this situation may not be considered a potential conflict of interest. Thus, you need to learn the guidelines and policies that are unique to your company's environment." Note that we modified the content to address this challenge because the course was almost completed. However, in a situation where we were earlier in the design process, we could have created 'space' in the course to use a cross-cultural learning object: One that acknowledged and specifically addressed the cultural norm of using relationships to one's advantage in business.

4. Language and Globalizing your Language

Using clear language is important in all courseware, but it is especially true for courses that will be translated and/or taken by non-native speakers. Language can be a content challenge, for a variety of reasons. For example, American courses are written in American English, which tends to include jargon, idioms, and colloquialisms. For anyone who has ever learned a second language, the challenges presented by such phrases is evident. Imagine yourself reading a book in a language you have just learned. You encounter a set of words that does not make sense to you. Each word, individually, has meaning, but as a group of words, they take on a unique meaning. Such phrases are not included in dictionaries and, while you can find them online or in specialized dictionaries, do you want to interrupt your reading and comprehension by searching for their meaning? Thus, it is important to replace idioms and other 'phrases of meaning' with singular words. For example, a business that was 'taken over' was 'acquired.' Instead of "You *have to* do this' you would say, "You must do this."

Non-native speakers also rely on good grammar and punctuation to facilitate meaning. Active versus passive sentences are clearer and shorter. For example instead of saying "We are a trusted and respected organization because each of us accepts the responsibility for upholding our values and enhancing our reputation," we changed the sentence to: "People trust and respect our organization because we all accept the responsibility of upholding company values."

Globalizing any language improves clarity and reduces word count. Here is an example of editing done in a module on Financial Integrity to eliminate wordiness, jargon, and unclear phrases:

- 37 words

I hope so because my instincts are telling me that there may already be some questions seeing as we are ahead of schedule in a country that is notorious for their delays and a lack of transparency.

- 30 words (assuming the phrase 'lack of transparency' is understood)

I hope so because I suspect that there will be issues - We are ahead of schedule in a country that is notorious for delays and lack of transparency.

- 27 words (replacing the transparency phrase)

I hope so because I suspect that there will be issues – We have progressed unusually quickly in a country that is notorious for delays and unclear regulations.

Communications, Language, and Cultural Norms

The most predominant example of culturally influenced language and communications in the modules was the expectation that learners would act individualistically. In the American culture, we promote individualism; thus, in the modules, statements encouraged learners to 'take action' when they encountered unethical practices. However, in other cultures, where hierarchy is important, indirect communication is the norm, and acting individually is uncommon, these statements were perceived as 'non-solutions'. Thus, we modified feedback along the lines of "If you are uncomfortable speaking directly to your superiors, use a method that is comfortable for you to bring this situation to the supervisor's attention as soon as possible."

In cultures where there is a hierarchy and being a member of an in-group is important, a cultural norm would be to avoid conflict and *not* report unethical behavior. Thus, we added language encourage learners to modify their usual behavior: "In other situations or companies [where you have worked], employees may not have been encouraged to raise concerns, or if they did, perhaps they were punished in some way. As we have stated previously, to maintain trust and confidence, we encourage all employees to voice their concerns, suggest solutions, and feel confident that their input is valued and will never be punished" and then we left space for the client to include specific instructions for reporting potentially unethical behavior.

Language for Translation

In the previous example, we decreased the number of words to be translated by 27%, and in addition, the client will not be spending money to have translators 'interpret' idioms or locate local translations for 'transparency.' In addition to the 27% saved in initial translation costs, the cost of translating sub-titles and voice-overs will be reduced, as well. Audio language concerns are addressed below.

There are many techniques for increasing the comprehension of written materials and decreasing the costs of translation, such as avoiding synonyms, which are discussed in a resource chapter in the back of the book.

Instructional Design or Teaching Concerns

Instructional Approach

One of the benefits of elearning is that instructional designers can create more than one instructional approach so that those employees with different learning styles can self-adapt. In this case, however, course modules were all designed in the same manner: Content was primarily introduced via problem-based learning (a short case followed by multiple choice questions and feedback) or by a video. Content was presented via feedback and in text/content areas of the modules. Activities, cases, and questions throughout the course were included for the purposes of interaction and content presentation; only the post-course final test (multiple choices) was used to assess learning and to confirm that an employee had successfully passed the module.

Overall, in this case, both American and European learners appear to have comfortably accepted this model, which may indicate that it aligns either to their expectations or to previous courseware experiences. In any event, however, we recommend always consulting with end users (targeted learners) during course design and in pilot testing. In our case, the content and context of the modules underwent more adaptation than did the instructional approaches. Recommendations were made as to how content could be better sequenced, but that was for future courses, since these were close to production. Most adaptations to instructional approach were scaffolding the content, rewriting feedback to create regional relevancy, and clarifying course instructions so learners realized how they would be evaluated (final test versus during the course).

Sequencing

At the beginning of most of the ethics and compliance modules, the learners were presented with a scenario and asked to identify appropriate (ethical) behaviors. For

Americans, this methodology stimulated interest and challenged the learners to select the best response(s) based on their experiences, almost like a contest or challenge. The feedback for correct and incorrect responses provided them with the information about which actions and behaviors were most appropriate and why. However, some learners, especially in the Asian group, expected 'content before questions'. In risk-averse cultures, learners appear to be more comfortable (and therefore more likely to learn effectively) if information is provided *before* they are required to respond to any questions. It was too late in the course design process to re-sequence activities so we simply added explanations that these particular questions did not 'count' towards their final score.

Scaffolding

As mentioned previously, scaffolding is relating a new concept to one with which the learners are likely familiar. In the ethics and compliance modules, this was done frequently with new content that needed robust explanations and with instructions. Here is an example:

We added text to the Introduction:

In some cases, these guidelines may be new or strange to you. In other cases, you may not understand why our company considers an action 'unethical' when you do not view it that way. However, successful companies have become successful because they have learned to 'act' in certain ways that make them – and their employees – more trustworthy and reliable. Thus, please pay careful attention to our explanations of ethical behaviour and try to see how such behaviours do, indeed, make us more trustworthy and reliable. In addition, we present information and guidelines to help YOU make decisions based on our company's values, which we expect you to uphold while working for us.

Assessments

Types and criticality of assessments are important to learners. As mentioned previously, we modified the course instructions to inform learners that only the post-module test 'counted' towards successful completion and that it was not 'critical' to respond correctly to all in-module questions. This made learners more comfortable with the case method and problem-based learning because they knew that their responses did not count against their success. We actually anticipate that learners may become more comfortable with these new approaches and even learn to enjoy them.

Throughout the modules, learners were asked questions about situations; presented with rules, laws, and guidelines; and given feedback as to why which responses were correct. However, the course was not structured to use these responses towards a final 'score' to pass the modules. In this case, having a single test at the end of the modules conformed to the expectations of learners in Europe and other regions, where this progression tended to mirror their classroom experiences.

Feedback is an important mechanism in these modules for relaying content and for helping learners discern ethical from non-ethical situations. As mentioned previously, though, feedback for the European version was often rewritten or supplemented with statements that acknowledged that the content could be in contrast to their cultural norms. For instance, in the Intellectual Property modules, we added:

In many countries, using the intellectual properties of others is a common way of conducting business (such as copying popular movies to sell them). However, in successful global businesses, these actions are considered unethical. By knowing that our employees respect our intellectual property, we maintain trust and confidence within the company.

We would expect that feedback would require similar modification for other regions, locales, or sub-groups. Thus, again, the use of cross-cultural learning objects could be beneficial.

In addition, feedback needs to be structured appropriately. For example, in many family and group-oriented cultures, the original response does NOT represent the cultural norm or expectation in most European countries:

Original feedback in Conflict of Interest module:

Your first obligation as an employee is to the company.

Amended comment:

When you work for our company, we expect you to be loyal to the company by not engaging in activities that we consider being conflicts of interest. In some cases, our expectations may differ from what you have experienced in other companies. However, when you work with us, we expect you to abide by our values and guidelines. For example, if someone... (continues).

Amended feedback is not an ultimate solution (perhaps also not politically or culturally correct), but at least it clarifies the corporate stance. We added similar clarifications throughout the modules on Financial Integrity, Intellectual Property, and so forth. However, as mentioned previously, addressing these expected differences through course design and the use of learning objects will greatly facilitate cultural adaptation.

Media and Technology Concerns

Images and Scenes

In this series of courses, we addressed several visual aspects of the course, from the scenes, as mentioned above, to

- The actual images of faces (did you know that people recognize Americans because of their very white, even teeth?) (Figure 5),
- The business attire (which is more sophisticated and formal outside of the U.S.),
- Various habits (eating fast food at your desk is very American and working from home is not common in all companies or industries), etc.

Metaphors and Analogies

Metaphors and analogies need to be global as well. The Apollo or U.S. moon landing in a module may not be relevant in Europe, especially if the targeted learners were too young to have been alive (another cultural difference – multigenerational differences!). In this case, none of the modules included inappropriate metaphors, but we did remove references to strictly American items, etc., like firefighters' calendars, eating fast food at one's desk, going 'green,' etc.

Audio

In these modules, the videos were originally prepared for subscripts and voiceover. However, after receiving the edited scripts and reviewing the cost of subscripts and

Figure 5. American smiles

voiceover, the clients opted for still frame images of scenarios for most modules, greatly increasing their ability to provide customized scenes and content for other cultures and significantly decreasing the anticipated cost of translation. In the few videos kept, learners quickly identified actors as Americans speaking with an accent; thus, do not expect to fool people!

In the case of some dialogues and video segments that were translated and then re-filmed (sometimes with video and sometimes with a static montage of images) for translation, the characters accents were such that the Latin American version, for example, had all character accents from Spain. While this may have appeared less "U.S.-centric", the new module suddenly seemed "Spain-centric", which was equally as problematic in terms of convincing local learners that this courseware was created for them. What may sound accurate to us could easily be inaccurate and thus, we should avoid assumptions about accents.

Other

Taboos, Errors, Red Flags

A local or in-country reviewer may be the best source of information on content that immediately seems erroneous. Online, there are many websites dedicated to cultural taboos. Even the most knowledgeable cultural consultant may be unfamiliar with all the nuances of a specific region or culture; thus, we always recommend further research, as well as validation, by a member of the targeted cultural group.

For example, in one module of our case, learners were addressed as members of the European Union, but not all countries in Europe are members, so minor modifications were made in the wording. There was also humor in some of the dialogues and images, but the situations portrayed would not have been acceptable in European business environments (such as a telecommuter working in pajamas, jokes alluding to American culture, etc.).

SOLUTIONS AND RECOMMENDATIONS

In summary, the following actions proved to be successful for adapting elearning courseware in ethics and compliance:

1. Conducting a systematic cultural analysis of content, instructional methodology, and media helps identify the majority of critical cultural differences. Cultural differences that could affect course design could be socio-economic,

geo-political, religious, gender related; or, related to communications, learning styles, respect (hierarchy) and etiquette, legal, etc.

2. Including the targeted learners (end-users) or their representatives, in courseware development, cultural analysis, and final review or pilot testing validates our proposed modifications.
3. Using local subject matter experts to confirm the validity and accuracy of content is critical to maintaining the integrity of the content.
4. Providing simple explanations of laws and rules may work well in a culture such as the U.S. (where people may feel that laws and rules must be enforced merely because the law or rule exists), but more robust explanations are typically required to provide greater context and additional justification for the value of such rules outside the U.S.
5. Customizing the courseware includes addressing cultural norms and expectations, which can be very different from those of the designing culture.
6. Being prepared to *creatively* modify cultural elements when detected late in the design process is the best approach for courseware already in production; however, we recommend building courseware with templates, editable content areas, and space to insert reusable learning objects as the most flexible course design format for multinational, multilingual courseware.
7. Conducting a final overview and pilot testing the final version of all courseware, before it goes into production ensures the integrity of content and values and the acceptability of instructional approaches and technologies by the target learners.

LESSONS LEARNED

From conducting the cultural analyses and working with our clients, we have also learned that:

- Subject matter experts (SMEs) tend to assume that content for their region and country is applicable in others. In addition, they tend to be unaware of which aspects of their content are uniquely American.
- Very few instructional designers are trained to do cultural adaptation or even recognize the need.
- Creative staff members, like producers and scriptwriters, tend to resist cultural modifications: Writers tend to feel that using global English strips their work of creativity, so they need to see revised versions to be convinced. Video producers are unconvinced that learners can detect 'Americanisms.'

- Stakeholders in the design are prone to letting their cultural values interfere with good design and accurate content (written and visual).
- Instructional designers tend to rely on what they know best - Western or American theories on adult learning and instructional design – and do not actively investigate what would work best for international learners.
- Globalizing and regionalizing a course after the instructional design process has been complete can be a successful approach but cultural adaptation is best incorporated into early design process.
  - Asking instructional designers outside of the U.S. to do the initial draft of the content is one way of ensuring that the elearning will meet local expectations – and it also provides key insight, when American instructional designers review the proposed materials, as to what makes certain materials or content feel "foreign".
  - Using experienced U.S. instructional designers with cross-cultural and international experience.
- Working with instructional designers, writers, and subject matter experts early in the courseware development process greatly decreases the need for editing, error correction, inappropriate course design, etc.

CURRENT, FUTURE, OR RELATED CHALLENGES

Obviously, in ethics and compliance courses, the content and context is extremely important to localize. The challenge will be to convince more organizations that are rolling out new elearning or engaging employees who are new to the U.S. corporate environment that cultural adaptation is necessary and makes good business sense – for them and for their learners.

For the moment, adapting a course to cultural regions works well for providers of elearnng courseware on ethics and compliance; however, creating courseware for more specific cultural groups will be on the horizon, as well.

In addition, many Americans, even experienced instructional designers, find it difficult to grasp the depth to which culture can affect learning. As a result, they are not likely to consider courseware adaptation simply because they are unaware of culture's impact.

Training designers and other development and creative staff to recognize cultural differences to make modifications at their level will be essential to integrating cultural adaptation into the instructional design process. For example, writers can be trained to use Global English. Instructional designers can learn to use templates, reusable or cross-cultural learning objects, and content sequencing to create courses that can be more readily adapted to another culture. Creative staff like artists, video producers, etc., can develop libraries of different scenes and characters from different countries.

In this case, the authors described the instructional design process, including analysis and modifications, which was used on various ethics and compliance courses to achieve a more global, regional, or country-specific applicability, including an overview of changes made to content and methodology. We hope this helps other ethics and compliance courseware developers to create culturally viable international versions.

REFERENCES

Edmundson, A. L. (2008). Cross-cultural learning objects (xclos). In Putnik, G. A., & Cunha, M. M. (Eds.), *Encyclopedia of networked and virtual organizations*. Hershey, PA: Idea Group, Inc. doi:10.4018/978-1-59904-885-7.ch049

eWorld Learning Inc. (2010). *e-World Learning*. Retrieved October 4, 2010, from www.eWorldLearning.com

Language and Culture Worldwide. (2010). *Language and culture worldwide*. Retrieved October 4, 2010, from www.LanguageandCultureWorldwide.com

Society for Human Resource Management (SHRM). (2009). *Firms need plans preventing violations of EU worker protections*. Retrieved October 4, 2010, from http://www.shrm.org/hrdisciplines/global/Articles/Pages/CMS_016549.aspx

This work was previously published in Cases on Globalized and Culturally Appropriate E-Learning: Challenges and Solutions, edited by Andrea Edmundson, pp. 263-279, copyright 2011 by Information Science Reference (an imprint of IGI Global).

Chapter 11
Culturally Significant Signs, Symbols, and Philosophical Belief Systems within E-Learning Environments

Caroline M. Crawford
University of Houston, Clear Lake, USA

Ruth Gannon Cook
DePaul University, USA

EXECUTIVE SUMMARY

Semiotic components, that of culturally representative signs and symbols, when thoughtfully included in the design of electronic learning (e-learning) environments could directly impact the viability of the e-learning environment and student success in that environment. In fact, when the instructor's and instructional designer's philosophies and model choices are embedded with cultural and historical symbolic representations, stories, and tools, including new technologies, there can be a positive impact upon the students in the semiotic e-learning environment (Del Rio & Alvarez, 1995; Dillon, 1996; Gallini, Seaman, & Terry, 1995; Gannon-Cook & Crawford, 2001; Salomon, 1997; Verene, 1993).Within an electronic learning environment, the semiotic and philosophical imperatives can culturally charge the students' impressions, communications, and interactions with a strong positive impact. The learner's consciousness, because of the subconscious comfort level with the embedded semiotic course elements, is then more open to the new content material. The cultural and social elements thus minimize cognitive load and positively impact

DOI: 10.4018/978-1-4666-1885-5.ch011

electronic learning, not only in courses, but in other environments where semiotics is thoughtfully embedded, such as video and gaming environments. These case studies help provide a chronicle of the lessons learned from the ongoing research on embedded semiotics in e-learning.

To more appropriately frame the book chapter discussion, it is appropriate to offer a short overview of the discussion. The crux of the problem, at least in part, seemed to reside in a number of students' inability to succeed in taking an online course, in learning how to navigate the course, and in getting used to the isolation of online courses. The goal of the study was to see if the inclusion of semiotic tools, signs, symbols, stories, and tools, could help students to feel more comfortable and whether that comfort could help them to persist in completing assignments and finishing the course.

The contextual backdrop of the problem and goal of the study are based within the framework that the researchers wanted to be sure that the courses were unique in their appropriateness to their respective cultures; but they also wanted to see if the course adaptations provided cultural values and perspectives that were fairly consistent and appropriate across cultures and nations. The methodology is qualitative in nature, specifically focused upon development design research and narrative inquiry. The findings suggest that there were several levels of concern: learner concerns; instructional design or teaching concerns; management and organizational concerns; and, technology concerns. This study has addressed the question "what lessons could be learned from semiotic and philosophical instructional imperatives inclusion within e-learning environments?" As such, the interpretation of the findings of the study shed light on the importance of simple mediation tools, such as signs, symbols, and stories. The implications of the findings indicate that more research could shed light on how to help students feel comfortable enough to follow through and complete their e-learning courses. In viewing best practices for e-learning, students' existent knowledge can be bridged with what they need to know by using a variety of the semiotic tools discussed in this study.

ORGANIZATION BACKGROUND

The two universities that were the focus of this study significantly differ in size, and situation, but with similar missions with respect to their commitment to student success. Each has also committed to the success of their electronic learning (e-learning) programs. The priorities within each of the organizations are the design, development and implementation of the e-learning environments and the successful integration of the subject matter for the learner. One of the aspects also considered critical to the program's success was the impact of the underlying philosophical belief systems of the instructional designers, the instructors, and the universities. All of these factors needed to congeal into cohesive interactive e-learning environments and the researchers discovered that this seemed to occur more readily when there was a concerted effort to integrate semiotic representations, specifically the metaphorical representations meant to frame and support the learner's conceptual framework of understanding within the e-learning environment.

The first university (University A) is a smaller regional public university in the southwestern area of the United States of America. The primary focus of University A, at this point in time, is primarily upon graduate studies. Its mission is noted as being:

... an upper-level educational institution with a distinct identity, whose primary role is to provide fair and equitable learning opportunities to graduate and undergraduate students. The University serves a diverse student population from the state, the nation and abroad... by offering programs on and off campus.

The University's faculty, staff, and administrators are committed to providing a humane, responsive, and intellectually stimulating environment for productive learning and working. The "University A" emphasizes (a) learning through teaching, research, scholarship, and professional and community service; (b) the advancement of knowledge; (c) delivery of educational opportunities through new instructional technologies and through distance learning; (d) a commitment to high academic standards; (e) sensitivity to the needs of the students and communities served by the institution; and (f) above all, integrity in all institutional functions. (University of Houston-Clear Lake, 2008, para. 1, 4)

The second university (University B) is a larger private university in the north central area of the United States of America. The primary focus of University B is upon student learning success within undergraduate and graduate studies. The mission is noted as being:

... in common with all universities, is dedicated to teaching, research, and public service. However, in pursuing its own distinctive purposes, among these three fundamental responsibilities this university places highest priority on programs of instruction and learning. All curricula emphasize skills and attitudes that educate students to be lifelong, independent learners.... provides sufficient diversity in curricular offerings, personal advisement, student services, and extracurricular activities to serve students who vary in age, ability, experience, and career interests.

Full-time and part-time students are accorded equivalent service and are held to the same academic standards.

In meeting its public service responsibility, the university encourages faculty, staff and students to apply specialized expertise in ways that contribute to the societal, economic, cultural and ethical quality of life in the metropolitan area and beyond. When appropriate ... develops service partnerships with other institutions and agencies. (DePaul University, 1991, para. 1, 4)

The two university missions demonstrate their underlying concerns associated with the developing importance of e-learning environments As such, the stated mission of each university offers a compatible starting point from which to view the information framed throughout the remaining of the discussion.

The researchers who combined their research in this study are faculty members at these universities who were interested in gaining more data on which factors seemed to work successfully with elearners within their university settings. The authors' understanding of the instructional environment, the underlying philosophical frameworks, as well as the semiotic support inherent within e-learning environments, have led towards the success of the authors within the instructional milieu. An example of their teaching effectiveness is exemplified in one of the authors having been awarded the 2009 Outstanding Professor Award by the university's Alumni Association and the other author's nomination for that award by her students. This may suggest that one of the reasons for both researchers' online e-learning success may be due to their focus upon researching which factors result in the highest student satisfaction and retention. Another reason could relate to their understanding of the need to underscore underlying philosophical frameworks that inherently impact the e-learning environment, as well as the subsequent design and integration of semiotic components so as to support the learner's understanding of the subject matter.

SETTING THE STAGE

In prior research conducted together, the researchers looked at the role of motivational beliefs and classroom contextual factors (Pintrich, Marx, & Boyle, 1993) in student attention and retention (Crawford & Gannon-Cook, 2008a,b), now the researchers also wanted to look at the underlying semiotic and philosophical frameworks that could inherently impact the e-learning environment, as well as the subsequent design and integration of semiotic components so as to support the learner's understanding of the subject matter.

The study of signs, metaphors, and symbols within a culturally representative environment is framed as the study of semiotics. "The world 'semiotics' comes from the Greek root, *seme*, as in *semeiotikos*, an interpreter of signs. Semiotics as a discipline is simply the analysis of signs or the study of the functioning of sign systems" (Cobley & Jansz, 2007, p. 4). Basically, one may suggest that the representative signs viewed throughout a culturally laden world offer underlying ideas, themes and understandings that may support and enhance one's representation of the world. "The crux of the matter concerns the difference between 'natural signs' (freely occurring throughout nature) and 'conventional' signs (those designed precisely for the purpose of the communication)" (Cobley & Jansz, 2007, p. 5). The primary interest within this discussion is upon the "conventional" signs that one may design into an electronic learning environment so as to support and enhance the learner's understanding of the subject matter.

If these signs are embedded in e-learning some research into the degree to which these semiotic tools may have influenced the learners, and how much learning is enhanced, are two primary reasons for conducting the research in this study.

Culture, Memories and Their Relevance to Learning

The suggested impact of the social world upon one's learning experience and working frame of knowledge that directly impacts the e-learning environment has historical precedent (Angelaki, 1999; Beasley-Murray, 1997; Bandera, 1986; Blair & Caine, 1995; Blumer, 1969; Crawford & Gannon Cook, 2008a, 2008b; Danesi, 1993; Davydov & Radzikhovskii, 1985; Del Rio & Alvarez, 1995; Dillon, 1996; Greene, 1997; Greeno & Hall, 1997; Hall & Wortham, 1997; Hayes,1996; Lee, 1985; Popkewitz, 1997; Salomon, 1997; Wertsch, 1985). Seminal experts in the field of education, such as Vygotsky, have held that:

Social interaction plays a fundamental role in the development of cognition. Vygotsky (1978) states: "Every function in the child's cultural development appears twice: first, on the social level, and later, on the individual level; first, between people (interpsychological) and then inside the child (intrapsychological). This applies equally to voluntary attention, to logical memory, and to the formation of concepts. All the higher functions originate as actual relationships between individuals." (p57). (Kearsley, n.d., para. 1)

Vygotsky's view of learning purports that the socio-cultural impact upon the learner directly enhances, corrects and supports the learner's integration of new knowledge and information into her or his own personal (and socially enhanced) conceptual framework of understanding (Vygotsky, 1935, 1962, 1978, 1981; Wertsch, 1985);

Vygotsky's views directly impact one's semiotic understanding, which may then support and frame the learner's understanding of new knowledge and information.

Also of interest is Vygotsky's body of work which included his belief that there was a zone of proximal development (ZPD) where learning could be scaffolded upon prior learning.

The socially laden impact upon on the learner must be realized. A second aspect of Vygotsky's theory is the idea that the potential for cognitive development depends upon the "zone of proximal development" (ZPD): a level of development attained when children engage in social behavior. Full development of the ZPD depends upon full social interaction. The range of skill that can be developedwith adult guidance or peer collaboration exceeds what can be attained alone. (Kearsley, n.d., para. 2)

Another aspect that directly impacts the learners within the e-learning environment is the underlying belief systems of the persons who design, develop and implement e-learning environments. This aspect is closely aligned with the semiotics focus, as the underlying elements of one's belief system regarding learning is directly supported and enhanced within a real world e-learning working environment by the chosen semiotic influences. One's underlying belief system regarding learning usually focuses upon four different learning theories that help explain how people understand new information: Behaviorism; Cognitivism; Constructivism; and, Connectivism.

Behaviorism is one of the earlier learning theories to be embraced within the educational milieu, wherein:

Behaviorism is a worldview that assumes a learner is essentially passive, responding to environmental stimuli. The learner starts off as a clean slate (i.e. tabula rasa) and behavior is shaped through positive reinforcement or negative reinforcement. Both positive reinforcement and negative reinforcement increase the probability that the antecedent behavior will happen again. In contrast, punishment (both positive and negative) decreases the likelihood that the antecedent behavior will happen again. Positive indicates the application of a stimulus; Negative indicates the withholding of a stimulus. Learning is therefore defined as a change in behavior in the learner. Much of the (early) behaviorist work was done with animals (e.g., Pavlov's dogs) and generalized to humans. (Learning-Theories.com, 2008a, para. 4)

Cognitivism is a learning theory that is focused upon the mind as the tool through which learning occurs, as noted:

The cognitivist revolution behaviorism in 1960s as the dominant paradigm. Cognitivism focuses on the inner mental activities – opening the "black box" of the human mind is valuable and necessary for understanding how people learn. Men-

tal processes such as thinking, memory, knowing, and problem-solving need to be explored. Knowledge can be seen as schema or symbolic mental constructions. Learning is defined as change in a learner's schemata.

A response to behaviorism, it posits that people are not "programmed animals" that merely respond to environmental stimuli; people are rational beings that require active participation in order to learn, and whose actions are a consequence of thinking. Changes in behavior are observed, but only as an indication of what is occurring in the learner's head. Cognitivism uses the metaphor of the mind as computer: information comes in, is being processed, and leads to certain outcomes. Learning-Theories.com, 2008c, para. 4-5)

Constructivism, in contrast, is focused upon the framing of information through social and contextual means:

A reaction to didactic approaches such as behaviorism and programmed instruction, constructivism states that learning is an active, contextualized process of constructing knowledge rather than acquiring it. Knowledge is constructed based on personal experiences and hypotheses of the environment. Learners continuously test these hypotheses through social negotiation. Each person has a different interpretation and construction of knowledge process. The learner is not a blank slate (tabula rasa) but brings past experiences and cultural factors to a situation. NOTE: A common misunderstanding regarding constructivism is that instructors should never tell students anything directly but, instead, should always allow them to construct knowledge for themselves. This is actually confusing a theory of pedagogy (teaching) with a theory of knowing. Constructivism assumes that all knowledge is constructed from the learner's previous knowledge, regardless of how one is taught. Thus, even listening to a lecture involves active attempts to construct new knowledge. (Learning-Theories.com, 2008b, para. 3-4)

Connectivism is the more recent of the learning theories, developing within the Digital Age constructs:

Connectivism is the integration of principles explored by chaos, network, and complexity and self-organization theories. Learning is a process that occurs within nebulous environments of shifting core elements – not entirely under the control of the individual. Learning (defined as actionable knowledge) can reside outside of ourselves (within an organization or a database), is focused on connecting specialized information sets, and the connections that enable us to learn more are more important than our current state of knowing.

Connectivism is driven by the understanding that decisions are based on rapidly altering foundations. New information is continually being acquired. The ability to draw distinctions between important and unimportant information is vital. The ability to recognize when new information alters the landscape based on decisions made yesterday is also critical. Principles of connectivism:

- Learning and knowledge rests in diversity of opinions.
- Learning is a process of connecting specialized nodes or information sources.
- Learning may reside in non-human appliances.
- Capacity to know more is more critical than what is currently known
- Nurturing and maintaining connections is needed to facilitate continual learning.
- Ability to see connections between fields, ideas, and concepts is a core skill.
- Currency (accurate, up-to-date knowledge) is the intent of all connectivist learning activities.
    - Decision-making is itself a learning process. Choosing what to learn and the meaning of incoming information is seen through the lens of a shifting reality. While there is a right answer now, it may be wrong tomorrow due to alterations in the information climate affecting the decision.

      (Siemens, 2004, para.21-23)

Through this framework of understanding, it is possible to delve into the world of underlying philosophical belief systems and semiotics, and their subsequent impact upon the learning environment.

Information Frameworks

Although online learning has been a priority within all realms of the instructional process for well over a decade, it is interesting to note that the primary focus during those years has been upon "getting the information into the environment" instead of focusing upon the information's framework within the e-learning environment. This has been a fundamental concern of the authors through the years, wherein semiotic and underlying philosophical frameworks of understanding (by the instructional designers, developers, instructors/facilitators, and learners) had not been taken seriously as an area of concern and study; however, within a current framework, the more "warm fuzzy," "high tech, high touch" (Naisbitt, 1982, p.2) impact upon the learner as begun to grow in interest as researchers expand their search for best e-learning practices.

As such, it is appropriate to focus upon the underlying factors associated with e-learning which include:

- The impact of semiotic components or aspects within e-learning environments, as relates to learner success.
- The impact of the instructional designer's and the e-learning instructor's philosophical framework of understanding upon the e-learning environment, as relates to the learner success.
- The culturally charged communications within e-learning environments, as relates to learner success.
- The socially charged communications within e-learning environments, as relates to learner success.
- The social impact of graphical, audio, video and gaming environments within e-learning environments, as relates to learner success.

Other important underlying factors, such as the differing philosophical belief systems that directly impact the e-learning environment, those of the instructional designer(s), instructor(s), multimedia expert(s), and learner(s), as well as social and cultural experiences that may impact the e-learning environment, merit investigation to search for answers to how much these factors do impact e-learning.

These factors, when reviewed, will likely raise additional questions such as what role the decision-makers play in the overall planning, implementation and management of learning? And, what is the impact of different players (decision-makers) within the e-learning oversight and within the learning environment? This question may include the content expert, the instructional designer(s), the graphic artist, multimedia expert(s), adjunct instructors who teach the course, and the learners. The differing underlying philosophical belief systems of the instructional designer(s), instructor who developed the course, adjunct instructor of the course (not the original subject matter expert who developed the course), multimedia expert(s), and learner(s) within the course environment milieu, can also directly impact the e-learning environment's viability and sense of socialization, as much as the social community of learning that should be built and enhanced throughout the course experience.

While considering these concerns, the possible alternatives, including pros and cons, facing the organizations when dealing with the focus upon semiotic and underlying philosophical belief systems may be delineated. The different semiotic understandings integrated within the e-learning environment may (or may not) impact the self-regulatory abilities of the learners, the "flow" of the learners within the course, the communicative abilities, the conceptual and underlying understandings of the knowledge base (towards higher order thinking skills), and the cognitive load of the learners within the e-learning environment.

Examples of How Semiotics Works: Case Studies and Examples

Case studies since the surge of e-learning have pointed to the underlying influence of culture and culturally-representative images and references (Erstad, Klevenberg, & Amstad, 2008; Gannon-Cook, 1998; Gannon-Cook & Crawford, 2001; Gayol, 1998; Popkewitz, 1997). In the Gayol research, the idea of technological transparency is treated as a mythology because it hides the tremendous social impact of computer-mediated communication because technology has a systemic, rather than instrumental, relation with individuals and society. The a systemic connection of human-artifacts-knowledge promulgated by computer use reconstitutes society under the premise of autonomous individual technological aims, in the process disintegrating anything that cannot be converted into technology. Computers mediated communication alters language structure, social relationships, space, and time, and reconceptualizes pedagogies, overcoming the reproduction of mythologies and overlooking the impact of society and culture in communications and in education.

In the Erstad research (2008), two upper secondary schools took part in ongoing initiatives using an interactive knowledge forum in Norway with a school in Spain. They were both part of a project called 'Students as researchers in science education' and was part of a collaborative longitudinal study taking place from 2007-2011. The theme of the project was'global warming'. As a trigger in the project the students in both Norway and Barcelona watched a film on global warming to gain a better understanding of how students from different cultures speaking different languages could share a dialog about a shared topic.

The Popkewitz research (1997) centers around with the systems of reason that govern educational policy and research related to pedagogy and teacher education, including historical, ethnographic and comparative studies conducted in Asia, Europe, Latin America, Southern Africa, and the U.S. and points to the ways that different countries and cultures have siloed educational topics excluding important cultural and historical aspects of students' prior informal educational experiences.

METHODOLOGY

Case Study Description

The researchers conducted a model research case study (Richey & Klein, 2007) on two university online courses that were offered through each of their universities to assess e-learning challenges and semiotic factors that could affect students' learning and retention. The premise of the case study was that the techniques of instructional design often are taken for granted in university settings, largely because there are standardized design processes, web management software programs that absorb the course designs and integrate the course content into universal e-learning systems within the university. The researchers were interested in best online course practices that were applicable to local student populations, but could also be explored across languages and cultures. The researchers wanted to be sure that the courses utilized in the study were unique in their appropriateness to their respective cultures; but they also wanted to see if the course adaptations provided cultural values and perspectives that were fairly consistent and appropriate across cultures and nations. They designed the study to include very strategically placed icons, symbols, graphics and electronic devices, such as podcasts, in specific course modules in order to see which modules would have the greatest number and highest quality of responses. The difficulty level of the modules were also balanced so that there would be no modules of greater difficulty in either the control modules or the semiotic-designed modules. The intent was to use development design research to assess whether there would be more substantive positive responses in the treatment modules and whether there might be less attrition in the courses that might be at least, in part, attributable to the strategic semiotic interventions. The researchers knew that in the latter case of attrition, while the final course participant numbers might reflect better retention, those may not necessarily be attributable to the use of strategic semiotics in the courses. If there was greater student retention in the courses, then future studies could explore this factor in greater detail.

One major concern was whether embedded signs and symbolic representations, and narratives would be relevant to the learners. The researchers elected to use simple, universal signs that would not be perceived as offensive in any way, such as a campfire, a sailboat, a stop sign, people eating and talking together (Appendix B), and the researchers used stories and testimonials, as evidenced in the student feedback (see Appendix A). Several metaphors were also implemented, such as cave walls, and chalk boards. While these representations worked well, the researchers were always mindful that there could be cultural misunderstandings with any signs or metaphors that could be viewed as culturally inappropriate.

The two researchers opted to use several types of qualitative research, development design research and also narrative inquiry, to assess the online course design as well as student satisfaction enrolled in those courses.

Development Design Research

Development design is "the systematic study of design, development and evaluation processes with the aim of establishing an empirical basis for the creation of instructional and non-instructional products and tools" (Richey & Klein, 2007, p.

I). It entails a host of assessments necessary throughout the process of design and delivery to be sure that the online course is presented with all of the elements necessary for effective conveyance of the course material. Since these courses were offered internationally, it was even more incumbent upon the researchers to delve more deeply into the needs of the students in the course and to be sure those needs were met by both the course and the instructor. There are six facets to instructional design: learners, context, nature of content and its sequencing, instructional strategies, the media and delivery systems used, and the designers themselves. In this study the researchers opted for model development research, a type of development design research that is particularly appropriate for case studies. "The object of this research is the production of new knowledge...it commonly examines design and development as it is practiced" (p. II).

Model development is the study of "the development, validation, and use of design and development models, leading primarily to generalized conclusions" (2007, p.158) research includes the development of the knowledge management system as well as covering rapid prototype development and maintenance to accommodate the students' needs. In model research the researchers incorporate the content material, development, learning management system and evaluation process in situ.

(The) field has not sufficiently employed scientific methods to facilitate (our) understanding of design and development processes. The need for research is especially critical with respect to the models and processes employed by designers and developers. Few models, design strategies, and tools employed in practice have been empirically tested and validated. This is the gap that design and development research seeks to address. (p.3)

Narrative Inquiry

Clandinin and Connelly (1980, 2000) define narrative inquiry as a method that uses the following field texts as data sources: stories, autobiography, journals, field notes, letters, conversations, interviews, family stories, photos (and other artifacts), and life experience. Narrative inquiry is often included in appreciative inquiry (AI) (Van der Haar & Hosking, 2004), which is the active investigation and inquiry into the practice of researching what strengthen a system's capacity to maximize its positive potential. In using experiential, embodied metaphors, the instructional designer as researcher can challenge knowledge as embodied and embedded in a culture based on narrative unity and maximize learner's potential receptivity to new learning.

The two researchers in this study were faculty members who were interested in gaining more data on which factors seemed to work more successfully with elearners within their university settings (Gannon Cook & Crawford, 2009). The authors felt that the instructional environments, the underlying philosophical frameworks, and the semiotic support systems within the e-learning environments, all contributed to the success of the students within their university settings, they wanted to see if they could parse out which factors might be controlled; since changes could not be made to the instructional environments, what remained were the philosophical frameworks and the semiotic support systems. They chose to study the effects of the semiotic support systems of each university to see what inferences could be made from studying modules with few or no semiotic tools, and compare them to modules that contained thematic semiotic tools and narratives. Their courses were both educational technology application courses with comparable assignments.

Since both universities purported that learner-centered, constructivist, philosophies guided their missions, the courses would rest upon those principles, but the researchers also hoped to study whether there were emergent themes of connectivism that emanated from the assignments and discussions of the students.

The researchers documented each course module and the students' reactions and responses to the modules, the instructor, and to each other. Since the courses were in university template format within the web management software, it was not possible to change these features; however, they were able to design the content and add graphic elements to the course modules. They designed the first module to help acclimate the students to the course; the next two modules to be almost exclusively text based, then embedded semiotic elements to the fourth and fifth modules. (All five modules were comparable in content and assignment difficulty). After module five they asked for feedback on the first five modules to see what the feedback would be, and found the students far preferred the fourth and fifth modules over the first three modules. The remaining five modules were interspersed with semiotic elements to make sure that the students were provided with optimum content and visual material. The researchers, from module five onward, made thick notes of where the students seemed to have problems and where some changes, such as the provision of additional clarification, or possibly some additional semiotic tools, might help minimize the problems encountered by the students. Their hope was that, in the future, these suggested changes might assuage some of the students' fears and help them to feel more comfortable so that they would continue through the course to complete it successfully.

The researchers had embedded simple signs and symbols into the courses with the hopes that the subconscious awareness of the common symbols, such icons of signposts, doors, and books, along with photos of smiling students, and students engaged in conversation or the use of laptops, to convey subliminal messages of recognition and comfort to the students. Symbols and metaphors render the process of relevance-making possible; cultural content emerges (from symbols) in the development of cultural systems (Cobley & Jansz, 2007;Dillon, 1997; Eisner, 1997; Gannon-Cook, 1998; Salomon, 1997). There was supporting research to support that semiotics bridges new and old knowledge and mediates between human consciousness and computers, providing a safety zone upon which new knowledge could be scaffolded (Dillon, 1996; Eisner, 1997; Greeno, 1997; Gayol, 1998, Hall, 1997; Lee, 1985; Popkewitz, 1997; Salomon, 1997).

Humans hold onto memories, and symbolic nostalgia that give meaning to our lives (Popkewitz, 1997). The findings of the student feedback revealed that, while students participated in the primarily text-based online courses, they seemed to prefer the course modules that were embedded with signs, symbols, and narrative, such as modules three and four, over those modules without them. The findings also revealed that there were students who lurked or hesitated throughout the course, and it was not clear whether they were experiencing severe cognitive overload or whether there were cultural differences that may have kept them from responding to the instructor and to each other. Interestingly, the one thing that seemed to draw those lagging students somewhat out of their hiding and into the course were the assignments that encouraged them to tell their own stories. The students seemed to become very engaged when they were encouraged to share their own experiences which again reinforced the use of semiotic narratives in e-learning course designs. Both researchers found very similar responses from the students in the online courses with respect to their willingness to share experiences through their narratives.

Learner Concerns

The student feedback on the first five modules indicated: in the first module, the students repeatedly mentioned concern over what was expected of them, despite clear explanations, rubrics, and explicit assignments; in the second module, they mentioned feeling a little better about the course what was expected of them; and by the third module they seemed to understand the expectations of the instructor for the assignments and felt more comfortable in the course. But there still remained some students who lurked in the shadows of the course, except in the instances where they were asked to share their own experiences. Since they were largely unfamiliar with the concept of cognitive load, there was little mention of feeling stressed because of online technology demands or navigational issues; the only mention of issues that related to cognitive load were tied to stress, but the students tied the stress more to the course assignments or to the work stress in their lives more than the technological or content issues of the online courses. (The qualitative documentation is offered in Appendix A).

Instructional Design or Teaching Concerns

Since there were fixed templates and course management systems in-place at both universities, the researchers were limited to the designs of the contents and the inclusion of semiotic tools within the course. As far as teaching concerns, both researchers taught the courses as well as serving as embedded researchers, dual roles that might be in conflict in other types of research, but very necessary in many types of qualitative research, such as action research (North Central Educational Research Laboratory, 2010), development design research (Richey & Klein, 2007), or appreciative narrative inquiry research (Van der Haar & Hosking2004).

One major concern was whether embedded signs and symbolic representations, and narratives would be relevant to the learners. So the researchers elected to use simple, universal signs that would not be perceived as offensive in any way, such as a campfire, a sailboat, a stop sign, people eating and talking together, (Appendix B) and they used stories and testimonials, as evidenced in the student feedback (see Appendix A). Several metaphors were also used, such as cave walls, and chalk boards. While these representations worked well, the researchers were always mindful that there could be cultural misunderstandings with any signs or metaphors that could be viewed as culturally inappropriate.

Management and Organizational Concerns

While the researchers understood that change occurs slowly and it may take a while for the lessons learned in their research to be understood and implemented on a larger scale than in the courses researched for the study, the results from the study could help influence management's e-learning design decisions, particularly with respect to students' retention. The concerns of management and organizations are most often the bottom line, so if changes can be economical and also have positive bottom line benefits, which in this case would be student retention, then the innovations have a better chance of adoption. Since there was little cost to management to implement the kinds of changes needed to create e-learning courses that would include semiotics and deeper philosophical instructional imperatives, and since these recommendations could be phased in with several beta-test courses coming online in the next year, the courses with these elements could be slated for inclusion in the next cycle of new online courses and further research could also be conducted to see if students in those courses experienced better assimilation of new course materials. The university could also review these courses to determine whether more students remained in the courses, and if so, see if they could directly attribute the retention to these factors: semiotics; deeper philosophical instructional imperatives; the importance of simple mediation tools, such as signs, symbols, and stories; e-learning design; and, e-learning management.

Technology Concerns

The researchers realized that the web management software and the university templates could not be changed, but the course itself and the contents could be changed, so they worked within the parameters they could control. They also could not control the technology, but the technology functioned adequately for the most part, and when it malfunctioned the students seemed resigned to the fact that occasionally technology fails. During those times the students complained a little, and some complaints showed up in the students' feedback responses. There were students in the course who were less technological, but the hope was that the modules they had designed with embedded semiotics had impacted the students sufficiently as to resonate with them in a very positive way, enough to dispel some of the newer technology users' fears. The students were asked to contact their teachers and the help desk for assistance on an ongoing basis, but the teachers as researchers also shored up the students by having at least two phone conferences during the course so that students could openly discuss their fears, including any technology concerns.

SOLUTIONS AND RECOMMENDATIONS

It is interesting to consider the potential solutions and recommendations associated with this subject, especially as focused upon recommendations of the researchers based on the findings of this study to the management of the organization. After reviewing the students' mid-course and final course evaluations the researchers had sufficient evidence that the modules with the strategic semiotic enhancements were preferred by more than eighty percent of the students. This finding provided input that, while technological tools require in-depth preparation to be sure the tools fit with the university's technological architectural and delivery systems, so too should the psychological tools of semiotics require in-depth planning to maximize the success of e-learning courses.

While there has been prior research (Clandinin & Connelly, 2000; Eisner, 1997; Salomon, 1997; GannonCook, & Crawford, 2001) that demonstrates the preference for graphics, narratives, and multi-media in online courses, there yet remains enough research to determine what the effects of strategically embedded semiotics could have in the design of online courses. This model research provides enough evidence to suggest that there is a need to explore which factors could enhance students' increased receptivity and retention in online courses.

There is no "final solution" that can be recommended at this point in time, as it is a relatively new and growing area within the e-learning milieu. However, after this study, there are suggested guidelines and approaches that may support, enhance and encroach upon the viable e-learning environment and these aspects must be further delineated. Recommendations for some online course standards should be proposed that would address the need for thoughtfully embedded semiotics in the design of online courses at their universities to provide a psychological learning bridge to students, particularly at-risk students, enrolled in those e-learning courses.

EXAMPLES OF THE CAVE TEACHERS

This study has addressed the question "what lessons could be learned from semiotic and philosophical instructional imperatives inclusion within e-learning environments?" The researchers investigated how the tools of semiotics could excavate sociocultural knowledge from learners and mediate with that knowledge to integrate it with new contents introduced in e-learning courses. Just like shining a light in an ancient cave revealed petroglyphs that revealed stories and lessons of ancestors, the findings of the study shed light on the importance of simple mediation tools, such as signs, symbols, and stories. The research also indicated that more research could shed light on how to help students feel comfortable enough to follow through and complete their e-learning courses. In viewing best practices for e-learning, students' existent knowledge can be bridged with what they need to know by using a variety of the semiotic tools discussed in this study.

Lessons Learned

The long range effects of this case are inherent towards the further understanding of social communities of learning within e-learning environments. The old idea of "build it and they will come" is no longer an option, as the first generation of e-learning environments may have embraced; today's e-learning realm must not only offer ease of use and viable textual and multimedia options, as is appropriate, but also must include factors that include the sociological, social and cultural milieu within the e-learning environment. Semiotic course elements must be embraced and understood beyond the current realm of consideration to help provide consistency and minimize cognitive overload for the students in online courses. Five lessons learned from this study are:

1. The impact of semiotics upon the e-learning environment are much more affective than previously considered;
2. The impact of the textual, graphical, audio, video, and gaming environments upon the e-learning environment could greatly impact the learners, so thoughtfulness should be given to their use;

3. The impact of underlying philosophical beliefs upon the e-learning product and e-learning environment can positively affect students' attitudes in e-learning environments; and,
4. Suggested strategies and recommendations towards addressing the design, development and implementation of successful social communities of learning within e-learning environments should be given much deeper thought and the stories and narratives of students encouraged in the design of online courses.
5. Ongoing monitoring of mediation tools should be kept as an integral part of the formative evaluation process of each university's online courses to insure the maximum success of the students enrolled in those courses.

CURRENT, FUTURE OR RELATED CHALLENGES

For now the challenge remains how to overcome skepticism from universities to spend more time in the thoughtful development of 21st Century electronic learning environments that incorporate historical and cultural artifacts to enhance learning. Most universities need to put as many courses online as possible to shore up their bottom lines and minimize costs. But those costs cannot be derived from short-changing students who need those semiotic tools to bridge the gap from what they know to what they need to learn. Prior e-learning courses were once viewed as the vanguard for environmental learning changes where students could take online courses in almost any subject. But as the research on the average completion rates of elearners revealed (National Center for Education Statistics, 2002), they did not always succeed, with attrition rates often exceeding 40%. While efforts of post-secondary institutions continue to try to improve the completion rates of students enrolled in online courses, the recognition that prior learning and historical-cultural artifacts could conjure positive memories and scaffold new learning could encourage greater efforts to include more semiotic elements to scaffold new educational experiences on students' cultural and historical understandings and reintroduce a respect for the lessons of our ancestors. Hopefully learning outcomes will not only produce higher online course completion rates, but emerge as virtual oracles of knowledge artifacts for the next generations of elearners.

REFERENCES

Anderson, L. W., & Krathwohl, D. (Eds.). (2001). *A taxonomy for learning, teaching and assessing: A revision of Bloom's taxonomy of educational objectives*. New York, NY: Longman.

Angelaki, J. (1999). Machinic modulations: New cultural theory and technopolitics. *Journal of the Theoretical Humanities*, *4*(2).

Bandera, A. (1986). *Social foundations of thought and action*. Englewood Cliffs, NJ: Prentice Hall.

Beasley-Murray, J. (1997). So here comes a book that makes everything easy: Towards a theory of intellectual history in the field of intellectual production. *Cultural Theory, 2*(7).

Blair, B., & Caine, R. (1995). Landscapes of change: Toward a new paradigm for education. In B. Blair & R. Caine (Eds.), *Integrative learning as the pathway to teaching holism, complexity and interconnectedness*. Lewiston, UK: EMText.

Bloom, B. S. (1956). *Taxonomy of educational objectives, handbook I: The cognitive domain*. New York, NY: David McKay Co Inc.

Bloom, B. S. (1984). *Taxomony of educational objectives*. Boston, MA: Allyn and Bacon.

Bloom, B. S., Englhart, M. D., Furst, E. J., Hill, W. H., & Krathwohl, D. R. (Eds.). (1956). *Taxonomy of educational objectives, the classification of educational goals. Handbook I: Cognitive domain*. New York, NY: Longman.

Blumer, H. (1969). *Symbolic interactionism: Perspective and method*. Englewood Cliffs, NJ: Prentice-Hall, Inc.

Chicago Press.

Churches, A. (2008). *Bloom's taxonomy blooms digitally.* Retrieved on April 22, 2008, from http://techlearning.com/shared/printableArticle.php?articleID=196605124

Clandinin, D. J., & Connelly, F. M. (1980). *Narrative inquiry* (3rd ed.). Chicago, IL: University of.

Clandinin, D. J., & Connelly, F. M. (2000). *Narrative inquiry: Experience and story in qualitative research.* San Francisco, CA: Jossey-Bass Publishers.

Clark, D. (2000). *Learning domains or Bloom's taxonomy*. Retrieved on February 5, 2005, from http://www.nwlink.com/~donclark/hrd/bloom.html

Cobley, P., & Jansz, L. (2007). *Introducing semiotics. Thriplow & Cambridge*. UK: Icon Books Ltd.

Crawford, C. M., & Gannon Cook, R. (2008a). Building autonomous and dynamic communities of learning within distance learning environments: Focusing upon making connections, knowledge creation and practice communities. *The International Journal of Technology, Knowledge and Society*, *4*(4), 47–58.

Crawford, C. M., & Gannon Cook, R. (2008b). Creating and sustaining communities of learning within distance learning environments: Focusing upon making connections, creating communities of learning, and responsibilities. *The International Journal of Learning*, *15*(2), 179–193.

Danesi, M. (1993). *Vico, metaphor, and the origin of language*. Bloomington, IN: Indiana University Press.

Davydov, V., & Radzikhovskii, L. (1985). Vygotsky's theory and the activity-oriented approach in psychology. In Wertsch, J. W. (Ed.), *Culture, communication and cognition*. Cambridge, UK: Cambridge University Press.

Del Rio, P., & Alvarez, A. (1995). Changing architectures of mind and agency. In Wertsch, J. (Ed.), *Sociocultural studies of mind*. Cambridge, UK: Cambridge University Press.

DePaul University. (1991). *University mission statement*. Retrieved on October 12, 2009, from http://mission.depaul.edu/mission/index.asp

Dillon, A. (1996). Myths, misconceptions and an alternative view of information usage and the electronic medium. In Jrouet, (Eds.), *Hypertext and cognition* (pp. 24–42). Mahwah, NJ: Erlbaum.

Eisner, E. W. (1997). Cognition and representation. *Phi Delta Kappan*, *78*(5), 349–353.

Erstad, O., Klevenberg, B., & Aamdal, G. (2008). *Negotiating otherness in knowledge building*. Summer Institute 2008, University of Oslo, Norway. Retrieved on February 22, 2010 from http://elevforsk.umb-sll.wikispaces.net/file/view/paper_Summer_Institute08.pdf

Gallini, J., Seaman, M., & Terry, S. (1995). Metaphors and learning new text. *Journal of Reading Behavior*, *27*(2), 187–191.

Gannon Cook, R. (1998). Semiotics in technology, learning and culture. *Bulletin of Science, Technology & Society*, *18*(2), 178–183.

Gannon Cook, R. (2009). Lessons learned from parietal art: Pansemiotics and e-learning. Paper presented at the CELDA Conference of IADIS held in November in Rome, Italy.

Gannon Cook, R., & Crawford, C. (2009). Exhuming cultural artifacts to embed and integrate deep adult e-learning. In the *Proceedings of the American Educational Communications and Technology Conference,* October, Louisville, KY.

GannonCook. R., & Crawford, C. M. (2001). Metaphorical representation within a distributed learning environment. In J. D. Price, D. A. Willis, N. Davis & J. Willis (Eds.), SITE 2001 Annual – *Society for Information Technology and Teacher Education* (pp.1086-1088). Charlottesville, VA: Association for the Advancement of Computing in Education (AACE).

Gayol, Y. (1998). Technological transparency: The myth of virtual education. *Bulletin of Science, Technology & Society, 18*(3), 180–186. doi:10.1177/027046769801800305

Greene, M. (1997). Metaphors and multiples: Representations and history. *Phi Delta Kappan, 78*(5), 387–394.

Greeno, J. G., & Hall, R. P. (1997). Practicing representation. *Phi Delta Kappan, 78*(5), 361–366.

Hall, G., & Wortham, S. (1997). Introduction: Authorizing culture – interdisciplinarity. *Journal of the Theoretical Humanities, 4*(2).

Hayes, B. (1996). Speaking of mathematics. *American Scientist, 84*(2-3), 110–113.

Kearsley, G. (n.d.). *Social development theory.* Retrieved on August 15, 2009 from http://tip.psychology.org/vygotsky.html

Learning-Theories.com. (2008a). *Behaviorism.* Retrieved on October 7, 2008, from http://www.learning-theories.com/behaviorism.html

Learning-Theories.com. (2008b). *Constructivism.* Retrieved on October 7, 2008, from http://www.learning-theories.com/constructivism.html

Learning-Theories.com. (2008c). *Cognitivism.* Retrieved on October 7, 2008, from http://www.learning-theories.com/cognitivism.html

Lee, B. (1985). Intellectual origins of Vygotsky's semiotic analysis. In Wertsch, J. W. (Ed.), *Culture, communication and cognition.* Cambridge, UK: Cambridge University Press.

Naisbitt, J. (1982). *Megatrends.* New York, NY: Warner Books.

National Center for Education Statistics (NCES). (2002). *A profile of participation in distance education: 1999-2000.* Retrieved January 15, 2002, from http://www.nces.ed.gov/pubs02/

North Central Regional Educational Laboratory. (2010). *Action research.* Retrieved on February 22, 2010, from http://www.ncrel.org/sdrs/areas/issues/envrnmnt/drug-free/sa3act.htm

Pintrich, P. R., Marx, R. W., & Boyle, R. A. (1993). Beyond cold conceptual change: The role of motivational beliefs and classroom contextual factors in the process of conceptual change. *Review of Educational Research, 63*(2), 167–199.

Popkewitz, T. S. (1997). A changing terrain of knowledge and power: A social epistemology of educational research. *Educational Researcher, 26*(9).

Richey, R., & Klein, J. (2007). *Design and development research.* Mahwah, NJ: Lawrence Erlbaum Associates.

Salomon, G. (1997). Of mind and media: How culture's symbolic forms affect learning and thinking. *Phi Delta Kappan, 78*(5), 375–380.

Siemens, G. (2004). *Connectivism: A learning theory for the digital age.* Retrieved on October 7, 2008, from http://www.elearnspace.org/Articles/connectivism.htm

Tangient, L. L. C. (2008). Educational origami: Bloom's and ICT tools. Retrieved on April 22, 2008, from http://edorigami.wikispaces.com/Bloom%27s+and+ICT+tools

University of Houston-Clear Lake. (2008). *Role and scope statement (mission).* Retrieved on October 12, 2009, from http://prtl.uhcl.edu/portal/page/portal/PRE/UHCL_MISSION_STATEMENT

University of Victoria Counseling Services. (2003). *Bloom's taxonomy.* Retrieved on October 23, 2006, from http://www.coun.uvic.ca/learn/program/hndouts/bloom.html

Van der Haar, D., & Hosking, D. M. (2004). Evaluating appreciative inquiry: A relational constructivist perspective. *Human Relations, 57*(8), 1017–1036. doi:10.1177/0018726704045839

Van der Haar, D., & Hosking, D. M. (2004). Evaluating appreciative inquiry: A relational constructivist perspective. *Human Relations, 57*(8), 1017–1036. doi:10.1177/0018726704045839

Verene, D. (1993). Metaphysical narration, science, and symbolic form. *The Review of Metaphysics, 47*, 115–132.

Vygotsky, L. S. (1935). *Mental development of children during education.* Moscow-Leningrad, Russia: Uchpedzig.

Vygotsky, L. S. (1962). *Thought and language.* Cambridge, MA: MIT Press. doi:10.1037/11193-000

Vygotsky, L. S. (1978). *Mind in society*. Cambridge, MA: Harvard University Press.

Vygotsky, L. S. (1981). The genesis of higher mental functions. In Wertsch, J. V. (Ed.), *The concept of activity in Soviet psychology*. Armonk, NY: Sharpe.

Wertsch, J. V. (1985). *Cultural, communication, and cognition: Vygotskian perspectives*. Cambridge, UK: Cambridge University Press.

KEY TERMS AND DEFINITIONS

Appreciative Inquiry: Is a qualitative research methodology that incorporates narrative, storytelling, and testimonials to encourage responses that look at issues to be addressed and solutions, not just point out problems.

Behaviorism: A learning theory that is focused upon viewing the learner as an "unfilled box" waiting to be filled with information; also referred to as a "blank slate" (tabulae rasa) upon which to add knowledge. The concept behind this theory is that the instructor is the "expert" and all information must travel through the instructor.

Connectivism: A learning theory that is focused upon realizing that all other learning theories are more of a "mash up" of ways through which the learners understand the knowledge that should be focused upon, with the instructor acting as the "expert" as well as the "guide on the side", as is most appropriate. The concept behind this theory is based upon the Digital Age, wherein information is readily available but that the learners must not only be able to understand the information represented but also to analyze the information for "truth" and appropriateness, as well as work within higher order thinking skills frameworks (Anderson & Krathwohl, 2001; Bloom, 1956, 1984; Bloom, Englhart, Furst, Hill, & Krathwohl, 1956; Churches, 2008; Clark, 2000; Tangient LLC, 2008; University of Victoria Counseling Services, 2008).

Constructivism: A learning theory that is based upon viewing the learner as the central focus of the learning process, wherein the learner knows what knowledge they need so as to more appropriately learn about the information desired. The instructor takes the role of the facilitator instead of leading "expert" within the classroom environment; instead of being the "all knowing" entity, a more appropriate representation is the "guide on the side".

Cognitivism: A learning theory that is focused upon viewing all learning as occurring through the reframing of the learner's cognitive ability; introducing and explaining the knowledge as focused upon the mind's processes. The concept behind this theory is that all learners are able to understand information if it is explained so that the mind can "take it in" appropriately.

E-Learning: A phrase that has developed over the past fifteen year period. The original term was "electronic learning", which was then shortened to "e-learning". This phrase is focused upon the online course that is developed within and supported through the course learning management system implemented within each university environment.

Instructional Designer: Designs and develops the learning environment structure, based upon the basic instructional design aspects of: analysis; design; development; implementation; and, evaluation. The majority of the time, the instructional design works in concert with other team members towards the design and development of a product; however, within this case study situation, the instructional designers are a "one person only" team who is also the subsequent course instructor of record.

Instructor: The leading entity within any learning environment, due to the desire to support the learner and facilitate the success of the learner within the learning environment.

Learner: The primary focus within any learning environment, due to the desire for the learner to understand and obtain information and then utilize the information towards meeting specific learning goals and objectives.

Semiotics: Is, simply stated, the study of signs, symbols, metaphors, and stories. The cultural implication, as well as cognitive and conceptual understanding of information within a learning environment, may be directly impacted by the semiotic integration.

APPENDIX A

Qualitative Documentation

(Sample Responses: University A)

Unsolicited Student Communications

Date: Sunday, February 14, 2010 9:04pm

Hi Caroline,

Thank you for being so understanding. I am surprised that you can tell from the online responses that I am so hard on myself! I am glad you reminded me because it helps me to slow down a bit and breathe.

You have been great in explaining everything! Because I am so happy to learn, I have had information overload and then all goes haywire, like when our computers have too much information and do not respond instantly when we would like them to.

Hopefully, I am somewhat on track now and will be able to attend to the Unit One Paper tomorrow at some point.

Sincerely,

[student name]

Date: Thursday, March 4, 2010 10:44pm

Caroline,

You don't know how thankful I am that you understand all that I went through. Computers that start and stop can make us go crazy, and I have to get started on a new computer very soon.

I will try to do what you said, delete and upload with a different name. That is quite an interesting web address I've got. Yes, I need to do something about that.

I really do appreciate your patience with me, because I flipped last night after my computer froze, as you can see. And I appreciate your kind words. Thank you.

Sincerely,

[student name]

Date: Wednesday, March 10, 2010 10:15pm

Caroline,

Thank you so much. You have been a wonderful teacher and a wonderful introduction to my first graduate course!

Sincerely,

[student name]

Date: 12.07.09 at 8:12 PM

Your courses are laid out so well that I could almost teach it to myself by following your outline provided as long as I have the materials that you will use. What do you mean step-up your instructional skills? You are the best teacher I have ever had at the college level! I have had a few others that I enjoyed working with, but none ever inspired me to go as far above and beyond as you did. Maybe, as you like to say, all you did was point me in the right direction, but you did a fantastic job of that.

[student name]

Date: Sunday, January 25, 2009 12:34 pm

Dr. Crawford,

After much thought and consideration, I have made the very difficult decision to drop this class. The spring testing season is the very busiest for me job-wise. I hold myself to very high expectations, and I know at this time I will not be able to devote the time and attention necessary to do my very best work. I'm not willing to sacrifice my best effort just to "get through it".

It may seem silly to make such a big deal out of this, but you are the kindest and most personable professor that I think I've ever had. I plan to pick this class back up in the summer, as schools are not in session and a very slow time for me. Please let me know if you are teaching it then. I would really like to complete it with you.

Thank you so much!

[Student name]

Date: Monday, March 16, 2009 1:19 pm

Dr. Crawford,

It was my pleasure to fill out the survey and I have submitted already. Indeed, this has been a wonderful experience to begin a new phase in life. You have made the course interesting, provocative, and insightful. I appreciate your contagious enthusiasm and your interest for each student. Will keep you up on what's going on.

Thank you very much,

[student name]

Date: Thursday, February 5, 2009 11:56 am

you are the best.

You TEACH! I think the layout of your research, expectations, enthusiasm and absolute hands-on PARTICULARLY in a web-class is EVERYTHING a Master's Level course should be. THANK YOU!!!

Now I must go. I should have taken a bigger leap at these lessons sooner. Coupled with my Thesis, I just can't do the work load.

Thank you so MUCH for the notes in my first assignment and giving me additional time. I value your expertise and desire for your students to excel.

I would love this class when it was longer - I want to enjoy the information as is ruminates in my head and heart space.

I would be happy to give you a glowing course evaluation if it is allowed, and you want me to.

As long as I can get into this space, I would like to get the rest of my lessons. I have printed off so much material and find it wonderful. Again - your research is worth the price for the course...which I am going to have to pay. I take solace in the learning of all lessons and will read these articles to soften the $$ blow.

Thank you again - I can be reached at mcrain@com.edu - or 888 258 8859 ext 689 which is my work number.

Be well, and keep up the phenominal work!! I look forward to our paths crossing again.

[student name]

Date: Monday, February 2, 2009 12:09 pm

I am REALLY impressed! You have put forth a tremendous amount of work. Yes, I want your offer to improve my work product and will endeavor to make this lesson LAST through the semester.

You are a great e-instructor. I have had several e-instructors and by far - you have done more to research and deliver to the student than anyone thus far - and you are really PRESENT on the web and in our work product.

Thank you again, for my extra chance ... I will make good.

[student name]

Date: Monday, February 9, 2009 7:19 pm

Dr. Crawford,

Thank you so much for your kind and encouraging words. I was very touched by your compassion. Again, I can't tell you how much I appreciate your consideration.

Sincerely,

[student name]

Date: Saturday, May 16, 2009 4:19 am

Caroline,

I know, but I panicked for a quick second! These last two semesters with you have been a wild ride to say the least. I have been exposed to such many things I had no concept of just a few months ago. I am still giddy with the excitement of putting it all into action in my classes. I look forward to my last two courses and internship this summer.

Thank you so much for your encouragement and awesome example of online distance instruction at it best.

[student name]

Date: Wednesday, June 10, 2009 7:32pm

Wow, I have to say I am very impressed I have taken these courses before and felt the teacher either did not have the knowledge to teach the course or did poorly at delivering actual information through the use of the online class but I have to say I am very impressed with your course. Glad to see that I will actually get some education this time around. Great Job ;-) Sorry if this sounds a bit weird but I don't run across people in this field that impress me very often.

[student name]

Date: 08.07.2009 at 03:23 PM

Page 2

Dr. Crawford was instrumental in my overall positive program experience, and not just during the internship. She was an advisor who actively engaged in my educational future from the very beginning. This comes from my experience with her as a classroom professor, advisor, independent study professor, and internship advisor. I can honestly say that this experience would have been much different if she had not been involved in the process.

[student name]

(Sample Responses: University B)

Unsolicited Student Communications

[Student T]

I have developed skills and abilities through a combination of class discussion, group collaboration, individual projects, reading assignments and instructor based guidance. I came in to this course a technology "novice" who was mostly familiar with MS Word and less familiar with other functions of technology, and I have since become something of a "techie initiate" who is familiar enough with most MS Products as to be functional in their use and effective in their application. Further, I entered this course expecting to be rather overwhelmed by unfamiliar and cumbersome technology that would leave me puzzled and confused. Instead, thanks to the graphic course aids, I have learned to embrace technology as a part of the educative

Figure 1.

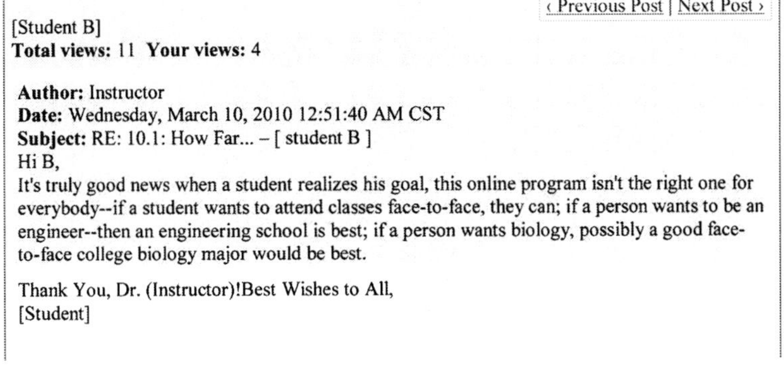

‹ Previous Post | Next Post ›

[Student B]
Total views: 11 **Your views:** 4

Author: Instructor
Date: Wednesday, March 10, 2010 12:51:40 AM CST
Subject: RE: 10.1: How Far... – [student B]
Hi B,
It's truly good news when a student realizes his goal, this online program isn't the right one for everybody--if a student wants to attend classes face-to-face, they can; if a person wants to be an engineer--then an engineering school is best; if a person wants biology, possibly a good face-to-face college biology major would be best.

Thank You, Dr. (Instructor)!Best Wishes to All,
[Student]

or "training" process in its useful application to human output and production. So my experiences have largely disproved my assumptions and the result has been learning and growth that has hopefully contributed to making me a better employee now and will continue to enhance my performance as an employee in future (see Figure 1).

[Student J]

Hello All, How quickly times goes by. When I first considered this class, my assumptions were that this was a course that would teach the fundamentals of creating instructional material. As the class unfolded, I saw that this was much more than I imagined. Through this course, I was able to see the entire planning process; I enjoyed reading the case studies and viewing the graphic course aids to walk me through the creation of the assignments. I saw this as an opportunity to improve my own work.

My only regret is not being able to take this course in person. While I did learn a great deal through the online experience, I think that I would have personally would have benefitted from a classroom environment.

Thank you Dr. R and thanks to the rest of the class for their help and commentary (see Figure 2).

[Student S]

Even though this course was challenging for me due to my pregnancy, I really did enjoy working with you Dr. R and all the students in this course.. I learned very much from everyone's submissions, and from Dr. R's timely feedback which was very detailed and helpful.. the study aids and course Q&A posts were also a huge plus for me.. whenever there was something I was not too sure about, I would find that someone else had the same question.. this helped reassure me that I was not

Figure 2.

Subject: V

Author: V
Date, November 15, 2009 6:08:17 PM CST

Next Post ›

I have enjoyed this class more than any other class that I have taken in a long time. The content related to my experiences as a corporate trainer, and really opened up new ideas for blended strategies of training.
I had fun viewing other students work and enjoyed the feedback that everyone has provided. This was my first experience taking an online class, I really enjoyed the convenience on this format. I think I will be taking more online classes than classroom versions now that I know I can do this. I have three children at home, two of them small. This format allows mw the flexibility that I needed.
The assignments are skills that we all came take away from this class and put into practice. Not all class assignments are applicable to everyday usage, these assignments were effective and beneficial.
I had a difficult time with the final assignment (webpage), this was the first time I have ever attempted to create a website, but I hope I did ok. Thank you to Dr. R. and to all of the students that have provided feedback to me, good luck to all and take care!

Figure 3.

Author: E Next Post ›
Posted date: Saturday, November 14, 2009 11:55:16 PM CST

Farewell Classmates and Professor,
Initially, I did not know that this class would be challenging, intriguing and fun at the same time. This class opened my eyes to alternative methods of presenting and teaching data, and since I currently work in an environment that constantly changes, it has been very beneficial. I also had to challenge myself to erase some of my old habits and embrace new ways of thinking, as well as executing projects. During our groups session, I mentioned this class could have helped me through several obstacles that I experienced in my career.

totally clueless, and I got the answer I needed quickly learning about technology and theories was very interesting as I mentioned before that I do not have any experience in these fields. I particularly got a lot out of the case studies which helped me to get an inside look at different situations and problems that I have not faced personally as a full time student… also, because I was not raised here in the US (I have only been here for about 2 years) many concepts were new to me, as we have very different laws back home in Saudi Arabia.

The individual work we each did was very beneficial in that it helped me be a bit more organized.. now I find myself always organizing and grouping related links together in folders to be more easily accessible and to think more critically as I never really put much thought into these topics before.. the final project really was the most challenging assignment I had to do this quarter (not just for this class).. all in all, I did learn so much more than I had anticipated at the beginning of the quarter, thank you Dr. R for your understanding and flexibility with some of us who had a hard time keeping up, and thank you to everyone in this class for your positive attitudes and knowledge.. happy holidays everyone! (refer to Figure 3)

[Student E]

APPENDIX B

Examples of Pictures as Semiotic Tools

(No podcasts or MP4s were used in these classes)

Breaking Bread (Courtesy Microsoft, 2010) (Figure 4)

Boat Navigation Metaphor (Courtesy Microsoft 2010) (Figure 5)

Figure 4.

Figure 5.

Figure 6.

Technology Can Be Easy Too (Courtesy CommonCraft.com 2010) (Figure 6)

Unsolicited Course Evaluation Commentary

Spring 2009

INST 5035.01: Creating Digital Resources

The following written comments were offered (verbatim):

- This course opens many doors for me. It enriches my information about many topics that related to technology and how I can apply them into my experience field. The instructor is very helpful. She is amazing.
- The course was not what I expected I took it in error and it was too late to change so I stuck it out with help from Dr. Crawford.
- Dr. Crawford is far too intelligent and good an instructor to work in this program. If she were ever to leave, you might as well shut the whole thing down. UHCL is extremely lucky to have her, particularly considering the (lack of) quality of the other INST instructors.

Spring 2009

INST 5131.21: Trends and Issues

The following written comments were offered (verbatim):

- I was nervous about starting a grad program online, but I was quickly put at ease. Thank you for a great learning experience.
- Dr. Crawford's use of assessment rubrics made it easy for students to understand the learning requirements for each assignment. I wish the course would go into more detail about the current trends in the education industry along with the future expectations for instructional technology.
- The reflection papers were an excellent method for encouraging and assessing my mastery of the material. The efolio tested my technology skills. The instructor's criticisms pushed me to improve my skills. What a rush!
- I have learned a great deal in this course and have improved skills because of it.Thank you to Dr. Crawford!
- What a pleasure it was to work with Dr. Crawford, a true professional in every sense of the word. This course ignited a spark that is lighting the way toward a new direction in my life. This was my first graduate course and very happy that I took it.

- The instructor was GREAT and knowledgeable. She provided quick responses to questions via email or discussion board. It was a positive experience for me just entering into my Masters degree. Thanks Dr. Crawford.

Summer 2009

INST 5035.11: Creating Digital Resources

The following written comments were offered (verbatim):

- Dr. Crawford is an amazing instructor! She included constructive criticism that motivated me to do better on future assignments. In addition to wanting to do great on each assignment, I also wanted to do a great job on each assignment just because she is such a great instructor. The only suggestion I have is that the assignment objectives be clearer and that a sample manuscript be provided at the beginning of the course. After taking this course, I know that I belong in grad school! It was definitely full of hard work, and I am so proud of myself for completing the course!

Summer 2009

INST 5131.40: Trends and Issues

The following written comments were offered (verbatim):

- This course was a great experience for myself. The course expectations were clearly outlined in the syllabus and rubric. This was probably one of the best courses that I have had the chance to take online at UHCL and it would be a great resource for other instructors wishing to do the same.
- To my own detriment, I should have taken this course during a fall or spring semester. This course should not be recommended for the 5-week summer session. The instructor was fabulous. She was encouraging and offered insight into topics. She tried to encourage more communication between the students and get them engaged.
- I have left this comment for other classes too. I think it would be very helpful if all instructors used a standard web page format to deliver the content. When taking multiple classes it gets confusing when the same type of information is kept in different areas (pages) ex.. due dates could all be on the calendar, assignment all on a page called assignments, etc.

Fall 2009

INST 5131.21: Trends and Issues

The following written comments were offered (verbatim):

- Dr. Crawford was most helpful in answering my questions; her support of students is unparalleled. This course was very well organized with unit instructions. Unit 6 (eFolio) could be improved by including example instructions on how to create html pages. It would be helpful to include a flow chart detailing the steps of first downloading a html software, then creating html files, then uploading the files, etc. Many external resources were included in the course but there are quite a few of broken links.
- This course was a far better experience than I expected it to be. The video "lectures" were excellent and really helped frame the discussion. The only thing I would suggest is letting students know in advance that they will be given a chance to revise their first paper. I didn't realize the situation applied to many people and really thought that I had done very poorly when it was not the case. Otherwise, a fantastic course. The BEST online class I have taken!
- Really enjoyed the course, instructor was very helpful with any questions. Very enthusiastic with explanations and uplifting comments throughout the course. Would recommend course to others.

This work was previously published in Cases on Globalized and Culturally Appropriate E-Learning: Challenges and Solutions, edited by Andrea Edmundson, pp. 44-72, copyright 2011 by Information Science Reference (an imprint of IGI Global).

Section 4
Instructional Globalization

Chapter 12
Collaborative Reflection in Globally Distributed Inter-Cultural Course Teams

Nicholas Bowskill
University of Glasgow, Scotland

David McConnell
Glasgow Caledonian University, Scotland

EXECUTIVE SUMMARY

This chapter looks at processes for conducting collaborative reflection in action and collaborative reflection on action. The authors examine this in the context of globally distributed inter-cultural course teams. From a review of the literature, they identify the significance of openness, structure and dialogue as factors that support collaborative reflection. The authors consider these factors in our own experience of global online teaching. They explore and focus upon one technique used in our collaborative inter-cultural reflective practice. This technique involves having one tutor maintain and share an online journal with the other tutors in the course team. This process combined reflective writing and discussion in action. The authors suggest that having one tutor author and share a learning journal may provide facilitation and structure that supports reflective dialogue in inter-cultural globally distributed teams. They consider the influence of cultural pedagogy on inter-cultural reflection. The authors' technique is culturally sensitive in that it respects the right of others to read the journal and to comment only if they wish. Finally, the authors close with a look at instrumentalist versus developmental collaborative reflective practice.

DOI: 10.4018/978-1-4666-1885-5.ch012

BACKGROUND

"As we move beyond the individual towards the social context then..... [w]e need to find ways of rehabilitating some key aspects of reflection that have been eroded through unthinking use while moving further to deal with these new issues. This is the challenge from professional practice that confronts us" (Boud, 2006).

Our own experiences as online tutors show us that collaborative reflection is helpful to develop and understand our practice(s). However, we also note a trend to working in an increasingly distributed manner. New processes are required to support collaborative reflection in globally distributed course teams. This chapter looks at the use of a learning journal, maintained by one tutor and shared online with the team, as a focus for collaborative reflection in action. This journal was shared in a group of six tutors working as one online team. The tutor team was distributed across China and across the United Kingdom (UK). The team used a tutor forum in a Moodle Virtual Learning Environment to support each other. To set this in a wider context, we begin with a view of the literature that relates to collaborative reflection.

David Boud (2006) has highlighted the need for tutors to reflect on their practice in teams. In the past, teachers typically worked alone. Today there is a greater emphasis on team teaching and working within team structures. This is particularly true in distance and e-learning contexts but finding a process for collaborative reflection is problematic. Finding a process for doing so in globally distributed inter-cultural online course teams is exponentially more difficult. This chapter reviews one experience that resulted in one particular approach to collaborative reflection. We speculate that such a process may have value both locally and globally.

Boud (2001) builds on the work of Schon (1983) articulating a reflective practice that includes reflection-in-action and reflection-on-action. Reflection-in-action involves thinking about events as they unfold relating them to existing knowledge and earlier experiences. Reflection-on-action looks back at completed events and draws upon available data in a dialogue with that experience. Collaborative reflection adds to this discussion with others. The authors of this chapter acknowledge that research into collaborative reflection in online course teams is becoming ever more urgent in local practices and innovative processes are required as new global inter-cultural pedagogical practices emerge.

Osguthorpe (1999) defines collaborative reflection as "prolonged joint work on the continual process of improving one's practice and the commitment to help others improve theirs." Castle et al (1995) believe that reflection involves a change in the whole person. They suggest that it is "complex and demanding", and that "it is not likely to occur in any depth unless those involved are willing to reflect on themselves and their practice and to set this reflection in a collaborative context."

Collaborative reflection offers different perspectives from within the group and this also provides checks and balances on private views. Independent reflection, usually through reflective writing, is believed to address only the early stages of the learning cycle typified by Kolb (1984). Collaborative reflection is said to potentially deepen that process and help develop broader thinking in support of learning and development. Enablers of collaborative reflection include attitudinal characteristics such as being open towards sharing and having an intention to learn together. Most agree the additional need for a clear structure to support reflection in groups (Platzer et al, 1997 provide an overview of models, barriers and enablers). In networked practice, the ability to view a record of your own interaction and to view the way other course tutors work online supports reflection amongst the course team. Again this requires a willingness to work openly as a member of a learning community of e-tutors (McConnell, 2006).

Conversely, barriers to collaborative sharing include personal issues, actions of other people involved and actions of tutors/facilitators (Johns, 1990 in Platzer et al, 1997). These personal issues include a lack of belief in the value of your own views and a lack of ability to articulate experience. It also includes a lack of confidence and a possible inability to identify relevant experience. The actions of others include situations where others might dominate discussions or disrupt the reflective process. It also includes a possible unwillingness to participate in a collaborative process. The actions of facilitators relates to their possible inability to facilitate the process. It also includes their perceptions regarding their role in the process.

Having a process for reflecting together can help avoid drawn out, casual or unfocused conversations (Castle et al, 1995). Processes for collaborative reflection typically include the use of written records (diaries, journals etc). These are sampled and shared with others who may or may not be directly involved in the event under review. Beginning with a consideration of learning journals, we can identify at least 4 functions of shared learning journals from the literature:

- They can contribute towards the development of identity in a holistic way and go beyond the learning of subject-matter
- They can provide an outlet for thoughts and feelings to be expressed which may be difficult to express elsewhere in the curriculum
- They are part of a sense-making process
- The may contribute towards a sense of community

A learning journal supports the development of a voice and the development of a personal and professional identity.

Successful reflective practice entails engaging in a continual rescripting of one's own practice, not in merely having it rescripted and played back by others. In 'practical' terms, keeping a journal (and sharing its content with others) is the key to this. (Usher, Bryant and Johnston, 1997, in Conway (1999).

Learning journals create a space for thoughts that may not find an outlet in other forms of pedagogical interaction such as seminars, tutorials and lectures. "E-journaling provides an opportunity for learners to express opinions, ideas, and concerns about the course materials that would not be shared otherwise" (Phipps, 2005). Learning journals, shared with others, help to make sense of experience and go beyond what might otherwise be descriptions and feelings. These descriptions and feelings are important to learning, particularly in new or complex settings, but may represent a shallow approach to reflection, "Reflective journal writing encouraged learners to process what they were learning and make sense of it by sharing it with an audience" (Andrusyszyn and Davie, 1997). Sharing online journals is a way of providing social glue and a sense of togetherness. Haberstroh et al (2005) used online journals to maintain contact between different professional trainees bringing them together "spatially and temporally" extending and complementing face to face discussion. The ability to read the journals of others helped create a sense of community and fed back into individual thinking.

Having briefly expanded on these four features of shared journals, there are three further things to say at this point. First, the use of learning journals has been mainly researched in student-learning contexts. Less is known about the use of shared journals amongst course tutors in higher education. How transferable are these student practices to course teams in support of reflection-in-action? Second, for reflection to be useful in a professional development context such as teaching, it has to be carried out in a critical way. Reflection without critique can be an ego enhancing activity. Critical reflection carried out in the company of others has powerful positive democratic consequences (Young 1992). Third, when tutors reflect upon online work it still tends to be done in a face to face context. With course teams becoming ever more distributed, how can collaborative reflection be supported within the online space? What role might journals have in a wider process of collaborative reflection for highly distributed tutors?

Castle et al (1995) describe collaborative reflection in and on action for a group of university tutors who kept a journal during a course in which they participated together as on-campus learners. Their individual journal entries were shared and read in preparation for a group meeting the day after each class. After the course was ended the reflective group met some time later to reflect on the data gathered. They arranged the data into the themes in the course using them as categories for analysis. The outcome was to write an article together to synthesise their learning.

More importantly, they viewed collaborative reflection as a process of holistic development and growth. They warned that reflection against criteria is reductive and supports a managerialist view of reflective practice.

Swinglehurst (2008) has provided some hint of collaborative reflection in an online context. Participants from different institutions reflected together in an online focus group sharing individual experiences of facilitating reflection online. They used the outcomes of that focus group to inform their own collaborative reflective practice. In what followed, it appears that one tutor kept a learning journal during an online course. This was shared at course review meetings and used as a basis for discussion. Also in an online context, McConnell (2006) describes how course participants reflect together within a course in which an online space, time and a structure are provided for groups to unpack their experience. There was also an online space for tutors to reflect-in-action. In that space tutors raised issues about their practice and supported each other as the course progressed. These tutors were mainly based in the same institution.

Course teams are becoming increasingly distributed. With this trend in mind, how can we support collaborative reflection in action by tutors in a globally distributed inter-cultural course context? There are several complicating factors to consider in answering such a question. The first issue relates to time zones. Participation may occur at different times of the day according to your whereabouts. Overnight it can mean that a good deal of activity has already passed before some tutors can catch up. This risks an issue being missed or by-passed or heightened. A second factor is also related to time zones but to do with the accommodation of reflective practices in a distributed tutor group. What kind of strategy might be used to record and co-ordinate reflection upon the issues as they arise? In a group of globally distributed tutors this is a non-trivial task. With each tutor supporting a different group in the course it is easy for the activities and tasks in those groups to overwhelm tutors or to take up so much time that there is little room or energy for reflection.

We would also highlight a third and possibly more important factor. How might collaborative reflection be effected by working in inter-cultural distributed course teams? Tutors in such teams may have a different pedagogical heritage and may therefore interpret and respond to the course differently. Meanings of events need to be negotiated and understood in the tutor group as they reflect together. Individual reflection may be broadly similar in different cultures but that collaborative reflection may be understood quite differently from one culture to another (Buckley, 1999). Western heritage is described by Buckley (1999) as an argument-based culture in contrast with American Indian culture (for example) where argument and lack of respect for elders are unacceptable. We also know that the cultures of Asia have a history of being teacher-led seeking harmony rather than disagreement in groups.

Of course, the idea of cultural difference is not set at national or regional boundaries. Cultural difference exists at a local level. The very idea of team teaching and collaborative reflection can be problematic amongst tutors in the same institution. Knights et al (2006) have noted that it may even be against the general culture of some tutors to collaborate at all. The way tutors from different cultures reflect together is therefore an issue for negotiation each time. How might this be organised? What would be the issues and benefits?

To explore these questions, we reflect on our experience of collaborative reflection in action. This experience is set in a globally distributed inter-cultural course team context. Our online course was delivered between tutors in three United Kingdom universities and in four universities in China. We worked as one tutor team in a course that was entirely online. Participants in the course were university tutors undertaking professional development experience of inter-cultural pedagogy and collaboration. The course and the groups within had broadly equal numbers based in UK and China. The first author of this chapter was one of the United Kingdom tutors and the other author provided management of the course team and made a significant contribution to the design of the course.

CASE DESCRIPTION

The online course was part of the e-China Inter-cultural Pedagogy Research Project based at Lancaster University in the United Kingdom. The project involved collaboration with two other universities in the United Kingdom and four universities across China. There were three parallel work programmes:

1. The collaborative production of an inter-cultural, professional development e-learning and teaching course, to be run online and offered to higher education staff in the United Kingdom and China. The course took place from October-December 2006 and involved the examination of inter-cultural (Sino-UK) conceptions of e-learning and e-tutoring.
2. Sino-UK collaboration on investigating new tools for supporting formative assessment and knowledge extraction in online group learning settings.
3. The development of a framework/model for planning and running inter-cultural professional development in e-learning, using innovative research methodologies.

The project developed an Inter-cultural professional development eLearning and eTeaching course that was run online and offered to higher education staff in the UK and China in late 2006. One of the main purposes of the Inter-cultural professional development course was to support participants in the development of their conceptions of e-learning.

The UK and Chinese partners collaborated on the design and delivery of the online course. The course was designed as a professional development event (at Masters level) that took place asynchronously over 11 weeks with 50 hours of study. Participants gained an understanding of Inter-cultural issues in e-learning by working together in an online learning community.

Key pedagogic features of the online course were:

- Fully virtual course using asynchronous and synchronous communication
- Inter-cultural learning design
- Online learning community
- Inter-cultural e-tutoring team
- Inter-cultural learning support
- Online tasks, activities & resources

The course activities included:

- Tutors and participants together as a community
- Participants as a parallel community
- Tutors as a parallel community
- Use of e-portfolios for accreditation

The course outcomes for the tutors included:

- An understanding of tutors' experiences
- Learning about inter-cultural collaborative design
- Learning about distributed inter-cultural team teaching
- An understanding of participants' experiences
- Learning about inter-cultural e-learning, professional development, collaborative online learning, group work, e-portfolios

CURRENT CHALLENGES

- How can collaborative reflection in action be developed in our inter-cultural course team?
- What are the processes that might support collaborative reflection in complex online settings such as ours?
- How does this relate to earlier reflection on action that looked at inter-cultural competence (Bowskill et al, 2007)?

Research Methods and Analysis

As part of the course, the first author chose to keep a journal of the shared experience and share it with the other course tutors. This was maintained in the shared tutor space. Over the time of the course other tutors commented upon the journal entries often resulting in an online discussion of issues and interpretations. This study reflects on the process and the data arising to identify and discuss reflective activities contained within this collaboration. For each area of reflection we attempt to raise questions around it for further research.

A grounded approach was taken to the study of the data (Strauss and Corbin, 1990; Charmaz, 2000). This involved a close reading of the journal archive to reveal emerging categories. Those categories then became the means by which the data was sorted. These were aspects of the experience that were collaboratively reflected upon by the tutors in practice. The categories that emerged are:

- Reflection on the Learning Journal as a Tool for Collaborative Reflection
- Reflections on Tutoring as an Inter-cultural Course Team
- Reflections on tutoring with Inter-cultural Participants
- Reflections on Personal-Previous e-Tutoring Practice

Reflection on the Learning Journal as a Tool for Collaborative Reflection Authoring the journal provided a means to make sense of the unique and complex tutoring experience by creating a narrative that was shared with others. The course experience became transformed and internalized through writing. It offered some sense of ownership and control for the author in what was a new area of practice. The sharing of the journal produced a closer relationship with the other tutors.

...initially the rhythm would probably come from the course, the other participants and the structure. It's all externally controlled. Later you will find your own rhythm that is created by you and your own context. That is internally controlled. I think one of the main techniques that helps you develop that control is the diary. Writing gives you authority over time. ... [Thursday, 21 December 2006, 12:41 PM]

...I am benefiting a lot from your diary in the way you set out in some detail your thinking as you deal with what is happening in your learning set. It is almost like a Mind Map ... So your 'thinking out loud' stuff really helps! [UK Tutor B - Tuesday, 14 November 2006, 01:56 PM]

To tell you something....I read your diaries whenever I access and it really helps me think. Thank you for this! [China Tutor A - Thursday, 16 November 2006, 01:50 PM]

Castle et al (1998) noted the tendency to move away from a focus to do with external events as their reflective discussion developed. Their dialogue began to reference issues raised amongst the group as the reflective process developed into a search for meaning. In many ways this was true in our context. This was a kind of group synthesis and a sense-making process.

There are many questions still to be explored here. To what extent are any new meanings shared across the team? Is reading the journal enough or does it require the discussion as well in order to develop these meanings? It is also likely that the discussions may not have taken place were it not for the journal. Looking at the sharing of the journal, what other functions does the shared journal have across the team? Is it a home for thinking? Is it a check for the team? Does the journal become a burden or a pressure on others to conform or follow it in some way? What are the rhythms and how significant would less frequent entries be on the team? Is there an ideal length or frequency of input for different inter-cultural groups? Certainly the shared journal seems to add value but what is the nature of that value to each member and to the team as a whole?

Reflections on Tutoring as an Inter-Cultural Course Team

Through the journal the course team became aware of themselves working in a unique configuration. The tutors were scattered across each country as well as between countries. Coordination amongst themselves and with the participants was always a challenge. As a team we were experiencing a global dimension to tutoring together and through the shared reflection we started to identify what this might mean for both practice and reflection.

Yes, I agree with you. So we are in a very special professional development ourselves in this inter-cultural e-tutoring team. Another interesting thing is that I like this across-time-zones way of working, because we can expect things to happen while we're sleeping. [China Tutor A -Thursday, 2 November 2006, 10:21 AM]

Thank you for sharing your diary. It is interesting that almost every.... hour one or more participants are online, so no one will feel lonely. When you are asleep, we continue the discussion. [China Tutor C - Friday, 3 November 2006, 10:08 AM]

This sense of working as one team fits in with the ideas about shared journals suggested by Haberstroh et al (2005) that noted the way sharing journals can create a sense of belonging. Through the journal it is clear that a sense of working as an inter-cultural course team is shared amongst the tutors. An inter-cultural course team is a concept that came to mean something distinct. This meaning emerged, in part, through collaborative reflection facilitated by the shared journal.

With regards to working as an inter-cultural course team, what is the significance of being on duty around the clock and around the world? What are the implications for the individuals involved in recognizing such a view? Does it put more pressure on the tutors to feel that the team is always in action or in a state of readiness? Alternatively, is this sense of togetherness generated by the combination of the shared journal and discussion, provide a platform that supports the team being constantly available? Does each member share the same level of feeling and do they interpret that feeling in the same way? How does it affect their inter-cultural and local practice(s)?

Reflections on tutoring with Inter-cultural Participants In this extract from the journal, the author recalls a standard repertoire for handling Skype phone calls. This was developed in previous local e-tutoring settings. The author is reflecting on how those once familiar practices need to be re-thought in new and complex settings.

[one of the participants] mentioned that she'd joined a Skype session at the start in the induction week but that part way through it all fell silent and then it was closed. It seemed as though she had something to say but wanted to be invited to speak and when an invite didn't come she just let it pass. Again this may be another aspect of inter-cultural work and the need to facilitate group phone conferences by going around the group asking them to give their views as a means of letting them speak. [Thursday, 7 December 2006, 03:20 PM]

As Buckley (1999) suggests we should not assume that others share our own understandings and practices. The extract below shows the use of the journal for problem solving through reflection in action. This produced a metaphor for 'building bridges.'

..you do need to shift your mindset to that of your...participants and to work in their culture once you have some sense of it. I think when there are more cultures involved then the task is to build bridges between them that allow for a critical view but framed within a harmonious context. How that is best achieved is my task and [our] task.... [Monday, 23 October 2006, 09:16 AM]

In consequence another tutor is prompted to consider metaphors for e-tutoring raised in the journal and they are used to compare their own metaphors and to do so within the context of this unique collaborative experience.

Very interesting metaphors! I like them! Actually I don't think I am a 'sage on the stage' in face-to-face classrooms. Never! I'm also waiting, fishing, shepherding ... There're many things I do aside from explaining language points. You're right in this point. To summarize the role of tutors or teachers in such a way is somewhat arbitrary. [China Tutor A - Monday, 18 December 2006, 11:39 AM]

What does 'bridge building' mean? Is this a new metaphor for this kind of context? How can we build bridges between online inter-cultural participants? Does 'bridge-building' add anything to ideas of facilitation? Is it distinct from 'sage on the stage' or 'guide on the side' so widely used in the literature? What are the most suitable metaphors? Do we need new metaphors for such complex practices? Are we highlighting an inadequacy of some much-used metaphors or engaged in a process of re-conceptualising and broadening those metaphors? Is it this kind of experience that really tests the utility of such metaphors?

Developing this to think about inter-cultural pedagogy, might shared journals be a useful tool for learners as well as for tutors? Is there anything about this application that makes it better suited to one group/culture than another?

Reflections on Previous e-Tutoring Practice The journal extract below shows a comparison of current practice in local distributed online teams with work in globally-distributed teams. The author reflects on different ways the tutors managed and supported themselves. This creates a reflective resource to assess the impact of being far apart as a comparison.

However my previous experience was on a course provided by a single institution. The tutoring team worked quite differently. In that earlier model there were 4 tutors and we each had a small group or learning set. We were in different buildings but we knew that we could meet together or separately any time.... What is interesting here is that we are very much further away from each other and the opportunity to discuss and react to things is very different. We are communicating across time zones and we only meet up once every few months. In fact we will only meet once during the course. [Wednesday, 1 November 2006, 11:07 AM]

Throughout the course, the tutors involved were engaged in conversations with their own practice, their previous experience and their own understandings of this unique and dynamic situation. What value has previous experience that is significantly different than the current context? How transferable is previous experience? What is it within previous experience that may be transferable? Does previous experience in one culture transfer to another culture? Is it practical ideas and techniques that transfer or is it different ways of thinking that might have greater utility?

LESSONS LEARNED

1. Openness, structure and dialogue are indicated as prerequisites to the process of collaborative reflection in local as well as Inter-cultural global contexts.
2. Greater flexibility is required for collaborative reflection in globally distributed inter-cultural course teams. Combining recording and reviewing in action is helpful to collaborative reflection in unique and complex online pedagogical settings. It also facilitates reflection on action.
3. The use of a shared journal as a basis for dialogue provides a process for collaborative reflection. In globally distributed inter-cultural course teams recording and review happen inter-changeably.
4. Through our experience of collaborative reflection, focused around the shared online journal, we generated holistic professional development, an outlet for expression difficult to obtain elsewhere, a sense-making process individually and collectively, and group cohesion. This is in line with findings in the literature such as those from Castle et al (1995). We can say this process is therefore able to deliver the same benefits in a globally distributed inter-cultural course team.
5. Local and Global teaching practices are brought into the collaborative reflection and both practices may be changed as a result of the reflective experience. This mixture of practices being shared creates the sense of a global practice as an inter-cultural hybrid.
6. The process may also provide a vehicle for collaborative reflection amongst co-located course teams. We see no reason why this online process should not be supportive of collaborative reflection for face to face teaching. It may even be a process that could be extended to student involvement.
7. Collaborative reflection amongst globally distributed inter-cultural course teams indicates a new area of research.

Our experience of collaborative reflection agrees with findings from the literature that the key requirements for this process are openness amongst the practitioners, a structure to the interaction and dialogue. Our task was to identify a process for accommodating such needs in unique and complex online settings. In our case one tutor was willing to maintain and share the developing learning journal with the other tutors. Developing the journal within the online space gave a structure and place for collaborative reflection. By inviting comments from the other tutors we created an opportunity for dialogue and a greater sense of togetherness.

In addition to meeting the needs for an open disposition, structure and dialogue we identified additional needs. Our globally distributed and inter-cultural teaching context meant that we needed to establish a process that could be flexible, that would model ways of reflecting together and that would be culturally-sensitive. We have firstly recognized the way the shared journal *combined* writing and discussion. This is in contrast to the more common practice of conducting those activities in separate phases. The journal became a structure around which dialogue about practice in action could unfold. It was a flexible structure because the team could expand and dwell on a particular point or just move on. This process is culturally-sensitive in that it allows everyone to respond to it individually. There was no requirement to read the journal entries or to comment upon them but it allowed the tutors to pick up points of dissonance and resonance and react according to their situation.

The process we adopted yielded 4 different areas upon which we reflected together:

- Reflections on Tutoring as an Inter-cultural Course Team
- Reflections on tutoring with Inter-cultural Participants
- Reflections on Previous e-Tutoring Practice
- Reflection on the Learning Journal as a Tool for Learning

Clearly, we have moved beyond the early stages of the reflective cycle and beyond simple descriptions of our experience. These four aspects are evidence of an emerging framework for development of our inter-cultural reflective practice. The outcomes of this reflection show individual local practices being considered and discussed alongside the emerging global practice. These two practices fed into each and informed the development of both of those practices. An inter-cultural practice is a hybrid practice in the global space derived from reflective conversations around those shared practices. This hybrid global practice creates new teaching techniques emerging as a combination of the team's local and global experience and knowledge.

The use of the shared online journal combined with discussion was an effective process for supporting collaborative reflective practice in unique and complex settings. It is a process that may also have applications in co-located course teams where spaces and opportunities for collaborative reflection are often difficult to find or use. It may also have further application with students working this way in groups with or without tutors. Our experience suggests a wide variety of possibilities that remain unexplored. There are clearly a number of areas for further work within the same team and for future teams.

What does our experience tell us and others about collaborative reflection in general? The literature on collaborative reflection reviewed at the start of this chapter refers to phases of written reflection and dialogue as a process to support learning about shared and individual practice. In our case, we saw these two processes happening together, rather than in sequence, as we reflected in action. As the entries were being made into the journal reflecting on one tutor's experience so the other tutors were reading and also reflecting. The tutors annotated the journal with their own observations and experience of the course and brought their own pedagogical knowledge and experiences into the process. This seems to be an effective strategy for professional development in inter-cultural global teams. At the same time it raises many questions for further research. Using a written text as the means of recording experience may not fit with all cultures and all participants. Writing in English for example may disadvantage tutors from China who may need time to translate it or construct a reply in English. Graphics and diagrams may be more appropriate or effective in inter-cultural collaborative reflection. Would shared diagrams be as expressive of the journal author's experience? Would the use of diagrams promote more or deeper discussions in inter-cultural online course team contexts?

Why did only one tutor pursue the idea of keeping a journal and sharing it? There was no requirement or obligation to keep a journal or to share it. It was down to a preference and interest of that tutor to learn from a unique situation. A disposition towards sharing the journal was engendered from a previous experience of working with a particular online course team. That earlier experience had engendered a spirit of openness and trust that persisted into this new setting. Would it be different if sharing the journal was a requirement akin to reflection-on-demand (Boud, 2006)? How much of previous experience of course teams influences later attitudes towards openness? How do previous experiences of teaching techniques compare with previous experience of attitudes?

Why did the other tutors not keep or share a journal? Certainly there was no requirement that anyone should keep a journal. Others may have had alternative approaches to reflective practice and alternative places for reflection. It would probably be impractical to try and track six different learning journals in action whilst working in such a complex environment. What we do know is that other tutors did keep a learning journal but preferred not to make it public to the other tutors. Comments were however posted about those other entries made in those other private journals. Is the process of keeping a journal perhaps something that fits more easily into Western culture, and less likely to be practised by tutors in other cultures? Does a shared journal offer Chinese colleagues opportunities to be more open about their practice and to feel empowered in talking about their practice, or about practice generally? This may apply equally to UK tutors too but could the concept of sharing practice be one that the journal helped Chinese colleagues to participate in a dialogue more easily than with UK colleagues? If so, then is this an indication of inter-cultural professional openness?

It may also be a cultural issue but other UK tutors did not keep or share a journal either. It did emerge that others were motivated to keep a journal themselves having read the shared online journal. In this respect, the shared journal functioned as a model for others. Is there a cultural heritage of reflective practice? Might it be that collaborative reflection was not culturally compatible for tutors from a non-Western pedagogical background? We do not know but certainly there is a cultural difference in pedagogical issues that may extend to and include reflective practices. This highlights the need for approaches to reflective practice to be negotiated each time with each different team. Again more research is required.

How does the combination of the journal as a living document, along with the author as one of the reflecting tutors, function in the reflective context? Could it be that the sharing of the learning journal by one tutor constituted a facilitative function for the inter-cultural tutor team to reflect together? In this way the journal provided a structure and the author was the facilitator of a dialogue around that document. With time zones and different patterns of participation amongst a highly distributed group finding a structure for shared reflection is difficult. The author is a host for the dialogue explaining, elaborating and questioning the entries. This way the author combines the structural requirements and the facilitative requirements for the reflecting practitioners. This combination allows time and space for individual reflection whilst allowing flexibility in the way the group reflects together. This dynamic process supports sense-making and cohesion amongst the tutor team as they record, discuss and digest their shared experience?

What difference does the number of tutors have on the process? At what number does it become impractical or ineffective? Might a team of 12 inter-cultural tutors reap as much benefit from a shared journal? What about increasing the number of shared journals from different tutors? We suggest that having one tutor share a journal is helpful to other tutors in providing a means and a focus for collaborative reflection in action within complex and inter-cultural online courses. There are technologies such as RSS that might support the easier sharing of multiple journals amongst the course team but we do not know what the effect of this might be on the sense of the tutor group as a learning community. Again further research is needed on these issues.

This experience has shown that collaborative reflection is possible and productive in extremely complex online tutoring configurations. We endorse the view by Castle et al (1995) that collaborative reflection is a form of professional development but we would add that inter-cultural, temporal and geographical issues along with a mix of technologies need to be factored into collaborative reflection in global pedagogy. We endorse the view of Buckley (1999) that collaborative reflection is influenced by culture (national, regional or individual) and that processes for reflection and understandings of terms and practices need to be negotiated and agreed each time.

Through this reflection on action we have identified elements of a research agenda related to collaborative reflective practice in inter-cultural global course teams. Further research is required to explore the issues and practices raised here. Other inter-cultural contexts, perhaps with other national cultures represented, warrant further investigation. Research may also be useful to explore the value of such an approach amongst a course team on the same campus. The use of an online shared journal combined with online discussion can provide the flexibility for collaborative reflection in action and on action. Ultimately, the task is not to learn how to deliver to people *from* other cultures but rather, how to deliver learning and teaching *with* people from other cultures.

As a parting comment, we reflect on Castle et al (1995) and their concern that reflection on action risks becoming a tool solely for management when conducted according to external competencies. This chapter follows-up on some earlier work collaboratively reflecting on the same course experience (Bowskill et al, 2007). In that earlier work, we applied an adaptation of Belisle's (2007) framework of Inter-cultural competence for e-tutors to our experience. That work concluded that the skills and competencies suggested by the framework were present in the team but that they were not evenly distributed. Nor did each member of the team have all the competencies suggested by the framework. As one would expect, each tutor brought different strengths and resources to the team. In that early work, we also assessed the utility and value of the framework itself. We concluded that it was indeed a useful tool to help support further reflection and dialogue. We build on it here, with a review of a process of collaborative reflection that contrasts with that competency-driven view. We are more aware that our thinking about practice is informed by our collective local and global practices shared and discussed online. Our reflection process is one very much grounded in our own experience that in turn very much informs our personal and professional growth.

REFERENCES

Andrusyszyn, M. A., & Davie, L. (1997). Facilitating reflection through interactive journals writing in an online graduate course: A qualitative study. *Journal of Distance Education*, *XII*(1/2), 103–126.

Belisle, C. (2007). *eLearning and inter-cultural dimensions of learning theories and teaching models*. Paper submitted to the FeConE (Framework for eContent Evaluation) Project, May 2007. Retrieved July 17, 2007, from http://www.elearningeuropa.info/files/media/media13022.pdf

Boud, D. (2001). Using journal writing to enhance reflective practice. In L. M. English & M. A. Gillen (Eds.), *Promoting journal writing in adult education. New directions in adult and continuing education no. 90* (pp. 9-18). San Francisco: Jossey-Bass.

Boud, D. (2006, July 3). *Relocating reflection in the context of practice: Rehabilitation or rejection?* Keynote Presentation, Professional lifelong learning: beyond reflective practice, One Day Conference, University of Leeds, UK.

Bowskill, N., McConnell, D., & Banks, S. (December, 2007, December 11-13). *Inter-cultural e-tutoring teams: The dynamics of new collaborations and new needs*. Society for Research in Higher Education, Annual Conference, University of Sussex, Brighton, UK.

Buckley, J. (1999, February 24-27). *Multicultural reflection*, Paper presented at the Annual Meeting of the American Association of Colleges for Teacher Education, 51st, Washington, DC.

Byram, M., Gribkova, B., & Starkey, H. (2002). *Developing the inter-cultural dimension in language teaching. A practical introduction for teachers.* Council of Europe, Strasbourg. Retrieved July 17, 2007, from http://lrc.cornell.edu/director/Inter-cultural.pdf

Campbell, E. (2002). Career management. *Nursing Spectrum Magazine*. Retrieved January 2, 2008, from http://community.nursingspectrum.com/MagazineArticles/article.cfm?AID=7981

Castle, J. B. (1995). Collaborative reflection as professional development. *Review of Higher Education, 18*(3), 243–263.

Charmaz, K. (2000). Grounded theory: Objectivist and constructivist methods. In N. Denzin & Y. S. Lincoln (Eds.), *The handbook of qualitative research* (pp. 509-535). Thousand Oaks, CA: Sage Pubs. Inc.

Conway, J. (1999). Multiple identities of an adult educator: A learning journal story. In B. Merrill (Ed.), *Proceedings of The Final Frontier. SCUTREA 29th Annual Conference, Standing Conference on University Teaching and Research in the Education of Adults, 1999.* (ERIC Document Reproduction Service No. ED 438 447)

Haberstroh, S., Parr, G., Gee, R., & Trepal, H. (2006). Interactive e-journaling in group work: Perspectives from counselor trainees. *Journal for Specialists in Group Work, 31*(4), 327–337. doi:10.1080/01933920600918840

Kerka, S. (2002). *Journal writing as an adult learning tool. Practice application, brief no. 22.* Retrieved January 2, 2008, from http://www.cete.org/acve/docs/pab00031.pdf

King, F. B., & LaRocco, D. J. (2006). E-journaling: A strategy to support student reflection and understanding. *Current Issues in Education, 9*(4). Retrieved January 2, 2008, from http://cie.asu.edu/volume9/number4/

Knights, S., Sampson, J., & Meyer, L. (2006, July 3). *"It's all right for you two, you obviously like each other": Recognizing the pitfalls and challenges in pursuing collaborative professional learning through team teaching.* Paper presented at the Professional lifelong learning: beyond reflective practice, One Day Conference, University of Leeds, UK.

Kolb, D. A. (1984). *Experiential learning experience as a source of learning and development.* Upper Saddle River, NJ: Prentice Hall.

McConnell, D. (2006). *E-learning groups and communities: Imagining learning in the age of the Internet.* OU Press.

Phipps, J. (2005). E-journaling: Achieving interactive education online. *Educause Quarterly, 2005*(1), 62-65. Retrieved January 2, 2008, from http://net.educause.edu/ir/library/pdf/EQM0519.pdf

Platzer, H., Blake, D., & Snelling, J. (1997). A review of research into the use of groups and discussion to promote reflective practice in nursing. *Research in Post-Compulsory Education, 2*(2), 193–204. doi:10.1080/13596749700200010

Schon, D. (1983). *The reflective practitioner.* New York: Basic Books.

Strauss, A., & Corbin, J. (1990). *Basics of qualitative research: Grounded theory procedures and techniques.* London: Sage.

Swinglehurst, D., & Russell, J. (2008). Peer observation of teaching in the online environment: An action research approach. *Journal of Computer Assisted Learning, 24*(5), 383–393. doi:10.1111/j.1365-2729.2007.00274.x

Young, R. (1992). *Critical theory and classroom talk.* Clevedon, UK: Multilingual Matters Ltd.

This work was previously published in Cases on Online Tutoring, Mentoring, and Educational Services: Practices and Applications, edited by Gary A. Berg, pp. 172-184, copyright 2010 by Information Science Reference (an imprint of IGI Global).

Chapter 13
A Multidisciplinary Project Integrating Marketing Research, Art and Spanish Language for Social Sciences

Manuel Cuadrado-García
University of Valencia, Spain

María-Eugenia Ruiz-Molina
University of Valencia, Spain

Lourdes Hernández-Martín
London School of Economics, UK

EXECUTIVE SUMMARY

In the framework of a collaboration agreement between the University of Valencia (UV) and the London School of Economics (LSE), students from both universities have had an opportunity to take part in an interdisciplinary project based on a real decision making process in the context of cultural management.

In this chapter we describe this interdisciplinary project focusing on the contribution in the teaching-learning process of students at the University of Valencia, in the context of the subject Marketing Research. Specifically, a series of photographs is selected in order to organize an exhibition in London and, to ensure the success of the exhibition, students of the subject Marketing Research have combined sources

DOI: 10.4018/978-1-4666-1885-5.ch013

of secondary and primary data, and have become familiar with databases of business information from the Library of the University of Valencia as well as with the commonly used software for data processing. In general, students have very much appreciated this activity as a facilitator of learning in the field.

ORGANIZATION BACKGROUND

An important trend in education in the last decades is a movement of the focus from that of teaching to that of learning (e.g. Bates, 1995; Oliver & Omari, 1999). An evidence of this change is the wide use of problem-based learning, an instructional learner-centered approach that empowers learners to conduct research, integrate theory and practice, and apply knowledge and skills to develop a viable solution to a defined problem (Savery, 2006). The learning effectiveness and the transfer of skills of problem-based learning requires activities valued in the real world (Bransford, Brown & Cocking, 2000).

In the present chapter, we assess the outcomes of a problem-based activity in a Content and Language Integrated Learning (CLIL) program. It is a project based on a multicultural, interdisciplinary and bilingual collaboration developed between two European universities, i.e. the University of Valencia (Spain) and the London School of Economics and Political Science (United Kingdom)

In this project, students have worked on linguistic aspects, economic and managerial contents as well as other social competences. In particular, the activity was held for LSE students taking an optional course such as Spanish Language and Society, which is oriented to non-Spanish-speaking students, and for students at UV taking a core course of the Business Administration degree (i.e. Marketing Research) in English, which is not the native language for most students. Students had to do several tasks in groups related to Business and Society (qualitative and quantitative research, including a survey, data collection and statistical analysis, and written reports). Language used by LSE students was Spanish, while UV students had to communicate in English.

A pinhole exhibition was proposed as a source of inspiration for multidisciplinary activities in Higher Education studies at the University of Valencia and the London School of Economics.

What is a pinhole photography? It is a photograph which is cooked inside a metal without lens, viewfinder and even without a shutter. The light enters through a tiny hole forming the image on a photosensitive paper. fotolateras.com

Thanks to a previous bilateral interuniversity agreement in force since 2006, the Marketing Department of University of Valencia (Spain) and the Spanish Section of the Language Centre in London School of Economics (UK), with the help of the photography artists Fotolateras.com[1], decided to implement several teaching-learning activities related to the subject of marketing research (for University of Valencia students) and Spanish language (for the London School of Economics students).

In order to assess the outcomes of this activity, both qualitative and quantitative approaches have been considered. Regarding the qualitative assessment, results have allowed us to conclude that this collaboration project enables students to obtain and to process information on other realities and to improve their language skills through a motivating online learning environment. In general, students' involvement and feedback seem to confirm the positive contribution of this problem-based, interdisciplinary and bilingual activity to the teaching-learning process.

Concerning quantitative analysis, a survey to measure the student assessment of this activity was performed among participants. In particular, the survey measured student assessment on the interest of this activity for the teaching-learning process, motivation, group interaction and use of technological tools. We also considered data about student participation in this activity and final grades. After statistical processing of student assessment, participation and grades, as well as the qualitative feedback obtained from student' comments, we obtained evidence supporting the relevance of this project in the teaching-learning process and its positive implication in students' results. Notwithstanding, the project failed at encouraging group interaction and involved difficulties in the use of technology. As a result, discussion about the importance of task definition and its influence on e-learning outcomes will need to be developed.

SETTING THE STAGE

Active learning environments, in comparison to traditional classrooms, have been associated with increased student motivation (Garcia & Pontrich, 1996, Stipek et al., 1998), contributing in this way to self-regulated learning (Young, 2005). In this sense, the cognitive theory states that student motivation and performance is influenced by the will to reach specific academic objectives, that can be learning-oriented or goal-oriented (Elliott & Dweck, 1988; Ames, 1992; Dupeyrat & Mariné, 2005). Additionally, student social motivations have been also proposed as antecedents of academic goal achievement (Wentzel, 1993; Urdan & Maehr, 1995; Covington, 2000; Humphrey, 2004). Thus, student motivation is closely related with participation (Martin, 2007).

To actively involve students in their learning process, Marketing lecturers have used various learning methods and activities such as team projects (Lilly & Tippins, 2002), documented class participation (Peterson, 2001), experiential learning exercises (Gremler et al., 2000), Internet-based projects (Siegel, 2000), case-study method (Kennedy et al., 2001) and, sharing certain characteristics with the latter, problem-based learning (Savery, 2006).

In particular, problem-based learning is an instructional approach focused on the student that develops the ability to carry out research, to integrate theory and practice, and to apply knowledge and skills to reach a viable solution to a problem (Savery, 2006). However, to ensure effective learning and transfer of skills, problem-based learning requires activities highly valued in the real world (Bransford et al., 2000). Mainly used in Medicine studies, this teaching-learning method has been applied successfully in the past decades and continues to gain acceptance in various disciplines. This method can be included among active and cooperative learning strategies that use students to help each other learn (Slavin, 1990).

CASE DESCRIPTION

A pinhole exhibition: Tinned Cities/Ciudades Enlatadas is part of the activities celebrating the 10-year anniversary of the LSE Language Centre and it is conceived as an inspiration for several multidisciplinary activities.

The project has been integrated in two courses in the academic year 2009-10:

- Marketing Research, core degree of the Business Administration degree, taught in English by Manuel Cuadrado-Garcia and María-Eugenia Ruiz-Molina, marketing lecturers at the University of Valencia.

In 2009-2010, students taking this course have developed a survey that has shown the real-life implementation of marketing research. Specifically, they have undertaken a quantitative research to select 23-black and white pinhole pictures by *fotolateras.com* to be shown in an exhibition at LSE in February 2010. Thus, students have fully understood the application of the theoretical concepts of Marketing Research (see Figure 1).

- Spanish Language and Society (Beginners) course coordinated by Lourdes Hernández-Martín, Assistant Language Co-ordinator (Spanish) at LSE.

In 2009-2010, as a part of Spanish Language and Society (Beginners), students have followed a 20-hours activity called *Still Spanish*, a workshop which aims

Figure 1. Torres de Serranos, Valencia. (© 2009, fotolateras.com. Used with permission.)

to provide students with a basic knowledge of documentary films. As their final product, students have been asked to create a multimedia essay using pictures, text and audio under the title *Cityscape*.

The 23-pictures of *Tinned Cities/Ciudades Enlatadas* by *fotolateras.com* to be shown at the exhibition have been used as material for several activities for *Still Spanish*. Among those activities, students have written the captions of the pictures for the exhibition (with a translation in English).

Students have participated in a workshop given by *fotolateras.com* on photographic techniques (see Figure 2).

All these activities have taken place in Spanish and they have been integrated into the curriculum of the course during Lent Term.

LSE students are exposed to research on cities through different programs or projects such as LSE Cities: Urban Age[2] or the Cities Programme[3]. Their work focuses on the problematic nature of 21st Century cities[4]. Politicians, investors, planners, architects, urban designers, engineers, public service workers and private sector leaders seem to be the only inhabitants of these complex spaces which need to be developed, organised, and managed.

Fotolateras.com and their collection *Tinned Cities/Ciudades Enlatadas* will bring a different narrative of the urban spaces to LSE. Witnesses of a society which watches everything but does not look, *fotolateras.com* wander the urban landscapes as *baudelarian flaneurs* "cooking" new images in their tins where past and present mixed in a singular manner. *fotolateras.com* reminds us that cities can still be lived in and experienced as romantic and mysterious landscapes.

Figure 2. Trafalgar Square, London. (© 2009, fotolateras.com. Used with permission.)

Aims of the Project

For the Marketing Department, Faculty of Economics, UV

The aims of this project are linked to the basic principles, competences and skills of the University of Valencia strategic plan and the Bologna principles. Among them: cooperation, exchange, languages, cultures, new technologies, critical thinking, etc. Focused on the UV students, the project aims

- To understand the role of marketing research in an organisation and in the society, and specifically in the context of arts.
- To develop individual and team working abilities, to improve informational and communicational skills, and to learn to search and analyse different types of information resources.
- To understand the problems or situations an organisation may face, and suggesting surveys and actions to start solving them.
- To make the teaching-learning process more interesting, motivating and satisfactory.
- To make students more aware of disciplines different to business, management and marketing.

For the Spanish Section, Language Centre, LSE

This project has offered the Spanish section a means to directly address some of LSE values and strategic priorities as stated in the *LSE Strategic Plan 2008-2013*[5]:

- To implement innovative ways of teaching and learning offering students educational experiences that are engaging and relevant.
- To address the whole student experience which encompasses their social, living, study and life experiences.
- To engage with the wider community through a diverse range of activities.

From a language point of view, this project fulfills fully the criteria of the Common European Framework of Reference for Languages (CEFR) for selecting language tasks which must be "purposeful and meaningful –perceived as real life[6] - for the learners, and involve them as fully as possible"[7].

The project has also provided students with an excellent opportunity to practise all their language skills through activities involving reception, production, interaction and mediation in real life.

The objectives of this project are linked to the basic principles, competences and skills of the Strategic Plan of the University of Valencia, as well as the key topics of the European Higher Education Area, among them being cooperation, exchange, languages, culture, information and communication technologies, critical thinking, etc.

Process/Stages

In order to achieve the above mentioned objectives, a real problem in cultural management is proposed to students to be solved. The following steps are followed:

21 September 2009- 15 December 2009

In the course Marketing Research in the International Group (taught in English) at the University of Valencia, students have carried out market research in order to select, among a large number of pinhole photographs by *fotolateras.com*, the most-liked 23 photographs to be shown in a public exhibition at LSE.

Qualitative and quantitative techniques have been developed to measure the level of attractiveness of the pictures. The research population, i.e. interviewees, has been potential visitors of an art exhibition in a university campus: students, administrative personnel and academics in the University of Valencia.

In particular, the University of Valencia students have developed six activities to conduct research from the research problem definition to survey, analyse data, and develop decision making skills. In order to provide a solution to the problem of choosing 23 photos out of 53, UV students had to conduct several activities:

- Define management problem and research problem,
- Define research questions,
- Conduct qualitative research using secondary sources of information (i.e. documents already available, not elaborated by the researchers, such as institutional websites and market research databases of the UV library, that involve generalization, analysis, synthesis or data evaluation).
- Conduct quantitative research through primary sources of information (i.e. first-hand information collected by researchers), that involved questionnaire elaboration and survey to collect data from 10 respondents by student,
- Conduct data analysis through statistical analysis software (SPSS version 17).

UV students had to deliver three written reports showing and explaining the results of their qualitative research (Report 1), data collection (Report 2) and data analysis (Report 3).

Report 1 consisted of a comparative study between United Kingdom (i.e. exhibition site) and Spain (country where the research is developed) about attendance to exhibitions, camera sales and additional data allowing inferences about the popularity of photography and cultural events related to this in United Kingdom and Spain. In order to complete this task, UV students made use of the databases available in the Virtual Library of the University of Valencia.

Report 2 involved for students to develop proposals of questionnaire that were later gathered by the lecturers to elaborate an official questionnaire that will be used by all the students in the field work. The objective of this questionnaire was to gather the assessment of a representative sample of members of the university community (i.e. target market of the exhibition) about the 53 pinhole photos with the final purpose of selecting 23 for the London exhibition. In order to achieve this aim, each student needed to collect 10 valid questionnaires.

Finally, Report 3 shows the results of the questionnaires once processed with the SPSS software. The students were invited to perform a series of statistical analyses that allow to choose the 23 most preferred pictures by respondents and to conclude the potential success of the pinhole exhibition to be celebrated in London.

For students at the University of Valencia, this project was proposed as a team and voluntary activity, whose full implementation might contribute to the student's final grade in a maximum of 1 point out of 10.

15 December 2009-10 January 2010

Fotolateras.com have organised the exhibition to be taken place in London according to the results of the research. In this sense, *Fotolateras.com* have sent copies of the 23 selected photographs via email to Lourdes Hernandez-Martin to be integrated in the activities of *Still Spanish.*

January 2010

Once the 23 photos were selected as a result of the research conducted by the students at the University of Valencia, the students of Spanish Language and Culture at the London School of Economics were invited to develop a caption and a text (in Spanish with a translation in English) to accompany each of the photographs in the exhibition in London, under the collaborative agreement between both the universities. The inter-university project was designed as a multicultural, interdisciplinary and bilingual project; each student at LSE was required to develop this task individually.

All activities have been performed in Spanish.

16-23 February

- Exhibition at LSE: Tinned Cities/Ciudades Enlatadas. Inauguration: 16 February 2010, Time: 19.30, Place: Atrium Gallery, Old Building.
- Workshop. The artists will give a 4-hours workshop to students of Spanish Language and Society (Beginners) in Spanish on photographic techniques focusing on pinhole techniques using tins.

Day: 17 February 2010, Time: 14.00-16.00

Weather permitted, students will have the opportunity "to *photo-tin*": 18 February 2010, Time: 9.00-11.00 (see Figure 3).

METHODOLOGY FOR ANALYZING TEACHING-LEARNING OUTCOMES

With these activities we expect to increase student motivation, comprehension of the contents of the respective subjects and the involvement in class activities. In order to assess these expected outcomes, we have combined both qualitative and quantitative data. Regarding the former, we have considered the quality of the tasks developed by the students during the course, as well as the feedback received.

Figure 3. 5th Ave., New York. (© 2009, fotolateras.com. Used with permission.)

Regarding quantitative inputs, we have conducted a survey among students to assess motivation, group interaction, use of technology, and the suitability of problem-based learning. The items of the questionnaire have been adapted from Hazari et al. (2009) and proposed by the authors; data have been processed through SPSS statistical software to obtain descriptive statistics and contingence tables.

To evaluate the results of this pilot activity for the UV students, the first consideration was student participation in this activity, both quantitatively and qualitatively. In this sense, although this activity was voluntary and its contribution to the student final grade was scarce (i.e. 10% maximum), almost all enrolled students took part in this project. In particular, 57 out of 64 students (i.e. 89.06%) submitted at least one of the three reports under this activity. Regarding the quality of the reports submitted, it is quite high, being the average grade "outstanding".

Second, on the last day of the class a questionnaire based on the proposal of Hazari et al. (2009) was administered in order to gather students' evaluation of their perception of the educational contribution of this activity, their motivation for problem-based learning activities, the ability of this activity to encourage interaction within the group and the use of technology tools such as databases of the Digital Library of the University of Valencia and the statistical software SPSS. Additionally, classification questions were included.

Respondents were asked to rank each statement in a 5-point Likert scale according to their level of agreement or disagreement (1 = I totally disagree, 2 = I disagree, 3 = neutral, 4 = I agree, 5 = I totally agree). Results for 56 valid questionnaires are shown in Table 1.

Regarding the assessment of the pinhole activity by the UV students, the results obtained are encouraging, since the scores exceed the midpoint of the 5-point Likert scale (i.e., 3) for all items considered. In particular, high scores are obtained for the items "I would recommend classes that use real problem-based activities to other students" (4.16), "Development of a real marketing research promoted collaborative learning" (3.96) and "The Pinhole Exhibition activities were overall easy to understand" (3.95). Notwithstanding, the questionnaire also shows as the worst rated items those relating to the use of technology tools: e.g. " Benefits of using the SPSS outweighed any technical challenges of its use" (3.27) and "Using SPSS was easy" (3.02).

Grouping the items in Table 1 in the four factors identified by Hazari et al. (2009), i.e., Learning/Pedagogy, Motivation, Group Interaction and Technology, we have estimated the average of the items included in each factors. Results are shown in Table 2.

The results obtained provide evidence in the sense that our problem-based activity is not encouraging group interaction as expected. Thus, although Reports 1 and 3 were to be developed in teams, it seems as if team members divided tasks and worked individually. This finding has relevant implications for task definition.

Furthermore, the resulting average for the Technology factor supports the difficulties experienced by some students with the technological tools used during the course. Notwithstanding, the high value of the standard deviation for this factor reflects the heterogeneity of the assessments expressed by students regarding this issue.

On the other hand, the high average scores for student motivation and the contribution of this activity to learning are encouraging. Therefore, the fact of conducting a real research project from the beginning to the end seems to have encouraged students to actively follow the course and to complete the different tasks, contributing positively to the assessment of their learning in this subject.Additionally, UV students were requested to contribute to this activity to improve their English command. Results of the comparison of their command at the completion of the project to the previous English command are shown in Table 3.

As a result, we observe that half of the students consider that taking part in this activity has positively contributed to the development of their communication skills in English. In particular, this improvement is assessed as more relevant to the improvement of the English command of the student. Therefore, we obtain evidence supporting a positive impact of the proposed problem-based activity on the teaching-learning of Marketing Research and on the student language skills.

Finally, the questionnaire included an open question -"Any additional comments? (such as what you liked MOST/LEAST about the Pinhole exhibition marketing research)"- inviting students to provide qualitative feedback about their experience in this problem-based activity. Results are shown in Table 4.

Table 1. Students' assessment of the pinhole activity contribution to the teaching-learning process

	Mean	St. Dev.
1. The Pinhole Exhibition activities were overall easy to understand	3.95	0.796
2. I liked interacting with other students in the Pinhole Exhibition activity	3.73	0.842
3. I would prefer classes that use problem-based activities over other classes that do not use this kind of activities	3.36	1.227
4. Using SPSS was easy	3.02	0.981
5. The Pinhole Exhibition activities aided me in achieving course objectives	3.59	0.813
6. I stayed on the task more because of the Pinhole Exhibition activities	3.36	0.841
7. I would like to see problem-based activities used in other courses	3.79	0.825
8. Benefit of the Pinhole Exhibition activities is worth the extra effort & time required to work on them	3.45	0.807
9. I participated in the assignment more because of this problem-based activity	3.47	0.690
10. Benefits of using the SPSS outweighed any technical challenges of its use	3.27	0.952
11. The Pinhole Exhibition activities helped me interact more with students	3.64	0.841
12. Technical features of SPSS helped enhance my learning	3.36	1.103
13. Because of working on a real problem-based activity, my group was able to come to a consensus faster	3.59	0.910
14. I will retain more material as a result of taking part in the Pinhole Exhibition activity	3.47	0.790
15. I would recommend classes that use real problem-based activities to other students	4.16	0.811
16. Compared to SPSS, the Euromonitor database was easier to use	3.87	1.090
17. Development of a real marketing research promoted collaborative learning	3.96	0.687
18. I learned more because of information shared with other students in the Pinhole Exhibition activities	3.36	0.749
19. The Pinhole Exhibition activity enhanced my interest in the course	3.66	0.837
20. I will continue to explore use of databases for education	3.63	0.964

Although this was the last question and was not as quick to answer as the preceding multiple choice or 5-point-scale questions, nearly a quarter of students developed and provided their impressions about this activity. In particular, 12.5% of students responded to this question with thankful and supporting comments, encouraging the lecturers to repeat this type of activity in further courses.

On the other hand, all negative comments were focused on complaints about the difficulties experienced with the use of SPSS software and the speed of computer processing. Regarding the latter, there were some problems with computers in some sessions due to a failure in the UV network. Notwithstanding, some students suggested the convenience of including an additional session to get familiar with the SPSS software before developing the required task and, thus, we shall take this idea into account for further courses.

Table 2. Students' assessment of the pinhole activity contribution to their English command

Factor	Items no.	Mean	St. dev.
Technology	1, 4, 10, 12, 16	3.48	0.557
Motivation	3, 6, 8, 15, 20	3.71	0.491
Group Interaction	2, 11, 13, 17, 18	3.13	0.435
Learning/Pedagogy	5, 7, 9, 14, 19	3.60	0.493

Table 3. Students' assessment of the pinhole activity contribution to their English command

English	Pinhole activity contribution to English command			Total
command	**None**	**Fair**	**Significant**	
Intermediate	2 3.6%	10 17.9%	1 1.8%	13 23.2%
Advanced	19 33.9%	10 17.9%	2 3.6%	31 55.4%
Proficiency	5 8.9%	5 8.9%	0 0.0%	10 17.9%
Native	2 3.6%	0 0.0%	0 0.0%	2 3.6%
Total	28 50.0%	25 44.6%	3 5.4%	56 100.0%

Chi-squared: 10.807 (p-value: 0.095)

Table 4. Students assessment of the pinhole activity contribution to their English command

Type of feedback	Number of students	%
Positive	7	12.5%
Positive & negative	1	1.8%
Negative	4	7.1%
None	45	78.6%

CONCLUSION, LIMITATIONS AND RECOMMENDATIONS

A problem-based learning approach was adopted to design a Marketing Research course activity to be developed sequentially to enable students to achieve course objectives in a more efficient way in comparison with traditional methods. Following the evidence obtained for the UV Marketing Research course, we consider that the interdisciplinary collaboration between UV and LSE through this project has involved positive effects on students' motivation, involvement and performance. In particular, we have obtained results supporting that, even if there is a low extrinsic reward for the student because of his/her participation, he/she becomes actively implicated in the activities proposed if he/she considers them as exciting, challenging and useful for solving a real-world problem. This result has implications for the design of attractive teaching-learning activities that may stimulate student's participation therefore contributing to improve his/her final results. This evidence is in the line of Deci & Ryan (1985), who assumed that the activation of intrinsic motivation is determined to a great extent by characteristics of the task. In this sense, we agree with Bergin (1992) regarding the existence of a relationship between motivation, academic activities and leisure that the lecturer must take advantage of in favour of the teaching-learning process.

All in all, the results obtained for the students of University of Valencia seem to support the positive influence of this interdisciplinary activity in the students' performance and the use of learning methods that facilitate active and cooperative learning through problem-based activities. The collaboration project allowed students from two different disciplines and different universities not only to meet the learning objectives of their corresponding courses, but also to get information on other realities (i.e. arts management) and to improve their foreign language skills. Both the qualitative and quantitative results seem to confirm the positive contribution of this interdisciplinary problem-based learning activity to the teaching-learning process and, according to previous literature, the convenience of the use of this method in Higher Education classrooms.

However, the evidence is not conclusive, as it has been an exploratory research and the activity should be replicated in further years and for different courses. Regarding the quantitative data, the results obtained could be biased because some students' work in groups for Reports 1 and 3 that may find an incentive to act as "free riders", since the grade for these reports was common for all team members. On the other hand, causality between participation indicators and student's final grade has not been explored. In this sense, do students have better results because of their participation in this problem-based learning activity? Or do the "best" students tend to participate in this activity more than others? "Best" students might be more intrinsically motivated by these class activities and vice versa. In this sense, considering the performance of students in other subjects and qualitative analysis – e.g. interviews with students – might contribute to shed additional light on the results of this research.

REFERENCES

Ames, C. (1992). Classrooms: Goals, structures, and student motivation. *Journal of Educational Psychology*, *84*(3), 261–271. doi:10.1037/0022-0663.84.3.261

Bates, A. (1995). *Technology, open learning and distance education*. New York, NY: Routledge.

Bergin, D. A. (1992). Leisure activity, motivation, and academic achievement in high school students. *Journal of Leisure Research*, *24*(3), 225–239.

Bransford, J. D., Brown, A. L., & Cocking, R. R. (2000). *How people learn: Brain, mind, experience, and school*. Washington, DC: National Academy Press.

Covington, M. V. (2000). Goal theory, motivation and school achievement: An integrative review. *Annual Review of Psychology*, *51*, 171–200. doi:10.1146/annurev.psych.51.1.171

Deci, E. L., & Ryan, R. M. (1985). *Intrinsic motivation and self-determination in human behavior*. New York, NY: Plenum.

Dupeyrat, C., & Mariné, C. (2005). Implicit of intelligence, goal orientation, cognitive engagement, and achievement: A test of Dweck's model with returning to school adults. *Contemporary Educational Psychology*, *30*(1), 43–59. doi:10.1016/j.cedpsych.2004.01.007

Elliot, E., & Dweck, C. (1988). Goals: An approach to motivation and achievement. *Journal of Personality and Social Psychology*, *54*(1), 5–12. doi:10.1037/0022-3514.54.1.5

Garcia, T., & Pontrich, P. R. (1996). The effects of autonomy on motivation and performance in the college classroom. *Contemporary Educational Psychology*, *21*(4), 477–486. doi:10.1006/ceps.1996.0032

Gremler, D. D., Hoffman, K. D., Keaveney, S. M., & Wright, L. K. (2000). Experiential learning exercises in services marketing courses. *Journal of Marketing Education*, *22*(1), 35–44. doi:10.1177/0273475300221005

Hazari, S., North, A., & Moreland, D. (2009). Investigating pedagogical value of Wiki technology. *Journal of Information Systems Education*, *20*(2), 187–198.

Humphrey, N. (2004). The death of the feel-good factor? *School Psychology International, 25*(3), 347–360. doi:10.1177/0143034304046906

Kennedy, E. J., Lawton, L., & Walker, E. (2001). The case for using live cases: Shifting the paradigm in marketing education. *Journal of Marketing Education, 23*(2), 145–151. doi:10.1177/0273475301232008

Lilly, B., & Tippins, M. J. (2002). Enhancing student motivation in marketing classes: Using student management groups. *Journal of Marketing Education, 24*(3), 253–264. doi:10.1177/0273475302238048

Martin, A. J. (2007). Examining a multidimensional model of student motivation and engagement using a construct validation approach. *The British Journal of Educational Psychology, 77*(2), 413–440. doi:10.1348/000709906X118036

Oliver, R., & Omari, A. (1999). Using online technologies to support problem based learning: Learners' responses and perceptions. *Australian Journal of Educational Technology, 15*(1), 58–79.

Peterson, R. M. (2001). Course participation: An active learning approach employing student documentation. *Journal of Marketing Education, 23*(3), 187–194. doi:10.1177/0273475301233004

Savery, J. R. (2006). Overview of problem-based learning: Definitions and distinctions. *The Interdisciplinary Journal of Problem-based Learning, 1*(1), 9–20.

Siegel, C. E. (2000). Introducing marketing students to business intelligence using project-based learning on the World Wide Web. *Journal of Marketing Education, 22*(2), 90–98. doi:10.1177/0273475300222003

Slavin, R. E. (1990). *Cooperative learning*. New Jersey: Prentice-Hall.

Stipek, D. J., Salmon, J. S., & Givven, K. B. (1998). The value of practices suggested by motivation research and promoted by mathematics education reformers. *Journal for Research in Mathematics Education, 29*(4), 465–488. doi:10.2307/749862

Urdan, T., & Maehr, M. L. (1995). Beyond a two-goal theory of motivation: A case for social goals. *Review of Educational Research, 65*(3), 213–244.

Wentzel, K. R. (1993). Does being good make the grade? Social behavior and academic competence in middle school. *Journal of Educational Psychology, 85*(2), 357–364. doi:10.1037/0022-0663.85.2.357

Young, M. R. (2005). The motivational effects of the classroom environment in facilitating self-regulated learning. *Journal of Marketing Education, 27*(1), 25–40. doi:10.1177/0273475304273346

ADDITIONAL READING

Albanese, M. A., & Mitchell, S. (1993). Problem-based learning: A review of the literature on its outcomes and implementation issues. *Academic Medicine*, *68*(1), 52–81. doi:10.1097/00001888-199301000-00012

Appleton-Knapp, S. L., & Krentler, K. A. (2006). Measuring Student Expectations and Their Effects on Satisfaction: The Importance of Managing Students Expectations. *Journal of Marketing Education*, *28*(3), 254–264. doi:10.1177/0273475306293359

Association of College & Research Libraries. (2000). Information Literacy Competency Standards for Higher Education. Retrieved February 13, 2010, from http://www.ala.org/ala/acrl/acrlstandards/informationliteracycompetencystandards.cfm.

Boekaerts, M. (1997). Self-regulated learning: A new concept embraced by researcher, policy makers, educators, teachers and students. *Learning and Instruction*, *7*(2), 161–186. doi:10.1016/S0959-4752(96)00015-1

Denton, B. G., Adams, C. C., Blatt, P. J., & Lorish, C. D. (2000). Does the introduction of problem-based learning change graduate performance outcomes in a professional curriculum? *Journal on Excellence in College Teaching*, *11*(2&3), 147–162.

Garcia, T., & Pontrich, P. R. (1996). The effects of autonomy on motivation and performance in the college classroom. *Contemporary Educational Psychology*, *21*(4), 477–486. doi:10.1006/ceps.1996.0032

Gremler, D. D., Hoffman, K. D., Keaveney, S. M., & Wright, L. K. (2000). Experiential learning exercises in services marketing courses. *Journal of Marketing Education*, *22*(1), 35–44. doi:10.1177/0273475300221005

Hmelo-Silver, C. E. (2004). Problem-based learning: What and how do students learn? *Educational Psychology Review*, *16*(3), 235–266. doi:10.1023/B:EDPR.0000034022.16470.f3

Hmelo-Silver, C. E., & Barrows, H. S. (2006). Goals and strategies of a problem-based learning facilitator. *Interdisciplinary Journal of Problem-based Learning*, *1*(1), 21–39.

Hsu, J. (2007). Innovative Technologies for Education and Learning. *International Journal of Information and Communication Technology Education*, *3*(3), 70–89. doi:10.4018/jicte.2007070107

Kirschner, P. A., Sweller, J., & Clark, R. E. (2006). Why minimal guidance during instruction does not work: an analysis of the failure of constructivist, discovery, problem-based, experiential, and inquiry-based teaching. *Educational Psychologist, 41*(2), 75–86. doi:10.1207/s15326985ep4102_1

Lilly, B., & Tippins, M. J. (2002). Enhancing student motivation in marketing classes: Using student management groups. *Journal of Marketing Education, 24*(3), 253–264. doi:10.1177/0273475302238048

Loranger, A. L. (1994). The study of strategies of successful high school students. *Journal of Reading Behavior, 26*(4), 347–360.

Merrill, M. D. (2002). A pebble-in-the-pond model for instructional design. *Performance Improvement, 41*(7), 39–44. doi:10.1002/pfi.4140410709

Peterson, R. M. (2001). Course participation: An active learning approach employing student documentation. *Journal of Marketing Education, 23*(3), 187–194. doi:10.1177/0273475301233004

Schmidt, H. G. (1993). Foundations of problem-based learning: some explanatory notes. *Medical Education, 27*(5), 422–432. doi:10.1111/j.1365-2923.1993.tb00296.x

Siegel, C. E. (2000). Introducing marketing students to business intelligence using project-based learning on the World Wide Web. *Journal of Marketing Education, 22*(2), 90–98. doi:10.1177/0273475300222003

Stinson, J. E., & Milter, R. G. (1996). Problem-based learning in business education: Curriculum design and implementation issues. In Wilkerson, L., & Gijselaers, W. H. (Eds.), *Bringing problem- based learning to higher education: Theory and practice. New Directions For Teaching and Learning Series, No. 68* (pp. 32–42). San Francisco, CA: Jossey-Bass.

Stipek, D. J., Salmon, J. S., & Givven, K. B. (1998). The value of practices suggested by motivation research and promoted by mathematics education reformers. *Journal for Research in Mathematics Education, 29*(4), 465–488. doi:10.2307/749862

Sweller, J. (1988). Cognitive load during problem solving: Effects on learning. *Cognitive Science, 12*(2), 257–285. doi:10.1207/s15516709cog1202_4

Sweller, J. (2006). The worked example effect and human cognition. *Learning and Instruction, 16*(2), 165–169. doi:10.1016/j.learninstruc.2006.02.005

Sweller, J., Van Merrienboer, J., & Paas, F. (1998). Cognitive architecture and instructional design. *Educational Psychology Review, 10*(3), 251–296. doi:10.1023/A:1022193728205

KEY TERMS AND DEFINITIONS

Content and Language Integrated Learning (CLIL): Lecturer and students of content subjects (e.g. History, Economics, Business, Political Sciences, etc.) use a foreign or second language as the medium of communication and instruction. In this sense, CLIL is a means of learning a language, and of introducing international aspects into the teaching of content subjects.

Cooperative Learning: Educational strategy through which students learn from others.

Problem-Based Learning: Instructional student-centered approach that empowers students to conduct research, integrating theory and practice, and applying knowledge and skills to develop a feasible solution to a problem proposed by the instructor.

ENDNOTES

1. For more information on their work, please visit the web page of the two artists http://www.fotolateras.com/.
2. http://www.urban-age.net/01_introduction/intro_idea.htm.
3. http://www.lse.ac.uk/collections/cities/.
4. In China, India, Africa, and Latin America, urban populations are exploding and cities are growing exponentially. At the same time, many developed cities are shrinking and being radically restructured as a result of shifting economic bases and new patterns of migration. (…)Urban policymakers are struggling to balance this massive growth in public and private investment with more sustainable forms of urban development. Questions regarding the shape, size, density and distribution of the city have become increasingly complex and politicised. …http://www.urban-age.net/01_introduction/intro_idea.html.
5. Planning and Corporate Policy Division, London School of Economics. LSE Strategic Plan 2008-2013. London, UK.
6. Common European Framework, http://www.coe.int/T/DG4/Portfolio/documents/Framework_EN.pdf, p.161.
7. Common European Framework, http://www.coe.int/T/DG4/Portfolio/documents/Framework_EN.pdf p. 153.

This work was previously published in Cases on Innovations in Educational Marketing: Transnational and Technological Strategies, edited by Purnendu Tripathi and Siran Mukerji, pp. 135-148, copyright 2011 by Business Science Reference (an imprint of IGI Global).

Chapter 14
ORIENT:
The Intercultural Empathy through Virtual Role-Play

Sibylle Enz
Otto-Friedrich-Universitaet Bamberg, Germany

Carsten Zoll
Otto-Friedrich-Universitaet Bamberg, Germany

Natalie Vannini
Julius-Maximilians Universität Würzburg, Germany

Mei Yii Lim
Heriot-Watt University, Edinburgh, UK

Wolfgang Schneider
Julius-Maximilians Universität Würzburg, Germany

Lynne Hall
University of Sunderland, UK

Ana Paiva
INESC-ID, Portugal

Ruth Aylett
Heriot-Watt University, Edinburgh, UK

EXECUTIVE SUMMARY

In a globalised world, cultural diversity is a challenge for everyone. Even for those staying "at home" cultural diversity enters their daily lives by people migrating from other regions of the world, sharing their social world. While intercultural encounters pose a great enrichment to one's experiences and perspectives, they also represent an immense challenge, confronting us with different languages, attitudes, habits, and social norms. The work presented in this chapter takes up this challenge by developing and evaluating a believable agent-based educational application ("ORIENT") designed to develop inter-cultural empathy for 12-14 year olds. The following chapter:

DOI: 10.4018/978-1-4666-1885-5.ch014

1. Discusses the approach to use the appealing character of games in order to foster social and emotional learning in the age group while drawing on effective pedagogical interventions like role-play that have previously been successfully used to trigger social and emotional learning in a variety of real-world contexts;

2. Introduces the development of ORIENT as an affective agent architecture modeling culturally-specific agent behavior, drawing on the psychological and pedagogical theories outlined;

3. Considers the role of novel interaction modalities in supporting an empathic engagement with culturally-specific characters as well as active engagement in collaborative learning within a group of learners; and

4. Presents and discusses results of preliminary evaluation studies based on an early prototype.

BACKGROUND

eCIRCUS (Education through Characters with emotional Intelligence and Role-playing Capabilities that Understand Social interaction)has developed a new approach in the use of ICT to support social and emotional learning within Personal and Social Education (PSE). This was achieved through virtual role-play with synthetic characters that establish credible and empathic relations with learners. eCIRCUS investigated educational role-play using autonomous synthetic characters and involving the child through affective engagement, including the use of standard and highly innovative interaction mechanisms. This has developed novel conceptual models based on theories of narrative and role-play from psychology and implemented them in affectively driven autonomous graphically embodied agents – actors with attitude. It has delivered early prototype showcases through a VLE for emotional and social learning, one on anti-bullying education and one on intercultural empathy.

SETTING THE STAGE

ORIENT (Overcoming Refugee Integration with Empathic Novel Technology) focuses on the domain of intercultural learning, aiming at the home community with the ultimate goal of improving the social integration of youths with migration background in European countries. ORIENT is a showcase developed for Personal and Social Education by the EU-funded project eCIRCUS, funded within its Framework VI program. It offers a virtual learning environment for a group of three learners who are interacting with autonomous artificial characters representing another species (the "Sprytes") on an alien planet called ORIENT, a distant planet under threat of destruction by a large meteor. Interacting with the ORIENT application, a small group of adolescent learners equipped with innovative interaction technology are asked to solve – as foreigners on the alien planet of ORIENT – story-based problems and learn by interacting with the software how to get into contact, communicate, and cooperate with others who are fundamentally different from themselves.

The virtual world of the Sprytes is represented on a large screen of the real-world interaction space of the three learners, allowing for interaction between the learners in the real-world context as well as for interaction between the learners and the virtual world of the Sprytes; interaction devices used include RFID tagged real-world objects and RFID reading mobile phones, a game mat for navigation in the virtual world, and a WiiMote controller. First participants are told about their role as applicants for an internship in Space Command who will travel to an alien planet called ORIENT to find out about the inhabitants, the so-called Sprytes, of whom only very little is known so far. Their mission goal is to find out about Spryte habits and ways, to allow Space Command to judge whether it would be safe to establish further contact with the Sprytes. Then they are allocated the three roles:

- Navigation officer, who navigates on ORIENT using the game mat and handles the ORA-CLE;
- Communication officer, who communicates with the Sprytes by using expert knowledge about Spryte gestures, using the WiiMote;
- Intelligence officer, who can exchange objects with the Sprytes and attract the Sprytes attention, using the mobile phone.

The team then "teleport" to ORIENT, which is displayed via projector on a wall of the room after the participants have moved to their respective places.

In the course of the role-play, the group of learners and the Sprytes gradually learn from each other and the learners share the engaging experience of cooperatively handling novel interaction technology, implemented to enable communication with the Sprytes. ORIENT as a semi-immersive graphical environment depicting an imaginary foreign culture thus couples social learning in a group with intercultural learning. Its development was guided by pedagogical and psychological theories to develop an existing affective agent architecture (Dias & Paiva, 2005; Paiva et al., 2005) into one that also models cultural behavior in its full range.

As far as the intercultural learning challenge is concerned, ORIENT first and foremost draws on contact theory (Allport, 1954), the idea that inter-group prejudice can be reduced through contact between different cultural groups under specific conditions, such as equal status between the groups in the situation, common goals, intergroup cooperation, and the support of authorities, law, or custom. Carefully trying to design a learning experience that takes up at least some of these situational characteristics, ORIENT provides the adolescent user with the experience of role-play within an unfamiliar culture in which problems have to be solved. By experiencing for themselves the stresses of dealing with an unfamiliar culture, we hope to trigger transfer in learners, ultimately empathizing with those in their own peer group going through the same process. Dangers that lie in using real cultures for this type of role-play e.g. relate to misrepresentation of the depth of a depicted human culture, or to specific prejudices that may be present in the host group. For these reasons it was decided ORIENT would take place on a distant planet populated by non-human aliens, carefully balancing these risks and dangers with the heightened challenge to secure transfer to real-world settings. What cultural theory can help in designing such an environment? Here the project drew on the cultural dimensions derived by Hofstede (1991, 2001) from empirical work with employees of IBM in a variety of countries.

CASE DESCRIPTION

ORIENT: A Novel Learning Application

In recent years, a diverse range of applications designed for education, training, therapy or entertainment purposes have been developed that rely more and more on technology to augment user experiences. For instance, believable autonomous synthetic characters (Core et al., 2006; Kenny et al., 2007; Paiva et al., 2005; Rossen et al., 2008; Rowe et al., 2007) that have been previously shown to enrich interaction with human users (Cassell et al., 2000) draw on the engagement of human-human interaction, trying to reproduce it. Particularly in areas where changes in attitude and behavior change are in the focus (i.e. in social and emotional learning) rather than pure acquisition of knowledge, autonomous synthetic characters may have good potential as a pedagogical instrument to change cognition, emotion, and behavior. Based on these considerations, synthetic characters may be designed to specifically trigger affective engagement through the creation of an empathic relationship between user and character, for instance based on psychological theories and models of cognitive appraisal (Ortony et al., 1988) and coping behavior (Lazarus, 1991).

The aim in the work presented in this case study is to develop characters with social and emotional capabilities for the application area of intercultural learning, with capabilities such as emotionally driven behavior including emotional expressivity, determined by emotional variables in their action-selection mechanisms. As a result different patterns of character behavior emerge which support e.g. the users ascribing personality to the characters when they interact with them.

Such characters seem particularly suitable for applications in which emotionally expressive behavior is required (Allbeck & Badler, 2004; Isbister, 2004; Koda et al., 2008; Rehm et al., 2007). In the application area of intercultural learning however, other factors than emotional expressivity come into focus. Being faced with the challenges of intercultural encounters, highly routinized behavioral reactions such as the unconscious application of stereotypes are rather common and persistent (as well as highly psychologically plausible), calling for a learning application that tackles cognitive as well as affective bases of behavior.

Another novelty of the approach presented in this chapter is to develop synthetic characters that are not only psychologically plausible due to their believable behavior and underlying action selection mechanism, but also act according to their cultural characteristics, thus specifically linking behavior to cultural standards and norms: not only their expressive behavior (including language and clothing, see e.g. Hall et al., 2006) is modified according to their cultural background, but they are considered as social actors within their respective cultural context. In ORIENT, characters' verbal and non-verbal behaviors are culturally mediated from a model-based perspective. While it is highly reasonable to assume that cultural ways and assumptions always play their role in the design of virtual worlds and believable characters inhabiting them (e.g. Rosis et al., 2004), ORIENT tries to create a new culture with which the learners are confronted, triggering reflection about similarities and differences and ultimately reinforcing the overcoming of prejudices and fears by learning more about each other as well as learning to cooperate. For these sensitive learning mechanisms, the virtual learning application offers a safe and secure as well as engaging environment to carefully open up for intercultural experiences.

The theoretical work behind ORIENT informs three different areas of development: (1) the change in attitude, emotion, and behavior in intercultural encounters; (2) the cultural specification of ORIENT and the implementation of a model that allows for representation of the cultural parameters impacting action-selection of the Sprytes; and (3) the modeling of the impact of the user interaction on the Sprytes behavior. Hence, the following chapter outlines the design process of ORIENT and the implementation of the underpinning theories on social and emotional learning (e.g. educational role-play) and on culture and intercultural learning which are then introduced in detail in subsequent section of the paper.

THE ORIENT APPLICATION: EMOTION, PERSONALITY, CULTURE

Designing the Spryte Culture along the Dimensions of Cultural Variability

Hofstede (1991, 2001) posited five dimensions to describe different cultures. These dimensions were used to design the artificial culture for the inhabitants of ORIENT. The following chapter first provides some basic information about the concept of culture, before the links with the modeling of culture in ORIENT, in particularly in the mind of the artificial agents that inhabit ORIENT is explained in more detail.

Culture has an effect on human cognition, affect and behavior. To define cultural differences in agents, variables which describe the cultural personality of an agent have to be defined. There are systematic similarities and differences across cultures that can be explained and predicted theoretically using dimensions of cultural variability (e.g. individualism-collectivism). Classifications of culture and dimensions of cultural variability have for example been provided by Hall (2001) or Hofstede (1991), who created a five factor cultural model. Hofstede (2001) defines culture as "the collective programming of the human mind that distinguishes the members of one human group from those of another. Culture in this sense is a system of collectively held values" (p. 9). Enculturation takes place during socialization, the time when children adopt orientation of a specific culture without further reflection. Based on work by Inkeles and Levinson (1969), Hofstede's empirical work carried out with IBM employees in a number of different cultures yielded five cultural dimensions that have since been widely used to describe a wide range of different cultures, with one of the characteristics within each dimension tending to predominate.

Individualism-Collectivism is the major dimension of cultural variability used to explain similarities and differences in communication across cultures. "Individualism pertains to societies in which the ties between individuals are loose: everyone is expected to look after himself or herself and his or her immediate family. Collectivism as its opposite pertains to societies in which people from birth onwards are integrated into strong cohesive in-groups, which throughout people's lifetime continue to protect them in exchange for unquestioning loyalty" (Hofstede, 1991, p. 51). One tendency tends to predominate in each culture, e.g. individualism in the United States, Canada, Australia, New Zealand, and northern Europe and collectivism in African, Arab, Latin, and southern European cultures (Gudykunst & Mody, 2002). As humans seek for autonomy and community, moderate or hybrid forms of individualism and collectivism have to be assumed. Individual-level characteristics, such as personality, individual values and self construals mediate the influence of cultural individualism-collectivism on individuals' communication and might explain variability in communication within cultures (Gudykunst & Mody, 2002). The individual's psychological needs, e.g. the need for affiliation, are influenced by parameters like community, collaboration, shared interests, harmony, traditions and public good being emphasized in collectivistic cultures and personal rights, responsibilities, privacy, freedom and self-expression in individualistic cultures. This provides a link from the general cultural stereotype to the intentions and behaviors of the individual agent (Kriegel et al., 2008).

The dimension of uncertainty avoidance describes the degree, to which members of a culture try to avoid uncertainty. In high uncertainty avoidance cultures (e.g. Japan, Mexico, France, Chile, Egypt), members have a lower tolerance for uncertainty and ambiguity, "which expresses itself in higher levels of anxiety and energy release, greater need for formal rules and absolute truth, and less tolerance for people or groups with deviant ideas or behavior" (Hofstede, 1979, p. 395) than members of low uncertainty avoidance cultures (e.g. Canada, Denmark, India, United States) which are more comfortable with ambiguous situations and unfamiliar risks.

Powers distance "is the extent to which the less powerful members of institutions and organizations accept that power is distributed unequally" (Hofstede & Bond, 1984, p. 419). Members of high power distance cultures tend to see and accept power as a part of society and make use of referent power (e.g. Egypt, Ethiopia, Nigeria, Venezuela), whereas members of low power distance cultures assume that power should only be used when legitimate and accordingly use more reward, legitimate, and expert power (e.g. Australia, Canada, Germany, United States).

Masculinity-Femininity: Masculine and feminine cultures are particularly differentiated through gender role distribution. In traditional-gender-oriented masculine cultures, distinct social gender roles (e.g. men are assertive and focused on material success, women are modest and concerned with the quality of life) can be identified. Individuals belonging to masculine cultures tend to organize information on the basis of their genders and to follow cultural definitions of appropriate behavior (Bem, 1993). In contrast, gender roles overlap in feminine cultures (e.g. both men and women might be modest, tender and concerned with the quality of life) (Hofstede, 1991).

Long term / short term orientation: While long-term oriented cultures value thrift and perseverance, short-term oriented cultures value respect for tradition, fulfilling social obligations, and "saving face".

These dimensions are linked with manifestations that have been described (Hofstede, 1991) as values (internal manifestations) on the individual level, and rituals, heroes, and symbols (external manifestations) on the societal level. A subset of the Hofstede dimensions discussed above served as guidelines for the design of an artificial culture for the people on ORIENT, with its tribal and hierarchical culture, the Sprytes. Hierarchy (power distance) values respect and age; the Sprytes are a

Figure 1. Spryte character

militarily active culture who believe in using force and power to influence others and to protect their habitat. They are a collectivistic culture (individualism-collectivism), being largely compassionate with each other, and living in groups where usually the majority holds power. Sprytes are highly traditional in their ways and view uncertainty as a threat (uncertainty avoidance). The hierarchy in Spryte culture has three layers: The top layer is represented by the Elder, followed by the members of its council (tribal elders, military generals and the like) and Spryte population. Gender is absent in the Spryte culture (masculinity-femininity), and their graphical representation, as seen for one character in Figure 1, is intentionally ambiguous.

In order to reinforce the believability of the characters and the sets, a large screen projection is used so that characters are close to life-size. The importance of close-to-life-size characters and world is that the users are put on a more equal footing, with their movements and actions in the real world serving as interaction modes with the virtual world. The learners' own bodies thus are in the focus of interaction. For this reason, keyboard interaction is replaced by other more novel interaction modalities designed to promote cooperation between the three users as well as more direct interaction with the characters. These are discussed below.

Baseline Architecture

The ORIENT agent architecture started from FAtiMA (Dias & Paiva, 2005; see Figure 2), an agent architecture used for synthetic agents in which emotions and personality take a central role in influencing behavior and thus achieving more believable agents. In FAtiMA emotions are based on the OCC cognitive theory of emotions (Ortony et al., 1988), which views the emotional process as based on appraisal, with the quality of emotions resulting from the appraisals of events.

In FAtiMA there are two main layers for the appraisal and coping processes: the Reactive Layer, which is responsible for the character's emotional reactions and reactive behavior, and the Deliberative Layer, responsible for the character's goal-oriented behavior. To appraise an event in the world, agents use their memories and knowledge about the world, stored in a knowledge base and in an autobiographic memory. The knowledge base is responsible for storing semantic knowledge, such as properties about the world and their relations, while the autobiographic memory contains information concerning past events in the character's personal experience. Every time the sensors of the agent perceive an event, that event is appraised, generating a set of emotions forming an emotional state.

Once the emotional state has been updated by the appraisal process, it is used by the reactive level to trigger action tendencies, generating the agent's emotional reactive behavior. In parallel the deliberative level (which includes a continuous planner; Aylett et al., 2006) selects the most appropriate goal and the most adequate coping strategies. Note that the event perceived will also be used to update existing plans triggering the goal activation process. Finally, after an action is selected for execution, it is performed in the virtual world through the agent's effectors.

While FAtiMA has been very successfully applied in the FearNot! application (Dias & Paiva, 2005) it is subject to certain disadvantages common to symbolically-represented cognitive appraisal architectures. The OCC taxonomy is extensive but still fails to capture significant outcomes of empathic processes, especially in relation to social behavior. FAtiMA in its original form also requires a substantial authoring effort in which goals, emotional reactions, actions and effects are all authored. For this reason, the architecture was extended for ORIENT by incorporating aspects of a needs driven architecture, PSI (Dörner et al., 2003).

Figure 2. Agent Architecture

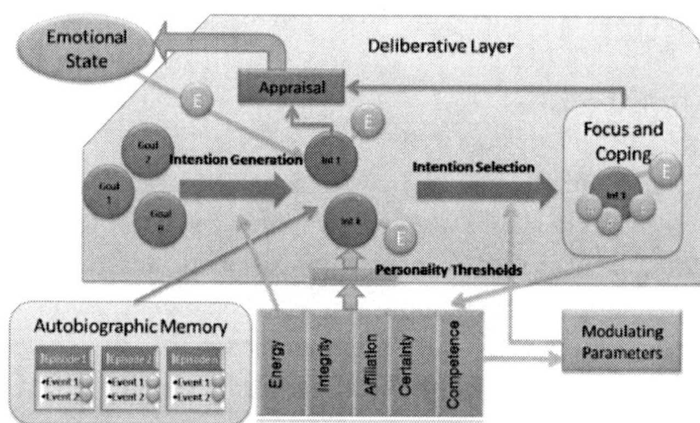

This is a comprehensive psychologically-grounded model of human-action regulation encompassing perception, motivation, cognition, memory, learning and emotions. It is based on a set of drives, such as existence-preserving, species-preserving, certainty, competence and affiliation (see also Figure 2). This seemed a good way of extending FAtiMA with a motivational structure that could allow goals to be dynamically managed rather than pre-set. The drives set was modified slightly and the five drives Energy, Integrity, Certainty, Competence and Affiliation were implemented (Lim et al, 2009). The strength of a drive ranges from 0 (complete deprivation) to 10 (complete satisfaction) and goals and actions are tagged with their expected contribution to Energy, Integrity and Affiliation, allowing their update. Competence is related to success in the environment and thus to goal achievement, so that goal outcomes change its value. Certainty is also related to goal success but less directly, since it represents the extent to which current knowledge about the outcomes of goals and actions are accurate. It is represented as an error prediction based on past successes and failures and thus as an exponential moving average. The need for certainty is not about avoiding those goals with high uncertainty but rather trying to reduce estimation errors; this may mean selecting uncertain goals in order to examine their outcome and reduce their uncertainty via trial-and-error.

This links naturally into the Autobiographic Memory component of the architecture which holds information about past successes and failures and thus acts as a mechanism for learning about the outcome of goals and actions.

The incorporation of aspects of the PSI architecture provides a flexible and context-sensitive goal-management system. A goal may satisfy one or more needs, and a need may be satisfied by different goals.

Symbols, Rituals and Culture

FAtiMA was also extended beyond the individual affective settings to allow for cultural adaptation of the agents via cultural dimension values for the culture of the character, cultural specific symbols, culturally specific goals and needs, and the rituals of the culture (Mascarenhas et al., 2009).

As outlined above, agents perceive the world based on their sensors. However, once an event is perceived, it is passed to a symbol translation process that captures specificities of communication in the culture of that agent. Thus, different cultures perceive events differently according to their symbols, so that the symbol translation process logically precedes the cognitive appraisal process relating events to individual goals. The architecture captures this by allowing for a specific culture parameterization of the symbols in a culture. Once the event has been identified by the agent, the appraisal process is triggered. The appraisal structure contains three variables associated with the OCC model. They are: desirability for the agent, desirability for others and praiseworthiness. The desirability for the agent is calculated based on the motivational system and thus depends on the agents' needs and drives. If an event is positive for the agent's needs, the desirability of the event is high, and vice versa.

The second variable in the appraisal structure is related to how good the event is for other agents, a social judgment, and so some of the aspects of the culture are taken into account in this appraisal using the Hofstede cultural dimension values. For example, in collectivist culture events that are good for others are appraised more positively than in an individualist culture.

Finally, the praiseworthiness of the event is considered as a cultural appraisal in that it captures the social norms of the culture that the agent is part of. For example, an event that shows that the agent is not following the steps of a ritual is appraised as negative. The appraisal component will then activate an emotion producing an update of the memory of the agent and starting the deliberation process. Once an action is chosen, symbol translation is invoked again, and the agent translates the action taking into account relevant symbols, before the action is performed by its actuators.

One other component included in the architecture is rituals capturing in an explicit way some specific rituals of that culture. A ritual is defined as a set of actions with symbolic value, the performance of which is prescribed by the culture.

Interaction in ORIENT

With culture being a social process it is vital to the success of the role-play in ORIENT that user interaction modalities reinforce the story-world and bring it into the real world.

For this reason, user interaction is based on real, physical and tangible objects surrounding them. In the real world the user can see, touch and manipulate objects whose material and shape may support intuitive use and represent real issues. These are always visible and ubiquitous, encouraging a pragmatic approach to problem-solving. Finally, movement in physical space supports social behavior (gestures, speech, movements) and full body interaction that are particularly important in supporting the social nature of culturally-specific interaction.

Appropriate interaction devices for ORIENT were based on a controlled study with 18 children exploring different multi-user settings for pervasive games (Leichtenstern et al., 2007). This study revealed that an appropriate distribution of interaction devices may have a positive effect on collaboration in role play. There was clear evidence that a setting where each user was assigned a role via an interaction device with a dedicated function helps organize interactions within a group, balances the level of interactivity and avoids dominant users. This setting promoted collaboration among users in a better way than a setting where just one interaction device was given to the whole group or a setting where each group member was equipped with an identical device. Based on this study, the assignment of roles in ORIENT is supported by the use of three different interaction devices: a game mat, a mobile phone and a WiiMote. Each interaction device has a different function and attached role, but all of them are necessary to accomplish the overall goal of the game.

Navigation within the ORIENT world is via walking on the spot using a game mat. The Sprytes speak a 'gibberish' generated on the fly related to the language output by the character minds, and this is represented in English (or German) text on the screen with the story-world explanation of a high-tech translator device embedded in a mobile phone carried by a second user. This phone also allows the user to speak 'magic words' that act as symbols within the culture and for SMS communication with the characters. It can recognize RFID tags attached to real world objects that also have an existence in the virtual world.

The third user carries a WiiMote, and this is used to replicate important gestures in order to successfully enter into greetings rituals for example. Figure 3 shows the devices used. The intention in using novel interaction devices was to incite the adolescents' curiosity and increase their motivation to learn more about the Spryte culture. In this vein, the adolescents are not only taken through the different stages of intercultural sensitivity (Bennett, 1986) by the story line, they may actively experience these stages by engaging in interactions with the characters. Addressing explicitly experiential learning approaches (Kolb, 1984), we make use of interaction devices that require bodily activity, such as the game mat and the WiiMote.

Figure 3. Interaction Devices

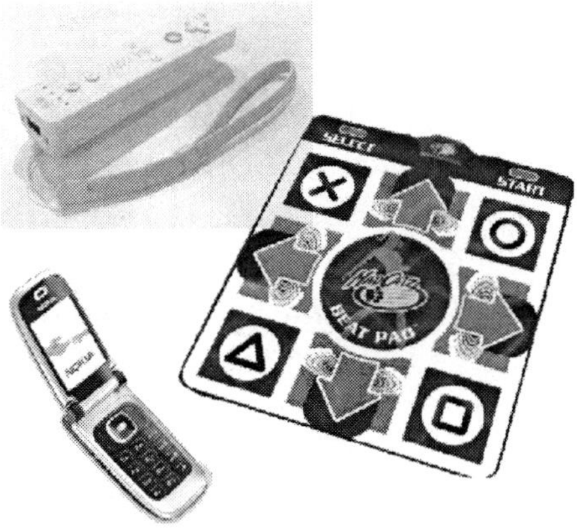

By employing interaction devices that are intuitive to use and support collaboration among the adolescents, we also hope to encourage intergroup collaboration which is one of the conditions of Contact Theory (Allport, 1954).

Furthermore, the ORA-CLE (Onboard Resource Agent for Cultural and Liaison Engagements), an embodied computer character, aims at enhancing learning in the game. It stimulates the learners' reflection on the events and outcomes of ORIENT by asking suitable questions, by encouraging the recording of both personal and collective diaries, and by commenting on the learners' actions. It also helps the transfer of learning to real-world situations, by carrying out a "debriefing" session with learners when they report back to the ORA-CLE with material collected during the mission. The ORA-CLE also fosters learner motivation and keeps them engaged by not disrupting the game flow, stimulating group collaboration (by suggesting participants to use cooperative actions when the team is in a deadlock), keeping players' focus on the task (by reminding them that time is passing by and the meteorite is arriving), and providing help during the mission. It has its own emotional status, which changes during the game according to the team's progress.

Learning in ORIENT: Theories and Outcomes

Social and Emotional Learning

Social and emotional learning (SEL) is defined by Elias et al. (1997) as a process through which learners "enhance their ability to integrate thinking, feeling, and behaving to achieve important life tasks" and embraces such competencies as recognition and management of emotions, establishing healthy relationships, setting of positive goals, meeting personal and social needs, and making responsible and ethical decisions. This can be achieved through different learning processes such as learning through the building of associations between experiences and emotional reactions (associative learning), e.g. due to appropriate reinforcement (e.g. Rotter, 1954; Seligman, 1972), as well as on learning through observation of models and their behavior (e.g. Bandura, 1973; Bandura & Adams, 1977).

One example of a successful didactical tool to foster SEL is role-play. Role-play can be used as training method for empathy in social interactions, experimenting with different reactions to a given situation and exploring experiences of self and other. Role-play thus supports experiential learning in which learners acquire and apply knowledge, skills and feelings in a specific setting, emphasizing the importance of a direct encounter with the subject of study "rather than merely thinking about the encounter [with the subject], or only considering the possibility of doing something about it" (Borzak, 1981). Role-play supports the creation of knowledge and meaning from concrete – though imagined – experiences and uses perspective-taking and empathy as mechanisms for a learner-centered constructivist approach. It is therefore an effective way of addressing intercultural learning as it will be outlined in the course of this chapter. The educational impact of virtual as well as real-life role-play draws on the willingness of participants to commit to the roles they have decided to play. In virtual role-play, believable characters are seen as fundamental both to producing the required social immersion in the story world and also to creating a specific social pressure to stay in role. Implementing role-play in virtual reality thus offers the possibility to combine a successful didactical tool to challenge cognition, emotion, and behavior in school as well as in therapeutic contexts and a virtual, and thus safe and secure learning environment that is fun to explore and to interact with. It helps learners to take over the perspective of the member of another culture, and to understand the similarities and differences in ways of feeling and thinking between their own and the other culture, which – on the one hand – leads to a reflection of their own cultural traditions and boundaries, and on the other hand helps them to alter their own behavior and attitudes in order to better match the challenges of complex (multicultural) social encounters.

Theories of social learning (e.g. Bandura, 1973; Bandura & Adams, 1977) and experiential learning (e.g. Kolb, 1984) suggest that a number of different aspects must be addressed in an application of this nature and help to establish generic requirements. Firstly, it is important that users can identify and acquire knowledge about "adequate" behavior options, and for this reason a cooperative task has been selected in which success depends on overcoming cultural differences. Secondly, scenarios should feature characters that are similar to and stories that are attractive to the target group. This is seen as both facilitating the learning process and representing the learner's own experience. Thirdly, the system should not only provide the learner with scenarios, but also allow them to act and interact with the characters, so that behavior options are not only witnessed but also carried out, producing role commitment.

In sum, the learning process prompted by ORIENT is social and emotional, since attitudes, emotions and behavioral reactions are prompted through the interaction members of the other culture that are reflected upon and discussed in a team of learners that collaboratively try to meet a common goal through understanding and empathizing with members of the other culture.

Collaborative Learning

ORIENT as a group-based learning application focuses on collaborative learning among a group of three adolescent learners. Collaborative learning in a group serves the enhancement of school achievement and the improvement of intergroup relations (Auernheimer, 2003). It is a specific form of small-group education, which emphasizes and structures the social processes during learning. While learners keep independent subtasks and merge them to an overall result of "cooperative learning", the collective development of a solution is in the focus of "collaborative learning"1 (e.g. Slavin, 1995; Roschelle & Teasley, 1995). Being characterized by the sharing of work as well as by the dependence between single tasks, collaborative learning ensures that learners work together during the whole learning process. Usually, a group for collaborative learning is composed heterogeneously concerning abilities, individual characteristics, gender, cultural background, social competence, native language, and learning styles (Weidner, 2006). Basic elements of collaborative learning (Johnson, Johnson & Holubec, 1993) are

- Positive mutual dependence: all members of the team feel involved based on the working for a shared aim. The team is only successful, if everyone makes a contribution to it.
- Individual accountability: every team-member feels responsible for the own and for the group learning processes and contributes to their achievement. The team-members consider it important to maximize the learning outcome of one another.
- Face-to-face interaction: to optimize communication and interaction processes, the members of a group sit close together and must additionally learn to think and act relating to one another. A consensus is gathered through discussion, negotiation, and balance of the arguments.
- Social and team-competence (social skills, such as to encourage, listen to, help, compliment one another better communication, trustfulness, negotiation ability, decision making, and appropriate conflict resolution strategies).
- Evaluation of group processes: the group members reflect and appraise their common efforts, to constantly ameliorate their cooperative competencies and working strategies.

By comparison, Slavin (1995) differentiates three principles, which control the setting: team rewards, individual accountability, and equal opportunity for success. Every advancement counts for the team, so that the individuals are stimulated to cooperate and mutually help each other, which means that from a motivational perspective, cooperative goal structures create a situation in which group members can only attain their personal goals if the group is successful. Each team-member brings in certain competencies or perceptions and is important to achieve the shared goal.

ORIENT aims at intercultural learning through collaboration. Considering the theories and models outlined above, the following principles are reflected in the design and development of ORIENT (Slavin, 1995):

- Interacting with ORIENT provides the learner with the possibility to get into contact with members of other cultures (virtual and/or real);
- The collaborative task allows for equal status roles for learners;
- It specifies different tasks for different learners and makes sure that each team-member brings in certain competencies or perceptions and is important to achieve the shared goal;
- The collaborative task also emphasizes a collective development of a solution.

Learning Outcomes of Social and Emotional Learning and Collaborative Learning

As described above, the personal developmental process comprises changes on the cognitive, affective and behavioral level (Grosch & Leenen, 1998) and needs to connect learning experiences on all three levels. On the cognitive level, the learning individual for example takes over other perspectives of interpretation, which are partly oppositional and conflictive to earlier beliefs. This perspective-taking leads to a better understanding of the thoughts and feelings of members of other cultures, in general as well as in specific situations. Particularly in cross-cultural encounters, where uncertainty (as far as the differences between self and other are concerned) and the resulting fears and anxieties represent cognitive and affective challenges to the "appropriate" behavioral choices, social and emotional learning is a suitable approach, because of its explicit aim of developing people's skills "to recognize and manage their emotions, appreciate the perspective of others, establish positive goals, make responsible decisions, and handle interpersonal situations effectively" (Greenberg et al., 2003, p. 468).

One outcome of collaborative learning is group cohesion (e.g. Carron et al., 1985) which can be defined as degree of commitment of group members concerning common standards and aims and additionally as degree of mutual positive feelings (Forgas, 1994). Those mutual positive feelings act as a reinforcement of learning in a group and are positively related to the group's performance, in particular in small groups and when the collaborative task is attractive and engaging (e.g. Mullen & Copper, 1994). However, the danger that comes with high group cohesion is a high conformity among the members of the group, resulting in the fact that divergent and creative ideas are not verbalized ("group think", Janis, 1982). While ORIENT focuses on other group interaction characteristics such as active engagement and collaboration among a team of learners, group cohesion is a phenomenon that might become more important when established groups of learners who know each other well continue to interact with the software over a longer period of time. For assessing the quality of group interaction within ORIENT teams, dimensions like those suggested by Bales (1976) seem more appropriate, which categorizes communication according to its perceived interpersonal goal, such as expressing social information and emotions (positive / negative socio-emotional dimensions), or inquiring about the task or procedure at hand (task-oriented questions dimension and a task-oriented answers/solutions dimension).

Behavior-related categories that are relevant for collaboration in groups are – among others – helping one another, sharing resources, valuing others and treating them respectfully. Moreover, communicative competence (e.g. to be a good listener, a good speaker, to interpret gestures and facial expression adequately, to give constructive feedback), conflict behavior (e.g. to accept differences, to handle and solve a conflict), and emotional competence (e.g. to identify, express and control one's own feelings, to show compassion, to empathize) are crucial (Weidner, 2006). These variables will be drawn on when it comes to developing novel methodologies for evaluating the ORIENT learning outcomes.

Intercultural Learning

As was outlined earlier, ORIENT draws on contact theory (Allport, 1954), the idea that inter-group prejudice can be reduced through contact between the groups under specific conditions, such as equal status between the groups in the situation, common goals, intergroup cooperation, and the support of authorities, law, or custom. Contact theory is controversial and some work agues against it, but a recent survey of existing studies (Pettigrew & Tropp, 2006) gives support to it and it has been applied with some success to the integration of child refugees (Cameron et al., 2006).

But mere contact to other cultures does not allow for an understanding of the learning process behind intercultural learning. According to Gudykunst et al. (1977), taking over a third-culture-perspective fosters cultural awareness as precondition for intercultural competence, and allows analyzing differences and similarities. Beside (cognitive) uncertainty, anxiety is assumed to be crucial in the cultural learning and adaptation process (Gudykunst et al., 1977). Due to the latter approach of anxiety/uncertainty management (AUM) theory, individuals should learn about the impact of anxiety and uncertainty on the development of intercultural empathy and how to cope with anxiety and uncertainty in a different culture. But how can such intercultural empathy develop? Based on empathy models (Davis, 1996) and Bennett's (1993) model of intercultural sensitivity which are both described below, we suggest that intercultural empathy is the ability to understand and share the thoughts and feelings of members of other cultures.

As far as empathy is concerned, Davis (1996) distinguishes in his organizational model between several processes within the mind of an empathic observer which can be organized according to the cognitive effort they consume. As outcomes of these empathic processes, affective and non-affective outcomes are identified. Af-

Table 1. Bennett's Development Model of Intercultural Sensitivity.

Ethno-centric Stages			Ethno-relative stages		
Denial	**Defense**	**Minimization**	**Acceptance**	**Adaptation**	**Integration**
There is no reason to know something about foreign cultures	My own culture is superior to foreign cultures in many respects	All human beings are similar despite some superficial differences	Differences among people are not a problem, they are of interest for me	I use different standards for the evaluation of situations in foreign cultural contexts	I almost feel as comfortable in another culture as I do in my own culture

fective outcomes are emotions that emerge in the observer, which can be parallel to the emotions detected in the target (emotional contagion, e.g. resulting from motor mimicry or conditioning), or reactive to them (empathic concern or personal distress).

As far as intercultural learning in cross-cultural contexts is concerned, Bennett (1986, 1993) conceptualizes it as a process of personal development, with changing attitudes, feelings and reactions towards own and foreign culture. His Developmental Model of Intercultural Sensitivity (Table 1) as a dynamic approach reflects "how individuals construe their world in terms of dealing with cultural differences between themselves and others as members of distinct groups" (Hesse & Goebel, 2003, p. 2). Because of a missing empirical foundation, this model must be understood as phenomenological and thus as an idealized description of personality development. Bennett (1993) assumes a continuum of intercultural sensitivity. Six stages of development represent different ways of experiencing difference and every stage indicates a particular cognitive structure that is expressed in certain kinds of attitudes and behavior related to cultural difference. The development leads from a more ethno-centrist view, especially considering the own culture, towards ethno-relativism, being characterized by tolerant and respectful openness towards other cultures.

In ORIENT, Bennett's developmental model of intercultural sensitivity was used to describe the stages that guide learners through the interaction with ORIENT as a result from a careful design of the application. Along Bennett's continuum they pass the stages of denial, defense, minimization, acceptance, adaptation, and integration (see Table 1).

Denial of cultural differences may occur, when "physical or social isolation precludes any contact at all with significant cultural differences" (Bennett, 1986, p. 182). Another more common form of denial is parochialism, emerging from a lower degree of contact with other cultures. In extreme cases, cultural differences may be attributed to subhuman status. An individual at this level of sensitivity either doesn't perceive difference at all, or uses wide categories in perceiving difference (e.g. "us"/"them").

Defense as second stage is characterized by strategies such as denigrating differences ("negative stereotyping") or assuming cultural superiority. Cultural differences are identified, but they appear to threaten the centrality of one's world view.

Minimization means that cultural differences are recognized, but considered insignificant or trivial. Instead, commonness is underlined, so that the own world view doesn't need to be questioned. "Minimization may serve the function of preserving for these people a kind of "enlightened ethnocentrism" that sounds interculturally sensitive while allowing them to avoid the sense of incompetence which might arise from confronting cultural unknowns" (Bennett, 1986, p. 190).

A major shift from an ethnocentric to an ethno-relative approach can be seen in the subjective re-construal of difference as a "thing" to difference as a "process", which means that people don't "have" patterns, but rather "behave". Learners change their attitudes, towards more openness and tolerance, and intercultural behavioral competence develops.

Acceptance leads over to ethno-relativism. Instead of appraising cultural differences as positive or negative, they are simply acknowledged in a value-free way. Bennett (1993) differentiates two major levels of acceptance: The acceptance of behavioral difference (language, communication style, and nonverbal patterns) and the acceptance of underlying cultural value differences. Individuals at this stage of intercultural sensitivity enjoy recognizing and exploring difference.

Adaptation to difference as the "heart of intercultural communication" (Bennett, 1986, p. 185) relates to the ability to act ethno-relatively and so the ability to act outside of the own native world view. New skills appropriate to a different world view are acquired in an additive process. Adaptation allows for consciously shifting the frame of reference, because two or more cultural orientation systems have been internalized.

Integration of difference means to apply ethno-relativism to one's own identity. According to Bennett (1986), an individual operating at an integrative level can construe differences as processes, can adapt to these differences, and can construe him or herself in various cultural ways. Phenomena are evaluated as relative to the cultural context and cultural difference is considered as an essential and joyful aspect of life. The achievement of this level normally implies long and intense contacts to different cultures.

The development of ORIENT is based on Bennett´s model in that it serves as a reliable guide to the stages the participants pass through on their way to intercultural sensitivity. The "tasks" (based on the interaction with the characters) that the users are confronted with progress according to the different stages of the model, e.g. the first level of ORIENT focuses on the promotion of users' awareness that it is important to learn about a given different cultural background in order to interact successfully in an intercultural context. However, not all of the stages are addressed: The focus

Table 2. Intercultural Learning in ORIENT.

ORIENT	Stage
Reflection of the meaning of culture and the own culture previous to the role-play.	Acceptance
Role-play as in-world activities.	Acceptance, Adaptation
Reflection (during and after the role play) to enhance learning outcome through learning from each other's experiences: what happened (cognition), how do the characters feel (affect), how would you react (behavior)?	Adaptation

lies on the exploration of another (virtual) culture and on the reflection of similarities and differences between the own and the foreign culture (stages of acceptance and adaptation). ORIENT thus is designed to lead the learner to understand how to explore a culture and to understand that thoughts and feelings are culturally driven (see Table 2). A danger attached to such a limitation can be seen in the assumption that the learner has already internalized the earlier stages, i.e. that they are motivated to, curious about and open towards interacting with another culture.

Learning Outcomes of Intercultural Learning

Intercultural competence as a learning outcome is the basis for efficient and successful behavior in cross-cultural encounters (Barmeyer, 2003). According to Hesse and Goebel (2003), intercultural competence is not simply about acquisition of knowledge about another culture or the ability to behave appropriately in that culture – it is about understanding and internalizing appropriate behavior which should emerge naturally in the respective cultural context. Hence, culture-general components (e.g. coping with stress; suspension of overhasty appraisals; consciousness of the culture dependence of cognition, interpretation and action; familiarity with mechanisms of intercultural communication and with principles of acculturation) as well as culture-specific components and abilities provide the basis for intercultural competence; the latter are abilities such as to achieve competences in a target culture, to gain mastery in ethnographic knowledge, and to get to know the world view and behavior in a specific culture. Moreover, Grosch, Groß and Leenen (2002) describe interculturally relevant general personality characteristics, such as resilience, uncertainty- and ambiguity tolerance, cognitive flexibility, emotional resilience, and personal autonomy. These skills that are closely linked to social and emotional learning outcomes lead to the next learning outcome – intercultural empathy – as a concept combining social and emotional learning with the challenges of cross-cultural encounters.

Intercultural Empathy is the core learning outcome of ORIENT; it builds on the general ability to empathize (Davis, 1996) that constitute empathy in the mind of an empathic observer, but it poses more challenges in that it focuses on targets that are less similar than members of the home culture: Building empathy to those who are dissimilar to us not only personality-wise but culture-wise thus should represent a greater challenge than empathizing with members of our own group or culture (Similarity Principle, e.g. Byrne, 1971). The components included in intercultural empathy are outlined in the following:

Firstly, intercultural empathy builds on self-reflection and mental flexibility: being aware of one's own cultural identity as well as being able to temporarily suppress it in order to understand the impact of culture on others (cognitive aspect: resilience, cognitive flexibility, and personal autonomy).

Secondly, they involve stress and ambiguity tolerance: not being afraid of others that seem to be different (affective aspect: uncertainty- and ambiguity tolerance, and emotional resilience). Finally, they involve communicative skills: being able to feed the shared experiences back to others.

ORIENT addresses adolescents being confronted with peers and classmates that are dissimilar to them, but with whom they have to get along and effectively cooperate, for instance in the classroom context. Because it is easier to empathize with those you we perceive as similar to us (e.g. Davis, 1996; Byrne, 1971), ORIENT has to carefully balance the challenge inherent in the experience of dissimilarity between self and other in intercultural contexts with positive reactions to ORIENT that could be provided by perceived similarity between own experiences and the content presented in the software.

HOW EFFECTIVE ARE VIRTUAL LEARNING APPLICATIONS?

General Considerations

Virtual worlds which provide opportunities for exploration, practice, experiments, and construction, have an enriching function to traditional learning tools. They allow for experiential learning (Kolb, 1984) in safe and secure learning environments, in particular for social and emotional learning in complex social situations, without the social risks (e.g. stigmatization, doing harm or being harmed) that the learner faces in real social situations. ORIENT represents a possibility for learners to experience encounters and relations with members of another culture. Moreover, the depicted virtual cultures that struggle with their own intercultural conflicts can act as coping model to the users.

Nevertheless, there is not much empirical evidence yet concerning the relation of learning in virtual worlds and the effectiveness and efficiency of knowledge acquisition (Schwan & Buder, 2002). Moreno et al. (2001) deduce from Vygotskys (1978) assumption of the learning process being routed in social processes in which communication plays an essential role, that an agent can represent the necessary characteristics of a social agent in the learning process. Once a positive relationship is established between agent and learner, it enhances motivation and interest and hence constructive learning. Motivation is critical, because it fosters a more intense occupation with the material as well as transfer activities: "More motivated students try harder to make sense of the presented material than do less motivated students. They are also more likely to form a coherent mental model that enables them to apply what they learned to challenging new problem solving situations." (Moreno et al., 2001, p. 193). The social relationship between learner and agent is the key mechanism to foster interaction and promote learning within a computer-based learning system (Baylor & Ryu, 2003). Baylor (2001) summarizes the main factors which influence the learner's development of confidence in agents: agent believability, motivational attachment to the agent(s), agent competence, and agent trustworthiness. Moreover, to assure quality and quantity of knowledge acquisition, a specific pedagogical arrangement is necessary, such as to choose appropriate tasks, to structure the learning process, to ensure meaningful operation alternatives, and to support the learner through feedback and reflection challenges. Especially in explorative learning environments, specific goals facilitate an integrative and elaborative data processing. Structuring the learning experience in single, clear steps can be realized through an adequate choice of tasks on the one hand (different, temporally short learning episodes for cognitive release, higher motivation, and flexible knowledge representation), as well as through an adequate creation of the virtual reality on the other hand. The former is realized in ORIENT through single scenarios, in which the users need to solve different tasks and conflicts with the Sprytes. However, to ensure the learning outcomes, the process of interacting with a virtual world should be embedded in sessions that serve to prepare and reflect upon the experiences in the virtual learning environment. Therefore, reflection circles before and after the role play are highly recommended to complement the ORIENT learning experience. A facilitator can support the learners by stimulating the discussions when needed, e.g. through helpful questions. Additionally, support is integrated in the virtual world via the ORA-CLE, which provides further information and help for the user. Apart from the carefully designed structure of the application and the inclusion of reflection cycles, the virtual learning environment offers innovative reinforcement for getting into contact with members of other cultures: exciting and highly activating interaction devices such as the WiiMote controller, a game mat or RFID technology will be used by the user to interact with the virtual world.

Results of Evaluating an Early Orient Prototype

ORIENT poses a number of different issues for evaluation: the user perspective focuses on a successful outcome in saving the planet while from the design team perspective, success involves both a resulting change in intercultural awareness and behavior (the pedagogical and psychological impact) as well as a high degree of user immersion, engagement and suspension of disbelief (interaction and technical impact). As has been discussed in the context of pervasive games (Vavoula et al., 2006), the use of the real world as part of the application and of novel interaction technology make some traditional forms of evaluation, especially of usability in its narrow sense, somewhat problematic. In the wider sense, the presence of a large number of interacting factors make it hard to evaluate which part of the overall design is responsible for which specific effects.

Evaluation of ORIENT itself is necessarily group-based and focused on qualitative rather than quantitative responses. The instruments used are incorporated into the role-play as Space Command debriefing and as support for the users' "mission" to gain greater awareness of the Spryte culture rather than being presented as an explicit evaluation. For instance, to show they are "qualified" for the internship in general and this mission in particular, participants fill in an applicant's form (demographic data) and the Cultural Intelligence Scale. This approach seeks to capture relevant data in an interesting and engaging way for users and to extend their sense of their role in the ORIENT scenarios.

ORIENT was evaluated in Germany and the UK with four groups in the first and three in the second, each interacting with ORIENT for around two hours. The German groups were all girls aged 13-14, while the UK groups included 6 boys and 3 girls and were somewhat younger, aged 12-13. A set of questionnaires were used, listed in Table 1, which were customized to fit in with the story-world being used as Space Command briefings and debriefings. Interaction behavior within the group of learners was observed in real-time: The technical evaluation team sat behind the team with two laptops and the projector, while the psychological evaluation team members sat in left and right corners of the room filling in the ORAT (Orient Rating process for the Assessment of the Team) and taking notes. The interaction was also videotaped by two cameras and attached microphones, placed in the remaining two corners of the room, directed towards the participants.

ORAT was used to assess whether ORIENT fosters cooperation, with team members coordinating their actions in order to reach their common goal of learning more about the Sprytes. On the whole teams were rated by independent observers as showing a high degree of solution orientation in their activities (UK and German groups), also a high degree of communication related to the content of the application, interaction, and cooperation (UK groups more than German groups).

In post-interaction discussions learners reported quite positive feedback about how they felt they had done. The post-interaction questionnaires showed differences between the UK and German groups in their knowledge of and attitude towards the Sprytes. The German girls found Sprytes friendlier, less advanced, younger, and more 'together' compared to their own culture, whereas the UK teenagers saw Sprytes as less friendly, more advanced, older though also more 'together' than their own culture. The UK groups felt significantly more negative (e.g. more threatened, more nervous, more alert, etc.) when interacting with the Sprytes than the German teenagers did. Finally, one significant difference from the Orient Evaluation Questionnaire was that the UK groups thought Sprytes considered them enemies whereas the German teenagers thought Sprytes considered them friends. This may of course have been related to gender rather than culture as only the UK groups contained boys. Despite the large similarities between the learners and the virtual culture of the Sprytes, all groups managed to see some similarities as well as differences between themselves and the Sprytes, suggesting the basis for empathy exists. The conclusion of this evaluation was that ORIENT lays the basis for the development of intercultural empathy. Far more story content needs to be developed however and the personalities of individual Sprytes need to be clearly established, as well as conflicts between them in which teenagers can intervene. The interaction technologies used were both a plus and a minus: they did indeed engage, but required far too much concentration on interaction mechanics, distracting from the Sprytes and their story. More intuitive and less cognitively demanding interaction is a priority in the further development of ORIENT.

CONCLUSION

The ORIENT application is an innovative character-based educational role-play aimed at developing inter-cultural empathy in participating users. A culture-specific character architecture has been developed based solidly on theories of cultural dimensioning and intergroup interaction. Initial evaluation shows that this architecture can meet the demands of the social process and story-world of ORIENT and that, combined with the novel interaction modalities discussed above, it offers a new approach to an increasingly important area of Personal and Social Education in which beliefs, attitudes and behaviors are necessarily the pedagogical focus. Evaluation has raised the interesting question of the relationship between personality and culture in synthetic character models and interaction, and further work will be carried out investigating this.

ACKNOWLEDGMENT

This work was partially supported by European Community (EC) and is currently funded by the eCIRCUS project IST-4-027656-STP with university partners Heriot-Watt, Hertfordshire, Sunderland, Warwick, Bamberg, Augsburg, Wuerzburg plus INESC-ID and Interagens. The authors are solely responsible for the content of this publication. It does not represent the opinion of the EC, and the EC is not responsible for any use that might be made of data appearing therein.

REFERENCES

Allbeck, J. M., & Badler, N. I. (2004). Creating Embodied Agents With Cultural Context. In Payr, S., & Trappl, R. (Eds.), *Agent Culture: Human-Agent Interaction in a Multicultural World* (pp. 107–126). London: Lawrence Erlbaum Associates.

Allport, G. W. (1954). *The nature of prejudice*. Reading, MA: Addison-Wesley.

Andersen, P. A. (2000). Explaining intercultural differences in nonverbal communication. In Samovar, L. A., & Porter, R. E. (Eds.), *Intercultural communication: A reader*. Belmont, CA: Wadsworth.

Auernheimer, G. (2003). *Einführung in die interkulturelle Pädagogik* [Introduction to Intercultural Pedagogy]. Darmstadt, Germany: Wiss. Buchges.

Aylett, R. S., Dias, J., & Paiva, A. (2006). An affectively-driven planner for synthetic characters. In *Proceedings of ICAPS, 2006*, 2–10.

Bailenson, J. N., Blascovich, J., & Guadagno, R. E. (2008). Self representations in immersive virtual environments. *Journal of Applied Social Psychology, 38*(11), 2673–2690. doi:10.1111/j.1559-1816.2008.00409.x

Bales, R. F. (1976). *Interaction process analysis: A method for the study of small groups*. Chicago: University Press.

Bandura, A. (1973). *Aggression: a social learning analysis*. Englewood Cliffs, NJ: Prentice-Hall.

Bandura, A., & Adams, N. E. (1977). Analysis of self-efficacy theory of behavioral change. *Cognitive Therapy and Research, 1*(4), 287–310. doi:10.1007/BF01663995

Barmeyer, C. (2003). Interkulturelles Coaching. [Intercultural Coaching] In Rauen, C. (Ed.), *Handbuch Coaching* (pp. 241–272). Göttingen: Hogrefe.

Baylor, A. L. (2001). Permutations of control: Cognitive considerations for agent-based learning environments. *Journal of Interactive Learning Research, 12*(4), 403–425.

Baylor, A. L., & Ryu, J. (2003). *Evidence that multiple agents facilitate greater learning. International Artificial Intelligence in Education*. Sydney, Australia: AI-ED.

Bem, S. (1993). *The lenses of gender*. New Haven, CT: Yale University Press.

Bennett, M. (1986). A developmental approach to training for Intercultural Sensitivity. *International Journal of Intercultural Relations, 10*(2), 179–195. doi:10.1016/0147-1767(86)90005-2

Bennett, M. (1998). Intercultural communication: a current perspective. In Bennett, M. (Ed.), *Basic Concepts of Intercultural Communication*. Yarmouth, MA: Intercultural Press.

Bennett, M. J. (1993). Towards enthnorelativism: A developmental model of intercultural sensitivity. In Paige, M. (Ed.), *Education for the intercultural experience*. Yarmouth, MA: Intercultural Press.

Borde, D. (2007). Psychosoziale Potentiale und Belastungen der Migranten – globale, institutionelle und individuelle Perspektiven. [Psycho-social potentials and burdens of migrants – global, instituational and individual perspectives] In Borde, D., & David, M. (Eds.), *Migration und psychische Gesundheit*. Frankfurt am Main, Germany: Mabuse.

Borzak, L. (1981) (ed.). *Field study: A source book for experiential learning*. Beverly Hills, CA: Sage Publications.

Byrne, D. (1971). *The attraction paradigm*. New York: Academic Press.

Cameron, L., Rutland, A., Brown, R., & Douch, R. (2006). Changing children's intergroup attitudes toward refugees: Testing different models of extended contact. *Child Development, 77*(5), 1208–1219. doi:10.1111/j.1467-8624.2006.00929.x

Carron, A. V., Widmeyer, W. N., & Brawley, L. R. (1985). The development of an instrument to assess cohesion in sport teams: The Group Environment Questionnaire. *Journal of Sport Psychology, 7*, 244–266.

Cassell, J., Sullivan, J., Prevost, S., & Churchill, E. (2000). *Embodied Conversational Agents*. Cambridge, MA: MIT Press.

Core, M., Traum, D., Lane, H. C., Swartout, W., Gratch, J., van Lent, M., & Marsella, S. (2006). Teaching negotiation skills through practice and reflection with vVirtual humans. *Simulation, 82*(11), 685–701. doi:10.1177/0037549706075542

Davis, M. H. (1996). *Empathy – a social psychological approach.* Madison, WI: Brown & Benchmark Publishers.

de Rosis, F., Pelachaud, C., & Poggi, I. (2004). Transcultural Believability in Embodied Agents: A Matter of Consistent Adaptation. In Payr, S., & Trappl, R. (Eds.), *Agent Culture: Human-Agent Interaction in a Multicultural World* (pp. 75–106). London: Lawrence Erlbaum Associates.

Dias, J., & Paiva, A. (2005). Feeling and reasoning: a computational model. In *Proceedings of the 12th Portuguese Conference on Artificial Intelligence*, EPIA 2005 (pp. 127-140). Berlin: Springer.

Dörner, D. (2003). The mathematics of emotions. In F. Detje, D.Dörner, & H. Schaub (Eds.), *Proceedings of the Fifth International Conference on Cognitive Modeling* (pp. 75–79). Bamberg, Germany: Universitäts-Verlag.

Elias, M. J., Zins, J. E., Weissberg, R. P., Frey, K. S., Greenberg, M. T., & Haynes, N. M. (1997). *Promoting social and emotional learning: Guidelines for educators.* Alexandria, VA: Association for Supervision and Curriculum Development.

Forgas, J. (1994). *Soziale Interaktion und Kommunikation* [Social interaction and communication]. Weinheim, Germany: Beltz.

Gratch, J., & Marsella, S. (2005). Evaluating a computational model of emotion. *Autonomous Agents and Multi-Agent Systems, 11*(1), 23–43. doi:10.1007/s10458-005-1081-1

Greenberg, M. T., Weissberg, R. P., O'Brien, M. U., Zins, J. E., Fredericks, L., Resnik, H., & Elias, M. J. (2003). Enhancing School-Based Prevention and Youth Development Through Coordinated Social, Emotional and Academic Learning. *The American Psychologist, 58*, 466–474. doi:10.1037/0003-066X.58.6-7.466

Grosch, H., Groß, A., & Leenen, W. R. (2002). Interkulturelle Kompetenz in der sozialen Arbeit [Intercultural competence in social work]. In G. Auernheimer (ed.), *Interkulturelle Kompetenz und pädagogische Professionalität.* Opladen, Germany: Leske + Budrich.

Grosch, H., & Leenen, W. R. (1998). Bausteine zur Grundlegung interkulturellen Lernens [Modules for intercultural learning]. In *Interkulturelles Lernen. Arbeitshilfen für politische Bildung.* Bonn, Germany: Bundeszentrale für politische Bildung.

Gudykunst, W. B., Hammer, M. R., & Wiseman, R. (1977). An analysis of an integrated approach to cross-cultural training. *International Journal of Intercultural Relations, 1*, 99–109. doi:10.1016/0147-1767(77)90045-1

Gudykunst, W. B., & Mody, B. (2002). *Handbook of international and intercultural communication*. Thousand Oaks, CA: Sage Publications.

Hall, E. T. (1990). *The silent language*. New York: Anchor Press.

Hall, E. T. (2001). *Understanding cultural differences*. Yarmouth, MA: Intercultural Press.

Hall, L., Vala, M., Hall, M., Webster, M., Woods, S., Gordon, A., & Aylett, R. (2006). FearNot's appearance: Reflecting children's expectations and perspectives. In J. Gratch, M. Young, R. Aylett, D. Ballin, & P. Olivier (eds.), *6th International Conference, IVA 2006* (pp. 407-419). Berlin: Springer.

Herskovits, M. (1955). *Cultural anthropology*. New York: Knopf.

Hesse, H.-G., & Göbel, K. (2003). *Evaluation and quantitative methods in global learning: A contribution from the field of intercultural sensitivity*. Paper presented at the Global Education Network Europe Seminar: Starting practice and theory in global education. Improving quality and raising standards through evaluation. University of Erlangen-Nürnberg, 29.03.2003.

Hinsch, R., & Pfingsten, U. (2002). *Gruppentraining Sozialer Kompetenzen (GSK)* [Group Training of Social Competencies]. Weinheim, Germany: BeltzPVU.

Hofstede, G. (1979). Value systems in forty countries. In Eckensberger, L., Lonner, W., & Poortinga, Y. (Eds.), *Cross-cultural contributions to psychology*. Amsterdam: Swets and Zeitlinger.

Hofstede, G. (1991). *Cultures and Organizations*. Thousand Oaks, CA: Sage Publications.

Hofstede, G. (2001). *Culture's consequences: Comparing values, behaviors, institution, and organizations across nations*. Thousand Oaks, CA: Sage Publications.

Hofstede, G., & Bond, M. (1984). Hofstede's culture dimensions. *Journal of Cross-Cultural Psychology, 15*, 417–433. doi:10.1177/0022002184015004003

Huntington, S. P. (2000). Cultures count (Foreword). In Harrison, L. E., & Huntington, S. (Eds.), *Culture Matters. How Values Shape Human Progress*. New York: Basic Books.

Inkeles, A., & Levinson, J. (1969). National character: The study of modal personality and sociocultural systems. In Lindzey, G., & Aronson, E. (Eds.), *Handbook of social psychology* (*Vol. 4*, pp. 418–506). Reading, MA: Addison-Wesley.

Isbister, K. (2004). Building bridges through the unspoken: Embodied agents to facilitate intercultural communication. In Payr, S., & Trappl, R. (Eds.), *Agent Culture: Human-Agent Interaction in a Multicultural World*. London: Lawrence Erlbaum Associates.

Janis, I. (1982). *Groupthink* (2nd ed.). Boston: Houghton-Mifflin.

Johnson, D. W., Johnson, R. T., & Holubec, E. J. (1993). *Cooperation in the classroom*. Edina, MN: Interaction Book Company.

Kanther, M. (2001). *Interkulturelles Lernen* [Intercultural learning]. Stuttgart, Germany: ibidem-Verlag.

Keesing, R. (1974). Theories of culture. *Annual Review of Anthropology*, *3*, 73–97. doi:10.1146/annurev.an.03.100174.000445

Kenny, P., Parsons, T., Gratch, J., Leuski, A., & Rizzo, A. (2007) Virtual patients for clinical therapist skills training. In *Proceedings of the 7th International Conference on Intelligent Virtual Agents* (pp. 197-210). Berlin: Springer.

Kluckhohn, C. (1962). *Culture and Behavior*. New York: The Free Press of Glencoe.

Koda, T., Rehm, M., & André, E. (2008). Cross-cultural evaluations of avatar facial expressions designed by Western Designers. In *Proceedings of Intelligent Virtual Agents IVA*, *2008*, 245–252.

Kolb, D. A. (1984). *Experiential learning: Experience as the source of learning and development*. Englewood Cliffs, NJ: Prentice Hall.

Kriegel, M., Lim, M. L., Nazir, A., Aylett, R., Cawsey, A., Enz, S., & Zoll, C. (2008). Culture-personality based affective model. Enculturating conversational interfaces by socio-cultural aspects of communication. In *Workshop on IUI 2008*, Canary Islands, Jan 13, 2008.

Kroeber, A., & Kluckhohn, C. (1952). *Culture*. New York: Meridian Books.

Lazarus, R. (1991). *Emotion and adaptation*. New York: Oxford University Press.

Leichtenstern, K., André, E., & Vogt, T. (2007). Role assignment via physical mobile interaction techniques in mobile multi-user applications for children. In *Proceedings of the Ambient Intelligence AmI*, *2007*, 38–54.

Lim, M. Y., Dias, J., Aylett, R., & Paiva, A. (2009) Intelligent NPCs for Educational Role Play Game. In *Proceedings of Agents for Games and Simulation Workshop, AAMAS 09*, Budapest, Hungary, May 10-15, 2009.

Lohaus, A., Jerusalem, M., & Klein-Heßling, J. (2006). *Gesundheitsförderung im Kindes- und Jugendalter* [Health promotion in education of children and adolescents]. Göttingen, Germany: Hogrefe.

Mascarenhas, S., Dias, J., Afonso, N., Enz, S., & Paiva, A. (2009) Using Rituals to Express Cultural Differences in Synthetic Characters. In *Proceedings of AAMAS 2009*, Budapest, May 10-15, 2009.

Moreno, R., Mayer, R. E., Spires, H., & Lester, J. (2001). The case for social agency in computer-based teaching: Do students learn more deeply when they interact with animated pedagogical agents? *Cognition and Instruction*, *19*, 177–213. doi:10.1207/S1532690XCI1902_02

Mullen, B., & Copper, C. (1994). The Relation between Group Cohesiveness and Performance: An Integration. *Psychological Bulletin*, *115*, 210–227. doi:10.1037/0033-2909.115.2.210

Ortony, A., Clore, G., & Collins, A. (1988). *The cognitive structure of emotions*. Cambridge: Cambridge University Press. doi:10.1017/CBO9780511571299

Paiva, A., Dias, J., Aylett, R., Woods, S., Hall, L., & Zoll, C. (2005). Learning by feeling: Evoking empathy with synthetic characters. *Applied Artificial Intelligence*, *19*, 235–266. doi:10.1080/08839510590910165

Pettigrew, T. F., & Tropp, L. R. (2006). A meta-analytic test of intergroup contact theory. *Journal of Personality and Social Psychology*, *90*, 751–783. doi:10.1037/0022-3514.90.5.751

Rehm, M., André, E., Bee, N., Endrass, B., Wissner, M., Nakano, Y., et al. (2007). The CUBE-G approach – Coaching culture-specific nonverbal behavior by virtual agents. In I. Mayer, & H. Mastik (eds.), *Organizing and Learning through Gaming and Simulation. Proceedings of ISAGA 2007,* (pp. 313-321). Delft: Eburon.

Roschelle, J., & Teasley, S. D. (1995). The construction of shared knowledge in collaborative problem solving. In O'Malley, C. E. (Ed.), *Computer-supported Collaborative Learning* (pp. 69–197). Berlin: Springer. doi:10.1007/978-3-642-85098-1_5

Rossen, B., Lok, B., Johnsen, K., Lind, S., & Deladisma, A. (2008). Virtual Humans Elicit Skin-Tone Bias Consistent with Real-World Skin-Tone Biases. In *Proceedings of Intelligent Virtual Agents IVA, 2008*, 237–244.

Rotter, J. B. (1954). *Social learning and clinical psychology*. New York: Prentice-Hall. doi:10.1037/10788-000

Rowe, J., McQuiggan, S., & Lester, J. (2007). Narrative Presence in Intelligent Learning Environments. In *Working Notes of the 2007 AAAI Fall Symposium on Intelligent Narrative Technologies* (pp. 126–133). Arlington, VA.

Schulz von Thun, F. (1001). *Miteinander reden 1: Störungen und Klärungen* [Talking to each other 1: interferences and clarifications]. Reinbek, Germany: Rowohlt.

Schwan, S., & Buder, J. (2002). Lernen als Wissenserwerb in virtuellen Realitäten. [Learning as knowledge acquisition in virtual realities] In Bente, G., Krämer, N., & Petersen, A. (Eds.), *Virtuelle Realitäten* (pp. 109–129). Göttingen, Germany: Hogrefe.

Seligman, M. E. P. (1972). Learned helplessness. *Annual Review of Medicine, 23*, 407–412. doi:10.1146/annurev.me.23.020172.002203

Slavin, R. E. (1995). *Cooperative Learning: theory, research and practice*. Boston: Allyn and Bacon.

Triandis, H. C. (1989). The self and social behavior in differing cultural contexts. *Psychological Review, 96*(3), 506–520. doi:10.1037/0033-295X.96.3.506

Tuckman, B. (1965). Developmental sequence in small groups. *Psychological Bulletin, 63*, 384–399. doi:10.1037/h0022100

Turner, J. C. (1987). *Rediscovering the social group*. Oxford, UK: Blackwell.

Vavoula, G., Meek, J., Sharples, M., Lonsdale, P., & Rudman, P. (2006). A lifecycle approach to evaluating MyArtSpace. In S. Hsi, Kinshuk, T. Chan, & D. Sampson (Eds.), *Proceedings of the 4th IEEE International Workshop on Wireless and Mobile Technologies in Education (WMUTE 2006)* (pp. 18-22). Athens, Greece: IEEE Computer Society.

Vygotsky, L. S. (1978). *Mind in society: The development of higher psychological processes*. Cambridge, MA: Harvard University Press.

Weidner, M. (2006). *Kooperatives Lernen im Unterricht* [Cooperative learning in school]. Seelze, Germany: Erhard Friedrich Verlag.

ADDITIONAL READING

Aylett, R., Paiva, A., Woods, S., Hall, L., & Zoll, C. (2005). Expressive Characters in Anti-Bullying Education. In Canamero, L., & Aylett, R. (Eds.), *Animating Expressive Characters for Social Interaction* (pp. 161–176). Amsterdam: John Benjamins.

Aylett, R. S., & Louchart, S. (2003). Towards a narrative theory of VR. *Virtual Reality Journal (Special Edition on Storytelling in Virtual Environments), 7* (1), 2-9.

Brna, P., Martins, A., & Cooper, B. (1999). My first story: Support for learning to Write Stories. In Cumming, G., Okamoto, T., & Gomez, L. (Eds.), *Advanced Research in Computers and Communications in Education* (*Vol. 1*, pp. 335–341). Amsterdam: IOS.

Dautenhahn, K. (1996). Embodiment in animals and artifacts. In *AAAI FS Embodied Cognition and Action* (pp. 27–32). AAAI Press.

de Vries, G. (1997). Involvement of School-aged Children in the Design Process. *Interaction*, *4*(2), 41–42.

Enz, S., & Brosch, S. (2008). Autonomous Agents with Personality. *International Journal of Psychology*, *43*(3/4).

Enz, S., Zoll, C., Vannini, N., Schneider, W., Hall, L., Paiva, A., & Aylett, R. (2007). E – Motional Learning in Primary Schools: FearNot! An Anti-bullying Intervention Based on Virtual Role-play with Intelligent Synthetic Characters. *Electronic Journal e-Learning, 6(2), 111 – 118.*

Hall, L., Woods, S., Dautenhahn, K., & Wolke, D. (2007). Implications of gender differences for the development of animated characters for the study of bullying behavior. *Computers in Human Behavior*, *23*(1), 770–786. doi:10.1016/j.chb.2004.11.018

Ho, W. C., & Watson, S. (2006). Autobiographic knowledge for believable virtual characters. In *Intelligent Virtual Agents 2006* (pp. 383–394). Springer. doi:10.1007/11821830_31

Louchart, S., & Aylett, R. (2004). Narrative theory and emergent interactive narrative. *International Journal of Continuing Engineering Education and Lifelong Learning*, *14*(6), 506–518. doi:10.1504/IJCEELL.2004.006017

Lyons, E., & Chryssochoou, X. (2000). Cross-cultural research methods. In Breakwell, G. M., & Hammond, S. a. (Eds.), *Research methods in psychology* (2nd ed., pp. 134–146). London, England: Sage Publishers Ltd.

KEY TERMS AND DEFINITIONS

Anxiety/Uncertainty: Strategies to cope with uncertainty and anxiety when being faced management with highly ambiguous situations, e.g. cross-cultural situations

Collaborative Learning: A specific form of small human group-education, which emphasizes and structures the social processes while learning

Emotional Learning: Their ability to integrate thinking, feeling, and behaving to achieve important life tasks"

Ethno-Centric: Learners are centered in their own cultural ways and habits.

Ethno-Relative: Learners change their attitudes, towards more openness and tolerance, and intercultural behavioral competence develops

FAtiMA: An architecture for the building of agents minds Social & Elias et al. (1997): "process through which children enhance

ORA-CLE: A device to help the players of ORIENT to structure their experience in the virtual world

ORAT: An assessment tool for behavioral observation of group interaction, developed by the project team.

ORIENT: A software prototype developed by the EU FP6 project eCIRCUS to help teenagers to overcome integration problems

Role-Play: A technique to acquire or perform behavior that is currently not available, either because it was not yet learned, or – if it has been learned – is for some reason not executed. It thus aims at the acquisition and rehearsal of new behavior as well as at the actualization of already acquired behavior

WiiMote: An interaction device to interact with virtual environments and computer games

ENDNOTE

1 In fact, both terms are often used interchangeably.

This work was previously published in Cases on Transnational Learning and Technologically Enabled Environments, edited by Siran Mukerji and Purnendu Tripathi, pp. 65-88, copyright 2010 by Information Science Reference (an imprint of IGI Global).

Chapter 15
Learning in Cross-Cultural Online MBA Courses:
Perceptions of Chinese Students

Xiaojing Liu
Indiana University Bloomington, USA

Richard J. Magjuka
Indiana University Bloomington, USA

EXECUTIVE SUMMARY

The rapid improvement in online communication technologies and the globalization of the economy have made offering transnational courses in online learning programs a popular trend. This chapter reports the findings of a case study that investigated the perceptions of international students regarding cultural challenges in their learning experiences during an online MBA program. The study revealed that international students faced cultural barriers, including time management, transition to different instruction styles, time zone differences, case-based learning, and academic integrity, which affected their engagement in online MBA courses. Recommendations are made at the end of the chapter on how to improve the quality of the international students' learning experiences in cross-cultural learning environments.

DOI: 10.4018/978-1-4666-1885-5.ch015

SITUATION BACKGROUND

Introduction

The advancement of Internet, computer-mediated communication and Web 2.0 technologies have made the world increasingly mutual and interconnected. These technologies have created an interactive learning environment, which allows students from multiple cultures to learn collaboratively and share knowledge. In his most recent book, Curt Bonk (2009) listed a variety of learning technologies that have helped to make the world of today a different educational environment than it was 10 or 20 years ago. These technologies include e-learning and blended learning, open source and free software, leveraged resources and open courseware, learning object repositories and portals, open information communities, electronic collaboration, alternate reality and real-time mobility and portability (Wadholm, 2009).

Business schools have been active leaders in online education. With the movement toward global education and increased competition in the domestic e-learning market, the delivery of blended or online international MBA programs has become a strategic mission for many business schools. Developing countries in East Asia, including China and India, have been the most attractive locations in which for many American schools to offer online degrees due to their rapid rise in economic development and enormous demands for higher education access.

Pinhey (1998) stated that the Internet has made possible a global education curriculum. However, institutions and instructors must be prepared to effectively deal with the demands of an international setting in order to be successful in their outreach to students abroad. Research has documented that students from different cultures may have varying levels of compatibility with certain learning styles, different social expectations of the instructor and student roles and different levels of cognitive abilities (Hofstede, 1984; Hannon, & D'Netto, 2007). Understanding and tolerance of cultural differences are needed in order to reach a successful learning outcome in a global learning environment (Lanham & Zhou, 2003; Hannon, & D'Netto, 2007).

Learning in a cross-cultural online environment is not without challenges. Shattuck (2005) observed that highly interactive learning environments cannot reduce online learners' feelings of "marginalization, or, sometimes even alienation" from the dominant American learner group (p. 186). Research suggests that cultural barriers affect the success of online students in distance education programs (Walker-Fernandez, 1999). For example, when pedagogical values in one culture are inappropriate in another, students may question knowledge or the merit of participation, may challenge the teacher's views and become disenfranchised in a learning process that does not fit their worldview (Australian Flexible Learning, 2004). As such, a distance education program needs to devise strategies by which to deal with these challenges in order to provide a satisfactory learning experience for global learners. However, due to limited published research "on the cultural aspects of online learning and teaching" (Gunawardena, Wilson, & Nolla, 2003, p. 770), online educators lack empirical evidence to guide their practices in delivering cross-cultural programs.

In this chapter, we will describe a case study that was used to investigate the perceptions of international students in an online MBA program regarding their transnational learning experiences. In particular, we explored and identified potential cultural barriers that may have affected the performance and satisfaction of the international student population. Two major questions were addressed in this study:

- What challenges do Chinese students perceive in a cross-cultural learning environment?
- What features do Chinese students recommend in order to design a culturally inclusive global course?

Cultural Challenges and Online Learning

Cultural discontinuity is defined as "a lack of [a] contextual match between the conditions of learning and a learner's socio-cultural experiences" (Wilson, 2001, p. 52). Jacobson (1996) recognized that learners experience cultural discontinuity when "outside of familiar meaning systems" and in "new" cultures, and, as such, "find themselves in situations where familiar ways of interpreting and acting are not reliable, yet others' ways of interpreting and acting are not fully accessible" (Jacobson, 1996, p. 16). Cultural discontinuity creates barriers that hinder students from being able to learn in a dominant culture different from their own culture. For example, research has found that different cultural communication patterns increased miscommunication, and that the greater the perception of cultural differences between the participants in an activity, the greater the incidents of miscommunication (Reeder, Macfadyen, & Chase, 2004).

Walker-Fernandez (1999) found that culture plays an important role in cross-cultural encounters for students in American distance education programs. The coupling of cultural perception differences with transactional distance creates a potential barrier to communication that could affect short-term success in distance education programs. In order to overcome this barrier, students cite the need for good communication as being essential in meeting students' needs, especially communication that is supportive, full of detail and context and from a primary source (i.e., directly from the professor). Some students appear to have developed "extended identities" which means that they acculturated in varying degrees in order to be successful in their program, but that their local cultural identity was not compromised in any way.

The language barrier has been a prevalent theme reported in existing studies of cross-cultural learning experiences of Chinese students in online education programs (Ku & Lohr, 2003; Gunawardena et al., 2007). Tu's (2001) study found that although all foreign students in the American must pass English competency tests before they can matriculate into American colleges, the Chinese students still found that using English to communicate with others was the major barrier affecting their communication and learning. Composing a message was a long and tedious process for these students due to unfamiliar communication forms and concerns about saving face. However, studies have also found that the Chinese students believe that they face fewer language barriers when taking asynchronous online courses than when taking face-to-face courses because of the increased time to read and understand course material as well as the dominant focus on writing (Zhao & McDougall, 2008).

Chinese students rely as heavily on direct feedback from online instructors in online courses as in traditional settings (Ku, & Lohr, 2003). Ku and Lohr (2003) found that Chinese students requested more initial support from their instructors in order to boost their confidence and motivation in online learning.

On the other hand, Zhao and McDougall (2008) found that Chinese students thought that the authoritative image of the instructor might limit the range of their thinking and prevent them from writing messages that conflict with the instructor's view. However, these same students also believe that the online environment reduces the instructor's apparent authority and, as such, they may present more contradictory opinions in class discussions.

As Chinese students tend to be conservative, modest and face-saving they often face challenges associated with these traits in online discussions. Research suggests that Chinese students are as much concerned with face saving in the online environment despite the absence of face-to-face contact and non-verbal cues as in a traditional classroom. Thompson and Ku (2005) observed that participants were less critical and opinionated in online discussions than their American peers. Tu (2001) found that Chinese students were concerned that the potential bad quality of their writing would cause them to lose face by conveying a bad impression when corresponding with an instructor or would demonstrate a lack of respect for the instructor. In addition, they often hesitated to ask questions and were reluctant to voice their opinions when their opinions conflicted with those of other participants (Zhao & McDougall, 2008).

However, studies also suggested that some Chinese students modified their personality characteristics and behaved differently online. They became more active and "talked more" (i.e., posted more messages) in their online courses than in their face-to-face courses. Most of the students stated that they might insist on and argue for their own opinions in an online learning environment than they would in a face-to-face learning environment (Zhao & McDougall, 2008).

Being ignorant of or misunderstanding Western social life or academic culture of education influenced international students' engagements in asynchronous online learning. For example, Goodfellow, Lea, Gonzalez and Mason (2001) found that unfamiliarity with the linguistic and academic culture of the UK negatively influenced non-native English speaking students' successes and academic performances.

In a study, Zhao and McDougall (2008) found that the Chinese students misconstrued some discussion messages, did not know when it was appropriate to "cut in" during a discussion and could not understand metaphors drawn from local social life due to their lack knowledge about Canadian social life. Consequently, they believed that they wrote fewer messages to the discussion board than they would have if they had understood Canadian culture better. The reduced participation affected their perception of their social presence, making them feel alienated from their learning community (Zhao & McDougall, 2008).

Cultures differ in regard to thinking patterns in the form of reasoning and approaches to problem solving. Depending on the worldviews and cultures through which the learners filter their perceptions, they may perceive the same object in different ways according to their culturally dominant thinking pattern (Bentley, Tinney, & Chia, 2005). Gunawardena et al. (2003) wrote that a noticeable characteristic of the Anglo-American communication style is that it is direct, which occurs because Anglo-American individuals think in linear patterns, whereas the characteristic of Eastern culture is circular, which occurs because individuals from Eastern culture tend to think in circular patterns. Differences in thinking patterns can lead to misunderstandings in intercultural communication and education because these differences influence students in how they interact with course content, in the assumptions that designers make in designing course content and in the students' expectations about what the courses offer and how to successfully complete them (Bentley et al., 2005).

SETTING THE STAGE

The case setting selected was an online MBA program at an accredited business school at a large Midwestern university. This program was founded in 1999 with only 14 students. The number of the students has subsequently increased more than 100 times. The majority of the students in the program are working professionals who wish to pursue a MBA degree in order to prepare for future career advancement.

During the 2007-2008 academic year, the program offered MBA and M.S. degree programs, as well as certificate programs. The student body contains approximately 1500 students, geographically located in every region of North America and around the world. The instructors, drawn from the business school, are all full-time, tenured faculty members.

As the demand for online MBA degrees becomes increasingly global, the program management felt the need to develop strategies to establish international partnerships with global companies in order to enroll increasing numbers of international students. This need arose for two reasons. First, the increasingly competitive domestic e-learning market put pressure on MBA student enrollment. Second, the globalization and internationalization of business industries demanded MBA students' gain skills that focus on dealing with cross-cultural issues in the business process. A cross-cultural learning environment provides opportunities for students to develop intercultural competencies.

In 2007, two international programs were established in partnership with two large Chinese companies. The students recruited for these programs were mainly from middle-level management groups in the companies who wished to pursue an advanced degree. They applied for the program through procedures similar to those used by other online MBA students in the program. They had to pass the TOFEL (Test of English as a Foreign Language) and GMAT (Graduate Management Admission Exam) exams in order to achieve an adequate level of English proficiency to enroll in the program. Except for the in-residence weeks, the enrolled students completed took all of the courses asynchronously online with the American students.

Except for the courses offered during the required on-campus visit, the courses were delivered entirely through the online ANGEL course management system. Similar to other MBA programs, case-based learning (CBL) and virtual teams were the two major instruction methods used in the online courses at the time of the study. Approximately half of the courses used CBL and four-fifths used virtual teams. Online asynchronous discussions were used in four-fifths of the courses as well. Email communications, announcements and participation in the asynchronous or synchronous discussions were the methods used most often by the online instructors to communicate with the students.

Since the partnership programs were the first of their kind for the business program, the program officials placed a strong emphasis on the quality of the online learning and the satisfaction of the international students' experiences in the program. A program coordinator worked with the students and companies in order to closely monitor the students' progress.

As part of the strategy to ensure a satisfactory experience for the international students, the program officials initiated a study aimed at investigating the emerging cross-cultural issues that influenced the experiences of the international students and identifying areas that need program support in implementing successful online transnational courses.

Chinese students from two global companies were solicited for interviews through email invitations. All, except for two, of the students agreed to participate in the study. Sixteen students participated in the interviews. The majorities of the participants were in their first year of study in the program and had never taken an online course prior to this experience. Nonetheless, many of the students had experience working with international customers.

Both the individual and focus group interviews were used to gather the students' perceptions about their learning experiences in the online courses. The interviews followed an open, free-flowing interview format in which the students were asked to describe the challenges and issues related to their learning experiences in the cross-culture online courses. The students were then asked to provide their perspectives on their preferred learning strategies in their courses. Each individual interview lasted approximately one hour, while the focus group interviews lasted two to three hours.

After the interviews, the interview data was transcribed and analyzed using Strauss and Dorbin's (1990) constant comparative method. According to Patton (1990), Strauss and Dorbin's constant comparison method is appropriate when analyzing different perspectives on questions by cross-case grouping of answers. Major cultural themes emerged as the data were summarized and categorized.

CASE DESCRIPTION

Cultural Challenges Faced by Chinese Students in Online Courses

Time Management. Previous research has documented that time management is among the top five factors that affect the success of an online learner (Kerr, Rynearson, & Kerr, 2006). A multi-cultural learning environment adds a level of complexity that further complicates time management in online courses. For example, unlike American companies, Chinese companies do not have fixed work schedules and may require employees to work after regular work hours without much or any prior notice. Additionally, some positions require employees to travel for business on a regular basis. These situations pose challenges for the Chinese students who are expected to follow a rigorous course schedule. As one student noted:

In western companies, employees usually just work for 8 hours. If they need to work after hours, they are usually told in advance and will be paid extra, but, in Chinese companies, we may need to work after hours at any time. This practice is common in Chinese companies. If the boss needs an employee to work after hours, he or she will be given tasks right away.

Another difficulty faced by the Chinese students was to find enough time to study each day. The students were expected to commit 12 to 15 hours per week on each course. With both family and work responsibilities, most of the Chinese students felt that it was a great challenge for them to allocate two to three hours on coursework every evening after a long day of work.

Further, the language difficulty prolonged the reading time. The students had to spend at least three times as much time on the required readings as the American students.

Instructional Design. Becoming accustomed to a learner-centered learning style was a great challenge for the Chinese students as they attempted to transition to case-based learning. The Chinese students noted that very few American courses had specific textbooks tied closely to the assignments. For the Chinese students, a textbook is the class bible by which basic structure is provided for the class learning.

According to one participant, Chinese textbooks are very clearly structured from easy to complex for an easy memorization of key theories and concepts, while American textbooks provide many resources for each case study, but do not contain a definite structure or explanations on key theories. The students noted that they sometimes felt lost within the wealth of information provided with the cases and examples.

In addition to the lack of textbooks, the students also indicated that they had difficulty processing the information presented in the online discussions without the instructor's assistance. According to the students, having been accustomed to Chinese instructors' ways of frequently summarizing key points and giving direct instructions on key content, the students felt overwhelmed with the large amount of information presented in online discussions.

Time Zone Differences. Time zone differences had an impact on the students' online participation in their courses. The students mentioned the time zone differences caused problems in their timely participation in both the synchronous and asynchronous discussions. For the synchronous discussions, most of the instructors were not willing to schedule two sets of synchronous chats for the same topic discussion. The Chinese students typically were not able to participate in the online synchronous discussions if they were scheduled during the evenings in the American because they had to be at work during the daytime in China.

The asynchronous discussions caused a problem in the group online discussions. Due to the 12 hour time difference, the Chinese students were delayed in providing feedback and, as such, their feedback was often ignored and sometimes even interpreted as not active participation in the group work. In the online discussions, some of the instructors requested that the students not repeat other students' viewpoints already made in previous posts. Some of the Chinese students reported that this instruction was difficult to follow, as it was hard to locate an unanswered question 12 hours after the discussion began.

Collaboration. According to the participants, the Chinese students exhibited modest, face-saving personalities in the group work, which affected their engagement in learning from the group interaction process. On the other hand, the American students were assertive and confident with an unpersuasive attitude that dominated the group interaction process. For example, a few of the students mentioned that in their groups, which consisted of both American and Chinese students, the American students normally acquired the leadership roles. They set-up the framework of and finalized the assignments. Consequently, the Chinese students had reduced participation due to their "politeness" and their lack of ability in regard to speaking or writing English fluently.

Problem-solving. The Chinese students noted that there were significant differences between the American and Chinese students in regard to the ways by which they would solve the problems in the simulations or cases. These differences sometimes caused serious conflicts within the teams if they were not appropriately managed. For example, when solving problems in the simulations or cases, the American students tended to follow a methodological (linear) method (e.g. following the formula or standard process) of solving the problems even when the results were intuitive and simple. One Chinese student mentioned that "sometimes I think that the American students are mechanical. I can immediately tell the results from the data given in the table. Yet, they were still trying to use the formula to do the calculation."

Case-based Instruction. The Chinese students mentioned that most of the cases used in the online courses did not contain international components. Therefore, they often had difficulty understanding the cases or examples as they were American based and the explanations did not provide sufficient resources to explain the local cultural context or terms. Culturally specific cases such as these place international students at a disadvantage in the learning process when compared to the American students. For example, one course used a case that concerned retirement plans and requested that the students interview five to eight people who currently had retirement plans in the American One student noted that he had difficulty completing the project, as he had neither knowledge of the plans nor access to such individuals in the American.

The Chinese students mentioned that a lack of close relationships existed between the case analyses and practical issues faced by their companies. They stated that they felt that the cases used in the courses were too distant from the reality of the Chinese work environment. Therefore, it was difficult for them to apply their newly acquired knowledge to their home working environment. For example, one student noted:

For example, in the course that focused on Organizational Change, the cases used, we think, were a bit too far from the environments in China.

For example, we hope that, in the future, the ED chooses to analyze cases in which companies in the business field have expanded from their home country to other countries. This might be better because we need to learn more about company operations.

Language Barrier. The biggest challenge that the Chinese students faced seemed to come from their language barriers. Although each of the students were required to passed the standard graduate admission examinations (i.e., TOEFL and GMAT), the majority of the students indicated that they still had great difficulty finishing the required reading and comprehending the content at the level necessary by which to achieve the desired level of understanding. For example, one student noted that "if the book had been written in Chinese, I may have only had to spend half an hour reading it. Instead, I had to spend several hours." Another student mentioned that "the students had difficulty with the English as we still have a translation process occurring in our minds. We have to first translate to Chinese what the instructor said and then respond, so there is a delay."

Accordingly, a lack of deep understanding caused by the language deficiency resulted in less effective communication of their opinions on the part of the Chinese students in the live interactions and passive participation in the online discussions. "For Business Law, we may have had a feeling about it after reading the chapters, but could not express our arguments or perspectives. The law itself was tough to understand. Being able to express it with an in-depth view was even more difficult for us."

Academic conduct. Several of the Chinese students expressed frustration at being severely punished for inappropriately citing others' work due to a lack of knowledge of the reference rules of the university. These students mentioned that what they did was an acceptable practice in the academia of their country. For example, one student commented:

When the professor pointed it out [my inappropriate citation], I immediately expressed an apology for my ignorance and committed to following it in the future. Regardless, I was reprimanded for academic dishonesty, which caused me to lose marks and end up with a lower grade. I personally feel that this would have been treated in a different way in India, where I probably would have received a warning for a future reprimand.

Recommendations by Students for Designing Culturally Appropriate Online Courses

Preplan in advance. The Chinese students noted that a well-defined and predictable course assessment schedule with regularly occurring learning or assessment activities (e.g. weekly discussions or quizzes) was particularly helpful for them in maintaining their continuous engagement with the course amid their busy professional lives. The students felt that it would be helpful to inform them of the course schedule in advance, so that they could adjust their work schedules accordingly in case unexpected work tasks came up. In addition, preparation in advance alleviated language barriers by allowing them to have more time to review course materials. For example, one student commented that "Considering the huge amount of reading materials, I hope that we can have some time to look up vocabulary, etc. in advance. " The benefit of having the course schedule in advance was noted by another student:

The earlier we are given the course schedule, the more helpful it will be for us. Knowing the course schedule in advance will help us to manage our time accordingly. We will not require the professors to change the course schedule. This advance notice allows us to make adjustments of our schedule.

Instruction scaffolding. Although the Chinese students appreciated the opportunities for the immediate application of the knowledge in the case-based learning, they sometimes felt overwhelmed with the unstructured learning materials and information overload in the online case discussions. They would like the instructors to provide more direct instructional support, such as providing advanced organizers at the beginning of each lesson and summaries at the conclusion of the lesson. In addition, they would like the instructors to weave and synthesize the online discussions. These strategies would help the Chinese students process the information effectively and facilitate their transition from a highly structured instruction style to a less structured style. As one student noted:

[I]n China, we are accustomed to the instructors' ways of recapping key points for us. Here, the instructors talk about a lot of things. They should let us know the most important things that we need to grasp in order to understand American laws.

Diversifying cases. The Chinese students would like to see a balanced use of local and global cases in the courses, including diversified cases from different cultures and closer relationships between the case analyses and practical issues faced by their companies. In addition, for the cases that the students are not familiar with, the instructors should provide more information on the cultural contexts or explanations of the culturally specific terms of the case. Tow students commented on the need for international cases:

Certainly, if [the program name] can add cases that address Chinese companies, that would be super. For example, they could use examples of both the successful and unsuccessful Chinese companies that operate in the American

For the course on organizational change, I did not like that there was a big gap between the knowledge and application. Rather, I hoped that I could apply the knowledge more directly and quickly. If the cases could include cases from China that will be great.

Language support. In order to help ease the language barriers, the students suggested that advance preparation was the key to effective learning. They appreciated that certain professors set up the course schedule and materials earlier than the start of the course or lessons in order to allow them additional time to better prepare for the course or lesson. For example, one student commented:

For example, before the beginning of the course, the instructor could provide the materials in advance, such as the relevant audio files, video clips, professional terms, etc., for those students who have language difficulties.

The students also appreciated those professors who made an effort to provide audio and video aids, which not only helped the students to understand the course content, but, also, allowed them to review the content repeatedly in order to overcome the language barriers. For example, one student noted: "… if audio materials were provided, that will be helpful. Then, we could listen to these materials again and again."

Multiple channels for communication. The Chinese students suggested that the combination of synchronous and asynchronous communication was helpful in establishing the multiple culture learning community. The synchronous communications provided vivid interactions, which allowed the students to get to know each other much better and quicker, whereas the asynchronous communications afforded flexibility in communication and allowed the students more time to think and provide feedback. Many of the students appreciated the instructors' use of a combination of both types of communication modes in order to offset the communication weaknesses of each type. For example, one student mentioned that his course used both discussion forums and live meetings in order to effectively engage students in different regions.

Multiple assessment methods. The interviewees mentioned that the assessment methods used in most of the courses were effective. For instance, many of the courses used multiple assessment methods (e.g., student participation in the discussions, projects, final exams, etc.) and spread the methods over the duration of the course instead of only having one or two large exams. The process-oriented assessment methods were perceived to be effective in engaging the students in online learning. Some of the interviewees noted that the assessment methods heavily focused on the application of knowledge and ignored the consolidation of theoretical knowledge. For example, one Chinese student commented on her preferences for multiple assessment methods:

[the] ideal assessment should include open-ended discussions and exams. One extreme would be to just use open-ended discussions. This extreme is not good because we lose the benefit of learning from textbooks and improving our theoretical knowledge. The other extreme would be to only use exams, especially those focusing on memorization. Neither of the extremes is good. The ideal format would be in the middle, including discussions and exams, providing us with opportunities to understand theories and apply them.

Simulation. The Chinese students appreciated the use of business simulations in the online courses. The simulated exercises provided them with the feeling of real-world experiences in a different culture. As one student noted:

Although there are theories in the book, you would not be able to learn a lot without practice.

With the simulations, our views were broadened. If we can introduce these simulations into China, let the senior managers learn this model and let their thinking become aligned with this model, it would change their old ways of thinking.

RECOMMENDATIONS

In summary, this case study revealed the challenges faced by Chinese students when learning in cross-cultural online MBA courses and the strategies recommended to counter those challenges. The study revealed that online instructors need to design courses in such a way as to remove potential cultural barriers, including time management, language barriers, time zone differences, differences in learning approaches, academic integrity issues and a lack of multicultural learning content, which may affect international students' learning performances.

Table 1. Summary of cultural themes and recommendations from the students

	Challenges	Recommendations
Time management	• No fixed work schedule in China's factories • Traveling on a regular basis • Having difficulty in committing 12-15 hours to study every week	• providing a well-defined and predictable course assessment schedule for preplanning • informing students of the course schedule in advance
Instruction design	Change from a highly structured, teacher-centered style to a less structured, more conversational and instructor-centered style	• more direct instructional support, such as providing advanced organizers at the beginning of each lesson and summaries at the conclusion of the lesson • weaving and synthesizing during online discussions
Time Zone differences	• Scheduling difficulty in synchronous discussions • Delayed feedback caused by the time differences	
Collaboration	• Reduced learning engagement in group interaction process due to the modest, face-saving Chinese personalities • Cultural differences in problem solving process	• awareness of cultural differences • using strategies such as assigning member roles and establishing communication rules to enable more equalized participation
Case-based learning	• No international components in the cases • A lack of sufficient resources to explain the local cultural context or terms. • Lack of close relationships existed between the case analyses and practical issues faced by their companies	• a balanced use of local and global cases • providing more information on the cultural contexts or explanations of the culturally specific terms of the case
Language barrier	• Having difficulty finishing the required reading and comprehending the content • A lack of deep understanding caused by the language deficiency • Less effective communication of their opinions	• advanced preparation for the course or lesson • providing audio and video aids
Academic conduct	frustrations at being charged with Plagiarism caused by the lack of knowledge of local academic culture	awareness of cultural contexts in plagiarism practices
		Preferences for diversity in instructional design • the combination of synchronous and asynchronous communication • multiple assessment methods and process-oriented assessment adaptive to different cultural styles • simulated exercises provided them with the feeling of real-world experiences in a different culture

The present case study indicates that an international program needs to address those challenges in order to ensure full participation by the international students in online courses. Based on the challenges and recommendations put forward by the participants in this study, the following recommendations were made to the program management in order to improve the quality of the cross-cultural learning experiences of the international students.

First, the findings suggest that Chinese students have a preference for a structured learning style that places an emphasis on textbooks. This preference reflects the value of China's educational culture, which has been strongly influenced by Confucianism, which emphasizes inter-relatedness and order in learning (Tang, 1996). Similar to the results of this study, other studies have reported significant differences between American and Chinese students in regard to learning style preferences (Wang, 1991; Zhang, 2009). Wang (1992) found that American students have a more social, interactive learning style, preferring to interact with peers and instructors, while Chinese students prefer to work with highly organized materials and engage in programs in which they determine the pace. Experiencing a change from a highly structured, direct learning style to a less structured, discovery learning style gives rise to a learning curve for most Chinese students. As suggested by the students, supplementing instructions with more detailed lecture notes, providing structured frameworks for the problem analyses and facilitating online discussions by summarizing or synthesizing the discussions can be effective ways by which to facilitate Chinese students' abilities to adapt to this new style of learning.

Hofstede's cultural theory can be used to explain cultural group behaviors that differ between Chinese and American students (Wang, 2007; Hofstede, 1991). According to this theory, Chinese culture features a collectivistic orientation in which people seek collaboration and harmony in order to avoid conflicts with others, while American culture features an individualistic orientation in which individuals tend to act independently and competitively. The negative impact caused by differences in cultural orientations on students' learning participation in group processes suggests a need to establish team process guidelines in order to help build healthy, collaborative and functioning teams. For example, creating clear team goals, member responsibilities and communication protocols can be useful when establishing an atmosphere for open exchanges and communication. Assigning roles can also make students more accountable for their behaviors and motivated to participate in team activities.

The findings of this study indicate a lack of cross-cultural adaptations in regard to content based on the needs of international students. In the short term, the adaptation of complex cases for global learning may be difficult, but should not prevent instructors from designing innovative ways by which to embed international components into curriculum. For example, instructors can design activities that can be used to facilitate cross-cultural conversations on the context of cases in which students are encouraged to share their personal cases or experiences from a cultural standpoint.

Both the lack of cultural considerations in course design and the dealing with the student academic conduct issues reflected a weak cultural sensitivity of the instructors. The case study indicates that an online MBA program that wishes to extend its global outreach needs a strategic plan to provide cross-cultural training support for both students and instructors. In order to increase the cultural awareness of the international students, an initial orientation to the cultural differences or simulated cultural exercises would be helpful in order to serve as a starting point for the development of cultural competencies.

The findings of this study indicate that the language barrier was a significant issue with the Chinese students, particularly at the beginning of their program study. Online instructors should be advised to combine the use of asynchronous and synchronous activities in order to allow the students to improve both their writing and communication skills. Developing audio and visual aids can alleviate language barriers and allow the students to have the ability to repeatedly review the materials. In addition, providing training on writing English and effective communication skills in cross-cultural environments could help the students to make a smoother transition to the program.

Finally, the findings of this study indicate that students' preferences for diversity and multiplicity in online pedagogy accommodate cultural variability. These preferences indicate a need for online instructors to foster the principles of flexibility in online courses, assume multiple supportive faculty roles and provide expertise (McLoughlin & Oliver, 2000; Collis, 1999). For example, if an international student is studying online for the first time, the need for dialogue and direction may be greatest at the initial stages of the course (McLoughlin & Oliver, 2000). Online instructors can conduct a quick learner analysis in order to get an understanding of the students' expectations and cultural backgrounds, so that they may adjust the diversity of the course in order to address the international audience accordingly.

LESSONS LEARNED

The international partnership was a new experience for the online international program in the study. The early experience was used as a test base for future expansions into new international programs in East Asia. Several key lessons were learned during the case study and can be summarized as follows.

First, international students who take online American courses from their home country are faced with additional challenges (e.g. time zone differences, language barriers, etc.) not faced by international students taking courses in the American These challenges can negatively influence the students' learning.

Second, the assessment of the international students' learning experiences is important for international program development. Due to a lack of empirical guidelines in developing effective cross-cultural learning environments, a targeted assessment and revision of the cross-cultural program warrants an improved learning experience for international students. For example, after the investigation, the program adopted several measures to support international students. First, a culture tutor was arranged to assist the student in understanding American culture. Also, an EPT (English Practical Training) course was developed to help students adjust to the Western style of communication and writing. Finally, a program coordinator assigned to the program was responsible for communicating with the international students regarding their concerns and suggestions for their learning.

Third, it is important for an instructor who is new to teaching online international students to be aware that their previous experiences with full-time international students may not apply to online students. Besides receiving cultural training and attending to the needs of the international students in the online courses, the online instructors need to consistently reflect on their work with the international student in order to be culturally sensitive and redesign the course to focus more on global learning.

Finally, for an international cohort program specifically developed for an organization, an online program can take advantage of the relationship developed with the organization, and encourage the organization to take pre-orientation measures and intensify English training so that the students can quickly adapt to the new environment.

As a program-level case study (Yin, 2002) based on a small sample size of participants, limitations exist in generalizing the results of this study to other contexts. However, we believe that the analysis of emerging cultural issues and recommendations raised in this study provide highly valuable information and insights that can be used to assist distance educators and policymakers of similar online MBA programs when making educational policies and practices for successful global online learning experiences.

FUTURE CHALLENGES

As technology advances, more learning technologies will become available by which to develop highly interactive learning environments. On one hand, these new technologies bear the potential to further decrease transactional distance in online learning. However, these technologies may also bring new challenges and problems that an online program will have to cope with in order to maintain its success. For example, the differences in technological infrastructure development in different cultures pose challenges in managing educational accessibility. Plagiarism may become more rampant with the convenience of additional advanced technology. A culturally sensitive program should always be alert to the potential impact of new technology on the program development and renew its strategies to adapt to the new challenges.

REFERENCES

Australian Flexible Learning Framework. (2004). *Cross-cultural issues in content development and teaching online*. Retrieved August 23, 2007, from http://www.flexiblelearning.net.au/flx/webdav/site/flxsite/users/kedgar/public/quick_guides/crosscultural.pdf

Bentley, J. P. H., Tinney, M. V., & Chia, B. H. (2005). Intercultural Internet-based learning: Know your audience and what it values. *Educational Technology Research and Development*, *53*(2), 117–127. doi:10.1007/BF02504870

Bonk, C. J. (2009). *The world is open: How Web technology is revolutionizing education*. San Francisco, CA: Jossey-Bass.

Collis, B. (1999). Designing for differences: Cultural issues in the design of WWW-based course-support sites. *British Journal of Educational Technology*, *30*(3), 201–215. doi:10.1111/1467-8535.00110

Goodfellow, R., Lea, M., Gonzales, F., & Mason, R. (2001). Opportunity and e-quality: Intercultural and linguistic issues in global online learning. *Distance Education*, *22*(1), 65–84. doi:10.1080/0158791010220105

Gunawardena, C. N., Nolla, A. C., Wilson, P. L., Lopez-Islas, J. R., Ramirez-Angel, N., & Megchun-Alpizar, R. M. (2002). A cross-cultural study of group process and development in online conferences. *Distance Education*, *22*(1), 85–121. doi:10.1080/0158791010220106

Gunawardena, C. N., Wilson, P. L., & Nolla, A. C. (2003). Culture and online education. In Moore, M. G., & Anderson, W. G. (Eds.), *Handbook of distance education* (pp. 753–775). Mahwah, NJ: Lawrence Earlbaum Associates.

Hannon, J., & D'Netto, B. (2007). Cultural diversity online: Student engagement with learning technologies. *International Journal of Educational Management*, *21*(5), 418–432. doi:10.1108/09513540710760192

Hofstede, G. (1984). *Culture's consequences: International differences in work-related values*. Newbury, CA: Sage Publications.

Jacobson, W. (1996). Learning, culture, and learning culture. *Adult Education Quarterly, 47*(1), 15–28. doi:10.1177/074171369604700102

Kerr, M. S., Rynearson, K., & Kerr, M. C. (2006). Student characteristics for online learning success. *The Internet and Higher Education, 9*(2), 91–105. doi:10.1016/j.iheduc.2006.03.002

Ku, H., & Lohr, L. L. (2003). A case study of Chinese students' attitude toward their first online learning experience. *Educational Technology Research and Development, 51*(3), 94–102. doi:10.1007/BF02504557

Lanham, E., & Zhou, W. (2003). Cultural issues in online learning–is blended learning a possible solution? *International Journal of Computer Proceeding of Original Languages, 16*(4), 275–292. doi:10.1142/S0219427903000930

Liang, A., & McQueen, R. J. (1999). Computer assisted adult interactive learning in a multi-cultural environment. *Adult Learning, 11*(1), 26–29.

McLoughlin, C., & Oliver, R. (2000). Designing learning environments for cultural inclusivity: A case study of indigenous on-line learning at tertiary level. *Australian Journal of Educational Technology, 16*(1), 58–72.

Pinhey, L. A. (1998). *Global education: Internet resources*. Eric Digest.

Pratt, D. D. (1999). *A conceptual framework for conducting cross-cultural research on teaching*, 40th Annual Adult Education Research Conference, Northern Illinois University, DeKalb, Illinois. Retrieved on March 13, 2002, from http://www.edst.educ.ubc.ca/faculty/pratt/DPconfra.html

Rooney, M. (2003, January 14). Report urges aggressive recruiting of international students at American colleges. *The Chronicle of Higher Education.* Retrieved January 14, 2009, from http://opendoors.iienetwork.org/?p=35053

Shattuck, K. (2002). Speaking personally. *American Journal of Distance Education, 16*(4), 259–263.

Shattuck, K. (2005). *Glimpses of the global coral gardens: Insights of international adult learners on the interactions of cultures in online distance education*. Unpublished doctoral dissertation, The Pennsylvania State University, University Park, PA.

Strauss, A., & Corbin, J. (1990). *Basics of qualitative research: Grounded theory procedures and techniques*. Newbury Park, CA: Sage Publications.

Tang, C. (1996). Collaborative learning: The latent dimension in Chinese students' learning. In Watkins, D. A., & Biggs, J. B. (Eds.), *The Chinese learner: Cultural, psychological and contextual influences* (pp. 183–204). Hong Kong: CERC and ACER.

Thompson, L., & Ku, H. (2005). Chinese graduate students' experiences and attitudes toward online learning. *Educational Media International, 42*(1), 33–47. doi:10.1080/09523980500116878

Tu, C. (2001). How Chinese perceive social presence: An examination of interaction in online learning achievement. *Educational Media International, 38*(1), 45–60. doi:10.1080/09523980010021235

Wadholm, R. R. (2009). The world is open. *Educational Technology Research and Development, 57*(3), 411–413. doi:10.1007/s11423-009-9114-0

Walker-Fernandez, S. E. (1999). *Toward understanding the study experience of culturally sensitive graduate students in American distance education programs.* Unpublished dissertation, Florida International University, Miami Beach, Florida.

Wang, M. (2007). Designing online courses that effectively engage learners from diverse cultural backgrounds. *British Journal of Educational Technology, 38*(2), 294–311. doi:10.1111/j.1467-8535.2006.00626.x

Wilson, M. S. (2001). Cultural considerations in online instruction and learning. *Distance Education, 22*(1), 52–64. doi:10.1080/0158791010220104

Yin, R. K. (2002). *Case study research: Design and methods* (3rd ed.). Thousand Oaks, CA: Sage.

Zhang, K. (2009). Online collaborative learning in a project-based learning environment in Taiwan: A case study on undergraduate students' perspectives. *Educational Media International, 46*(2), 123. doi:10.1080/09523980902933425

Zhao, N., & McDougall, D. (2008). Cultural influences on Chinese students' asynchronous online learning in a Canadian university. *Journal of Distance Education, 22*(2), 59–80.

ADDITIONAL READING

Abrams, Z. (2005). Asynchronous CMC, Collaboration and the development of critical thinking in a graduate seminar in applied linguistics. *Canadian Journal of Learning Technology, 31*(2), 23–47.

Auyeung, P., & Sands, J. (2009). A cross-cultural study of the learning style of accounting students. *Accounting and Finance*, *36*, 261–274. doi:10.1111/j.1467-629X.1996.tb00310.x

Collis, B., Vingerhoets, J., & Moonen, J. (1997). Flexibility as a key construct in European training: Experiences from the TeleScopia Project. *British Journal of Educational Technology*, *28*(3), 199–217. doi:10.1111/1467-8535.00026

Gunawardena, C. N., Nolla, A. C., Wilson, P. L., Lopez-Islas, J. R., Ramirez-Angel, N., & Megchun-Alpizar, R. M. (2002). A cross-cultural study of group process and development in online conferences. *Distance Education*, *22*(1), 85–121. doi:10.1080/0158791010220106

Hofstede, G. (1984). *Culture's Consequences*. Beverly Hills, CA: Sage.

Hofstede, G. (1991). *Cultures and Organizations: Software of the Mind*. New York: McGraw Hill.

Hoft, N. (1995). *International Technical Communication: How to Export Information about High Technology*. New York: John Wiley.

Reeves, T. (1992). Effective dimensions of interactive learning systems. *Proceedings of Information Technology for Training and Education Conference* (ITTE '92) (pp. 99-113). St. Lucia, Brisbane: University of Queensland.

Rogers, P. C., Graham, C. R., & Mayes, C. T. (2007). Cultural Competence and instructional design: Exploration research into the delivery of online instruction cross-culturally. *Educational Technology Research and Development*, *55*, 197–217. doi:10.1007/s11423-007-9033-x

Shih, Y. D., & Cifuentes, L. (2003). Taiwanese intercultural phenomena and issues in a United States-Taiwan telecommunications partnership. *Educational Technology Research and Development*, *51*(3), 82–90. doi:10.1007/BF02504555

UNESCO & Council of Europe. (2000). Code of Good Practice in the Provision of Transnational Education. Retrieved Oct 10, 2009, from http://www.cepes.ro/hed/recogn/groups/transnat/code.htm.

Wang, H. (1992). A descriptive study of the learning styles of Chinese and American graduate students and Professors. Unpublished doctoral dissertation, Mississippi State University, Mississippi.

Wang, M. (2007). Designing online courses that effectively engage learners from diverse cultural backgrounds. *British Journal of Educational Technology*, *38*(2), 294–311. doi:10.1111/j.1467-8535.2006.00626.x

Wild, M., & Henderson, L. (1997). Contextualising learning in the World Wide Web: accounting for the impact of culture. *Education and Information Technologies*, *2*(3), 179–192. doi:10.1023/A:1018661213335

Williams, M. (2004). *Exploring the effects of a multimedia case-based learning environment in pre-service science teacher education in Jamaica.* Unpublished doctoral dissertation, University of Twente, Enschede, The Netherlands.

KEY TERMS AND DEFINITIONS

Case-Based Learning: An instructional approach in which learners develop complex problem-solving skills by investigating contemporary issues in real-life contexts by collecting resources, analyzing situations and evaluating alternative solutions.

Cross-Cultural Learning: A learning situation in which learners from different cultural backgrounds learn together.

Culture: A set of values, norms, beliefs, perceptions and behavior patterns shared among a group of people, which distinguishes the members of the group from those of other groups.

Cultural Awareness: The ability of an individual to develop an awareness of one's own culture in order to assist in communications with other cultures.

E-Learning: Any learning experience that involves electronic means to support the learning process.

Online MBA Program: A MBA (Masters of Business Administration) program delivered primarily through Web technologies.

Transnational Courses: Courses taken by learners in which the learners are in a country other than the one in which the awarding institution is based.

This work was previously published in Cases on Globalized and Culturally Appropriate E-Learning: Challenges and Solutions, edited by Andrea Edmundson, pp. 168-186, copyright 2011 by Information Science Reference (an imprint of IGI Global).

Section 5
Institutional Globalization

Chapter 16
Integrated Cross-Cultural Virtual Classroom Exchange Program:
How Adaptable Public Schools are in Korea and the USA?

Eunhee Jung O'Neill
Center for International Virtual Schooling, USA

EXECUTIVE SUMMARY

As information and communication technology (ICT) evolves, the scope of social interactions expands globally through the Web, and knowledge has become a key source for economic production. The capacity to understand diverse cultures and the ability to utilize ICT for knowledge acquisition and application have become critical to increasing and sustaining global solidarity, peace and development. Accordingly, society expects educational institutions to provide students with cultural learning opportunities and ICT skills. In an effort to address these issues, a cross-cultural virtual classroom exchange program using an online course management system was introduced to public schools in Korea and the USA. By investigating technological, pedagogical, and organizational factors, this paper analyzes the adaptability of public schools in Korea and the USA with respect to integrating cross-cultural virtual exchange activities within their respective curricula. Ultimately, this case recommends solutions for increasing adaptability, and invites international collaboration among education stakeholders to disseminate the cross-cultural virtual learning worldwide.

DOI: 10.4018/978-1-4666-1885-5.ch016

ORGANIZATION BACKGROUND: PUBLIC SCHOOLS AND ICT POLICY

The Republic of Korea (South Korea)'s public K-12 schools are composed of six-year elementary schools, three-year middle schools, and three-year high schools. The K–12 curriculum is centralized at the national level. Since 1954, the Korean Ministry of Education (currently renamed as Ministry of Education, Science and Technology: MEST) has developed and advanced the national curriculum every eight to ten years. The centralized national curriculum reflects the governments' political and economic stances. For example, the government put great emphasis on education as an engine of the nation's economic growth in the 1970's. Diverse research and reports have disclosed the power of Korea's education as related to its rapid economic development (Korea Education & Research Information Service, 2008; Morris, 1996; UNESCO, 1993). Accordingly, science, mathematics, and technical education have been core subjects. Since 1997, with an emphasis on globalization, the English language has been taught from the third grade and has become one of the biggest interests of Korean society.

By providing the vision for adapting education to the Information Age (Korea Education & Research Information Service, 2000), MEST has directed educators to participate in and follow school innovation using ICT. There is a very structured and linear connection between the central department of education, local office of education, and each level of public schools.

The policies for the informatization of education were introduced in two stages. In the First Comprehensive Plan (1997–2000), all elementary and middle schools were provided with ICT hardware, one PC with high-speed Internet connection, a large screen TV projector per every classroom, and one or two computer laboratories. The Second Stage Plan started in 2001 and focused on developing ICT software, such as digital online content materials. The Korean Education & Research Information Service (KERIS) led the development of ICT content material and its distribution. KERIS also supplied ICT resources for teachers and students including cyber learning services and the promotion of public education through the Internet (KERIS, 2004).

The central administration and its policy systematically planned and supported the provision of public schools' ICT equipment and contents materials. Since funding amounts were based on school size, i.e., the number of students, classrooms, and facilities, all public schools in Korea were set up equally with ICT infrastructures (KERIS, 2001). The plan for adapting ICT in elementary and secondary education has been continuously implemented. Emphasizing educational welfare and information culture, MEST has focused on "narrowing the education gap" since 2006. Also, MEST enacted Regulations for the Center of Safe On-line Learning, which requested schools to teach the ethics of information and communications, and to install software that blocks students from any harmful information (MEST & KERIS, 2007, p. 19).

The United States of America (USA) has a decentralized educational system. The U.S. Department of Education (DOE) is not responsible for the whole nation's education, instead, each state DOE is accountable for their state's education. Thus, the U.S. DOE makes overarching educational policy and provides an educational technology plan as suggestions and recommendations, and the state level departments set the concrete plans for implementation. This decentralized structure brings a dynamic quality of education according to a state's unique environment and policies. Typically, states follow either a 5-3-4 compulsory education system (five years of elementary school, three years of junior high school, and four years of high school), or a 6-3-3 system. Since the American school in this case study is located in Virginia, reviewing the respective educational ICT policy will be appropriate.

Under the No Child Left Behind Act of 2001 (White House, 2002) whereby public schools are required to administer a state-wide standardized test to all students every year to enhance academic achievement, the U.S. DOE announced a national technology plan to inform and guide policy makers to implement ICT in education (Culp, Honey & Mandinach, 2003). In addition, since the Enhancing Education Through Technology (EETT) Act of 2001 was passed by Congress, the Virginia Department of Education established the Educational Technology Plan for Virginia: 2003–2009 (State Board of Education, 2003). This plan addresses technology integration, professional development and support programs, connectivity, educational application, and accountability. It aims to ensure that "all students develop the technology skills and knowledge to realize their potential as leaders in a technology-supported information economy." The plan emphasizes "long-range, effective, statewide integration of educational technology into teaching, learning, and school management." (State Board of Education, 2003, p. v)

Unlike South Korea where the government established a nationwide ICT infrastructure equally, the Virginia plan diagnosed that "all public schools and school division offices in Virginia do not have the same level of connectivity to local and outside resources. Infrastructures vary widely from school division to school division and even among schools in the same division" (State Board of Education, 2003, p. 53). The Virginia State Board of Education suggests a standardization of schools' connectivity, thus allowing all classrooms to be networked through the high-speed Internet connections. Educational funding in the U.S. is based on regional tax rates, and each school applies to a district office of education for any additional project funding.

SETTING AND PARTICIPANTS

Three elementary schools in Seoul (Korea) and one elementary school in Virginia (USA) performed International Virtual Elementary Classroom Activities (IVECA) activities for a whole semester. As shown in Figure 1, participants of this case study include six classrooms of total 154 students, six classroom teachers (T), ten support teachers (ST), four school administrators (P) in four public elementary schools in both countries. In particular, in the one American school, there were two 5th grade Reading and Writing in English (RWE) classes (indicated with the codes, Class1 and Class2, respectively in Figure 1.), their teachers (T1 and T2), one 6th grade RWE class (Class3) and their teacher (T3), four technological and instructional support teachers (ST1– ST4) and a school administrator (P1). The data collection sources in the three Korean schools were three regular 6th grade classes (Class 1– Class 3), their teachers (T1–T3), two support teachers (ST1 and ST2) in each school, and three school principals (P1– P3). A cross-cultural virtual classroom exchange program, IVECA, consists of three virtual classrooms. Each virtual classroom was paired with one American classroom and one Korean classroom.

CASE DESCRIPTION

This case study aims to discuss the adaptability of public schools in Korea and USA in a cross-cultural virtual classroom exchange program for their students. The ultimate goal of this paper is to recommend international collaboration for the dissemination of cross-cultural virtual classroom exchanges in public schools worldwide. Thus, it is important to first understand the inclusive context of this educational effort.

Figure 1. Setting and participants (T: Teacher, ST: Support Teacher, P: Principal)

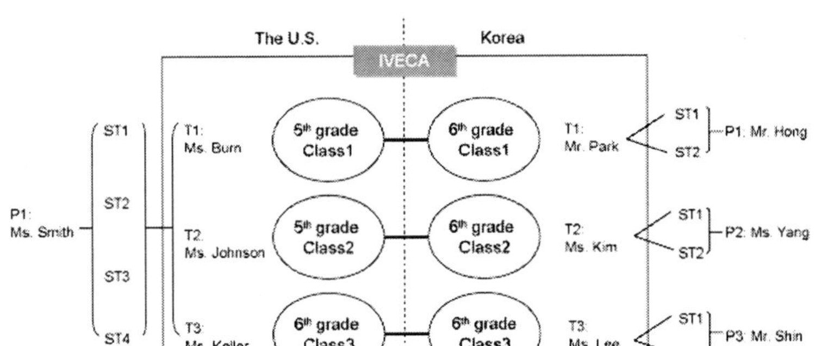

Introduction to an integrated cross-cultural classroom exchange program will demonstrate the value of analyzing the adaptability of public schools and will serve as a guide to problems in this case study. The subsequent three narrative sections will illustrate realistic situations of the public schools in Korea and the USA during their adaptation processes of the cross-cultural virtual exchange program.

Contextual Background

Rapid evolution of information and communication technologies (ICT) has globally networked diverse societies and economies. Economic trade and social interaction occur in virtual spaces without limitations of physical boundaries and distance between nations. Infinite information and knowledge introduced through ICT has become a key source of economic production (Asian Development Bank, 2003; Bloom, 2004). Due to the unprecedented scale of globalization, people frequently encounter others from different cultures of distant regions or overseas. However, differences in culture, including language and religion, have often resulted in conflict due to intolerance, prejudice, and misunderstandings among peoples and nations (UNESCO, 2006a).

Intercultural competence is the ability to work appropriately and effectively in international and multicultural working environment with others who are linguistically and culturally different from oneself in collaboration (Fantini, 2006; Lasonen, 2006). Intercultural competence develops most effectively as people communicate and interact directly with others in environments of different cultures and diverse languages (Fantini, 2000). At this point, the means of fostering interculturally situated communication opportunities into school curriculum become an issue.

Fortunately, ICT has evolved enough to facilitate direct and regular intercultural interaction among students around the world through their respective school systems. Emphasizing the benefits of ICT for vitalizing societies, Burke addressed the uses of ICT for students' intercultural learning when featured at the 2003 Intercultural Education Summit as the keynote speaker:

... I see the dramatically-increasing availability of tools and resources other than that of the school-room (or even of the established information media).... in the way information and communication technology (ICT) is enhancing the abilities of even small communities to survive without having no submerge themselves in larger, more powerful cultures, ... it has also become urgent that we find ways to inform students about modes of thought other than that of their own locality. The world is already too interconnected for us to continue in the old isolationist paradigm. Nowhere is now too 'far away' to matter. It is no longer acceptable in a world of proximity, to ignore the views of other cultures. Fortunately, the same technology that has given rise to this complication also provides means to deal with it (Burke, 2003, pp. 2-3).

International Virtual Elementary Classroom Activities (IVECA) was thus designed to provide cross-cultural learning opportunities by using ICT to effectively develop intercultural competence through public school curricula.

Integrated Cross-Cultural Classroom Exchange Program: IVECA

IVECA is an online classroom exchange program where K-12 school students in different countries share their thoughts and ideas through a web based, course management system (CMS). Its curriculum was developed by integrating local curricula with the framework of improving intercultural competence. With the school curricula integrated with the IVECA program, students in different countries perform individual and group projects in their classrooms according to the weekly activity topics provided in the IVECA program. The topics consist of activities such as personal introductions, comparison of school lives and cultures, discussions of cause and effect, and finding solutions regarding international issues. Completed projects are posted using the CMS communication and collaboration tools. Students from each country share their ideas, collaborate, and search and exchange information with each other every week. Depending on the needs and objectives of local schools, communication and collaboration platforms may include mainly discussion board and optionally blogs, wikis, and other images, not excluding podcasting and videocasting as well as synchronous audio and video interactions. The following vignette illustrates how IVECA is integrated in a public school classroom.

Monday afternoon after all students went back home, American English teacher Ms. Medlin visits her international virtual classroom on the web to see what activities are planned for this Thursday. The first page of the site shows an announcement describing this week's teaching and learning topic. The topic of this week is "what do you think about this issue?" The objective is to teach students how to search for events or news related to the U.S. and Korea, and logically write and talk about the cause and effect of the events. The goal of the discussion activities of this topic is to make students realize that there are different viewpoints in understanding an issue according to their cultural background and to cultivate open-mindedness and flexibility to these differences.

Since writing cause-effect sentences are the objectives in the English class, Ms. Medlin easily makes the connection between her English class objectives and the virtual classroom topic and starts designing lesson plans for this week. From her standard of learning objectives, she selects relevant local teaching materials to use as an introduction on how to find cause and effect in a story and how to use supporting ideas to write about the relationship. She feels that the first unit of this week would work with the materials. Thinking of the next English unit, she wants to prepare more interesting activities. "Let me see what is in the virtual classroom resource menu…," she says as she clicks on the course material menu on the virtual classroom website. She checks through all the relevant links and materials, and she finds that some very interesting events happened between the U.S. and Korea. She wants to use the material for this week's discussion with Korean students. Some creative ideas come to her mind. She thinks that it will be great to do some role-play with the story, to exchange the video clip, and then to share student ideas about the causes and effects of the events. Thinking that maybe the role-play itself might reveal different student perspectives and understanding of the events, she is getting excited about the activities.

However, wondering how the Korean teacher will design this activity and whether or not she will like her idea, Ms. Medlin opens her mail box and types a message to the virtual administrator about her idea. While waiting for a response, she keeps opening other resources that the virtual classroom website provided. "Wow…. um….. really?" Finding other news and events currently happening in Korea, she realizes how differently Korean society understands and solves certain problems.

When Ms. Medlin returns home, she finds an email response from the virtual administrator. The message says that the Korean teacher is also very excited about the idea and agrees to follow the suggested lesson plans of Ms. Medlin. In addition, the Korean teacher provides some additional stories in their textbook, which are relevant to the events that Ms. Medlin wants to use for the exchange activity. The additional materials will be helpful for both Korean and U.S. students, as well as for the teachers, in understanding the background of the events.

On Wednesday, she brings her students to the class library and reads the events she selected for the students. After studying some difficult words together, Ms. Medline lets them find and share the causes and effects of the events. Also, they share their supporting ideas about why they think the events caused the results and brought about those effects. When students return to their seats, they start writing cause and effect paragraphs in their notes. Also, she allows them to ask questions when they do not clearly understand the situation and bring ideas they want to share with the Korean students. Also they write about what they need to ask Korean students to have a better understanding of the events. Thereafter, the teacher gives students time to plan the role-play with the events.

On the exchange day, Thursday, Ms. Medlin distributes hand-outs including additional stories that the Korean teacher provided a few days ago. At first, each student reads the stories and shares his/her idea with a partner and jots down the reflection of his/her readers' response. In the classroom library, students volunteer to present their notes while others give feedback, including compliments and suggestions to the readers. Now Ms. Medlin takes out the school digital video camera and sets up the role-play stage in the open space at the back of the classroom. Students are very concentrated on the role-play preparation. While seeing her students work so hard and even enjoy what they are doing, Ms. Medline is very satisfied....

Multiple studies on IVECA in public elementary schools in Korea and the USA have proved its effectiveness in improving students' intercultural competence. Students attain knowledge about diverse cultures including their own, open their minds to accepting and adjusting to cultural differences, interact appropriately with people in different cultures and communicate effectively—share information, ideas and feelings—with others who have culturally and linguistically different backgrounds. In addition, IVECA has a positive influence on students' writing skills, it helps students broaden their worldviews by overcoming prejudice, misunderstandings, and racism, and it motivates students to learn (O'Neill, 2007; 2008). Below is the final voluntary posting of a Korean sixth grade student regarding her IVECA experience. It shows the potential impact of intercultural education in reducing world conflicts and contributing to peace and solidarity.

...I think IVECA activities are really great for students to develope [develop] their ways of thinking. It's hard to explain but, this is the way. If you continue to share stories with foreign countries, you students naturally get used to think widely. What I mean is that their thoughts and the basic structure and ways they think will become based on the whole world not only their own country. And if that happens, all students would care about overseas friends and further more, the danger and worries about war between each countries would decrease as well. The International Virtual Elementary Classroom Activities are the first start of all those great stuff. I fill [feel] proud and honorable for being the first class to experience it. I believe this activity would spread to more countries and help students all over the world develope [develop] themselves.

As the student envisioned, the impact of IVECA will be greater when it is diffused widely around the world and when it is implemented sustainably in public school systems. Now, the question is whether or not public schools worldwide can adapt to such transnational and intercultural learning environments facilitated by ICT. Seeking the answer to this question, this paper first investigates the adaptability of public schools in Korea and the USA. The following problems will guide finding the solution.

Problem Statement

How adaptable are public schools in Korea and the USA with respect to implementing IVECA, an integrated cross-cultural virtual classroom exchange program?

1. What technological concerns arise when the public schools in Korea and the USA implement IVECA?
2. How do teachers and students perform IVECA in their teaching and learning at school?
3. What are the organizational issues that influence IVECA integration in the public school systems of both nations?

Data Collection and Analysis

Data was collected during the previously conducted research on the implementation of IVECA. It included direct observation (recorded classroom video reviews for the Korean site), participant observation as a virtual administrator, student journals, interviews with students, teachers, support teachers and principals, informal talk with American teachers before, during, and after their IVECA class hours, instant messaging with Korean teachers, email exchanges, and archived postings of students in the Moodle discussion boards. Documents including each school's educational goals, curricula, American teacher pacing guides, Korean teacher guide books, class schedules, computer lab schedules, and school event calendar were also collected. American state standards of learning objectives and Korea's national curriculum were also obtained.

Miles and Huberman's (1994) analytic technique was used for the data analysis. Corpuses of data were reduced by coding and categorizing events and episodes into major themes. Patterns and relationships among the themes and role players (students, teachers, and administrators) were explored and analyzed by displaying the data through the forms of charts, graphs, matrices, and networks. Answers to the questions of this case study were concluded and verified throughout the continuous analytic comparison of data.

Technology Components and Implementation Procedure

While IVECA was integrated as a part of local classroom activities, its transnational exchange activities were performed through Moodle, an open source online content management system. With the guidance of the teachers, students searched information from the Internet and inserted relevant images into their postings. On special occasions, such as introducing themselves or conducting role-play through audio/video message, either students or teachers used multimedia production tools. Video/still cameras and multimedia editing software were utilized for the activities. Paint, iPhoto, Movie Maker, and iMovie, which were installed as default programs on PC and Mac computers, were used for the image and video editing. Also, microphones for audio recording were sometimes used. Especially for Korean teachers, a commercial web video conference system, WebEx, was used for the IVECA teacher training sessions at a distance. Teachers Room, a Moodle discussion board created for teachers, was used as the basic communication and discussion channel among the teachers in both countries; email was also used. Communication channels of the students were two Moodle discussion boards—one was for formal weekly discussions and the other was for informal daily conversations. For the communication with the investigator (virtual administrator), both email and instant messaging were used in addition to Moodle's Teachers Room.

IVECA weekly topics/activities were introduced to the public school teachers and instructional coordinators. Once each of the schools revised and approved the IVECA curriculum based on their respective curricula's pace/schedule, a final syllabus was posted and distributed through the IVECA classrooms in Moodle. Teachers in both nations were trained through both face-to-face meetings and online training using Moodle. Before beginning IVECA weekly activities, teachers of each nation introduced IVECA to their students and trained them how to use the computer keyboard and Moodle system. IVECA was implemented for a whole school semester.

Three major issues—technological, pedagogical, and organizational factors—influenced adaptability of public schools in Korea and the USA in their integration of IVECA. The following sections relevant to each issue are presented in narrative form in order to illustrate realistic situations of adaptation of IVECA in the public schools. Each scene is based on observation field notes, interviews, informal talk, instant messaging, and journals. There was also a need to pay attention to the conflicts, ineffectiveness, and incoherency of the situations and perspectives of the key players in order to determine the specific problems in this case. Also, searching for positive potentials or alternatives should reveal solutions to the problems. In these narrative sections, the investigator speaks in the first person and appears as a virtual administrator providing instructional consultation, technological training and support.

Technological Issue: What Were the Technological Concerns?

"Didn't we have Movie Maker on our school laptops?"

American school technology specialist, Ms. Thorne was talking on the phone with a city technology officer. While examining the programs and capacity of the school laptops in preparation for IVECA, Ms. Thorne and I could not find Movie Maker in the program menu. The city officer informed her that unnecessary programs had been blocked to prevent students from playing with the programs in their classes.

"Well, let's schedule to meet this week or next week. I will come by your school and unblock any programs your school needs," said the officer. Ms. Thorne typed all programs and multimedia tools that would be required for IVECA activities in the technology check-up request form and submitted it to the city technology officer by email.

"Is it very hard to unblock the path to the programs?"

Ms. Thorne answered my question, "I doubt it, but we are not allowed to change the setting by ourselves. You need to have a security password. The city office manages all computers distributed to the city schools. I guess, if a school messes up something while manipulating their computer settings, it makes harder to get it fixed later on. So, that's why I think the city office wants to have the control over the city school computers maintenance."

In the evenings, while setting up the American school computers with the city technology officer, I also communicated with Korean schools via email and instant messages to check their technology capacity and availability. Each school technology assistant provided information about their computer systems and multimedia production tools. Unlike the American school, where students and teachers used both Mac (at the computer lab) and PC (laptops in this school), the Korean schools only used PC desktop computers. Teachers and students could access all programs on the school PCs—each school was managing their computers. The Korean schools had digital video and still camera for recording school events. However, they did not have multimedia production equipment for students use.

Ms. Kim, the Korean Class 2 teacher, said, "I am not worried. These days, many students have their own digital still or video cameras at home. You know, still camera also can take quite considerable amount of video. I am sure we will figure out how to make video with my students. My students know technology better than me."

As for Internet access, some schools in Korea have installed software to limit students' Internet searches if they use inappropriate keywords such as "sex" or "nude." Korean public schools teach students how to use the Internet appropriately and productively. Consequently, the school computers were basically open to any sites on the World Wide Web.

About a month later, with the help of Ms. Thorne and the American school media specialist, Ms. Laura, the teacher training session was set up at the school. Both Mac and PC computers, video/still cameras, mini DV tapes, microphones were prepared. I asked them,

"Were you able to find the Firewire cables with both 6-4 pins and 4-4 pins?"

A few weeks ago, Ms. Laura and I found that their PCs and Macs had different types of Firewire ports, and that the school did not have the two types of Firewire cables. Ms. Laura expressed her frustration while realizing that her school has multimedia tools, but they are neither compatible with each other, nor are they fully set up for a whole multimedia production process. However, Ms. Laura answered with a big smile,

"Yes, we got it through the city office media center. All our equipment will finally work together!"

Shortly after her excitement, in the middle of the training session, however, I began to hear,

"The page does not open!"

"You might need to wait for a while. The page might have a lot of images."

"No, no, I have been waiting forever. I don't think the site works."

Ms. Perkins, a city office instructional technology teacher, commented,

"Ah, you know what? The site might be blocked by the school network system. We are trying to protect our students from harmful video clips on the web, but it sometimes blocks things too much, you know."

I was introducing the teachers to a website to show some example video clips that will be helpful for their activities on video production of the day. I also planned to provide the teachers with an additional option using a secured web platform to upload students' videos and make them appear in the Moodle system. However, for the day, I emphasized that teachers should be careful in helping their students produce only short-length video clips, which can be handled in Moodle system. Ms. Perkins and I also decided to have another meeting to continue our discussion.

The same training course that the American school teachers took was provided for Korean teachers, but it was delivered only through the online video-conference system, WebEx. Since the teacher training module was designed and offered through the Moodle system as a distance learning course, Korean teachers were also able to follow all the course work with minimum guidance. The participating homeroom teacher in each school attended the session with their support teachers—either a school technology assistant or a technologically competent peer teacher. When asked her reflection on the training experience, Ms. Lee, the Korean Class 3 teacher, answered,

"I am not so proficient in using technologies like this. So I was afraid if I might not be able to follow these required activities, but I feel more confident now. I think I can perform my task. In addition, I have my peer teacher who I can ask a help if I forget how to do this again"

In fact, it was observed through the web conference system that she and her support teacher were laughing together as they worked on their joint video production. They also completed their tasks in the given time. However, Ms. Kim and her school technology assistant imported their video clips with Korean multimedia software. Due to codec incompatibility, the clips would not play properly through Windows Media Player on the American site. Thus, teachers were instructed to use only default multimedia tools as guided in the training module.

The training session was very intensely delivered in four hours instead of two weeks as was initially planned, since the teachers could not find *time* to attend the training together. Although the teachers were enthusiastic and clearly enjoyed experiencing IVECA activities, posting messages, creating video messages, and practicing Moodle functions, I was sorry that they could not have sufficient time to practice collaborating on an actual lesson plan. At the end of the session, Ms. Johnson, the America's Class 2 teacher walked to me and said,

"I really enjoyed today's activities and presentations… I am not still so confident about dealing with the technology and I'm a bit confused about how I should teach my kids and how my students' exchange will happen in Moodle. However, I think I am getting it gradually and I would like to learn more. Let me keep practicing it through the online materials and tutorials you provided, and I hope you would keep helping me to play my work right"

I did not realize at the time the significance of her comment until the end of the IVECA intervention when the program was over.

Pedagogical Application: Did Teachers and Students use IVECA Effectively?

I like IVECA but feel like I haven't really gotten to know anyone because no one's written back to me yet. (Journal)

At the early stage of IVECA implementation, an American Class 2 student, Sara, wrote in her journal that she felt disengaged since she actually had not exchanged messages with any specific counterpart student. I found that her postings were typically posted close to the last one in each discussion thread. Students tended to read messages from the top and reply to the messages as they read. Usually, the computer lab hour was not long enough for students to read and reply to all messages posted. In one of our conversations, Ms. Kim, the Korean Class 2 teacher asked,

"Should I tell my kids to reply to all messages? I am trying to guide my kids to reply as evenly as possible for all American kids' messages, but they usually read the first few postings from the top and it is hard for them to know who is replying to which messages."

While Ms. Kim was trying to find effective ways to engage more students in message exchanges, Ms. Johnson, her counterpart teacher, showed a lack of understanding in how to use Moodle for the exchange activities,

"Are we posting our message this time [at the follow-up's week] or replying to the Korean kids' messages?"

Ms. Keller, the American Class 3 teacher, was also having difficulty guiding her students where to post their messages for the follow-up week activities. Ms. Keller was with one of the students and was trying to guide him:

"Yes, they are gonna reply… If you guys reply in the What's Up board in week three, and they are gonna… is it right [looking at me, investigator]?"

What's Up board allowed students to exchange informal notes about their daily life at anytime. Somehow, she thought that the board was for follow-up activities, which gave additional time for students to edit and complete their unfinished messages, discuss similarities and differences between the two countries' information, and or reply to counterpart student messages. I later found that in the weekly discussion boards from her class, some students had replied to some of the Korean's postings while others had posted new messages in the What's Up board.

After half way through the implementation, Ms. Keller, however, began to integrate her RWE class time with computer lab hour. During her RWE class hours, she showed the IVECA topic announcement page to her students through a projector she checked out in advance. She helped her students have enough time to grasp the objectives and activities of the week's writing topic. She handed out worksheets that she redesigned, based on the IVECA weekly activity guides. Using the worksheet, her students brainstormed in groups what to prepare and to write for the week's postings. A few days later, on the day her class was assigned to use the computer lab, she brought her students to the lab. Students took out their worksheets including the information they had gathered over the week. Ms. Keller made multiple groups with the students and guided them as they discussed and completed their final postings as a group on the IVECA discussion board.

The following week, after the Korean students had posted their messages, Ms. Keller grouped her students again and assigned each group to a certain number of Korean postings. The group members read, discussed, and replied together to the assigned postings first and then freely read and replied to either Koreans' or their own classmates' postings. However, since she had not asked her students to list their names as a group on each posting, there was some misunderstanding among the Korean students:

IVECA activities are very good experience to learn USA's cultures and English. I satisfied with most things, but I was disappointed to a friend who writes a letter very careless [carelessly]. There are kind of cheater who write a letter same with their friends. Think of it, when you did a very good work with your best with very long time, but someone cheat your great ideas! When I'm victim, I will miss a fun to write my idea. Without that, IVECA was very good activity that I have ever done... (Journal)

Since the American students posted the paired group work individually, the same messages were being posted under different author names so that Korean students thought one of them had "cheated" by copying someone else's response. When I was recalling this incident with teachers at the end of the program, Ms. Johnson commented,

I mean it is an experience matter. If you experienced this beforehand, it would be easier. If I do this again, I will be definitely better. I think knowing ahead of time about how I could implement it will be great. (Interview)

While each class lessons were getting formulated over the implementation period, Ms. Keller was often observed reserving the computer lab for IVECA activities. However, it was also observed that she was spending quite a lot of time in checking whether any projectors were available and she would borrow projectors spontaneously. Also, she occasionally asked her students to bring laptops from other classrooms during the RWE class hour. Ms. Burn who participated in IVECA a second time commented on the differences between having a complete technology package set up in one place and having each piece in different locations.

Last year the laptop that we used had the projector on the cart with the computers. So, it was just easy to pull out the projector and put it on the screen. Now, the projector is in another room. It's like when I was thinking about checking out, I just feel like.. Before, it was right there, I just could use it. Now, it's really pathetic excuses....But, I think at this point, it's kind of shame that every classroom doesn't have projector everyday to use. I mean for the kids to read Social Studies books, they can be reading off the Internet and teachers should be showing where to go. (Interview)

In the other site, Mr. Park, the Class 1 teacher in Korea, was showing weekly activities through the built-in projector in his classroom before bringing his students to the computer lab. He integrated many of his subject classes with IVECA activities whenever the topics were relevant to the subject matter.

I once had an objective in my Korean class; Students can identify the organization of the writing and can demonstrate their understanding in the writing through comparison and contrast. I've been emphasizing that we need to be aware of differences between their posting and ours on IVECA. And, it's good chance to apply what they learned about stanza in their Korean class and also good for interdisciplinary learning and application. They have been enjoying learning about other countries in their social studies class also. Well, I design my classes from interdisciplinary approach. For example, we have unit on Internet manner in our practical course subject. I've tried to integrate that unit in IVECA activities. I'm trying to integrate any other related subject matters rather than stick to certain one subject.... (Interview)

Ms. Lee also used the large screen TV in her classroom, which had been distributed to all public school classrooms under the Ministry of Education Information Age project. She used a computer lab for students' actual computing activities—searching for information and relevant images, and posting and replying to messages on IVECA discussion boards. During the week, she took advantage of the TV projector to view IVECA announcement pages at anytime, she guided students in brainstorming topics, and she assigned homework ahead of time.

For the preparative homework assignments, Ms. Kim utilized her class homepage and let her students gradually upload the information they found over the week to use it collaboratively for the IVECA weekly activities. When asked about her teaching strategies, Ms. Kim commented,

Korean students have learned how to use computer software like Microsoft Word, PowerPoint and Hangul and they know even better than teachers in using the Internet, playing with images, multimedia and so on. You know computer education is a required curriculum in public schools in Korea...But, of course, there are some kids who left behind than others. But they teach and learn with each other. I actually didn't do much with technology for IVECA. My students did follow the IVECA instruction. I just guided them to understand the value of this cultural learning, help them to grasp topics and find the appropriate contents for them to write effectively. As we used to use our homepage for the class homework submission, I guided them to use it for IVECA preparation, too. It is just like my Korean language education class. (Interview)

As Ms. Kim mentioned, the Korean students easily found relevant images and embedded them into most of their postings. The American students showed their excitement when they read the Korean's messages including images:

Bruce was concentrated on reading each message from the beginning of the class. As he saw pictures of dessert, "Wow~", he smiled with his friend, Walt. Bruce found another picture [in the Korean students' postings], "Look at this" John responded, "Oh, my god"... "Woah... hahaha"

Bruce and John are talking about images of vegetables. When they scrolled down and read another message, "Oh, they like steak... Wohoo!!!" They read every single message carefully and expressed their excitement and surprise. Tom was looking at John's screen. Carol was not even looking around as she read the Korean students' messages and replied to their messages (Field note)

Such images also helped the Korean students understand the American students' messages written in English. When Donsuk was asked about what he learned through the activities. He answered,

Culture. But I could not fully understand. I could guess the meanings by looking at pictures. [And then] friends who are good at English told me the [exact] meanings. (Interview)

Since students enjoyed using images, which were helpful for communications as well as increased students' interests, they were motivated to use images appropriate for their counterparts. The Korean teachers allowed their students to search image files on the Internet, and the students were able to attach them once their teacher guided them through the process. However, the American students had restricted Internet access. The school technology specialist, Ms. Thorne, usually found images and stored them on the school sever in advance and students could only use images from this pool in their postings.

As the implementation progressed, it was often observed that many American students were typing messages with only one finger or just one hand. They gradually showed improvement in typing and some of the students said that IVECA motivated them to practice typing faster. However, a few students who had poor typing skills and very low writing proficiency reported that throughout the entire program, typing made it difficult for them to perform writing tasks for IVECA.

I mean the only part I really didn't like was the typing part.... But to actually talk to them and actually read what they have to say, because they do have like pretty cool stuff, I actually liked that part.... And like other people [his close friends who had the same problem in typing with poor writing skill] it's the same way and like I think it's just because of the typing because they don't really like to do it [typing] and it get's really boring. (Interview)

Knowing that America also emphasize technological literacy, I wondered why these kids had not yet been trained in typing, at school. I asked one of the American teachers about the possible reasons. One of the answers led me to further explore the school's policies and administrative functions.

Teachers and schools are very focused on students' academic achievement. We have State level tests. School's major interest is whether or not our students will pass the standard of learning. Keyboarding? It is not included in the test. Our students begin to learn typing from 6th grade. (Informal talk)

Organizational Influence: How were the Schools Managed?

"Oh, I am sorry. We could not post anything yesterday."

"No, no, you don't need to apologize. What happened?"

"All 6th grade students had to take SOL test prep at the time we normally use for IVECA, and I could not change my computer lab hour ahead of time"

When I encountered Ms. Keller in the cafeteria during her lunch time, she explained why her students could not post any messages to that week's IVECA board. I sat down next to her and asked about how she was doing with IVECA and whether she had any difficulties. She said,

"No, I am enjoying IVECA. Remember? At the beginning, my students were like, I-don't-know-what-to-write, why-do-we-write-this... kind of attitude. But now they write a couple of paragraphs much faster and their writings make sense better than before. I think they also try to get attention from Korean kids, and you know what? As a matter of fact, my kids were sort of open their mind because they could see Korean kids use two languages and some of the Korean kids' life styles are better than their lives, and foods and traditions are so rich and interesting to them. My kids are realizing that they have not known well even their own culture, the meaning of the flag and history and so on. I think IVECA is really good for them to learn not only different culture but also their own culture. They learn from the students overseas. So, how interesting it is! Ha-ha-ha..."

Ms. Keller kept going on and on about IVECA, but finally she began to talk about her concerns.

"These weeks, we had not enough time for IVECA preparation because of SOL preparation. My kids' level is low, so I had to pay attention to their SOL test score.... It will be good if the principal let public to know this program will be good, this is pretty cool, and how we integrate teaching with our kids. I think it would be a good role as a principal."

She reminded me of a conversation with Ms. Burn in the computer lab. She said,

Ms. Johnson and I were talking about this the other day. You know kids are doing NCLB thing and take test. But this [IVECA] is much meaningful activity. They have reasons why they are writing and enjoy it. And they express something they could do by going there for the people [Korean kids]. Won't you need go and let principal know this? This is real experience and meaningful. They need to do this at RWE mainly! (informal talk)

When Ms. Keller had almost finished her lunch, I asked her if she had informed her Korean counterpart of when her students would be able to do the weekly activities. I was concerned since the Korean students could move to the next week activities based on American students' postings this week. Furthermore, I had seen some messages from some Korean kids, at the What's Up board, wondering why their American friends had not been posting. Ms. Keller said she hadn't and explained that it was because of her busyness at school due to the test preparation. I told her that I would check with Korean teacher about the pacing adjustment.

Later that evening, I left a message in the virtual Teacher Room to inform Ms. Keller's counterpart, Ms. Lee, about the situation in the American site and suggested an alternative pacing option. Although I did not receive a response from Ms. Lee, I saw that her students had moved on to the next week's activities. In the mean time, I received an email from Ms. Lee. She understood the American school situation and mentioned that her school would be very busy over the next a couple of weeks since they had a very important school function to attend to.. Much later, when the program ended, I found out how busy she really was those days. She explained,

My principal Mr. Shin does not know much about this activity. He is more interested in Art. He devoted his whole career to Art education. Since my school is a model school, I had to turn in activity reports of seven different topics with my 6th graders. To be honest, my formal vice-principal introduced me to IVECA, but (after he moved to another school) neither the principal nor new vice-principal were interested in IVECA....As my class is the only one for IVECA, I felt isolated from other classes. (Interview)

I responded to her email by asking if it would be hard to follow the IVECA pace during school hours. I suggested that she encourage her students to keep interacting with American kids freely through the What's Up board. I also suggested encouraging individual participation in weekly discussions before the whole class could come back to the topic. She agreed to my suggestions and left a message for Ms. Keller regarding her school situation and activity plan, in the Teacher Room.

I also observed that the number of students' postings in Korean Class 2 had been decreasing over the last two weeks and the consistency of postings was not as good as that of previous weeks. As a result, many of the American student postings did not have any replies. Since in the Teacher Room I could not find any messages written by Ms. Kim regarding a pacing problem, I proposed an on-line meeting with her. At the end of the school day, when she became available online, she began to type messages:

"I just came back to my classroom from school playfield. How are you?"

"Pretty good thanks. What's going on in your school?"

"It's autumn sports festival season. It's been so crazy these couple of weeks. Because all of our 6th grade students will be doing a Taekon-Dance performance in the festival next week, we have to rehearse during class time. It has been hard to find time for any activity including IVECA because of these practices."

"Ah… that's why I could not see your student postings as usual. You know kids are very sensitive about the replies. They might wonder if the Korean kids do not like to talk to them anymore"

"Oh, they might, I know. My kids are also eager to receive replies. I should've informed Ms. Johnson. I've been just so pre-occupied. But you know my kids love IVECA. Actually they have been asking when we are going to computer lab for the activities all the time. Next week, once the festival is over, I am sure my kids will be able to go back to normal pace."

So, I suggested that she do another follow-up activity the following week instead of working on next week's topic. I also conveyed the pacing adjustment to Ms. Johnson through the Teacher Room.

When I was about to log-off from the instant messaging application, Mr. Park sent me a text message saying his kids might not be able to do IVECA because they had a mid-term exam and would be going on a field trip after the exam. I told him that I wished he could have included some questions related to IVECA activities in the exam questionnaire. Along with a smile emoticon, he said that he thought it should be that way and that it would be possible if all 6th grader teachers participated in IVECA together. He further noted that in elementary schools in Korea, teachers develop their exam questionnaire based on the national curriculum objectives. I also asked him if IVECA had been too much work. He said,

Since IVECA bulletin board has clear instructions on it and is well managed, students can use it without calling out for help. Thus, it's not been a big burden to teachers. Honestly, I don't think I've done anything. Rather, it lightened the burden on the teacher-discretion class [Da-neem Jai-riang class that teacher can run the class curriculum as they want], which we need to utilize computer in my class. (Interview)

I asked him if his principal, Mr. Hong, had ever talked about IVECA with him. Mr. Park said that Principal Hong was very interested in IVECA, and in fact it was the principal introduced who had introduced him to IVECA. Whenever the principal saw Mr. Park, he would check to see how he was doing with IVECA and offer encouragement. Mr. Park commented that his principal's encouragement reaffirmed that he was doing the right thing for his students. After the project ended, I visited the principal and learned that the he was linking IVECA to English education and cultural learning integrated with other relevant subject matters:

[Through IVECA] we not only learn other language but also can pick up the culture and apply that in using that language. Since learning the language helps students learn about the culture automatically, it would help them in communicating with foreigners. We call it an interdisciplinary subject. It would be great to use the subject in which computers, English, or other subject matter are integrated. (Interview)

Mr. Hong additionally commented that IVECA fits perfectly with Korean society's interest in globalization, English education, and the missions of his school—producing global citizens, promoting English proficiency and cultural understanding, and utilizing ICT in education.

Near the end of the program, as suggested by American teachers during the project period, I also tried to convey the value of IVECA to the school administration. First, I met with the instructional coordinator, Ms. Spreen. She is a school leadership team member as well as one of the IVECA support teachers. I asked how she saw IVECA with respect to the Standards of Learning (SOL) and No Child Left Behind (NCLB) issues at school. She very confidently expressed her perspective on IVECA:

I think that, to me, the biggest piece of the IVECA is the exchange of cultures. But within exchange of culture then can you weigh up infuse what we are required by the State to teach. So, you know, when we are thinking about skills, that skills is going back into a piece of literature or an article and picking up some details or answering some questions, and then we could use the articles that they read or maybe they are summarizing and giving their opinions back to somebody else. Those are good skills and that something that our kids need to know.... And then we will be pointing out to the teachers how this is not a stand-alone, this is not something in addition to what you have to do. This could be in places something and maybe pointing out where our standards are really in there. (Interview)

She also added that it could be about whether or not teachers can make the link between the State requirement and IVECA activities. In fact, Ms. Spreen could not attend the initial training course due to schedule conflicts. Nor was she observed giving any instructional support for teachers over the program implementation period, which is why, she explained, most IVECA teachers had not come to her for help. Nevertheless, her perception about IVECA made me think that other IVECA teachers should have worked with her earlier. I wondered what the principal would want to say about IVECA.

"How are you? Ms. Smith. We are all done with IVECA this semester. Have you had a chance to hear about the program from anyone?"

"No, actually not, I think Ms. Spreen is the person who communicates with the teachers."

"Oh, then you might have talked with Ms. Spreen about IVECA."

"Well… no, we had not had a chance to talk about it specifically. This is my first semester as a principal. The leadership team has had to dealt with many things, haha. But I know which teachers were working on the project and what the program is about"

Ms. Smith commented on her perception of IVECA,

Everybody says these days… is global economy and world are spread everything, but I do think it is true. My students need to be able to understand other cultures and communicate with people of all different types. (Interview)

To the question about the goals and mission of her school, Ms. Smith clearly stressed that the mission of the school was to facilitate students' high achievement in SOL test scores, and to conform with the NCLB Act regulations. She also described how IVECA is related to the school goal and RWE curriculum.

I think the project like this fits in because there was a still teacher choice in how you deliver the curriculum so a project like this that has a strong writing component to it where the kids have written it fits perfectly in for our RWE class because we are doing concentration on reading and writing during the two hour block...I think that like anything needs to fit. Teachers need to see this as something well the children in learning communication skills, writing skills, thinking about how they want to formulate their idea to communicate fits into my RWE program. (Interview)

Consequently, I did not need to explain the benefit of IVECA to her, since Ms. Smith was of a like mind. However, I did need to tell the IVECA teachers what the principal thought.

In light of the issues set forth in the narrative sections above, what needs to be done?

CURRENT CHALLENGES FACING THE ORGANIZATION

As illustrated above, the study revealed that technological, pedagogical, and organizational issues affected the adaptability of public schools in both Korea and America in integrating cross-cultural virtual learning activities, IVECA. Additionally, schools faced challenging issues for further adoptions of IVECA.

Specific Problems Addressed

Technologically, the American school needed to set up all the different types of equipments to be compatible and access to the required programs needed to be unblocked. Both American and Korean schools had to make sure they used common multimedia software so that the created video files could be viewable in both countries. All participating teachers should be trained how to utilize online course management system (CMS) and how to produce diverse types of communication forms including text, audio, and video. This is also related to pedagogical issues.

To provide effective instruction and interculturally meaningful learning opportunities for students, teachers needed to be familiar with how IVECA exchange processes work and how IVECA is integrated with local curricula. Efficient and easy access to technologies helped teachers effectively adapt integration of IVECA with their class activities. While Korean classrooms were equipped with built-in projectors and large screen televisions, American schools needed to check out the equipment ahead of time. Technological competence of the students also influenced the implementation of IVECA. The Korean teachers let their students handle image files and allowed them to utilize the Internet for their activities. American students had a technology specialist assist them in the use of image files, and their Internet searches were relatively restricted. Some American students had difficulties in typing for IVECA activities. A school's organizational management based on state or national policy affected these differences.

Korea's public elementary schools are required to teach computer education from the first grade. While the Virginia emphasizes technology utilization in schools, at the local level, schools are more focused on SOL testing, which does not test computer skills. Official approval of IVECA integration by school principals was desired by participant teachers in both Korea and American schools in managing their time to adapt IVECA. The benefits of IVECA need to be connected to a principal's educational focus and a school's mission, state/national learning objectives, and national curriculum goals. However, communication and sharing perspectives between the teachers and administrators need to be established for adapting IVECA effectively under the support of school administration.

Challenges and Current Status

After the project was completed, participant teachers and administrators discussed with the investigator how they could continue to implement and integrate IVECA into their school activities.

American school teachers suggested that classrooms be set up in a way that teachers do not need to plan for and check out technology equipment in advance, bring it to classrooms and set it up in their classroom every time. The teachers agreed they should at least be able to view the IVECA website in any class hour for effective integration and efficient class time management. However, Principal Smith stated that her school does not have enough funds to install such equipment in every classroom nor set up an additional room with a full set of multimedia and computing equipment. Ms. Smith said that someone at school level should persuade the school board or city office. A principal may suggest the need for technology funding, but actual decision making for granting the funds comes out of the board. Alternatively, an investigator from a university and school members could write up grant proposal to obtain funding from an educational technology fund resource or state/federal level grant program. Ms. Smith said someone should be dedicated to such work.

All American participating teachers thought IVECA had high-quality activities and were willing to rejoin the project in the future. However, they were not sure if it would be possible to have all of the same-grade teachers join IVECA to make it fully adapted to their school. They said that since the pressure from SOL testing is heavy, most teachers tend to avoid implementing creative teaching. To meet the state and school requirements, they preferred to drill students in content and test-taking skills. Helping such teachers understand that IVECA is integrated with their curriculum and training them to be capable for IVECA utilization seemed challenging. Along with it, providing students with computer education from younger grade would become a challenge.

As for the matter of having all same-grade teachers participate in IVECA, Korean teachers were rather positive. Since Korean teachers already tend to work collaboratively with the same-grade teachers, they thought it would make their schools more adaptable to IVECA integration. If some teachers did not know how to use technology, they said other teachers would help them. However, one of the participant teachers expressed a concern that older teachers might be hesitant to join because of their limited English proficiency. The other two teachers pointed out that this issue would be also resolved by working together with the same-grade teachers.They also commented that students could be used for the communication. English could be a problem, but they agreed it would simply be a matter of how to provide training for those hesitant teachers to take advantage of IVECA and the collaborative work from peer teachers.

One of the growing problems in using the Internet was also pointed out. Korean students are very exposed to cyber games, such that child Interent addiction has become a significant social issue. In 2007, Korea Agency for Digital Opportunity and Promotion reported degree of elementary students' Intenet addition—1.2% (high risk) and 11.0% (potentially at-risk) (MEST & KERIS, 2007). During the IVECA impelementation, a student who thought he was addicted to Internet gaming reported that he did not pay attention during the program. He found out too late that there were, in fact, some very interesting activities. However, he said that he could not resist his desire to play games when sitting at the computer lab. Developing the instructional strategies to engage such children in IVECA and helping them overcome such addiction would be one of the next challenging tasks for Korean schools.

Currently, the American school installed a projector and an electronic white-board in every classroom and they are connnected to the teacher's computer. City office of education supported the installations so that the school's adaptability of technology infrastructure has been improved dramatically over a year. This American school is planning to join IVECA and interact with several schools in Korea elementary schools soon.

SOLUTIONS AND RECOMMENDATIONS

As described above, investigating technological, educational, and organizational issues identifies specific problems determining public schools adaptability of cross-cultural classroom exchange activities (in this study, IVECA). The problems that schools can resolve internally are not an issue. However, the challenges come from problems that schools cannot find any alternatives to, or that they have difficulties adopting a solution. In an attempt to provide schools with a solution guide, this section first clarifies the factors that influence public school adaptability. Second, solutions to the challenges schools faced will be discussed in economic, social, cultural and political contexts. Ultimately, this paper will provide recommendations to diffuse further cross-cultural virtual classroom exchange programs integrated with pubic school systems.

Adaptability Factors as Solution Guides

Figure 2 presents the primary factors and its subordinate elements of public schools adaptability to IVECA.

Figure 2. Adaptability factors in public school. Integration with cross-cultural classroom exchange programs

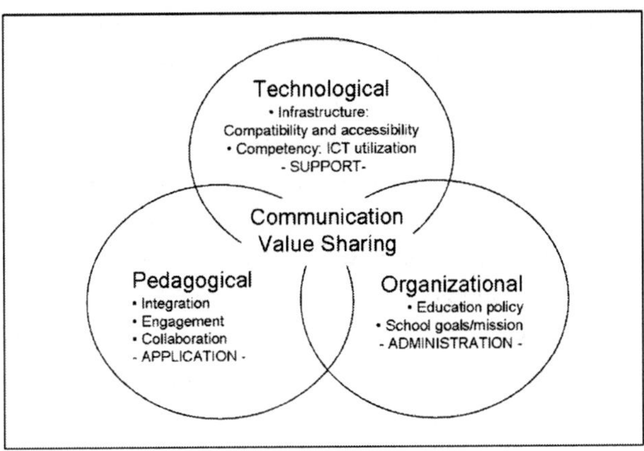

The technological factor consists of two elements—technological infrastructure and competency of ICT users (key players: students, teachers, and resource teachers) in schools. Although schools have technologies for online activities and multimedia production, all equipments and computer systems need to be compatible in the system. In addition, the easier it is for users to access the technologies, the more adaptable schools are. Research has also addressed the positive relationship between easy access to technologies and technology integration in teaching (Williams, Coles, Richardson, Wilson, & Tuson, 2000; Dexter, 2002). Additionally, schools are more adaptable to IVECA when the teachers and students are competent in using ICT including online content management systems, typing, diverse media tools, and software. This factor is about how school infrastructure and key players are technologically supportive to the implementation process.

The pedagogical factor is related to how well teachers integrate IVECA with their classroom activities. Teachers in a decentralized curriculum system need to be proficient in grasping the relationship between IVECA topics/activities and state learning objectives. Teachers in a centralized curriculum system can link IVECA topics/activities to relevant subject unit objectives. They can also use their textbooks for IVECA activity content material. Appropriate engagement skills for intercultural exchange are critical to successful cross-cultural learning. Teacher intercultural sensitivity influences student intercultural understanding (Van Hook, 2005). Teachers need to have instructional strategies when applying student group projects, thereby enabling each member to contribute to achieving the goal of the group cooperatively. The more group projects promote collaboration with counterparts, the more successful the adaptation to IVECA will be. In addition, collaborative teaching with peer teachers increases the adaptability.

Since state and national education policy governs the goals, missions and curricula of local public schools, the organizational factor significantly affects a schools' adaptability. When school administrators find the connection between the benefit of IVECA and emphases of education policy, schools become more adaptable to IVECA. However, appropriate managerial strategies of school administrators are required in fostering the adaption processes of schools. For example, establishing clear communication channels among teachers, resource teachers, and leadership teams help them know that school authorizes IVECA. This facilitates the adoption of IVECA as part of school curricula. Such communication channels include meetings to enhance pedagogical and technological adaptation. Such meetings provide teachers with opportunities to collaborate and to share experiences and insights that could enhance adaptability. As Rogers (2003) also emphasizes, sharing the benefits of innovation (IVECA) among adopters (teachers) expedites its adaptation.

Additionally, to adopt IVECA as a formal school curriculum, public schools under a strictly centralized system need authorization from local offices of education in the context of education policy established by a Ministry of Education. Thus, the adaptability of such public schools has greater influence from higher level organizations and national education policy. However, once it is approved, the scope of IVECA dissemination becomes large and schools' adaptability can dramatically increase.

The factors clarified above will guide local schools in solving the specific problems identified in this case study. The following section discusses solutions for the current challenges that the schools faced in broader context. Recommendation of the solutions will be provided beyond local school level to the economical, cultural and political context.

Solutions and Recommendations

The challenges that the public schools met in further adapting IVECA include: 1) obtaining funds or support from State/National offices of Education to construct technological infrastructure 2) helping teachers avoid limiting their teaching due to the SOL test, 3) promoting teacher competency and collaboration, and 4) engaging students addicted to Internet gaming.

The first challenge involves technological policy matters in terms of distributing technologies to schools. The second challenge also is relevant to educational policy along with professional development issues. The third challenge pertains to pedagogical and organizational aspects of teacher preparation. The last challenge is related to pedagogical and technological issues. Overall, these challenges are related to educational technology policy, teacher preparation and professional development. Thus, the solutions lie in identifying the roles of key players, policy makers and higher education teacher educators.

Recommendation one: Policy makers increase educational technology budgets to enhance technological infrastructure for public schools in order to promote adaptability of cross-cultural virtual exchange activities worldwide. Such support would foster social and economic potential as well as educational advancement.

The theme of this case study—public school adaptability in cross-cultural virtual classroom exchange program integration—implies a relationship with political, cultural, technological, and educational issues. Elucidation of these relationships should provide policy makers with sufficient reason to act on this recommendation. Society demands that education facilitate cultural understanding among people and nations. The use of information and communication technology (ICT) as means to that end is very promising. Furthermore, the utilization of ICT in education will contribute to society's economic growth due to the nature of our global knowledge-based economy.

Recently, international organizations have paid marked attention to promoting mutual understanding and respect for cultural differences among nations and culturally different groups of people. Established in 2005, United Nations Alliance of Civilizations (AoC) identified four main fields of action—*education, youth, migration, and media*—to resolve cultural conflicts around the world (United Nations, 2007; 2008). AoC addresses the significance of improving "mutual respect and understanding through the positive experiences resulting from increasingly direct encounters between people of diverse cultures" (Kerim, 2007). Since 2006, the United Nations Global Alliance for ICT and Development has been dedicated to enhancing world harmony and facilitating co-development through the use of ICT (UNGAID, 2009). Asia-Europe Meeting also emphasizes "promoting dialogue among cultures and civilizations and mutual understanding between people of Asia and Europe" (Xinhua News, 2008).

Such international organizations and academia agree that education plays a critical role in producing global citizens who are respectful of cultural differences and capable of interacting and cooperating with people from other countries and cultures. Reimers (2006) stresses that schools should cultivate students to possess global citizenship by teaching them how to communicate in peaceful and constructive ways across-cultural differences. He also posits that schools need to inculcate global values in their students through curriculum. At the UNESCO Expert Meeting on Intercultural Education, scholars underscored the need to implement intercultural education in all levels of education to help students become interculturally competent global citizens (UNESCO, 2006b).

Currently, due to the increased rates of international marriages, illegal immigrants, North Korean refugees, and international trainees, Korean society has become more multicultural. Educators and society in general are urged to develop best practices in multicultural education, and to that end, the use of an e-learning format is considered to be the most promising (Park & O'Neill, 2009).

In response to America's economic crisis, an emphasis has been placed on education as a fundamental resource for long-term and sustainable development of the nation. In the American Recovery and Reinvestment Act of 2009, investment for education technology was underscored by the motto of Education for the 21st Century. It was to ensure economic competitiveness of the next generation (House of Representatives, 2009). Exchange programs of "online learning for teachers and children around the world" were also specifically suggested as ways to promote development and preserve different cultural value through education (New York Times, 2009).

Cross-cultural virtual classroom exchange programs, such as IVECA, promote children's intercultural competence and provide them with opportunity to utilize and develop ICT skills (e.g. information searches, creating electronic projects, and utilizing information for international exchanges). By exchanging ideas, discussing issues, and sharing thoughts and feelings with classmates and international counterparts, students develop analytic and critical thinking, and communicative strategies. These skills are essential to being a competent human resource for 21st century global society. Most importantly, IVECA helps students broaden their worldview and grow as global citizens by providing them with ways and means to define their own cultural identity and overcome racism and prejudice through the acquisition of global knowledge and values in diverse cultures (O'Neill, 2007; 2008).

It is certain that cross-cultural virtual classroom exchange activities fulfill social, economic, cultural needs. Therefore, policy makers need to plan immediate actions to help public schools adapt to cross-cultural virtual exchange activities through their regular school curricula and provide financial support at the state and national levels. The wider such cross-cultural learning opportunities are diffused, the greater the impact on society and the economy will be.

Recommendation two: Teacher educators in higher education need to internationalize teacher education programs and provide intercultural dialogues among pre-service teachers through the Web. Internationalized interdisciplinary teacher education programs integrated with educational technology and intercultural/multicultural education will produce quality teachers required for adapting cross-cultural virtual classroom exchanges in schools.

Studies have stressed the importance of the teacher's role in promoting intercultural learning in second/foreign language students (Byram, 2001). Genuine engagement strategies based on intercultural sensitivity and competence are known to positively influence minority student performance (Nel, 1992) and increase the effectiveness of intercultural virtual classroom exchange (O'Neill, 2008).

The effectiveness of teacher technology competence on students learning has been addressed. Albee (2003) focuses on increasing pre-service teachers' technology skill preparedness in stating teachers' technology competence increases the effectiveness of teaching. Experienced teachers also have recommended that pre-service teacher education programs include technology competence development (Fisher, 1997). Teachers who experienced IVECA also noted the importance of developing technological proficiency in online classroom activities and multimedia communication.

IVECA teachers testified they could better grasp how cross-cultural learning can be integrated with their curriculum after they experienced the activities over the course of a semester. Kearsley (1998) posits that teacher training should be planned in the form of long term, on-going and experience-based training. He also stresses that the training focus should be on instructional applications of the technologies and contents.

Therefore, pre-service teachers need realistic opportunities to develop their intercultural competence and their utilization of technology for cross-cultural virtual classroom exchange activities. By linking interdisciplinary teacher education programs overseas through the Internet, teacher education programs should facilitate pre-service teachers' real experience in cross-cultural virtual exchange activities. As a result, pre-service teachers will be able to enhance their intercultural understanding and will be trained how to utilize technologies for online cross-cultural learning. Developing student teaching programs in local schools will promote sustainable adaptability to cross-cultural exchange activities. At the same time, continued scholarly discourse and research through this exchange program would advance the quality of cross-cultural classroom exchange programs benefiting not only students and society in each nation but also global society.

Furthermore, state and national offices of education can collaborate with universities in providing professional development courses for cross-cultural virtual classroom exchanges. In addition, it will be more practical if policy makers establish a teacher education and employment policy that credits such pre- and in-service teachers, who took the training course or experienced cross-cultural virtual classroom exchange activities.

Naturally, these two recommendations will require systematic collaboration. The vision is that such collaborative efforts will increase the adaptability of local schools in cross-cultural classroom exchange activities, and ultimately produce an international virtual schooling system. As more students can join such schools, there will be greater reduction in cultural conflicts and a collaborative development of a world economy. Universities and nonprofit organizations in Korea and America have established and are seeking further international collaboration from academia, ministries, technology firms, and international organizations. The nature of such collaboration supports the long-standing efforts of the United Nations and UNESCO to create a better world.

The education of the young and exchanges of young people and of ideas in a spirit of peace, mutual respect and understanding between peoples can help to improve international relations and to strengthen peace and security (General Assembly resolution 2037 (XX) of 7 December 1965).

REFERENCES

Albee, J. (2003). A Study of Preservice Elementary Teachers Technology Skill Preparedness and Examples of How It Can Be Increased. *Journal of Technology and Teacher Education*, 11.

Asian Development Bank. (2003). *Key Indicators: Education for Global Participation*. Retrieved from http://www.adb.org/Documents/Books/Key_Indicators/2003/pdf/theme_paper.pdf

Bloom, D. E. (2004). Globalization and Education: An Economic Perspective, In M. Suarez-Orozco & D. Qin-Hillard, (Ed.), *Globalization: Culture and Education in the New Millennium.* (pp. 58-77). Ewing, NJ: University of California Press.

Burke, J. (2003). *Intercultural Education Summit Keynote.* Retrieved from http://people.ucsc.edu/~pmmckerc/IEA.html

Byram, M., Nichols, A., & Stevens, D. (Eds.). (2001). *Developing Intercultural Competence in Practice: Languages for Intercultural Communication and Education.* Multilingual Matters, Ltd.

Culp, K. M., Honey, M., & Mandinach, E. (2003). *A Retrospective on Twenty Years of Education Technology Policy.* Washington, DC: Center for Children and Technology Education Development Center, U.S. Department of Education, Office of Educational Technology.

Dexter, S. (2002). eTIPS-Educational Technology Integration Principles. *Designing instruction for technology-enhanced learning.* Hershey, PA: Idea Group Publishing.

Fantini, A. E. (2000). A CENTRAL Concern: Developing Intercultural Competence. In *SIT Occasional Papers Series,* (1). Brattleboro, VT: School for International Training.

Fantini, A. E. (2006). *Final Report of a Research Project conducted by the Federation of The Experiment in International Living with funding support from the Center for Social Development at Washington University, St. Louis, Missouri* (The Initial Phase of An Extended Project to Explore and Assess Intercultural Outcomes in Service Program Participants Worldwide). Brattleboro, VT: Federation EIL

Fisher, M. (1997). The Voice of Experience: Inservice Teacher Technology Competency Recommendations for Preservice Teacher Preparation. *Journal of Technology and Teacher Education*, *5*(2-3), 139–147.

Kearsley, G. (1998). Educational Technology: A Critique. *Educational Technology*, *38*(2), 47–51.

Kerim, S. (2007, September). *Statement of the 62nd Session of the United Nations General Assembly at the Ministerial Meetings of Group of Friends of the Alliance of Civilizations*, New York. Retrieved from http://www.unaoc.org/images/articles/min_pga.pdf

Korea Education & Research Information Service. (2000-2004). *White Paper: Adapting Education to the Information Age.* Seoul: Korea, Retrieved from http://english.keris.or.kr/etc/whitepaper.jsp

Korean Culture and Information Service Ministry of Culture. (2008). *Facts about Korea.* Korean Government Publication.

Lasonen, J. (2006). *Expert Meeting on Intercultural Education: Intercultural Education in the Context of Internationalization, Localization and Globalization*. Paris: UNESCO Headquarters.

MEST & KERIS. (2007). 2007Adapting Education to the Information Age. Seoul, Korea: Ministry of Education, Science and Technology & Korea Education and Research Information Service. Retrieved from http://www.keris.or.kr/download/data/2007-WhitePap.pdf

Morris, P. (1996). Asia's Four Little Tigers: a comparison of the role of education in their development. *Comparative Education*, *32*(1), 95–109. doi:10.1080/03050069628948

Nel, J. (1992). The Empowerment of Minority Students: Implications of Cummins. *Action in Teacher Education*, *14*(3), 38–45.

New York Times. (2009, June 4). Obama's Speech in Cairo. *New York Times*. Retrieved June 4, 2009, from http://www.nytimes.com/2009/06/04/us/politics/04obama.text.html?pagewanted=7

O'Neill, E. J. (2007). Implementing International Virtual Elementary Classroom Activities for Public Schools Students in the U.S. and Korea. *Electronic Journal e-Learning, 5*(3), 207-218.

O'Neill, E. J. (2008). *Intercultural Competence Development: Implementing International Virtual Elementary Classroom Activities for Public Schools Students in the U.S. and Korea.* Doctoral dissertation, University of Virginia.

Park, N., & O'Neill, E. J. (2009). *Adapting to Cultural Diversity: Policy to Promote Intercultural Education Policy in Korea.* Paper presented at 2009 World Civic Forum, Seoul, Korea.

Reimers, F. (2006, September). Citizenship, Identity and Education: Examining the public purposes of schools in an age of globalization. *Prospects*, *36*(3).

Rogers, E. M. (2003). *Diffusion of Innovations (5th ed.)*. New York: Simon and Schuster.

State Board of Education. (2003). *Educational Technology Plan for Virginia: 2003-2009.* Virginia Department of Education.

Tellis, W. (1997). Introduction to Case Study. *Qualitative Report*, *3*(2).

UNESCO. (1993). *World Education Report,* Paris: UNESCO Publishing.

UNESCO. (2006a). *Guideline on International Education*. Paris: UNESCO Headquarters.

UNESCO. (2006b). *Expert Meeting on Intercultural Education.* Paris: UNESCO Headquarters.

United National Global Alliance for ICT and Development. (2009). *Our Mission.* Retrieved June 3, 2009, from http://www.un-gaid.org/About/OurMission/tabid/893/language/en-US/Default.aspx

United Nations. (1965). *Declaration on the Promotion among Youth of the Ideals of Peace, Mutual Respect and Understanding between Peoples*. Retrieved April 22, 2007, from http://www.unhchr.ch/html/menu3/b/65.htm

United Nations. (2006, November). *Alliance of Civilizations Report of the High-level Group.* New York: U.S. from http://www.unaoc.org/repository/HLG_Report.pdf

United Nations. (2007, September). *UN High Representative for Alliance of Civilizations: Address to the AoC Group of Friends (Ministry Level).* New York: U.S., ECOSOC Chamber, Retrieved from http://www.unaoc.org/images/articles/hr_final_remarks.pdf

United Nations. (2008, January). *The First Alliance of Civilization Forum, Madrid.* New York: U.S., Alliance of Civilization. Retrieved from http://www.unaoc.org/images/aoc%20forum%20report%20madrid%20complete.pdf

Van Hook, C. W. (2005). Preparing Teachers for the Diverse Classroom: A Developmental Model of Intercultural Sensitivity. *University of Illinois at Urbana-Champaign: Clearinghouse on Early Education and Parenting (CEEP), Early Childhood and Parenting (ECAP). Collaborative, 22*(6), 67–72.

White House. (2002, September). Remarks on Implementation of the No Child Left Behind Act of 2001. *Weekly Compilation of Presidential Documents, 38*(36), 1482-1486. Washington, DC: US Government Printing Office, Retrieved from http://www.gpo.gov/fdsys/pkg/WCPD-2002-09-09/html/WCPD-2002-09-09-Pg1482.htm

Williams, D., Coles, L., Richardson, A., Wilson, K., & Tuson, J. (2000). Integrating Information and Communications Technology in Professional Practice: an Analysis of Teachers' Needs Based on a Survey of Primary and Secondary Teachers in Scottish Schools. *Technology, Pedagogy and Education, 9*(2), 167–182. doi:10.1080/14759390000200089

Xinhua News. (2008, October 25). ASEM Resolves to Further Promote Interfaith Understanding and Exchanges. In *the news of 7th Asia-Europe Meeting.* Retrieved January 9, 2009 from http://news.xinhuanet.com/english/2008-10/26/content_10252340.htm

ADDITIONAL READING

Bennett, J. M., & Bennett, M. J. (2001). Developing Intercultural Sensitivity: An Integrative Approach to Global and Domestic Diversity. *Paper delivered to the Diversity Symposium, Diversity Collegiums, Bentley College, Waltham, MA.*

Davis, N., & Cho, M. O. (2005). Intercultural competence for future leaders of educational technology and its evaluation. *Interactive Educational Multimedia, 10*, 1–22.

Davis, N., & Niederhauser, D. S. (2007). Virtual Schooling. *Learning & Leading with Technology, 34*(7), 6.

Dawes, L. (2001). What stops teachers using new technology. *Issues in teaching using ICT.* New York: Routledge Falmer.

Earle, R. S. (2002). The integration of instructional technology into public education: Promises and challenges. *Educational Technology, 42*(1), 5–13.

Elbaum, B., McIntyre, C., & Smith, A. (2002). *Essential Elements: Prepare, Design, and Teach Your Online Course*. Madison: Atwood Pub.

Fantini, A. E. (1995). Introduction-language, culture and world view: Exploring the nexus. *International Journal of Intercultural Relations, 19*(2), 143–153. doi:10.1016/0147-1767(95)00025-7

Grant, A. C. (2006). *The development of global awareness in elementary students through participation in an online cross-cultural project.* Unpublished Ph.D., Louisiana State University and Agricultural & Mechanical College, United States -- Louisiana.

Guiherme, M. (2002). Critical citizens for an intercultural world: Foreign Language Education as Cultural Politics: LICE: Language for Intercultural Communication and Education

Hammer, M. R., Bennett, M. J., & Wiseman, R. (2003). Measuring intercultural sensitivity: The intercultural development inventory. *International Journal of Intercultural Relations, 27*(4), 421–443. doi:10.1016/S0147-1767(03)00032-4

Hanvey, R. G. (1982). An Attainable Global Perspective. *Theory into Practice, 21*(3), 162–167. doi:10.1080/00405848209543001

Harms, C. M., Niederhauser, D. S., Davis, N. E., Roblyer, M. D., & Gilbert, S. B. (2006). Educating Educators for Virtual Schooling: Communicating Roles and Responsibilities. *The Electronic Journal of Communication, 16*(1-2).

Huang, Y., Rayner, C., & Zhuang, L. (2003). Does intercultural competence matter in intercultural business relationship development? *International Journal of Logistics, 6*(4), 277–288. doi:10.1080/13675560310001626963

Kincaid, T., & Feldner, L. (2002). Leadership for Technology Integration: The Role of Principals and Mentors. *Educational Technology & Society, 5*(1).

Korhonen, K. (2002). *Intercultural competence as part of professional qualifications: A training experiment with Bachelor of Engineering students*. Unpublished doctoral dissertation, Jyvaskylan Yliopisto, Finland.

Kozma, R. B. (Ed.). (2004). Technology, Innovation, and Educational Change, A Global Perspective, A Report of the Second Information Technology in Education Study (SITES) Module 2, A Project of the International Association for the Evaluation of Educational Achievement (IEA). Eugene: International Society for Technology in Education (ISTE).

Law, N., & Plomp, T. (2003). Curriculum and Staff Development for ICT in Education. Cross-national Information and Communication Technology Policies and Practices in Education.

Mahlstedt, A. (2003). Global Citizenship Education in Practice: An Exploration of Teachers in the United World Colleges. *Monograph, International Comparative Education, School of Education, Stanford University.*

O'Dowd, R. (2009). Online Intercultural Exchange--An Introduction for Foreign Language Teachers. *ELT Journal*, *63*(1), 81–84. doi:10.1093/elt/ccn065

Pieterse, J. N. (2009). *Globalization and culture: Global mélange* (2nd Ed). New York: Rowman & Littlefield Publishers.

Suarez-Orozco, M. M., & Qin-Hilliard, D. (2004). *Globalization: Culture and education in the new millennium*. Berkley and LA: University of California Press.

Tearle, P. (2004). Implementation of ICT in UK secondary schools. *Final Report: February 2004*. Devon: University of Exeter.

Thorne, S. L., & Payne, J. S. (2005). Evolutionary Trajectories, Internet-mediated Expression, and Language Education. *CALICO Journal*, *22*(3), 371–397.

Williams, T. R. (2005). Exploring the Impact of Study Abroad on Students' Intercultural Communication Skills: Adaptability and Sensitivity. *Journal of Studies in International Education*, *9*(4), 356. doi:10.1177/1028315305277681

KEY TERMS AND DEFINITIONS

Course Management System (CMS): Web-based software platform allowing instructors to create online courses, manage course content, track student performance, and offer online collaboration and diverse means of communication.

Global Knowledge-based Economy: An economy wherein knowledge and information-based digital products are produced and traded through virtual market spaces that depend on ICT. In this economy, a firm's productivity relies on the quality of information and the promptness of obtaining and utilizing information for customer needs.

Intercultural Competence: Ability to interact appropriately, communicate effectively, and work collaboratively in international and multicultural environments, with others who are linguistically and culturally different from oneself. Intercultural competence is composed of five dimensions: knowledge, skills, attitudes, awareness, and language proficiency.

Information and Communication Technology (ICT): All sorts of technologies that enable people to obtain, share, and utilize information and knowledge, and to communicate with each other. It includes technologies for communicating through text, audio, voice, images, or videos. In the field of education, ICT refers to digital and computing technologies that allow access to the Internet, facilitate the construction of knowledge, and manipulation of diverse digitized information through a wide range of networks. ICT also includes wireless mobile technologies such as cellular telephones or PDAs.

International Virtual Elementary/Secondary Classroom Activities (IVECA): Online intercultural classroom exchange programs providing elementary and or secondary school students with opportunities to learn cultural similarities and differences through direct communication with students in different countries via virtual learning spaces. The intercultural exchange activities are integrated with the curricula of local participating schools so that IVECA becomes a part of their school curricula—not as an add-on special project.

International Virtual Schooling: A form of intercultural schooling in which schools in multiple countries are connected through ICT and use cross-cultural classroom exchanges as a part of their curricula.

Moodle: Free open-source course/content management system such as Sakai's Collaboration and Learning Environment, ILIAS, etc..

This work was previously published in Cases on Technological Adaptability and Transnational Learning: Issues and Challenges, edited by Siran Mukerji and Purnendu Tripathi, pp. 284-310, copyright 2010 by Information Science Reference (an imprint of IGI Global).

Chapter 17
International Collaboration in Distance Education in Sub-Saharan Africa:
Trends, Trials and Tomorrow's Thrusts

Gbolagade Adekanmbi
University of Botswana, Botswana

Bopelo Boitshwarelo
University of Botswana, Botswana

EXECUTIVE SUMMARY

This chapter examines international collaboration in distance education in Sub-Saharan Africa (SSA), focusing on efforts aimed at utilizing technology. It identifies a number of significant collaborative endeavors. The collaborative efforts observed have a similar goal of pooling together ICT resources and expertise towards improving educational outcomes. The prevalence of teacher education and training across the initiatives, in the context of the Millennium Development Goals, is noted. Institutions outside Africa are actively involved in the funding and provision of expertise. Also, the AVU consortium model seems to be a viable approach to collaboration, with notable results seen. With the challenges facing technology-focused collaboration, such as a lack of enabling policies and the digital divide, the chapter suggests that African countries and institutions should pursue a culture of change and be more flexible. More formal training in distance education, utilizing Africans in the Diaspora and promoting dialogue across international spectrums are also recommended.

DOI: 10.4018/978-1-4666-1885-5.ch017

BACKGROUND

The main motivation for the introduction of distance education in sub-Saharan Africa in the early 19th century, apart from the sub continent's problem of unsatisfied educational demands, was the need to utilize an available international educational innovation. In this early thrust, distance education institutions which awarded the first set of qualifications were based on foreign soil, the tutors and the content of instruction were mostly foreign, and the course materials were developed outside the continent. Even when local initiatives were first seen, in the activities of individual entrepreneurs and university centres and departments, external organizations and outside agencies provided the needed technical and technological support, and helped in organizing training programmes for the personnel involved (Adekanmbi, 2002). Government involvement in distance education did not reduce the thrust of international activities. Rather, it assisted in the establishment of the Commonwealth of Learning in 1988. Over the years, international collaboration has taken new turns, with collaboration addressing such issues as programme development, research and publications, technology-based collaborative initiatives and among others, the promotion of digitization.

This paper examines the trends observable in distance education development in Africa. It discusses the nature of international collaboration in distance education in Africa and examines the trials and challenges it faces. It also investigates the extent to which international collaboration could have an impact on the use of technology in distance education on the continent. The paper further explores the rationale for integrating ICTs in distance education and identifies some of the existing collaborative efforts in the area of ICT-supported Open and Distance Learning (ODL). Of particular interest, among others, is the African Virtual University (AVU) and the role it has played in increasing access to quality ICT-supported ODL programmes through its unique collaborative model. The paper further analyses the nature of these efforts and identifies what the challenges and prospects are. It also examines future directions for collaborative initiatives in distance education on the continent, against the backdrop of problems which affects many collaborative initiatives. This is with a view to suggesting strategies through which Africa could further benefit from international collaboration in ICT-supported distance education.

The thesis of this paper is that international collaboration plays a major role in the development of distance education in sub-Saharan Africa and can influence, among others, the desire for ICT integration in distance education practices on the continent.

SETTING THE STAGE

Distance Education: Trends and Trials in Africa

The initial global attempts in tertiary distance education in Africa had its landmark in the early days of distance education in the UK (1840's), Canada (1919), Australia (1914), USA (1728) France and Germany (1856), and other parts of the developed world. From about 1915, British journals circulated the advertisements of leading British colleges such as Wolsey Hall, University Correspondence College, Rapid Results College, Foulks and Lynch and others (Harris, 1971). The colleges helped Africans to prepare for university based examinations set by the Universities of London, Oxford and Cambridge. Then known as colonial examinations, nationalists were later to query such offerings, referring especially to the foreign content as "problems of possible indoctrination and mental enslavement." Such was the nature of the beginning of distance education and the internationalization of higher education in many African countries.

Although the initial entry of tertiary distance education reflected the promotion of foreign content, the emergence of conventional universities in the new African states affected the nature of programmes offered. At the Ahmadu Bello University in Nigeria in 1967, the focus was on teacher education, and in other places, the liberal arts were common. The model of instruction was generally dual or integrated and conventional course offerings were generally replicated. At a later stage, open universities emerged in Nigeria, Tanzania, and Zimbabwe, although it must be noted that many decades earlier, the University of South Africa (UNISA) was established as Africa's first open university.

It is noteworthy though that since its first African University Day celebrations in 1995, the Association of African Universities (AAU) has dedicated two themes to distance education, with universities organizing seminars around such themes. *Distance Education and African Universities* and *Cross Border Provision of Higher Education* were themes in 2003 and 2004 respectively (AAU, 2007). The Association for the Development of Education in Africa (ADEA) Working Group on Distance Education has also been active while the African Council for Distance Education (ACDE) is also making strides in the promotion of distance education.

On programme thrusts, teacher training initiatives at a distance have been prevalent. The findings on Zimbabwe (Chivore, 1992), Kenya (Kinyanjui, 1992), Tanzania (Chale, 1992), Nigeria and other parts of former British West Africa (Omolewa, 1978; 1982); reflect this assertion. Also, Adekanmbi's submissions (Adekanmbi, 2008; 2002; 1998), Aderinoye's writings (Aderinoye, 1992), and a host of others on

Anglophone Africa, give some insight into the use of this field for teacher training. This has had its indirect impact on the promotion of basic education, which the World Bank has championed over the years. While distance education has helped to open up access, its use in the promotion of science and technology was late in coming.

The use of distance education as a strategy for promoting education for refugees, has been discussed by Thomas (1996). In this respect, its use at primary, secondary, tertiary, technical, professional, vocational education and training levels, including non-formal education and training are noted. Thomas (1996) also provides bibliographic details and advice on various institutional providers.

The examination of the development orientation of distance education programmes in Africa shows that the field appears to replicate old paradigms while its development orientation has been limited (Adekanmbi, 1998). Distance education may have emphasized entrance qualifications common in conventional education and not specifically addressed alternative routes to social development.

On training and development in the field, most formal training routes for practitioners have for a long time relied extensively on foreign programmes and Internet-based courses. The work of the Commonwealth of Learning (COL), since its establishment has however been significant in promoting the training of practitioners. Also, in-house training programmes, supported occasionally by outside agencies are also growing in the distance education departments and units in tertiary education institutions. There has also been a great reliance on foreign publications and research aimed at promoting development in the field.

A convergence of commercialization, technology use and the impact of globalisation on the fortunes of distance education is being observed. For example, many African universities may have started using distance education to improve their revenue base. In a submission, Bennel (1998) has noted that tertiary distance education in Africa is becoming an internationally tradable commodity, and this, in the context of an increasingly competitive global market (cited by Saint, 1999). In the context of globalization, courses are now moving from being limited to the traditional teacher training turf to include science, engineering, vocational and computing courses among others. Methods and media are slowly adopting a digital frame, open universities are increasing and cross border education is growing. In 1996, a third of all tertiary level enrolments in South Africa were distance education students (Saint, 1999).

Related to the above, some developments aimed primarily at improving the quality of operations and attempting to utilize new technology have been noted. A few examples reflected in Adekanmbi (2007) include the following:

- Publication of a Code of Ethics by National Association of Distance Education Organisations (NADEOSA) for its member institutions (NADEOSA, 2005)
- Establishment of the African Council for Distance Education
- The research and collaborative initiatives of the Distance Education Association of Southern Africa (DEASA)
- Publication of the *Quality Criteria for Distance Education in South Africa* (Welch and Reed, 2005) with specific expectations relating to policy and planning, learners, quality assurance, information dissemination and results, among others.
- The drive by staff of distance education institutions to obtain the International Computer Drivers' Licence
- The case of Namibian College of Open and Distance Learning (NAMCOL) and Botswana College of Distance and Open Learning(BOCODOL) who have carried out Quality Assessment Audits of each institution's activities between them.
- The setting up of free toll lines by distance education organizations for students, a practice being utilised by NAMCOL for its students.
- UNISA's practice of distributed messages to its students
- The University of Botswana's utilisation of video conferencing, and in its conventional programmes, the partial use of web-based instruction.
- Development of vital policy documents to enhance practices and synergy between mainstream providers and conventional faculty practices. To this end, the University of Botswana Council has approved the University's *Distance Education Mainstreaming Policy* while the University of Namibia's Centre for External Studies now has a Policy Document on Open and Distance Learning in place.
- International conferences, especially technology-based conferences geared towards developing distance education practitioners have been reported (Wright 2007).

There have been a variety of challenges facing distance education in Africa. Two are worth highlighting here as they hint at the need for some degree of collaboration.

The first is the problem of staff retention in African universities, the subject of a major submission by Tettey (2006) to the World Bank. In the report, the loss rate of African university intellectuals is in the neighbourhood of 23000 a year, with countries such as Egypt, Kenya, Nigeria, Ghana and South Africa greatly affected (The Chronicle of Higher Education, November 2, 2001:A63). The report covers the Universities of Botswana, Ibadan, Kwazulu Natal, Ghana and the Makerere University. Among the difficulties cited are staff recruitment, attrition due to poor service conditions, the problem of an ageing professoriate, and the fact that many of the universities operated below capacities. Tettey (2006) also notes that appointment procedures were cumbersome, with the resultant loss of potential employees. Procedures for promotion were also stressful. Workload problems were due to mostly large classes which reflect an enrolment expansion policy without an accompanying capacity. The result is that very often, the gaps have been difficult to fill.

The second challenge generally facing tertiary education in Africa, but more so, facing distance education, is that of digital divide. Adekanmbi (2008) while citing the International Telecommunications Union (2004) notes:

- The digital divide between the developed countries and the developing nations was 11 times more in 1994 with respect to fixed telephones lines per 100 inhabitants. In 2004, it was only 4 times more.
- For mobile phone subscription, the divide was 27 times more in 1994, but in 2004 it was 4 times more.
- For Internet users per 100 inhabitants, the divide in 1994 was 73 times more, but in 2004, it was 8 times more.
- The overall Internet penetration by region in 2004 was 1.8% for Africa while Europe enjoyed a 30.6% position and the Americas had 30.5.

Digital divide refers to the gaps between individuals, communities and nations in their capacity to utilize, and the extent to which they have access to or own various forms of Information and Communication Technologies (ICTs). This also refers to imbalances which occur as a result of the availability or non-availability of resources or skills which individuals require to operate new technologies (Wikipedia, 2007). Selwyn et al (2006) have observed that these gaps may often be based on class, gender, age levels, socio-economic groupings, poverty and other disparities in knowledge or opportunities to educational facilities, means or structures. It has been seen that the digital divide in Africa has 'a spatial dimension, an educational dimension, a social dimension, and an income dimension' (Nwuke, 2003: p.36). The writer also cites the ITU, which reports that 80% of phone users in Africa are located in only six countries. For those who have the Internet, a great probability exists that 'a substantial number of computers in Africa is owned by the expatriate community' who, probably, account for 'much of the Internet usage' (Nwuke, 2003, p.36). No doubt, this has posed a major challenge to Africa's drive to utilize new technology in its distance education operations.

Given these and other challenges, collaboration becomes a useful strategy for moving the fortunes of distance education forward in the Continent.

CASE DESCRIPTION

International Collaboration in Distance Education

Collaboration is the pooling together of resources, human, material and physical, with the aim of building capacity, promoting efficiency, meeting institutional goals and ensuring a fair distribution of meager available resources. It has been seen to facilitate opportunities for local, regional and international cooperation as well increase clientele participation in activities. Adekanmbi (2004) has identified the following as problems which collaboration further addresses, especially in African distance education institutions: course material development, limitation in library and information resources, programme implementation delay, obsolescence in knowledge, inadequate training capacity, and copyright issues. In addressing these, collaboration thus takes various forms, including direct intervention, shared market, shared resources, association and the eclectic models, among others (Adekanmbi, 2004).

Distance education institutions in Africa also collaborate to address the problems of production delays, inappropriate expertise, inadequate technical training, conversion of programmes and aiding of other technology-oriented applications. Also addressed are resource sharing, space utilisation, adoption and adaptation of courses and joint research and publication initiatives. Perhaps a major area is the mitigation of the effects of low technology as most distance education outfits in Africa still wear predominantly a 'print gown'.

Over the years various organizations have promoted practices and sponsored distance education in the region. Examples include the International Extension College, British Council, Commonwealth of Learning (COL), USAID, and the German Foundation for International Development. For advocacy, organisation of conferences and the promotion of training, the International Council for Open and Distance Education (ICDE), Distance Education Association of Southern Africa, National Association of Distance Education Organisations in Southern Africa, the West African Distance Education Association, and of course COL, among others, have been actively involved. For documentation, material development and research, the International Centre for Distance Learning, and the COL have been very active. For example, COL has sponsored initiatives for DEASA members in media related training and the Certificate for Practitioners in Distance Education programme, among other local collaborative efforts within the region.

It is appropriate to say that COL is one of the most active, if not the most active organizations providing access to and support for training in distance education in Africa. Apart from publishing a *Directive of Courses and Materials for Training in Distance Education* (COL, 1995), the level of documentations available through its web site is very high (see, for example, the COL website/ col.org.). Also, the level of involvement of COL in making available information on courses across the globe is high. Since inception, COL has had sponsored numerous fellowships through the assistance of the Government of British Columbia. This has enabled many university lecturers to benefit from educational exchanges across Commonwealth countries, thus improving the standards of distance education practice in local institutions. Also, through COL, many professionals have traveled overseas from the British Columbia to make their skills available through consultancy work. Information available on COL website shows new developments in this area. Notably too, a lot of research support has been indirectly provided by the International Centre for Distance Learning, an arm of the Open University of the UK, through its documentation services.

Challenges to International Collaboration

Elliot (2001) warns against the rhetoric of collaboration, suggesting that so often, there is much talk about collaboration with little actual success seen on the ground. This perhaps is why Woodrow et al (cited in Woodrow and Thomas, 2002:3) write:

Collaboration is widely perceived as an essential component of policies to widen participation by under represented groups, but evidence on the relative merits of different forms of collaboration is not easy to find. Almost there is an impression that to collaborate at all is the most important thing and that how it is done is largely incidental. Hence the structures and strategies employed sometimes appear to have developed almost incidentally, rather than as the result of any conscious and informed choice between alternative patterns of collaboration.

Also, other writers have explored the nature of bottlenecks collaboration faces which must be avoided if it is to achieve desired results. For example, Moran and Mugridge (1993) and King (1996) have noted such issues as lack of mission clarity of organizations involved, absence of a clear funding policy, and the lack of effective leadership, among others.

Although there are sometimes problems in collaboration, a concept Johnston (1997) has noted to be ‘full of uncharted territories, ambiguities and institutional complexities’ (cited in Schultz and Abbey, 2001, p.160), the gains far outweigh the problems. Based on the foregoing, collaboration will enhance learner success in programmes; distance education professionals would be able to work out minimum standards of practice; and the possibility of the utilisation of technology for collaborate training, would be greater. Dialogue between practitioners will also grow.

Technology Concerns

Rationale for ICT Use in Distance Education

In the various collaborative initiatives on the continent, the one linked to technology use has been of great concern. One major reason is that technology-oriented collaboration appears geared towards addressing the stigma that sub-Saharan African distance education systems wear a predominantly print gown. Thus recent moves to pursue a technology-oriented distance education provision in various parts of Africa have been reported in the literature (Adekanmbi, 2008; Saint, 1999; Daniel, 2005). While some distance education organizations have been attempting to adapt to technology-oriented changes to improve their practices, there are questions to which answers are required. For example, what rationales drive technology use in higher education in Africa, what forms has international collaboration taken in the promotion of technology in distance education? What challenges are faced in the process? How can these challenges be reduced to ensure proper utilization of technology in distance education?

There are a variety of reasons why information and communications technologies are used in education, particularly ODL. Debande and Ottersten (2004) identify four rationales for integrating technology in education in general. The first, *social rationale* is concerned with the role that ICTs play particularly with regards to communication and interaction between people. Second, the *economic and vocational rationale* is based on the requisite of ensuring that learners are prepared for the job market which requires ICT skills. Third is *pedagogical rationale* which recognizes the role ICT plays in improving the quality of teaching and learning. Fourth, the *cost effectiveness rationale,* which recognizes that ICT can reach far and wide even to the most disadvantaged communities in a cost-effective way. With specific reference to distance education in Africa, all these rationales apply. However, it seems the reasons that feature prominently are the fact that ICTs can increase access to distance education and the quality thereof (Mackintosh 2005; Lewin, 2003; Daniel & Menon, 2005). In other words the cost-effectiveness and pedagogy rationale reign supreme.

Following from the above, international collaboration in distance education in Africa is therefore driven mainly by these two notions of increasing access to and enhancing quality of education. As a result, initiatives that are geared towards integrating ICTs in education have grown in recent years both from within and outside Africa. An investigation into the literature reveals a few notable examples and these are discussed in the next sub-section.

African Initiatives of Collaborative ICT Utilization in Education

There is generally a consensus that ICTs hold a tremendous hope for the African continent in terms of educational development hence the growing numbers of projects and initiatives geared towards harnessing their potential (Mackintosh, 2005). For example, in its advertisement for its first ever-international conference on ICT for Development held in May 2006, E-learning Africa (2005) recognised the efforts that were already being made by the various stakeholders to take up e-Learning. It acknowledged the emergence of an African community of practitioners in e-Learning which has begun to "address the issues that are related to the efficient use of advanced modern technologies..." Specifically, the initiatives briefly discussed here are those with an international collaborative dimension, comprehensive in nature, widespread in reach and having a degree of impact regarding STEP factors.

SchoolNet Africa

SchoolNet Africa (SNA) is one notable initiative which provides support to practitioners, education policy makers, teachers and learners in a significant number of African counties (E-learning Africa, 2005). It is an African learning network set up to support national schoolnets to enhance learning and teaching through effective use of ICT. SNA which was founded in July 2000 has at least 10 SSA countries participating in it to date. It is an Africa-led initiative and is non-governmental in nature. It is driven by the philosophy that ICTs have a significant potential to enhance education in Africa (ThinkQuestAfrica, 2002). One of the significant projects of SNA is the African Teachers Network (ATN) whose aim is to be an active community of practice of teachers from all over Africa (http://www.schoolnetafrica.org/english/at_centre.html). The network's mission includes building capacity through collaborative projects, sharing resources, participation in different forums, and organization of professional development programmes of a diverse nature. The ATN envisions an improved teaching practice in the continent of Africa. Through its other various programs, the SNA has reportedly managed to:

- Facilitate many African schools' access to the Internet and other ICT tools,
- Continuously build and reinforce capabilities on the use of ICTs among teachers and students,
- Organise campaigns to promote ICT use at different teaching levels as well as develop activities that bring together different sectors and stakeholders into partnerships with the education community,
- Develop educational materials and,

- Carry out other projects that include the Global Teenager Project (GTP) which gets pupils and teachers to discuss contemporary issues online. It currently involves at least 20 countries (SchoolNet Africa, 2007).

DFID Imfundo Project

Recognizing that the use of technology in education is imperative for Africa's economic growth, the British government through the Department for International Development (DFID) set up a millennium education initiative in 2000 called the Imfundo*: Partnership for IT in Education* (Selinger, 2002). This is '…an initiative in DFID which considers ways in which Information and Communication Technology can be used to support Education in Sub-Saharan Africa (Info Dev. 2009).' This is with the view that ICTs can play a major role in extending information and knowledge to the poor and marginilised of the continent. Its major role is to create partnerships to contribute to the delivery of universal primary education and gender equality in Africa. The programme had a particular focus on teacher training and improving the professional development in general (Selinger, 2002) but with a more specific emphasis on improving access to and quality of primary education. A key feature of this project was to invite and coordinate contributions of resources from various stakeholders in different sectors. It was also to develop a Resource Bank and identify, through *liaison partners,* activities in the concerned African countries where these resources could be efficiently utilized (Unwin, 2005). In addition the project worked with *local partners* to ensure that appropriate and sustainable activities are implemented meaningfully and in context. This initiative ran in Ethiopia, Ghana, Kenya and South Africa. While this project was short-lived apparently due to its ambitious nature which went beyond the core agenda of the DFID, it received accolades from its beneficiaries in Africa. It also provided a useful framework for partnerships involving the used of ICTs in education. One of the significant achievements of the project is the Knowledge Bank of reference materials which is used to share information on the use of ICTs in education in Africa. Additionally, the Resource Bank mentioned above brings together all kinds of resources including expertise and ideas from the business community (Department for International Development, 2009).

COL Initiative of VUSSC

The Virtual University for Small States of the Commonwealth (VUSSC) can be traced back to a meeting of the Commonwealth Ministers of Education that was held in Halifax, Nova Scotia, Canada in 2000. At that Conference, ministers from small states expressed a common concern about the lack of critical mass in expertise and resources to engage with online learning in an autonomous fashion. This challenge emanated from the fact that these countries were small either territory-wise or demographically. Consequently, they either have limited resources and/or limited skilled manpower. While this initiative involves a number of countries from a number of regions of the world a significant number of countries from mainland Africa and islands states from around the continent are part thereof. Specifically, the countries from SSA are Botswana, The Gambia, Lesotho, Namibia, Sierra Leone, and Swaziland. Details of this initiative are contained in a document developed by COL and Government interlocutors (2007). The plan for the VUSSC was approved in 2003, and in 2005, representatives from 22 countries agreed to form the VUSSC. As a consortium, VUSSC would "develop capacity, develop and share learning content and courses, and work toward establishing a standards and credit transfer mechanism". This would be underpinned by the following:

- Members would share resources, expertise and experiences towards quality education and training for learners of various needs;
- COL would handle coordination, quality assurance and facilitate networking; and
- Members would have regular consultations as they developed and implemented their programmes as well as participating and availing resources towards quality learning environments.

Rather than attempt to create a new institution, the intention of this initiative was to augment efforts in the various post-secondary institutions so as to combat the challenges faced by the member states. The VUSSC initiative was to ensure that member countries build capacity to provide quality educational programmes using various technologies.

Membership has since increased quite significantly and to date, the VUSSC has engaged extensively in cooperative material development using online technologies where countries like Botswana and Namibia have participated (West, 2007; Daniel &West, 2008). This is done through training and materials development workshops called "boot camps". However, increasingly online collaborative methods of development are being used as capacity grows. Additionally, the VUSSC has decided to establish a Transnational Qualifications Framework (TQF) which will assist in formalising the working arrangements among member states and their respective institutions as well as ensure credibility of courses and programmes internationally. As the VUSSC looks ahead, the member states are encouraged to adapt and meaningfully make use of VUSSC initiatives by putting in place local institutional arrangements to reach their goals (Daniel, 2008). The latest information on VUSSC is that it now has several courses in a variety of areas and other materials, toolkits, resources and guides (VUSSC, 2009).

The African Virtual University

The African Virtual University (AVU) was established in 1997 in response to the problems facing the higher education sector (Shrestha, 2000). It is geared towards promoting alternative modes of the delivery of tertiary education with a view to complementing the efforts of existing institutions of higher learning. The AVU is described in its website as a "Pan African Inter-governmental organisation whose aim is to increase access to higher education and training through the innovative use of Information and communication technologies" (www.avu.org). The AVU headquarters are situated in Nairobi and it currently operates in about 27 countries, with a total of 55 technology-based learning centres. These centres are equipped with the necessary cabling and hardware and receive digital satellite transmissions. The AVU offers certificate, diploma and degree programs in a variety of programmes, particularly science and technology, IT and business studies. Specifically sponsored by the African Bank, teacher education and training has also become part of its menu. The AVU is essentially a network of ICT e-learning meant to avail educational resources and content in specific areas to partner institutions in Africa. These resources come from other universities in the continent and also from top universities overseas. In addition to educational resources, the AVU seeks to improve e-learning capacity in training ODL professionals and as well as physical resources. Courses are predominantly done through either asynchronous videotaped classes or synchronous satellite video feeds where students can ask questions telephonically. Essentially AVU is a kind of open university run in consortium style and as mentioned in its website it "builds and manages large consortia".

A detailed analysis of a specific case of AVU operations is done by Juma (2006) where the author describes the experience of Kenyatta University's participation in this initiative. This Kenyan University which started its partnership with the AVU in 1997, is one of the most notable examples and as such its experience offers a number of lessons. These are discussed by Juma and they include the need:

- To promote University ownership of AVU;
- To have community awareness campaigns about the AVU, including the business community;
- To have adequate learner support materials and equipment particularly ICT facilities;
- For skilled manpower;
- To have committed leadership for both the project and the partner university;
- To increase capacity building particularly in ICT skills and
- For delivery of quality academic programmes so that they can attract higher enrolments and have value for money.

Overall, the AVU has been successful with the number of partner institutions still on the rise. However, there is reportedly more uptake in Anglophone than Francophone Africa due to lower use of ODL methods in the latter (Juma, 2006).

Observation and Analysis

From the four cases above a number of observations seem to emerge. First, it is clear that international collaboration in Africa with regard to educational ICTs has only emerged, in a serious way, in the last twelve years. The AVU has been the first notable initiative to be developed. This is clearly understandable as around the time of setting it up, ICTs were becoming increasingly available in Africa.

Second, a similar set of aims run through these "collaborative endeavours". This is their objective of bringing together ICT resources and expertise for improving the quality and quantity of educational outcomes, particularly in post-secondary education. There is also the added objective of building capacity in the area of e-Learning for the region. This resonates with the pedagogical and the cost effectiveness rationale for using ICTs in education. However, it also, perhaps indirectly, touches on the other rationales: vocational/economic rationale as using modern technologies to educate learners prepares them for the global work market and; social because collaborative methods of learning foster the social dimension of education and prepares learners to function in society in a cohesive way. Thus there is clear indication that these efforts have sought to meet Social, Technological, Economic and Political (STEP) demands to varying extents.

Third, an emphasis on teacher education and training is evident. This seems to be a consequence of a response to the Millennium Development Goals (MDGs) on education by sponsoring organizations. By training teachers using modern technologies, these initiatives and others recognize the role of teachers in preparing the current generation of young people for technology-driven economies. A fourth observation is that these collaboration initiatives, except perhaps SNA, are initiated, funded or coordinated by international institutions and/or governments. This may be attributable to the fact that financial, technological and appropriate human resources reside predominantly outside the African continent.

Lastly in all these collaborative endeavours the consortium approach to collaboration is clearly visible with the AVU standing out prominently in this regard on several counts: The AVU is:

- Pan African and intergovernmental in nature;
- Has the highest membership of countries participating and benefiting from it;
- Brings together both institutions from within and without Africa and

- Has a strategic focus making it a sustainable endeavour; to date it has trained thousands of students in various fields particularly at the Kenyatta University.

The AVU has thus played a significant role over the last decade in increasing access to quality ICT-supported ODL programmes through its unique collaborative model.

CURRENT CHALLENGES

With particular reference to AVU, the Kenyatta University case, though a success story has reportedly faced a number of challenges (Juma, 2006). First, there are administrative challenges which emanate from the fact that the administration and management of a virtual university is different from a face-to-face university. Decision-making processes are usually slow and inflexible in the conventional institution while dealing with a virtual educational environment requires quicker, more creative and flexible decision-making processes. Secondly, capacity building, particularly with reference to academic staff's need to appreciate and use ICT in learning is a challenge as massive change such as this is never easy. Thirdly, owing to the fact that bureaucratic procedures of conventional systems are usually slow, cooperation can be difficult to formalize.

As a general observation, the over dependence of collaborative endeavors on external sponsors has generally led to non-sustainability as the programmes tend to stall if the support stops. It would seem therefore that strong partnerships with local institutions can ensure a high degree of sustainability. The AVU has generally been successful as its approach has been to integrate its interventions into the strategic intentions of the local partner institutions and focus on building capacity. This is a demand driven approach which is widely advocated for by Unwin (2005). Unwin in his exploration of partnerships for ICT for Development in Africa came to the following conclusion that partnerships, particularly of an international nature should concentrate not just on the supply aspects of the collaborative relationship but also on the demand side (the local implementation environment). This approach allows for initiatives to sufficiently appreciate the realities of the demand side with all its complexities and constraints.

Unwin (2005) also places emphasis on transparency among partners in terms of their contributions and what they expect to benefit from the partnership. The Imfundo project was exemplary as it outlined ethical guidelines, benefits framework and memorandums of understanding. This way, its activities were guided by a set of core principles and an acknowledgement of the different interests of the partners in terms of what they will contribute and benefit.He further recommended that partnerships should be multi-sector in nature involving partners from different sectors rather just having numerous stakeholders from a single sector.

In a study on e-learning, commissioned in 2004 by SNA in partnership with other organisations such as COL, the use of ICT in both pre-service and in-service teacher education in African countries was examined. Menon and Daniel (2005) have identified the following as one of the significant challenges: the lack of a comprehensive pan-African framework to inspire the development of local technological models and local teacher training content for building teachers' ICT capabilities.

SOLUTIONS AND RECOMMENDATIONS

As we envisage the future of collaboration, the following should further assist in ensuring the full utilization of collaborative initiatives in African distance education practices, especially in the context of promoting technology oriented distance education practices.

As evident from the discussion thus far, ICTs are necessary for the realization of wider access to quality tertiary education in Africa. However, given the challenges of infrastructure and limited capacities, international collaboration in ICT-use in education becomes imperative. The continent therefore will need to strengthen existing partnerships and if needs be create new and more innovative ones. The AVU has proved to be a viable initiative which many SSA countries can use to widen provision of quality higher and professional education. However institutions will need to be flexible in their operations, innovative in their thinking and generally have a culture that welcomes change if they are to fully benefit from such an endeavour. Similarly the VUSSC can be tapped into by African member states. While the VUSSC has promoted a bottom-up approach to its operations, it is also formalizing its arrangements so that the courses and programmes it helps develop will have a local relevance while having credibility at an international level. Seeing that a consortium arrangement seems to have good prospects in terms of sustainability and effectiveness similar initiatives in the context of ODL that address a variety of educational needs are possible. Apart from consortium arrangements, other initiatives and activities can be carried out to promote collaboration in the region, as further discussed below.

During international conferences, distance education practitioners in Africa can exchange ideas, collaborate with colleagues and develop new synergies which assist them in utilizing their best ideas. In recent times, the University of Pretoria and the University of Botswana engaged in the sharing of expertise and experience in joint organization of digital scholarship conferences. To date, two of such conferences have been held, in 2007 and 2008 in Gaborone and Pretoria respectively, while a third one is in the process of being planned for 2010. The DEASA is also encouraging and promoting technology-oriented collaboration among its members through its conferences and workshops. In West Africa, East Africa and Central Africa, this idea can be further promoted in the various regional associations. It is also right to call attention to the wide range of international conferences on educational technology, with a long list of such provided every year by Clayton Wright (Wright 2007). Such collaborative initiatives will no doubt enhance the development of useful ideas in ICT integration in distance education.

The absence of technology policies in many countries in Africa is a major hindrance to the contextual use of technology in distance education. Among other things, clear policies help to identify users, provide opportunities for linkages and identify possible areas of collaboration among many users within regions and local educational landscape. Such policies not only provide useful contexts for distance education to thrive, they also enhance the extension of pedagogical information access to rural areas. In addition, they encourage the collaboration of various stakeholders within national contexts to derive the best benefits from policy implementation. Related to this, Government provision of electricity to rural areas in Africa will also facilitate the growth of technology-enhanced educational initiatives, with distance education benefiting in the process. It is therefore imperative that all African countries develop ICT policies.

African scholars in Diaspora can be encouraged to return home on occasions and help utilize new skills in technology in local distance education projects. Ite (2004) used the term 'Return to sender' in a chapter on globalization, where he suggests that scholars from the African continent who have benefitted from exposure to new ways of doing things should from time to time return to their countries or institutions of origin. This is to provide needed assistance. ICT use is one way where such assistance is greatly needed, especially in distance education. The Federal Government of Nigeria has actually taken the 'Return to sender' phenomenon to a new level where its National Universities Commission has developed a system that facilitates the return of citizen lecturers from their places of abode abroad to Nigeria for short terms of academic engagement. Such interventions not only allow for the use of the expertise of the citizen concerned, but may open up new opportunities for institutional collaboration in distance education.

The promotion of the discipline of distance education is another area worth exploring. The training of practitioners in distance education, at the beginning was late in coming. Initial reliance on training was limited to the use of trainers from the International Extension College in the UK, local training initiatives and at a later stage, the participation in Masters and higher degree programmes where distance education was carried out by research. Recently, a Certificate Programme for Practitioners in distance education collaboratively done by the Commonwealth of

Learning and DEASA has been used to promote skills development in the field. The enhancement of the curriculum of such programmes by incorporating technology based units of instruction will further promote the use of ICTs in distance education. For collaborative purposes, joint development of programmes between institutional providers of distance education is also needed. Related to this, the identification of centers of excellence in various parts of Africa, especially of institutions that have achieved more in technology-oriented practices will further help the new institutions which lag behind further promote their distance education practices.

It has been observed that many business corporations have adopted successful technological practices that help enhance corporate practices for broad financial gains. Collaboration between the institutional providers of distance education and the corporate sector should be encouraged to promote growth in the field. The sharing of such experiences with local tertiary institutions will further ensure that technology is used to maximum benefit.

Most distance education institutions in Africa are working towards widening the access and promoting the growth of student numbers. The growth of open universities in the region is a realisation of this, in some measure. But access also has to be widened with respect to the offering of courses in technology related programmes for students in distance education programmes.

Generally, its is expected that institutions offering distance education must be in the fore front of innovation promotion, ICT policy implementation, promotion of a vibrant mentoring scheme for staff and students and the pursuit of collaborative research in various areas of their operation, especially in the field of ICT. The provision of support for distance learners through the use of technology enhanced practices is also crucial.

REFERENCES

Abramson, M., Bird, J., & Stennet, A. (1996). Introduction. In M. Abramson, J. Bird, & A. Stennet (Eds.), *Further and higher education partnerships: The future for collaboration* (pp.1-3). Buckingham, UK: Open University Press.

Adekanmbi, G. (1998). Development orientation of distance education programmes in Africa: A preliminary submission. *Ghana Educational Media and Technology Association (GEMTA). Journal, 2*, 59–70.

Adekanmbi, G. (2002). A comment on the education and training of distance education practitioners in Africa. *Open and Distance Learning Association of Australia (ODLAA) Papers,* (pp. 1-11).

Adekanmbi, G. (2004). Collaborative strategies for implementing continuing education programmes in Botswana. In D. Sanders & K. Brosnan et al. (Eds.), *Learning transformations: Changing learners, organizations and communities* (pp. 87-95). London: FACE.

Adekanmbi, G. (2007). Quantitative aspirations, qualitative considerations and technological imperatives: Collaborating for progress in African distance education. *Journal of Sociology and Education in Africa*, *6*(1), 1–12.

Adekanmbi, G. (2008). *The neo liberal ideology and the future of higher education in Africa: Lessons for Nigeria.* The Second Annual Professor (Mrs) Grace Mbipom Foundation Lecture, University of Calabar, Nigeria, 4 June 2008.

Aderinoye, R. (1992). *Retention and failure in distance education: the experience of the National Teachers' Institute, (NTI) Kaduna.* Unpublished Doctoral Thesis, University of Ibadan, Nigeria.

Chale, E. M. (1992). Application and cost effectiveness of distance education in teacher preparation: A case study of Tanzania. In P. Murphy and A. Zhiri (Eds.), *Distance Education in Anglophone Africa* (pp.123-136). Washington, DC: The World Bank.

Commonwealth of Learning. (1995). *Directory of courses and materials for training in distance education.* Vancouver: Commonwealth of Learning.

Commonwealth of Learning and the VUSSC government interlocutors. (2007). *A business strategy for the Virtual University for small states of the Commonwealth (2007–2013).* Retrieved June 7, 2009, from http://www.col.org/sitecollectionDocument/VUSSC.Business_Plan_20070220.doc

Daniel, J. (2005). Open and distance learning in Africa. In *15 CCEM mid-term review for Africa and Europe*, Freetown, Sierra Leone, 14 November 2005.

Daniel, J., & Menon, M. (2005). *ODL and ICTs for teacher development in Sub-Saharan Africa: The experience of the Commonwealth of Learning.* Retrieved 12 November, 2005, from http://www.col.org/speeches/JD_0509BOCODOL.htm

Daniel, J., & West, P. (2008). *The virtual university for small states of the Commonwealth: What is it for? How is it doing? Where is it going?* Retrieved June 7, 2009, from http://www.col.org/resources/speeches/2008presentations/2008-VUSSC/Pages/articleVUSSC.aspx

Debande, O., & Ottersten, E. K. (2004). Information and communication technologies: A tool for empowering and developing the horizon of the learner. *Higher Education Management and Policy, 16*(2), 31–61. doi:10.1787/hemp-v16-art15-en

Department for International Development. (2009). *Imfundo: Partnership for IT in education.* Retrieved September 20, 2009, from http://imfundo.digitalbrain.com/imfundo/

eLearning Africa. (2005). *1st International conference on ICT for development, education and training, UNCC, Addis Ababa, Ethiopia May 24-26, 2006.* Retrieved 12 November, 2005, from http://www.elearning-africa.com/conference.php

Elliott, A. (2001). Introduction. In M. Richards, A. Eliot, V. Woloshyn, & C. Mitchell (Eds.), *Collaboration uncovered: the forgotten, the assumed, and the unexamined in collaborative education.* Westport, CT: Bergin and Garvey.

Harris, W. J. A. (1971). Education by post (England). In O. Mackenzie & E.L. Christensen (Eds.), *The changing world of correspondence study* (pp. 299-302). University Park, PA: Pennsylvania State University Press.

InfoDev. (2009). *Quick guide: ICT and education at DFID.* Retrieved 07 June, 2009, from http://74.125.77.132/search?q=cache:i8YkiIxFsaIJ:www.infodev.org/en/Publication.146.html

Ite, U. (2004). *Return to sender: using the African intellectual disapora to establish academic links.*

ITU, International Telecommunications Union. (2007). *Measuring Village ICT in Sub-Saharan Africa.* Retrieved December 11, 2007, from http://www.itu.int/ITU-D/ict/statistics/material/Africa_Village_ICT_2007.pdf

Juma, M. N. (2006). Kenyatta University-African Virtual University, Kenya. In D. Antoni (Ed.), The virtual university: Models and messages/ lessons from case studies. Paris: UNESCO.

King, R. (1996). Competition or co-operation? In *Universities in the Twenty-first Century, Education in a Borderless World Conference*, Singapore, 13-14 August, IDP Education Australia.

Kinyanjui, P. (1992). The organization of teacher training at a distance with particular reference to Kenya. In P. Murphy and A. Zhiri (Eds.), *Distance education in Anglophone Africa: Experience with secondary education and teacher training* (pp. 117-122). Washington, DC: The World Bank.

Lewin, K. M. (2000). New technologies and knowledge acquisition and use in developing countries. *Compare*, *30*(3), 313–321. doi:10.1080/713657464

Mackintosh, W. (2005). Can you lead from behind? Critical reflections on the rhetoric of e-learning, open distance learning and, ICTs for development in Sub- Saharan Africa (SSA). In A. A. Carr-Chellman (Ed.). *Global Perspectives on e- learning: Rhetoric and reality* (pp.222-240). Thousand Oaks, California: SAGE Publications.

Moran, L., & Mugridge, I. (Eds.). (1993). *Collaboration in distance education: International case studies.* New York: Nicholas Publishing.

Nwuke, K. (2003). Higher education, economic growth, and information technology in Africa: some challenges and issues. In Beebe, M., Kouakou, K., Oyeyinka-Oyelaran, B. & Rao, M. (Eds.), *Africa Dot Edu: IT opportunities and higher education in Africa* (pp.17-42). New Delhi: Tata McGraw-Hill Publishing Company Limited.

Omolewa, M. (1978). Oxford University Delegacy of Local Examinations and Secondary School Education in Nigeria, 1929-1937. *Journal of Educational Administration and History*, *10*(2), 39–44. doi:10.1080/0022062780100205

Omolewa, M. (1982). Historical antecedents of distance education in Nigeria, 1887-1960. *Adult Education in Nigeria*, *7*(December), 7–26.

Saint, W. (1999). *Tertiary distance education and technology in sub-Saharan Africa.* Washington, DC: The World Bank.

Saint, W. (1999). *Tertiary distance education and technology in sub-Saharan Africa.* Washington DC: The World Bank.

SchoolNet Africa. (2007). *African education knowledge warehouse*. Retrieved on July 20, 2009, from http://www.schoolnetafrica.org/english/index.htm

Schutz, A., & Abbey, S. (2001). Collaborative mentoring: insights from a university research centre. In M. Richards, A. Elliott, V. Woloshyn, & C. Mitchell (Eds.), *Collaboration uncovered: the forgotten, the assumed, and the unexamined in collaborative education* (pp.219-235). Westport, CT: Bergin and Garvey.

Selinger, M. (2002). *Education and skills development in sub-Saharan Africa.* Paper presented at the ASET Conference on Untangling the Web: Establishing Learning Links, 7-10th July, Melbourne, Australia.

Selwyn, N., Gorard, S., & Furlong, J. (2006). *Adult learning in the digital age.* London and New York: Routledge.

Shrestha, G. (2000). *Utilization of information and communications technology for education in Africa.* Addis Ababa, Ethiopia: UNESCO, IICBA.

Tettey, W. (2006). *Staff retention in African universities: elements of a sustainable strategy.* Washington DC: The World Bank.

Thinkquest. (2002). *About SchoolNet Africa.* Retrieved November 14, 2005, from http://www.thinkquestafrica.org/about_sna.shtm

Thomas, J. (1996). *Distance education for refugees: The experience of using distance and* open learning with refugees in Africa, 1980-1995 with guidelines for action and a directory of information. Cambridge, UK: International Extension College.

Unwin, T. (2005). *Partnerships in development practice: Evidence from multi-stakeholder ICT4D partnerships practice in Africa.* Paris: UNESCO.

VUSSC. (2009). *A virtual university for small states of the Commonwealth (VUSSC).* Retrieved on 24 July 2009 from http://www.vussc.info/

West, P. G. (2007). The virtual university becomes a reality. *Educational Technology, 67*(6), 38–40.

Wikipedia. (2007). *Digital divide.* Retrieved December 11, 2007, from http://en.wikipedia.org/wiki/Digital_divide

Woodrow, M., & Thomas, L. (2002). Pyramids or spiders? Cross-sector collaboration to widen participation, learning from international experiences. In L. Thomas, M. Cooper, & J. Quinn (Eds.), *Collaboration to widen participation in higher education* (pp. 3-28). Stoke on Trent: Trentham Books.

Wright, C. (2007, June 15). *Educational technology conferences for 2007-2008.*

Zeleza, P., & Olukoshi, A. (Eds.). *African universities in the twenty-first century Vol. 1.* Dakar, Senegal: CODESRIA.

ADDITIONAL READING

Adei, S. (2004). Overview of university level education in Africa. In M. Beebe, K. Kouakou, B. Oyeyinka-Oyelaran & M. Rao (Eds.), *Africa Dot Edu: IT Opportunities and Higher Education in Africa* (pp. 90). New Delhi: Tata McGraw-Hill Publishing Company Limited.

Altbach, P. (2008). Globalization and forces for change in higher education. *Industry and Higher Education, 50*(Winter), 2.

Ayoubi, R. M., & Al-Habaibeh, A. (2006). An investigation into international business collaboration in higher education organizations. *International Journal of Educational Management, 20.* Retrieved 18 May 2009 from http://www.emeraldinsight.com/Insight/ViewContentServlet?Filename+Published

Eastmond, D. (2000). Realizing the promise of distance education in low technology countries. *ETR & D, 48*(2), 100–111. doi:10.1007/BF02313405

Farrell, G. (Ed.). (2003). *A virtual university for small states of the Commonwealth.* Vancouver, Canada: The Commonwealth of Learning.

Hanna, E., Donald, , & Latchem, C. (2002). Beyond national borders: Transforming higher education institutions. *Journal of Studies in International Education, 6,* 115–133. doi:10.1177/1028315302006002003

Isaacs, S., Broekman, I., & Mogale, T. (2004). Contextualizing Education in Africa: the role of ICTs. In T. James (Ed.), *Information and communication technologies for development in Africa: Volume 3, Networking institutions of Learning --SchoolNet* (Vol. 3, pp. 1-23). Ottawa, Canada: CODESRIA/IDRC.

Naidoo, V. (April 2003). *ICT in education policy- Reflecting on key issues.* Paper presented at the Pan-African workshop focusing on using ICT to support the education systems in Africa, organized by the Ministry of Education (Botswana), SchoolNet and Commonwealth of Learning in partnership with other agencies, Gaborone, Botswana.

Oduaran, A., & Bhola, H. (2006). *Widening access to education as social policy: essays in honor of Michael Omolewa.* Dordrecht: Springer.

Organization for Economic Cooperation and Development. (2007). *Qualification Systems: bridges to lifelong learning.* Paris: OECD.

Selwyn, N., Gorard, S., & Furlong, J. (2006). *Adult learning in the digital age.* London and New York: Routledge.

UNESCO. (2005). *Global education digest.* Montreal: UNESCO Institute for Statistics.

UNESCO. (2006). *Education for all global monitoring report.* Paris: UNESCO.

Varghese, N. (Ed.). (2006). *Growth and expansion of private higher education in Africa.* Paris: International Institute for Educational Planning (IIEP).

KEY TERMS AND DEFINITIONS

Collaboration: The working together of two or more entities, governments or institutions, with the aim of sharing resources to achieve common goals.

Digital Divide: The gap between individuals, contexts or sections of the population that have access to, or ability to utilize the Internet and other digital technologies and those that do not.

Diaspora: A dispersion or movement of any population sharing a common ethnic identity from their territory to other far removed areas

Globalization: A phenomenon in which nations and people become more interlinked, with broad implications for political, social, economic and technological integration

Information and Communication Technologies: Technologies used to create, manage and distribute information as well as facilitate communication.

Sub-Saharan Africa: The African countries located south of the Sahara Desert. The term is used in opposition to North Africa which is mostly inhabited by Arabs.

Virtual University: A tertiary institution that provides higher education programs through electronic media.

This work was previously published in Cases on Interactive Technology Environments and Transnational Collaboration: Concerns and Perspectives, edited by Siran Mukerji and Purnendu Tripathi, pp. 39-55, copyright 2010 by Information Science Reference (an imprint of IGI Global).

Compilation of References

Abramson, M., Bird, J., & Stennet, A. (1996). Introduction. In M. Abramson, J. Bird, & A. Stennet (Eds.), *Further and higher education partnerships: The future for collaboration* (pp.1-3). Buckingham, UK: Open University Press.

Adekanmbi, G. (2002). A comment on the education and training of distance education practitioners in Africa. *Open and Distance Learning Association of Australia (ODLAA) Papers,* (pp. 1-11).

Adekanmbi, G. (2004). Collaborative strategies for implementing continuing education programmes in Botswana. In D. Sanders & K. Brosnan et al. (Eds.), *Learning transformations: Changing learners, organizations and communities* (pp. 87-95). London: FACE.

Adekanmbi, G. (2008). *The neo liberal ideology and the future of higher education in Africa: Lessons for Nigeria.* The Second Annual Professor (Mrs) Grace Mbipom Foundation Lecture, University of Calabar, Nigeria, 4 June 2008.

Adekanmbi, G. (1998). Development orientation of distance education programmes in Africa: A preliminary submission. *Ghana Educational Media and Technology Association (GEMTA). Journal, 2*, 59–70.

Adekanmbi, G. (2007). Quantitative aspirations, qualitative considerations and technological imperatives: Collaborating for progress in African distance education. *Journal of Sociology and Education in Africa, 6*(1), 1–12.

Aderinoye, R. (1992). *Retention and failure in distance education: the experience of the National Teachers' Institute, (NTI) Kaduna.* Unpublished Doctoral Thesis, University of Ibadan, Nigeria.

Akintunde, M. (2006). Diversity.Com: Teaching an online course on white racism and multiculturalism. *Multicultural Perspectives, 8*(2), 35–45. doi:10.1207/s15327892mcp0802_7

Albee, J. (2003). A Study of Preservice Elementary Teachers Technology Skill Preparedness and Examples of How It Can Be Increased. *Journal of Technology and Teacher Education*, 11.

Albers-Miller, N. D., Straughan, R. D., & Prenshaw, P. J. (2001). Exploring innovative teaching among marketing educators: Perceptions of innovative activities and existing reward and support programs. *Journal of Marketing Education, 23*(3), 249–259. doi:10.1177/0273475301233010

Al-Lamki, S. (2000). Omanization: A three tier strategic framework for human resource management and training in the Sultanate of Oman. *Journal of Comparative International Management*, *1*(3).

Al-Lamki, S. (2002). Higher education in the Sultanate of Oman: The challenge of access, equity and privatization. *Journal of Higher Education Policy and Management*, *24*(1), 75–86. doi:10.1080/13600800220130770

Allbeck, J. M., & Badler, N. I. (2004). Creating Embodied Agents With Cultural Context. In Payr, S., & Trappl, R. (Eds.), *Agent Culture: Human-Agent Interaction in a Multicultural World* (pp. 107–126). London: Lawrence Erlbaum Associates.

Allen, I. E., & Seaman, J. (2007). *Online nation: Five years of growth in online learning*. Needham, MA: The Sloan Consortium. Retrieved September 22, 2008 from http://www.sloan-c.org/publications/survey/pdf/online_nation.pdf

Allport, G. W. (1954). *The nature of prejudice*. Reading, MA: Addison-Wesley.

Ames, C. (1992). Classrooms: Goals, structures, and student motivation. *Journal of Educational Psychology*, *84*(3), 261–271. doi:10.1037/0022-0663.84.3.261

Andersen, P. A. (2000). Explaining intercultural differences in nonverbal communication. In Samovar, L. A., & Porter, R. E. (Eds.), *Intercultural communication: A reader*. Belmont, CA: Wadsworth.

Anderson, L. W., & Krathwohl, D. (Eds.). (2001). *A taxonomy for learning, teaching and assessing: A revision of Bloom's taxonomy of educational objectives*. New York, NY: Longman.

Andrusyszyn, M. A., & Davie, L. (1997). Facilitating reflection through interactive journals writing in an online graduate course: A qualitative study. *Journal of Distance Education*, *XII*(1/2), 103–126.

Angelaki, J. (1999). Machinic modulations: New cultural theory and technopolitics. *Journal of the Theoretical Humanities*, *4*(2).

Aragon, S. R., Johnson, S. D., & Shaik, N. (2003). The influence of learning style preferences on student success in online versus face-to-face environments. *American Journal of Distance Education*, *16*(4), 227–243. doi:10.1207/S15389286AJDE1604_3

Ash, R. (1999). The Sapir-Whorf hypothesis. New York, NY: Payne. Retrieved 14 July, 2010, from http://www.angelfire.com/journal/worldtour99/sapirwhorf.html

Asian Development Bank. (2003). *Key Indicators: Education for Global Participation*. Retrieved from http://www.adb.org/Documents/Books/Key_Indicators/2003/pdf/theme_paper.pdf

Asmar, C. (1999). Is there a gendered agenda in academia? The research experience of female and male PhD graduates in Australian universities. *Higher Educator*, *38*(3), 255–273. doi:10.1023/A:1003758427027

Aspden, L., & Helm, P. (2004). Making the connection in a blended learning environment. *Educational Technology Research and Development*, *41*(3), 245–252.

Attewell. (2001). The first and second digital divides. *Sociology of Education*, *74*(3), 252-259.

Auernheimer, G. (2003). *Einführung in die interkulturelle Pädagogik* [Introduction to Intercultural Pedagogy]. Darmstadt, Germany: Wiss. Buchges.

Auré, L. (2010). Lisibilité des sites Web. In *All for Design*. Retrieved 4 April, 2010, from http://all-for-design.com/afd-le-theme

Australian Flexible Learning Framework. (2004). *Cross-cultural issues in content development and teaching online*. Retrieved August 23, 2007, from http://www.flexiblelearning.net.au/flx/webdav/site/flxsite/users/kedgar/public/quick_guides/crosscultural.pdf

Australian Government Department of Education. Employment and Workplace Relations. (August 19, 2009). *Media release: Measures to safeguard education for overseas students studying in Australia.* Retrieved September 23, 2009, from http://www.deewr.gov.au/ministers/gillard/media/releases/pages/article_090819_113519.aspx

Aylett, R. S., Dias, J., & Paiva, A. (2006). An affectively-driven planner for synthetic characters. In *Proceedings of ICAPS, 2006*, 2–10.

Babu, D. R. S. (2008). Digital divide: Educational disparities in India. *ICFAI Journal of Public Administration, 4*(3), 68–81.

Bailenson, J. N., Blascovich, J., & Guadagno, R. E. (2008). Self representations in immersive virtual environments. *Journal of Applied Social Psychology, 38*(11), 2673–2690. doi:10.1111/j.1559-1816.2008.00409.x

Bales, R. F. (1976). *Interaction process analysis: A method for the study of small groups*. Chicago: University Press.

Bandera, A. (1986). *Social foundations of thought and action*. Englewood Cliffs, NJ: Prentice Hall.

Bandura, A. (1973). *Aggression: a social learning analysis*. Englewood Cliffs, NJ: Prentice-Hall.

Bandura, A., & Adams, N. E. (1977). Analysis of self-efficacy theory of behavioral change. *Cognitive Therapy and Research, 1*(4), 287–310. doi:10.1007/BF01663995

Bannan-Ritland, B. (2003). The role of design in research: The integrative learning design framework. *Educational Researcher, 32*(1), 21–24. doi:10.3102/0013189X032001021

Barmeyer, C. (2003). Interkulturelles Coaching. [Intercultural Coaching] In Rauen, C. (Ed.), *Handbuch Coaching* (pp. 241–272). Göttingen: Hogrefe.

Bates, A. (1995). *Technology, open learning and distance education*. New York, NY: Routledge.

Bateson, G. (2002). *Mind and nature. A necessary unity*. New Jersey: Hampton Press.

Baylor, A. L. (2001). Permutations of control: Cognitive considerations for agent-based learning environments. *Journal of Interactive Learning Research, 12*(4), 403–425.

Baylor, A. L., & Ryu, J. (2003). *Evidence that multiple agents facilitate greater learning. International Artificial Intelligence in Education*. Sydney, Australia: AI-ED.

Bearden, W. O., Scholder, P. E., & Netemeyer, R. G. (2000). Challenges and prospects facing doctoral education in marketing. *Marketing Education Review, 10*(1), 1–14.

Beasley-Murray, J. (1997). So here comes a book that makes everything easy: Towards a theory of intellectual history in the field of intellectual production. *Cultural Theory, 2*(7).

Beckman, M. (1990). Collaborative learning: Preparation for the workplace and democracy. *College Teaching, 38*(4), 128–133.

Bejerano, A. R. (2008). The genesis and evolution of online degree programs: Who are they for and what have we lost along the way? *Communication Education*, *1*(3), 408 – 414.

Belisle, C. (2007). *eLearning and intercultural dimensions of learning theories and teaching models*. Paper submitted to the FeConE (Framework for eContent Evaluation) Project, May 2007. Retrieved July 17, 2007, from http://www.elearningeuropa.info/files/media/media13022.pdf

Bell, M., & Farrier, S. (2008). Measuring success in e-learning–a multi-dimensional approach. *Electronic Journal of e-learning*, *6*(2), 99-109.

Bem, S. (1993). *The lenses of gender*. New Haven, CT: Yale University Press.

Bender, T. (2003). *Rethinking learning theory within in the online class. Discussion-based online teaching to enhance students learning* (pp. 16–33). Sterling, VA: Stylus Publishing.

Bennett, R. (2007). *Omnium five-stage process for online collaborative creativity (OCC)*. Omnium Research Group. Retrieved August 28, 2008, from http://www.omnium.net.au/research

Bennett, M. (1986). A developmental approach to training for Intercultural Sensitivity. *International Journal of Intercultural Relations*, *10*(2), 179–195. doi:10.1016/0147-1767(86)90005-2

Bennett, M. (1998). Intercultural communication: a current perspective. In Bennett, M. (Ed.), *Basic Concepts of Intercultural Communication*. Yarmouth, MA: Intercultural Press.

Bennett, M. J. (1993). Towards enthnorelativism: A developmental model of intercultural sensitivity. In Paige, M. (Ed.), *Education for the intercultural experience*. Yarmouth, MA: Intercultural Press.

Bentley, J. P. H., Tinney, M. V., & Chia, B. H. (2005). Intercultural Internet-based learning: Know your audience and what it values. *Educational Technology Research and Development*, *53*(2), 117–127. doi:10.1007/BF02504870

Berge, Z. (2000). New roles for learners and teachers in online higher education. In Heart, G. (Ed.), *Readings and resources in global online education* (pp. 3–9). Melbourne, Australia: Whirlgig Press.

Bergin, D. A. (1992). Leisure activity, motivation, and academic achievement in high school students. *Journal of Leisure Research*, *24*(3), 225–239.

Bernard, M. (2006). *Optimal Web design*. Retrieved 28 Sep, 2006, from http://psychology.wichita.edu/optimalweb/international.htm

Bischoff, A. (2000). The elements of effective online teaching: Overcoming the barriers to success. In White, K. W., & Whight, B. H. (Eds.), *The online teaching guide: A handbook of attitudes strategies, and techniques for the virtual classroom* (pp. 57–72). Boston, MA: Allyn and Bacon.

Blackburn, W. R. (2007). *The sustainability handbook*. Washington, DC: Environmental Law Institute.

Blair, B., & Caine, R. (1995). Landscapes of change: Toward a new paradigm for education. In B. Blair & R. Caine (Eds.), *Integrative learning as the pathway to teaching holism, complexity and interconnectedness*. Lewiston, UK: EMText.

Blond, M.-V., Marcellin, O., & Zerbib, M. (2009). *Lisibilité des sites Web*. Paris, France: Eyrolles.

Bloom, D. E. (2004). Globalization and Education: An Economic Perspective, In M. Suarez-Orozco & D. Qin-Hillard, (Ed.), *Globalization: Culture and Education in the New Millennium.* (pp. 58-77). Ewing, NJ: University of California Press.

Bloom, B. S. (1956). *Taxonomy of educational objectives, handbook I: The cognitive domain*. New York, NY: David McKay Co Inc.

Bloom, B. S., Englhart, M. D., Furst, E. J., Hill, W. H., & Krathwohl, D. R. (Eds.). (1956). *Taxonomy of educational objectives, the classification of educational goals. Handbook I: Cognitive domain*. New York, NY: Longman.

Blumer, H. (1969). *Symbolic interactionism: Perspective and method.* Englewood Cliffs, NJ: Prentice-Hall, Inc.

Bonk, C. J. (2009). *The world is open: How Web technology is revolutionizing education*. San Francisco, CA: Jossey-Bass.

Bonk, C., & Graham, C. (Eds.). (In press). *Handbook of blended learning: Global perspectives, local designs*. San Francisco, CA: Pfeiffer Publishing.

Borde, D. (2007). Psychosoziale Potentiale und Belastungen der Migranten – globale, institutionelle und individuelle Perspektiven. [Psycho-social potentials and burdens of migrants – global, instituational and individual perspectives] In Borde, D., & David, M. (Eds.), *Migration und psychische Gesundheit*. Frankfurt am Main, Germany: Mabuse.

Borzak, L. (1981) (ed.). *Field study: A source book for experiential learning.* Beverly Hills, CA: Sage Publications.

Boud, D. (2001). Using journal writing to enhance reflective practice. In L. M. English & M. A. Gillen (Eds.), *Promoting journal writing in adult education. New directions in adult and continuing education no. 90* (pp. 9-18). San Francisco: Jossey-Bass.

Boud, D. (2006, July 3). *Relocating reflection in the context of practice: Rehabilitation or rejection?* Keynote Presentation, Professional lifelong learning: beyond reflective practice, One Day Conference, University of Leeds, UK.

Bourne, R. (2000). Ivory towers or driving forces for change: The development role of Commonwealth universities in the 21st Century. *The Round Table*, *356*, 451–458. doi:10.1080/003585300225025

Bowskill, N., McConnell, D., & Banks, S. (December, 2007, December 11-13). *Intercultural e-tutoring teams: The dynamics of new collaborations and new needs*. Society for Research in Higher Education, Annual Conference, University of Sussex, Brighton, UK.

Boyle, T. (2005). A dynamic, systematic method for developing blended learning. *Education Communication and Information*, *5*(3), 221–232. doi:10.1080/14636310500350422

Bransford, J. D., Brown, A. L., & Cocking, R. R. (2000). *How people learn: Brain, mind, experience, and school.* Washington, DC: National Academy Press.

Bridges, C. M., & Wilhelm, W. B. (2008). Going beyond green: The why and how of integrating sustainability into the marketing curriculum. *Journal of Marketing Education*, *30*(1), 33–46. doi:10.1177/0273475307312196

Briguglio, C. (2000). Language and cultural issues for English-as-a-second/foreign language students in transnational educational settings. *Higher Education in Europe*, *25*(3), 425–434. doi:10.1080/713669286

Brown, A. L. (1992). Design experiments: Theoretical and methodological challenges in creating complex interventions. *Journal of the Learning Sciences*, *2*(2), 141–178. doi:10.1207/s15327809jls0202_2

Brown, J. S., Collins, A., & Duguid, P. (1989). Situated cognition and the culture of learning. *Educational Researcher*, *18*(1), 32–42.

Brown, S., & Jones, E. (2007). Introduction: Values, valuing and value in an internationalised higher education context. In Jones, E., & Brown, S. (Eds.), *Internationalising higher education* (pp. 1–6). Abingdon, Oxon, UK: Routledge.

Brown, S., & Joughin, G. (2007). Assessment and international students: Helping clarify puzzling processes. In Jones, E., & Brown, S. (Eds.), *Internationalising higher education* (pp. 57–71). Abingdon, Oxon, UK: Routledge.

Buchanan, R. (2004). Human-centered design: Changing perspectives on design education in the East and West. *Design Issues*, *20*(1), 30–39. doi:10.1162/074793604772933748

Buckley, J. (1999, February 24-27). *Multicultural reflection*, Paper presented at the Annual Meeting of the American Association of Colleges for Teacher Education, 51st, Washington, DC.

Burbules, N. C. (2000). Does the Internet constitute a global educational community? In Burbules, N. C., & Torres, C. (Eds.), *Globalization and education: Critical perspectives* (pp. 323–355). New York: Routledge.

Burke, J. (2003). *Intercultural Education Summit Keynote.* Retrieved from http://people.ucsc.edu/~pmmckerc/IEA.html

Byram, M., Gribkova, B., & Starkey, H. (2002). *Developing the inter-cultural dimension in language teaching. A practical introduction for teachers.* Council of Europe, Strasbourg. Retrieved July 17, 2007, from http://lrc.cornell.edu/director/Inter-cultural.pdf

Byram, M., Nichols, A., & Stevens, D. (Eds.). (2001). *Developing Intercultural Competence in Practice: Languages for Intercultural Communication and Education.* Multilingual Matters, Ltd.

Byrne, D. (1971). *The attraction paradigm.* New York: Academic Press.

Cameron, L., Rutland, A., Brown, R., & Douch, R. (2006). Changing children's intergroup attitudes toward refugees: Testing different models of extended contact. *Child Development*, *77*(5), 1208–1219. doi:10.1111/j.1467-8624.2006.00929.x

Campbell, E. (2002). Career management. *Nursing Spectrum Magazine*. Retrieved January 2, 2008, from http://community.nursingspectrum.com/MagazineArticles/article.cfm?AID=7981

Campbell, N. (2003). So you want to teach online? It won't happen overnight but it can happen. *Computers in New Zealand Schools*, *15*(1), 11-13, 25.

Campbell, N. (1998). Learning to teach online: A case for support. *Computers in New Zealand Schools*, *10*(1), 11–13.

Carlisle, W. (July 27, 2009). Transcript: Holy cash cows. *Australian Broadcasting Corporation, Four Corners.* Retrieved September 23, 2009, from http://www.abc.net.au/4corners/content/2009/s2637800.htm

Carnes, L. W., Awang, F., & Marlow, J. (2003). Can instructors ensure the integrity and quality of online courses? *Delta Pi Epsilon Journal, 45*, 162–172.

Carron, A. V., Widmeyer, W. N., & Brawley, L. R. (1985). The development of an instrument to assess cohesion in sport teams: The Group Environment Questionnaire. *Journal of Sport Psychology, 7*, 244–266.

Carson, J., & Nelson, G. (1996). Chinese students' perceptions of ESL peer response group interaction. *Journal of Second Language Writing, 5*(1), 1–19. doi:10.1016/S1060-3743(96)90012-0

Cassell, J., & Tversky, D. (2005). The language of online intercultural community formation. *Journal of Computer-Mediated Communication, 10*(2). Retrieved September 12, 2007, from http://jcmc.indiana.edu/vol10/issue2/cassell.html

Cassell, J., Sullivan, J., Prevost, S., & Churchill, E. (2000). *Embodied Conversational Agents*. Cambridge, MA: MIT Press.

Castle, J. B. (1995). Collaborative reflection as professional development. *Review of Higher Education, 18*(3), 243–263.

Cavanaugh, J. (2003). Teaching online-a time comparison. *Online Journal of Distance Learning Administration, 3*(1). Retrieved April 25, 2008, from http://www.westga.edu/~distance/ojdla/spring81/cavanaugh81.htm

Chale, E. M. (1992). Application and cost effectiveness of distance education in teacher preparation: A case study of Tanzania. In P. Murphy and A. Zhiri (Eds.), *Distance Education in Anglophone Africa* (pp.123-136). Washington, DC: The World Bank.

Charmaz, K. (2000). Grounded theory: Objectivist and constructivist methods. In N. Denzin & Y. S. Lincoln (Eds.), *The handbook of qualitative research* (pp. 509-535). Thousand Oaks, CA: Sage Pubs. Inc.

Chen, F. J. (2001). Analysis of Lu Xun used the dialectics: Dialectic among

Chen, A., Mashhadi, A., Ang, D., & Harkrider, N. (1999). Cultural issues in the design of technology-enhanced learning systems. *British Journal of Educational Technology, 30*(3), 217–230. doi:10.1111/1467-8535.00111

Cheong, P. H. (2008). The young and techless? Internet use and problem solving behaviors among young adults in Singapore. *New Media & Society, 10*(5), 771–791. doi:10.1177/1461444808094356

Chiang, F. (2005). A critical examination of Hofstede's thesis and its application to international reward management. *International Journal of Human Resource Management, 16*(9), 1545-1563.

Chicago Press.

China Mobile Limited. (2009). *Customer data for August 2009.* Retrieved October 3, 2009, from http://www.chinamobileltd.com/

Choi, B., Lee, I., Kim, J., & Jeon, Y. (2005). *A qualitative cross-national study of cultural influences on mobile data service design.* Paper presented at the Conference on Human Factors in Computing Systems, Portland, OR.

Christiansen, E. (2005). *Boundary objects, please rise! On the role of boundary objects in distributed collaboration and how to design for them*. Retrieved September 2, 2009, from http://redesignresearch.com/chi05/EC%20Boundary%20Objects.pdf

Churches, A. (2008). *Bloom's taxonomy blooms digitally*. Retrieved on April 22, 2008, from http://techlearning.com/shared/printableArticle.php?articleID=196605124

Cimbala, S. J. (2002). Can teaching be saved? *International Journal of Public Administration, 25*(9-10), 1079–1095. doi:10.1081/PAD-120006126

Clandinin, D. J., & Connelly, F. M. (1980). *Narrative inquiry* (3rd ed.). Chicago, IL: University of.

Clandinin, D. J., & Connelly, F. M. (2000). *Narrative inquiry: Experience and story in qualitative research*. San Francisco, CA: Jossey-Bass Publishers.

Clark, D. (2000). *Learning domains or Bloom's taxonomy*. Retrieved on February 5, 2005, from http://www.nwlink.com/~donclark/hrd/bloom.html

Clark, G. (2007). Evolution of the global sustainable consumption and production policy and the United Nations environment programme's (UNEP) supporting activities. *Journal of Cleaner Production, 15*, 492–498. doi:10.1016/j.jclepro.2006.05.017

Cobb, P., Confrey, J., diSessa, A., Lehrer, R., & Schauble, L. (2003). Design experiments in educational research. *Educational Researcher, 32*(1), 9–13. doi:10.3102/0013189X032001009

Cobley, P., & Jansz, L. (2007). *Introducing semiotics. Thriplow & Cambridge*. UK: Icon Books Ltd.

Collins, A. (1992). Towards a design science of education. In Scanlon, E., & O'Shea, T. (Eds.), *New directions in educational technology* (pp. 15–22). Berlin, Germany: Springer. doi:10.1007/978-3-642-77750-9_2

Collins, A., Joseph, D., & Bielaczyc, K. (2004). Design research: Theoretical and methodological issues. *Journal of the Learning Sciences, 13*(1), 15–42. doi:10.1207/s15327809jls1301_2

Collis, B. (1999). Designing for differences: Cultural issues in the design of WWW-based course-support sites. *British Journal of Educational Technology, 30*(3), 201–215. doi:10.1111/1467-8535.00110

Commonwealth of Learning and the VUSSC government interlocutors. (2007). *A business strategy for the Virtual University for small states of the Commonwealth (2007– 2013)*. Retrieved June 7, 2009, from http://www.col.org/sitecollectionDocument/VUSSC.Business_Plan_20070220.doc

Commonwealth of Learning. (1995). *Directory of courses and materials for training in distance education*. Vancouver: Commonwealth of Learning.

Cong, Y. (2008). *The impact of Chinese culture in online learning: Chinese tertiary students' perceptions*. Unpublished master's thesis, University of Waikato, New Zealand.

Connaughton, S. L., & Shuffler, M. (2007). Multinational and multicultural distributed teams: A review and future agenda. *Small Group Research, 38*, 397–412. doi:10.1177/1046496407301970

Converge. (2009, 8 July). Podcast projects promote literacy. *Converge Magazine*. Retrieved from http://www.convergemag.com/literacy/Podcast-Projects-Promote-Literacy.html

Conway, J. (1999). Multiple identities of an adult educator: A learning journal story. In B. Merrill (Ed.), *Proceedings of The Final Frontier. SCUTREA 29th Annual Conference, Standing Conference on University Teaching and Research in the Education of Adults, 1999*. (ERIC Document Reproduction Service No. ED 438 447)

Cook, J., & Finlayson, M. (2005). The impact of cultural diversity on Web site design. *Advanced Management Journal, 70*(3), 15–45.

Cooper, J. (1990). Cooperative learning and college teaching: Tips from the trenches. *Teaching Professor, 4*(5), 1–2.

Core, M., Traum, D., Lane, H. C., Swartout, W., Gratch, J., van Lent, M., & Marsella, S. (2006). Teaching negotiation skills through practice and reflection with vVirtual humans. *Simulation, 82*(11), 685–701. doi:10.1177/0037549706075542

Covington, M. V. (2000). Goal theory, motivation and school achievement: An integrative review. *Annual Review of Psychology, 51*, 171–200. doi:10.1146/annurev.psych.51.1.171

Craig, C., & Douglas, S. (2000). *International marketing research*. Wiley.

Crawford, C. M., & Gannon Cook, R. (2008a). Building autonomous and dynamic communities of learning within distance learning environments: Focusing upon making connections, knowledge creation and practice communities. *The International Journal of Technology, Knowledge and Society, 4*(4), 47–58.

Crawford, C. M., & Gannon Cook, R. (2008b). Creating and sustaining communities of learning within distance learning environments: Focusing upon making connections, creating communities of learning, and responsibilities. *The International Journal of Learning, 15*(2), 179–193.

Cruickshank, K., Newell, S., & Cole, S. (2003). Meeting English language needs in teacher education: A flexible support model for non-English speaking background students. *Asia-Pacific Journal of Teacher Education, 31*(3), 239–247. doi:10.1080/0955236032000149373

Cudmore, G. (2005). Globalization, internationalization, and the recruitment of international students in higher education, and in the Ontario colleges of applied arts and technology. *Canadian Journal of Higher Education, 35*(1), 37–60.

Culp, K. M., Honey, M., & Mandinach, E. (2003). *A Retrospective on Twenty Years of Education Technology Policy*. Washington, DC: Center for Children and Technology Education Development Center, U.S. Department of Education, Office of Educational Technology.

Currie, J., Harris, P., & Thiele, B. (2000). Sacrifices in greedy universities: Are they gendered? *Gender and Education, 12*(3), 269–291. doi:10.1080/713668305

Curtiss, R. H. (1995, July/August). Oman: A model for all developing nations. *The Washington Report on Middle East Affairs*. Retrieved August 21, 2009, from http://www.wrmea.com/backissues/0795/9507049.htm

Danesi, M. (1993). *Vico, metaphor, and the origin of language*. Bloomington, IN: Indiana University Press.

Daniel, J. (2005). Open and distance learning in Africa. In *15 CCEM mid-term review for Africa and Europe*, Freetown, Sierra Leone, 14 November 2005.

Daniel, J., & Menon, M. (2005). *ODL and ICTs for teacher development in Sub-Saharan Africa: The experience of the Commonwealth of Learning*. Retrieved 12 November, 2005, from http://www.col.org/speeches/JD_0509BOCODOL.htm

Daniel, J., & West, P. (2008). *The virtual university for small states of the Commonwealth: What is it for? How is it doing? Where is it going?* Retrieved June 7, 2009, from http://www.col.org/resources/speeches/2008presentations/2008-VUSSC/Pages/articleVUSSC.aspx

Davies, J., & Harcourt, E. (2007). No shonky, cappuccino courses here, mate. UK perspectives on Australian higher education. *Perspectives*, *11*(4), 116–122.

Davis, M. H. (1996). *Empathy – a social psychological approach*. Madison, WI: Brown & Benchmark Publishers.

Davydov, V., & Radzikhovskii, L. (1985). Vygotsky's theory and the activity-oriented approach in psychology. In Wertsch, J. W. (Ed.), *Culture, communication and cognition*. Cambridge, UK: Cambridge University Press.

de Rosis, F., Pelachaud, C., & Poggi, I. (2004). Transcultural Believability in Embodied Agents: A Matter of Consistent Adaptation. In Payr, S., & Trappl, R. (Eds.), *Agent Culture: Human-Agent Interaction in a Multicultural World* (pp. 75–106). London: Lawrence Erlbaum Associates.

De Vita, G. (2007). Taking stock: An appraisal of the literature on internationalising HE learning. In Jones, E., & Brown, S. (Eds.), *Internationalising higher education* (pp. 154–168). Abingdon, Oxon, UK: Routledge.

De Vita, G., & Case, P. (2003). Rethinking the internationalisation agenda in UK higher education. *Journal of Further and Higher Education*, *27*(4), 383–398. doi:10.1080/0309877032000128082

Debande, O., & Ottersten, E. K. (2004). Information and communication technologies: A tool for empowering and developing the horizon of the learner. *Higher Education Management and Policy*, *16*(2), 31–61. doi:10.1787/hemp-v16-art15-en

Deci, E. L., & Ryan, R. M. (1985). *Intrinsic motivation and self-determination in human behavior*. New York, NY: Plenum.

Del Rio, P., & Alvarez, A. (1995). Changing architectures of mind and agency. In Wertsch, J. (Ed.), *Sociocultural studies of mind*. Cambridge, UK: Cambridge University Press.

Deng, Y. (2004). Network-based distance education in Chinese universities. *The UKEU reports*. UK eUniversities Worldwide Limited. Retrieved June 27, 2007 from http://www.matic-media.co.uk/ukeu/UKEU-r04-china-2005.doc

Dengler, M. (2008). Classroom active learning complemented by an online discussion forum to teach sustainability. *Journal of Geography in Higher Education, 32*(3), 481–494. doi:10.1080/03098260701514108

Denis, B. (2003). A conceptual framework to design and support self-directed learning in a blended learning programme. A case study: The DES-TEF. *Journal of Educational Media, 28*(2-3), 115–127. doi:10.1080/1358165032000165626

Dennen, V. P. (2005). From message posting to learning dialogues: Factors affecting learner participation in asynchronous discussion. *Distance Education, 26*(1), 127–148. doi:10.1080/01587910500081376

Department for International Development. (2009). *Imfundo: Partnership for IT in education.* Retrieved September 20, 2009, from http://imfundo.digitalbrain.com/imfundo/

DePaul University. (1991). *University mission statement.* Retrieved on October 12, 2009, from http://mission.depaul.edu/mission/index.asp

Dexter, S. (2002). eTIPS-Educational Technology Integration Principles. *Designing instruction for technology-enhanced learning.* Hershey, PA: Idea Group Publishing.

Dey, A. (2002). *An accessibility audit of WebCT.* Retrieved 20 Sept, 2009, from http://ausweb.scu.edu.au/aw02/papers/refereed/alexander/paper.html

Dhanarajan, G. (2001). Distance education: Promise, performance and potential. *Open Learning, 16*(1), 61–68. doi:10.1080/02680510124465

Dias, J., & Paiva, A. (2005). Feeling and reasoning: a computational model. In *Proceedings of the 12th Portuguese Conference on Artificial Intelligence*, EPIA 2005 (pp. 127-140). Berlin: Springer.

Dillon, A. (1996). Myths, misconceptions and an alternative view of information usage and the electronic medium. In Jrouet, (Eds.), *Hypertext and cognition* (pp. 24–42). Mahwah, NJ: Erlbaum.

DiPaola, S., Dorosh, D., & Brandt, G. (2004). *Ratava's line: Emergent learning and design using collaborative virtual worlds.* Retrieved October 22, 2007, from http://www.digitalspace.com/papers/sig2004-paper-ratava/index.html

Doctoroff, T. (2007). *Young digital mavens.* Beijing: IAC-JWT Worldwide.

Donaghy, A., McGee, C., Ussher, B., & Yates, R. (2003). *Online teaching and learning: A study of teacher education students' experiences.* Hamilton, New Zealand: The University of Waikato.

Doo, M. Y. (2006). A problem in online interpersonal skills training: do learners practice skills? *Open Learning, 21*(3), 263–272. doi:10.1080/02680510600953252

Dörner, D. (2003). The mathematics of emotions. In F. Detje, D.Dörner, & H. Schaub (Eds.), *Proceedings of the Fifth International Conference on Cognitive Modeling* (pp. 75–79). Bamberg, Germany: Universitäts-Verlag.

Dunn, P., & Marinetti, A. (2005). Cultural adaptation: Necessity for global e-learning. *New Economy e-Magazine.* Retrieved June 21, 2009, from www.linezine.com/7.2/articles/pdamca.htm

Dupeyrat, C., & Mariné, C. (2005). Implicit of intelligence, goal orientation, cognitive engagement, and achievement: A test of Dweck's model with returning to school adults. *Contemporary Educational Psychology, 30*(1), 43–59. doi:10.1016/j.cedpsych.2004.01.007

Dutton, W. H., & Cheong, P. H. & Park, N. (2004b). The social shaping of a virtual learning environment: The case of a university-wide course management system. *Electronic Journal of e-Learning, 2*(1), 69-80.

Dutton, W. H., Cheong, P. H., & Park, N. (2004). An ecology of constraints on e-learning in higher education: The case of a virtual learning environment. *Prometheus, 22*(2), 131–149. doi:10.1080/08109020420 00218337

Duverneuil, B. (2007). *Webdesign: Passé, present, et…présent*, p.3. World Wide Web Consortium SlideShare presentation. Retrieved 3 April, 2010, from http://www.slideshare.net/bduverneuil/webdesign-passe-present-et-present-part3

Earl, S. K., & Ball, T. (2007). *Roles for discussion. An update of one of Nola Campbell's online class activities. Unpublished document for class use in PROF521 and PROF522.* New Zealand: School of Education, University of Waikato.

Edmundson, A. (2009). Culturally accessible e-learning: An overdue global business imperative. *ASTD's Learning Circuits.*

Edmundson, A. (2007). *Globalized e-learning cultural challenges*. Hershey, PA: Information Science Publishing.

Edmundson, A. L. (2008). Cross-cultural learning objects (xclos). In Putnik, G. A., & Cunha, M. M. (Eds.), *Encyclopedia of networked and virtual organizations*. Hershey, PA: Idea Group, Inc.doi:10.4018/978-1-59904-885-7.ch049

Edwards, R., Crosling, G., Petrovic-Lazarovic, S., & O'Neill, P. (2003). Internationalisation of business education: Meaning and implementation. *Higher Education Research & Development, 22*(2), 183–192. doi:10.1080/07294360304116

Eisner, E. W. (1997). Cognition and representation. *Phi Delta Kappan, 78*(5), 349–353.

eLearning Africa. (2005). *1st International conference on ICT for development, education and training, UNCC, Addis Ababa, Ethiopia May 24-26, 2006.* Retrieved 12 November, 2005, from http://www.elearning-africa.com/conference.php

Elias, M. J., Zins, J. E., Weissberg, R. P., Frey, K. S., Greenberg, M. T., & Haynes, N. M. (1997). *Promoting social and emotional learning: Guidelines for educators*. Alexandria, VA: Association for Supervision and Curriculum Development.

Elliot, E., & Dweck, C. (1988). Goals: An approach to motivation and achievement. *Journal of Personality and Social Psychology, 54*(1), 5–12. doi:10.1037/0022-3514.54.1.5

Elliott, A. (2001). Introduction. In M. Richards, A. Eliot, V. Woloshyn, & C. Mitchell (Eds.), *Collaboration uncovered: the forgotten, the assumed, and the unexamined in collaborative education*. Westport, CT: Bergin and Garvey.

Ellis, R., & Calvo, R. (2004). Learning through discussions in blended environments. *Educational Media International*, *41*(3), 263–274. doi:10.1080/09523980410001680879

Engvig, M., & White, M. (2006). The students' perspectives. In Engvig, M. (Ed.), *Online learning: All you need to know to facilitate and administer online courses* (pp. 37–84). Cresskill, NJ: Hampton Press.

Enoch, Y., & Soker, Z. (2006). Age, gender, ethnicity and the digital divide: University students' use of Web-based instruction. *Open Learning*, *21*(2), 99–110. doi:10.1080/02680510600713045

Erstad, O., Klevenberg, B., & Aamdal, G. (2008). *Negotiating otherness in knowledge building.* Summer Institute 2008, University of Oslo, Norway. Retrieved on February 22, 2010 from http://elevforsk.umb-sll.wikispaces.net/file/view/paper_Summer_Institute08.pdf

Ess, C., & Sudweeks, F. (2005). Culture and computer-mediated communication: Toward new understandings. *Journal of Computer-Mediated Communication*, *11*(1), 179–191. doi:10.1111/j.1083-6101.2006.tb00309.x

eWorld Learning Inc. (2010). *e-World Learning*. Retrieved October 4, 2010, from www.eWorldLearning.com

Faiola, A., & Matei, S. (2005). Cultural cognitive style and Web design: Beyond a behavioral inquiry into computer-mediated communication. *Journal of Computer-Mediated Communication*, *11*(1), 18. doi:10.1111/j.1083-6101.2006.tb00318.x

Fantini, A. E. (2000). A CENTRAL Concern: Developing Intercultural Competence. In *SIT Occasional Papers Series,* (1). Brattleboro, VT: School for International Training.

Fantini, A. E. (2006). *Final Report of a Research Project conducted by the Federation of The Experiment in International Living with funding support from the Center for Social Development at Washington University, St. Louis, Missouri* (The Initial Phase of An Extended Project to Explore and Assess Intercultural Outcomes in Service Program Participants Worldwide). Brattleboro, VT: Federation EIL

Fisher, M. (1997). The Voice of Experience: Inservice Teacher Technology Competency Recommendations for Preservice Teacher Preparation. *Journal of Technology and Teacher Education*, *5*(2-3), 139–147.

Flew, T. (2008). *New media: An introduction.* (3rd ed.). New York, NY: Oxford.

Forgas, J. (1994). *Soziale Interaktion und Kommunikation* [Social interaction and communication]. Weinheim, Germany: Beltz.

Foucault, M. (1972-1977). In Gordon, C. (Ed.), *Power/Knowledge: Selected interviews & other writings*. New York, NY: Pantheon.

Gallini, J., Seaman, M., & Terry, S. (1995). Metaphors and learning new text. *Journal of Reading Behavior*, *27*(2), 187–191.

Gannon Cook, R. (2009). Lessons learned from parietal art: Pansemiotics and e-learning. Paper presented at the CELDA Conference of IADIS held in November in Rome, Italy.

Gannon Cook, R., & Crawford, C. (2009). Exhuming cultural artifacts to embed and integrate deep adult e-learning. In the *Proceedings of the American Educational Communications and Technology Conference,* October, Louisville, KY.

Gannon Cook, R. (1998). Semiotics in technology, learning and culture. *Bulletin of Science, Technology & Society, 18*(2), 178–183.

GannonCook. R., & Crawford, C. M. (2001). Metaphorical representation within a distributed learning environment. In J. D. Price, D. A. Willis, N. Davis & J. Willis (Eds.), SITE 2001 Annual – *Society for Information Technology and Teacher Education* (pp. 1086-1088). Charlottesville, VA: Association for the Advancement of Computing in Education (AACE).

Gao, G., & Ting-Toomey, S. (1998). *Communicating effectively with the Chinese.* Thousand Oaks, CA: Sage.

Garcia, T., & Pontrich, P. R. (1996). The effects of autonomy on motivation and performance in the college classroom. *Contemporary Educational Psychology, 21*(4), 477–486. doi:10.1006/ceps.1996.0032

Gayol, Y. (1998). Technological transparency: The myth of virtual education. *Bulletin of Science, Technology & Society, 18*(3), 180–186. doi:10.1177/027046769801800305

Gerbic, P. (2005). *Chinese learners and computer mediated communication: Balancing culture, technology, and pedagogy.* Paper presented at the ASCILITE Conference 2005: Balance, Fidelity, Mobility: Maintaining the Momentum? Queensland University of Technology, December 4-7 2005. Retrieved 24 September, 2009, from http://www.ascilite.org.au/conferences/brisbane05/blogs/proceedings/27_Gerbic.pdf

Ghailani, J. (2002, December 24). Quality of secondary education and labour market requirements. *Oman Daily Observer, Supplement,* (p. 3).

Giles, J., & Middleton, T. (1999). *Studying culture: A practical introduction.* Malden, MS: Blackwell Publishers.

Gill, C. (1997). Hands-on language learning through drama. In R. Ballantyne, J. Bain, & J. Packer (Eds.), *Reflecting on university teaching academics' stories* (pp. 1-12). Canberra, Australia: Commonwealth of Australia.

Gliddon, G. (September 12, 2009). Gillard calms Indian student fears. *Melton Leader.* Retrieved September 23, 2009, from http://melton-leader.whereilive.com.au/news/story/gillard-calms-indian-student-fears/

Goodfellow, R., Lea, M., Gonzales, F., & Mason, R. (2001). Opportunity and e-quality: Intercultural and linguistic issues in global online learning. *Distance Education, 22*(1), 65–84. doi:10.1080/0158791010220105

Gratch, J., & Marsella, S. (2005). Evaluating a computational model of emotion. *Autonomous Agents and Multi-Agent Systems, 11*(1), 23–43. doi:10.1007/s10458-005-1081-1

Greenberg, M. T., Weissberg, R. P., O'Brien, M. U., Zins, J. E., Fredericks, L., Resnik, H., & Elias, M. J. (2003). Enhancing School-Based Prevention and Youth Development Through Coordinated Social, Emotional and Academic Learning. *The American Psychologist, 58,* 466–474. doi:10.1037/0003-066X.58.6-7.466

Greene, M. (1997). Metaphors and multiples: Representations and history. *Phi Delta Kappan, 78*(5), 387–394.

Greeno, J. G., & Hall, R. P. (1997). Practicing representation. *Phi Delta Kappan, 78*(5), 361–366.

Gremler, D. D., Hoffman, K. D., Keaveney, S. M., & Wright, L. K. (2000). Experiential learning exercises in services marketing courses. *Journal of Marketing Education, 22*(1), 35–44. doi:10.1177/0273475300221005

Grosch, H., & Leenen, W. R. (1998). Bausteine zur Grundlegung interkulturellen Lernens [Modules for intercultural learning]. In *Interkulturelles Lernen. Arbeitshilfen für politische Bildung*. Bonn, Germany: Bundeszentrale für politische Bildung.

Grosch, H., Groß, A., & Leenen, W. R. (2002). Interkulturelle Kompetenz in der sozialen Arbeit [Intercultural competence in social work]. In G. Auernheimer (ed.), *Interkulturelle Kompetenz und pädagogische Professionalität*. Opladen, Germany: Leske + Budrich.

Gu, Q. (2005). Enjoy loneliness-understanding voices of the Chinese learner. *Humanising Language Teaching, 7*(6). Retrieved September 24, 2009, from, http://www.hltmag.co.uk/nov05/mart01.htm

Gudykunst, W. B., Hammer, M. R., & Wiseman, R. (1977). An analysis of an integrated approach to cross-cultural training. *International Journal of Intercultural Relations, 1*, 99–109. doi:10.1016/0147-1767(77)90045-1

Gudykunst, W. B., & Mody, B. (2002). *Handbook of international and intercultural communication*. Thousand Oaks, CA: Sage Publications.

Gunawardena, C. N., Nolla, A. C., Wilson, P. L., Lopez-Islas, J. R., Ramirez-Angel, N., & Megchun-Alpizar, R. M. (2002). A cross-cultural study of group process and development in online conferences. *Distance Education, 22*(1), 85–121. doi:10.1080/0158791010220106

Gunawardena, C. N., Wilson, P. L., & Nolla, A. C. (2003). Culture and online education. In Moore, M. G., & Anderson, W. G. (Eds.), *Handbook of distance education* (pp. 753–775). Mahwah, NJ: Lawrence Earlbaum Associates.

Guo, S., & Jamal, Z. (2007). Nurturing cultural diversity in higher education: a critical review of selected models. *Canadian Journal of Higher Education, 37*(3), 27–49.

Haberstroh, S., Parr, G., Gee, R., & Trepal, H. (2006). Interactive e-journaling in group work: Perspectives from counselor trainees. *Journal for Specialists in Group Work, 31*(4), 327–337. doi:10.1080/01933920600918840

Hall, A. (2009). *Designing online learning environments for local contexts, as exemplified in the sultanate of Oman*. EdD thesis, Faculty of Education, University of Wollongong. Retrieved April 20, 2009, from http://ro.uow.edu.au/theses/272

Hall, L., Vala, M., Hall, M., Webster, M., Woods, S., Gordon, A., & Aylett, R. (2006). FearNot's appearance: Reflecting children's expectations and perspectives. In J. Gratch, M. Young, R. Aylett, D. Ballin, & P. Olivier (eds.), *6th International Conference, IVA 2006* (pp. 407-419). Berlin: Springer.

Hall, E. (1976). *Beyond culture*. New York, NY: Anchor Books.

Hall, E. T. (1966). *The hidden dimension*. Garden City, NY: Anchor Press.

Hall, E. T. (1976). *Beyond culture*. New York, NY: Anchor Press-Doubleday.

Hall, E. T. (1990). *The silent language*. New York: Anchor Press.

Hall, E. T. (2000). Context and meaning. In Samovar, L. A., & Porter, R. E. (Eds.), *Intercultural communication: A reader* (9th ed., pp. 34–43). Belmont, CA: Wadsworth Publishing Co.

Hall, E. T. (2001). *Understanding cultural differences*. Yarmouth, MA: Intercultural Press.

Hall, G., & Wortham, S. (1997). Introduction: Authorizing culture – interdisciplinarity. *Journal of the Theoretical Humanities*, *4*(2).

Hannon, J., & D'Netto, B. (2007). Cultural diversity online: Student engagement with learning technologies. *International Journal of Educational Management*, *21*(5), 418–432. doi:10.1108/09513540710760192

Harasim, L. (2000). Shift happens: Online education as a new paradigm of learning. *The Internet and Higher Education*, *3*(1-2), 41–61. doi:10.1016/S1096-7516(00)00032-4

Hargittai, E. (2002). Second-Level Digital Divide: Differences in People's Online Skills. *First Monday*, *7*(4), Retrieved Sep.2002 from http://firstmonday.org/issues/issue7_4/hargittai/index.html

Harris, W. J. A. (1971). Education by post (England). In O. Mackenzie & E.L. Christensen (Eds.), *The changing world of correspondence study* (pp. 299-302). University Park, PA: Pennsylvania State University Press.

Harris, P. R., & Moran, R. T. (1987). *Managing cultural differences* (2nd ed.). Houston, TX: Gulf.

Havelock, E. (1986). *The muse learns to write: Reflections on orality and literacy from antiquity to the present*. New Haven, CT: Yale University Press.

Hayes, B. (1996). Speaking of mathematics. *American Scientist*, *84*(2-3), 110–113.

Hazari, S., North, A., & Moreland, D. (2009). Investigating pedagogical value of Wiki technology. *Journal of Information Systems Education*, *20*(2), 187–198.

Hernandez, S. (2002). Team learning in a marketing principles course: Cooperative structures that facilitate active learning and higher level thinking. *Journal of Marketing Education*, *24*(1), 73–85. doi:10.1177/0273475302241009

Hernandez-Serrano, J., & Jonassen, D. H. (2003). The effects of case libraries on problem solving. *Journal of Computer Assisted Learning*, *19*(1), 103–111. doi:10.1046/j.0266-4909.2002.00010.x

Herskovits, M. (1955). *Cultural anthropology*. New York: Knopf.

Hesse, H.-G., & Göbel, K. (2003). *Evaluation and quantitative methods in global learning: A contribution from the field of intercultural sensitivity*. Paper presented at the Global Education Network Europe Seminar: Starting practice and theory in global education. Improving quality and raising standards through evaluation. University of Erlangen-Nürnberg, 29.03.2003.

Hewling, A. (2005). Culture in the online class: Using message analysis to look beyond nationality-based frames of reference. *Journal of Computer-Mediated Communication*, *11*(1), 337–356. doi:10.1111/j.1083-6101.2006.tb00316.x

Hinsch, R., & Pfingsten, U. (2002). *Gruppentraining Sozialer Kompetenzen (GSK)* [Group Training of Social Competencies]. Weinheim, Germany: BeltzPVU.

Hofstede, G. (2003). Geert Hofstede™ cultural dimensions. Retrieved March 31, 2009, from http://www.geert-hofstede.com/

Hofstede, G. (1979). Value systems in forty countries. In Eckensberger, L., Lonner, W., & Poortinga, Y. (Eds.), *Cross-cultural contributions to psychology*. Amsterdam: Swets and Zeitlinger.

Hofstede, G. (1980). *Culture's consequences: International differences in work-related values*. Beverly Hill, CA: Sage.

Hofstede, G. (1984). *Culture's consequences: International differences in work-related values*. Newbury, CA: Sage Publications.

Hofstede, G. (1991). *Cultures and Organizations*. Thousand Oaks, CA: Sage Publications.

Hofstede, G. (1997). *Cultures and organizations: Software of the mind* (Rev. Ed.). New York: McGraw-Hill.

Hofstede, G. (2001). *Culture's consequences: Comparing values, behaviors, institution, and organizations across nations*. Thousand Oaks, CA: Sage Publications.

Hofstede, G. (2001). *Culture's consequences: Comparing values, behaviours, institutions and organizations across nations* (2nd ed.). Thousand Oaks, CA: Sage.

Hofstede, G., & Bond, M. (1984). Hofstede's culture dimensions. *Journal of Cross-Cultural Psychology, 15*, 417–433. doi:10.1177/0022002184015004003

Holzl, A. (1999). Designing for diversity in online learning environments. In *ASCILITE Proceedings*, Brisbane, Australia. Rertrived 23 March, 2010, from http://www.ascilite.org.au/conferences/brisbane99/papers/holzl.pdf

Horrigan, J., & Jones, S. (2008). *When technology fails*. Retrieved Nov. 15, 2008 from: http://www.pewinternet.org/pdfs/PIP_Tech_Failure.pdf

Huff, T. E. (2006). The big shift. *Society, 43*(4), 30–34. doi:10.1007/BF02687532

Humphrey, N. (2004). The death of the feel-good factor? *School Psychology International, 25*(3), 347–360. doi:10.1177/0143034304046906

Huntington, S. P. (2000). Cultures count (Foreword). In Harrison, L. E., & Huntington, S. (Eds.), *Culture Matters. How Values Shape Human Progress*. New York: Basic Books.

InfoDev. (2009). *Quick guide: ICT and education at DFID*. Retrieved 07 June, 2009, from http://74.125.77.132/search?q=cache:i8YkiIxFsalJ:www.infodev.org/en/Publication.146.html

Inkeles, A., & Levinson, J. (1969). National character: The study of modal personality and sociocultural systems. In Lindzey, G., & Aronson, E. (Eds.), *Handbook of social psychology* (*Vol. 4*, pp. 418–506). Reading, MA: Addison-Wesley.

Isbister, K. (2004). Building bridges through the unspoken: Embodied agents to facilitate intercultural communication. In Payr, S., & Trappl, R. (Eds.), *Agent Culture: Human-Agent Interaction in a Multicultural World*. London: Lawrence Erlbaum Associates.

Ite, U. (2004). *Return to sender: using the African intellectual disapora to establish academic links*.

ITU, International Telecommunications Union. (2007). *Measuring Village ICT in Sub-Saharan Africa*. Retrieved December 11, 2007, from http://www.itu.int/ITU-D/ict/statistics/material/Africa_Village_ICT_2007.pdf

Ja, C., & Symons-Brown, B. (September 14, 2009). Gillard kicks off student roundtable. *Brisbane Times*. Retrieved September 23, 2009, from http://news.brisbanetimes.com.au/breaking-news-national/gillard-kicks-off-student-roundtable-20090914-fnct.html

Jacobson, W. (1996). Learning, culture, and learning culture. *Adult Education Quarterly*, *47*(1), 15–28. doi:10.1177/074171369604700102

Jahan, K., & Mehta, Y. (2007). Sustainability across the curriculum. *International Journal of Engineering Education*, *23*(2), 209–217.

Janis, I. (1982). *Groupthink* (2nd ed.). Boston: Houghton-Mifflin.

Jardine, D. W., Friesen, S., & Clifford, P. (2006). *Curriculum in abundance*. Mahwah, NJ: Lawrence Erlbaum.

Jelfs, A., Nathan, R., & Barrett, C. (2004). Scaffolding students: Suggestions on how to equip students with the necessary study skills for studying in a blended environment. *Journal of Educational Media*, *29*(2), 85–96. doi:10.1080/1358165042000253267

Johnson, D. W., Johnson, R. T., & Holubec, E. J. (1993). *Cooperation in the classroom*. Edina, MN: Interaction Book Company.

Jonassen, D. (1998). Designing constructivist learning environments. In Reigeluth, C. M. (Ed.), *Instructional theories and models* (2nd ed., pp. 215–239). Mahwah, NJ: Erlbaum.

Juma, M. N. (2006). Kenyatta University-African Virtual University, Kenya. In D. Antoni (Ed.), The virtual university: Models and messages/ lessons from case studies. Paris: UNESCO.

Kanata, T., & Martin, J. N. (2007). Facilitating dialogues on race and ethnicity with technology: Challenging "Otherness" and promoting a dialogic way of knowing. *Journal of Literacy and Technology*, *8*(2), 1–40.

Kanther, M. (2001). *Interkulturelles Lernen* [Intercultural learning]. Stuttgart, Germany: ibidem-Verlag.

Kapiszewski, A. (2000). *Population, labour and education dilemmas facing GCC states at the turn of the century*. Paper presented at the Crossroads of the New Millennium, Abu Dhabi, UAE.

Kearsley, G. (n.d.). *Social development theory*. Retrieved on August 15, 2009 from http://tip.psychology.org/vygotsky.html

Kearsley, G. (1998). Educational Technology: A Critique. *Educational Technology*, *38*(2), 47–51.

Keesing, R. (1974). Theories of culture. *Annual Review of Anthropology*, *3*, 73–97. doi:10.1146/annurev.an.03.100174.000445

Kelley, C. A. (2007). Assessing the trends and challenges of teaching marketing abroad: A delphi approach. *Journal of Marketing Education*, *29*(3), 201–209. doi:10.1177/0273475307306885

Kelley, E. P. (1971). Marketing's changing social/environmental role. *Journal of Marketing*, *35*(3), 1–2.

Kelly, H. F., Ponton, M. K., & Rovai, A. P. (2007). A comparison on student evaluations of teaching between online and face-to-face courses. *The Internet and Higher Education, 10*(2), 189–101. doi:10.1016/j.iheduc.2007.02.001

Kennedy, E. J., Lawton, L., & Walker, E. (2001). The case for using live cases: Shifting the paradigm in marketing education. *Journal of Marketing Education, 23*(2), 145–151. doi:10.1177/0273475301232008

Kenny, P., Parsons, T., Gratch, J., Leuski, A., & Rizzo, A. (2007) Virtual patients for clinical therapist skills training. In *Proceedings of the 7th International Conference on Intelligent Virtual Agents* (pp. 197-210). Berlin: Springer.

Kerckhoff, A. C. (1995). Institutional Arrangements and Stratification Processes in Industrial Societies. *Annual Review of Sociology, 21*, 323–347. doi:10.1146/annurev.so.21.080195.001543

Kerim, S. (2007, September). *Statement of the 62nd Session of the United Nations General Assembly at the Ministerial Meetings of Group of Friends of the Alliance of Civilizations*, New York. Retrieved from http://www.unaoc.org/images/articles/min_pga.pdf

Kerka, S. (2002). *Journal writing as an adult learning tool. Practice application, brief no. 22*. Retrieved January 2, 2008, from http://www.cete.org/acve/docs/pab00031.pdf

Kerres, M., & de Witt, C. (2003). A didactical framework for the design of blended learning arrangements. *Journal of Educational Media, 28*(2-3), 101–113. doi:10.1080/1358165032000165653

Kerr, M. S., Rynearson, K., & Kerr, M. C. (2006). Student characteristics for online learning success. *The Internet and Higher Education, 9*(2), 91–105. doi:10.1016/j.iheduc.2006.03.002

Khan, N. (2007). The business of education. *Education*. Retrieved April 5, 2007, from http://www.apexstuff.com/bt/200703/education.asp

Kim, J., & Lee, K. (2005). *Cultural difference and mobile phone interface design: Icon recognition according to level of abstraction.* Paper presented at the Conference on Human Factors in Computing Systems, Portland, OR.

Kim, K., & Bonk, C. J. (2002). Cross-cultural comparisons of online collaboration. *Journal of Computer-Mediated Communication, 8*(1).

Kinash, S. (2006). *Seeing beyond blindness*. Greenwich, CT: Information Age.

King, F. B., & LaRocco, D. J. (2006). E-journaling: A strategy to support student reflection and understanding. *Current Issues in Education, 9*(4). Retrieved January 2, 2008, from http://cie.asu.edu/volume9/number4/

King, R. (1996). Competition or co-operation? In *Universities in the Twenty-first Century, Education in a Borderless World Conference*, Singapore, 13-14 August, IDP Education Australia.

Kinyanjui, P. (1992). The organization of teacher training at a distance with particular reference to Kenya. In P. Murphy and A. Zhiri (Eds.), *Distance education in Anglophone Africa: Experience with secondary education and teacher training* (pp. 117-122). Washington, DC: The World Bank.

Kirkley, S. E., & Kirkley, J. R. (2004). Creating next generation blended learning environments using mixed reality, video games and simulations. *TechTrends*, *49*(3), 42–89. doi:10.1007/BF02763646

Kluckhohn, C. (1962). *Culture and Behavior*. New York: The Free Press of Glencoe.

Knights, S., Sampson, J., & Meyer, L. (2006, July 3). *"It's all right for you two, you obviously like each other": Recognizing the pitfalls and challenges in pursuing collaborative professional learning through team teaching*. Paper presented at the Professional lifelong learning: beyond reflective practice, One Day Conference, University of Leeds, UK.

Koda, T., Rehm, M., & André, E. (2008). Cross-cultural evaluations of avatar facial expressions designed by Western Designers. In *Proceedings of IVA, 2008*, 245–252.

Kolb, D. A. (1984). *Experiential learning experience as a source of learning and development*. Upper Saddle River, NJ: Prentice Hall.

Kolb, D. A. (1984). *Experiential learning: Experience as the source of learning and development*. Englewood Cliffs, NJ: Prentice Hall.

Konur, O. (2007). Computer-assisted teaching and assessment of disabled students in higher education: The interface between academic standards and disability rights. *Journal of Computer Assisted Learning*, *23*(3), 207–219. doi:10.1111/j.1365-2729.2006.00208.x

Korea Education & Research Information Service. (2000-2004). *White Paper: Adapting Education to the Information Age*. Seoul: Korea, Retrieved from http://english.keris.or.kr/etc/whitepaper.jsp

Korean Culture and Information Service Ministry of Culture. (2008). *Facts about Korea*. Korean Government Publication.

Kotler, P., & Zaltman, G. (1971). Social marketing: An approach to planned social change. *Journal of Marketing*, *35*(3), 3–12. doi:10.2307/1249783

Kriegel, M., Lim, M. L., Nazir, A., Aylett, R., Cawsey, A., Enz, S., & Zoll, C. (2008). Culture-personality based affective model. Enculturating conversational interfaces by socio-cultural aspects of communication. In *Workshop on IUI 2008*, Canary Islands, Jan 13, 2008.

Kroeber, A., & Kluckhohn, C. (1952). *Culture*. New York: Meridian Books.

Ku, H., & Lohr, L. L. (2003). A case study of Chinese students' attitude toward their first online learning experience. *Educational Technology Research and Development*, *51*(3), 94–102. doi:10.1007/BF02504557

Language and Culture Worldwide. (2010). *Language and culture worldwide*. Retrieved October 4, 2010, from www.LanguageandCultureWorldwide.com

Lanham, E., & Zhou, W. (2003). Cultural issues in online learning–is blended learning a possible solution? *International Journal of Computer Proceeding of Original Languages*, *16*(4), 275–292. doi:10.1142/S0219427903000930

Lasonen, J. (2006). *Expert Meeting on Intercultural Education: Intercultural Education in the Context of Internationalization, Localization and Globalization*. Paris: UNESCO Headquarters.

Laurillard, D. (2002). *Designing teaching materials. Rethinking university teaching* (pp. 181–198). London, UK: Routledge Falmer. doi:10.4324/9780203304846

Lazarus, B. D. (2003). Teaching courses online: How much time does it take? *Journal of Asynchronous Learning Networks*, *7*(3), 47–54.

Lazarus, R. (1991). *Emotion and adaptation*. New York: Oxford University Press.

Lazarus, W., & Mora, F. (2000). *Online content for low-income and underserved Americans: The digital divide's new frontier*. CA: The Children's Partnership.

Learning-Theories.com. (2008a). *Behaviorism*. Retrieved on October 7, 2008, from http://www.learning-theories.com/behaviorism.html

Learning-Theories.com. (2008b). *Constructivism*. Retrieved on October 7, 2008, from http://www.learning-theories.com/constructivism.html

Learning-Theories.com. (2008c). *Cognitivism*. Retrieved on October 7, 2008, from http://www.learning-theories.com/cognitivism.html

Leask, B. (2007). International teachers and international learning. In Jones, E., & Brown, S. (Eds.), *Internationalising higher education* (pp. 86–94). Abingdon, Oxon, UK: Routledge.

LeCompte, M. D., & Schensul, J. J. (1999). The ethnographic tool kit: *Vol. 5. Analyzing and interpreting ethnographic data*. Walnut Creek, CA: AltaMira Press.

Lee, B. (1985). Intellectual origins of Vygotsky's semiotic analysis. In Wertsch, J. W. (Ed.), *Culture, communication and cognition*. Cambridge, UK: Cambridge University Press.

Lee, W. O. (1996). The cultural context for Chinese learners: Conceptions of learning in the Confucian tradition. In David, W. A., & John, B. B. (Eds.), *The Chinese learner: Cultural, psychological and contextual influences*. Hong Kong: Comparative Education Research Centre.

Lee, Y., & Nguyen, H. (2007). Get your degree from an Educational ATM: An empirical study in online education. *International Journal on E-Learning*, *6*(1), 31–40.

Leichtenstern, K., André, E., & Vogt, T. (2007). Role assignment via physical mobile interaction techniques in mobile multi-user applications for children. In *Proceedings of the AmI, 2007*, 38–54.

Lewin, K. M. (2000). New technologies and knowledge acquisition and use in developing countries. *Compare*, *30*(3), 313–321. doi:10.1080/713657464

Liang, A., & McQueen, R. J. (1999). Computer assisted adult interactive learning in a multi-cultural environment. *Adult Learning*, *11*(1), 26–29.

Liddicoat, A. (2005). Teaching languages for intercultural communication. In Cunningham, D., & Hatoss, A. (Eds.), *An international perspective on language policies, practices and proficiencies* (pp. 201–214). Belgrave, Australia: Fédération Internationale des Professeurs de Langues Vivantes.

Lilly, B., & Tippins, M. J. (2002). Enhancing student motivation in marketing classes: Using student management groups. *Journal of Marketing Education*, *24*(3), 253–264. doi:10.1177/0273475302238048

Lim, M. Y., Dias, J., Aylett, R., & Paiva, A. (2009) Intelligent NPCs for Educational Role Play Game. In *Proceedings of Agents for Games and Simulation Workshop, AAMAS 09*, Budapest, Hungary, May 10-15, 2009.

Liu, J. N. K., & Cheng, X. (2008). An evaluation of the learning of undergraduates using e-learning in a tertiary institution in China. *International Journal on E-Learning, 7*(3), 427–447.

Lohaus, A., Jerusalem, M., & Klein-Heßling, J. (2006). *Gesundheitsförderung im Kindes- undJugendalter* [Health promotion in education of children and adolescents]. Göttingen, Germany: Hogrefe.

Long, P. D., & Ehrmann, S. C. (2005). Future of the learning space: Breaking out of the box. *EDUCAUSE Review, 40*(4), 42–58.

Luna, D., Peracchio, L., & de Juan, M. (2002). Cross-cultural and cognitive aspects of website navigation. *Journal of the Academy of Marketing Science, 30*(4), 397–410. doi:10.1177/009207002236913

Lu-Xun's Fetchtism. *Guangxi Business College Journal, 4.* Retrieved May 26, 2008, from http://scholar.ilib.cn/Abstract.aspx?A=gxsygdzkxxxb200104018

MacDonald, J., & Mcateer, E. (2003). New approaches to supporting students: Strategies for blended learning in distance and campus based environments. *Journal of Educational Media, 28*(2-3), 129–146. doi:10.1080/1358165032000165662

Mackie, C., Macfadyen, L., Reeder, K., & Roche, J. (2002). Inter-cultural challenges in networked learning: Hard technologies meet soft skills. *First Monday, 7*(8). Retrieved September 12, 2007, from http://firstmonday.org/issues/issue7_8/chase/index.html

Mackintosh, W. (2005). Can you lead from behind? Critical reflections on the rhetoric of e-learning, open distance learning and, ICTs for development in Sub- Saharan Africa (SSA). In A. A. Carr-Chellman (Ed.). *Global Perspectives on e- learning: Rhetoric and reality* (pp.222-240). Thousand Oaks, California: SAGE Publications.

Mahbubani, K., & Myers, J. J. (2004). *Can Asians think? Understanding the divide between East and West.* Carnegie Council for Ethics in International Affairs. Retrieved August 29, 2009, from http://www.cceia.org/resources/transcripts/123.html

Mandernach, B. J., Gonzales, R. M., & Garrett, A. L. (2006). *Journal of Online Learning and Teaching, 2*(4). Retrieved February 23, 2009 from http://jolt.merlot.org/vol4no1/Vol2_No4.htm

Mao, L. (1994). Beyond politeness theory: Face revisited and renewed. *Journal of Pragmatics, 21*, 451–486. doi:10.1016/0378-2166(94)90025-6

Marcus, A., & Gould, E. (2000). Crosscurrents: Cultural dimensions and global Web user-interface design interactions. *ACM, 7*(4), 32–46.

Marginson, S. (2006). Dynamics of national and global competition in higher education. *Higher Education, 52*, 1–39. doi:10.1007/s10734-004-7649-x

Marick, B. (2003). *Boundary objects.* Retrieved September 2, 2009, from http://citeseerx.ist.psu.edu/viewdoc/download?doi=10.1.1.110.3934&rep=rep1&type=pdf

Martin, A. J. (2007). Examining a multidimensional model of student motivation and engagement using a construct validation approach. *The British Journal of Educational Psychology, 77*(2), 413–440. doi:10.1348/000709906X118036

Martin, J. N., & Davis, O. Idriss. (2001). Conceptual foundations for teaching about Whiteness in Intercultural Communication courses. *Communication Quarterly, 50*, 298–313.

Martin, J. N., & Nakayama, T. K. (1999). Thinking dialectically about culture and communication. *Communication Theory, 9*, 1–25. doi:10.1111/j.1468-2885.1999.tb00160.x

Mascarenhas, S., Dias, J., Afonso, N., Enz, S., & Paiva, A. (2009) Using Rituals to Express Cultural Differences in Synthetic Characters. In *Proceedings of AAMAS 2009*, Budapest, May 10-15, 2009.

McArthur, I. (2008). *East-West collaboration in online education*. Conference Proceedings, DesignEd 2008, 9-10 Dec 2008. School of Design, Hong Kong Polytechnic University.

McArthur, I., McIntyre, S., & Watson, K. (2007). *Preparing students for the global workplace: An examination of collaborative online learning approaches*. ConnectEd Conference Proceedings. The University of New South Wales, Australia.

McBurnie, G. (2000). Pursuing internationalization as a means to advance the academic mission of the university: An Australian case study. *Higher Education in Europe, 25*(1), 63–73. doi:10.1080/03797720050002215

McConnell, D. (2006). *E-learning groups and communities: Imagining learning in the age of the Internet*. OU Press.

McCool, M. (2006). Information architecture: Intercultural human factors. *Technical Communication, 53*(2), 167–183.

McCorkle, D. E., Reardon, J., Alexander, J. F., Kling, N. D., Harris, R. C., & Vishwanathan, I. R. (1999). Undergraduate marketing students, group projects, and teamwork: The good, the bad, and the ugly? *Journal of Marketing Education, 21*(2), 106–117. doi:10.1177/0273475399212004

McCracken, G. (1988). Lois Roget: Curatorial consumer in a modern world. In *Culture and consumption* (pp. 44–56). Bloomington, IN: Indiana University Press.

McDonald, S., Oates, C. J., Young, C. W., & Hwang, K. (2006). Toward sustainable consumption: Researching voluntary simplifiers. *Psychology and Marketing, 23*(6), 515–534. doi:10.1002/mar.20132

McLoughlin, C., & Luca, J. (2000). *Cognitive engagement and higher order thinking through computer conferencing: We know why but do we know how?* 9th Annual Teaching Learning Forum. Retrieved September 20, 2008, from http://lsn.curtin.edu.au/tlf/tlf2000/mcloughlin.html

McLoughlin, C. (1999). Culturally responsive technology use: Developing an on-line community of learners. *British Journal of Educational Technology, 30*(3), 231–243. doi:10.1111/1467-8535.00112

McLoughlin, C., & Oliver, R. (2000). Designing learning environments for cultural inclusivity: A case study of indigenous on-line learning at tertiary level. *Australian Journal of Educational Technology, 16*(1), 58–72.

Meiras, S. (2004). International education in Australian universities: Understandings, dimensions and problems. *Journal of Higher Education Policy and Management, 26*(3), 371–380. doi:10.1080/136008004200029 0212

Menon, A., & Menon, A. (1997). Enviropreneurial marketing strategy: The emergence of corporate environmentalism as marketing strategy. *Journal of Marketing, 61*, 51–67. doi:10.2307/1252189

Merryfield, M. (2003). Like a veil: Cross-cultural experiential learning online. *Contemporary Issues in Technology & Teacher Education, 3*(2), 146–171.

Merryfield, M. M. (2001). The paradoxes of teaching a multicultural education course online. *Journal of Teacher Education, 52*(4), 283–299. doi:10.1177/002248710105200 4003

MEST & KERIS. (2007). 2007Adapting Education to the Information Age. Seoul, Korea: Ministry of Education, Science and Technology & Korea Education and Research Information Service. Retrieved from http://www.keris.or.kr/download/data/2007-WhitePap.pdf

Mestre, L. (2006). Accommodating diverse learning styles in an online environment, (Guest Editorial). *Reference and User Services Quarterly, 46*(2), 27–32.

Michael, L. (2002). Reformulating the Sapir-Whorf hypothesis: Discourse, interaction, and distributed cognition. Austin, TX: University of Texas. Retrieved 14 July, 2010, from http://studentorgs.utexas.edu/salsa/proceedings/2002/papers/michael.pdf

Midgeley, W. (2009). We are, he is and I am: The adjustment accounts of two male Saudi Arabian nursing students at an Australian university. *Studies in Learning, Evaluation. Innovation and Development, 6*(1), 82–97.

Miles, M. B., & Huberman, A. M. (1994). *Qualitative data analysis*. Thousand Oaks, CA: Sage.

Miller, P., & Doherty, B. (June 1, 2009). Indian anger boils over. *The Age*. Retrieved September 23, 2009, from http://www.theage.com.au/national/indian-anger-boils-over-20090531-brrm.html

Miller, H. (1995). States, economies and the changing labour process of academics: Australia, Canada and the United Kingdom. In Smyth, J. (Ed.), *Academic work: The changing labour* (pp. 40–59). Buckingham, UK: Open University Press.

Miller, L., Lietz, P., & Kotte, D. (2002). On decreasing gender differences and attitudinal changes: Factors influencing Australian and English pupils' choice of a career in science. *Psychology Evolution & Gender, 4*(1), 69–92. doi:10.1080/1461666021000013670

Min-Sun, K. (2007). Our culture, their culture and beyond: Further thoughts on ethnocentrism in Hofstede's discourse. *Journal of Multicultural Discourses, 2*(1), 26–31. doi:10.2167/md051c.2

Mont, O., & Plepys, A. (2008). Sustainable consumption progress: Should we be proud or alarmed? *Journal of Cleaner Production, 16*(4), 531–537. doi:10.1016/j.jclepro.2007.01.009

Moore, M. G. (2005). Editorial: Blended learning. *American Journal of Distance Education, 19*(3), 129–132. doi:10.1207/s15389286ajde1903_1

Moran, L., & Mugridge, I. (Eds.). (1993). *Collaboration in distance education: International case studies.* New York: Nicholas Publishing.

Moreno, R., Mayer, R. E., Spires, H., & Lester, J. (2001). The case for social agency in computer-based teaching: Do students learn more deeply when they interact with animated pedagogical agents? *Cognition and Instruction, 19*, 177–213. doi:10.1207/S1532690XCI1902_02

Morris, M. W., Leung, K., Ames, D., & Lickel, B. (1999). Views from inside and outside: Integrating EMIC and ETIC insights about culture and justice judgment. *Academy of Management Review, 24*(4), 781–796.

Morris, P. (1996). Asia's Four Little Tigers: a comparison of the role of education in their development. *Comparative Education, 32*(1), 95–109. doi:10.1080/03050069628948

Morrow, V. (1999). It's cool… 'cos you can't give us detentions and things, can you?!: Reflections on research with children. In Carolin, B., & Milner, P. (Eds.), *Time to listen to children: Personal and professional communication* (pp. 203–215). London, UK: Routledge.

Motteram, G., & Forrester, G. (2005). *Become an online distance learner: What can be learned from students' experiences of induction to distance programmes?* ProQuest.

Moulton, G., Huyler, L., Hertz, J., & Levenson, M. (2002). *Accessible technology in today's business: Case studies for success.* Redmond, WA: Microsoft.

Mullen, B., & Copper, C. (1994). The Relation between Group Cohesiveness and Performance: An Integration. *Psychological Bulletin, 115*, 210–227. doi:10.1037/0033-2909.115.2.210

Murray, D., & Dollery, B. (2005). Institutional breakdown? An exploratory taxonomy of Australian university failure. *Prometheus, 23*(4), 385–398. doi:10.1080/08109020500350237

Naisbitt, J. (1982). *Megatrends.* New York, NY: Warner Books.

Napier, J. (2009, 10 July). Breaking language barriers. *Converge Magazine*. Retrieved from http://www.convergemag.com/literacy/Breaking-Language-Barriers.html

National Center for Education Statistics (NCES). (2002). *A profile of participation in distance education: 1999-2000.* Retrieved January 15, 2002, from http://www.nces.ed.gov/pubs02/

Natriello, G. (2001). Bridging the second digital divide: What can sociologists of education contribute? *Sociology of Education, 74*(3), 260–265. doi:10.2307/2673278

Nel, J. (1992). The Empowerment of Minority Students: Implications of Cummins. *Action in Teacher Education, 14*(3), 38–45.

New York Times. (2009, June 4). Obama's Speech in Cairo. *New York Times*. Retrieved June 4, 2009, from http://www.nytimes.com/2009/06/04/us/politics/04obama.text.html?pagewanted=7

Ngor, A. (2001). The prospects for using the Internet in collaborative design education with China. *Higher Education, 42*, 47–60. doi:10.1023/A:1017529624762

North Central Regional Educational Laboratory. (2010). *Action research*. Retrieved on February 22, 2010, from http://www.ncrel.org/sdrs/areas/issues/envrnmnt/drugfree/sa3act.htm

Norton, P., & Hathaway, D. (2008). Exploring two teacher education online learning designs: A classroom of one or many? *Journal of Research on Technology in Education*, *40*(4), 475–495.

Nwuke, K. (2003). Higher education, economic growth, and information technology in Africa: some challenges and issues. In Beebe, M., Kouakou, K., Oyeyinka-Oyelaran, B. & Rao, M. (Eds.), *Africa Dot Edu: IT opportunities and higher education in Africa* (pp.17-42). New Delhi: Tata McGraw-Hill Publishing Company Limited.

O'Neill, E. J. (2007). Implementing International Virtual Elementary Classroom Activities for Public Schools Students in the U.S. and Korea. *Electronic Journal e-Learning, 5*(3), 207-218.

O'Neill, E. J. (2008). *Intercultural Competence Development: Implementing International Virtual Elementary Classroom Activities for Public Schools Students in the U.S. and Korea.* Doctoral dissertation, University of Virginia.

O'Neill, A. M., & O'Neill, J. (2007). How the official curriculum shapes teaching and learning. In St. George, A., Brown, S., & O'Neill, J. (Eds.), *Facing the big questions in teaching: Purpose, power and learning* (pp. 3–113). Melbourne, Victoria, Australia: Cengage.

O'Toole, J. M., & Absalom, D. J. (2003). The impact of blended learning on student outcomes: Is there room on the horse for two? *Journal of Educational Media*, *28*(2-3), 179–190. doi:10.1080/1358165032000165680

Oates, C., McDonald, S., Alevizou, P., & Hwang, K. (2008). Marketing sustainability: Use of information sources and degrees of voluntary simplicity. *Journal of Marketing Communications*, *14*(5), 351–365. doi:10.1080/13527260701869148

Olaniran, B. A. (2001). The effects of computer-mediated communication on transculturalism. In Milhouse, V. H., Asante, M. K., & Nwosu, P. O. (Eds.), *Transcultural realities: Interdisciplinary perspectives on cross-cultural relations* (pp. 83–105). Thousand Oaks, CA: Sage. doi:10.4135/9781452229430.n5

Olaniran, B. A., & Agnello, M. F. (2008). Globalization, educational hegemony, and higher education. *Multicultural Education & Technology Journal*, *2*(2), 68–86. doi:10.1108/17504970810883351

Oliver, R., & Omari, A. (1999). Using online technologies to support problem based learning: Learners' responses and perceptions. *Australian Journal of Educational Technology*, *15*(1), 58–79.

Omolewa, M. (1978). Oxford University Delegacy of Local Examinations and Secondary School Education in Nigeria, 1929-1937. *Journal of Educational Administration and History*, *10*(2), 39–44. doi:10.1080/0022062780100205

Omolewa, M. (1982). Historical antecedents of distance education in Nigeria, 1887-1960. *Adult Education in Nigeria*, *7*(December), 7–26.

ONA. (2005, March 1). Sulaimi: Constant increase in schools, students, teachers. *Times of Oman,* (p. 1).

Ong, W. J. (1982). *Orality and literacy: The technologizing of the world.* London, UK: Routledge. doi:10.4324/9780203328064

Organizing Committee of China International Distance Education. (2007). *Conference invitation.* Retrieved 28 May, 2008 from http://www.chinaonlineedu.com/2007/English.asp

Ortony, A., Clore, G., & Collins, A. (1988). *The cognitive structure of emotions.* Cambridge: Cambridge University Press. doi:10.1017/CBO9780511571299

Osguthorpe, R., & Graham, C. (2003). Blended learning environments: Definitions and directions. *Quarterly Review of Distance Education, 4*(3), 227–233.

Osland, G. E. (1990). Doing business in China: A framework for cross-cultural understanding. *Marketing Intelligence & Planning, 8*(4), 4–14. doi:10.1108/02634509010141194

Paiva, A., Dias, J., Aylett, R., Woods, S., Hall, L., & Zoll, C. (2005). Learning by feeling: Evoking empathy with synthetic characters. *Applied Artificial Intelligence, 19,* 235–266. doi:10.1080/08839510590910165

Paladino, A. (2008). Creating an interactive and responsive teaching environment to inspire learning. *Journal of Marketing Education, 30*(3), 185–188. doi:10.1177/0273475308318075

Palloff, R. M., & Pratt, K. (1999). *Building learning communities in cyberspace: Effective strategies for the online classroom.* San Francisco, CA: Jossey-Bass.

Palloff, R. M., & Pratt, K. (2001). *Working with in the virtual student. Lessons from the cyberspace classroom* (pp. 107–124). San Francisco, CA: Jossey-Bass.

Palloff, R. M., & Pratt, K. (2003). *Who is the virtual student? The virtual student: A profile and guide to working with online learners* (pp. 3–14). San Francisco, CA: Jossey-Bass.

Panda, S. (2005). Higher education at a distance and national development: Reflections on the Indian experience. *Distance Education, 26*(2), 205–225. doi:10.1080/01587910500168868

Park, N., & O'Neill, E. J. (2009). *Adapting to Cultural Diversity: Policy to Promote Intercultural Education Policy in Korea.* Paper presented at 2009 World Civic Forum, Seoul, Korea.

Patron, M. C. (2007). Culture and identity in study abroad contexts: After Australia, French without France. In Chambers, H. (Ed.), *Cultural identity studies* (*Vol. 4*). Oxford, UK: Peter Lang.

Patron, M. C. (2009). *Diary of a French girl: Surviving intercultural encounters.* Gold Coast, Australia: Bond University Press.

Paulsen, M. (2003). *Global e-learning in a Scandinavian perspective.* Oslo, Norway: NKI Forlaget.

Pedró, F. (2005). Comparing traditional and ICT-enriched university teaching methods: Evidence from two empirical studies. *Higher Education in Europe, 30*(3/4), 399–411. doi:10.1080/03797720600625937

Peters, O. (1999). The paradigm shift in distance education and its meaning for teacher training. *Indian Journal of Open Learning, 8*(1), 5–7.

Peterson, R. M. (2001). Course participation: An active learning approach employing student documentation. *Journal of Marketing Education*, *23*(3), 187–194. doi:10.1177/0273475301233004

Pettigrew, T. F., & Tropp, L. R. (2006). A meta-analytic test of intergroup contact theory. *Journal of Personality and Social Psychology*, *90*, 751–783. doi:10.1037/0022-3514.90.5.751

Phipps, J. (2005). E-journaling: Achieving interactive education online. *Educause Quarterly*, *2005*(1), 62-65. Retrieved January 2, 2008, from http://net.educause.edu/ir/library/pdf/EQM0519.pdf

Pinhey, L. A. (1998). *Global education: Internet resources*. Eric Digest.

Pintrich, P. R., Marx, R. W., & Boyle, R. A. (1993). Beyond cold conceptual change: The role of motivational beliefs and classroom contextual factors in the process of conceptual change. *Review of Educational Research*, *63*(2), 167–199.

Pittinsky, M. S. (2003). *The wired tower: Perspectives on the impact of the internet on higher education.* Upper Saddle River, NJ: Financial Times Prentice Hall. Poole, D. (2001). Moving towards professionalism: The strategic management of international education activities at Australian universities and their faculties of business. *Higher Education*, *42*, 395-435.

Platzer, H., Blake, D., & Snelling, J. (1997). A review of research into the use of groups and discussion to promote reflective practice in nursing. *Research in Post-Compulsory Education*, *2*(2), 193–204. doi:10.1080/13596749700200010

Pollack, K. M. (1998). *Arab culture and Arab military performance: Tracing the transmission mechanism*. Ideas, Culture and Political Analysis Workshop. Retrieved October 14, 2002, from http://www.ciaonet.org/conf/ssr01/ss01af.html

Popkewitz, T. S. (1997). A changing terrain of knowledge and power: A social epistemology of educational research. *Educational Researcher*, *26*(9).

PorosityC8. (2009). e-SCAPE studio. Retrieved August 28, 2009, from http://porosity.c8.omnium.net.au/outline/

Postman, N. (2003). Questioning media. In M. S. Pittinsky (Ed.), *The wired tower: Perspectives on the impact of the Internet on higher education* (pp. 181-200). Upper Saddle River, NJ: Financial Times Prentice Hall.

Powell, G. (1997). On being a culturally sensitive instructional designer and educator. *Educational Technology*, *37*(2), 6–14.

Pratt, D. D. (1999). *A conceptual framework for conducting cross-cultural research on teaching*, 40th Annual Adult Education Research Conference, Northern Illinois University, DeKalb, Illinois. Retrieved on March 13, 2002, from http://www.edst.educ.ubc.ca/faculty/pratt/DPconfra.html

Price, L. L., Arnould, E. J., & Folkman, C. C. (2000). Older consumers' disposition of special possessions. *The Journal of Consumer Research*, *27*(2), 179–201. doi:10.1086/314319

Pryor, S., & Grossbart, S. (2005). Ethnography of an American main street. *International Journal of Retail and Distribution Management*, *33*(11), 806–823. doi:10.1108/09590550510629400

Randaree, K., & Narwani, A. (2009). Managing change in higher education: An exploration of the role of training in ICT enabled institutions in the United Arab Emirates. *The International Journal of Learning, 16*(4), 447–456.

Rankine, L. (2009). *Personal e-mail* from E-Learning Manager, Univ of Western Sydney Teaching Development Unit, 22 September, 2009.

Rankine, L., & Malfroy, J. (2006). *The WebCT 100 project*. Retrieved 20 September, 2009, from http://tdu.uws.edu.au/elearning/referencesheets/TheWebCT100Project.pdf

Reeves, P. M., & Reeves, T. C. (2008). Design considerations for online learning in health and social work education. *Learning in Health and Social Care, 7*(1), 46–58. doi:10.1111/j.1473-6861.2008.00170.x

Reeves, T. (2000). Socially responsible educational technology research. *Educational Technology, 40*(6), 19–28.

Rehm, M., André, E., Bee, N., Endrass, B., Wissner, M., Nakano, Y., et al. (2007). The CUBE-G approach – Coaching culture-specific nonverbal behavior by virtual agents. In I. Mayer, & H. Mastik (eds.), *Organizing and Learning through Gaming and Simulation. Proceedings of ISAGA 2007,* (pp. 313-321). Delft: Eburon.

Reimers, F. (2006, September). Citizenship, Identity and Education: Examining the public purposes of schools in an age of globalization. *Prospects, 36*(3).

Reitmanova, S. (2008). Unequal treatment of international students in Canada: Handling the case of health insurance coverage. *College Quarterly, 11*(2), 10–10.

Richey, R., & Klein, J. (2007). *Design and development research*. Mahwah, NJ: Lawrence Erlbaum Associates.

Rodríguez, L., & Cano, F. (2006). The epistemological beliefs, learning approaches and study orchestrations of university students. *Studies in Higher Education, 31*(5), 617–636. doi:10.1080/03075070600923442

Rogers, E. M. (2003). *Diffusion of Innovations (5th ed.)*. New York: Simon and Schuster.

Rooney, M. (2003, January 14). Report urges aggressive recruiting of international students at American colleges. *The Chronicle of Higher Education*. Retrieved January 14, 2009, from http://opendoors.iienetwork.org/?p=35053

Roschelle, J., & Teasley, S. D. (1995). The construction of shared knowledge in collaborative problem solving. In O'Malley, C. E. (Ed.), *Computer-supported Collaborative Learning* (pp. 69–197). Berlin: Springer. doi:10.1007/978-3-642-85098-1_5

Rose, D. H., & Meyer, A. (2002). *Teaching every student in the digital age: Universal design for learning*. Alexandria, VA: ASCD.

Rose, D. H., & Meyer, A. (Eds.). (2006). *A practical reader in universal design for learning*. Cambridge, MA: Harvard Education Press.

Rose, D. H., Meyer, A., & Hitchcock, C. (Eds.). (2005). *The universally designed classroom: Accessible curriculum and digital technologies*. Cambridge, MA: Harvard Education Press.

Rose, G., Evaristo, R., & Straub, D. (2003). Culture and consumer responses to Web download time: A four-continent study of mono and polychronism. *IEEE Transactions on Engineering Management, 50*(1), 31–44. doi:10.1109/TEM.2002.808262

Rossen, B., Lok, B., Johnsen, K., Lind, S., & Deladisma, A. (2008). Virtual Humans Elicit Skin-Tone Bias Consistent with Real-World Skin-Tone Biases. In *Proceedings of IVA, 2008*, 237–244.

Rossiter, D. (2007). Whither e-learning? Conceptions of change and innovation in higher education. *Journal of Organisational Transformation and Social Change*, *4*(1), 93–107. doi:10.1386/jots.4.1.93_1

Rotter, J. B. (1954). *Social learning and clinical psychology*. New York: Prentice-Hall. doi:10.1037/10788-000

Rowe, J., McQuiggan, S., & Lester, J. (2007). Narrative Presence in Intelligent Learning Environments. In *Working Notes of the 2007 AAAI Fall Symposium on Intelligent Narrative Technologies* (pp. 126–133). Arlington, VA.

Said, E. (1978). *Orientalism*. New York, NY: Pantheon.

Saint, W. (1999). *Tertiary distance education and technology in sub-Saharan Africa.* Washington DC: The World Bank.

Salmon, G. (2002). Creating e-tivities. *eTivities the key to active online learning* (pp.87-105). London, UK: Kogan Page School of Education. (2002) *Postgraduate certificate in e-education*, version 5/4/02. Unpublished new qualification proposal, University of Waikato, New Zealand.

Salomon, G. (1997). Of mind and media: How culture's symbolic forms affect learning and thinking. *Phi Delta Kappan*, *78*(5), 375–380.

Santovec, M. L. (2003). A model for evaluating online courses. *Distance Education Report*, *7*(8), 7–8.

Savery, J. R. (2006). Overview of problem-based learning: Definitions and distinctions. *The Interdisciplinary Journal of Problem-based Learning*, *1*(1), 9–20.

Scheel, N. P., & Branch, R. C. (1993). The role of conversation and culture in the systematic design of instruction. *Educational Technology*, *33*, 7–18.

Schon, D. (1983). *The reflective practitioner*. New York: Basic Books.

SchoolNet Africa. (2007). *African education knowledge warehouse*. Retrieved on July 20, 2009, from http://www.schoolnetafrica.org/english/index.htm

Schulz von Thun, F. (1001). *Miteinander reden 1: Störungen und Klärungen* [Talking to each other 1: interferences and clarifications]. Reinbek, Germany: Rowohlt.

Schutz, A., & Abbey, S. (2001). Collaborative mentoring: insights from a university research centre. In M. Richards, A. Elliott, V. Woloshyn, & C. Mitchell (Eds.), *Collaboration uncovered: the forgotten, the assumed, and the unexamined in collaborative education* (pp.219-235). Westport, CT: Bergin and Garvey.

Schwan, S., & Buder, J. (2002). Lernen als Wissenserwerb in virtuellen Realitäten. [Learning as knowledge acquisition in virtual realities] In Bente, G., Krämer, N., & Petersen, A. (Eds.), *Virtuelle Realitäten* (pp. 109–129). Göttingen, Germany: Hogrefe.

Schwartzman, R. (2007). Refining the question: how can online instruction maximize opportunities for all students? *Communication Education*, *56*(1), 113–117. doi:10.1080/03634520601009728

Scollon, R., & Scollon, S. W. (2001). *Intercultural communication: A discourse approach* (2nd ed.). Oxford, UK: Blackwell Publishers.

Seligman, M. E. P. (1972). Learned helplessness. *Annual Review of Medicine*, *23*, 407–412. doi:10.1146/annurev.me.23.020172.002203

Selinger, M. (2002). *Education and skills development in sub-Saharan Africa.* Paper presented at the ASET Conference on Untangling the Web: Establishing Learning Links, 7-10th July, Melbourne, Australia.

Selwyn, N., Gorard, S., & Furlong, J. (2006). *Adult learning in the digital age.* London and New York: Routledge.

Selwyn, N. (2004). Reconsidering Political and Popular Understandings of the *Digital Divide. New Media & Society*, *6*(3), 341–362. doi:10.1177/1461444804042519

Shattuck, K. (2005). *Glimpses of the global coral gardens: Insights of international adult learners on the interactions of cultures in online distance education*. Unpublished doctoral dissertation, The Pennsylvania State University, University Park, PA.

Shattuck, K. (2002). Speaking personally. *American Journal of Distance Education*, *16*(4), 259–263.

Shea-Schultz, H., & Fogarty, J. (2002). *Online learning today: Strategies that work*. San Francisco, CA: Berrett-Koehler.

Shih, C. (2009). *The Facebook era: Tapping online social networks to build better products, research new audiences, and sell more stuff.* Boston, MA: Pearson Education, Inc.

Shkodriani, G. M., & Gibbons, J. L. (1995). Individualism and collectivism among university students in Mexico and the United States. *The Journal of Social Psychology*, *135*(6), 765–780. doi:10.1080/00224545.1995.9713979

Shrestha, G. (2000). *Utilization of information and communications technology for education in Africa*. Addis Ababa, Ethiopia: UNESCO, IICBA.

Sieber, J. E. (2005). Misconceptions of and realities about teaching online. *Science and Engineering Ethics*, *11*, 329–340. doi:10.1007/s11948-005-0002-7

Siegel, C. E. (2000). Introducing marketing students to business intelligence using project-based learning on the World Wide Web. *Journal of Marketing Education*, *22*(2), 90–98. doi:10.1177/0273475300222003

Siemens, G. (2004). *Connectivism: A learning theory for the digital age*. Retrieved on October 7, 2008, from http://www.elearnspace.org/Articles/connectivism.htm

Sims, J., Vidgen, R., & Powell, P. (2008). E-learning and the digital divide: Perpetuating cultural and socio-economic elitism in higher education. *Communications of the Association for Information Systems*, *22*, 429–442.

Siritongthaworn, S., Krairit, D., Dimmitt, N. J., & Paul, H. (2006). The study of e-learning technology implementation: A preliminary investigation of universities in Thailand. *Education and Information Technologies*, *11*(2), 137–160. doi:10.1007/s11134-006-7363-8

Skyrme, G. R. (2005). *The reflective learner: Chinese international students' use of strategies to enhance university study*. Paper presented at the International Conference: Reflective Practice - The key to innovation in international education, Council for Research in International Education, Auckland, NZ, (23-26 June 2005). Retrieved 24 September 2009, from http://www.crie.org.nz/research_paper/G.Skyrme%20WP%2016.pdf

Slavin, R. E. (1990). *Cooperative learning*. New Jersey: Prentice-Hall.

Slavin, R. E. (1995). *Cooperative Learning: theory, research and practice*. Boston: Allyn and Bacon.

Smith, A., Dunckley, L., French, T., Minocha, S., & Chang, Y. (2003). A process model for developing usable cross-cultural websites. *Interacting with Computers*, *16*(1), 63–91. doi:10.1016/j.intcom.2003.11.005

Smith, K. A. (1986). Cooperative learning groups. In Schmoberg, S. F. (Ed.), *Strategies for active teaching and learning in university classrooms*. Minneapolis, MN: Office of Educational Development Programs, University of Minnesota.

Society for Human Resource Management (SHRM). (2009). *Firms need plans preventing violations of EU worker protections*. Retrieved October 4, 2010, from http://www.shrm.org/hrdisciplines/global/Articles/Pages/CMS_016549.aspx

Stacey, E., & Gerbic, P. (2007). Teaching for blended learning–research perspectives from on-campus and distance students. *Education and Information Technologies*, *12*, 165–174. doi:10.1007/s10639-007-9037-5

Stanford-Bowers, E. (2008). Persistence in online classes: As study of perceptions among community college stakeholders. *Journal of Online Learning and Teaching, 4*(1). Retrieved February 23, 2009 from http://jolt.merlot.org/vol4no1/stanford-bowers0308.htm

Stanley, L. D. (2003). Beyond Access: Psychosocial Barriers to Computer Literacy. *The Information Society*, *19*, 407–416. doi:10.1080/715720560

Star, S. L., & Griesemer, J. R. (1989). Institutional ecology, translations and boundary objects: Amateurs and professionals in Berkeley's Museum of Vertebrate Zoology, 1907-39. *Social Studies of Science*, *19*, 387–420. doi:10.1177/030631289019003001

State Board of Education. (2003). *Educational Technology Plan for Virginia: 2003-2009.* Virginia Department of Education.

Steyaert, J. (2005). Web-based higher education: The inclusion/exclusion paradox. *Journal of Technology in Human Services*, *23*(1/2), 67–78. doi:10.1300/J017v23n01_05

Stipek, D. J., Salmon, J. S., & Givven, K. B. (1998). The value of practices suggested by motivation research and promoted by mathematics education reformers. *Journal for Research in Mathematics Education*, *29*(4), 465–488. doi:10.2307/749862

Straker, D. (2008). *Changing minds*. London, UK: Syque.

Strauss, A., & Corbin, J. (1990). *Basics of qualitative research: Grounded theory procedures and techniques*. London: Sage.

Strauss, A., & Corbin, J. (1990). *Basics of qualitative research: Grounded theory procedures and techniques*. Newbury Park, CA: Sage Publications.

Swinglehurst, D., & Russell, J. (2008). Peer observation of teaching in the online environment: An action research approach. *Journal of Computer Assisted Learning*, *24*(5), 383–393. doi:10.1111/j.1365-2729.2007.00274.x

Tang, C. (1996). Collaborative learning: The latent dimension in Chinese students' learning. In Watkins, D. A., & Biggs, J. B. (Eds.), *The Chinese learner: Cultural, psychological and contextual influences* (pp. 183–204). Hong Kong: CERC and ACER.

Tang, C., & Biggs, J. (1996). How Hong Kong students cope with assessment. In David, W. A., & John, B. B. (Eds.), *The Chinese learner* (pp. 159–182). Hong Kong: Comparative Education Research Centre.

Tangient, L. L. C. (2008). Educational origami: Bloom's and ICT tools. Retrieved on April 22, 2008, from http://edorigami.wikispaces.com/Bloom%27s+and+ICT+tools

Taylor, A. S. (2000). The UN convention on the rights of the child: Giving children a voice. In Lewis, A., & Lindsay, G. (Eds.), *Researching children's perspectives* (pp. 21–33). Buckingham, UK: Open University Press.

Teaching Development Unit. (2009). *Teaching @UWS 2009*. Retrieved 21 September, 2009, from http://tdu.uws.edu.au/qilt/01_teachinguws/docs/Teaching@UWS.pdf

Tellis, W. (1997). Introduction to Case Study. *Qualitative Report*, *3*(2).

Ter-Minasova, S. (2005). Linguistic aspects of intercultural communication. In Cunningham, D., & Hatoss, A. (Eds.), *An international perspective on language policies, practices and proficiencies* (pp. 215–224). Belgrave, Australia: Fédération Internationale des Professeurs de Langues Vivantes.

Tettey, W. (2006). *Staff retention in African universities: elements of a sustainable strategy.* Washington DC: The World Bank.

The Design-Based Research Collective. (2003). Design-based research: An emerging paradigm for educational inquiry. *Educational Researcher*, *32*(1), 5–8. doi:10.3102/0013189X032001005

Thinkquest. (2002). *About SchoolNet Africa*. Retrieved November 14, 2005, from http://www.thinkquestafrica.org/about_sna.shtm

Thomas, J. (1996). *Distance education for refugees: The experience of using distance and* open learning with refugees in Africa, 1980-1995 with guidelines for action and a directory of information. Cambridge, UK: International Extension College.

Thompson, L., & Ku, H.-Y. (2005). Chinese graduate students' experiences and attitudes toward online learning. *Educational Media International*, *42*(1), 33–47. doi:10.1080/09523980500116878

Thorpe, K. (2006). *Report on responding to the needs of the Chinese learner in higher education: Internationalising the university.* Paper presented at the 2nd Biennial International Conference, University of Portsmouth, (15th & 16th July 2006). Retrieved September 24, 2009, from http://www.lass.soton.ac.uk/education/CLearnConfRpt.doc.

Toffler, A. (1991). *Future shock*. New York, NY: Bantam Books.

Tomlinson, C. (2002). Invitations to learn. *Educational Leadership*, *60*(1), 6–10.

Triandis, H. C. (1979). *The handbook of cross-cultural psychology*. Boston, MA: Allyn and Bacon.

Triandis, H. C. (1989). The self and social behavior in differing cultural contexts. *Psychological Review*, *96*(3), 506–520. doi:10.1037/0033-295X.96.3.506

Trompenaars, F. (1998). *Riding the waves of culture: Understanding cultural diversity in global business* (2nd ed.). New York, NY: McGraw Hill.

Tsui, A. (1996). Reticence and anxiety in second language teaching. In Bailey, K., & Nunan, D. (Eds.), *Voices from the language classroom* (pp. 145–167). Cambridge, UK: Cambridge University Press.

Tu, C. (2001). How Chinese perceive social presence: An examination of interaction in online learning achievement. *Educational Media International*, *38*(1), 45–60. doi:10.1080/09523980010021235

Tuckman, B. (1965). Developmental sequence in small groups. *Psychological Bulletin*, *63*, 384–399. doi:10.1037/h0022100

Turner, J. C. (1987). *Rediscovering the social group*. Oxford, UK: Blackwell.

Twigg, C. (2003). *Expanding access to learning: The role of virtual universities*. Retrieved June 14, 2004, from http://www.center.rpi.edu/PewSym/mono6.html

Tylee, J. (2002). *Cultural issues and the online environment*. Retrieved 4 May, 2006, from http://www.csu.edu.au/division/celt/resources/cultural_issues.pdf

UNESCO. (1993). *World Education Report*, Paris: UNESCO Publishing.

UNESCO. (2004). *Quality education in Oman*. Retrieved March 21 2009, from http://www.ibe.unesco.org/International/ICE47/English/Natreps/reports/oman_part_2.pdf

UNESCO. (2006a). *Guideline on International Education*. Paris: UNESCO Headquarters.

UNESCO. (2006b). *Expert Meeting on Intercultural Education*. Paris: UNESCO Headquarters.

UNESCO-UIE. (2002). *Literacy exchange: World resources on literacy: Oman*. March 21, 2004, from http://www.rrz.uni-hamburg.de/UNESCO-UIE/literacyexchange/oman/omandata.htm

United National Global Alliance for ICT and Development. (2009). *Our Mission*. Retrieved June 3, 2009, from http://www.un-gaid.org/About/OurMission/tabid/893/language/en-US/Default.aspx

United Nations. (1965). *Declaration on the Promotion among Youth of the Ideals of Peace, Mutual Respect and Understanding between Peoples*. Retrieved April 22, 2007, from http://www.unhchr.ch/html/menu3/b/65.htm

United Nations. (2006, November). *Alliance of Civilizations Report of the High-level Group*. New York: U.S. from http://www.unaoc.org/repository/HLG_Report.pdf

United Nations. (2007, September). *UN High Representative for Alliance of Civilizations: Address to the AoC Group of Friends (Ministry Level)*. New York: U.S., ECOSOC Chamber, Retrieved from http://www.unaoc.org/images/articles/hr_final_remarks.pdf

United Nations. (2008, January). *The First Alliance of Civilization Forum, Madrid*. New York: U.S., Alliance of Civilization. Retrieved from http://www.unaoc.org/images/aoc%20forum%20report%20madrid%20complete.pdf

University of Houston-Clear Lake. (2008). *Role and scope statement (mission)*. Retrieved on October 12, 2009, from http://prtl.uhcl.edu/portal/page/portal/PRE/UHCL_MISSION_STATEMENT

University of Victoria Counseling Services. (2003). *Bloom's taxonomy*. Retrieved on October 23, 2006, from http://www.coun.uvic.ca/learn/program/hndouts/bloom.html

Unwin, T. (2005). *Partnerships in development practice: Evidence from multi-stakeholder ICT4D partnerships practice in Africa*. Paris: UNESCO.

Urdan, T., & Maehr, M. L. (1995). Beyond a two-goal theory of motivation: A case for social goals. *Review of Educational Research*, *65*(3), 213–244.

Van der Haar, D., & Hosking, D. M. (2004). Evaluating appreciative inquiry: A relational constructivist perspective. *Human Relations*, *57*(8), 1017–1036. doi:10.1177/0018726704045839

van Dijk, J. (2005). *The Deepening Divide*. Thousand Oaks, CA: Sage.

Van Hook, C. W. (2005). Preparing Teachers for the Diverse Classroom: A Developmental Model of Intercultural Sensitivity. *University of Illinois at Urbana-Champaign: Clearinghouse on Early Education and Parenting (CEEP), Early Childhood and Parenting (ECAP)*. *Collaborative*, *22*(6), 67–72.

Vavoula, G., Meek, J., Sharples, M., Lonsdale, P., & Rudman, P. (2006). A lifecycle approach to evaluating MyArtSpace. In S. Hsi, Kinshuk, T. Chan, & D. Sampson (Eds.), *Proceedings of the 4th IEEE International Workshop on Wireless and Mobile Technologies in Education (WMUTE 2006)* (pp. 18-22). Athens, Greece: IEEE Computer Society.

Venkatachary, R., Vasan, M. L., & Freebody, P. (2009). Training for learner-centred pedagogy and curriculum design agendas in staff development for problem-based learning (PBL). *Kritika Kultura*, *12*, 81–99.

Verene, D. (1993). Metaphysical narration, science, and symbolic form. *The Review of Metaphysics*, *47*, 115–132.

Versluis, A. (2004). Virtual education and the race to the bottom. *Academic Questions*, *17*(3), 38–51. doi:10.1007/s12129-004-1017-2

VUSSC. (2009). *A virtual university for small states of the Commonwealth (VUSSC)*. Retrieved on 24 July 2009 from http://www.vussc.info/

Vygotsky, L. S. (1935). *Mental development of children during education*. Moscow-Leningrad, Russia: Uchpedzig.

Vygotsky, L. S. (1962). *Thought and language*. Cambridge, MA: MIT Press. doi:10.1037/11193-000

Vygotsky, L. S. (1978). *Mind in society*. Cambridge, MA: Harvard University Press.

Vygotsky, L. S. (1978). *Mind in society: The development of higher psychological processes*. Cambridge, MA: Harvard University Press.

Vygotsky, L. S. (1981). The genesis of higher mental functions. In Wertsch, J. V. (Ed.), *The concept of activity in Soviet psychology*. Armonk, NY: Sharpe.

Wadholm, R. R. (2009). The world is open. *Educational Technology Research and Development*, *57*(3), 411–413. doi:10.1007/s11423-009-9114-0

Walker-Fernandez, S. E. (1999). *Toward understanding the study experience of culturally sensitive graduate students in American distance education programs*. Unpublished dissertation, Florida International University, Miami Beach, Florida.

Wang, T. (2006). *Understand Chinese culture and learning.* Paper presented at Conference of the Australian Association for Research in Education, Melbourne, Australia. Retrieved February 1, 2008, from http://search.informit.com.au.ezproxy.waikato.ac.nz:2048/search;action=doSearch

Wang, M. (2007). Designing online courses that effectively engage learners from diverse cultural backgrounds. *British Journal of Educational Technology, 38*(2), 294–311. doi:10.1111/j.1467-8535.2006.00626.x

Wang, Q. (2007). Evaluation of online courses developed in China. *The Asian Journal of Distance Education, 5*(2), 4–12.

Warschauer, M. (2003). *Technology and Social Inclusion: Rethinking the Digital Divide*. Cambridge, MA: MIT Press.

Waters, J., & MacBean, N. (May 29, 2009). Anger grows over Indian student bashings. *ABC News.* Retrieved September 23, 2009, from http://www.abc.net.au/news/stories/2009/05/29/2583942.htm

Waves, C. - Collabor8. (2008). *Omnium research group*. Retrieved August 28, 2008, from http://creativewaves.omnium.net.au/c8/

WebCT Australia and New Zealand. (2004). *A unified approach to e-learning at the University of Western Sydney*. Retrieved from http://www.webct.com/au_nz

Wedge, C. C., & Kearns, T. D. (2005). Creation of the learning space: Catalysts for envisioning and navigating the design process. *EDUCAUSE Review, 40*(4), 32–38.

Wegerif, R. (1998). The social dimension of asynchronous learning networks. *Journal of Asynchronous Learning Networks, 2*(1), 34–49.

Weidner, M. (2006). *Kooperatives Lernen im Unterricht* [Cooperative learning in school]. Seelze, Germany: Erhard Friedrich Verlag.

Wentzel, K. R. (1993). Does being good make the grade? Social behavior and academic competence in middle school. *Journal of Educational Psychology, 85*(2), 357–364. doi:10.1037/0022-0663.85.2.357

Wertsch, J. V. (1985). *Cultural, communication, and cognition: Vygotskian perspectives*. Cambridge, UK: Cambridge University Press.

West, P. G. (2007). The virtual university becomes a reality. *Educational Technology, 67*(6), 38–40.

White House. (2002, September). Remarks on Implementation of the No Child Left Behind Act of 2001. *Weekly Compilation of Presidential Documents, 38*(36), 1482-1486. Washington, DC: US Government Printing Office, Retrieved from http://www.gpo.gov/fdsys/pkg/WCPD-2002-09-09/html/WCPD-2002-09-09-Pg1482.htm

Whorf, B. (1956). *Language, thought, and reality: Selected writings of Benjamin Lee Whorf* (Carroll, J., Ed.). Cambridge, MA: MIT Press.

Wikipedia. (2007). *Digital divide*. Retrieved December 11, 2007, from http://en.wikipedia.org/wiki/Digital_divide

Wiley, D. A. (2000). Connecting learning objects to instructional design theory: A definition, a metaphor, and a taxonomy. In Wiley, D. A. (Ed.), *The instructional use of learning objects: Online version.*

Williams, D. L., Beard, J. D., & Rymer, J. (1991). Team projects: Achieving their full potential. *Journal of Marketing Education, 13*(2), 45–53. doi:10.1177/027347539101300208

Williams, D., Coles, L., Richardson, A., Wilson, K., & Tuson, J. (2000). Integrating Information and Communications Technology in Professional Practice: an Analysis of Teachers' Needs Based on a Survey of Primary and Secondary Teachers in Scottish Schools. *Technology, Pedagogy and Education, 9*(2), 167–182. doi:10.1080/14759390000200089

Williams-Green, J., Holmes, G., & Sherman, T. (1997). Culture as a decision variable for designing computer software. *Journal of Educational Technology, 26*(1), 3–18.

Williams, R. (1958). Culture is ordinary. In McKenzie, N. (Ed.), *Convictions* (pp. 74–92). London, UK: MacGibbon and Kee.

Wilson, M. S. (2001). Cultural considerations in online instruction and learning. *Distance Education, 22*(1), 52–64. doi:10.1080/0158791010220104

Witkin, H. A., Moore, C. A., Goodenough, D. R., & Cox, P. W. (1977). Field-dependent and field-independent cognitive styles and their educational implications. *Review of Educational Research, 47*(1), 1–64.

Wolfe, J.M., Butcher, S., Lee, C., & Hyle, M. (2003). Changing your mind: On the contributions of top-down and bottom-up guidance in visual search for feature singletons. *Journal of Experimental Psychology, 29*(2), 483–502.

Wong, R. (July 13, 2009). Problems in Australia's overseas student program. *New Mandala.* Retrieved September 23, 2009, from http://rspas.anu.edu.au/rmap/newmandala/2009/07/13/problems-in-australias-overseas-student-program/

Wong, V. (2009). China's new focus on design. *Business Week.* Retrieved October 9, 2009, from http://www.businessweek.com/

Woodrow, M., & Thomas, L. (2002). Pyramids or spiders? Cross-sector collaboration to widen participation, learning from international experiences. In L. Thomas, M. Cooper, & J. Quinn (Eds.), *Collaboration to widen participation in higher education* (pp. 3-28). Stoke on Trent: Trentham Books.

World Bank. (2001). *The Sultanate of Oman cost effectiveness study for the education sector*. Muscat, Oman: World Bank.

World News Australia. (July 29, 2009). Government to crack down on student rip-offs. Retrieved September 23, 2009, from http://www.sbs.com.au/news/article/1061322/Government-to-crack-down-on-student-rip-offs

Wright, C. (2007, June 15). *Educational technology conferences for 2007-2008.*

Wu, W. P. (1994). *Guanxi and its managerial implications for western firms in China: A case study.* Paper presented at the International Conference on Management Issues for China in the 1990s. University of Cambridge, UK.

Wurtz, E. (2005). A cross-cultural analysis of websites from high-context cultures and low-context cultures. *Journal of Computer-Mediated Communication, 11*(1). Retrieved 18 July, 2006, from http://jcmc.indiana.edu/vol11/issue1/wuertz.html

Wu, S.-Y., & Rubin, D. L. (2000). Evaluating the impact of collectivism and individualism on argumentative writing by Chinese and North American college students. *Research in the Teaching of English*, *35*(2), 148–179.

Xinhua News. (2008, October 25). ASEM Resolves to Further Promote Interfaith Understanding and Exchanges. In *the news of 7th Asia-Europe Meeting*. Retrieved January 9, 2009 from http://news.xinhuanet.com/english/2008-10/26/content_10252340.htm

Xinhua. (2008, April). *China's Internet users hit 221m, rank world's first*. Retrieved May 27, 2008, from http://www.chinadaily.com.cn/china/2008-04/24/content_6641838.htm

Yin, R. K. (2002). *Case study research: Design and methods* (3rd ed.). Thousand Oaks, CA: Sage.

Young, J. R. (2005, August 12). Professors give mixed reviews of Internet's educational impact. *Chronicle of Higher Education*. Retrieved August 21, 2005 from http://chronicle.com/weekly/v51/i49/49a03201.htm

Young, R. (1992). *Critical theory and classroom talk*. Clevedon, UK: Multilingual Matters Ltd.

Young, M. R. (2005). The motivational effects of the classroom environment in facilitating self-regulated learning. *Journal of Marketing Education*, *27*(1), 25–40. doi:10.1177/0273475304273346

Young, S. (2006). Student views of effective online teaching in higher education. *American Journal of Distance Education*, *20*(2), 65–77. doi:10.1207/s15389286ajde2002_2

Yunzhong, Y. (1996). How to be an effective teacher in China: A Chinese teacher's insight. In *Amity Teachers Program Handbook, Nanjing University of Traditional Chinese Medicine*. Retrieved June 21, 2003, from http://www.amityfoundation.org/page.php?page=512

Zaharna, R. S. (1995). Bridging cultural differences: American public relations practices & Arab communication patterns. *Public Relations Review*, *21*(3), 241–255. doi:10.1016/0363-8111(95)90024-1

Zahed, F., Van Pelt, W., & Song, J. (2001). A conceptual framework for international Web design. *IEEE Transactions on Professional Communication*, *44*(2), 83–103. doi:10.1109/47.925509

Zeleza, P., & Olukoshi, A. (Eds.). *African universities in the twenty-first century Vol. 1*. Dakar, Senegal: CODESRIA.

Zembylas, M., & Vrasidas, C. (2007). Listening for silence in text-based, online encounters. *Distance Education*, *28*(1), 5–24. doi:10.1080/01587910701305285

Zhang, J. (2007). A cultural look at information and communication technologies in Eastern education. *Educational Technology Research and Development*, *55*(3), 301–314. doi:10.1007/s11423-007-9040-y

Zhang, K. (2009). Online collaborative learning in a project-based learning environment in Taiwan: A case study on undergraduate students' perspectives. *Educational Media International*, *46*(2), 123. doi:10.1080/09523980902933425

Zhao, N., & McDougall, D. (2008). Cultural influences on Chinese students' asynchronous online learning in a Canadian university. *Journal of Distance Education*, *22*(2), 59–80.

Zhao, W., Massey, B., Murphy, J., & Fang, L. (2003). Cultural dimensions of website design and content. *Prometheus*, *21*(1), 74–84. doi:10.1080/0810902032000051027

Ziguras, C. (1999). *Cultural diversity and transnational flexibility delivery*. ASCILITE Conference, Brisbane, Australia.

Ziguras, C. (2001). Education technology in trans-national higher education in South East Asia: The cultural politics of flexible learning. *Education Technology and Society*, *4*(4). Retrieved September 12, 2007, from http://globalism.rmit.edu.au/publications/CZ_EducationalTechnology.pdf

Zulkey, E. (2009). *Risk management for law firms: From policy to practice, Chapter 4: Managing professional liability–a ten-point approach*. (pp. 27-31). Ark Group in association with Managing Partner.

About the Contributors

Andrea Edmundson, CPLP is the Global Learning Strategist and CEO of eWorldLearning, Inc., (www.eWorldLearning.com). She is an expert in designing *culturally appropriate* training courses and materials (online or in classroom) in order to increase their effectiveness in other cultures and countries. She created the research-based Cultural Adaptation Process (CAP) Model, a unique process that helps instructional designers to align courses – content, instructional approach, and multimedia - to the cultural characteristics and preferences of targeted learners. She also founded the Global eLearning Community, an online membership association for professionals whose work encompasses culture, learning, and technology. She authored the pioneering book, *Globalized eLearning Cultural Challenges (2007)* and introduced the concept of *Cross-Cultural Learning Objects (XCLOs).* Dr. Edmundson served 3 terms as President of the American Society for Training and Development (Greater Tucson Chapter). She teaches graduate courses on distance learning and educational technology for several online universities. During her 25-year career in training and development, she has provided training courses - in the classroom and online - in 30+ countries for thousands of learners.

***

Gbolagade Adekanmbi has Ph.D. in Adult Education, specialising in Principles and Methods of Adult Education, with a focus on distance education. From 1987, he taught courses in adult education at the University of Ibadan and joined the Centre for Continuing Education (CCE) University of Botswana in 1995. His research interests include trends in distance education development in Africa, continuing education, self directed learning and biographies in adult education. He has published articles in the *FID Review, Open Learning* and the *Journal of the African Association for Literacy and Adult Education*, among others. He is currently the Acting Director, Centre for Continuing Education, University of Botswana.

Ray Archee is a Lecturer in Communication at the University of Western Sydney, where he teaches classes in professional/technical writing and communication research. He has been a Primary School teacher, and has worked in Education for over 30 years. His research interests are in mediated communication, and e-learning issues. Ray also works as a computer journalist, a technical writer, a technical consultant, and a luthier of handmade jazz, acoustic and classical guitars. He has an undergraduate degree in Arts, a Masters in Psychology, a diploma in Adult Education and a PhD in Communication.

Ruth Aylett (www.macs.hw.ac.uk/~ruth) is a Professor of Computer Science at Heriot-Watt University in Edinburgh, UK, where she leads the research group VIS&GE – Vision, Interactive Systems and Graphical Environments. She researches the overlap between AI and interactive graphics and specifically affective agent architectures and interactive narrative. She coordinated the EU-funded project eCIRCUS in which the ORIENT system was developed and is now a partner in an EU project LIREC – Living with Robots and Interactive Characters. Dr. Aylett has more than 170 publications at refereed conferences, in journals and book chapters.

Gem Baltazar is a talent management professional with extensive experience in leading global professional services organizations. She is currently a Director with McGladrey responsible for creating and driving the Industry learning and professional development strategy in partnership with the firm's industry business leaders. Prior to McGladrey, she held knowledge and talent management roles at global law firm Baker & McKenzie. As Global Talent Manager, she led and managed a variety of programs supporting the Development Framework for its lawyers worldwide. Gem also gained considerable competency modeling, learning plan and instructional design experience with Arthur Andersen's worldwide learning organization. She has an M.Ed. with focus on Adult and Corporate Instructional Management from the Loyola University Chicago, and a B.A. Psychology from the University of the Philippines, Diliman, Quezon City.

Bopelo Boitshwarelo, PhD in Education with specialization in Instructional Technology and Flexible Learning is coordinating the development and delivery of distance education programs and training of academic staff in the area of Instructional design for e-learning at the Centre for Continuing Education at the University of Botswana. His research interests are online communities of practice, blended learning, course design and development, quality assurance issues in online learning and the use of activity theory in learning settings.

Nicholas Bowskill is an active researcher and lecturer in the area of online learning since 1992. He has worked on a host of e-learning projects including those concerned with computer supported collaborative group work and the networked librarian. Most recently Nicholas was a researcher and online tutor in the e-China project, based at Lancaster University, undertaking fieldwork in China and exploring interculturality in online pedagogy. Previously he has worked at a variety of UK universities. He was a tutor in the online MSc in eLearning at the University of Sheffield for several years. Nicholas has also published book chapters and articles on different aspects of online learning. He is currently undertaking a doctoral study in the area of 'collaborative reflection' as part of a project at University of Glasgow concerned with technology and discussion.

Pauline Hope Cheong is associate professor of New Media and Intercultural Communication in the Hugh Downs School of Human Communication at Arizona State University, USA. She is also an affiliate faculty member in the School of Justice and Social Inquiry, and the Department of Film & Media Studies. Her research interests focus on the social implications of communication technologies, including issues of access and power for minority and marginalized communities. She has published multiple articles on E-learning and the digital divide in national and international journals, including *New Media and Society, Journal of Computer-Mediated Communication, and Information, Communication and Society.*

Yan Cong is a graduate from University of Waikato with Master's in Education. She also has a diploma in primary school teaching and bachelor in Chinese literature from China. After five-years primary teaching in Nanjing (China), she travelled to New Zealand and studied towards her Master's degree for professional development as well as personal academic pursuit. Since completing her Master's thesis Yan has worked as a teaching assistant for an undergraduate paper (Bachelor of Teaching Primary degree programme) at the University of Waikato, and as a research assistant for a literature review contract project titled, "eLearning and New Zealand schools: A literature Review" funded by the New Zealand Ministry of Education. Alongside her thesis work she has been involved in developing articles for publication and a conference presentation (New Zealand Association for Research in Education). Her interests are cultural study and eLearning.

Ruth Gannon Cook, Ed.D., is an Assistant Professor at DePaul University in Chicago, Illinois. Dr. Gannon Cook earned her doctorate from the University of Houston in 2003; further, she earned a Certificate for Advanced Studies from Queens College, Cambridge, United Kingdom, with an emphasis in Change Diffusion and Technology Integration. Her M.S. Ed. in Educational Administration and B. A. in

Business are both from Loyola University, New Orleans. She currently serves on the Board of Trustees for the Cordell Hull Foundation for International Education, New York, and is a Judging Panel Coordinator for the International Student Media Festival of AECT.

Caroline M. Crawford, Ed.D., is an Associate Professor of Instructional Technology at the University of Houston-Clear Lake in Houston, Texas, USA. At this point in Dr. Crawford's professional career, her main areas of interest focus upon the appropriate and successful integration of technologies into the learning environment, no matter whether the learning environment be face-to-face, web-enhanced, online, virtual world or otherwise. Dr. Crawford may be contacted through her e-mail address, crawford@uhcl.edu.

Susan Crichton is an associate professor and Graduate Program Director at the University of Calgary - Faculty of Education, where she teaches in the Bachelor of Education program as well as the graduate specialization of Educational Technology. Her research explores the design and development of ICT enhanced learning environments and the use of digital approaches for qualitative research.

Manuel Cuadrado-García is an Associate Professor in the Department of Marketing and Market Research, University of Valencia, and is responsible for the International Exchange Office at the Faculty of Economics. He has been leading several research projects and teams of teaching-learning innovation. His projects have been financed by the Spanish Ministry of Education as well as by the University of Valencia. The results of his research have been published in several international journals and presented in global conferences. His current research interests are the outcomes of e-learning, as well as consumer behaviour in cultural settings.

Kerry Earl is lecturer in the Department of Professional Studies in Education, Faculty of Education at The University of Waikato, New Zealand. Kerry taught with Nola Campbell in the Post Graduate Certificate in eEducation. She was also a Co-Director for the Flexible Learning Leaders in New Zealand (FLLinNZ) Project 2005-2006. Kerry's background is primary (elementary) teaching and she has worked on a number of case study projects with the focus on research on innovation in education including the use of Information Communication Technologies, eEducation and the implementation of change. She teaches face-to-face and fully online undergraduate papers in eEducation, curriculum and assessment, and the professional practice of teachers. Kerry also teaches a graduate paper titled 'Learning and Leadership in the Communication Age'. Her supervision fields are the use of ICT in teaching and learning, eEducation and teacher practice.

Sibylle Enz studied Psychology and Andragogy at the University of Bamberg. She has worked as a research fellow at the department for diagnostics and personality psychology at the University of Bamberg before she became a research fellow at the department for general psychology, also at the University of Bamberg. She was research associate in the EU FP 5 project VICTEC, in the FP 6 project eCIRCUS, and in the FP 7 project LIREC. In early 2009 she has finished a Ph.D. on the role of empathy in conflicts at the workplace. Her research interests focus on empathy, self-presentation, and social conflict.

Veronique Guilloux (Ph.D. I.A.E. de Poitiers) is an Assistant Professor of Marketing at Université Paris XII. Her research interests include business education methods, new communication technologies, and consumer behavior.

Myra Gurney has taught in tertiary education for 20 years and is a full time staff member of the School of Communication Arts at the University of Western Sydney. She teaches professional writing, communication research and communication theory and practice. Her job also includes assisting international postgraduate students improve their academic writing. Her research interests include e-learning, language and political communication. She has a BA (Hons) and Diploma in Education (University of Sydney), MA (Communication and Cultural Studies) (UWS) and is currently studying for a PhD at UWS researching the relationship between modern political communication strategies in Australia and the language and discourse of the climate change debate.

Andrea Hall is an Educational Consultant & Designer at Sultan Qaboos University in the Sultanate of Oman. She has worked as a biomedical scientist, taught Pacific Islanders in a Paramedical Training Centre in New Zealand, Omani students in Oman, and more recently provides educational support for organizations and teachers in the design of e-learning courses. She has lived in Oman for nearly 20 years, and her experience in Oman and with Omani students resulted in a research motivation in the area of effective pedagogical approaches in learning and teaching for learners from Arabic cultural backgrounds. She has a B Sc. in Microbiology, a post graduate Diploma in Teaching English as a Second Language, and both a Masters and Doctorate in Education. She lives in Oman with her husband and children.

Lynne Hall is a Principal Lecturer in the Faculty of Applied Sciences at the University of Sunderland and has had over 50 academic papers published. Lynne has special interests in emphatic engagements, technology enhanced learning. She also specialises in personal, social and emotional learning.

Lourdes Hernández-Martín is Assistant Coordinator for Spanish and responsible for Arabic at the Language Centre, London School of Economics (London). She is part of the Spanish in Motion Team/ Language Centre project (http://spanishinmotion.wordpress.com/). Her research focuses on how the use of cinema techniques and global simulations can contribute towards enhancing motivation and learning during the acquisition of Spanish as a modern foreign language for specific purposes (i.e. social, political, and economic sciences).

Eunhee Jung (O'Neill) is the founder of the Center for International Virtual Schooling (C4IVS), Dr. Jung (O'Neill) is dedicated to formalizing an International Virtual Schooling (IVS) system by diffusing an intercultural program, International Virtual Elementary/Secondary Classroom Activities (IVECA), to public schools around the world in collaboration with universities, technology firms, NGOs, and international organizations. Her research on IVECA won the 21st Century Best Practice for Excellence in Distance Learning Award 2009 from the United States Distance Learning Association. Her expertise and research interests are in intercultural competence development, cross-cultural online classroom exchange for global knowledge-based societies, the use of ICT in education for intercultural understanding and capacity building, and the internationalization of teacher education and professional development of teachers. Dr. Jung (O'Neill) obtained her Ph.D. and M.Ed. in instructional technology from the Curry School of Education at the University of Virginia where she is currently a visiting scholar. She earned her B.A. in Elementary Education with concentration in Science Education from Seoul National University of Education in Korea.

Shelley Kinash is the Director of Quality, Teaching, and Learning at Bond University. Prior to Bond, Shelley taught as a Visiting Academic to the Faculty of Education at University of Southern Queensland. Shelley was an Academic in the Faculty of Education at the University of Calgary for 12 years. Shelley earned her PhD in Educational Technology in 2004. Her dissertation topic was Blind Online Learners, which she authored as one of her three books published by Information Age - Seeing Beyond Blindness. Shelley remains research active. Her current research topics are - closing the loop in online student evaluation of teaching, approaches to blended learning in higher education, research and co-authoring academic publications with children, international academics, and Web 2.0 technologies. Shelley's immediate family includes her husband Stan, daughter Kirsten, son Josh, and dog Jasper. They love the natural environment of their Gold Coast hinterland home.

Mei Yii Lim was born in Malaysia. She has Diploma and Advanced Diploma in Computer Science from Tunku Abdul Rahman College, Malaysia. She has also studied BSc in Computer Science from University of Campbell, USA and graduated in June 2002 with Summa Cum Laude. She completed her MSc with distinction in Virtual Environments from University of Salford, UK in July 2004. In 2007, she got her doctorate degree in Computing entitled Emotions, Behaviour and Belief Regulation in An Intelligent Guide with Attitude from Heriot-Watt University, Scotland. Currently, she is a research associate for the EU FP7 project LIREC. Her research is focused on Emotional Models, Emotional Memories, Intelligent Virtual Agents, Narrative, Mobile Technologies and Multimodal Interaction Interface.

Xiaojing Liu is a senior research analyst at Kelley Direct Program in the Kelley School of Business at Indiana University, Bloomington. Her research interest focuses on online learning, computer-supported collaborative learning, case-based learning, communities of practices, and knowledge management. She received her Ph.D. in instructional systems technology from Indiana University. Her work has appeared in academic journals such as British Journal of Education Technology, Quarterly Review of Distance Education, Education Technology and Society, and International Journal of E-learning. She can be contacted at: xliu@indiana.edu. 1275 E. 10th Street Suit 3011H, Bloomington, IN 47405.

Richard J. Magjuka is a professor of business administration in the Kelley School of Business. He has been the faculty chair of Kelley Direct since its inception. His primary research interests are the design and delivery of effective online education and in online pedagogy. He received his undergraduate degree from the University of Notre Dame and his Ph.D. from the University of Chicago. He can be contacted at: rmagjuka@indiana.edu. 1275 E. 10th Street Suit 3100, Bloomington, IN 47405.

Judith N. Martin is professor of Intercultural Communication in the Hugh Downs School of Human Communication at Arizona State University, USA. Her research interests focus on the role of culture in online communication; interethnic and interracial communication, as well as sojourner adaptation and reentry. She has published numerous research articles in Communication journals as well as other disciplinary journals and has co-authored three textbooks in intercultural communication with Thomas K. Nakayama: *Intercultural Communication in Contexts*, *Experiencing Intercultural Communication*, and *Readings in Intercultural Communication*. She has developed and taught various communication courses (including intercultural communication) online for the past 10 years.

Ian McArthur During 30 years professional practice as artist, designer and design educationalist Ian has held a range of leadership roles in vocational and higher education in Australia and South East Asia. From 2001 - 2003 Ian was

Program Director of Graphic Design, La Salle DHU International Design College (now Raffles Design Institute) at Donghua University, Shanghai, China. Ian holds a Master of Design (Middlesex University, UK) and two education degrees (UTS, Sydney). Ian's research focuses on the development of culturally adaptive art and design pedagogies using technology to create vibrant multifaceted learning communities. In 2003/2004 Ian McArthur initiated The Collabor8 Project to foster multidisciplinary projects online between design education programs in different institutions, and specifically between universities in China and Australia. Ian currently coordinates COFA Online's Undergraduate online program and lectures in the School of Design studies at The College of Fine Art (UNSW).

David McConnell is Professor of Learning Innovation in Glasgow Caledonian University, Scotland, and Visiting Professor in South China Normal University. Professor McConnell's academic interests include adult and continuing education, the potential of the Internet for learning and teaching, open and distance learning, professional development and interculturality. He has written extensively on teaching, learning and assessment in higher education and has published over 80 papers in refereed journals and co-authored several books. His most recent book is E-Learning Groups and Communities, Maidenhead, OU/SRHE Press.

Ana Paiva is a research group leader at INESC-ID and a professor at Instituto Superior Técnico, Technical University of Lisbon. She is well known in the area of Intelligent Agents, User Modeling and Artificial Intelligence Applied to Education. Her research is focused on the affective elements in the interactions between users and computers and in particular in the interaction with synthetic characters. Her areas of application range from education, entertainment computing to virtual storytelling. She has (co)authored over 80 publications in refereed journals, conferences and books. Prof. Paiva coordinated the participation of INESC within several Portuguese and European projects, such as the Storyteller (Portuguese Science Foundation), IDEALS (funded under the Telematics program), NIMIS (an I3-ESE project), DiViLab, Safira, VICTEC and COLDEX (IST- 5th Framework), among others. Ana Paiva has been Chair of number of important international conferences and workshops.

Iryna Pentina is an Assistant Professor of Marketing at the University of Toledo. Dr. Pentina's research interests include marketing pedagogy, consumer behavior, Internet marketing, and marketing communications.

María-Eugenia Ruiz-Molina is an Assistant Professor in the Department of Marketing and Market Research, University of Valencia, and consultant at Catalonia Open University (UOC). Together with Professor Manuel Cuadrado, she has been teaching in several Marketing courses in English. Dr. Ruiz-Molina's current research interests are the effects of the use of technology in language and marketing teaching-learning process, as well as consumer behaviour in retailing.

Wolfgang Schneider is currently Professor of Psychology at the Department of Psychology, University of Würzburg, Germany. He received his PhD in Psychology from the University of Heidelberg. His research interests include the development of memory and metacognition, giftedness and expertise, the development of reading and spelling, as well as the prevention of reading and math difficulties. He was Vice-president and President of the German Psychological Society (2000-2004), and has been Vice-president of the University of Würzburg since 2004. Dr. Schneider is author and (co-) editor of about 30 books, including the volume co-authored with Michael Pressley on "Memory Development between Two and Twenty", and (co-) authored about 350 journal articles and book chapters. He is currently President-Elect of the International Society for the Study of Behavioural Development (ISSBD).

Randall Stieghorst is a senior partner with Language & Culture Worldwide, where for the past 10 years he has provided instructional design and facilitation of cross-cultural learning for global organizations, as well as translation and localization project management, specifically related to ethics and compliance. A returned Peace Corps volunteer, Randall received his MBA from the University of Chicago. Currently based in Chicago, Randall has also lived and worked extensively in the Dominican Republic, Spain, Latvia, Brazil, and Argentina.

Natalie Vaninni has Dipl.-Psych. and she is a research fellow at the Institute of Educational Psychology at the University of Wuerzburg. She studied Psychology at the University of Amsterdam and the Humboldt-University of Berlin. Recently, she has worked for the eCircus project (http://www.e-circus.org) and is currently working on her PhD. Her scientific interests centre on social-emotional learning, virtual learning environments and evaluation.

Carsten Zoll works as a research fellow at the department for general psychology at the University of Bamberg. He studied psychology and computer science. Before joining the department for general psychology, he worked at the professorship for economic and social psychology at the Technical University of Chemnitz. In his dissertation he investigated decision making processes among experts of the financial markets. His scientific work focuses on simulation of humanlike behaviour, modelling the human mind, empathy, evaluation, decision making and behavioural finance.

Index

D

E

F

G

H

I

K

L

M

N

O

P

CPSIA information can be obtained at www.ICGtesting.com
Printed in the USA
BVOW081717210612

293269BV00005B/3/P

9 781466 618855